D0908290

Selected Writings

of

NICHIREN

Selected Writings

of

NICHIREN

Translated by
Burton Watson and others

Edited with an Introduction by
Philip B. Yampolsky

Columbia University Press
New York

Columbia University Press
New York   Oxford
Copyright © 1990 Nichiren Shoshu International Center
All rights reserved

Library of Congress Cataloging-in-Publication Data

Nichiren, 1222–1282.
   [Selections. English. 1990]
   Selected writings of Nichiren / translated by Burton Watson and
others ; edited with an introduction by Philip B. Yampolsky.
      p.   cm. — (Translations from the Oriental classics)
   Selections from: The major writings of Nichiren Daishonin,
1979–1988.
   Includes bibliographical references.
   ISBN 0-231-07260-0 (alk. paper) : $45.00
   1. Nichiren (Sect)—Doctrines—Early works to 1800.
I. Yampolsky, Philip B. II. Title. III. Series.
BQ8349.N573E5 1990
294.3'928—dc20   90-1367
                                       CIP

Casebound editions of Columbia University Press books are Smyth-sewn
and printed on permanent and durable acid-free paper

Book Design by Susan Phillips

Printed in the United States of America
c 10 9 8 7 6 5 4 3 2 1

Translations from the Oriental Classics

EDITORIAL BOARD

Wm. Theodore de Bary, Chairman

C. T. Hsia
Barbara Stoler Miller
Burton Watson
Donald Keene
Philip B. Yampolsky

CONTENTS

PREFACE

Nichiren (1222–1282) was one of a remarkable group of dedicated and creative Buddhist leaders who worked to make Mahayana Buddhism more readily available to the population as a whole by simplifying its practices in various ways and by stressing its message of universal salvation. To assist him in propagating his ideas, Nichiren produced a large body of writings in both Chinese and Japanese, known collectively as the *Gosho*. Some of them were lengthy doctrinal treatises; some were exhortations addressed to government officials; others were informal letters of advice, consolation, and encouragement directed toward his followers. Nichiren is of particular importance in the history of thought and religion because, although he may not originally have intended that result, his teachings in time came to constitute a separate sect of Buddhism, known as the Nichiren sect, the only major Buddhist sect to have its origin in Japan.

The purpose of the present work is to introduce to readers of English a sampling of the most important and influential of Nichiren's writings. It includes the "Five Major Works of Nichiren," his best known doctrinal writings, as well as a famous autobiographical piece and miscellaneous letters to believers.

In the late 1970s the Nichiren Shoshu International Center in Tokyo, which is allied with that sect of Nichiren Buddhism known as Nichiren Shoshu, began preparing English translations of Nichiren's writings, mainly for the use of its overseas followers. The translations were prepared by Burton Watson and the members of the Gosho Translation Committee of the Center, and have been published by the Center under the title *The Major Writings of Nichiren Daishonin*. So far five volumes of translations have appeared, and further volumes are in preparation.

The translations in the present work were drawn from the first four of these volumes. But in order to adapt them to the needs of general readers, certain changes have been made by Philip Yampolsky in the translations, the explanatory material accompanying them, and in the annotations to the texts.

To a large extent the translations as found in the original texts of the *Major Writings* have been followed. These translations are based on the texts as found in the *Nichiren Daishōnin Gosho Zenshū* published in 1952. Numerous variant texts exist for many of Nichiren's writings, but no attempt has been made either to reconcile them or to note the textual variants. In the translations, however, in several instances, changes have been made to conform with what has been the generally accepted rendition of a term by writers and translators of Buddhist materials. Thus the terms for the Ten Worlds, Three Bodies, and so forth have been given in the conventional rendition. These changes and their alternate forms are given in both the notes and the glossary. In some other instances the form used in the *Major Writings* has been maintained: for example, Former, Middle, and Latter Day of the Law, in place of the conventional Three Periods of the Law, i.e., the True, Simulated, and Degenerate periods (*shōbō, zōhō,* and *mappō*). Nichiren is himself referred to by the honorary title, *shōnin,* sage, in most Nichiren schools, and by the title, *daishōnin,* great sage, in Nichiren Shoshu. These titles have been dropped in the present work.

The aim of this work is to present, in translation, the major thought and teachings of Nichiren. Thus the introduction is intentionally brief and avoids mention and discussion of the many problems and intricacies of Kamakura Buddhism. Much scholarly work has been done in this area in the West and in Japan, but the inclusion of this material would make for a cumbersome and weighty introduction not in consonance with the aims of this work. Thus the reader will find little reference to contemporary academic scholarship. The notes, too, are in general confined to an explication of terms and an identification of sources. We have attempted to allow Nichiren to speak for himself and have refrained from elaborate doctrinal discussion. As it developed, the Nichiren sect divided into several schools descended from Nichiren's major disciples. Divergent interpretations of Nichiren's writings gave rise to certain doctrinal differences among the various schools. No attempt is made here to reconcile these differences; they center largely on the relative importance of different sections of the Lotus Sutra, interpretations of the concept of the Three Bodies of the Buddha, the Three Great Secret Laws, and so forth. The bibliography is confined to a brief listing of Western sources, and an identification of the Buddhist materials of which Nichiren made use.

In most instances the conventions established by the original translations have been followed. Inasmuch as these translations were made over a period of years, variations in these conventions have at times occurred, so that occasional inconsistencies are present. All personal names are given in accordance with the nationality of the individual, with the exception of Sanskrit names where the original is unknown, and figures in the sutras who have no historical existence. Nichiren frequently refers to priests and lay officials by posthumous names and titles and these have for the most part been maintained, even though Western works generally use the more common name. Thus Chih-i is always T'ien-t'ai, Chan-jan is Miao-lo, Saichō is Dengyō, and so forth. Book titles for Buddhist works are always given their Japanese readings even when the work is Chinese in origin, again with the exception of those works that are conventionally rendered in English. Diacritical marks have been entered for words in all languages, despite the awkward appearance of some Sanskrit words. For certain often-repeated names that are fairly familiar to readers of Buddhist materials, the diacritical marks have been omitted; thus Hinayana, Mahayana, Tathagata, etc. appear without marks. By convention Shakyamuni always appears as such. Sutra names are italicized with the exception of those that have English titles and those that use proper names (i.e., Vimalakirti) or widely known terms in their titles (i.e., Nirvana).

On the assumption that this book will not be read through at one sitting, footnotes are very often repeated under each specific title, and little attempt is made to cross reference similar notes that appear in different texts. A glossary is provided for the various names, technical terms, and more frequently encountered book titles. Appendixes give the Japanese equivalent of Sanskrit and Chinese names.

In compiling the notes and introductory materials much use was made of the *Dictionary of Buddhist Terms and Concepts* (1983) and the *Nichiren Daishōnin Gosho Jiten* (1977), as well as the material in the *Major Writings* itself.

ABBREVIATIONS

DDZ   *Dengyō Daishi Zenshū*. 5 vols. Reprint edition.
DNBZ *Dai-Nihon Bukkyō Zensho*. 150 vols. Original edition.
T   *Taishō Shinshū Daizōkyō*. 100 vols.
ZZ   *Zoku Zōkyō*. Kyoto. 150 cases.

Selected Writings

of

NICHIREN

INTRODUCTION

Historical Background

Nichiren (1222–1282) makes his appearance in the Kamakura period (1185–1333), a time of great turmoil and change in Japan. Throughout the several centuries of the preceding Heian period (794–1185) the imperial court, located in Kyoto, had dominated the country. The court aristocracy, however, had become more and more concerned with artistic and cultural endeavors, and paid less and less attention to the mundane details of running the country. This allowed for the rise of a new group: warriors who maintained estates in the remoter parts of the country. These warriors opened new lands to cultivation and sought the protection of local Buddhist temples or powerful families as a means of lessening their dependence on the Kyoto government and avoiding the obligation to remit taxes. Gradually local clans gained significant power and the new military leaders entrusted the farming to the peasantry and concentrated their efforts in developing their capabilities for warfare.

For a time these provincial clans made no attempt to concern themselves with affairs in the capital city. The imperial court had come to be dominated by the all-powerful Fujiwara clan, who monopolized all high governmental offices, married their daughters to the emperors, and installed and deposed child emperors at will. Different branches of the Fujiwara family in time came to rival each other in power and eventually to turn to the military lords in the outlying areas for support. Thus these military leaders gradually acquired a significant influence in the capital city. Eventually the military clan known as the Taira gained ascendancy and Taira no Kiyomori (1118–1181) became virtual dictator of Japan. The Taira clan, whose original base was the Inland Sea area, soon involved itself with the aristocratic court society, and lost its commitment to military goals. The death of Kiyomori in 1181 served to inspire other military leaders in outlying areas to seek control of the country.

Eventually the Taira were forced to flee Kyoto, driven out by other warrior clans headed by the Minamoto from eastern Japan. In 1185 the Taira forces were annihilated at the battle of Dannoura. The Minamoto, led by Minamoto no Yoritomo (1147–1199), seeking to avoid the errors of the previous rulers, chose Kamakura in eastern Japan, near to present-day Tokyo, as the seat of the new military government. While continuing to honor the Kyoto court and render it respect, Yoritomo in turn demanded recognition from the court, obtaining from it the title of shogun, or military leader. He appointed *shugo* or constables to maintain control in the outlying provinces and *jitō* or stewards to supervise both public and private estates. Although these officials were charged only with supervising the affairs of the warrior class they soon gained virtual autonomy in the areas under their control. Yoritomo passed away in 1199 and was succeeded by his son Yoriie, who was eighteen at the time. While nominally shogun, control of governmental affairs came into the hands of his maternal grandfather, Hōjō Tokimasa (1138–1215). From this time until the end of the Kamakura period in 1333, the Hōjō family held control of the government.

Buddhism

Buddhism was introduced to Japan in the mid-sixth century; at least this is what tradition holds. Various schools of Buddhism flourished particularly among the upper classes in Nara, the capital city since 710. Early in the Heian period (794–1185) two new schools entered Japan from China: T'ien-t'ai or Tendai, brought back by Saichō (767–822), known also by his posthumous name Dengyō Daishi, and Shingon, or esoteric Buddhism, brought in by Kūkai (774–835), otherwise called Kōbō Daishi. These new schools of Buddhism, in order to distance themselves from the court which had moved to Heian-kyō, present-day Kyoto, established themselves on mountains somewhat removed from the seat of government. Saichō opened a temple complex on Mt. Hiei, to the northeast of the capital; Kūkai founded his temple on Mt. Kōya in a then remote area in the northern portion of the province of Kii, to the south of where modern Osaka stands.

These new centers of Buddhism flourished greatly. The complex on Mt. Hiei became a major center of Buddhist studies. Virtually all monks from throughout Japan who sought to learn Buddhism were educated there. Indeed almost all of the monks who established new forms of Buddhism in the Kamakura period studied first at this mountain. By the late Heian period, however, Japan was undergoing substantial changes. Not only were the military clans gaining power, but major changes were taking place in the Buddhist religious establishment. Tendai, which centered its teaching on the Lotus Sutra, had early on surrendered to the attractions of esoteric doctrines and incorporated them into its own. But the methods of Buddhist education on Mt. Hiei had by this time become stagnant and moribund and very often failed to satisfy the demands and expectations of the monks who came to study. In addition, a concept that the world had entered into a degenerate age was widely accepted. Buddhist texts taught that after the death of Shakyamuni Buddha the world would pass through three different cycles or eras: the first when the True Law *(shōbō* or Former Day of the Law) would flourish, a second in which Buddhism would lapse into formality *(zōhō* or Middle Day of the Law), and a third, the degenerate age, or *mappō,* when Buddhism would decline altogether. *Mappō,* rendered here as the Latter Day of the Law, was calculated in various ways, but it was generally believed that the year 1052 marked the beginning of this age of decline. This belief was strengthened by the degeneration of the fortunes of the court, by warfare that engulfed the country, and by the numerous natural disasters that occurred at this time.

Both Tendai and Shingon stressed the possibility of the individual attaining enlightenment, but the conviction that the Latter Day of the Law had already arrived strengthened the fear that this attainment might no longer be possible. In the Tendai monastery at Mt. Hiei there arose a belief that reliance on an outside power might now be the only means of obtaining enlightenment. This belief was fostered by a faith in the saving power of the Buddha Amida and the possibility of rebirth in his Western Paradise or Pure Land. This concept was widely held in China, although no organized school of Pure Land Buddhism existed in that country at this time. In Japan, however, during the later days of the Heian period, faith in Amida Buddha attracted a great number of followers among Buddhist priests on Mt. Hiei and elsewhere and gained a great popularity with the aristocrats as well. With the appearance of the charismatic leader, Hōnen (1133–

1212), these Pure Land or Jōdo teachings spread to the general populace throughout the country. Jōdo held that it was no longer possible to rely on one's own efforts for salvation, but that by faith in the Buddha Amida and by calling his name, the practice called *Nembutsu*, one might at death be reborn in his Western Paradise.

The new military leaders in Kamakura embraced these Pure Land teachings to a certain extent, but at the same time were attracted to Zen Buddhism that had recently been imported from China. Monks went to China to study Zen, which by this time had come to dominate Buddhism in that country, and Chinese monks, refugees from the Mongol Yüan dynasty, came to Japan to teach. While Zen acknowledged that this was indeed a degenerate age, the Latter Day of the Law, it held that by the practice of meditation under the guidance of a teacher, one might still attain enlightenment through one's own efforts. This new form of Buddhism held a great appeal for the warrior class, and spread rapidly among them, as well as among the aristocratic courtiers in Kyoto.

Nichiren, of whom we will speak shortly in more detail, was well aware of these new forms of Buddhism. Throughout his writings we will see detailed condemnation of Jōdo (Pure Land), Zen, Shingon, Tendai as it was practiced after the days of its founder, Saichō, and other forms of Buddhism. Although Nichiren centered his activities in Kamakura and may have known less of Buddhist affairs in Kyoto, it is instructive to make note of the particular figures of whom he wrote. Hōnen is excoriated throughout Nichiren's writings, along with a host of local Pure Land monks. Shinran (1173–1262), founder of the True Pure Land or Jōdo Shin sect, is not mentioned at all. Among Zen monks no reference whatsoever is made to Eisai (or Yōsai, 1141–1215), generally regarded as the founder of the Rinzai Zen school, and Dōgen (1200–1253), founder of the Sōtō sect. This is probably because Eisai was more closely associated with the Tendai school than with Zen, and Dōgen was scarcely a significant figure when he first introduced his teachings. Instead Nichiren makes mention of Lan-ch'i Tao-lung (Rankei Dōryū, 1213–1278), a celebrated Chinese master who was greatly honored by the Hōjō rulers in Kamakura, and passing reference to Enni Ben'en (Shōitsu Kokushi, 1202–1280), founder of a famous Kyoto temple. Most frequently mentioned is Dainichi Nōnin (d. 1196?), an eccentric Zen monk, about whom little is known, but who was obviously of great importance in the early history of Japanese Zen. Nōnin was a self-enlightened Zen master who sent disciples to China with a written statement of his understanding. He was successful in gaining the sanction of a prominent Chinese monk, and proceeded to promulgate a brand of Zen that rejected adherence to the precepts and emphasized a connection with the teachings of the first Chinese Zen patriarch, Bodhidharma. This school of Zen, which was referred to as Nihon Daruma-shū, persisted for some time and was to a certain degree taught also by the followers of Dōgen.

Nichiren

It was in this age of new Buddhist teachings, social unrest, and natural catastrophes that Nichiren made his appearance. Nichiren was born on the sixteenth day of the second month of 1222 in Kominato, a small fishing village in the province of Awa in what is now Chiba Prefecture. Nichiren himself has written that he was born to the lowest class, the son of a fisherman. Some have argued, however, that the very fact that Nichiren was sent to a temple to be educated was an indication that his father was a minor functionary in a small fishing group within the local manor.

At any rate, at the age of twelve he arrived at Seichō-ji (known also as Kiyosumi-dera) in the mountains in Kominato. Seichō-ji belonged to the Sammon school of the Tendai sect and Nichiren studied both the Tendai and Shingon teachings that this school propounded. His teacher was Dōzen-bō, to whom Nichiren had a lifelong attachment. Dōzen-bō taught his young acolyte basic Tendai doctrines and a particular reverence for the Lotus Sutra. At the same time Nichiren undertook the study of Chinese, the language in which virtually all Buddhist texts available in Japan were written. The main object of worship at the Seichō-ji was the Bodhisattva Kokūzō (Ākāśagarbha), an important figure in the Shingon Womb Realm mandala, and Nichiren prayed before the statue to be made the "wisest man in Japan."

In 1237 when he was sixteen he was ordained by Dōzen-bō and was given the name Zeshō-bō Renchō. Soon, however, he became dissatisfied with the limitations of the knowledge that his teacher could give him and he set out for Kamakura, where he spent four years studying various forms of Buddhism, including Jōdo and Zen, which had recently been established in this new center of government. His old teacher, although of an esoteric Tendai background, had been a devotee of Pure Land Buddhism and a worshipper of Amida Buddha. Nichiren soon found these teachings unsatisfactory for his needs and he rejected them, as his writings so vividly demonstrate. In 1242 he returned briefly to Seichō-ji, but left shortly afterwards for western Japan.

He went first to Mt. Hiei, the Tendai center near Kyoto, where he gave himself to a study of the sutras and their commentaries. It is probable that his lowly birth precluded study with the more eminent teachers at Mt. Hiei, who were more concerned with the education of monks of aristocratic descent. Nichiren visited Mt. Kōya and temples in the Nara area, studying various forms of Buddhism. But he was soon convinced that the Lotus Sutra represented the true teachings of Buddhism; it was, after all, the culmination of the sutras preached by Shakyamuni and Nichiren felt assured that all teachings that preceded it were inferior. The Lotus Sutra stood at the heart of the original Tendai teaching; Nichiren believed at the time that he was reforming Tendai Buddhism as it was taught in his day and not necessarily establishing a new doctrine.

Returning to Seichō-ji early in 1253, Nichiren found himself ready to expound his teachings. On the twenty-eighth day of the fourth month he preached his doctrines before his teacher and other assembled priests. He chanted his homage to the Lotus Sutra, Nam-myoho-renge-kyo, changed his name to Nichiren, and declared that the Lotus Sutra was superior to all other sutras. With these pronouncements he soon occasioned the antagonism of Tōjō Kagenobu, the steward in charge of the area, who was a devout follower of the Pure Land teachings. Tōjō attempted to have Nichiren arrested but Dōzen-bō, although he was not converted to Nichiren's teachings, helped Nichiren to escape.

In 1253 Nichiren took up residence in an area known as Matsubagayatsu in southeast Kamakura. He began to proselytize and convert others to his teachings, frequently visiting Pure Land temples to debate with the resident priests. He attacked both Pure Land and Zen, angering not only religious leaders but government officials who supported these schools of Buddhism. Around this time a series of disasters began to strike the country in successive years. Droughts, famine, storms, floods, fires, typhoons, earthquakes, epidemics, and strange astronomical portents such as comets and eclipses devastated and terrified the country. To Nichiren the reason for these disasters was obvious: it was the failure to uphold the teachings of the Lotus

Sutra and the practice of giving honor to other sutras. In 1258 he moved to Jissō-ji in Iwamoto in present-day Shizuoka Prefecture where he could consult scriptural writings and seek out the true reasons for the disasters that were afflicting the country.

On the sixteenth day of the seventh month of 1260 he presented to Hōjō Tokiyori (1227–1263), a former regent who had retired to a Zen temple, but who still held decisive power, a manuscript entitled *"Risshō Ankoku Ron,"* "Establishment of the Legitimate Teaching for the Protection of the Country." The essay is a dialogue between a learned Buddhist and his guest. Here Nichiren attributes the disasters that had befallen Japan to slanders against the Lotus Sutra and to reliance on the teachings of Pure Land Buddhism and the worship of Amida Buddha. He quotes various sutras that describe the disasters that will strike a country that turns against true Buddhism. Of the disasters described in the sutras only two, internal disorder and foreign invasion, had not struck Japan. Nichiren predicted that if his teachings were not followed, these disasters were bound to occur.

It does not appear that the authorities paid any attention whatsoever to Nichiren's treatise. The Jōdo believers, however, heard of his attack on their religion and were outraged. They stormed his hut in Kamakura and Nichiren barely escaped with a few of his followers, making his way to Shimōsa Province, where a local samurai gave him shelter. But in 1261 he was back in Kamakura, preaching his message once more. Thereupon Pure Land priests, upset by the number of followers he was attracting, contrived to have him banished to the isolated area of the Izu Peninsula on the twelfth day of the fifth month, 1261. Although this region was a stronghold of Pure Land Buddhism, Nichiren found supporters in a small fishing village and spent a relatively easy two years of exile. During this time he continued to read the Lotus Sutra and found new significance in passages that seemed related directly to his own personal situation, passages that predicted the appearance of enemies who would obstruct the votary of the Lotus Sutra, for example, by persuading the authorities to have him exiled. Then in the second month of 1263 he was pardoned and he returned to Kamakura once more.

Some time later, in the eighth month of 1264, Nichiren returned to Kominato for his first visit in ten years. His father had died in the interim and he found his mother seriously ill. He was able to convert several villagers, although he was apparently unsuccessful in convincing his first teacher, Dōzen-bō, of the validity of his teachings.

Meanwhile his old enemy Tōjō Kagenobu heard of his return and determined to destroy him. Tōjō and his followers attacked Nichiren and a group of fellow monks in a place called Komatsubara, killing two of his followers and wounding several others. Nichiren himself sustained a broken hand and a cut on the forehead. Again he was obliged to flee, spending several years in nearby provinces. In 1268 he was back in Kamakura, continuing his teaching. In this year the invasion by foreign forces that Nichiren had predicted in his *"Risshō Ankoku Ron"* seemed about to materialize. A letter from the Mongol ruler Kublai Khan demanded the payment of tribute with the threat of invasion if none was forthcoming. The Japanese made efforts to strengthen their defenses, particularly in the area of northern Kyushu where an attack was expected. But they made no reply to the Mongol demand for tribute. Meanwhile Nichiren sent a series of letters to eleven high officials and religious leaders in Kamakura restating the predictions he had made in his essay, and warning that they would come true unless the government gave honor to his teachings. His warnings were ignored.

Almost two years after the first threatening letter from the Mongols was received, a second letter, renewing their demands, was brought by envoys from Korea. Nichiren reacted by making another copy of his *"Risshō Ankoku Ron,"* sending it to a high government official with the request that it be brought to the attention of Hōjō Tokimune (1251–1284), the regent at the time. Again the government did not respond. A severe drought struck the nation in 1271 and the government ordered the highly regarded Shingon-Ritsu priest Ryōkan (also known as Ninshō, 1217–1303) to offer prayers for rain. Nichiren, hearing of these orders, challenged Ryōkan to a test of his capacity to produce rain, declaring that he would become Ryōkan's disciple if the latter were successful, and requiring that Ryōkan should accept the teachings of the Lotus Sutra should he fail. Ryōkan gathered together a large number of priests, but the services they conducted produced no rain. Not only did Ryōkan not become Nichiren's disciple, but also developed into one of his most implacable enemies. At this time Nichiren continued his attacks on the Pure Land teachings and strongly condemned Zen practices as well. Charges were brought against him and his followers accusing them of a variety of misdeeds that, in addition to condemnations for attacks on other forms of Buddhism, included accusations of arming themselves with weapons and slandering prominent members of the Hōjō clan.

On the twelfth day of the ninth month soldiers seized Nichiren and he was ordered banished to the island of Sado. Nichiren and his followers were escorted out of Kamakura, destined for the town of Echi, where a pause in the journey had been scheduled. The road led past the execution grounds at Tatsunokuchi and Nichiren was convinced that he was to be beheaded here. He has written in his "Various Actions of the Priest Nichiren," translated here, the details of this harrowing experience and his interpretations of the event. In the tenth month of 1271 Nichiren and his escorts and a few loyal followers crossed over the Japan Sea to the island of Sado, where he was obliged to make his home in a dilapidated temple, exposed to the elements, and always wanting for food, clothing, and fire, in a place known as Tsukahara, where the bodies of criminals were abandoned. Gradually, however, followers came to his aid, providing food, clothing, and firewood, and he was enabled to devote time to his writings. It was during this time that he wrote two important works, also translated here: "The Opening of the Eyes" and "The True Object of Worship."

On the eleventh day of the second month in 1272, internal dissension within the Hōjō family erupted when Hōjō Tokimune discovered that his elder half-brother was plotting against him. The rebels were soon exposed and executed, but the incident served to support Nichiren's prediction that internal strife would strike the rulers of the country. Whether or not Nichiren's predictions significantly impressed the rulers is not known, but following the rebellion there was a noticeable lessening of the restrictions against Nichiren and his followers. Nichiren moved to the town of Ichinosawa where he was able to gain several converts. Finally, on the fourteenth day of the second month, 1274, Nichiren was pardoned, and he returned to Kamakura on the twenty-sixth day of the third month; he had been in exile for two years and five months.

The threat of a Mongol invasion was still imminent and Nichiren was summoned by the government to express his views. He declared that an invasion should be expected within the year. An important way to combat this threatened attack, he asserted, was through prayer, and he was fully convinced that prayer led by priests of the Shingon school would be to no avail. Nichiren was not listened to, however, and following the traditional Chinese maxim that a sage withdraws when his words are not heeded for the third time—first with the "Risshō Ankoku Ron," second at the time of his arrest and near execution, and third on his return to Kamakura—Nichiren left Kamakura on the twelfth day of the fifth month, 1274, to live in retirement.

Eventually he settled at Mount Minobu in the province of Kai in a small hermitage built for him by a local lord. Believers provided him with food and clothing and many gathered to hear his teaching and be trained by him. In the tenth month of 1274 the long-awaited Mongol attack took place, two small islands were overrun, and enemy troops landed in northern Kyushu. A typhoon that many felt had been divinely inspired by the constant prayers, destroyed the Mongol fleet, sending it back to Korea where preparations for another invasion were at once begun.

Nichiren continued his teaching and writing, but those who had converted to his beliefs suffered frequently from attacks by the more firmly established schools. Followers were seized and tortured; some were executed, but his school gradually gained strength. Late in the spring of 1281 the second Mongol invasion took place. The nation was now better prepared, fortifications had been installed, soldiers trained, and a small defense fleet assembled. Then once again a typhoon fortuitously arose, and when it was finally spent the Mongol fleet had again been destroyed. Since 1277 Nichiren had been in ill health, his body gradually weakened by disease. On the eighth day of the ninth month, 1282, Nichiren left Minobu, bound for the hot springs at Hitachi. He never reached his destination, passing away on the thirteenth day of the tenth month at Ikegami, in present-day Tokyo.

RISSHŌ ANKOKU RON

Introduction

In 1253 Nichiren returned to Kamakura and undertook a quiet propagation of his teachings in his own home and in nearby temples. He was convinced that the doctrine he was expounding represented a return to the Tendai teachings of T'ien-t'ai (Chih-i), Miao-lo (Chan-jan), and Dengyō Daishi; thus Tendai monks became a suitable audience for his preaching. He had also a lay following among the lower-rank government officials, and they contributed to his support.

Soon after his arrival Kamakura and the country as a whole faced a series of disasters that served to emphasize his conviction that the Latter Day of the Law had indeed been entered upon. On the sixth day of the eighth month of 1256 gale force winds and torrential rains caused floods and landslides, destroying crops and devastating much of Kamakura. In the ninth month of the same year an epidemic swept through the city, taking the lives of the shogun and other important officials. During the fifth, eighth, and eleventh months of 1257 violent earthquakes rocked the city and the sixth and seventh months witnessed a disastrous drought. The eighth month of the next year, 1258, saw storms destroy crops throughout the nation and floods in Kamakura drowned numerous people. On the sixteenth day of the tenth month of the same year Kamakura was visited by heavy rains and severe floods. In the first month of 1258 fires consumed the Jufuku-ji and the Hachiman shrine at Tsurugaoka, and in the eighth month of 1259 a violent rainstorm decimated crops. Throughout this year and the following, 1260, famine and frequent plagues devastated the country. The era-name was changed five times in the five years from 1256 to 1261. An era-name was usually changed only on the accession of a new emperor or when some natural disaster of severe proportions occurred; the frequency of the changes during this period attests to the magnitude of the disasters that struck Japan.

Nichiren sought answers to the cause of these disasters in the scriptural writings, and he found them in such sutras as the *Ninnō, Yakushi, Daijuku,* and *Konkōmyō*. He quotes passages from these sutras in the present text, the *"Risshō Ankoku Ron,"* or "Establishment of the Legitimate Teaching for the Protection of the Country," chronologically the first of his five major works.

The work was originally written in classical Chinese and submitted to Hōjō Tokiyori through the good offices of his majordomo, Yadoya Mitsunori, on the sixteenth day of the seventh month, 1260. Tokiyori was then living in retirement but still remained the most influential member *(tokusō)* of the Hōjō family. The work occasioned no immediate reaction and no official response was made to Nichiren. But the members of the government were incensed at the violent attack that the work made on the Pure Land teachings of Hōnen and his followers. Government officials and Pure Land followers apparently encouraged an attack made on Nichiren's home on the twenty-seventh day of the eighth month. Nichiren managed to escape and made his way to the province of Shimōsa to stay at the home of a follower. He returned to Kamakura early in the following year, 1261. He remained continually under the threat of persecution, and was summarily banished to Izu on the twelfth day of the fifth month of the same year.

This work consists of a dialogue between a host and a visitor who has stopped by. We may assume that Nichiren is the host and the visitor represents Hōjō Tokiyori or some other high government official. At the outset the host lays the blame for the disasters that have befallen the country on the belief in an erroneous religion, the Pure Land teachings of Hōnen. Presented are numerous scriptural references to disasters that will befall a nation that follows false teachings. Nichiren puts particular emphasis on a passage in the *Yakushi* Sutra that describes seven kinds of disasters that will strike a nation. Of these calamities, Nichiren points out, five have already occurred and two, the "calamity of invasion from foreign lands" and the "calamity of revolt within one's own domains" have yet to occur. Nichiren cautions that these will come about if the doctrines of the Lotus Sutra are not followed.

"Risshō Ankoku Ron" is not only the earliest of Nichiren's major works, but the most direct and least detailed. At this time Nichiren had perhaps not formalized the basic elements of his teachings and was directing his attention to a reformation of society as a whole through an appeal to the most powerful members of the government. That his appeal was ignored only gave emphasis to a contin-

ued unremitting effort to propagate his commitment to the primacy of the Lotus Sutra.

Once there was a traveler who spoke these words in sorrow to his host:

In recent years, there are unusual disturbances in the heavens, strange occurrences on earth, famine and pestilence, all affecting every corner of the empire and spreading throughout the land. Oxen and horses lie dead in the streets, the bones of the stricken crowd the highways. Over half the population has already been carried off by death, and in every family someone grieves.

All the while some put their whole faith in the "sharp sword"[1] of the Buddha Amida and intone this name of the lord of the Western Paradise; others believe that the Buddha Yakushi will "heal all ills,"[2] and recite the sutra that describes him as the Tathagata of the Eastern Region. Some, putting their trust in the passage in the Lotus Sutra that says, "Illness will vanish immediately, and he will find perpetual youth and eternal life,"[3] pay homage to the wonderful words of that sutra; others, citing the passage in the Ninnō Sutra that reads: "The seven calamities vanish, the seven blessings at once appear,"[4] conduct ceremonies at which a hundred preachers expound the sutra at a hundred places.[5] There are those who follow the secret teachings of the Shingon sect and conduct rituals by filling five jars with water;[6] and others who devote themselves entirely to Zen-type meditation and perceive the emptiness of all phenomena as clearly as the moon. Some write out the names of the seven guardian spirits[7] and paste them on a thousand gates, others paint pictures of the five mighty bodhisattvas[8] and hang them over ten thousand thresholds, and still others pray to the gods of heaven and the deities of earth in ceremonies conducted at the four corners of the capital and on the four boundaries of the nation;[9] others, taking pity on the plight of the common people, make certain that government on the national and local levels is carried out in a benevolent manner.

But despite all these efforts, they merely exhaust themselves in vain. Famine and disease rage more fiercely than ever, beggars are everywhere in sight, and scenes of death fill our eyes. Cadavers pile up in mounds like observation platforms, dead bodies lie side by side like planks on a bridge.

If we look about, we find that the sun and moon continue to move in their accustomed orbits, and the five planets[10] follow the proper course. The three treasures of Buddhism[11] continue to exist, and the period of a hundred reigns [during which the Bodhisattva Hachiman vowed to protect the nation][12] has not yet expired. Then why is it that the world has already fallen into decline and that the laws of the state have come to an end? What is wrong? What error has been committed?

The host then spoke: I have been brooding alone upon this matter, indignant in my heart, but now that you have come, we can lament together. Let us discuss the question at length.

When a man leaves family life and enters the Buddhist way, it is because he hopes to attain Buddhahood through the teachings of the Dharma. But attempts now to move the gods fail to have any effect, and appeals to the power of the Buddhas produce no results. When I observe carefully the state of the world today, I see people who in their ignorance [of Buddhism] will cause doubt in those who come later. They look up at the heavens and mouth their resentment, or gaze down at the earth and sink deep into anxiety.

I have pondered the matter carefully with what limited resources I possess, and have searched rather widely in the scriptures for an answer. The people of today all turn their backs upon what is right; to a man, they give their allegiance to evil. This is the reason that the benevolent deities have abandoned the nation, that sages leave and do not return. And in their stead come devils and demons, disasters and calamities that arise one after another. I cannot keep silent on this matter. I cannot suppress my fears.

The guest said: These disasters that befall the empire, these calamities of the nation—I am not the only one pained by them; the whole populace is weighed down with sorrow. Now I have been privileged to enter your home and to listen to these enlightening words of yours. You speak of the gods and sages taking leave and of disasters and calamities arising side by side—upon what sutras do you base your views? Could you describe for me the passages of proof?

The host said: There are numerous passages that could be cited and a wide variety of proofs. For example, in the *Konkōmyō* Sutra we read: "[The Four Heavenly Kings said to the Buddha,] 'Though this sutra exists in the nation, the rulers have never allowed it to be propagated. In their hearts they turn away from it, and they take no pleasure in hearing its teachings. They do not serve it, respect it, or sing its praises. Nor are they willing to respect . . . or give material support to the four kinds of Buddhists[13] who embrace the sutra. In the end, they have made it impossible for us and the countless other heavenly beings who are our followers to hear the teachings of this profound and wonderful Dharma. They have deprived us of the sweet dew of its words and cut us off from the flow of the True Law, so that our majesty and strength are drained away. Thus the number of beings who occupy the four evil paths increases and the number who enjoy the human and heavenly states decreases. People fall into the river of birth and death and turn their backs on the road to nirvana.

" 'World-Honored One, we, the Four Heavenly Kings, as well as our various followers and the *yakṣas*[14] and other beings, observing this state of affairs, have decided to abandon this nation, for we have no more heart to protect it. And it is not we alone who cast aside these rulers. All the great benevolent deities who guard and watch over the countless different regions of the country will also invariably reject them. And once we and the others have abandoned and deserted this nation, then many different types of disasters will occur in the country and the rulers will fall from power. Not a single person in the entire population will possess a heart of goodness; there will be nothing but binding and enslaving, killing and injuring, anger and contention. Men will slander each other or fawn upon one another, and the laws will be twisted until even the innocent are made to suffer. Pestilence will become rampant, comets will appear again and again, two suns will come forth side by side and eclipses will occur with unaccustomed frequency. Black arcs and white arcs will span the sky as harbingers of ill fortune, stars will fall, the earth will shake, and noises will issue from the wells. Torrential rains and violent winds will come out of season, there will be constant famine, and grains and fruits will not ripen. Marauders from many other regions will invade and plunder the nation, the people will suffer all manner of pain and affliction, and there will be no place where one may live in safety.' "[15]

The *Daijuku* Sutra says: "When the principles of Buddhism truly become obscured and lost, then people will all let their beards, hair, and fingernails grow long, and the laws of the world will be forgotten and ignored. At that time, loud noises will sound in the air and the earth will shake; everything in the world will begin to move as though it were a waterwheel. City walls will split and tumble, and all houses and dwellings will collapse. Roots, branches, leaves, petals, and fruits will lose their medicinal properties. With the exception of the five highest heavens in the world of form, all the regions of the worlds of form and desire[16] will become deprived of the seven flavors[17] and the three essences[18] that nourish life and human society, until nothing remains alive any more. All the good discourses that lead men to emancipation will at this time disappear. The flowers and fruits that grow in the earth will become few and will lose their flavor and sweetness. The wells, springs, and ponds will all go dry, the land everywhere will turn brackish and will crack open and warp into hillocks and gullies. All the mountains will be swept by fire and the heavenly dragons will no longer send down rain. The crops will all wither and die, all living creatures will perish, and even the grass will cease to grow any more. Dust will rain down until all is darkness and the sun and the moon no longer shed their light.

"All the four directions will be afflicted by drought, and evil omens will appear again and again. The ten kinds of evil behavior[19] will increase greatly, particularly greed, anger, and stupidity, and people will think no more of their fathers and mothers than does the roe deer. Living beings will decline in numbers, in longevity, physical power, and enjoyment. They will become estranged from the pleasures of human and heavenly existence and all will fall into the evil states of existence. The wicked rulers and monks who perform these ten kinds of evil behavior will destroy the True Law of the Buddha and make it impossible for sentient beings to be born in the human and heavenly states of existence. At that time the various benevolent deities and heavenly rulers, who would ordinarily take pity on living beings, will abandon this nation of confusion and evil and all will make their way to other regions."[20]

The *Ninnō* Sutra states: "When a nation becomes disordered, it is the spirits which first show signs of rampancy. Because these spirits become rampant, all the people of the nation become disordered. Invaders come to plunder the country and the common people face annihilation. The ruler, the high ministers, the heir apparent, and the other princes and government officials all quarrel with each other over right and wrong. Heaven and earth manifest prodigies and strange occurrences; the twenty-eight constellations,[21] the stars, the sun, and the moon appear at irregular times and in irregular positions, and numerous outlaws rise up."

The same sutra also states: "When I look at the three ages of past, present, and future with the five types of vision, I see that all the rulers of nations were able to attain the position of emperor or king because in past existences they served five hundred Buddhas. And this is the reason that all the various sages and arhats are born in their nations and are assisting them to gain great advantage. But if a time should come when the good fortune of these rulers runs out, then all the sages will abandon them and depart. And once the sages have departed, then the seven disasters are certain to arise."[22]

The *Yakushi* Sutra states: "If disasters and calamities should befall members of the ruling *kṣatriya*[23] class and anointed kings,[24] such disasters will be as follows: the calamity of disease and pestilence among the populace; the calamity of invasion and plunder from foreign lands; the calamity of revolt within one's own domain; the calamity of irregularities and strange occurrences among the stars and constellations; the calamity of eclipses of the sun and moon; the calamity of unseasonable wind and rain; and the calamity of rain that fails to fall even when the season for it has come and gone."[25]

In the *Ninnō* Sutra, the Buddha addresses [King Prasenajit][26] in these words: "Great King, the region where my teachings now hold sway consists of a hundred billion Sumeru worlds[27] with a hundred billion suns and moons. Each of these Sumeru worlds comprises four great continents. In the empire of the south, which is Jambudvīpa, there are sixteen great nations, five hundred medium-sized nations, and ten thousand small nations. In these nations, there are seven types of fearful calamities that may occur. All the rulers of these nations agree that these are indeed calamities. What, then, are these calamities?

"When the sun and moon depart from their regular courses, when the seasons come in the wrong order, when a red sun or a black sun appears, when two, three, four, or five suns appear at the same time,[28] when the sun is eclipsed and loses its light, or when one, two, three, four, or five coronas appear around the sun, this is the first calamity.

"When the twenty-eight constellations do not move in their regular courses, when the Metal Star, the Broom Star, the Wheel Star, the Demon Star, the Fire Star, the Water Star, the Wind Star, the Ladle

Star, the Southern Dipper, the Northern Dipper, the great stars of the Five Garrisons,[29] and all the many stars that govern the ruler, the three high ministers, and the hundred other officials—when each of these stars manifests some peculiar behavior, this is the second calamity.

"When huge fires consume the nation and the people are all burned to death, or when there are outbreaks of demon fire, dragon fire, heavenly fire, mountain god fire, human fire, tree fire, or bandit fire[30]—when these prodigies appear, this is the third calamity.

"When huge floods drown the population, when the seasons come out of order and there is rain in winter, snow in summer, thunder and lightning in the winter season, and ice, frost and hail in the sixth month, when red, black, or green rain falls, when mountains of dirt and stones come raining down, or when it rains dust, sand, or gravel, when the rivers and streams run backward, when mountains are afloat and boulders are washed away—when freakish happenings of this kind occur, this is the fourth calamity.

"When huge winds blow the people to their death and the lands, the mountains and rivers and the trees and forests are all at one time wiped out, when great winds come out of season or when black winds, red winds, green winds, heavenly winds, earthly winds, fire winds, and water winds blow—when prodigies of this kind occur, this is the fifth calamity.

"When heaven and earth and the whole country are stricken by terrible heat so that the air seems to be on fire, when the hundred plants wither and the five grains[31] fail to ripen, when the earth is red and scorched and the inhabitants all perish—when prodigies of this kind occur, this is the sixth calamity.

"When enemies rise up on all four sides and invade the nation, when rebels appear both within the ruler's family and without, when there are fire bandits, water bandits, wind bandits, and demon bandits[32] and the population is subjected to devastation and disorder, and fighting and plundering break out everywhere—when prodigies of this type occur, this is the seventh calamity."[33]

The *Daijuku* Sutra says: "Though the ruler of a state may have for countless existences in the past practiced the giving of alms, observed the precepts and abided by the principles of wisdom, if he sees that my Law, the Dharma of the Buddha, is in danger of perishing and stands idly by without doing anything to protect it, then all the inestimable store of good causes that he has accumulated through the practices just mentioned will be entirely wiped out, and his country will become the scene of three inauspicious occurrences. The first is high grain prices, the second is warfare, and the third is pestilence. All the benevolent deities will abandon the country, and although the king may issue commands, the people will not obey them. The country will constantly be invaded and vexed by neighboring nations. Violent fires will rage out of control, evil winds and rains will abound, the waters will swell and overflow, and the inhabitants will be blown about by winds or swept away by floods. The paternal and maternal relatives of the ruler will join in plotting revolt. Before long, the ruler will fall gravely ill, and after his life has come to an end, he will be reborn in one of the major hells. . . . And the same fate will befall the ruler's consort, his heir, the high ministers of the state, the lords of cities, the village heads and generals, the magistrates of districts, and the government officials."[34]

The passages I have quoted from these four sutras are perfectly clear—what person in ten thousand could possibly doubt their meaning? And yet the blind and the deluded trust to heretical doctrines and fail to recognize the correct teachings. Therefore, throughout the empire these days people are inclined to turn away from the Buddhas and the sutras and no longer endeavor to protect them. In turn, the benevolent deities and sages abandon the nation and leave their accustomed places. As a result, demons and followers of heretical doctrines create disaster and inflict calamity upon the populace.

The guest thereupon flushed with anger and said: Emperor Ming of the Later Han dynasty, having comprehended the significance of his dream of a golden man, welcomed the teachings of Buddhism brought to China by missionaries leading white horses.[35] Prince Shōtoku,[36] having punished Mononobe no Moriya for his opposition to Buddhism, proceeded to construct temples and pagodas in Japan. Since that time, from the supreme ruler down to the numberless masses, people have worshiped the Buddhist statues and devoted their attention to the scriptures. As a result, in the monasteries of Mount Hiei[37] and of the southern capital at Nara, at the great temples of Onjō-ji and Tō-ji,[38] throughout the land within the four seas, in the five areas adjacent to the capital,[39] and the seven outlying regions, Buddhist scriptures have been ranged like stars in the sky and halls of worship have spread over the land like clouds. Those who belong to the lineage of Śāriputra meditate on the moon atop Eagle Peak,[40] while those who adhere to the traditions of Haklenayaśas transmit the teachings of Mount Kukkuṭapāda.[41] How, then, can anyone say that the doctrines of Shakyamuni are despised or that the three treasures of Buddhism are neglected? If there is evidence to support such a contention, I would like to hear all the facts!

The host, anxious to clarify his words, replied: To be sure, Buddha halls stand rooftop to rooftop and sutra storehouses are ranged eave to eave. Priests are as numerous as bamboo plants and rushes, monks as common as rice and hemp seedlings. The temples and priests have been honored from centuries past, and every day respect is paid them anew. But the monks and priests today are fawning and devious, and they confuse the people and lead them astray. The ruler and his ministers lack understanding and fail to distinguish between truth and heresy.

The *Ninnō* Sutra, for example, says: "Evil monks, hoping to gain fame and profit, in many cases appear before the ruler, the heir apparent, or the other princes and take it upon themselves to preach doctrines that lead to the violation of the Buddhist Law and the destruction of the nation. The rulers, failing to perceive the truth of the situation, listen to and put faith in such doctrines, and proceed to create regulations that are perverse in nature and do not accord with the rules of Buddhist discipline. In this way they bring about the destruction of Buddhism and of the nation."[42]

The Nirvana Sutra states: "Bodhisattvas, have no fear in your hearts because of such things as wild elephants. But evil friends— they are what you should fear! If you are killed by a wild elephant, you will not fall into any of the three evil paths. But if evil friends lead you to your death, you are certain to fall into them!"[43]

The Lotus Sutra says: "There will be monks in that evil age with perverse views and hearts that are fawning and crooked who will say they have attained what they have not attained, being proud and boastful in heart. Or there will be forest-dwelling monks wearing clothing of patched rags and living in retirement who will claim they are practicing the true Way, despising and looking down on the rest of mankind. Greedy for profit and nourishment, they will preach the Dharma to white-robed laymen and will be respected and revered by the world as though they were arhats who possess the six supernatural powers.[44] . . . Constantly they will go about among the populace, seeking in this way to slander us. They will address the rulers, high ministers, Brahmans, and great patrons of Buddhism as well as the other monks, slandering and speaking evil of us, saying, 'These are men of perverted views who preach the doctrines of heretical sects!' . . . In a muddied kalpa, in an evil age there will be many different things to fear. Demons will take possession of others and through them curse, revile and heap shame on us. . . . The evil monks of that muddied age, failing to understand the Buddha's expedient means, how he preaches the Dharma in accord with what is appropriate, will confront us with foul language and angry frowns; again and again we will be banished."[45]

In the Nirvana Sutra, the Buddha says: "After I have passed away and countless hundreds of years have gone by, all the sages of the four stages[46] will also have passed away. After the Former Day of the Law has ended and the Middle Day of the Law has begun, there will be monks who will give the appearance of abiding by the rules of monastic discipline. But they will scarcely ever read or recite the sutras, and instead will crave all kinds of food and drink to nourish their bodies. Though they wear the robes of a monk, they will go about searching for alms like so many huntsmen, spying sharply and stalking softly. They will be like a cat on the prowl for mice. And constantly they will reiterate these words: 'I have attained the state of arhat!' Outwardly they will seem to be wise and good, but within they will harbor greed and jealousy. [And when they are asked to preach the Dharma,] they will conceal it, like Brahmans who have taken a vow of silence. They are not true monks—they merely have the appearance of monks. Consumed by their erroneous views, they slander the True Law."[47]

When we look at the world in the light of these passages of scripture, we see that the situation is just as they describe it. If we do not admonish the evil monks, how can we hope to do good?

The guest, growing more indignant than ever, said: A wise monarch, by acting in accord with heaven and earth, perfects his rule; a sage, by distinguishing between right and wrong, brings order to the world. The monks and priests of the world today enjoy the confidence of the entire empire. If they were in fact evil monks, then the wise ruler would put no trust in them. If they were not true sages, then men of worth and understanding would not look up to them. But now, since worthies and sages do in fact honor and respect them, they must be nothing less than paragons of their kind. Why then do you pour out these wild accusations and dare to slander them? To whom are you referring when you speak of "evil monks"? I would like an explanation!

The host said: In the reign of Emperor Gotoba there was a priest named Hōnen who wrote a work entitled the *Senchaku Shū*.[48] He contradicted the sacred teachings of Shakyamuni and brought confusion to people in every direction. The *Senchaku Shū* states: "The Chinese priest Tao-ch'o[49] distinguished between the *Shōdō* or Sacred Way teachings and the *Jōdo* or Pure Land teachings[50] and urged men to abandon the former and immediately embrace the latter. First of all, there are two kinds of Sacred Way teachings, [the Mahayana and the Hinayana]. Judging from this, we may assume that the esoteric Mahayana doctrines of Shingon and the true Mahayana teachings of the Lotus Sutra are both included in the Sacred Way. If that is so, then the present-day sects of Shingon, Zen, Tendai, Kegon, Sanron, Hossō, Jiron, and Shōron—all these eight schools are included in the Sacred Way that is to be abandoned.

"The priest T'an-luan[51] in his *Ōjō Ron Chū* states: 'I note that Nāgārjuna's *Jūjūbibasha Ron* says: "There are two ways by which the bodhisattva may reach the state in which there is no retrogression. One is the Difficult-to-Practice Way, the other is the Easy-to-Practice Way."'

"The Difficult-to-Practice Way is the same as the Sacred Way, and the Easy-to-Practice Way is the Pure Land Way. Students of the Pure Land sect should first of all understand this point. Though they may previously have studied teachings belonging to the Sacred Way, if they wish to become followers of the Pure Land school, they must discard the Sacred Way and give their allegiance to the Pure Land teachings."

Hōnen also says: "The Chinese priest Shan-tao[52] distinguished between correct and sundry practices and urged men to embrace the former and abandon the latter. Concerning the first of the sundry practices, that of reading and reciting sutras, he states that, with the exception of the recitation of the *Kammuryōju* Sutra and the other Pure Land sutras, the embracing and recitation of all sutras, whether Mahayana or Hinayana, exoteric or esoteric, is to be regarded as a sundry practice. Concerning the third of the sundry practices, that of worshiping, he states that, with the exception of worshiping the Buddha Amida, the worshiping or honoring of any of the other Buddhas, bodhisattvas, or deities of the heavenly and human worlds is to be regarded as a sundry practice. In the light of this passage, it is clear that one should abandon such sundry practices and concentrate upon the practice of the Pure Land teaching. What reason would we have to abandon the correct practices of the Pure Land teaching, which insure that, out of a hundred persons, all one hundred will be reborn in the Western Paradise, and cling instead to the various sundry practices and procedures, which could not save even one person in a thousand? Followers of the Way should ponder this carefully!"

Hōnen further states: "In the *Jōgen Nyūzō Roku*[53] we find it recorded that, from the six hundred volumes of the *Daihannya* Sutra[54] to the *Hōjōjū* Sutra,[55] the exoteric and esoteric sutras of Mahayana Buddhism total 637 works in 2,883 volumes. All of these should now be replaced by the recitation of the single Mahayana phrase, [the Nembutsu]. You should understand that, when the Buddha was preaching according to the capacity of his various listeners, he for a time taught the two methods of concentrated meditation and unconcentrated meditation.[56] But later, when he revealed his own enlightenment, he ceased to teach these two methods. The only teaching that, once revealed, shall never cease to be taught, is the single doctrine of the Nembutsu."

Again Hōnen states: "The passage which says that the practitioner of the Nembutsu must possess three kinds of mind[57] is found in the *Kammuryōju* Sutra. In the commentary on that sutra,[58] we read: 'Someone asked: "If there are those who differ in understanding and practice from the followers of the Nembutsu, persons of heretical and mistaken belief, how can one make certain that their perverse and differing views will not cause trouble?" ' We also see that these persons of evil views with their different understanding and different practices are compared to a band of robbers who call back the travelers who have already gone one or two steps along their journey. In my opinion, when these passages speak of different understanding, different practices, varying doctrines, and varying beliefs, they are referring to the teachings of the Sacred Way."

Finally, in a concluding passage, Hōnen says: "If one wishes to escape quickly from the sufferings of birth and death, one should confront these two superior teachings and then proceed to put aside the teachings of the Sacred Way and choose those of the Pure Land. And if one wishes to follow the teachings of the Pure Land, one should confront the correct and sundry practices and then proceed to abandon all those that are incorrect and devote one's entire attention to those that are correct."

When we examine these passages, we see that Hōnen quotes the erroneous explanations of T'an-luan, Tao-ch'o, and Shan-tao, and establishes the categories he calls Sacred Way and Pure Land, Difficult-to-Practice Way and Easy-to-Practice Way. He then takes all the 637 works in 2,883 volumes that comprise the Mahayana sutras of the Buddha's lifetime, including those of the Lotus Sutra and Shingon, along with all the Buddhas, bodhisattvas, and deities of the heavenly and human worlds, and assigns them all to the Sacred Way, the Difficult-to-Practice Way and the sundry practices categories, and urges men to "discard, close, ignore, and abandon" them. With these four injunctions, he leads all people astray. And on top of that, he groups together all the sage monks of the three countries[59] of India, China, and Japan as well as the students of Buddhism of the ten directions, and calls them a "band of robbers," causing the people to insult them!

In doing so, he turns his back on the passages in the three Pure Land sutras,[60] the sutras of his own sect, which contain Amida's vow to save everyone "except those who commit the five cardinal sins or slander the True Law."[61] At the same time, he shows that he fails to understand the warning contained in the second volume of the Lotus Sutra, the most important sutra expounded in the five preaching periods[62] of the Buddha's life, which reads: "One who refuses to take faith in this sutra and instead slanders it. . . . After he dies, he will fall into the hell of incessant suffering."[63]

And now we have come to this later age, when men are no longer sages. Each enters his own dark road, and all alike forget the direct way. How pitiful, that no one cures them of their blindness! How painful, to see them vainly lending encouragement to these false beliefs! And as a result, everyone from the ruler of the nation down to the humblest peasant believes that there are no true sutras outside the three Pure Land sutras, and no Buddhas other than the Buddha Amida with his two attendants.[64]

Once there were men like Dengyō, Gishin,[65] Jikaku and Chishō who journeyed ten thousand leagues across the waves to acquire the sacred teachings, or visited all the mountains and rivers of Japan to acquire Buddhist statues which they held in reverence. In some cases they built holy temples on the peaks of high mountains in which to preserve those scriptures and statues; in other cases they constructed sacred halls in the bottoms of deep valleys where such objects could be worshiped and honored. As a result, the Buddhas Shakyamuni and Yakushi[66] shone side by side, casting their influence upon present and future ages, while the Bodhisattvas Kokūzō and Jizō[67] brought benefit to the living and the dead. The rulers of the nation contributed counties or villages so that the lamps might continue to burn bright before the images, while the stewards of the great estates offered their fields and gardens [to provide for the upkeep of the temples].

But because of this book by Hōnen, this *Senchaku Shū,* the Lord Buddha Shakyamuni is forgotten and all honor is paid to Amida, the Buddha of the Western Land. The Lord Buddha's transmission of the Law is ignored, and Yakushi, the Buddha of the Eastern Region, is neglected.[68] All attention is paid to the three works in four volumes of the Pure Land scriptures, and all the other wonderful teachings that Shakyamuni proclaimed throughout the five periods of his preaching life are cast aside. If temples are not dedicated to Amida, then people no longer have any desire to support them or pay honor to the Buddhas enshrined there; if monks do not chant the Nembutsu, then people quickly forget all about giving those monks alms. As a result, the halls of the Buddha fall into ruin, scarcely a wisp of smoke rises above their mossy tiles; and the monks' quarters stand empty and dilapidated, the dew deep on the grasses in their courtyards. And in spite of such conditions, no one gives a thought to protecting the Law or to restoring the temples. Hence the sage monks who once presided over the temples leave and do not return, and the benevolent deities who guarded the Buddhist teachings depart and no longer appear. This has all come about because of this *Senchaku Shū* of Hōnen. How pitiful to think that, in the space of a few decades, hundreds, thousands, tens of thousands of people have been deluded by these devilish teachings and in so many cases confused as to the true teachings of Buddhism. If people favor perverse doctrines and forget what is correct, can the benevolent deities be anything but angry? If people cast aside doctrines that are all-encompassing and take up those that are incomplete, can the world escape the plots of demons? Rather than offering up ten thousand prayers for remedy, it would be better simply to outlaw this one evil doctrine that is the source of all the trouble!

This time the guest was truly enraged and said: In the ages since our original teacher, the Buddha Shakyamuni, preached the three Pure Land sutras, the priest T'an-luan had originally studied the four treatises[69] but abandoned them and put all his faith in the Pure Land teachings. Similarly, the priest Tao-ch'o ceased to spread the multifarious doctrines of the Nirvana Sutra[70] and devoted all his attention to the practices of the Western Region. The priest Shan-tao discarded the sundry practices and concentrated on the single practice of the Pure Land, and the priest Eshin collected passages from various sutras to form his work, stressing the importance of a single practice, the Nembutsu.[71] Such was the manner in which these men honored and respected the Buddha Amida, and uncountable numbers of people as a result were able to gain rebirth in the Pure Land.

Of particular note was the venerable Hōnen, who as a child entered the monastery on Mount Hiei. By the time he was seventeen, he had worked his way through all sixty volumes of Tendai literature[72] and had investigated all the eight sects[73] and mastered their essentials. In addition, he had read through the entire body of sutras and treatises seven times, and exhausted all the works of exegesis and biography. His wisdom shone like the sun and moon, and his virtue exceeded that of the earlier teachers.

In spite of all this, he was in doubt as to the proper path to salvation and could not make out the true meaning of nirvana. Therefore he read and examined all the texts he could, pondered deeply and considered every possibility, and in the end put aside all the sutras and concentrated on the single practice of the Nembutsu. In addition, he received confirmation of his decision when Shan-tao miraculously appeared to him in a dream,[74] and he proceeded to spread his doctrines among friends and strangers in all four corners of the land. Thereafter, he was hailed as a reincarnation of the Bodhisattva Seishi, or was revered as Shan-tao reborn. In every quarter people of eminent and lowly birth alike bowed their heads in respect, and men and women from all over Japan sought him.

Since that time, the springs and autumns have succeeded each other and the years have accumulated. And yet you insist upon putting aside the venerable teachings of Shakyamuni Buddha contained in the Pure Land sutras and willfully speak evil of the writings concerning the Buddha Amida. Why do you try to blame the sacred age of Hōnen for the disasters of recent years, going out of your way to slander the former teachers of Pure Land doctrine[75] and to heap abuse on a sage like Hōnen? You are, as the saying goes, deliberately blowing back the fur and hunting for flaws in the leather, deliberately piercing the skin in hopes of drawing blood. From ancient times to the present, the world has never seen such a speaker of evil! You had better learn a little caution and restraint. When you pile up such grave offenses, how can you hope to escape punishment? I am afraid even to sit here in your company. I must take up my staff and be on my way!

The host, smiling, restrained his guest and said: Insects that live on smartweed forget how bitter it tastes; those who stay long in privies forget how foul the smell is. Here you listen to my good words and think them wicked, point to a slanderer like Hōnen and call him a sage, mistrust a true teacher and take him for an evil monk. Your confusion is great indeed, and your offense anything but light. Listen to my explanation of how this confusion arose and let us discuss the matter in detail.

The doctrines that Shakyamuni Buddha preached in the course of his lifetime can be assigned to five distinct preaching periods. The order in which they were preached can be established, and they can be divided into provisional and true teachings. But T'an-luan, Tao-ch'o, and Shan-tao embraced the provisional teachings and forgot about the true ones, went by what had been taught in the earlier period of the Buddha's life and discarded what was taught later. They were not the kind of men who delve into the deep places of Buddhist doctrine.

Hōnen in particular, though he followed the practices advocated by these earlier men, was ignorant as to the source from whence they came. How do we know this? Because he lumped together all the 637 Mahayana scriptures with the 2,883 volumes of text, and along with them all the various Buddhas and bodhisattvas and the deities of the heavenly and human worlds, and urged people to "discard, close, ignore, and abandon" them, with these four injunctions corrupting the hearts of all people. Thus he poured out perverted words of his own invention and took absolutely no cognizance of the explanations put forth in the Buddhist scriptures. His is the worst kind of baseless talk, a clear case of defamation. There are no words to describe it, no way to censure it that is not too mild. And yet men all put faith in this baseless talk of his, and without exception pay honor to his *Senchaku Shū*. As a consequence, they revere the three sutras of the Pure Land and cast all the other sutras aside; they look up to one Buddha alone, Amida of the Land of Bliss, and forget about the other Buddhas. A man such as Hōnen is in truth the archenemy of the Buddhas and the scriptures, and the foe of sage monks and ordinary men and women alike. And now his heretical teachings have spread throughout the eight regions of the country; they have penetrated every one of the ten directions.

You became quite horrified when I blamed an earlier period[76] for the disasters that have occurred in recent years. Perhaps I should cite a few examples from the past to show you that you are mistaken in your feelings.

The second volume of the *Maka Shikan* quotes a passage from the *Shih Chi* or *Records of the Historian* which says: "In the closing years of the Chou dynasty, there were persons who let their hair hang down, went about naked to the waist, and did not observe the rites and regulations."[77] The *Guketsu* commentary on the *Maka Shikan*, in the second volume, explains this passage by quoting from the *Tso Chuan* as follows: "When King P'ing of the Chou first moved his capital east to Lo-yang, he saw men by the Yi River who let their hair hang down and performed sacrifices in the fields. Someone who had great understanding said: 'In less than a hundred years the dynasty will fall, for the rites are already neglected.' "[78] From this it is evident that the portent appears first, and later the disaster itself comes about.

The *Maka Shikan* passage goes on to say: "Juan Chi[79] of the Western Chin dynasty was a man of extraordinary talent, but he let his hair grow like a mass of brambles and left his belt undone. Later, the sons of the aristocracy all imitated him, until those who behaved in a churlish and insulting manner were thought to be acting quite naturally, and those who were restrained and proper in their behavior were ridiculed as mere peasants. This was a sign that the Ssu-ma family, the rulers of the Chin dynasty, would meet with their downfall."

Similarly, the *Nittō Junrei Ki* or *Record of a Pilgrimage to China in Search of the Law* by Jikaku Daishi records that in the first year of the Hui-ch'ang era (841), Emperor Wu-tsung of the T'ang dynasty commanded the priest Ching-shuang of Chang-ching temple to transmit the Nembutsu teachings of the Buddha Amida in the various temples. Ching-shuang spent three days in each temple, going about from one temple to another without ever ceasing.[80]

In the second year of the same era, soldiers from the land of the Uighurs invaded the borders of the T'ang empire. In the third year of the same era, the regional commander in the area north of the Yellow River suddenly raised a revolt. Later, the kingdom of Tibet once more refused to obey orders from China, and the Uighurs repeatedly seized Chinese territory. On the whole, the conflicts and uprisings were like those that prevailed at the time when the Ch'in dynasty and the military leader Hsiang Yü were overthrown, and the towns and villages were devastated by fire and other disasters. What was even worse, Emperor Wu-tsung carried out a vast campaign to wipe out Buddhist teachings and destroyed a great many temples and monasteries. He was never able to put down the uprisings, and died in agony shortly after. (This is the essence of Jikaku's original passage.)

In view of these events, we should consider the fact that Hōnen was active during the reign of Emperor Gotoba, around the Kennin era (1201–1203). And what happened to Gotoba is evident before our very eyes.[81] Thus China provided an earlier example of how the Pure Land teachings brought about the fall of an emperor, and our own country offers similar proof. You should not be in doubt about the matter or consider it strange. The only thing to do now is to abandon evil ways and take up those that are good, to cut off this affliction at the source, to cut it off at the root!

The guest, looking somewhat mollified, said: Though I have not yet probed deeply into the matter, I believe I understand to some degree what you are saying. Nevertheless, both in Kyoto, the capital, and in Kamakura, the headquarters of the shogun, there are numerous eminent Buddhist leaders and key figures in the clergy. And yet none of them has so far appealed to the shogun concerning this affair or submitted a memorial to the throne. You, on the other hand, a person of humble position, think nothing of spewing out offensive accusations. Your assertions are open to question and your reasoning lacks authority.

The host said: Though I may be a person of little ability, I have reverently given myself to the study of the Mahayana. A blue fly, if it clings to the tail of a thoroughbred horse, can travel ten thousand miles, and the green ivy that twines around the tall pine can grow to a thousand feet. I was born as the son of the one Buddha, Shakyamuni, and I serve the king of scriptures, the Lotus Sutra. How could I observe the decline of the Buddhist Law and not be filled with emotions of pity and distress?

Moreover, the Nirvana Sutra states: "If even a good priest sees someone slandering the Law and disregards him, failing to reproach him, to oust him or to punish him for his offense, then that priest is betraying Buddhism. But if he takes the slanderer severely to task, drives him off or punishes him, then he is my disciple and one who truly understands my teachings."[82]

Although I may not be a "good priest," I certainly do not want to be accused of "betraying Buddhism." Therefore, in order to avoid such charges, I have cited a few general principles and given a rough explanation of the matter.

Long ago in the Gennin era (1224), petitions to the throne were submitted time and again by the two temples of Enryaku-ji on Mount Hiei and Kōfuku-ji in Nara, and as a result an Imperial command and a letter of instruction from the shogunate were handed down, ordering that the wood blocks used in printing Hōnen's *Senchaku Shū* be confiscated and brought to the Great Lecture Hall of Enryaku-ji. There they were burned in order to repay the debt owed to the Buddhas of the past, present, and future. In addition, orders were given that the menials who are attached to the Gion Shrine should dig up and destroy Hōnen's grave in Kyoto. Then, Hōnen's disciples Ryūkan, Shōkō, Jōkaku, Sasshō[83] and others were condemned by the government to exile in distant regions, and were never pardoned.

In view of these facts, how can you say that no one has submitted a complaint to the authorities concerning these matters?

The guest, continuing to speak in a mild manner, replied: One could hardly say that Hōnen is the only one who disparages sutras and speaks ill of other priests, [since you do the same thing yourself]. However, it is true that he takes the 637 Mahayana scriptures with their 2,883 volumes of text, along with all the Buddhas and bodhisattvas and the deities of the heavenly and human worlds, and urges people to "discard, close, ignore, and abandon" them. There is no doubt that these four injunctions are his very words; the meaning of the passage is quite clear. But you keep harping on this one little "flaw in the jewel" and severely slandering him for it. I do not know whether he spoke out of delusion or out of true enlightenment. Between you and Hōnen, I cannot tell which is wise and which is foolish, or determine whose assertions are right and whose are wrong.

However, you assert that all the recent disasters are to be traced to the *Senchaku Shū* of Hōnen, speaking quite volubly on that point and elaborating on the meaning of your assertion. Now surely the peace of the world and the stability of the nation are sought by both ruler and subject and desired by all the inhabitants of the country. The nation achieves prosperity through the Buddhist Law, and the validity of the Law is proven by the people who embrace it. If the nation is destroyed and the people are wiped out, then who will continue to pay reverence to the Buddhas? Who will continue to have faith in the Law? Therefore one must first of all pray for the safety of the nation and then work to establish the Buddhist Law. Now if you know of any means whereby disasters can be prevented and troubles brought to an end, I would like to hear about it.

The host said: There is no doubt that I am the foolish one—I would never dare claim to be wise. However, I would just like to quote a few passages from the scriptures. Concerning the means for insuring order in the nation, there are numerous passages in both Buddhist and non-Buddhist texts, and it would be difficult to cite them all here. Since taking up the study of Buddhism, however, I have frequently given thought to this matter, and it seems to me that prohibiting those who slander the Law and paying respect to monks who follow the Correct Way is the best way to assure stability within the nation and peace in the world at large.

In the Nirvana Sutra we read: "The Buddha said, 'With the exception of one type of person, you may offer alms to all kinds of persons and everyone will praise you.'

"Cunda[84] said, 'What do you mean when you speak of "one type of person?" '

"The Buddha replied, 'I mean the type described in this sutra as violators of the precepts.'

"Cunda spoke again, saying, 'I am afraid I still do not understand. May I ask you to explain further?'

"The Buddha addressed Cunda, saying: 'By violators of the precepts I mean the *icchantika*. In the case of all other types of persons, you may offer alms, everyone will praise you, and you will achieve great rewards.'

"Cunda spoke once more, asking, 'What is the meaning of the term *icchantika?'*

"The Buddha said, 'Cunda, suppose there should be monks or nuns, lay men or women who speak careless and evil words and slander the True Law, and that they should go on committing these grave acts without ever showing any inclination to reform or any sign of repentance in their hearts. Persons of this kind I would say are following the path of the *icchantika.*

" 'Again there may be those who commit the four grave offenses[85] or are guilty of the five cardinal sins, and who, though aware that they are guilty of serious faults, from the beginning have no trace of fear or contrition in their hearts, or if they do, give no outward sign of it. When it comes to the True Law, they show no inclination to establish it and help to protect it over the ages, but rather speak of it with malice and contempt, their words replete with error. Persons of this kind too I would say are following the path of the *icchantika*. With the exception of this one group of people called *icchantika,* however, you may offer alms to all others and everyone will praise you.' ''[86]

Elsewhere in the same sutra, the Buddha spoke in these words: "When I recall the past, I remember that I was the king of a great state in this continent of Jambudvīpa. My name was Sen'yo, and I loved and venerated the Mahayana scriptures. My heart was pure and good and had no trace of evil, jealousy or stinginess. Men of devout faith, at that time I cherished the Mahayana teachings in my heart. Once, when I heard the Brahmans slandering these teachings, I had them put to death on the spot. Men of devout faith, as a result of that action, I never thereafter fell into hell."[87]

In another passage it says: "In the past, when the Tathagata was the ruler of a nation and practiced the way of the bodhisattva, he put to death a number of Brahmans."

Again it says: "There are three degrees of killings: the lower, middle, and upper degrees. The lower degree constitutes the killing of any humble creature, from an ant to any of the various kinds of animals. (Only the killing of a bodhisattva who has deliberately chosen to be born in animal form is excluded.) As a result of a killing of the lower degree, one will fall into the realm of Hell, Hungry Ghosts, or Animals, and will suffer all the pains appropriate to a killing of the lower degree. Why should this be? Because even the animals and other humble creatures possess the roots of goodness, insignificant though those roots may be. That is why a person who kills such a creature must suffer full retribution for his offense.

"Killing any person from an ordinary mortal to an *anāgāmin*[88] constitutes what is termed the middle degree. As a consequence of such an act of killing, one will fall into the realm of Hell, Hungry Ghosts, or Animals, and will suffer all the pains appropriate to a killing of the middle degree. The upper degree of killing refers to the killing of a parent, an arhat, a person who has reached the state of *engaku,* or a bodhisattva who has completed his efforts and will never retrogress. For such a crime one will fall into the hell of incessant suffering. Men of devout faith, if someone were to kill an *icchantika,* that killing would not fall into any of the three categories just mentioned. Men of devout faith, the various Brahmans that I have said were put to death—all of them were in fact *icchantika.*"[89]

In the *Ninnō* Sutra we read: "The Buddha announced to King Prasenajit, 'Thus I entrust the protection of my teachings to the ruler of the nation rather than to the monks and nuns. Why do I do so? Because the monks and nuns do not possess the kind of power and authority that the king has.' "[90]

The Nirvana Sutra states: "Now I entrust the True Law, which is unexcelled, to the rulers, the ministers, the high officials, and the four kinds of Buddhists. If anyone should vilify the True Law, then the high officials and four kinds of Buddhists should reprimand him and bring him to order."[91]

It also states: "The Buddha said, 'Kashō,[92] it is because I was a defender of the True Law that I have now been able to attain this diamond-like body.[93] . . . Men of devout faith, defenders of the True Law need not observe the five precepts[94] or practice the rules of proper behavior. Rather they should carry knives and swords, bows and arrows, prongs and lances.' "[95]

Again the Buddha said: "Even though there may be those who observe the five precepts, they do not deserve to be called practitioners of the Mahayana. But even if one does not observe the five precepts, if he defends the True Law, then he may be called a practitioner of the Mahayana. Defenders of the True Law ought to arm themselves with knives and swords, weapons and staves. Even though they carry swords and staves, I would call them men who observe the precepts."

The Buddha likewise said: "Men of devout faith, in past ages in this very city of Kuśinagara a Buddha appeared whose name was Kangi Zōyaku Nyorai or the Buddha Joy Increasing. After this Buddha passed away, the True Law that he had taught remained in the world for countless millions of years. Finally, only forty more years were left before the Law was due to come to an end.

"At that time there was a monk named Kakutoku who observed the precepts. There were many monks at this time who violated the precepts, and when they heard this monk preaching, they all conceived evil designs in their hearts and, arming themselves with swords and staves, attacked this teacher of the Law.

"At this time the ruler of the kingdom was named Utoku. He received reports of what was happening and, in order to defend the Law, he went at once to the place where the monk was preaching the Law and fought with all his might against the evil monks who did not observe the precepts. As a result, the monk who had been preaching the Law was able to escape grievous injury. But the king received so many wounds from the knives and swords, prongs and lances, that there was not a spot on his body the size of a mustard seed that remained unharmed.

"At this time the monk Kakutoku praised the king, saying, 'Splendid, splendid! You, O king, are now a true defender of the True Law. In ages to come, this body of yours will surely become a boundless vessel of the Law!'

"At that time, the king had already heard the teachings of the Law, and he felt great joy in his heart. Thereupon his life came to an end, and he was reborn in the land of the Buddha Ashuku, where he became the principal disciple of the Buddha. Moreover, all the military leaders, citizens, and associates of the king who had fought beside him or had rejoiced in his effort were filled with an unflagging determination to achieve enlightenment, and when they died, all of them were reborn in the land of the Buddha Ashuku.

"Later, the monk Kakutoku also died, and he too was reborn in the land of the Buddha Ashuku, where he became second among the disciples who received the direct teachings of the Buddha. Thus, if the True Law is about to come to an end, this is the way one ought to support and defend it.

"Kashō, the king who lived at that time, was I myself, and the monk who preached the Law was the Buddha Kashō.[96] Kashō, those who defend the True Law enjoy this kind of boundless reward. As a consequence, I have been able to obtain the distinguishing characteristics that I possess today, to adorn myself with them, and to put on the Dharma Body that can never be destroyed."

Then the Buddha declared to the Bodhisattva Kashō: "For this reason, lay believers who wish to defend the Law should arm themselves with swords and staves and protect it in this manner.

"Men of devout faith, in the age of confusion and evil after I have passed away, the nation will fall into neglect and disorder, men will plunder and steal from one another, and the common people will be reduced to starvation. Because of hunger, many men at that time will declare their determination to leave their families and become monks. Men such as these may be called shavepates. When this crowd of shavepates see anyone who is attempting to protect the True Law, they will chase after him and drive him away, or perhaps even kill him or do him injury. That is why I now give permission for monks who observe the precepts to associate and keep company with laymen who bear swords and staves. For even though they carry swords and staves, I would call them men who observe the precepts. But although they may carry swords and staves, they should never use them to take life."

The Lotus Sutra says: "One who refuses to take faith in this sutra and instead slanders it immediately destroys the seeds for becoming a Buddha in this world. . . . After he dies, he will fall into the hell of incessant suffering."[97]

The meaning of these passages from the sutras is perfectly clear. What need is there for me to add any further explanation? If we accept the words of the Lotus Sutra, then we must understand that slandering the Mahayana scriptures is more serious than committing the five cardinal sins. Therefore one who does so will be confined in the great fortress of the hell of incessant suffering and cannot hope for release for countless kalpas. According to the Nirvana Sutra, even though you may give alms to a person who has committed one of the five cardinal sins, you must never give alms to a person who has slandered the Law. He who kills so much as an ant will fall into the three evil paths, but he who helps to eradicate slander of the Law will ascend to the state from which there can be no retrogression. Thus the passage tells us that the monk Kakutoku was reborn as the Buddha Kashō, and that King Utoku was reborn as the Buddha Shakyamuni.

The Lotus and the Nirvana sutras represent the very heart of the doctrines that Shakyamuni preached during the five periods of his teaching life. Their warnings must be viewed with the utmost gravity. Who would fail to heed them? And yet those people who forget about the Correct Way and slander the Law put more trust than ever in Hōnen's *Senchaku Shū* and grow blinder than ever in their stupidity.

Thus some of them, remembering how their master looked in life, fashion sculptures and paintings of him, while others, putting faith in his perverse teachings, carve wood blocks with which to print his offensive words. These images and writings they scatter about throughout the area within the seas,[98] carrying them beyond the cities and into the countryside until, wherever honor is paid, it is to the practices of this school, and wherever alms are given, it is to the priests of this sect.

As a result, we see people cutting off the fingers of the images of Shakyamuni and refashioning them to form the gesture appropriate to Amida, or renovating temples formerly dedicated to Yakushi, the Buddha of the Eastern Region, and fitting them with statues of Amida, the lord of the Western Land. Or we find the ceremony of copying the Lotus Sutra, which has been carried out for over four hundred years on Mount Hiei, being suspended and the copying of the three Pure Land sutras substituted in its place, or the annual lectures[99] on the doctrines of the Great Teacher T'ien-t'ai being replaced by lectures on the teachings of Shan-tao. Indeed, the slanderous people and their associates are too numerous to count! Are they not destroyers of the Buddha? Are they not destroyers of the Law? Are they not destroyers of the Priesthood? And all their heretical teachings derive from the *Senchaku Shū!*

Alas, how pitiful, that others should turn their backs on the enlightened prohibitions of the Buddha! How tragic, that they should heed the gross and deluded words of this ignorant monk! If we hope to bring order and tranquility to the world without further delay, we must put an end to these slanders of the Law that fill the country!

The guest said: If we are to put an end to these people who slander the Law and do away with those who violate the prohibitions of the Buddha, then are we to condemn them to death as described in the passages from the sutras you have just cited? If we do that, then we ourselves will be guilty of inflicting injury and death upon others, and will suffer the consequences, will we not?

In the *Daijuku* Sutra, the Buddha says: "If a person shaves his head and puts on clerical robes, then, whether that person observes the precepts or violates them, both gods and men should give him alms. In doing so, they are giving alms and support to me, for that person is my son. But if men beat and abuse that person, they are beating my son, and if they curse and insult him, they are reviling me."[100]

If we stop to consider, we must realize that, regardless of whether one is good or bad, right of wrong, if he is a priest or a monk, then he deserves to have alms and nourishment extended to him. For how could one beat and insult the son and still not cause grief and sorrow to the father? The Brahmans who beat the Buddha's disciple Maudgalyāyana to death with their staves have for a long time been sunk in the hell of incessant suffering. Because Devadatta murdered the nun Utpalavarna, he has gone on and on choking in the flames of the Avīci Hell.[101] Examples from earlier ages make the matter perfectly clear, and later ages fear this offense most of all. You speak of punishing those who slander the Law, but to do so would violate the

Buddha's prohibitions. I can hardly believe that such a course would be right. How can you justify that?

The host said: You have clearly seen the passages from the sutras that I have cited, and yet you can ask a question like that! Are they beyond the power of your mind to comprehend? Or do you fail to understand the reasoning behind them? I certainly have no intention of censuring the sons of the Buddha. My only hatred is for the act of slandering the Law. According to the teachings of the Buddhas who lived prior to Shakyamuni, slanderous priests would have incurred the death penalty. But in the sutras preached since the time of Shakyamuni, priests of this type have merely been prevented from receiving alms. Now if all the four kinds of Buddhists within the four seas and the ten thousand lands would only cease giving alms to wicked priests and instead all come over to the side of the good, then how could any more troubles rise to plague us or disasters come to confront us?

With this the guest moved off his mat in a gesture of respect, straightened the collar of his robe, and said: The Buddhist teachings vary greatly and it is difficult to investigate each doctrine in full. I have had many doubts and perplexities and have been unable to distinguish right from wrong.

Nevertheless, this work by the venerable Hōnen, the *Senchaku Shū*, does in fact exist. And it lumps together all the various Buddhas, sutras, bodhisattvas, and deities and says that one should "discard, close, ignore, and abandon" them. The meaning of the text is perfectly clear. And as a result of this, the sages have departed from the nation, the benevolent deities have left their dwelling places, hunger and thirst fill the world, and disease and pestilence spread abroad.

Now, by citing passages from a wide variety of scriptures, you have clearly demonstrated the rights and wrongs of the matter. Therefore I have completely forsaken my earlier mistaken convictions, and my ears and eyes have been opened on point after point.

There can be no doubt that all men, from the ruler down to the common people, rejoice in and desire the stability of the nation and the peace of the world. If we can quickly put an end to the alms that are given to these *icchantika* and insure that continuing support is instead given to the host of true priests and nuns, if we can still these "white waves"[102] that trouble the Ocean of the Buddha and cut down these "green groves" that overgrow the Mountain of the Law, then the world may become as peaceful as it was in the golden ages of Fu

Hsi and Shen Nung, and the nation may flourish as it did under the sage rulers Yao and Shun.[103] After that, there will be time to dip into the Waters of the Law and to decide which are shallow doctrines and which are deep, and to pay honor to the pillars and beams that support the House of the Buddha.

The host exclaimed with delight: As the proverb says, the dove has changed into a hawk, the sparrow into a clam![104] How gratifying! You have transformed yourself through your association with me, and like the bramble growing in the hemp field, you have learned to stand up straight! If you will truly give consideration to the troubles I have been describing and put entire faith in these words of mine, then the winds will blow gently, the waves will be calm, and in no time at all we will enjoy bountiful harvests.

But a person's heart may change with the times, and the nature of a thing may alter with its surroundings. Just as the moon on the water will be tossed about by the waves, or the soldiers in the vanguard will be cowed by the swords of the enemy, so, although at this moment you may say you believe in my words, I fear that later you will forget them completely.

Now if we wish first of all to bring security to the nation and to pray for our present and future lives, then we must hasten to examine and consider the situation and take measures as soon as possible to remedy it.

Why do I say this? Because, of the seven types of disasters described in the passage from the *Yakushi* Sutra that I cited earlier, five have already occurred. Only two have yet to appear, the "calamity of invasion from foreign lands" and the "calamity of revolt within one's own domain." And of the three calamities mentioned in the passage from the *Daijuku* Sutra, two have already made their appearance. Only one remains, the "disaster of warfare."

The different types of disaster and calamity enumerated in the *Konkōmyō* Sutra have arisen one after the other. Only that described as "bandits and marauders from other regions invading and plundering the nation" has yet to materialize. This is the only trouble that has not yet come. And of the seven calamities listed in the *Ninnō* Sutra, six are now upon us in full force. Only one has not yet appeared, the calamity that occurs "when enemies rise up on all four sides and invade the nation."

Moreover, as the *Ninnō* Sutra says, "When a nation becomes disordered, it is the spirits which first show signs of rampancy. Because these spirits become rampant, all the people of the nation become disordered."[105]

Now if we examine the present situation carefully in the light of this passage, we will see that the various spirits have for some time been rampant, and many of the people have perished. If the first predicted misfortune in the sutra has already occurred, as is obvious, then how can we doubt that the later disasters will follow? If, in punishment for the evil doctrines that are upheld, the troubles that have yet to appear should fall upon us one after the other, then it will be too late to act, will it not?

Emperors and kings have their foundation in the state and bring peace and order to the age; ministers and commoners hold possession of their fields and gardens and supply the needs of the world. But if bandits come from other regions to invade the nation, or if revolt breaks out within the domain and people's lands are seized and plundered, how can there be anything but terror and confusion? If the nation is destroyed and families are wiped out, then where can one flee for safety? If you care anything about your personal security, you should first of all pray for order and tranquility throughout the four quarters of the land, should you not?

It seems to me that, when people are in this world, they all fear what their lot may be in the life to come. So it is that some of them put their faith in heretical teachings, or pay honor to those who slander the Law. It distresses me that they should be so confused about right and wrong, and at the same time I feel pity that, having embraced Buddhism, they should have chosen the wrong kind. With the power of faith that is in their hearts, why must they vainly give credence to heretical doctrines? If they do not shake off these delusions that they cling to but continue to harbor false ideas, then they will quickly leave the world of the living and fall into the hell of incessant suffering.

Thus the *Daijuku* Sutra says: "Though the ruler of a state may have for countless existences in the past practiced the giving of alms, observed the precepts, and abided by the principles of wisdom, if he sees that my Law, the Dharma of the Buddha, is in danger of perishing and stands idly by without doing anything to protect it, then all the inestimable store of good causes that he has accumulated through the practices just mentioned will be entirely wiped out. . . . Before long, the ruler will fall gravely ill, and after his life has come to an end, he will be reborn in one of the major hells. . . . And the same fate will befall the ruler's consort, his heir, the high ministers of the state, the lords of cities, the village heads and generals, the magistrates of districts, and the government officials." [106]

The *Ninnō* Sutra states: "If a man destroys the teachings of the Buddha, he will have no filial sons, no harmony with his close relatives, and no aid from the heavenly deities. Disease and evil spirits will come day after day to torment him, disasters will descend on him incessantly, and misfortunes will dog him wherever he goes. And when he dies, he will fall into one of the three realms of Hell, Hungry Ghosts, or Animals. Even if he should be reborn as a human being, he will be destined to become a slave in the army. Retribution will follow as an echo follows a sound or a shadow follows a form. A person writing at night may put out the lamp, but the words he has written will still remain. It is the same with the destiny we create for ourselves in the threefold world." [107]

The second volume of the Lotus Sutra says: "One who refuses to take faith in this sutra and instead slanders it. . . . After he dies, he will fall into the hell of incessant suffering." And in the *Fukyō* chapter in the seventh volume, it says: "For a thousand kalpas they dwelt in the hell of incessant suffering and underwent great pain and torment." [108]

In the Nirvana Sutra we read: "If a man separates himself from good friends, refuses to listen to the True Law and instead embraces evil teachings, then as a result he will sink down into the hell of incessant suffering, where he will experience indescribable torment." [109]

When we examine this wide variety of sutras, we find that they all stress how grave a matter it is to slander the Law. How pitiful, that all men should go out of the gate of the True Law and enter so deep into the prison of these perverse dogmas! How stupid, that they should fall one after another into the snares of these evil doctrines, and remain for so long entangled in this net of slanderous teachings! They lose their way in these mists and miasmas, and sink down amid the raging flames of hell. How they must grieve! How they must suffer!

Therefore you must quickly reform the tenets that you hold in your heart and embrace the one true vehicle, the single good doctrine of the Lotus Sutra. If you do so, then the threefold world will all become the Buddha land, and how could a Buddha land ever decline? The regions in the ten directions will all become treasure realms, and how could a treasure realm ever suffer harm? If you live in a country that knows no decline or diminution, in a land that suffers no harm or disruption, then your body will find peace and security and your mind will be calm and untroubled. You must believe my words, heed what I say!

The guest said: Since it concerns both this life and the lives to come, who could fail to be cautious in a matter such as this? Who could fail to agree with you? Now when I examine the passages you have cited from the sutras and see exactly what the Buddha has said, I realize that slandering is a very grave offense indeed, that violating the Law is in truth a terrible sin. I have put all my faith in one Buddha alone, Amida, and rejected all the other Buddhas. I have honored the three Pure Land sutras and set aside the other sutras. But this was not due to any distorted ideas of my own conception. I was simply obeying the words of the eminent men of the past. [110] And the same is true of all the other persons in the ten directions who follow the Pure Land teachings.

But now I realize that to do so means to exhaust oneself in futile efforts in this life, and to fall into the hell of incessant suffering in the life to come. The texts you have cited are perfectly clear on this point and their arguments are detailed—they leave no room for doubt. With your kind instruction to guide me, I have been able bit by bit to dispel the ignorance from my mind.

Now I hope we may set about as quickly as possible taking measures to deal with these slanders against the Law and to bring peace to the world without delay, thus insuring that we may live in safety in this life and enjoy good fortune in the life to come. But it is not enough that I alone should accept and have faith in your words—we must see to it that others as well are warned of their errors!

RATIONALE FOR WRITING THE "RISSHŌ ANKOKU RON"

Introduction

In the first month of 1268, envoys from Kublai Khan arrived at the Dazaifu government offices in Kyushu. Proceeding to Kamakura, they presented the shogunate with a message from the Khan demanding, in veiled terms, that Japan acknowledge fealty to the Mongol Empire. The envoys were sent back without an answer, and the government began taking steps to defend the country against foreign attack.

At this time, Nichiren wrote the short work known as "The Rationale for Writing the *Risshō Ankoku Ron*" *("Ankoku Ron Gokan Yurai")* and sent it to a man named Hōkan-bō. Little is known about this man; his name indicates that he was a Buddhist priest, but he would appear to have been active in government circles. Nichiren explains the circumstances that led to his writing of the *"Risshō Ankoku Ron"* eight years earlier and points out that the arrival of the Mongol emissaries with their threatening message substantiates the prophecy of foreign invasion that he had made in that treatise.

In the tenth month of the same year, Nichiren sent letters to eleven high-ranking political and religious leaders, including the regent Hōjō Tokimune (1251–1284), the Chinese Zen priest Lanch'i Tao-lung (Rankei Dōryū, 1213–1278) of Kenchō-ji, and the Ritsu priest Ryōkan Ninshō (1217–1303) of Gokuraku-ji, pointing out that the predictions in his *"Risshō Ankoku Ron"* were now being fulfilled and demanding the opportunity to demonstrate the validity of his teachings in public religious debate. He failed to receive any response to his letters.

In the first year of the Shōka era (1257), when the reverse marker of Jupiter was in the sector of the sky with the cyclical sign *hinoto-mi*, on the twenty-third day of the eighth month, at the time when the hour of the Dog gives way to the hour of the Boar (9:00 P.M.), there occurred an earthquake of unprecedented magnitude. In the second year of the same era (1258), cyclical sign *tsuchinoe-uma*, on the first day of the eighth month, there was a great wind. In the third year (1259), cyclical sign *tsuchinoto-hitsuji*, a major famine occurred. In the first year of the Shōgen era (1259), cyclical sign *tsuchinoto-hitsuji*, disease was rampant, and throughout the four seasons of the second year (1260), cyclical sign *kanoe-saru*, the sickness continued to rage without abating. By this time more than half the ordinary citizens of the nation had been laid low by death. The rulers of the country, alarmed at this state of affairs, turned to the scriptures of Buddhism and the non-Buddhist writings for help, ordering that various prayers be offered. These, however, failed to produce the slightest effect. On the contrary, famine and disease raged more fiercely than ever.

I, Nichiren, observing this state of affairs, proceeded to consult the various Buddhist scriptures. There I discovered the reason why these prayers are without effect and on the contrary actually make the situation worse, along with passages of proof to support it. In the end I had no other recourse than to compile a work to present my findings, entitling it *"Risshō Ankoku Ron."* In the first year of the Bunnō era (1260), cyclical sign *kanoe-saru*, on the sixteenth day of the seventh month, at the hour of the Dragon (7:00–9:00 A.M.), I handed it to the lay monk Yadoya for presentation to His Lordship, the late lay priest of Saimyō-ji.[1] This I did solely that I might repay the debt of gratitude that I owe to my native land.

The essence of my work, the *"Risshō Ankoku Ron,"* is as follows. Long ago it was said that this country of Japan would be ruled by seven heavenly deities, five earthly deities, and a hundred kings, reigning one after the other in succession. During the reign of Emperor Kimmei, the thirtieth of the human sovereigns, Buddhism was for the first time introduced from the kingdom of Paekche.[2] From that time until the reign of Emperor Kammu, a period of some 260 years that saw the reigns of fifty or more sovereigns, all the various Buddhist scriptures were brought to Japan, as well as the six sects[3] of Buddhism. At this time, however, the Tendai and Shingon sects had not yet been introduced.

During the reign of Emperor Kammu, there was a young priest named Saichō, who was a disciple of Priest Gyōhyō of Yamashina Temple.[4] (He later came to be known by the title Great Teacher Dengyō.[5]) He made a thorough study of the six sects that had been introduced to Japan earlier, as well as of the Zen sect, but none of these seemed to satisfy him. Some forty years earlier, in the reign of Emperor Shōmu, a Chinese monk named Chien-chen[6] had come to Japan and brought with him the commentaries of the Great Teacher T'ien-t'ai. When Saichō read these for the first time, he came to understand in essence the true meaning of Buddhism.

In the fourth year of the Enryaku era (785), Saichō founded a temple on Mount Hiei[7] in order to insure the continuance of peace in heaven and on earth. Emperor Kammu paid honor to the new establishment, designating it as a place of worship where prayers could be offered to the guardian star of the ruler. He ceased to heed the teachings of the six sects and instead gave wholehearted allegiance to the perfect doctrines of the Tendai sect.

In the thirteenth year of the Enryaku era (794), the emperor moved the capital from Nagaoka to the city of Heian.[8] In the twenty-first year of the same era (802), on the nineteenth day of the first month, the emperor summoned fourteen learned scholars of the six sects from the seven great temples of Nara, including such priests as Gonsō and Chōyō,[9] to the temple called Takao-dera, and ordered them to engage Saichō in debate.[10] These enlightened masters of the six sects were not able to hold their own against Saichō even for a single exchange of opinions, but shut their mouths so tightly one might have mistaken them for noses. The "Five Teachings" of the Kegon sect, the "Three Periods" of the Hossō sect, the "Two Storehouses" and "Three Periods" propounded by the Sanron sect[11]—all of these doctrines were demolished by Saichō. The doctrines of the six sects not only were refuted, but in fact served to reveal that the other debaters were all guilty of slandering the Law. On the twenty-ninth day of the same month, the emperor handed down an edict criticizing the fourteen monks who had opposed Saichō. The fourteen monks in turn drew up a letter apologizing for their conduct and submitted it to the emperor.

Thereafter, one sovereign after another paid allegiance to Mount Hiei, treating it with even greater deference than a filial son shows toward his father and mother, regarding it with greater awe than the common people manifest before the might of the ruler. At times the rulers issued edicts to honor it, at other times they were obliged to give their approval to its unjust demands. We may note in particular that Emperor Seiwa [12] was able to ascend the throne as a consequence of the powerful prayers of Priest Eryō of Mount Hiei. The emperor's maternal grandfather, the Kujō Minister of the Right, for this reason submitted a written pledge of his fidelity to Mount Hiei. Minamoto no Yoritomo, the founder of the Kamakura shogunate, it will be recalled, was a descendant of Emperor Seiwa. And yet the government authorities in Kamakura, though they may or may not be following the right course in their administration, ignore and turn their back on Mount Hiei. Have they no fear of the punishment of Heaven?

Later, in the time of the Retired Emperor Gotoba, during the Kennin era (1201–1204), there appeared two men, Hōnen and Dainichi, [13] who in their arrogance believed that their understanding surpassed that of all others. Their bodies were possessed of devils, and they went about deluding the people of both high and low station throughout the country, until everyone had become a Nembutsu believer or else was hastening to join the Zen sect. Those who continued to pay respect to Mount Hiei became surprisingly few and lacking in ardor, and throughout the country, the priests who were authorities on the Lotus Sutra or the Shingon teachings found themselves ignored and rejected.

As a result, the deities Tenshō Daijin, Hachiman, and the gods of the seven shrines of the Sannō, who guard and protect Mount Hiei, as well as the other benevolent deities who protect the different parts of the nation, were no longer able to taste the flavor of the Dharma. Their power and brilliance waned, and they abandoned the country. Thus the demons were able to gain access to the nation and to bring about disasters and calamities. These disasters, as I stated [in my "Risshō Ankoku Ron"], were omens signifying that our country would in the end be destroyed by a foreign nation.

Later, in the first year of the Bun'ei era (1264), cyclical sign *kinoene,* on the fifth day of the seventh month, a comet appeared in the east, and its light shown over the whole country of Japan. This is an evil portent such as has never been seen before since the beginning of history. None of the authorities on the Buddhist scriptures or the secular writings could understand what had brought about such an ill omen. I became even more grieved and distressed. Now, nine years after I presented my work, [the *"Rissho Ankoku Ron"*], to the authorities, in the intercalary first month of this year (1268), this letter has arrived from the great kingdom of the Mongols. The events that have occurred match the predictions made in my work as exactly as do the two halves of a tally.

The Buddha left this prediction, saying: "More than one hundred years after my passing, a ruler known as the Great King Aśoka will appear in the world and will spread my relics far and wide." In the reign of King Chao, the fourth ruler of the Chou dynasty, the Grand Historian Su Yu made this prediction: "One thousand years from now, the teachings [of the Buddha] will be spread throughout this country." Crown Prince Shōtoku predicted: "After my death, when two hundred years or more have passed, the city of Heian will be established in the province of Yamashiro." And the Great Teacher T'ien-t'ai predicted: "Two hundred years or more after my death, a person will be born in an eastern country who will spread my Correct Law." All of these predictions were fulfilled to the letter.

When I, Nichiren, observed the great earthquake of the Shōka era, and the great wind and famine that occurred in the same era, as well as the major outbreak of disease that took place in the first year of the Shōgen era (1259), I made a prediction, saying: "These are omens indicating that this country of ours will be destroyed by a foreign nation." I may seem to be congratulating myself on having made such a prediction, though in fact, of course, if our country should be destroyed, it would most certainly mean the destruction of the Buddhist teachings as well.

The eminent Buddhist priests of our time seem to be of one mind with those who slander the Law. In fact, they do not even understand the true meaning of the teachings of their own sects. It is certain that, if they should receive an Imperial command or instructions from the government authorities to offer prayers in an effort to avert the evils that beset the nation, they would only make the Buddhas and deities angrier than they are already, and then the nation could not help but face ruin.

I, Nichiren, understand the steps that should be taken to remedy the situation. Other than the sage of Mount Hiei,[14] I am the only person in all of Japan who does. Just as there are not two suns or two moons, so two sages are not to be found standing side by side. If these words of mine are false, then may I be punished by the Ten Goddesses *(rākṣasī)*, the ten daughters of the demon mother who protect this Lotus Sutra that I embrace. I say all this solely for the sake of the nation, for the sake of the Law, for the sake of others, not for my own sake. I will be calling upon you in person, and so I am informing you of this. If you do not heed my advice, you will surely regret it later.

Respectfully,
Nichiren

Bun'ei era, fifth year (1268), cyclical sign tsuchinoe-tatsu, *fourth month, fifth day*

POSTSCRIPT TO THE "RISSHŌ ANKOKU RON"

Introduction

In 1269, Mongol emissaries once more arrived at the Dazaifu, the government headquarters in Kyushu, pressing for an answer to their earlier demands. Nichiren is believed to have sent off another round of letters to high officials, which again failed to elicit a response. The brief "Postscript to the *'Risshō Ankoku Ron'* " (*Risshō Ankoku Ron Okugaki*) which follows, dated the eighth day of the twelfth month of 1269, was appended to a copy of the *"Risshō Ankoku Ron"* which he wrote out himself, and warns that the prophecies set forth in that document more than nine years earlier are now coming true.

I compiled the above work in the first year of the Bunnō era (1260), when the reverse marker of Jupiter was in the sector of the sky with the cyclical sign *kanoe-saru*. That is, I began the work during the Shōka era (1257–1258) and completed it in the first year of the Bunnō era.

In the first year of the Shōka era (1257), cyclical sign *hinoto-mi,* on the twenty-third day of the eighth month, at the time when the hour of the Dog gives way to the hour of the Boar (9:00 P.M.), there was a severe earthquake. Observing the event, I began compiling the work. Later, in the first year of the Bunnō era (1260), cyclical sign *kanoe-saru,* on the sixteenth day of the seventh month, I presented it to His Lordship, the late lay monk of Saimyō-ji, by way of Yadoya Zemmon. Still later, in the first year of the Bun'ei era (1264), cyclical sign *kinoe-ne,* on the fifth day of the seventh month, when a great comet appeared, I became even more certain of the origins of these disasters. Then, on the eighteenth day of the intercalary first month of the fifth year of the Bun'ei era (1268), cyclical sign *tsuchinoe-tatsu,* nine years after the first year of the Bunnō era, when I submitted the *"Risshō Ankoku Ron,"* a letter came from the great kingdom of the Mongols that lies to the west, threatening to attack our country. Again, in the sixth year of the same era (1269), a second letter arrived. Thus the prediction that I made in my memorial [the *"Risshō Ankoku Ron"*] has already proved to be true. In view of this, we may suppose that the predictions I made will continue to come true in the future as well.

This work of mine has now been substantiated by fact. But this has in no regard happened because of my powers. Rather it has come about as a response to the true words contained in the Lotus Sutra.

Copied on the eighth day of the twelfth month of the sixth year of the Bun'ei era (1269), cyclical sign tsuchinoto-mi.

THE OPENING OF THE EYES

Introduction

Completed in the second month of 1272, "The Opening of the Eyes" *(Kaimoku Shō)* is, in terms of chronology, the second of Nichiren's five major works. The eyes that are to be opened are those of the blind person, or humanity as a whole; what they are to be opened to are the true teaching and its true teacher. The work describes the role Nichiren played in championing the supremacy of the Lotus Sutra and the part he played in spreading its teachings, as he himself envisioned and experienced it.

The work was written on Sado Island to which he had been exiled after the Tatsunokuchi Persecution of 1271. His life on this forbidding island was full of hardship; his hut was open to wind and snow and he lacked food, clothing, and writing materials. In addition to his physical suffering he was greatly troubled by the news that many of his followers in Kamakura had abandoned their faith. Feeling himself constantly haunted by the shadow of death, he wrote this treatise to encourage his disciples as though it were his last will and testament.

Nichiren later described his motivations for writing the work in his "On Various Actions of the Priest Nichiren" *(Shuju Onfurumai Gosho):* "After everyone had gone, I began to put into shape a work in two volumes, called 'The Opening of the Eyes,' which I had been working on since the eleventh month of the previous year. I wanted to record the wonder [of my enlightenment] in case I should be beheaded. The essential message in this work is that the destiny of Japan depends solely upon me. A house without pillars collapses and a person without a soul is dead. I am the soul of the people of Japan."

Nichiren begins this essay with the words: "There are three categories of people that all men and women should respect. They are the sovereign, the teacher, and the parent." These three categories are equated with the three virtues that are the attributes of the sovereign, teacher, and parent and in turn are the qualifications of a Buddha. The virtue of the sovereign is the ability to protect all living beings; the virtue of the teacher is the ability to lead all to enlightenment, and the virtue of the parent is the possession of a compassion that will nurture and maintain them. These three virtues constitute a theme that runs throughout this essay and at the conclusion of the second volume of this work Nichiren declares: "I, Nichiren, am sovereign, teacher, father, and mother to all the people of Japan."

At the outset Nichiren discusses Confucianism, Taoism, Brahmanism, Hinayana Buddhism, and provisional Mahayana Buddhism, and then moves on to the Lotus Sutra. He attributes the disasters ravaging Japan to the failure by others to recognize the supremacy of the Lotus Sutra. Here he distinguishes the theoretical teaching (the first half of the sutra) and the essential teaching (the latter half of the sutra), in which Shakyamuni Buddha proclaims that he first attained enlightenment in an unfathomably remote past. Nichiren states that the Buddha himself predicted that the Lotus Sutra was "the most difficult to believe and the most difficult to understand." Nichiren was convinced that he himself must propagate the Lotus Sutra in spite of the persecution that he knew he would incur. He realized that his followers might doubt him because of the failure of the gods to protect a votary of the Lotus Sutra. Therefore he emphasized that: "This doubt lies at the heart of the pieces I am writing. And because it is the most important concern of my entire life, I will raise it again and again here and emphasize it more than ever, before I attempt to answer it."

The second part of "The Opening of the Eyes" discusses the *Yujutsu* and the *Juryō* (fifteenth and sixteenth) chapters of the Lotus Sutra, where Shakyamuni reveals that he had attained enlightenment in the indescribably remote past, and that all the other Buddhas of other sutras are his emanations and all the bodhisattvas his disciples. This occasions great doubt and consternation among those who are listening to him. Just as Shakyamuni was doubted by his disciples, so Nichiren is doubted by his followers who cannot understand why he has been exiled and suffered so many persecutions.

Nichiren explains that each sutra has its own claim to excellence; he gives examples of statements within the sutras that claim superiority to other works. But the Lotus Sutra alone declares that it is supreme among all sutras, and Nichiren reconfirms its supremacy. The Lotus Sutra speaks of three powerful enemies of the sutra and prophesies opposition and hostility toward the sutra. All this Nichiren had himself encountered; all this is predicted in the sutra. He writes: "Let the gods forsake me. Let all persecutions assail me. Still I will give my life for the sake of the Law. . . . I will be the Pillar of Japan. I will be the Eyes of Japan. I will be the Great Ship of Japan. This is my vow and I will never forsake it!" He is concerned only with being able to carry out his mission.

At the conclusion of this treatise Nichiren explains that there are two ways to propagate the Lotus Sutra: *shōju,* or gentle arguments, and *shakubuku,* or strict refutation. Here Nichiren argues that both methods should be used, because there are two kinds of countries, those whose people are ignorant, and those whose people deliberately go against the Law. But Japan, as a nation that slanders the Lotus Sutra, requires the *shakubuku* method.

PART ONE

There are three categories of people that all men and women should respect. They are the sovereign, the teacher, and the parent. There are three types of doctrines that are to be studied. They are Confucianism, Brahmanism, and Buddhism.

Confucianism describes the Three Rulers, the Five Emperors, and the Three Kings,[1] which it calls the Heaven-Honored Ones. These men are depicted as the heads of the government officials and the pillars of the populace. In the age before the Three Rulers, people lived like animals and did not even know who their own fathers were. But from the time of the Five Emperors on, they learned to identify both their father and mother and to treat them according to the dictates of filial piety. Thus Shun, the last of the Five Emperors, served his father with reverence, though the latter was stubborn and hard-headed. Also, the governor of P'ei, after he became the first emperor of the Han dynasty, continued to pay great respect to his father, the Venerable Sire. King Wu[2] of the Chou dynasty made a wooden image of his father, the Earl of the West, and Ting Lan[3] fashioned a statue of his mother. All of these men are models of filial piety.

The high minister Pi Kan,[4] seeing that the Yin dynasty was on the path to ruin, strongly admonished the ruler, though it cost him his head. Hung Yen,[5] finding that his lord, Duke Yi, had been killed, cut open his own stomach and inserted the duke's liver in it before he died. These men may serve as models of loyalty.

Yin Shou was the teacher of Emperor Yao, Wu Ch'eng was the teacher of Emperor Shun, T'ai-kung Wang[6] was the teacher of King Wen, and Lao Tzu was the teacher of Confucius.[7] These teachers are known as the Four Sages. Even the Heaven-Honored Ones bow their heads to them in respect, and all people press their palms together in reverence. Sages such as these have left behind writings that run to over three thousand volumes in such works as the *Three Records, Five Canons,* and *Three Histories.*[8] But all these writings in the end do not advance beyond the three mysteries. The first of the three mysteries is Being. This is the principle taught by the Duke of Chou and others. The second mystery is Non-Being, which was expounded by Lao Tzu. The third is Both Being and Non-Being, which is the mystery set forth by Chuang Tzu. Mystery denotes darkness. Some say that, if we ask what existed before our ancestors were born, we will find that life was born out of the primal force, while others declare that eminence and obscurity, joy and sorrow, right and wrong, gain and loss occur simply as part of the natural order.

These are theories that are cleverly argued, but which fail to take cognizance of either the past or the future. Mystery, as we have seen, means darkness or obscurity, and it is for this reason that it is called mystery. It is a theory that deals with matters only in terms of the present. Speaking in terms of the present, the Confucians declare that one should abide by the principles of benevolence and righteousness[9] and thereby insure safety to oneself and peace and order to the state. If one departs from these principles, they say, then one's family will be doomed and one's house overthrown. But although the wise and worthy men who preach this doctrine are acclaimed as sages, they know nothing more about the past than an ordinary person unable to see his own back, and they understand as little about the future as a blind man who cannot see what lies in front of him.

If, in terms of the present, one brings order to his family, carries out the demands of filial piety, and practices the five constant virtues of benevolence, righteousness, propriety, wisdom, and good faith, then his associates will respect him and his name will become known throughout the country. If there is a wise ruler on the throne, he will invite such a man to become his minister or his teacher, or may even cede his position to him. Heaven too will come to protect and watch over such a man. Such were the so-called Five Elders[10] who gathered about and assisted King Wen and King Wu of the Chou dynasty, or the twenty-eight generals of Emperor Kuang-wu of the Later Han, who were likened to the twenty-eight constellations of the sky.[11] But since such a man knows nothing about the past or the future, he cannot assist his parents, his sovereign, or his teacher in making provisions for their future lives, and he is therefore unable to repay the debt he owes them. Such a person is not a true wise man or sage.

Confucius declared that there were no wise men or sages in his country, but that in the land to the west there was one named Buddha who was a sage.[12] This indicates that non-Buddhist teachings should be regarded as the first step toward Buddhist doctrine. Confucians first taught the doctrine of propriety and music[13] so that, when the Buddhist writings were brought to China, the concepts of the precepts, meditation, and wisdom[14] could be more readily grasped. They taught the ideals of ruler and minister so that the distinction between superior and subordinate could be made clear, they taught the ideal of parenthood so that the importance of filial piety could be appreciated, and they explained the ideal of the teacher so that men might be taught to follow.

The Great Teacher Miao-lo writes: "The propagation of Buddhism truly depends on this. The doctrines of propriety and music must first be set forth, after which the principles of truth can be introduced."[15] T'ien-t'ai states: "In the *Konkōmyō* Sutra it is recorded that 'All the good teachings that exist in the world derive from this sutra. To have a profound knowledge of this world is itself Buddhism.' "[16] In the *Maka Shikan* we read: "I, the Buddha, have sent three sages to teach the people of China."[17] In the *Guketsu,* Miao-lo's commentary on the *Maka Shikan,* we read: "The *Shōjōhōgyō* Sutra states that Bodhisattva Gakkō appeared in that land under the name Yen Hui, Bodhisattva Kōjō appeared there as Confucius, and Bodhisattva Kashō appeared as Lao Tzu. Since the sutra is speaking from the point of view of India, it refers to China as 'that land.' "[18]

Secondly, we come to the non-Buddhist teachings of India. In Brahmanism we find the two deities Śiva, who has three eyes and eight arms, and Viṣṇu. They are hailed as the loving father and compassionate mother of all living beings and are also called Heaven-Honored and sovereign. In addition, there are three men, Kapila, Ulūka, and Ṛṣabha,[19] who are known as the three ascetics. These ascetics lived somewhere around eight hundred years before the time of the Buddha. The teachings expounded by the three ascetics are known as the Four Vedas, and number sixty thousand works.

Later, in the time of the Buddha, there were the six non-Buddhist teachers,[20] who studied and transmitted these various non-Buddhist scriptures and acted as tutors to the kings of the five regions of India.[21] Their teachings split into ninety-five or ninety-six different lines, forming sect after sect. The banners of their pride were lifted up higher than the highest heaven of the threefold world, and their dogmatic rigidity was harder than metal or stone. But in their skill and depth of understanding, they surpassed anything known in Confucianism. They were able to look into the past and perceive two, three, or even seven existences, a period of eighty thousand kalpas, and they could likewise know what would happen eighty thousand kalpas in the future. As the fundamental principle of their doctrine, some of these sects taught that causes produce effects, others taught that causes do not produce effects, while still others taught that causes both do and do not produce effects. Such were the basic doctrines of these non-Buddhist schools of thought.

The devout followers of the non-Buddhist teachings observe the five precepts[22] and the ten good precepts,[23] practice a lesser form of meditation and, ascending through the worlds of form and formlessness,[24] believe they have attained nirvana when they reach the highest level of the threefold world. But although they make their way upward bit by bit like an inchworm, they fall back from the highest level and descend instead into the three evil paths. Not a single one succeeds in remaining on the level of Heaven, though they believe that once a person has attained that level, he will never descend from it. Each approves and practices the doctrines taught by his teacher and stoutly abides by them. Thus some of them bathe three times a day in the Ganges even on cold winter days, while others pull out the hairs on their head, fling themselves against rocks, expose themselves to fire, burn their bodies, or go about stark naked. Again there are those who believe they can gain good fortune by sacrificing many horses, or who burn grasses and trees, or make obeisance to every tree they encounter.

Erroneous teachings such as these are too numerous to be counted. Their adherents pay as much respect and honor to the teachers who propound them as the various deities pay to the god Taishaku or the court ministers pay to the ruler of the empire. But not a single person who adheres to these ninety-five types of higher or lower teachings ever escapes from the cycle of birth and death. Those who follow teachers of the better sort will, after two or three rebirths, fall into the evil states of existence, while those who follow evil teachers will fall into the evil states in their very next rebirth.

And yet the final conclusion of these non-Buddhist teachings constitutes an important means of entry into Buddhism. Some of them state, "A thousand years from now, the Buddha will appear in the world,"[25] while others state, "A hundred years from now, the Buddha will appear in the world."[26] The Nirvana Sutra remarks: "All scriptures or teachings, from whatever source, are ultimately the revelation of Buddhist truth. They are not non-Buddhist teachings."[27] And in the Lotus Sutra it is written, "They will display the three poisons and appear to cherish wrong views. In this way, by skillful means, my disciples save the people."[28]

Thirdly, we come to Buddhism. One should know that the Enlightened One, the Buddha, is a Great Teacher for all living beings, a Great Eye for them, a Great Pillar, a Great Helmsman, a Great Field of Good Fortune.[29] The Four Sages and Three Ascetics of the Confucian and Brahmanical scriptures and teachings are referred to as sages, but in fact they are no more than common mortals who have not yet been able to eradicate the three categories of illusion.[30] They are referred to as wise men, but in fact they are no more than children who cannot understand the principles of cause and effect. With their teachings for a ship, could one ever cross over the great sea of birth and death? With their teachings for a bridge, could one ever escape from the maze of the six paths? But the Buddha, our Great Teacher, has advanced beyond even the higher states of rebirth,[31] let alone the lower cycle of birth and death. He is able to wipe out the very root of fundamental ignorance,[32] let alone the petty delusions of thought and desire that are like branches and leaves.

This Buddha, from the time of his enlightenment at the age of thirty until his entry into nirvana when he was eighty, expounded his sacred teachings for a period of fifty years. Each word, each phrase he spoke is the truth; not a sentence, not a verse was uttered in error. The words of the sages and wise men preserved in the scriptures and teachings of Confucianism and Brahmanism, as we have noted, are free of error, and the words match the spirit in which they were spoken. But how much more true is this in the case of the Buddha, who from countless kalpas in the past has never spoken in error! In comparison to the non–Buddhist scriptures and teachings, the doctrines that he expounded over a period of fifty years represent the Great Vehicle, the true words of the Great Man. Everything that he preached, from the dawn of his enlightenment until the evening that he entered into nirvana, is none other than the truth.

The doctrines that the Buddha taught over a period of fifty years number eighty thousand.[33] They fall into various categories such as Hinayana works and Mahayana works, provisional and true sutras, exoteric and esoteric teachings, detailed and rough discourses, truths and fallacies, correct and incorrect views. But among these, the Lotus Sutra represents the correct teachings of Shakyamuni Buddha, the true words of the Buddhas of the ten directions in the past, present, and future. The sutras, numerous as the sands of the Ganges, that the Buddha preached during the first forty or so years of his teaching life, belong to the time when, as the Buddha said, he had "not yet revealed the truth."[34] The eight years during which he preached the Lotus Sutra he called the time when he "now must reveal the truth."[35] Thus Tahō Buddha came forth from the earth to testify that "All that you have expounded is the truth,"[36] and the Buddhas that are emanations of Shakyamuni gathered together and extended their tongues up to the Brahma Heaven in testimony.[37] These words are perfectly clear, perfectly understandable, brighter than the sun on a clear day or the full moon at midnight. Look up to them and believe them, and when you turn away, cherish them in your heart!

The Lotus Sutra contains two important teachings.[38] The Kusha, Jōjitsu, Ritsu, Hossō, and Sanron sects have never heard even so much as the name of these teachings. The Kegon and Shingon sects, on the other hand, have surreptitiously incorporated these doctrines and made them the heart of their own teachings. The doctrine of *ichinen sanzen* is found in only one place, hidden in the depths of the *Juryō* chapter of the essential teaching of the Lotus Sutra. The Bodhisattvas Nāgārjuna and Vasubandhu were aware of it but did not bring it forth into the light. The Great Teacher T'ien-t'ai alone embraced it and kept it ever in mind.

The concept of *ichinen sanzen* begins with an understanding of the mutual possession of the Ten Worlds or states of existence. But the Hossō and Sanron sects speak only of eight worlds[39] and know nothing of the entirety of the Ten Worlds, much less of the concept of their mutual possession. The Kusha, Jōjitsu, and Ritsu sects derive their teachings from the *Agon* sutras. They are aware only of the six worlds, the six lower states of existence, and know nothing of the other four worlds that represent the higher levels of existence. They declare that in all the ten directions there is only one Buddha, and do not preach that there is a Buddha in any of the ten directions. Of the principle that "All sentient beings possess the Buddha nature,"[40] they of course say nothing at all. They refuse to acknowledge that even a single person possesses the Buddha nature. In spite of this, one will sometimes hear members of the Ritsu and Jōjitsu sects declaring that there are Buddhas in all the ten directions or that all beings possess the Buddha nature. This is because, at some time since the passing away of the Buddha, the men of these sects have appropriated these doctrines of Mahayana Buddhism and incorporated them into the teachings of their own sect.

Similarly, in the period before the appearance of Buddhism, the proponents of Brahmanism were not so bound up in their own views. But after the appearance of the Buddha, when they had listened to and observed the Buddhist religion, they became aware of the short-comings of their own teachings. They then conceived the clever idea of appropriating Buddhist teachings and incorporating them into the doctrines of their own sect, and as a result they fell into even deeper error than before. These are examples of the type of heretical teachings known as *fubukkyō* and *gakubuppōjō*.[41]

The same thing occurred in the case of China. Before Buddhism was brought to China, Confucianism and Taoism were rather naive and childish affairs. But in the Later Han, Buddhism was introduced to China and challenged the native doctrines. In time, as Buddhism became more popular, there were certain Buddhist monks who, be-cause they had broken the precepts, were forced to return to secular life, or who elected to join forces with the native creeds. Through such men, Buddhist doctrines were introduced and surreptitiously incorporated by the Confucian and Taoist sects.

In volume five of the *Maka Shikan* we read: "These days there are many devilish monks who renounce their vows and return to lay life. Fearing that they will be punished for their action, they then go over to the side of the Taoists. Hoping to gain fame and profit, they speak extravagantly of the merits of Lao Tzu and Chuang Tzu, usurping Buddhist concepts and reading them into the Taoist scriptures. They twist what is lofty and force it into a mean context, they destroy what is exalted and drag it down among the base, striving to put the two on an equal level."[42]

Miao-lo, in his *Guketsu,* comments on this passage as follows: "Though they are monks, they destroy the teachings of Buddhism. Some renounce their vows and return to lay life, as Wei Yüan-sung[43] did. Then, as laymen, they work to destroy the teachings of Buddhism. Men of this kind steal and usurp the correct teachings of Buddhism and use them to supplement and bolster the heretical writings. The passage on 'twisting what is lofty . . . ,' means that, adopting the outlook of the Taoists, they try to place Buddhism and Taoism on the same level, to make equals of truth and falsehood, though reason tells us that this could never be. Having once been followers of Buddhist teachings, they steal what is correct and use it to bolster what is erroneous. They twist the lofty doctrines of the twelve divisions[44] and eighty thousand writings of the Buddhist canon and force them into the mean context of Lao Tzu's two chapters and five thousand words, using them to interpret the base and erroneous words of that text. This is what is meant by 'destroying what is exalted and dragging it down among the base.' "[45] These comments should be carefully noted, for they explain the meaning of the foregoing description of events.

The same sort of thing happened within Buddhism itself. Buddhism was introduced to China during the Yung-p'ing era (58–75 A.D.) of the Later Han dynasty, and in time replaced the Confucian and Taoist teachings as the orthodox doctrine of the land. But differences of opinion developed within the orthodox doctrine, resulting in the so-called three schools of the south and seven schools of the north,[46] which sprang up here and there like so many orchids or chrysanthemums. In the time of the Ch'en and Sui dynasties, however, the Great Teacher T'ien-t'ai overcame these various schools and returned Buddhism once more to its primary objective of saving all living beings.

Later, the Hossō and Shingon schools of Buddhism were introduced from India, and the Kegon school also made its appearance. Among these schools, the Hossō school set itself up as an arch rival of the T'ien-t'ai school, because their teachings are contradictory to each other like fire and water. Later, when Hsüan-tsang and Tz'u-en,[47] the founders of the Hossō school in China, closely examined the works of T'ien-t'ai, they came to realize that the views of their own school were in error. Although they did not openly repudiate their own school, it appears that in their hearts they switched their allegiance to the T'ien-t'ai teachings.

From the beginning the Kegon and Shingon schools were both provisional schools based upon provisional sutras. But Shan-wu-wei and Chin-kang-chih,[48] who introduced the esoteric teachings to China, usurped the T'ien-t'ai doctrine of *ichinen sanzen* and made it the core of the teachings of their school, adding the practice of mudras and mantras and convincing themselves that their teachings surpassed T'ien-t'ai's. As a result, students of Buddhism, unaware of the real facts, came to believe that the doctrine of *ichinen sanzen* was to be found in the *Dainichi* Sutra that had been brought from India. Similarly, in the time of the Kegon patriarch Ch'eng-kuan,[49] the T'ien-t'ai doctrine of *ichinen sanzen* was surreptitiously incorporated and used to interpret the passage in the *Kegon* Sutra that reads, "The mind is like a skilled painter."[50] People are unaware that this is what happened.

In the case of our own country of Japan, Kegon and the other sects that comprised the six Nara sects were introduced to Japan before the Tendai and Shingon sects. The Kegon, Sanron, and Hossō sects argued and contended, as inimical to one another as water and fire. When the Great Teacher Dengyō appeared in Japan, he not only exposed the errors of the six Nara sects, but also made it clear that the Shingon sect had stolen the principles of the Lotus Sutra as expounded by T'ien-t'ai and made them the heart of the teachings of its own sect. The Great Teacher Dengyō called upon the leaders of the other sects to set aside their arbitrary views and interpretations and to examine matters solely in the light of the scriptures themselves. As a result, he was able to defeat eight eminent monks of the six Nara sects, then twelve monks, then fourteen, then over three hundred, including the Great Teacher Kōbō.[51] Soon there was not a single person in all Japan who did not acknowledge allegiance to the Tendai sect, and the great temples of Nara, the Shingon temple Tō-ji in Kyoto, and other temples throughout all the provinces became subordinate to the head temple of the Tendai sect at Mount Hiei. The Great Teacher Dengyō also made it clear that the founders of the various other sects of Buddhism in China, by acknowledging allegiance to the doctrines of the Great Teacher T'ien-t'ai, had escaped committing the error of slandering the true teachings of Buddhism.

Later, however, conditions in the world declined and men became increasingly shallow in wisdom. They no longer studied or understood the profound doctrines of the Tendai sect, and the other sects became more and more firmly attached to their prejudiced views.

Eventually, the six Nara sects and the Shingon sect turned upon and attacked the Tendai sect. The latter, growing ever weaker, in the end found that it was no match for the other sects. To aggravate the situation, absurd new sects such as Zen and Jōdo appeared and began attacking the Tendai sect as well, and more and more of its lay believers transferred their allegiance to these unorthodox teachings. In the end, even those monks who were looked up to as the most eminent leaders of the Tendai sect all admitted defeat and lent their support to the heretical sects. Not only Tendai but Shingon and the six Nara sects as well were forced to yield their lands and estates to the new heretical sects, and the true teachings [of the Lotus Sutra] fell into oblivion. As a result, the Sun Goddess, the God Hachiman, the Mountain King of Mount Hiei, and the other benevolent deities who guard the nation, no longer able to taste the flavor of the true teachings, departed from the land. Demons came forward to take their place, and it became apparent that the nation was doomed.

Here I would like to state my humble opinion that the teachings expounded by the Buddha Shakyamuni during the first forty or so years of his teaching differ markedly from those expounded in the Lotus Sutra during the last eight years of his life. Contemporary scholars have already expressed the opinion, and it is my conviction as well, that the chief difference lies in the fact that the Lotus Sutra teaches that persons in the two realms of *shōmon* and *engaku* can attain Buddhahood, and that the Buddha Shakyamuni in reality attained enlightenment at an inconceivably distant time in the past.

When we examine the Lotus Sutra, we see that it predicts that Śāriputra will become the Flower Light Tathagata, that Mahākāśyapa will become the Light Bright Tathagata, Subhūti will become the Wonderful Form Tathagata, Kātyāyana will become the Jāmbunada Golden Light Tathagata, Maudgalyāyana will become the Tamālapattra Sandalwood Fragrance Buddha, Pūrṇa will become the Law Bright Tathagata, Ānanda will become the Mountain Sea Wisdom Unrestricted Power King Buddha, Rāhula will become the Stepping on Seven Treasure Flowers Tathagata,[52] the five hundred and seven hundred *shōmon* disciples will become the Universal Brightness Tathagatas, the two thousand *shōmon* who have more to learn or do not have more to learn will become the Treasure Form Tathagatas, the nuns Mahāprajāpatī and Yaśodharā will become the Tathagatas Gladly Seen by All Sentient Beings and Form Resplendent with Ten Million Lights respectively.[53]

Thus, if we examine the Lotus Sutra, we will realize that these persons are worthy of great honor. But when we search through the scriptures containing the teachings expounded in the periods previous to the Lotus Sutra, we find to our regret that the situation is far different.

The Buddha Shakyamuni, the World-Honored One, is a man of truthful words. Therefore he is designated the Sage and the Great Man. In the non-Buddhist scriptures of India and China there are also persons called worthy men, sages, or heavenly ascetics because they speak words of truth. But because the Buddha surpasses all these, he is known as the Great Man.

When he expounded the Lotus Sutra, the Buddha said that "the Buddhas appear in this world for one great reason."[54] He also said, "In these more than forty years I have not yet revealed the truth,"[55] that "The World-Honored One has long expounded his doctrines and now must reveal the truth," and that, "Honestly discarding the provisional teachings, I will expound the supreme Way."[56] Tahō Buddha added his testimony to the words of the Buddha, and the emanations of the Buddha put forth their tongues as a token of assent. Who, then, could possibly doubt that Śāriputra will in the future become the Flower Light Tathagata, that Mahākāśyapa will become the Light Bright Tathagata, or that the other predictions made by the Buddha will come true?

Nevertheless, all the sutras preceding the Lotus Sutra also represent the true words of the Buddha. The *Kegon* Sutra states: "The Great Medicine King Tree, which is the wisdom of the Buddha, has only two places where it will not grow and bring benefit to the world. It will not grow if it falls into the vast void which is the deep pit of the *shōmon* and the *engaku,* or if it is drowned in the profoundly heretical and passion-bound waters of those unworthy beings who destroy the roots of goodness within themselves."[57]

This passage may be explained as follows. In the Himalaya there is a huge tree that has numberless roots. It is called the Great Medicine King Tree and is the monarch of all the trees that grow in the continent of Jambudvīpa.[58] It measures 168,000 *yojana*[59] in height. All the other trees and plants of Jambudvīpa depend upon the roots, branches, flowers, and fruit of this tree to attain their own flowering and fruition. Therefore this tree is employed as a metaphor for the Buddha nature, and the various other trees and plants stand for all the sentient beings of the world. But this great tree will not grow in a fiery pit or in the watery circle. The fiery pit is used as a metaphor for the state of mind of the *shōmon* and the *engaku,* and the watery circle[60] is used as a metaphor for the life-condition of men of incorrigible disbelief *(icchantika).* The scripture is saying that these two categories of beings will never attain Buddhahood.

The *Daijuku* Sutra states: "There are two types of persons who are destined to die and not to be reborn, and who in the end will never be able to understand or repay their obligations. One is the *shōmon* and the other is the *engaku.* Suppose that a person falls into a deep pit. That person will be unable to benefit himself or to benefit others. The *shōmon* and the *engaku* are like this. They fall into the pit of nirvana and can benefit neither themselves nor others."[61]

The more than three thousand volumes of Confucian and Taoist literature of China on the whole stress two principles, namely, filial piety and loyalty to the sovereign. But loyalty is nothing more than an extension of filial piety. Filial piety may be described as lofty. Though heaven is lofty, it is no loftier than the ideal of filial piety. Filial piety may be called deep. Though earth is deep, it is no deeper than filial piety. Sages and worthy men are the product of filial piety. It goes without saying, therefore, that persons who study the teachings of Buddhism must also observe the ideal of filial piety and understand and repay their obligations. The disciples of the Buddha must without fail understand the four types of obligation[62] and know how to repay them.

In addition, Śāriputra, Mahākāśyapa and the other disciples, who belonged to the two realms of *shōmon* and *engaku,* carefully observed the two hundred and fifty precepts[63] and the three thousand rules of conduct,[64] practiced the three types of meditation,[65] carried out the teachings of the *Agon* sutras, and freed themselves from the illusions of thought and desire in the threefold world. They should therefore have been models in the understanding and repaying of obligations.

And yet the Buddha declared that they were men who did not understand obligation. He said this because, when a man leaves his parents and home and becomes a monk, he should always have as his goal the salvation of his father and mother. But these men belonged to the two realms of *shōmon* and *engaku,* and although they thought they had attained nirvana for themselves, they did nothing to benefit others. And even if they had done a certain amount to benefit others, they had led their parents to a path whereby they could never attain Buddhahood. Thus, contrary to what one might expect, they became known as men who did not understand their obligations.

In the Vimalakirti Sutra we read: "Vimalakīrti once more questioned Monju, saying, 'What are the seeds of Buddhahood?' Monju replied, 'All the delusions and defilements are the seeds of Buddhahood. Even though a person commits the five cardinal sins and is condemned to the hell of incessant suffering, he is still capable of aspiring to the lofty status of Buddhahood.' "

The same sutra also says: "Good listeners, let me give you a metaphor. The plains and highlands will never bring forth the stems and blossoms of the lotus or the water lily. But the muddy fields that are low-lying and damp—that is where you will find these flowers growing."

It also says: "One who has already become an arhat and achieved the level of truth that goes with arhatship[66] can never conceive the desire to attain Buddhahood or to realize the Buddha nature in himself. He is like a man who has destroyed the five sensory organs and therefore can never again enjoy the five delights that go with them."[67]

The point of this sutra is that the three poisons of greed, anger, and stupidity can become the seeds of Buddhahood, and the five cardinal sins of killing one's father, etc., can likewise become the seeds of Buddhahood. Even if the high plains should bring forth lotus flowers, the two states of *shōmon* and *engaku* would never lead to Buddhahood. The text is saying that, when the goodness of these two states is compared with the evils of the state of common delusion, it will be found that, though the evils of common delusion can lead to Buddhahood, the virtue of the *shōmon* and the *engaku* never can. The various Hinayana sutras censure evil and praise virtue. But this sutra, the Vimalakirti, condemns the virtue of the *shōmon* and the *engaku* and praises the evil of the common mortal. It would almost appear that it is not a Buddhist scripture at all, but rather the teachings of some non-Buddhist school. But the point is that it wants to make absolutely clear that the *shōmon* and the *engaku* can never become Buddhas.

The *Hōdō Darani* Sutra states: "Monju said to Śāriputra, 'Can a withered tree put forth new blossoms? Can a mountain stream turn and flow back to its source? Can a shattered rock join itself together again? Can a scorched seed send out sprouts?' Śāriputra replied, 'No.' Monju said, 'If these things are impossible, then why do you come with joy in your heart and ask me if Buddhahood has been predicted for you in the future?' "[68]

The passage means that, just as a withered tree puts forth no blossoms, a mountain stream never flows backward, a shattered rock cannot be joined, and a scorched seed cannot sprout, so those in the two states of *shōmon* and *engaku* can never attain Buddhahood. In their case the seeds of Buddhahood have been scorched.

In the *Daibon Hannya* Sutra we read: "All you heavenly beings, if you have not yet conceived a desire for Buddhahood, now is the time to do so. If you should once enter the realm of *shōmon,* you would no longer be capable of conceiving such a desire for Buddhahood. Why is this? Because you would be outside the world of birth and death."[69] This passage indicates that the Buddha is not pleased with the persons in the two realms of *shōmon* and *engaku* because they do not conceive the desire for Buddhahood, but he is pleased with the heavenly beings because they do conceive such a desire.

The *Shuryōgon* Sutra states: "If a person who has committed the five cardinal sins should hear of this resolute meditation and should conceive the desire for the highest enlightenment, then, contrary to what you might believe, he would be capable of attaining Buddhahood. But, World-Honored One, an arhat who has cut off all desires is like a broken vessel. He will never be worthy or capable of receiving this meditation."[70]

The Vimalakirti Sutra says: "Those who give alms to you are cultivating for themselves no field of fortune. Those who give support to you will instead fall into the three evil paths."[71] This passage means that the human and heavenly beings who give support to the sage monks such as Mahākāśyapa and Śāriputra will invariably fall into the three evil paths. Sage monks such as these, one would suppose, must be the eyes of the human and heavenly worlds and the teachers of all beings, second only to the Buddha himself. It must have been very much against common expectation that the Buddha spoke out time and again against such men before the great assemblies of human and heavenly beings, as we have seen him do. Was he really trying to scold his own disciples to death? In addition, he employed countless different metaphors in expressing his condemnation of the *shōmon* and the *engaku,* calling them donkey milk as compared to the cow's milk [of the bodhisattva], clay vessels as compared to vessels of gold, or the glimmer of a firefly as compared to the light of the sun.

He did not speak of this in one word or two, in one day or two, in one month or two, in one year or two, or in one sutra or two, but over a period of more than forty years, in countless sutras, addressing himself to great assemblies of countless persons, condemning the *shōmon* and the *engaku* without a single extenuating word. Thus everyone learned that his condemnation was true. Heaven learned it and earth learned it, not merely one or two persons but a billion learned and heard of it, as did all the human and heavenly beings, the *shōmon* and the *engaku,* and the great bodhisattvas gathered in assembly from the worlds of the ten directions, the worlds of form and formlessness, the six heavens of the world of desire, the four continents, and the five regions of India, and the heavenly beings, the dragon kings, and the *asuras* of the threefold world.[72] Then each of these beings returned to his own land, explaining the teachings of the Buddha of the *saha* world one by one to the inhabitants of his respective land, so that there was not a single being in the countless worlds of the ten directions who did not understand that Mahākāśyapa, Śāriputra and those like them would never attain Buddhahood and that it was wrong to give them alms and support.

In the Lotus Sutra preached during the last eight years of his life, however, the Buddha suddenly retracted his earlier position and instead taught that persons in the two stages of *shōmon* and *engaku* can in fact attain Buddhahood. Could the human and heavenly beings gathered in the great assembly to listen to him be expected to believe this? Would they not rather reject it, and in addition, begin to entertain doubts about all the sutras preached in the earlier periods? They would wonder if all the teachings put forward in the entire fifty years of the Buddha's preaching were not, in fact, empty and erroneous doctrines.

To be sure, there is a passage in the *Muryōgi* Sutra that says, "In these more than forty years, I have not yet revealed the truth." Nevertheless, one might wonder if the devil had not taken on the Buddha's form and preached this sutra of the last eight years, the Lotus Sutra. In the sutra, however, the Buddha describes quite specifically how his disciples in the *shōmon* and the *engaku* realms will attain Buddhahood and reveals the time and the lands in which they will appear, the names they will bear, and the disciples they will teach. Thus it becomes apparent that there is a contradiction in the words of the Buddha. This is what people mean when they say that his own sayings are at variance with themselves. This is why the Brahmanists laugh at the Buddha and call him the great prevaricator.

But just as the human and heavenly beings in the great assembly were feeling downcast in the face of this contradiction, Tahō Buddha, who dwells in the world of Treasure Purity in the east, appeared in a stupa decorated with seven kinds of gems[73] and measuring five hundred *yojana* high and two hundred and fifty *yojana* wide. The human and heavenly beings in the great assembly accused the Buddha of contradicting his own words, and although the Buddha answered in one way or another, he was in considerable embarrassment, being unable to dispel their doubts, when the Treasure Tower emerged out of the ground before him and ascended into the sky. It came forth like the full moon rising from behind the eastern mountains in the dark of night. The Treasure Tower ascended into the sky, clinging neither to the earth nor to the roof of the heavens, but hanging in midair, and from within the stupa a pure resounding voice issued, speaking words of testimony. As the Lotus Sutra describes it: "At that time a loud voice issued from the Treasure Tower, speaking in praise, 'Excellent, excellent! Shakyamuni, World-Honored One, for the sake of the multitude you skillfully preach the Lotus Sutra, the great wisdom to save all beings equally, which is the Law taught to the bodhisattvas and the doctrine cherished and guarded by the Buddhas. It is as you say. Shakyamuni, World-Honored One, all that you have expounded is the truth!' "[74]

Elsewhere the Lotus Sutra says: "At that time the World-Honored One manifested his great spiritual powers[75] in the presence of Monju and the other hundreds of thousands of billions of bodhisattvas who had from past times lived in the *saha* world, . . . as well as the human beings and nonhuman beings. He extended his long broad tongue till it reached upward to the Brahma Heaven. Then he emitted light from all his pores until it reached the worlds of the ten directions, and all the other Buddhas seated on the lion king thrones under the jewel trees throughout the universe did the same, extending their long broad tongues and emitting innumerable rays of light."[76]

And in another chapter it says: "All the Buddhas who had gathered from the ten directions of the universe returned to their respective lands, . . . and the Buddha ordered that the Treasure Tower of Tahō Buddha return to its original place."[77]

In the past, when the Buddha preached for the first time after attaining enlightenment,[78] the Buddhas of the ten directions appeared to counsel and encourage him, and various great bodhisattvas were dispatched to him. When he preached the *Hannya* Sutra, he covered the major world system[79] with his long tongue, and a thousand Buddhas appeared in the ten directions. When he preached the *Konkōmyō* Sutra, the four Buddhas[80] appeared in the four directions, and when he preached the *Amida* Sutra, the Buddhas of the six directions[81] covered the major world system with their tongues. And when he preached the *Daijuku* Sutra, the Buddhas and bodhisattvas of the ten directions gathered in the Great Treasure Chamber that stands on the border between the worlds of form and desire.

But when we compare the auspicious signs that accompanied these sutras with those accompanying the Lotus Sutra, we find that they are like a yellow stone compared to gold, a white cloud to a white mountain, ice to a silver mirror, or the color black to the color blue —a person with clear vision can distinguish one from the other, but the bleary-eyed, the squint-eyed, the one-eyed, and the wrong-viewed will be likely to confuse them.

Since the *Kegon* Sutra was the first sutra to be preached, there were no previous words of the Buddha for it to contradict, and so it naturally raised no doubts. In the case of the *Daijuku* Sutra, *Hannya* Sutra, *Konkōmyō* Sutra, and *Amida* Sutra, the Buddha, in order to censure the Hinayana ideal of the *shōmon* and *engaku* realms, described the pure lands of the ten directions, and thereby inspired bodhisattvas and common mortals to aspire to attain them. Thus he caused the *shōmon* and *engaku* to abandon the ideal of Hinayana.

Again, because there are certain differences between the Hinayana sutras and the Mahayana sutras mentioned above, we find that in some cases Buddhas appeared in the ten directions, in others great bodhisattvas were dispatched from the ten directions, or it was made clear that the particular sutra was expounded in the worlds of the ten directions, or that various Buddhas came from the ten directions to meet in assembly. In some cases, it was said that Shakyamuni Buddha covered the major world system with his tongue, while in others it was the various Buddhas who put forth their tongues. All of these statements are intended to combat the view expounded in the Hinayana sutras that in the worlds of the ten directions there is only one Buddha.

But in the case of the Lotus Sutra, it differs so greatly from the previous Mahayana sutras that Śāriputra and the other *shōmon* disciples, the great bodhisattvas, and the various human and heavenly beings, when they heard the Buddha preach it, were led to think, "Is this not a devil who has taken on the Buddha's form?"[82] And yet those bleary-eyed men of the Kegon, Hossō, Sanron, Shingon, and Nembutsu sects all seem to think that their own particular sutras are exactly the same as the Lotus Sutra. That is what I call wretched perception indeed!

While the Buddha was still in this world, there were undoubtedly those who set aside the sutras he had taught during the first forty or more years of his teaching life and embraced the Lotus Sutra. But after he passed away, it must have been difficult to find persons who would open and read this sutra and accept its teachings. To begin with, the sutras preached earlier run to countless words, while the Lotus Sutra is limited in length. The earlier sutras are numerous, but the Lotus Sutra is no more than a single work. The earlier sutras were preached over a period of many years, but the Lotus Sutra was preached in a mere eight years.

Moreover, the Buddha, as we have seen, has been called the great liar, and therefore one can hardly be expected to believe his words. If one makes a great effort to believe the unbelievable, he can perhaps bring himself to believe in the earlier sutras but not in the Lotus Sutra. Nowadays, there are many persons who appear to believe in the Lotus Sutra, but in fact they do not really believe in it. It is only when someone assures them that the Lotus Sutra is the same as the *Dainichi* Sutra, or that it is the same as the *Kegon* Sutra or the *Amida* Sutra, that they are pleased and place their faith in it. If someone tells them that the Lotus Sutra is completely different from all the other sutras, they will not listen to him, or even if they should listen, they would not think that the person was really speaking the truth.

Nichiren has this to say. It is now over seven hundred years since Buddhism was introduced to Japan.[83] During that time, only the Great Teacher Dengyō truly understood the Lotus Sutra, but no one is willing to heed this fact which Nichiren has been teaching. It is just as the Lotus Sutra says: "To seize Mount Sumeru and fling it far off to the measureless Buddha lands—that is not difficult. . . . But in the evil times after the Buddha's passing to be able to preach this sutra—that is difficult indeed!"[84]

The teachings I am expounding are in complete accord with the sutra itself. But as the Nirvana Sutra, which was designed to propagate the Lotus Sutra, says: "In the troubled times of the Latter Day of the Law, those who slander the True Law will occupy all the land in the ten directions, while the supporters of the True Law will possess no more land than can be placed on top of a fingernail."[85] What do you think of that? Would you say that the people of Japan who oppose me can be squeezed into the space of a fingernail? Would you say that I, Nichiren, occupy the ten directions? Consider the matter carefully.

In the reign of a wise king, justice will prevail, but when a foolish king reigns, then injustice will have supremacy. One should understand that, in similar fashion, when a sage is in the world, then the true significance of the Lotus Sutra will become apparent.

In my remarks here, I have been contrasting the early sutras with the theoretical teaching of the Lotus Sutra, and it would appear as though the early sutras are in a position to prevail. But if they really win out over the theoretical teaching of the Lotus Sutra, then it means that Śāriputra and the others who are in the two realms of *shōmon* and *engaku* will never be able to attain Buddhahood. That would surely be lamentable!

I turn now to the second important teaching of the Lotus Sutra.[86] Shakyamuni Buddha was born in the Kalpa of Continuance, in the ninth small kalpa,[87] when the span of human life was diminishing and measured a hundred years. He was the grandson of King Siṁhahanu and the son and heir of King Śuddhodana. As a boy he was known as Crown Prince Siddhārtha, or the Bodhisattva All Goals Completed. At the age of nineteen he became a monk, and at thirty he achieved Buddhahood. At Buddhagayā, his place of enlightenment, he first revealed the ceremony of Vairocana Buddha of the Lotus Treasury World and expounded the ten mysteries, the six forms,[88] and the profound and subtle great law for immediate attainment of the ultimate fruit. At that time the Buddhas of the ten directions appeared before him, and all the bodhisattvas gathered about like clouds. In view of the place where Shakyamuni preached, the capacity of the listeners, the presence of the Buddhas, and the fact that it was the first sermon, is there any reason the Buddha could have concealed or held back the supreme law? Therefore the *Kegon* Sutra says: "He displayed his power at will and expounded a sutra of true perfection."[89]

The work, which consists of sixty volumes, is indeed a sutra of true perfection in its every word and phrase. It may be compared to the wish-granting gem which, though it is a single gem, is the equal of a countless number of gems. For the single gem can rain down ten thousand treasures which are equal to the treasures brought forth by ten thousand gems. In the same way, one word of the *Kegon* Sutra contains all the meaning encompassed in ten thousand words. The passage that expounds the identity of "mind, Buddha, and all living beings" represents not only the core of Kegon teachings, but of the teachings of the Hossō, Sanron, Shingon, and Tendai sects as well.

In such a superb sutra, how could there be any truths that are hidden from the hearer? And yet we find the sutra declaring that persons in the two realms of *shōmon* and *engaku* and those who belong to the category of incorrigible disbelief *(icchantika)* can never attain Buddhahood. Here is the flaw in the gem. Moreover, in three places the sutra speaks of Shakyamuni Buddha as attaining enlightenment for the first time in India. It thus hides the fact that, as revealed in the *Juryō* chapter of the Lotus Sutra, Shakyamuni Buddha actually attained enlightenment in the remote past. Thus, the *Kegon* Sutra is in fact a chipped gem, a moon veiled in clouds, a sun in eclipse. How incomprehensible!

The *Agon, Hōdō, Hannya,* and *Dainichi* sutras, since they were expounded by the Buddha, are splendid works, and yet they cannot begin to compare with the *Kegon* Sutra. Therefore one could hardly expect that doctrines concealed even in the *Kegon* Sutra would be revealed in these sutras. Thus we find that the *Zō-agon* Sutra speaks of Shakyamuni Buddha as having "attained enlightenment for the first time in India,"[90] the *Daijuku* Sutra says, "It is sixteen years since the Buddha first attained enlightenment,"[91] and the Vimalakirti Sutra states, "For the first time the Buddha sat beneath the tree and through his might conquered the devil."[92] Likewise, the *Dainichi* Sutra describes the Buddha's enlightenment as having taken place "some years ago when I sat in the place of meditation,"[93] and the *Ninnō Hannya* Sutra refers to it as an event of "twenty-nine years ago."[94]

It is hardly surprising that these sutras should speak in this fashion. But there is something that is an astonishment to both the ear and the eye. This is the fact that the *Muryōgi* Sutra also speaks in the same way. In the *Muryōgi* Sutra, the Buddha denies the *Kegon* Sutra concept of the phenomenal world as created by the mind alone, the *Daijuku* Sutra concept of the ocean-imprint *samādhi*[95] and the *Hannya* Sutra concept of the identity and non-duality of all beings when he declares, "I have not yet revealed the truth." The *Muryōgi* Sutra regards the practices taught in the previous sutras as the "kalpa after kalpa of training" that the bodhisattva must undergo in order to attain Buddhahood. However, the same sutra says, "Previously I went to the place of meditation and sat upright beneath the Bodhi tree, and after six years, I was able to attain the supreme enlightenment,"[96] using the same type of language as the *Kegon* Sutra when it talks of Shakyamuni Buddha having "attained enlightenment for the first time in India."

Strange as this may seem, we may suppose that, since the *Muryōgi* Sutra is intended to serve as an introduction to the Lotus Sutra, it deliberately refrains from speaking about doctrines to be revealed in the Lotus Sutra itself. But when we turn to the Lotus Sutra itself, we find that, in the sections where the Buddha discusses in both abbreviated and expanded form the three realms of *shōmon, engaku,* and bodhisattva as provisional goals,[97] he says: "The true aspect of all phenomena (dharmas) can only be understood and shared between Buddhas."[98] "The World-Honored One has long expounded his doctrines and now must reveal the truth,"[99] he says elsewhere, and, "Honestly discarding the provisional teachings, I will expound the supreme Way."[100] Moreover, Tahō Buddha testifies to the verity of the eight chapters[101] of the theoretical teaching in which these passages occur, declaring that these are all true. We would suppose, therefore, that in them there would be nothing held back or concealed. Nevertheless, the Buddha hides the fact that he attained enlightenment countless kalpas ago, for he says: "When I first sat in the place of meditation and gazed at the tree and walked about it, . . ."[102] This is surely the most astounding fact of all.

In the *Yujutsu* chapter, a multitude of bodhisattvas who had not been seen previously in the more than forty years of the Buddha's preaching life suddenly appear, and the Buddha says, "I taught them, and caused them for the first time to aspire to enlightenment."[103] Bodhisattva Miroku, puzzled by this announcement, says: "World-Honored One, when you were crown prince, you left the palace of the Śākyas and sat in the place of meditation not far from the city of Gayā, where you attained the supreme enlightenment. A mere forty years or so have passed since then. In that short period of time, how could you have accomplished so much great work as a Buddha?"[104]

In order to dispel this doubt and puzzlement, the Buddha then preaches the *Juryō* chapter. Referring first to the version of the events presented in the earlier sutras and the theoretical teaching of the Lotus Sutra, he says: "All the human and heavenly beings and the *asuras* at present believe that Shakyamuni Buddha, after leaving the palace of the Śākyas, sat in the place of meditation not far from the city of Gayā and there attained the supreme enlightenment."[105] But then, in order to dispel their doubts, he says: "However, men of devout faith, the time is limitless and boundless — a hundred, thousand, ten thousand, hundred thousand, nayuta kalpas — since I in fact attained Buddhahood."[106]

All the provisional sutras such as the *Kegon, Hannya,* and *Dainichi* not only conceal the fact that people in the two realms of *shōmon* and *engaku* can attain Buddhahood, but they also fail to make clear that the Buddha attained enlightenment countless kalpas in the past. These sutras have two flaws. First, because they teach that the ten worlds of existence are separate from one another, they fail to move beyond the provisional doctrines and to reveal the doctrine of *ichinen sanzen* as it is expounded in the theoretical teaching of the Lotus Sutra. Second, because they teach that Shakyamuni Buddha attained enlightenment for the first time in India and do not explain his true identity, they fail to reveal the fact, stressed in the essential teaching, that the Buddha attained enlightenment countless kalpas ago. These two great doctrines are the core of the Buddha's lifetime teachings and the very heart and marrow of all the sutras.

The *Hōben* chapter, which belongs to the theoretical teaching, expounds the doctrine of *ichinen sanzen,* making clear that persons in the two realms of *shōmon* and *engaku* can achieve Buddhahood. It thus avoids committing one of the two errors perpetrated in the earlier sutras. But it nevertheless fails to reveal that the Buddha attained enlightenment countless kalpas ago. Thus the true doctrine of *ichinen sanzen* remains unclear and the attainment of Buddhahood by persons in the two realms is not properly affirmed. Such teachings are like the moon seen in the water, or rootless plants that drift on the waves.

When we come to the essential teaching of the Lotus Sutra, then the belief that Shakyamuni obtained Buddhahood for the first time in India is demolished, and the effects of the four teachings[107] are likewise demolished. When the effects of the four teachings are demolished, the causes[108] are likewise demolished. Thus the cause and effect of the ten worlds of existence as expounded in the earlier sutras and the theoretical teaching of the Lotus Sutra are wiped out, and the cause and effect of the Ten Worlds in the essential teaching are revealed. This is the doctrine of original cause and original effect. It reveals that the nine other worlds are all present in the beginningless Buddhahood, and that the Buddhahood is inherent in the beginningless nine other worlds. This is the true mutual possession of the Ten Worlds, the true hundred worlds and thousand factors, the true *ichinen sanzen*.

When we consider the matter in this light, we can see that the Vairocana Buddha described in the *Kegon* Sutra, the Shakyamuni described in the *Agon* sutras, and the provisional Buddhas described in the *Hōdō* and *Hannya* sutras such as the *Konkōmyō, Amida,* and *Dainichi* sutras are no more than reflections of the Buddha of the *Juryō* chapter, like reflections of the moon that float on the surfaces of various large and small bodies of water. The scholars of the various schools of Buddhism, confused by the doctrines of their own school and unaware of the teachings of the *Juryō* chapter of the Lotus Sutra, mistake the reflection in the water for the actual moon, some of them entering the water and trying to grasp it in their hands, others to snare it with a rope. As T'ien-t'ai says, "They know nothing of the moon in the sky, but gaze only at the moon in the pond."[109]

Nichiren has this to remark. Though the Lotus Sutra teaches that persons in the two realms of *shōmon* and *engaku* can attain Buddhahood, this view tends to be overshadowed by the opposite view propounded in the sutras that precede the Lotus Sutra. How much more so is this the case with the doctrine that the Buddha attained enlightenment countless kalpas ago! For in this case, it is not the Lotus Sutra as a whole that stands in contradiction to the earlier sutras, but the essential teaching of the Lotus Sutra that stands in contradiction both to the earlier sutras and to the first half or theoretical teaching of the Lotus Sutra. Moreover, of the chapters of the Lotus Sutra that deal with the essential teaching, all of them with the exception of the *Yujutsu* and *Juryō* chapters retain the view that Shakyamuni Buddha attained enlightenment for the first time in India.

The forty volumes of the Nirvana Sutra, preached by the Buddha on his deathbed in the grove of sal[110] trees, as well as the other Mahayana sutras except the Lotus Sutra, have not one single word to say about the fact that the Buddha attained enlightenment countless ages ago. They speak of the *hosshin* or Dharma body of the Buddha as being without beginning and without end, but they do not reveal the true nature of the other two bodies, the *hōshin* or reward body, and the *ōjin* or manifested body.[111] How, then, can we expect people to cast aside the vast body of writings represented by the earlier Mahayana sutras, the Nirvana Sutra, and the major portion of the theoretical and essential teachings of the Lotus Sutra, and put all their faith simply in the two chapters *Yujutsu* and *Juryō?*

If we examine the origins of the school called Hossō, we find that, nine hundred years after Shakyamuni passed away in India, there was a great teacher of doctrine called Asaṅga.[112] At night, he entered the halls of Tuṣita,[113] where he came before Bodhisattva Miroku and resolved his doubts concerning the teachings propounded by the Buddha during his lifetime. In the daytime, he worked to propagate the Hossō doctrines in the state of Ayodhyā.[114] Among his disciples were various great scholars such as his younger brother Vasubandhu, Dharmapāla, Nanda, and Śīlabhadra.[115] The great ruler, King Śīlāditya,[116] converted to his teachings, and in time the people of all the five regions of India abandoned their arrogance and declared themselves followers of his teaching.

The Chinese monk Hsüan-tsang[117] journeyed to India, spending seventeen years visiting one hundred and thirty or more states in India. He rejected all the other teachings of Buddhism, but brought back the doctrines of the Hossō school to China and presented them to the wise sovereign, Emperor T'ai-tsung of the T'ang. Hsüan-tsang numbered among his disciples such men as Shen-fang, Chia-shang, P'u-kuang, and K'uei-chi.[118] He preached his teachings in the great temple in the capital city of Ch'ang-an called Tz'u-en-ssu and spread them through more than three hundred and sixty districts of China.

In the reign of Emperor Kōtoku, the thirty-seventh sovereign of Japan, the monks Dōji and Dōshō[119] went to China and studied these doctrines, and on their return preached them at Yamashina Temple.[120] In this way, the Hossō sect became the leading sect of Buddhism throughout all three lands of India, China, and Japan.

According to this sect, in all the teachings of the Buddha, from the *Kegon* Sutra, the earliest of the sutras, to the Lotus and Nirvana sutras that were preached last, it is laid down that those who do not possess the innate nature of any enlightenment and those predestined for the two vehicles can never become Buddhas. The Buddha, they say, never contradicts himself. Therefore, if he has once declared that these persons will never be able to attain Buddhahood, then, even though the sun and moon may fall to the earth and the great earth itself may turn upside down, that declaration can never be altered. In the earlier sutras those who do not possess the innate nature of any enlightenment or those predestined for the realms of *shōmon* and *engaku* were said to be incapable of attaining Buddhahood. Therefore, even in the Lotus or Nirvana Sutra it is never said that they can in fact do so.

"Close your eyes and consider the matter," the members of the Hossō school would say. "If it had in fact been plainly stated in the Lotus and Nirvana sutras that those who do not possess the innate nature of any enlightenment or those predestined for the two realms can actually attain Buddhahood, then why would not the great scholars such as Asaṅga and Vasubandhu or eminent monks such as Hsüan-tsang and Tz'u-en have taken notice of this fact? Why did they not mention it in their own writings? Why did they not accept the belief and transmit it to later ages? Why did not Asaṅga question Bodhisattva Miroku about it? People like you, Nichiren, claim that you are basing your assertions on the text of the Lotus Sutra, but in fact you are simply accepting the biased views of men like T'ien-t'ai, Miao-lo, and Dengyō and interpreting the text of the sutra in the light of their teachings. Therefore you claim that the Lotus Sutra is as different from the earlier sutras as fire from water."

Again, there are the Kegon and Shingon schools, which are incomparably higher in level than the Hossō and Sanron schools. They claim that the doctrines that persons in the realms of *shōmon* and *engaku* may attain Buddhahood and that the Buddha achieved enlightenment countless kalpas ago are to be found not only in the Lotus Sutra, but in the *Kegon* and *Dainichi* sutras as well.

According to these schools, the Kegon patriarchs Tu-shun, Chih-yen, Fa-tsang and Ch'eng-kuan,[121] and the Shingon masters Shan-wu-wei, Chin-kang-chih, and Pu-k'ung[122] were far more eminent than T'ien-t'ai or Dengyō. Moreover, they claim that Shan-wu-wei's teachings descend in an unbroken line from the Buddha Mahāvairocana. How could men like this, who are manifestations of the Buddha, possibly be mistaken, they ask. They point to the passage in the *Kegon* Sutra that reads: "Some people perceive that an inestimable number of kalpas have passed since the Buddha Shakyamuni attained enlightenment,"[123] or the passage in the *Dainichi* Sutra that says: "I am the source and beginning of all things."[124] Why, they ask, would anyone claim that it is the *Juryō* chapter of the Lotus alone that expounds the doctrine that the Buddha attained enlightenment long ago? Persons who do so are like frogs at the bottom of a well who have never seen the great sea, or ignorant hill folk who know nothing of the capital. "You people look only at the *Juryō* chapter and know nothing of the *Kegon, Dainichi,* and the other sutras! Do you suppose that in India and China and Silla and Paekche[125] people believe that these two doctrines are limited to the Lotus Sutra alone?"

As we have seen, the Lotus Sutra, which was preached over a period of eight years, is quite different from the earlier sutras preached over a period of some forty years. If one had to choose between the two, one ought by rights to choose the Lotus Sutra, and yet the earlier sutras in many ways appear to carry greater weight.

While the Buddha was still alive, there would have been good reasons for choosing the Lotus Sutra. But in the ages since his passing, the teachers and scholars have in most cases shown a preference for the earlier sutras. Not only is the Lotus Sutra itself difficult to believe, but in addition, the Former and the Middle Days of the Law are coming to an end, sages and worthy men grow fewer and fewer, and deluded persons constantly increase in number. People are prone to make mistakes even in shallow, worldly affairs, so how much more likely are they to be mistaken about the profound Buddhist teachings that lead to enlightenment?

Vatsa and the ascetic, Vaipulya,[126] were keen and perceptive, but still they confused the Hinayana and Mahayana sutras. Vimalamitra and Mādhava[127] were very clever by nature, but they could not distinguish properly between the provisional teachings and the true teachings. These men lived during the thousand-year period known as the Former Day of the Law, not far removed in time from the Buddha himself, and in the same country of India, and yet they fell into error, as we have seen. How much more likely, therefore, that the people of China and Japan should do so, since these countries are far removed from India and speak different languages from it?

Now men have grown increasingly dull by nature, their life span diminishes steadily,[128] and the poisons of greed, anger, and stupidity continue to multiply. Many centuries have passed since the Buddha's death, and the Buddhist scriptures are all misunderstood. Who these days has the wisdom to interpret them correctly?

Therefore the Buddha predicted in the Nirvana Sutra: "In the Latter Day of the Law, those who abide by the true teachings will occupy no more land than can be placed on top of a fingernail, while those who slander the true teachings will occupy all the lands in the ten directions."[129]

In the *Hōmetsujin* Sutra we find this passage: "Those who slander the true teachings will be as numerous as the sands of the Ganges, but those who abide by the true teachings will be no more than one or two pebbles."[130] Though five hundred or a thousand years go by, it will be difficult to find even a single person who believes in the true teachings. Those who fall into the evil states of existence because of secular crimes will be as insignificant in number as the space of a fingernail, but those who do so because of violations of the Buddhist teachings will occupy all the lands in the ten directions. More monks than laymen, and more nuns than laywomen, will fall into the evil paths.

Here Nichiren considers as follows: Already over two hundred years have passed since the world entered the Latter Day of the Law. I was born in a remote land far from India, a person of low station and a priest of humble learning. During my past lifetimes through the six paths, I have perhaps at times been born as a great ruler in the human or heavenly worlds, and have bent the multitudes to my will as a great wind bends the branches of the small trees. And yet at such times I was not able to become a Buddha.

I studied the Hinayana and Mahayana sutras, beginning as an ordinary practitioner with no understanding at all and gradually moving upward to the position of a great bodhisattva. For one kalpa, two kalpas, countless kalpas I devoted myself to the practices of a bodhisattva, until I had almost reached the state where I could never fail to attain Buddhahood. And yet I was dragged down by the powerful and overwhelming influence of evil, and I never attained Buddhahood. I do not know whether I belong to the third group[131] of those who heard the preaching of the sixteenth son of Daitsū Buddha and failed to attain enlightenment again during the lifetime of Shakyamuni Buddha, or whether I faltered and fell away from the teachings which I heard [long before Daitsū Buddha,] at *gohyaku-jintengō*,[132] [and thus have been reborn in this form].

While one is practicing the teachings of the Lotus Sutra, he may surmount all kinds of difficulties occasioned by the evil forces of worldly life, or by the persecutions of rulers, non-Buddhists, or the followers of the Hinayana sutras. And yet he may encounter someone like Tao-ch'o, Shan-tao, or Hōnen,[133] monks who seemed thoroughly conversant with the teachings of the provisional and the true Mahayana sutras but who were in fact possessed by devils. Such men seem to praise the Lotus Sutra most forcefully, but in fact they belittle the people's ability to understand it, claiming that "its principles are profound but human understanding is slight."[134] They mislead others by saying, "Not a single person has ever attained Buddhahood through that sutra" or "Not one person in a thousand [can reach enlightenment through its teachings]."[135] Thus, over a period of countless lifetimes, men are deceived more often than there are sands in the Ganges, until they [abandon their faith in the Lotus Sutra and] descend to the teachings of the provisional Mahayana sutras, abandon these and descend to the teachings of the Hinayana sutras, and eventually abandon even these and descend to the teachings and scriptures of the non-Buddhist doctrines. I understand all too well how, in the end, men have come in this way to fall into the evil states of existence.

I, Nichiren, am the only person in all Japan who understands this. But if I utter so much as a word concerning it, then parents, brothers, and teachers will surely criticize me and the government authorities will take steps against me. On the other hand, I am fully aware that if I do not speak out, I will be lacking in compassion. I have considered which course to take in the light of the teachings of the Lotus and Nirvana sutras. If I remain silent, I may escape harm in this lifetime, but in my next life I will most certainly fall into the hell of incessant suffering. If I speak out, I am fully aware that I will have to contend with the three obstacles and the four devils. But of these two courses, surely the latter is the one to choose.

If I were to falter in my determination in the face of government persecutions, however, I would not be able to fulfill my course. In that case, perhaps it would be better not to speak out. While thinking this over, I recalled the teachings of the Hōtō chapter on the six difficult and nine easy acts.[136] Persons like myself who are of paltry strength might still be able to lift Mount Sumeru and toss it about; persons like myself who are lacking in spiritual powers might still shoulder a load of dry grass and yet remain unburned in the fire at the end of the kalpa of decline;[137] and persons like myself who are without wisdom might still read and memorize as many sutras as there are sands in the Ganges. But such acts are not difficult, we are told, when compared to the difficulty of embracing even one phrase or verse of the Lotus Sutra in the Latter Day of the Law. Nevertheless, I vowed to summon up a powerful and unconquerable desire for the salvation of all beings, and never to falter in my efforts.

It is already over twenty years since I began proclaiming my doctrines. Day after day, month after month, year after year I have been subjected to repeated persecutions. Minor persecutions and annoyances are too numerous even to be counted, but the major persecutions number four. Among the four, twice I have been subjected to persecutions by the government itself.[138] The most recent one has come near to costing me my life. In addition, my disciples, my lay followers, and even those who have merely listened to my teachings have been subjected to severe punishment and treated as though they were guilty of treason.

In the *Hosshi* chapter of the Lotus Sutra we read: "Since hatred and jealousy abound even during the lifetime of the Buddha, how much worse will it be in the world after his passing!"[139] The *Hiyu* chapter states: "They will despise, hate, envy, and bear grudges against those who read, recite, transcribe, and embrace this sutra."[140] And the *Anrakugyō* chapter says: "The people will resent [the Lotus Sutra] and find it extremely difficult to believe."[141] The *Kanji* chapter states: "There will be many ignorant people who will curse and speak ill of us," and, "They will address the rulers, high ministers, Brahmans and great patrons of Buddhism . . . slandering and speaking evil of us, saying, 'These are men of perverted views.' " It is also stated in the *Kanji* chapter: "Again and again we will be banished,"[142] and, in the *Fukyō* chapter, "They would beat him with sticks and staves, and stone him with rocks and tiles."[143]

The Nirvana Sutra records: "At that time there were a countless number of non-Buddhists who plotted together and went in a group to King Ajātaśātru of Magadha and said, 'At present there is a man of incomparable wickedness, a monk called Gautama. All sorts of evil persons, hoping to gain profit and alms, have flocked to him and become his followers. They do not practice goodness, but instead use the power of spells and magic to win over men like Mahākāśyapa, Śāriputra, and Maudgalyāyana.' "[144]

T'ien-t'ai says: "It will be 'much worse' in the future because [the Lotus Sutra] is so hard to teach."[145] Miao-lo says: "Those who have not yet freed themselves from impediments are called 'hostile ones,' and those who take no delight in listening to the doctrine are called 'jealous ones.' "[146] The leaders of the three schools of the South and seven schools of the North[147] of Buddhism in China, as well as the countless other scholars of China, all regarded T'ien-t'ai with resentment and animosity. Thus Tokuitsu said: "See here, Chih-i, whose disciple are you? With a tongue less than three inches long you slander the teachings that come from the Buddha's long broad tongue!"[148]

Priest Chih-tu writes in his work *Tōshun:* "Someone questioned me, saying, 'While the Buddha was in the world, there were many who were resentful and jealous of him. But now, in the years after his passing, when we preach the Lotus Sutra, why are there so many who try to make trouble for us?' I replied, 'It is said that good medicine tastes bitter. This sutra, which is like good medicine, dispels attachments to the five vehicles and establishes the one supreme teaching. It reproaches common mortals and censures sages, denies provisional Mahayana and refutes Hinayana. It speaks of the heavenly devils as poisonous insects and calls the non-Buddhists evil demons. It censures those who cling to Hinayana beliefs, calling them mean and impoverished, and it dismisses bodhisattvas as beginners in learning. For this reason, heavenly devils hate to listen to it, non-Buddhists find their ears offended, persons in the *shōmon* and *engaku* realms are dumbfounded, and bodhisattvas flee in terror. That is why all these types of persons try to make trouble for us. The Buddha was not speaking nonsense when he predicted that we would face "much hatred and jealousy." ' " [149]

The Great Teacher Dengyō in his *Kenkai Ron* writes: "The superintendents of priests [in the capital of Nara] submitted a memorial to the throne, saying: 'Just as in the Western Hsia land of Central Asia there was an evil Brahman named Devil Eloquence who deceived people, so now in this eastern realm of Japan there is a shave-pated monk who spits out crafty words. Creatures like this will attract to themselves those who are of like mind and will deceive and mislead the world.' I replied to these charges by saying: 'Just as in the Ch'i dynasty of China we heard of the [arrogant] superintendent of priests, Hui-kuang, so now in our own country we see these six superintendents of priests [who oppose me]. How true was [the Buddha's prediction in] the Lotus Sutra: "How much worse will it be [in the world after the Buddha's passing]!" ' " [150]

In the *Hokke Shūku*, the Great Teacher Dengyō also says: "The propagation of the true teaching will begin in the age when the Middle Day of the Law ends and the Latter Day opens, in a land to the east of T'ang and to the west of Katsu, among people stained by the five impurities who live in a time of conflict. The sutra says, 'Since hatred and jealousy abound even during the lifetime of the Buddha, how much worse will it be in the world after his passing?' There is good reason for this statement." [151]

When a little boy is given moxibustion treatment, he will hate his mother for a time; when a seriously ill person is given good medicine, he will complain without fail about its bitterness. And we meet with similar complaints [about the Lotus Sutra], even in the lifetime of the Buddha. How much more severe is the opposition after his passing, especially in the Middle and Latter Days of the Law and in a far-off country like Japan? As mountains pile upon mountains and waves follow waves, so do persecutions add to persecutions and criticisms augment criticisms.

During the Middle Day of the Law, one man alone, the Great Teacher T'ien-t'ai, understood and expounded the Lotus Sutra and the other sutras. The other Buddhist leaders of both northern and southern China hated him for it, but the two wise sovereigns, Emperor Wen of the Ch'en dynasty and Emperor Yang of the Sui, gave him an audience to establish the correctness of his views in debate with his opponents. Thus in time he ceased to have any more opponents. At the end of the Middle Day of the Law, one man alone, the Great Teacher Dengyō, grasped the Lotus Sutra and the other sutras just as the Buddha had expounded them. The seven great temples of Nara rose up like hornets against him, but the two worthy sovereigns, Emperor Kammu and Emperor Saga, gave him the opportunity to make clear the correctness of his views, and thereafter there was no further trouble.

It is now over two hundred years since the Latter Day of the Law began. The Buddha predicted that conditions would be much worse after his passing, and we see the portents of this in the quarrels and wranglings that go on today because unreasonable doctrines are prevalent. And as proof of the fact that we are living in a muddied age, [the priests of the Shingon and other sects] are not called together [for doctrinal debates with me, so that the rulers may settle the matter fairly,] but instead I am sent into exile and my very life is imperiled.

When it comes to understanding the Lotus Sutra, I have only a minute fraction of the vast ability that T'ien-t'ai and Dengyō possessed. But though it is presumptuous for me to say so, my ability to endure persecution and the wealth of my compassion far surpasses theirs. [As a votary of the Lotus Sutra,] I firmly believe that I should come under the protection of the gods, and yet I do not see the slightest sign of this. On the contrary, I fall under growing accusation for the crimes I am said to commit. In view of this, am I perhaps then not a votary of the Lotus Sutra after all? Or have the numerous benevolent deities of heaven who vowed to protect the votary of the Lotus Sutra perhaps taken leave and departed from this land of Japan? I find myself in much perplexity.

But then I recall the twenty lines of verse in the *Kanji* chapter of the fifth volume of the Lotus Sutra [in which the eighty myriads of millions of nayutas of bodhisattvas describe the persecutions they will endure after the Buddha's death for the sake of the Lotus Sutra]. If I, Nichiren, had not been born in this land of Japan, then the words of the Buddha predicting such persecutions would have been a great prevarication, and those eighty myriads of millions of nayutas of bodhisattvas would have been guilty of the same crime as that of Devadatta, of lying and misleading others.

The *Kanji* chapter says: "There will be many ignorant people who will curse and speak ill of us, and will attack us with swords and staves, with rocks and tiles."[152] Look around you in the world today —are there any monks other than Nichiren who are cursed and vilified because of the Lotus Sutra or who are attacked with swords and staves? If it were not for Nichiren, the prophecy made in this verse of the sutra would have been sheer falsehood.

The same passage says: "There will be monks in that evil age with perverse views and hearts that are fawning and crooked,"[153] and, "They will preach the Dharma to white-robed laymen and will be respected and revered by the world as though they were arhats who possess the six supernatural powers."[154] If it were not for the teachers of the Nembutsu, Zen, and Ritsu sects of our present age, then Shakyamuni Buddha, who uttered these prophecies in the sutra, would have been a teller of great untruths.

The passage likewise says: "Constantly going about among the populace, . . . they will address the rulers, high ministers, Brahmans and great patrons of Buddhism . . . slandering and speaking evil of us." If the monks of today did not slander me to the authorities and condemn me to banishment, then this passage in the sutra would have remained unfulfilled.

"Again and again we will be banished," says the sutra. But if Nichiren had not been banished time and again for the sake of the Lotus Sutra, what would these words "again and again" have meant? Even T'ien-t'ai and Dengyō were not able to fulfill this prediction, that they would be banished "again and again," much less was anyone else. But because I have been born at the beginning of the Latter Day of the Law, the "fearful and evil age" described in the sutra, I alone have been able to live these words.

As other examples of prophecies that were fulfilled, in the *Fuhōzō* Sutra it is recorded that Shakyamuni Buddha said, "One hundred years after my passing, a ruler known as the Great King Aśoka will appear."[155] In the *Māyā* Sutra he said, "Six hundred years after my passing, a man named Bodhisattva Nāgārjuna will appear in southern India."[156] And in the *Daihi* Sutra he said, "Sixty years after my passing, a man named Madhyāntika will establish his base in the Dragon Palace."[157] All of these prophecies came true. Indeed, if they had not, who would have faith in the Buddhist teachings?

Thus the Buddha decided the time [when the votary of the Lotus Sutra should appear], describing it as a "fearful and evil age," "a latter age," "a latter age when the Law will disappear," and "the final five hundred years," as attested by both the two Chinese versions of the Lotus Sutra, *Shō-hokke Kyō* and *Myōhō-renge-kyō*.[158] At such a time, if the three powerful enemies predicted in the Lotus Sutra did not appear, then who would have faith in the words of the Buddha? If it were not for Nichiren, who could fulfill the Buddha's prophecies concerning the votary of the Lotus Sutra? The three schools of southern China and seven schools of northern China, along with the seven great temples of Nara, were numbered among the enemies of the Lotus Sutra in the time of the Middle Day of the Law. How much less can the Zen, Ritsu, and Nembutsu priests of the present time hope to escape a similar label?

With this body of mine, I have fulfilled the prophecies of the sutra. The more the government authorities rage against me, the greater is my joy. For instance, there are certain Hinayana bodhisattvas, not yet freed from delusion, who draw evil karma to themselves by their own compassionate vow. Thus, if one of them sees that his mother and father have fallen into hell and are suffering greatly, he will deliberately create the appropriate karma in hopes that he too may fall into hell and take their suffering upon himself. To suffer for the sake of others is a joy to him. It is the same with me in fulfilling the prophecies. Though at present I must face trials that I can scarcely endure, I rejoice when I think that in the future I will escape being born into the evil paths.

And yet the people doubt me, and I too have doubts about myself. Why do the gods not assist me? Heavenly gods and other guardian deities made their vow before the Buddha. Even if the votary of the Lotus Sutra were an ape rather than a man, if he announced that he was a votary of the Lotus Sutra, then I believe the gods should rush forward to fulfill the vow they made before the Buddha. Does their failure to do so mean that I am in fact not a votary of the Lotus Sutra?

This doubt lies at the heart of this piece I am writing. And because it is the most important concern of my entire life, I will raise it again and again here and emphasize it more than ever, before I attempt to answer it.

Prince Chi-cha[159] in his heart had promised to give the Lord of Hsü the precious royal sword that he wore. Therefore, [when he later found that the Lord of Hsü had died,] he placed the sword on his grave. Wang Shou,[160] having drunk water from a river, carefully tossed a gold coin into the water as payment. Hung Yen, finding that his lord had been killed, cut open his stomach and inserted his lord's liver in it before he died. These were worthy men, and they knew how to fulfill their obligations. How much more so, then, should this be the case with great sages like Śāriputra and Mahākāśyapa, who observed every one of the two hundred and fifty precepts and the three thousand rules of conduct, and had cut themselves off from the illusions of thought and desire[161] and separated themselves from the threefold world? They are worthy to be the teachers of Bonten, Taishaku and the other gods of Heaven, and the eyes of all living beings. During the first forty or more years of the Buddha's preaching, these men, [because they belonged to the *shōmon* and *engaku* realms,] were disliked and pushed aside with admonitions that they could "never attain Buddhahood." But when they had tasted the medicine of immortality in the Lotus Sutra, they were like scorched seeds that sprout, a shattered rock joined together again, or withered trees that put forth blossoms and fruit. Through the Lotus Sutra, it was revealed that they would attain Buddhahood after all, though they had yet to enter the eight phases of a Buddha's existence.[162] Why, then, do they not do something to repay their obligation to the sutra? If they do not do so, they will show themselves to be inferior to the worthy men I have mentioned earlier, and in fact be no more than animals who have no understanding of obligation.

The turtle that Mao Pao[163] saved did not forget to repay the obligation of the past. The great fish of the K'un-ming Pond,[164] in order to repay the man who had saved his life, presented a bright pearl in the middle of the night. Even these creatures understood how to fulfill their obligations, so why shouldn't men who are great sages?

Ānanda was the second son of King Droṇodana,[165] and Rāhula was the grandson of King Śuddhodana. Both men were born into very distinguished families but, because they had attained the level of arhat, they were prevented from ever reaching Buddhahood. And yet, during the eight-year assembly at Eagle Peak when the Lotus Sutra was preached, it was revealed that Ānanda would become the Mountain Sea Wisdom [Unrestricted Power King] Buddha and that Rāhula would become the Buddha Stepping on Seven Treasure Flowers. No matter what great sages these men were or how distinguished their families, if it had not been for the revelation in the Lotus Sutra, who would have paid respect to them?

Emperor Chieh of the Hsia dynasty and Emperor Chou of the Yin dynasty[166] were lords of an army of ten thousand chariots and commanded the allegiance of the entire populace of their kingdoms. But because they governed despotically and brought about the downfall of their dynasties, people speak of Chieh and Chou as the epitome of evil men. Even a beggar or a leper, if he is likened to Chieh and Chou, will be enraged at the insult. [Thus we see that power and position alone do not necessarily insure that one will be respected.]

If it had not been for the Lotus Sutra, then who would ever have heard of the twelve hundred shōmon[167] and the countless other shōmon [who would attain Buddhahood through the sutra], and who would have listened to their voices? No one would have read the Buddhist sutras compiled by the thousand shōmon disciples,[168] nor would there be any paintings or statues of them set up and worshiped. It is entirely due to the power of the Lotus Sutra that these arhats are revered and followed. If these shōmon were to separate themselves from the Lotus Sutra, they would be like a fish without water, a monkey without a tree, a baby without the breast, or a people without a ruler. Why, then, do they abandon the votary of the Lotus Sutra?

In the sutras that precede the Lotus Sutra, the shōmon are depicted as acquiring the Heavenly Eye and the Wisdom Eye in addition to their physical eyes. In the Lotus Sutra, we are told that they are also provided with the Dharma Eye and the Buddha Eye.[169] Their eyesight can penetrate any of the worlds in the ten directions. How then could they fail to see me, the votary of the Lotus Sutra, right here in the saha world? Even if I were an evil man who had said a word or two against them, or even if I cursed and reviled the shōmon for a year or two, a kalpa or two, or a countless number of kalpas, and went so far as to threaten to take up swords and staves against them, so long as I maintain my faith in the Lotus Sutra and act as its votary, then they should never abandon me.

A child may curse his parents, but would the parents for that reason cast him aside? The young owls eat their mother, but the mother nevertheless does not abandon them. The *hakei*[170] beast kills its father, but the father does nothing to prevent this. If even animals behave like this, then why should great sages like the *shōmon* abandon the votary of the Lotus Sutra?

The four great *shōmon* disciples[171] of the Buddha, in the passage that deals with their belief and understanding, proclaimed: "Now have we become true *shōmon*,[172] for we take the voice *(shō)* of the Buddha's Way and cause it to be heard *(mon)* among all beings. Now have we become true arhats, for among all the gods, men, demons, and Bontens of the various worlds, everywhere in their midst we deserve to receive offerings. The Buddha in his great beneficence makes use of a rare thing[173] to comfort and teach us and bestow benefit upon us. In countless millions of kalpas, who could ever repay him? Though men offer him their hands and feet,[174] bow their heads to the ground in obeisance, and present him with all manner of alms, none of them could repay him. Should they bear him on the crown of their heads or carry him on their two shoulders, through kalpas numerous as the sands of the Ganges exhausting their hearts in reverence; should they offer him delicious foods, numberless jeweled garments and articles of bedding, potions and medicines of every kind; should they use oxhead sandalwood and all kinds of rare gems to erect a stupa shrine, spreading jeweled garments over the ground; should they perform these acts and use these things as offerings through kalpas numerous as the sands of the Ganges, still they could never repay him."[175]

In the various sutras preached during the earlier period of the Buddha's life, which have been compared to the first four flavors,[176] the *shōmon* disciples were depicted on countless occasions as subjected to all kinds of abuse and shamed before the great assembly of human and heavenly beings. Thus we are told that the sound of Mahākāśyapa's weeping and wailing echoed through the major world system,[177] that Subhūti was so dumbfounded that he almost went off and left the alms bowl[178] he had been carrying, that Śāriputra spat out the food he was eating,[179] and that Pūrṇa was berated for being the kind who would put filth in a precious jar.[180]

When the Buddha was at the Deer Park, he extolled the *Agon* sutras and enjoined men to observe the two hundred and fifty precepts, warmly praising those who did so, and yet before long, as we have seen, he turned about and began condemning such men. He is guilty, we would have to say, of making two different and completely contradictory pronouncements.

Thus, for example, the Buddha cursed his disciple Devadatta, saying, "You are a fool who licks the spit of others!" Devadatta felt as though a poison arrow had been shot into his breast, and he cried out in anger, saying, "Gautama is no Buddha! I am the eldest son of King Droṇodana, the elder brother of Ānanda and a cousin of Gautama. No matter what kind of evil conduct I might be guilty of, he ought to admonish me in private for it. But to publicly accuse me of faults in front of this great assembly of human and heavenly beings— is this the behavior appropriate to a Great Man or a Buddha? He showed himself to be my enemy in the past when he stole the woman I intended to marry,[181] and he has shown himself my enemy at this gathering today. From this day forward, I vow to look upon him as my greatest enemy for lifetime after lifetime and age after age to come!"[182]

When we stop to consider, we note that, of the *shōmon* disciples, some were originally from Brahman families who followed non-Buddhist doctrines, or were leaders of various non-Buddhist schools who had converted kings to their teachings and were looked up to by their followers. Others were men of aristocratic families or the possessors of great wealth. But they abandoned their exalted positions in life, lowered the banners of their pride, cast off everyday clothing and wrapped their bodies in the humble, dingy-hued robes of a Buddhist monk. They threw away their white fly whisks, their bows and arrows, and took up a solitary alms bowl, becoming like paupers and beggars and following the Buddha. They had no dwellings to protect them from the wind and rain, and very little in the way of food or clothing by which to sustain life. Moreover, all the people of the five regions of India and the four seas were disciples or supporters of the non-Buddhist religions, so that even the Buddha himself was on nine occasions forced to suffer major hardships.

Thus, for example, Devadatta hurled a great stone at him, King Ajātaśatru loosed a drunken elephant on him, and King Ajita for a period of ninety days would give him and his followers nothing but horse fodder to eat. At a Brahman city, he was offered stinking rice gruel, and a Brahman woman named Ciñcamāṇavikā, tying a bowl to her belly, claimed to be pregnant with his child.[183]

Needless to say, the Buddha's disciples were likewise forced to suffer frequent hardships. Thus, countless numbers of the Shakya clan were killed by King Virūḍhaka, and ten million of the Buddha's followers were trampled to death by drunken elephants that were set upon them. The nun Utpalavarṇā was killed by Devadatta, the disciple Kālodāyin was buried in horse dung, and the disciple Maudgalyāyana was beaten to death by members of a Brahman group named Bamboo Staff.[184] In addition, the six non–Buddhist teachers banded together and slandered the Buddha before King Ajātaśatru and King Prasenajit, saying, "Gautama is the most evil man in the whole continent of Jambudvīpa. Wherever he may be, his presence heralds the onset of the three calamities and the seven disasters. As the numerous rivers gather together in the great sea and the groves of trees cluster on the great mountains, so do crowds of evil men gather about Gautama. The men called Mahākāśyapa, Śāriputra, Maudgalyāyana, and Subhūti are examples. All those who are born in human form should place loyalty to the sovereign and filial piety above all else. But these men have been so misled by Gautama that they disregard the lessons of their parents, abandon their families and, defying the commandments of the king, go to live in the mountain forests. They should be expelled from this country. It is because they are allowed to remain that the sun, moon, and stars manifest sinister phenomena and many strange happenings occur in the land."[185]

The *shōmon* disciples did not know how they could possibly bear this slander. Then, as if to add to their hardship, [the Buddha himself began to denounce them]. They found it difficult to follow him. Now and then, hearing him condemn them repeatedly in great assemblies of human and heavenly beings, and not knowing how to behave, they only became more confused.

On top of all this, they had to face the greatest hardship of all, as revealed in the Vimalakirti Sutra, when the Buddha addressed the *shōmon* disciples, saying: "Those who give alms to you are cultivating for themselves no field of fortune. Those who give support to you will instead fall into the three evil paths."[186] According to this passage, these words were spoken in the gardens of Ambapāli [in the city of Vaiśālī]. There Bonten, Taishaku, the deities of the sun and moon, the Four Heavenly Kings, and the various gods of the three-fold world, along with earth gods, dragon gods, and other beings as numerous as the sands of the Ganges, had gathered in a great assembly, when the Buddha said, "The human and heavenly beings who give alms to Subhūti and the other monks will fall into the three evil paths." After the human and heavenly beings had heard this, would they be likely to go on giving alms to the *shōmon* disciples? It would almost appear as though the Buddha were deliberately attempting through his words to inflict death upon those who were in the two realms of *shōmon* and *engaku*. The more sensible persons in the assembly were no doubt repelled by the Buddha's action. Nevertheless, the *shōmon* disciples were able to obtain enough of the alms given to the Buddha to keep themselves alive, meager though the amount was.

When I consider the situation, it occurs to me that, if the Buddha had passed away after preaching the various sutras delivered in the first forty or more years of his teaching life, and had never lived to preach the Lotus Sutra in the later eight years, then who would ever have offered alms to these *shōmon* disciples? They would have fallen alive into the realm of Hungry Ghosts.

But after more than forty years of preaching various sutras, it was as though the bright spring sun appeared to melt the frigid ice, or a great wind arose to dispel the dew from countless grasses. With one remark, in one moment, the Buddha wiped away his earlier pronouncements, saying, "I have not yet revealed the truth." Like a great wind scattering the dark clouds or the full moon in the vast heavens, or like the sun shining in the blue sky, he proclaimed, "The World-Honored One has long expounded his doctrines and now must reveal the truth."[187] With the brilliance of the sun or the brightness of the moon, it was revealed in the Lotus Sutra that Śāriputra would become the Flower Light Tathagata and Mahākāśyapa would become the Light Bright Tathagata. Because of the Lotus Sutra, which is a phoenix among writings, and a mirror that reflects the teachings after the Buddha's passing, these *shōmon* disciples were looked up to by the human and heavenly supporters of Buddhism as though they were actual Buddhas.

If the water is clear, then the moon will not fail to be reflected there. If the wind blows, then the grass and trees will not fail to bow before it. And if there is a true votary of the Lotus Sutra, then the sages, the *shōmon* disciples, should not fail to go to his side, though they might have to pass through a great fire to do so, or make their way through a great rock. Though Mahākāśyapa may be deep in meditation, he should not ignore the circumstances.[188] Why does he do nothing about the situation? I am completely perplexed. Is this not the period of "the fifth five hundred years"? Is the prediction that the Lotus Sutra will be widely declared and spread[189] mere nonsense? Is

Nichiren not the votary of the Lotus Sutra? Are the *shōmon* disciples protecting those who disparage the Lotus Sutra as a mere written teaching and who put forth their great lies about what they call a "special transmission"?[190] Are they guarding those who write "Discard! close! ignore! abandon!,"[191] urging men to put an end to the teachings of the Lotus Sutra and to throw away the texts, and who cause the ruin of the temples where they are taught? The *shōmon* disciples and the various deities of Heaven swore before the Buddha to protect the votary of the Lotus Sutra, but now that they see how fierce are the great persecutions of this age of chaos, have they decided to withhold their aid? The sun and the moon are still up in the sky. Mount Sumeru has not collapsed. The sea tides ebb and flow and the four seasons proceed in their normal order. Why then is there no sign of aid for the votary of the Lotus Sutra? My doubts grow deeper than ever.

In the sutras preached before the Lotus Sutra, the Buddha is shown predicting that various great bodhisattvas and heavenly and human beings will attain Buddhahood in the future. But trying to realize such predictions is like trying to grasp the moon in the water, like mistaking the reflection for the actual object—it has the color and shape of the object but not the reality. Likewise, the Buddha would seem to be displaying profound kindness in making such predictions, but in fact it is little kindness at all.

When Shakyamuni had first attained enlightenment and had not yet begun to preach, more than sixty great bodhisattvas, including Dharma Wisdom, Forest of Merits, Diamond Pennant, and Diamond Storehouse, appeared from the various Buddha lands of the ten directions and came before the Buddha. There, at the request of the bodhisattvas Chief Wise, Moon of Deliverance,[192] and others, they preached the doctrines of the ten stages of security, the ten stages of practice, the ten stages of devotion, the ten stages of development,[193] etc. The doctrines that these great bodhisattvas preached were not learned from Shakyamuni Buddha. At that time, Bonten and other deities of the worlds of the ten directions came together and preached the Dharma, but again it was not something they had learned from Shakyamuni.

These great bodhisattvas, deities, dragons, etc. who appeared at the assembly described in the *Kegon* Sutra were beings who had dwelt in "inconceivable liberation"[194] since before Shakyamuni. Perhaps they were disciples of Shakyamuni Buddha when he was carrying out bodhisattva practices in previous incarnations, or perhaps they were disciples of previous Buddhas of the worlds of the ten directions. In any event, they were not disciples of the Shakyamuni who was born in India and who attained enlightenment at the age of thirty.

It was only when the Buddha set forth the four types of teachings[195] in the *Agon, Hōdō,* and *Hannya* sutras that he finally acquired disciples. And although these were doctrines preached by the Buddha himself, they were not his own. Why do I say this? Because the *bekkyō* and *engyō,* the two higher types of teachings, as set forth in the *Hōdō* and *Hannya* sutras, do not differ in meaning from the *bekkyō* and *engyō* as set forth in the *Kegon* Sutra. The *bekkyō* and *engyō* teachings given in the *Kegon* Sutra are not the *bekkyō* and *engyō* teachings of Shakyamuni Buddha. They are the *bekkyō* and *engyō* teachings of Hōe, or Dharma Wisdom, and the other great bodhisattvas mentioned earlier. These great bodhisattvas may appear to most people to have been disciples of Shakyamuni Buddha, but in fact it would be better to call them his teachers. Shakyamuni listened to these bodhisattvas preaching and, after gaining wisdom and understanding, proceeded to set forth the *bekkyō* and *engyō* teachings of the *Hōdō* and *Hannya* sutras. But these differ in no way from the *bekkyō* and *engyō* teachings of the *Kegon* Sutra.

Therefore we know that these bodhisattvas were the teachers of Shakyamuni. These bodhisattvas are mentioned in the *Kegon* Sutra, where they are called *zenchishiki* or men of "good influence." To call a person a *zenchishiki*[196] means that he is neither one's teacher nor one's disciple. The two types of teachings called *zōkyō* and *tsūgyō* are offshoots of the *bekkyō* and *engyō* teachings. Anyone who understands the *bekkyō* and *engyō* teachings will invariably understand the *zōkyō* and *tsūgyō* teachings as well.

A teacher is someone who teaches his disciples things that they did not previously know. For example, in the ages before the Buddha, the heavenly and human beings and followers of Brahmanism were all disciples of the two deities and the three ascetics.[197] Though their doctrines branched off to form ninety-five different schools, these did not go beyond the views of the three ascetics. Shakyamuni also studied these doctrines and for a time became a disciple of the Brahmanic teachers. But after spending twelve years in various painful and comfortable practices,[198] he came to understand the principles of suffering, emptiness, impermanence, and non-ego. Therefore he ceased to call himself a disciple of the Brahmanic teachings and instead proclaimed himself the possessor of a wisdom acquired from no teacher at all. Thus in time the heavenly and human beings came to look up to him as a great teacher.

It is clear, therefore, that during the teaching period of the first four flavors, Shakyamuni Buddha was a disciple of Hōe and the other great bodhisattvas. Similarly, he was the ninth disciple of Bodhisattva Monju.[199] This is also the reason why the Buddha repeatedly declares in the earlier sutras, "I never preached a single word."

When Shakyamuni Buddha was seventy-two, he preached the *Muryōgi* Sutra on Eagle Peak in the kingdom of Magadha. At that time he denied all the sutras he had preached during the previous more than forty years, and all the fragmentary teachings derived from those sutras, saying, "In these more than forty years, I have not yet revealed the truth." At that time, the great bodhisattvas and the various heavenly and human beings hastened to implore the Buddha to reveal the true doctrine. In fact, in the *Muryōgi* Sutra he mentioned one teaching that appeared to be true, but he did not elaborate on it. It was like the moment when the moon is about to rise. The moon is still hidden behind the eastern hills, and though its glow begins to light the western hills, people cannot yet see the body of the moon itself.

In the *Hōben* chapter of the Lotus Sutra, when the Buddha first briefly explained the principle of opening the three vehicles to reveal the one vehicle, he also briefly explained the concept of *ichinen sanzen,* speaking the true thoughts that were in his mind. But because this was the first time he had touched on the subject, it was only dimly apprehended, like the first note of the cuckoo heard by someone drowsy with sleep, or like the moon appearing over the rim of the hill but veiled in thin clouds. Śāriputra and the others, startled, called the deities, dragon gods, and great bodhisattvas together, begging for instruction. As the sutra says: "The various deities and dragon gods were numberless as the sands of the Ganges; the various bodhisattvas seeking to be Buddhas were great in number, eighty thousand. And from the myriads of millions of lands the wheel-turning kings[200] arrived. With palms pressed together and reverent minds, all wished to hear the teaching of perfect endowment."[201]

The passage indicates that the persons requested to hear a doctrine such as they had not heard in the previous more than forty years, one that differed from the four flavors and the three teachings. With regard to the line "they wish to hear the teaching of perfect endowment," it may be noted that the Nirvana Sutra states: "*Sad* indicates perfect endowment."[202] The *Daijō Shiron Gengi Ki* states: "*Sad* connotes six. In India the number six implies perfect endowment."[203] In his annotation on the Lotus Sutra, Chi-tsang[204] writes: "*Sad* is translated as perfect endowment." In the eighth volume of his *Hokke Gengi,* T'ien-t'ai remarks, "*Sad* is a Sanskrit word, which is translated as *myō*."[205] Bodhisattva Nāgārjuna, in the heart of his thousand-volume *Daichido Ron,* comments, "*Sad* signifies six."[206] (Nāgārjuna was thirteenth in the lineage of the Buddha's successors, the founder of the Shingon, Kegon, and the other schools, a great sage who had ascended to the forty-first stage of bodhisattva practice and whose true identity was the Tathagata Hōun Jizaiō.)

The title *Myōhō-renge-kyō* is of course Chinese. In India, the Lotus Sutra is called *Saddharmapuṇḍarīka-sūtra.* The following is the mantra concerning the heart of the Lotus Sutra composed by Shan-wu-wei:

> Nōmaku sammanda bodanan (Hail to the universal Buddha)
> on (the three-bodied Tathagata)
> a a annaku (who opens, shows, enlightens, causes us to enter)
> saruba boda (all the Buddha's)
> kinō (wisdom and)
> sakishubiya (understanding)
> gyagyanō samsoba (so that we understand the empty nature)
> arakishani (and display a departure from defilement)
> satsuri daruma (the correct Dharma)
> fundarikya (white lotus)
> sotaran (sutra)
> ja (enters)
> un (everywhere)
> ban (causing us to dwell)
> koku (in joy)
> bazara (with steadfast)
> arakishaman (protection,)
> un (void, without form, without desire)
> sohaka (absolutely achieved)[207]

This mantra, which expresses the heart of the Lotus Sutra, was found in the iron tower in southern India.[208] In this mantra, the words *satsuri daruma* mean "correct Dharma." *Satsu* means *shō* (correct). *Shō* is the same as *myō* (mystic), *myō* is the same as *shō*. *Shōhokke* is the same as *Myōhokke*. And when the two syllables *Namu* are prefixed to the title *Myōhō-renge-kyō,* we have the formula Nam-myōhō-renge-kyō. [209]

Myō means *gusoku* (perfect endowment). Six refers to the six types of practices leading to perfection. [210] When the persons ask to hear the teaching of perfect endowment, they are asking how they may gain the perfect endowment of the six practices of the bodhisattvas. In the word *gusoku,* the element *gu* (possession) refers to the mutual possession of the Ten Worlds, while the element *soku* (perfect) means that, since there is mutual possession of the Ten Worlds, then any one world contains all the other worlds, indicating that this is "perfect." This Lotus Sutra is a single work consisting of eight volumes, twenty-eight chapters, and 69,384 characters. To each and every character is attached the word *myō* or "mystic," making it a Buddha endowed with the thirty-two distinguishing features and eighty physical characteristics. [211] Each of the Ten Worlds manifests its own fruit of Buddhahood. As Miao-lo writes, "If even the Buddha nature is present in all the Ten Worlds, then all the other worlds will of course be present, too." [212]

[According to the *Hōben* chapter,] the Buddha replied to the request of his listeners by saying that all Buddhas desire "to cause all beings to open the Buddha wisdom." [213] The term "all beings" here refers to Śāriputra and it also refers to *icchantika,* men of incorrigible disbelief. It also refers to the nine worlds, thus fulfilling the words of the Buddha, "All beings are numberless—I vow to save them." [214] As the Buddha says [in the *Hōben* chapter], "At the start I pledge to make all people perfectly equal to me, without any distinction between us. By now the original vows that I made have already been fulfilled." [215]

All the great bodhisattvas, heavenly beings and others, when they had heard the doctrine of the Buddha and comprehended it, said: "From past times we have heard the World-Honored One preach on various occasions, but we have never heard anything to match the profoundness and wonder of this superior Dharma!" [216]

The Great Teacher Dengyō comments: " 'From past times we have heard the World-Honored One preach on various occasions' refers to the fact that they had heard him preach the great doctrines of the *Kegon* Sutra and other sutras in the time previous to the preaching of the Lotus Sutra. 'We have never heard anything to match the profoundness and wonder of this superior Dharma' means that they had never heard the doctrine of the unique, supreme Buddha vehicle propounded in the Lotus Sutra."[217]

They understood, that is, that none of the previous Mahayana sutras such as the *Kegon, Hōdō, Hannya, Jimmitsu,*[218] and *Dainichi,* which are numerous as the sands of the Ganges, had ever made clear the great principle of *ichinen sanzen,* which is the core of all the teachings of the Buddha's lifetime, or the bone and marrow of those teachings, the doctrines that those in the two realms of *shōmon* and *engaku* shall achieve Buddhahood and that the Buddha attained enlightenment countless kalpas ago.

PART TWO

From this time forward, the great bodhisattvas as well as Bonten, Taishaku, the gods of the sun and moon, and the Four Heavenly Kings, became the disciples of Shakyamuni Buddha. Thus, in the *Hōtō* chapter of the Lotus Sutra, the Buddha treats these great bodhisattvas as his disciples, admonishing and instructing them in these words: "I say to the great assembly: After I have passed away, who can protect and embrace, read and recite this sutra? Now in the presence of the Buddha let him come forward and speak his vow!"[1] This was the solemn way he addressed them. And the great bodhisattvas in turn were, in the words of the sutra, "like the branches of small trees when a great wind blows them." Like the *kusha* grass[2] bending before a great wind or like rivers and streams drawn to the great ocean, so were they drawn to the Buddha.

But it was still a relatively short time since the Buddha had begun to preach the Lotus Sutra on Eagle Peak, and what he said seemed to his listeners dreamlike and unreal. The Treasure Tower had first appeared to confirm the correctness of the theoretical teaching in the first part of the Lotus Sutra, and after that the Treasure Tower prepared the way for the expounding of the essential teaching. The Buddhas of the ten directions gathered in assembly, Shakyamuni Buddha announcing that "all of these are emanations of my being." The Treasure Tower hung in the air, with Shakyamuni and Tahō seated side by side in it, as though both the sun and the moon had appeared side by side in the blue sky. The great assembly of human and heavenly beings were ranged about the sky like stars, and the

Buddhas who were emanations of Shakyamuni Buddha were on the ground, seated on their lion king thrones[3] under jewel trees.

In the Lotus Treasury World described in the *Kegon* Sutra, the Buddhas in their reward bodies all dwell in their separate lands. Buddhas of other worlds do not come to this world and call themselves emanations of Shakyamuni, [as happened in the case of the Lotus Sutra,] nor do Buddhas of this world go to other worlds. Only Hōe and the others of the four bodhisattvas[4] come and go.

As for the Nine Honored Ones of the Eight Petaled Lotus and the Thirty-seven Honored Ones,[5] described in the *Dainichi* and *Kongōchō* sutras, although they appear to be transformation bodies of the Buddha Dainichi or Mahāvairocana, they are not Buddhas enlightened since the remote past nor endowed with the three bodies.

The thousand Buddhas described in the *Daibon Hannya* Sutra and the Buddhas of the six directions represented in the *Amida* Sutra never assembled in this world, [as did the Buddha's emanations in the Lotus Sutra]. The Buddhas who are described in the *Daijuku* Sutra as assembling in this world, on the other hand, were not emanations of Shakyamuni. Similarly, the four Buddhas of the four directions[6] depicted in the *Konkōmyō* Sutra are merely their own transformation bodies.[7]

Thus, in the various sutras other than the Lotus Sutra, Shakyamuni does not assemble Buddhas who carry out different austerities and practices and who possess the three bodies, nor does he identify them as emanations of himself. [Only in the *Hōtō* chapter of the Lotus Sutra does he do so.] This chapter, then, is intended as an introduction to the *Juryō* chapter that follows later. Shakyamuni Buddha, who was believed to have attained enlightenment for the first time only some forty or more years previously, calls together Buddhas who had become enlightened as long ago as one or even ten kalpas in the past, and declares that they are emanations of himself. This is a far cry indeed from the Buddha's usual preaching on the equality of all Buddhas [in their Dharma bodies], and in fact a cause of great astonishment. If Shakyamuni had attained enlightenment for the first time only some forty years earlier, there could hardly have been so many beings in the ten directions who had received his instruction. And even if he was privileged to possess emanations, there would have been no benefit in his showing them to his listeners. T'ien-t'ai, describing what went on in the astonished minds of the assembly, says:

"It was evident to them that Shakyamuni Buddha possessed numerous emanations. Therefore they understood that he must have attained enlightenment in the far distant past."[8]

In addition, a multitude of great Bodhisattvas of the Earth appeared, rising up out of the ground. Even Fugen and Monju, who had been regarded as the leading disciples of Shakyamuni, could not compare to them. The great bodhisattvas described in the assemblies in the *Kegon, Hōdō,* and *Hannya* sutras and the *Hōtō* chapter of the Lotus Sutra, or Kongōsatta and the others of the sixteen great bodhisattvas of the *Dainichi* Sutra, when compared with these newly arrived bodhisattvas, seemed like a pack of apes or monkeys, with the new bodhisattvas appearing among them like so many Taishakus. It was as though great ministers of court should mingle with humble mountain folk. Even Miroku, who was to be the next Buddha after Shakyamuni, was perplexed by them, to say nothing of the lesser personages in the assembly.

Among these innumerable great bodhisattvas there were four great sages called Jōgyō, Muhengyō, Jōgyō, and Anryūgyō. In the presence of these four, the other bodhisattvas suspended in the air or seated on Eagle Peak could not bear to gaze on them face to face or try to match the workings of their minds. Even the four bodhisattvas of the *Kegon* Sutra,[9] the four bodhisattvas of the *Dainichi* Sutra,[10] or the sixteen great bodhisattvas of the *Kongōchō* Sutra,[11] when in the presence of these four, were like bleary-eyed men trying to peer at the sun, or like humble fishermen appearing in audience before the emperor. These four were like T'ai-kung Wang and the others of the Four Sages of ancient China,[12] who towered above the multitude. They were like the Four White-haired Recluses of Mount Shang[13] who assisted Emperor Hui of the Han dynasty. Solemn, dignified, they were beings of great and lofty stature. Aside from Shakyamuni Buddha, Tahō Buddha and the emanations of Shakyamuni Buddha from the ten directions, they were worthy of acting as teachers to all beings.

Then Bodhisattva Miroku began to consider the matter in his mind. He said to himself, "Since Shakyamuni Buddha was a crown prince, and during the forty-two years since he gained enlightenment at the age of thirty up until this gathering on Eagle Peak, I have known all the bodhisattvas of this world, and all the great bodhisattvas that have come from the worlds of the ten directions to attend this assembly. Moreover, I have visited all the pure and impure lands of the ten directions, sometimes as the Buddha's emissary, at other times on my own initiative, and I have become acquainted with all the great bodhisattvas of those various countries. Now who are these great bodhisattvas who have appeared from the earth, and what kind of Buddha is their teacher? Surely he must be a Buddha who surpasses even Shakyamuni, Tahō, and the emanations from the ten directions! From the violence of the rain, you can judge the greatness of the dragon that caused it to fall; from the size of the lotus flower, you can tell the depth of the pond that produced it. [14] Now from what country did these great bodhisattvas come, under what Buddha did they study, and what great Dharma do they practice?" [15]

Thus did Miroku wonder to himself, becoming so puzzled that he was unable to utter a sound. But, perhaps through the Buddha's power, he was at last able to put his doubts into words, saying: "The incalculable thousands of myriads of millions of bodhisattvas in a great multitude such as the past has never seen . . . This great, majestic, vigorously advancing multitude of bodhisattvas . . . who preached the Dharma for their sake, instructing them and leading them to their present state? As whose followers did they first turn to the Way? What Buddha's teachings do they proclaim? . . . World-Honored One, from past times I have never seen their like! I beg you to explain where they come from, the name of the land. Though I am constantly visiting other countries, I have never seen the likes of them! Within all this multitude, I do not recognize a single person. Suddenly they have come out of the ground—I beg you to explain the reason!" [16]

T'ien-t'ai comments on this: "From the time immediately after his enlightenment when Shakyamuni preached the *Kegon* Sutra up until the present gathering on Eagle Peak, bodhisattvas had continuously come from the ten directions to gather in assembly. Their numbers were unlimited, but Miroku, with the wisdom and power appropriate to the Buddha's successor-to-be, had seen and come to know them all. And yet among the newly arrived multitude, he did not recognize a single person—this in spite of the fact that he had traveled in the ten directions, had served various Buddhas, and was well known among the multitude." [17]

Maio-lo comments: "Wise men can see omens and what they foretell, as snakes know the way of snakes." [18]

The meaning of these passages of scripture and commentary is perfectly clear. In effect, from the time of Shakyamuni's enlightenment up until the assembly on Eagle Peak in this land, in all the lands of the ten directions, no one had ever seen or heard of these bodhisattvas that came forth from the earth.

The Buddha, replying to Miroku's doubts, said: "Ajita,[19] . . . these persons whom you and the others have never seen before, they are bodhisattvas whom I converted and guided after I had attained supreme enlightenment in this *saha* world. I tamed their hearts and caused them to develop a longing for the Way."[20]

He also said: "When I was in the city of Gayā,[21] seated beneath the Bodhi tree, I attained the highest form of enlightenment and turned the wheel of the unparalleled Law. Thereafter I taught them, and caused them for the first time to aspire to enlightenment. And now all dwell in the stage where they will never backslide. . . . Ever since the long distant past I have been teaching and guiding the members of this multitude."

But Miroku and the other great bodhisattvas were further perplexed by these words of the Buddha. When the Buddha preached the *Kegon* Sutra, Hōe and countless other great bodhisattvas appeared in the assembly. Miroku and the others wondered who they could be, but the Buddha said, "They are my good friends," and they thought this must be true. Later, when the Buddha preached the *Daijuku* Sutra at the Great Treasure Chamber[22] and the *Daibon Hannya* Sutra at the White Heron Lake,[23] great bodhisattvas appeared in the assembly and Miroku and the others supposed that they too were friends of the Buddha.

But these great bodhisattvas who had newly appeared out of the earth were older and more distinguished-looking than those earlier bodhisattvas. One might conclude that they were the teachers of the Buddha, and yet he had "caused them for the first time to aspire to enlightenment,"[24] and, when they were still immature, had converted them and made them his disciples. It was this that Miroku and the others found so profoundly perplexing.

Prince Shōtoku[25] of Japan was the son of Emperor Yōmei, the thirty-second sovereign of Japan. When he was six years old, elderly men came to Japan from the states of Paekche and Koguryŏ in Korea and from the land of China. The six-year-old prince thereupon exclaimed, "These are my disciples!" and the old men in turn pressed their palms together in reverence and said, "You are our teacher!" This was a strange happening indeed.

There is a similar story found in a secular work. According to this work, a man was walking along a road when he saw by the roadside a young man of about thirty who was beating an old man of about eighty. When he asked the reason, the young man replied, "This old man is my son."[26]

Bodhisattva Miroku, continuing to doubt, said, "World-Honored One, when you were crown prince, you left the palace of the Shakyas and sat in the place of meditation not far from the city of Gayā, where you attained the supreme enlightenment. A mere forty years or so have passed since then. In that short period of time, how could you have accomplished so much great work as a Buddha?"[27]

The various bodhisattvas who had attended the numerous assemblies held in the forty-some years since the Buddha preached the *Kegon* Sutra had raised doubts at each assembly. The Buddha dispelled these doubts for the benefit of the multitude. But this present doubt [concerning the bodhisattvas who had appeared out of the earth] was the greatest doubt of all. It surpassed even the doubt entertained by Daishōgon and the others of the eighty thousand bodhisattvas described in the *Muryōgi* Sutra when the Buddha, after declaring in the previous forty-some years of his teaching that enlightenment was something that required countless kalpas to attain, now announced that it could be attained in a very short time.[28]

According to the *Kammuryōju* Sutra, King Ajātaśatru, led astray by Devadatta, imprisoned his father and was on the point of killing his mother, Lady Vaidehī. Reprimanded by the court ministers Jīvaka and Candraprabhā, however, he spared his mother's life. At that time she had an interview with the Buddha and began by posing this question: "What sin have I committed in the past that I should have given birth to this evil son? And, World-Honored One, through what cause have you come to be related to a person as evil as your cousin Devadatta?"[29]

Of the two doubts raised here, the second is the more perplexing, the question of why the Buddha should be related to an evil person like Devadatta. A wheel-turning king, we are told, is never born into the world along with his enemies, nor is the god Taishaku to be found in the company of demons. The Buddha had been a merciful personage for countless kalpas. Yet the fact that Shakyamuni was born together with his archenemy might make one doubt whether he was indeed a Buddha at all. The Buddha, however, did not answer the question of Lady Vaidehī. Therefore, if one reads only the *Kammuryōju* Sutra and does not examine the *Devadatta* chapter of the Lotus Sutra, he will never know the truth of the matter. [30]

In the Nirvana Sutra, Bodhisattva Kashō posed thirty-six questions to the Buddha, but even these cannot compare to this question [concerning the bodhisattvas who appeared from the earth]. If the Buddha had failed to dispel the doubts concerning this matter, the sacred teachings of his entire lifetime would have amounted to no more than froth on the water, and the members of the multitude would have remained tangled in the snare of doubt. That was why it was so important for him to preach the *Juryō* chapter.

Later, when the Buddha preached the *Juryō* chapter, he said: "All the human and heavenly beings and the *asuras* at present believe that Shakyamuni Buddha, after leaving the palace of the Shakyas, sat in the place of meditation not far from the city of Gayā and there attained the supreme enlightenment." This passage expresses the view held by all the great bodhisattvas and the rest of the multitude from the time when Shakyamuni first attained enlightenment until the preaching of the *Anrakugyō* chapter of the Lotus Sutra. "However, men of devout faith," the Buddha continued, "the time is limitless and boundless—a hundred, thousand, ten thousand, hundred thousand, nayuta kalpas—since I in fact attained Buddhahood." [31]

Three places in the *Kegon* Sutra the Buddha said: "I have attained enlightenment for the first time." In the *Agon* sutras he speaks of having "for the first time attained enlightenment"; in the Vimalakirti Sutra he says, "For the first time the Buddha sat beneath the tree"; in the *Daijuku* Sutra, "It is sixteen years since the Buddha first attained enlightenment"; in the *Dainichi* Sutra, "some years ago when I sat in the place of meditation"; in the *Ninnō* Sutra, "twenty-nine years since my enlightenment"; in the *Muryōgi* Sutra, "previously I went to the place of meditation"; and in the *Hōben* chapter of the Lotus Sutra, "when I first sat in the place of meditation." But now all these passages have been exposed as gross falsehoods by this single pronouncement in the *Juryō* chapter.

When Shakyamuni Buddha revealed that he had gained enlightenment in the far distant past and had since then been constantly in the world, it became apparent that all the other Buddhas were emanations of Shakyamuni. When the Buddha preached the earlier sutras and the first half, or theoretical teaching, of the Lotus Sutra, the other Buddhas present were pictured as practicing various religious austerities and disciplines side by side with Shakyamuni Buddha. Therefore the people who pay devotion to one or another of these Buddhas as the object of worship customarily look down on Shakyamuni Buddha. But now it becomes apparent that Vairocana Buddha of the *Kegon* Sutra and the various Buddhas of the *Hōdō, Hannya,* and *Dainichi* sutras are all in fact followers of Shakyamuni Buddha.

When Shakyamuni gained enlightenment at the age of thirty, he seized the *saha* world away from Bonten and the Devil of the Sixth Heaven, who had ruled it previously, and made it his own. In the earlier sutras and the first half of the Lotus Sutra, he called the regions of the ten directions "pure lands" and spoke of the present world as an "impure land." But now he has reversed this in the *Juryō* chapter, revealing that this world is the true land and the so-called pure lands of the ten directions are impure lands, mere provisional lands.

Since the Buddha of the *Juryō* chapter is revealed as the eternal Buddha, it follows that the great bodhisattvas such as Monju and Miroku, and the great bodhisattvas from other realms are in fact disciples of Shakyamuni Buddha. If, among all the numerous sutras, this *Juryō* chapter should be lacking, it would be as though there were no sun and moon in the sky, no supreme ruler in the nation, no gems in the mountains and rivers, and no spirit in man.

Nevertheless, Ch'eng-kuan, Chia-hsiang, Tz'u-en, Kōbō, and others, seemingly learned men of provisional sects such as Kegon and Shingon, in order to praise the various sutras upon which their provisional doctrines are based, go so far as to say, "The Buddha of the *Kegon* Sutra is the Buddha in his reward body, while the Buddha of the Lotus Sutra is merely the Buddha in his manifested body."[32] Or they say, "The Buddha of the *Juryō* chapter of the Lotus Sutra is in the region of darkness, while the Buddha of the *Dainichi* Sutra occupies the position of enlightenment."[33]

As clouds obscure the moon, so calumnious ministers can obscure the man of true worth. A yellow stone, if people praise it, may be mistaken for a jewel, and ministers who are skilled in flattery may be mistaken for worthy men. In this impure age we live in, scholars and students are confused by the slanderous assertions of the kind of men I have mentioned above, and they do not appreciate the true worth of the jewel of the *Juryō* chapter. Even among the men of the Tendai sect there are those who have become so deluded that they cannot distinguish the gold of the Lotus Sutra from the mere stones that are the earlier sutras.

One should consider the fact that, if the Buddha had not attained enlightenment in the distant past, there could not have been so many disciples who were converted and instructed by him. The moon is not stingy with its shining, but if there is no water to catch its rays, then its reflection will not be seen. The Buddha may be very anxious to convert all people, but if the connection between them is not strong enough, then he cannot go through the eight phases[34] of a Buddha's existence. Thus, for example, the shōmon disciples attained the first stage of security [of bekkyō] and the first stage of development [of engyō—the stages where they could teach others],[35] but so long as they followed the teachings that preceded the Lotus Sutra and sought only to regulate and save themselves, they had to postpone the attainment of the eight phases of a Buddha's existence to some future lifetime.

If Shakyamuni Buddha had actually attained enlightenment for the first time at the age of thirty, then when he preached the Lotus Sutra, Bonten, Taishaku, the gods of the sun and moon, and the Four Heavenly Kings who have ruled the present world since the beginning of the kalpa would have been disciples of Shakyamuni Buddha for no longer than a period of forty-some years. During the eight years when he preached the Lotus Sutra, the beings who assembled to listen to him would have been unable to accept as their master a person who had so recently come to prominence and would have deferred instead to Bonten, Taishaku, and the other deities who had from ages past been the lords of this world.

But now that it has become apparent that Shakyamuni Buddha attained enlightenment countless kalpas ago, then the Bodhisattvas Nikkō and Gakkō, who attend the Buddha Yakushi of the eastern region, the Bodhisattvas Kannon and Seishi, who attend the Buddha Amida of the western region, along with the disciples of all the Buddhas of the worlds of the ten directions and the great bodhisattvas who are disciples of the Buddha Dainichi as they are shown in the Dainichi and Kongōchō sutras—all of these beings are disciples of Shakyamuni Buddha. Since the various Buddhas themselves are emanations of Shakyamuni Buddha, it goes without saying that their disciples must be disciples of Shakyamuni. And of course the various deities of the sun, moon, and stars, who have dwelt in this world since the beginning of the kalpa, must likewise be disciples of Shakyamuni Buddha.

Nevertheless, the sects of Buddhism other than Tendai have gone astray concerning the true object of worship. The Kusha, Jōjitsu, and Ritsu sects take as their object of worship the Shakyamuni Buddha who eliminated illusions by practicing thirty-four kinds of spiritual purification.[36] This is comparable to a situation in which the heir apparent of the supreme ruler of a state mistakenly believes himself to be the son of a commoner. The four sects of Kegon, Shingon, Sanron, and Hossō are all Mahayana schools of Buddhism. Among them the Hossō and Sanron sects worship a Buddha who is comparable to the Buddha in the superior manifested body.[37] This is like the heir of the supreme ruler supposing that his father was a member of the samurai class. The Kegon and Shingon sects look down upon Shakyamuni Buddha and declare that Vairocana or Dainichi Buddha should be the true object of worship. This is like the heir looking down upon his own father, the supreme ruler, and paying honor to one who is not even related to him by blood simply because that person pretends to be the Dharma King. The Jōdo sect considers itself to be most closely related to the Buddha Amida, who is an emanation of Shakyamuni, and abandons Shakyamuni himself. The Zen sect behaves like a person of low birth who makes much of his small achievements and despises his father and mother. Thus the Zen sect looks down upon both the Buddha and the sutras. All of these sects are misled concerning the true object of worship. They are like the people who lived in the age before the Three Rulers of ancient China and did not know who their own fathers were. In that respect, the people of that time were no different from birds and beasts.

The men of these sects who are ignorant of the teachings of the *Juryō* chapter are similarly like beasts. They do not understand to whom they are obligated. Therefore Miao-lo states: "Among all the teachings of the Buddha's lifetime, there is no place [other than the *Juryō* chapter] where the true longevity of the Buddha is revealed. A person ought to know how old his father and mother are. If a son does not even know how old his father is, he will also be in doubt as to what lands his father presides over. Though he may be idly praised for his talent and ability, he cannot be counted as a son at all!"[38]

The Great Teacher Miao-lo lived in the T'ien-pao era (742–755) in the latter part of the T'ang dynasty. He is saying that if one makes a deep and thorough examination of the Sanron, Kegon, Hossō, and Shingon schools and the sutras upon which they are based, but fails to become acquainted with the Buddha of the *Juryō* chapter, he is no more than a talented animal who does not even know what lands his father presides over. "Though he may be idly praised for his talent and ability" refers to men like Fa-tsang and Ch'eng-kuan of the Kegon school or Shan-wu-wei of the Shingon school. These teachers had talent and ability, yet they were like sons who do not even know their own father.

The Great Teacher Dengyō was the patriarch of both esoteric and exoteric Buddhism in Japan.[39] In his *Hokke Shūku* he writes: "The sutras that the other sects are based upon give expression in certain measure to the mother-like nature of the Buddha. But they convey only a sense of love and are lacking in a sense of fatherly sternness. It is only the Tendai sect, based upon the Lotus Sutra, that combines a sense of both love and sternness. The sutra is a father to all the worthy men, sages, those in the stages of learning and beyond learning, and those who have awakened in themselves the mind of the bodhisattva."[40]

The sutras that form the basis of the Shingon and Kegon sects do not even contain the terms "sowing," "maturing," and "harvest," much less the doctrine [of the sowing of the seeds of Buddhahood, the maturing of the seeds, and the eventual attainment of Buddhahood] to which these terms refer. When the sutras of the Kegon and Shingon sects assert that their followers will enter the first stage of development and achieve Buddhahood in their present body and in the same lifetime, they are putting forth the teachings of the provisional sutras alone, teachings that conceal [the seeds sowed in] the past.[41] To expect to attain fruition without knowing the seed first sowed is like the eunuch Chao Kao attempting to seize Imperial power in China or the monk Dōkyō trying to become emperor of Japan.[42]

The various sects argue with one another, each claiming that its sutra contains the true seeds of enlightenment. I do not intend to enter the argument. I will let the sutras speak for themselves. Thus the Bodhisattva Vasubandhu, speaking of the seeds of enlightenment implanted by the Lotus Sutra, designates them "the seeds without peer."[43] And these seeds of enlightenment are the doctrine of *ichinen sanzen* as expounded by the Great Teacher T'ien-t'ai.

The seed of enlightenment of the various Buddhas described in the *Kegon* Sutra, the *Dainichi* Sutra, and the other various Mahayana sutras, is the one doctrine of *ichinen sanzen*. And the Great Teacher T'ien-t'ai was the only person who was capable of perceiving the truth of this doctrine. Ch'eng-kuan of the Kegon sect usurped the doctrine of *ichinen sanzen* and used it to interpret the passage in the *Kegon* Sutra that reads: "The mind is like a skilled painter." [44]

The *Dainichi* Sutra of the Shingon sect contains no mention of the fact that the *shōmon* and *engaku* can attain Buddhahood, that the Buddha Shakyamuni achieved enlightenment countless kalpas ago, or of the doctrine of *ichinen sanzen*. But after Shan-wu-wei came to China, he had occasion to read the *Maka Shikan* by T'ien-t'ai and came to gain wisdom and understanding. He then usurped the doctrine of *ichinen sanzen,* using it to interpret the passages in the *Dainichi* Sutra on "the reality of the mind" or that which reads, "I am the source and beginning of all things," [45] making it the core of the Shingon teachings but adding to it the practice of mudras and mantras. And in comparing the relative merits of the Lotus Sutra and the *Dainichi* Sutra, he declared that while the two agree in principle, the latter is superior in practice. The mandalas of the two worlds [46] symbolize the attaining of Buddhahood by the *shōmon* and *engaku* and the mutual possession of the Ten Worlds, but are these doctrines to be found anywhere in the *Dainichi* Sutra? [Those who claim so] are guilty of the grossest deception!

Therefore the Great Teacher Dengyō writes: "The school of Shingon Buddhism that has recently been brought to Japan deliberately obscures how its transmission was falsified in the recording [by I-hsing, who was deceived by Shan-wu-wei], while the Kegon school that was introduced earlier attempts to disguise the fact that it was influenced by the doctrines of T'ien-t'ai." [47]

Suppose someone were to go to some wild region like the island of Ezo (Hokkaido) and recite the famous poem:

> How I think of it—
> dim, dim in the morning mist
> of Akashi Bay,
> that boat moving out of sight
> beyond the islands. [48]

If the person told the ignorant natives of Ezo that he himself had composed the poem, they would probably believe him. The Buddhist scholars of China and Japan are equally gullible.

The Chinese priest Liang-hsü [49] [of the T'ien-t'ai school] writes: "The doctrines of the Shingon, Zen, Kegon, Sanron . . . can at best serve as a kind of introduction to the Lotus Sutra." [50] We are told that Shan-wu-wei was subjected to punishment by Emma, the King of

Hell, no doubt because of his mistaken view [that the *Dainichi* Sutra is superior to the Lotus Sutra]. Later he had a change of heart and became an enthusiastic supporter of the Lotus Sutra, which is why he was spared further punishment. As evidence, when he, Pu-k'ung, and the others devised mandalas to symbolize the teachings of the Shingon school, they placed the Lotus Sutra in the center of the two worlds as the supreme ruler, with the Womb Realm mandala of the *Dainichi* Sutra and the Diamond Realm mandala of the *Kongōchō* Sutra to the left and right as ministers to the ruler.

When Kōbō of Japan drew up a theoretical statement of the Shingon teachings, he was attracted by the Kegon sect and assigned [the *Kegon* Sutra to the ninth stage of advancement and] the Lotus Sutra to the eighth stage. [51] But when he taught the practices and ceremonies to his disciples Jitsue, Shinga, Enchō, Kōjō, [52] and the others, he placed the Lotus Sutra in a central position, between the two realms of the Womb and the Diamond as Shan-wu-wei and Pu-k'ung had done.

In a similar case, Chia-hsiang of the Sanron school, in his ten-volume *Hokke Genron,* assigned the Lotus Sutra to the fourth of the five periods of teachings, [53] claiming that it opened the way of the bodhisattva to the *shōmon* and *engaku*. Later, however, he became converted to the teachings of T'ien-t'ai. He ceased giving lectures, dismissed his disciples, and instead served the Great Teacher T'ien-t'ai for a period of seven years, personally carrying T'ien-t'ai on his back [when T'ien-t'ai mounted an elevated seat for preaching].

Again, Tz'u-en, the founder of the Hossō school, in his seven-volume and twelve-volume *Daijō Hōon Girin Jō,* [54] states: "The One Vehicle doctrine set forth in the Lotus Sutra is a mere expedient; the Three Vehicle doctrine represents the truth." He also makes many similarly absurd pronouncements. But in the fourth volume of the *Hokke Genzan Yōshū,* [55] he is represented as saying that "both doctrines are to be accepted," thus bringing flexible interpretation to the tenets of his own sect. Although he said that both doctrines were acceptable, in his heart he supported the T'ien-t'ai teachings on the Lotus Sutra.

Ch'eng-kuan of the Kegon school wrote a commentary on the *Kegon* Sutra in which he compared the *Kegon* and Lotus sutras and seems to have declared that the Lotus Sutra is a mere expedient doctrine. But later he wrote: "I believe that the teachings of the T'ien-t'ai school represent the truth. In doctrine and principle they agree completely with those of my own school."[56] From this it would appear, would it not, that he regretted his earlier pronouncement.

Kōbō is a similar example. If one has no mirror, he cannot see his own face, and if one has no opponents, he cannot learn of his own errors. The scholars of the Shingon and the other various sects were unaware of their errors. But after they were fortunate enough to encounter the Great Teacher Dengyō, they became conscious of the mistakes of their own particular sects.

The various Buddhas, bodhisattvas, and heavenly and human beings described in the sutras that preceded the Lotus may seem to have gained enlightenment through the particular sutras in which they appear. But in fact they attained enlightenment only through the Lotus Sutra. The first of the general vows taken by Shakyamuni and the other Buddhas to "save the countless sentient beings" finds fulfillment through the Lotus Sutra. That is the meaning of the passage in the *Hōben* chapter of the Lotus Sutra in which Shakyamuni declares: "By now the original vows that I made have already been fulfilled."[57]

In view of these facts, I believe that the devotees and followers of the various [provisional] sutras such as the *Kegon, Kammuryōju,* and *Dainichi* sutras will undoubtedly be protected by the Buddhas, bodhisattvas, and heavenly beings of the respective sutras that they uphold. But if the votaries of the *Dainichi, Kammuryōju,* and other sutras should set themselves up as the enemies of the votary of the Lotus Sutra, then the Buddhas, bodhisattvas, and heavenly beings will abandon them and will protect the votary of the Lotus Sutra. It is like the case of a filial son whose father opposes the ruler of the kingdom. The son will abandon his father and support the ruler, for to do so is the height of filial piety.

The same thing applies to Buddhism. The Buddhas, bodhisattvas, and the Ten Goddesses described in the Lotus Sutra lend their protection to Nichiren, the votary of the Lotus. And in addition, the Buddhas of the six directions and the twenty-five bodhisattvas of the Jōdo sect,[58] the 1,200 venerable ones of the Shingon sect,[59] and the various venerable ones and benevolent guardian deities of the seven sects[60] also protect Nichiren. It is like the case of the Great Teacher Dengyō, who was protected by the guardian deities of the seven sects.

I, Nichiren, think as follows. The gods of the sun and moon and the other deities were present in the two places and three assemblies[61] when the Lotus Sutra was preached. If a votary of the Lotus Sutra should appear, then, like iron drawn to a magnet or the reflection of the moon appearing in the water, they will instantly come forth to take on his sufferings for him and thereby fulfill the vow that they made in the presence of the Buddha. But they have yet to come and inquire of my well-being. Does this mean that I am not a true votary of the Lotus Sutra? If that is so, then I must examine the text of the sutra once more in the light of my conduct and see where I am at fault.

Question: What eyes of wisdom allow you to perceive that the Nembutsu, Zen, and other sects of our time are the enemies of the Lotus Sutra and evil companions who are ready to mislead all people?

Answer: I do not state personal opinions, but merely hold up the mirror of the sutras and commentaries so that the slanderers of the Law may see their ugly faces reflected there and perceive their errors. But, blind men that they are, it is beyond my power.

In the *Hōtō* chapter in the fourth volume of the Lotus Sutra we read: [62] "At that time Tahō Buddha in the Treasure Tower gave half of his seat to Shakyamuni Buddha. . . . At that time, the great multitude saw the two Buddhas seated with legs crossed on the lion throne in the tower of seven treasures. . . . Shakyamuni Buddha addressed the four categories of Buddhists in a loud voice, saying, 'Who among you will propagate the Lotus Sutra throughout the *saha* world? Now is the time to do so! Before long, the Buddha will enter nirvana. The Buddha hopes there is someone to whom he can entrust this Lotus Sutra.' "

This is the first pronouncement of the Buddha.

Again the chapter reads: "At this time the World-Honored One, wishing to repeat the announcement that he had just made, spoke in verse:

'The Sainted Lord, World-Honored One [Tahō Buddha],
though he passed into nirvana long ago,
seats himself in the Treasure Tower,
coming here for the sake of the Law.
You people, why then do you also
not strive for the sake of the Law? . . .
My emanations,
these numberless Buddhas
who are like the sands of the Ganges,
they have come, desiring to hear the Law . . .
Each has abandoned his precious land

as well as his host of disciples,
the heavenly and human beings, dragons and gods,
and all the offerings they give him—
to make certain that the Law will long endure,
they have come to this place . . .
It is like the branches of small trees
when a great wind blows them.
Through this expedient means
they make certain that the Law will long endure.
So I say to the great assembly:
After I have passed away,
who can protect and maintain,
read, and recite this sutra?
Now in the presence of the Buddha
let him come forward and speak his vow!' "

This is the second proclamation of the Buddha. The passage continues:

" 'Tahō Buddha, myself
and the emanations of myself
who have gathered here—
they know the intention of my words . . .
Men of devout faith,
each of you must consider carefully!
This is a difficult matter—
it is proper that you take a great vow.
The other sutras
number as many as the sands of the Ganges,
but though you expound them all,
that is not worthy to be considered difficult.
To seize Mount Sumeru
and fling it far off
to the measureless Buddha lands—
that too is not difficult . . .
But after the Buddha's passing,
in the time of evil,
to be able to preach this sutra—
that is difficult indeed! . . .
When the fires come at the end of the kalpa,
to load dry grass on one's back
and enter the fire without being burned—
that is not difficult.
But after my passing,

to be able to preserve this sutra
and expound it to even one person—
that is difficult indeed! . . .
Men of devout faith,
after my passing,
who can receive and embrace,
read and recite this sutra?
Now in the presence of the Buddha
let him come forward and speak his vow!' "

This is the third admonition from the Buddha. The fourth and
fifth admonitions are found in the *Devadatta* chapter and I will deal
with them later.

The meaning of these passages from the sutra is right before our
eyes, obvious as the sun suspended in the blue sky or a mole on a
white face. And yet the blind ones, those with perverse eyes, the one-
eyed, those who believe no one but their own teachers, and those
who cling to biased views cannot see it!

For those who have set their hearts on the Truth, in spite of all
difficulties, I will try to demonstrate [what these passages mean]. But
they must understand that the Truth is more rarely met with than the
peaches of immortality that grow in the garden of the Queen Mother
of the West, or the udumbara flower that blooms only once every
three thousand years in the age of a wheel-turning monarch. [63] Moreover, the conflict [between Nichiren and the various sects] surpasses
the eight years of warfare when Liu Pang and Hsiang Yü[64] battled
for the empire of China, the seven years when Minamoto no Yoritomo and Taira no Munemori[65] fought for the islands of Japan, the
struggles between Taishaku and the *asuras,* or between the dragon
kings and the *garuḍa* birds at the Icy Lake. [66]

This Truth that I am speaking of has made its appearance twice in
the country of Japan. You should understand that it appeared once
with the Great Teacher Dengyō and again with Nichiren. But the
sightless ones doubt this, and it is beyond my power to convince
them. Shakyamuni Buddha, Tahō Buddha, and the Buddhas of the
ten directions gathered together and judged the relative merits of all
the sutras of Japan, China, India, the palace of the Dragon King, the
heavens, and all the other worlds of the ten directions, and this is the
sutra they chose.

Question: Do sutras such as the *Kegon, Hōdō, Hannya, Jimmitsu,*

Ryōga, Dainichi, and Nirvana belong to the "nine easy acts" group or the "six difficult acts" group?[67]

Answer: Tu-shun, Chih-yen, Fa-tsang, and Ch'eng-kuan of the Kegon school, who were all masters of the three divisions of the canon, stated that both the Lotus Sutra and the *Kegon* Sutra belong to the "six difficult acts" category. Though in name they are two different sutras, they are identical in their teachings and principles. It is similar to the statement, "Though the four perceptions of reality are separate, the truth they point to is identical."[68]

The Tripitaka Master Hsüan-tsang and the Great Teacher Tz'u-en of the Hossō school state that the *Jimmitsu* Sutra and the Lotus Sutra both expound the Consciousness-Only doctrine. They date from the third period of the Buddha's teaching[69] and belong to the "six difficult" category.

Chia-hsiang of the Sanron school asserts that the *Hannya* Sutra and the Lotus Sutra are different names for a single entity, two sutras that preach one Truth.

The Tripitaka masters Shan-wu-wei, Chin-kang-chih, and Pu-k'ung of the Shingon school say that the *Dainichi* Sutra and the Lotus Sutra are identical in principle and that both belong to the "six difficult" category. But the Japanese Shingon leader Kōbō says that the *Dainichi* Sutra belongs neither to the "six difficult" nor the "nine easy" category. The *Dainichi* Sutra, according to him, stands apart from all the other sutras preached by Shakyamuni Buddha, since it was preached by Dainichi Buddha, the Buddha in his Law body. Likewise, some persons assert that, since the *Kegon* Sutra was preached by the Buddha in his reward body, it stands outside the categories of "six difficult" and "nine easy."

Such, then, are the views put forth by the founders of these four schools. The thousands of followers of these schools likewise subscribe to the same views.

I must observe sadly that, although it would be simple enough to point out the error of the views put forward by these men, if I did so, the people of today would not even look in my direction, much less listen to me. They would go on in their erroneous ways, and in the end would slander me to the rulers of the country and put my life in jeopardy. Nevertheless, our merciful father Shakyamuni Buddha, when he faced his end in the grove of sal trees, stated as his dying instructions that we are to "rely on the Law and not upon persons."[70]

"Not relying upon persons" means that, when persons of the first, second, third, and fourth ranks[71] preach, even though they are bodhisattvas such as Fugen or Monju whose enlightenment almost approaches that of the Buddha, if they do not preach with the sutra in hand, following its teachings faithfully, then they are not to be accepted.

It is also laid down that one should "rely on the sutras that are complete and final and not on those which are not complete and final."[72] We must therefore look carefully among the sutras to determine which are complete and final and which are not, and put our faith in the former. Bodhisattva Nāgārjuna in his *Jūjūbibasha Ron* states: "Do not rely on treatises that distort the sutras; rely only on those that are faithful to the sutras."[73] The Great Teacher T'ien-t'ai says: "That which accords with the sutras is to be accepted and heeded. But put no faith in anything that in word or meaning fails to do so."[74] The Great Teacher Dengyō says: "Depend upon the preachings of the Buddha and do not put faith in traditions handed down orally."[75] Enchin or the Great Teacher Chishō says: "In transmitting the teachings, rely on the written words."[76]

To be sure, the leaders of the various sects whose opinions I have quoted above all appear to base themselves on some groups of sutras and treatises in attempting to establish which teachings are the most superior. But these men all cling firmly to the doctrines of their own sect and perpetuate the erroneous views handed down from their predecessors, so that their judgments are characterized by "twisted interpretations and personal feelings." Their doctrines are no more than private opinions that have been dressed up and glorified.

The non-Buddhist schools of such men as Vatsa and Vaipulya, which appeared in India after the Buddha's death, are even more wrong in their views and more cunning in their doctrines than their counterparts before the Buddha [because they borrowed ideas from Buddhism]. Similarly, since the introduction of Buddhism to China in the Later Han dynasty, non-Buddhist views and writings have become even more wrong and cunning than the pre-Buddhist writings of Confucianism that deal with the Three Rulers and Five Emperors of antiquity. Also the leaders of the Kegon, Hossō, Shingon, and other schools, jealous of the orthodox teachings of the T'ien-t'ai school, brazenly interpret the words of the true sutra [i.e., the Lotus Sutra] in such a way that they will accord with the provisional teachings.

Those who seek the truth of Buddhism, however, should reject such one-sided views, transcending disputes between one's own sect and others, and should not treat others with contempt.

In the *Hosshi* chapter of the Lotus Sutra, the Buddha says: "Among all the sutras I have preached, now preach, and will preach, this Lotus Sutra is the most difficult to believe and the most difficult to understand."[77]

Miao-lo remarks: "Though other sutras may call themselves the king among sutras, there is none that announces itself as foremost among all the sutras preached in the past, now being preached, or to be preached in the future."[78] He also says: "Faced with this wonderful sutra that surpasses all those of past, present, and future, there are those who persist in going astray. They commit the grave fault of slandering the Truth and for many long kalpas are condemned to hell."[79]

Startled by these passages in the sutra and its commentaries, I examined all the sutras and the expositions and commentaries of the various teachers, and found that my doubts and suspicions melted away. But now those foolish Shingon priests rely upon their mudras and mantras and believe that the Shingon sect is superior to the Lotus Sutra, simply because the Great Teacher Jikaku and their other teachers have assured them that Shingon is superior. Their views are not worthy of discussion.

The *Mitsugon* Sutra says: "The *Jūji, Kegon, Daiju, Jinzū, Shōman,* and the other sutras all derive from this sutra. Thus the *Mitsugon* Sutra is the greatest of all sutras."[80]

The *Daiun* Sutra states: "This sutra is the wheel-turning monarch among all sutras. Why is this? Because in this sutra is set forth the doctrine of the constancy of the Buddha nature as the true nature of all beings."[81]

The *Rokuharamitsu* Sutra says: "All the correct teachings expounded by the countless Buddhas of the past and the eighty-four thousand wonderful laws that I have now expounded are in this sutra and may as a whole be divided into five categories: 1. sutra; 2. vinaya; 3. abhidharma; 4. prajñāparamitā; 5. dhāraṇī. The works in these five collections will instruct sentient beings. Among sentient beings there may be those who cannot accept and abide by the sutras, vinaya, abhidharma, and prajñāparamitā, or there may be sentient beings who commit various evil acts such as the four grave offenses, the eight grave offenses, or the five cardinal sins that lead to the hell of incessant suffering, [82] or slander the Mahayana sutras and disbelieve Buddhism itself. In order to wipe out such crimes, give rapid release to the offenders and allow them to enter into nirvana at once, I preached for their sake this collection of *dhāraṇīs*.

"These five divisions of the Dharma are compared to the flavors of milk, cream, curdled milk, butter, and ghee respectively, with ghee as the finest. The division containing the *dhāraṇīs* compares to ghee. Ghee has the finest and most subtle flavor among the five substances enumerated above and is capable of curing various sicknesses and easing the minds and bodies of sentient beings. Similarly, the *dhāraṇī* division stands foremost among the five divisions of the teachings because it can do away with grave offenses." [83]

The *Gejimmitsu* Sutra states: "At that time the Bodhisattva Shōgishō addressed the Buddha, saying, 'World-Honored One, in the first period of your teaching when you were in the Deer Park in Vārāṇaśi, for the sake of those who wished merely to embark upon the way of the *shōmon,* you expounded the doctrine of the four noble truths, [84] in this way turning the wheel of the Correct Law. This was a very wonderful thing, a very rare thing. No heavenly or human being in any of the countless worlds had ever been able to expound such a doctrine as this before. And yet the wheel of the Law that you turned at that time left room for improvement, left room for doubt. It was not yet final in meaning and offered ample opportunity for dispute.

" 'Then, World-Honored One, in the second period of your teaching, for the sake of those who wished merely to practice the way of the Great Vehicle, [85] you taught that all phenomena are without distinctive natures of their own, that there is no birth or death, that all things are basically in a state of quietude, and that the nature of beings as they exist constitutes nirvana. You turned the wheel of the Correct Law, although you did not reveal the whole truth. This was even more wonderful, an even rarer thing. But the wheel of the Law that you turned at that time left room for improvement, left room for doubt. It was not yet final in meaning and offered ample opportunity for dispute.

" 'Now, World-Honored One, in the third period of your teaching, for the sake of those who wish to practice the vehicle that saves all beings, you taught that all phenomena are without distinctive natures, that there is no birth or death, that all things are basically in a state of quietude, and that the nature of beings as they exist constitutes nirvana—and then you have taught that the "nature" you spoke of itself lacks anything that can be called a nature. You have turned the wheel of the Correct Law and expounded these doctrines in their perfect form. This is most wonderful, the rarest thing of all. This wheel of the Law that you have turned leaves no room for improvement, no room for doubt. It is truly complete and final in meaning and offers no opportunity for dispute.' "[86]

The *Daihannya* Sutra says: "By listening to the laws of the secular world and Buddhism, all beings may through expedient means be brought to understand and embrace the profound principles of *prajñā* or wisdom. And they will also come to understand and embrace the truth that, through *prajñā,* all actions carried out in the present world can be seen to partake of the Dharma nature, and that there is nothing whatsoever that is outside the Dharma nature."[87]

The first volume of the *Dainichi* Sutra states, "Master of Secrets, there is a Great Vehicle practice which arouses the mind that is unrelated to things and leads one to understand that all phenomena are without individual natures. Why is this? Because in past times those who practiced this way were able to observe the *ālaya-*consciousness[88] within the five aggregates, and to realize that individual natures are illusory."

The same sutra also says, "Master of Secrets, these men in this way cast aside the concept of egolessness and came to realize that the mind exists in a realm of complete freedom and that the individual mind has from the beginning never known birth [or death]."

It also says: "Emptiness is by nature removed from the sense organs and their objects. It has no form nor boundaries, but is a kind of void that transcends all theory. It represents the ultimate in the absence of individual nature."

It also says, "The Buddha Dainichi or Mahāvairocana addressed the Master of Secrets, saying, 'Master of Secrets, what is the meaning of enlightenment? It means to understand one's own mind as it truly is.' "[89]

The *Kegon* Sutra states, "Among the various beings of all the different worlds, there are few who seek to practice the vehicle of the *shōmon.* There are still fewer who seek that of the *engaku,* and those who seek the Great Vehicle are extremely rare. To seek the Great Vehicle is relatively easy to do, but to have faith in the doctrines of this sutra is difficult in the extreme. And how much more difficult is it to accept this sutra, keep its teachings correctly in mind, practice them as directed, and understand their true meaning.

"To take the major world system and hold it on the top of your head without moving for the space of a kalpa is not such a difficult thing to do. But to have faith in the doctrines of this sutra is difficult in the extreme. For the space of a kalpa to offer musical instruments to all the sentient beings who are as countless as the dust particles of the major world system will not gain you much merit. But to have faith in the doctrines of this sutra will gain you merit in great quantity. To hold ten Buddha lands in the palm of your hand and remain stationary in the midst of the air for the space of a kalpa is not so difficult to do. But to have faith in the doctrines of this sutra is difficult in the extreme. For the space of a kalpa to offer musical instruments to all the sentient beings who are as countless as the dust particles of those ten Buddha lands will not gain you much merit. But to have faith in the doctrines of this sutra will gain you merit in great quantity. For the space of a kalpa you may honor and give alms to the various Buddhas who are as countless as the dust particles of those Buddha lands. But if you can accept and abide by the doctrines of this chapter, you will gain vastly greater merit."[90]

The Nirvana Sutra says, "Although [belief in] the various Mahayana sutras will bring inestimable merit, there is no way to describe how much greater is the merit gained by [belief in] this sutra. It is a hundred times, a thousand times, a billion times greater, greater in a way that is beyond calculation or simile. Men of devout faith, milk comes from the cow, cream is made from milk, curdled milk is made from cream, butter is made from curdled milk, and ghee is made from butter. Ghee is the finest of all. He who eats it will be cured of all illnesses, just as if all kinds of medicinal properties were contained in it. Men of devout faith, the Buddha is like this. The Buddha brought forth the twelve divisions of the sacred writings. From among these twelve divisions he brought forth the sutras, from among the sutras he brought forth the Mahayana sutras, from the Mahayana sutras he brought forth the *Hannyaharamitsu* sutras, and from the *Hannyaharamitsu* sutras he brought forth the Nirvana Sutra. The Nirvana Sutra is comparable to ghee. Ghee here is a metaphor that stands for the Buddha nature."[91]

When we compare these sutras that I have just quoted with the Lotus Sutra, the greatest of "past, present, and future" with its "six difficult and nine easy acts," it stands out like the bright moon beside the tiny stars, or Mount Sumeru, highest of all mountains, beside the other eight mountain ranges which surround it.[92] And yet Ch'eng-kuan of the Kegon school, Tz'u-en of the Hossō school, Chia-hsiang of the Sanron school, and Kōbō of the Shingon sect, all men who were believed to possess the Buddha eye of wisdom, did not understand the above phrases [of the Lotus Sutra]. How then could the ordinary scholars of the time, who appear to be quite blind, be expected to judge the difference between the Lotus Sutra and the other ones! This difference is as plain as black and white, or Mount Sumeru side by side with a mustard seed, yet these men go astray. It is hardly surprising, therefore, that they are also confused by the principles as vast as the sky. Unless one can perceive the relative profundity of the various writings, he cannot judge the worth of the principles that derive from them.

The teachings of the sutras often differ from volume to volume and the texts must be understood in their proper order. Since it is therefore difficult to judge the worth of these teachings, I will quote further passages and try to help the ignorant to understand.

When it comes to kings, there are great kings and minor kings, and in any matter whatsoever, there are parts and there is the whole. We have talked about the simile of the five flavors of milk, cream, curdled milk, butter, and ghee, but we must understand when this simile is being applied to Buddhist teachings as a whole and when it is being applied to one part of those teachings.

The *Rokuharamitsu* Sutra teaches that sentient beings can attain enlightenment, but it says nothing about the enlightenment of *icchantika*. And of course it mentions nothing about the doctrine that Shakyamuni Buddha attained enlightenment countless ages in the past.

[The *Rokuharamitsu* Sutra claims that the *dhāraṇīs* are comparable to ghee,] but they cannot in fact even compare with the Nirvana Sutra, which compares itself with ghee, much less with the theoretical and essential teachings of the Lotus Sutra. And yet the Great Teacher Kōbō of Japan, misled by this sutra, assigned the Lotus Sutra to the fourth category, comparing it to the flavor of butter. If the so-called ghee of the *dhāraṇīs* cannot even match the so-called ghee of the Nirvana Sutra, then how could he possibly make such an obvious mistake? And yet he writes that "the teachers of China in their competition have stolen the ghee!,"[93] calling T'ien-t'ai and others thieves. And in a boastful vein he writes, "What a pity it is that the worthy men of ancient times were not able to taste this ghee!"[94]

Putting all this aside, I will point out the truth for the sake of my followers. If others do not choose to believe it now, they will form a reverse relationship. By tasting a single drop, one can tell the flavor of the great ocean, and by observing a single flower in bloom, one can predict the advent of spring. One does not have to cross the water to far-off China, spend three years traveling to Eagle Peak in India,[95] enter the palace of the Dragon King the way Nāgārjuna did, encounter the Bodhisattva Miroku the way Asaṅga did,[96] or be present at the two places and three assemblies when Shakyamuni preached the Lotus Sutra, in order to judge the relative merits of the Buddha's teachings. It is said that snakes can tell seven days in advance when a flood is going to occur. This is because they are akin to dragons, who make the rain fall. Crows can tell what lucky or unlucky events are going to take place throughout the course of a year. This is because in a past existence they were diviners. Birds are better at flying than human beings. And I, Nichiren, am better at judging the relative merits of sutras than Ch'eng-kuan of the Kegon school, Chia-hsiang of the Sanron school, Tz'u-en of the Hossō school, and Kōbō of the Shingon sect. That is because I follow in the footsteps of the teachers T'ien-t'ai and Dengyō. But Ch'eng-kuan and the others, because they did not heed the teachings of T'ien-t'ai and Dengyō, could not avoid committing the error of slandering the Law.

I, Nichiren, am the richest man in all of present-day Japan. I have dedicated my life to the Lotus Sutra, and my name will be handed down in ages to come. If one is lord of the great ocean, then all the gods of the various rivers will obey him. If one is king of Mount Sumeru, then the gods of the various other mountains cannot help but serve him. If one can understand the doctrine of the "six difficult and nine easy acts" of the Lotus Sutra, then, without reading the other sutras, he should [understand the superiority of the Lotus and] follow it.

In addition to the three pronouncements of the Buddha in the *Hōtō* chapter of the Lotus Sutra, the *Devadatta* chapter contains two enlightening admonitions. [The first reveals that Devadatta will attain Buddhahood.] Devadatta was a man of incorrigible disbelief, of the type called *icchantika,* and yet it is predicted that he will in the future become a Buddha called Heavenly King. The forty volumes of the Nirvana Sutra [state that all beings, including the *icchantika,* possess the Buddha nature,] but the actual proof of that is found in this chapter of the Lotus Sutra. There are countless other persons such as the monk Sunakṣatra or King Ajātaśatru[97] who have committed the five cardinal sins and slandered the Law, but Devadatta is cited as one example to represent all the countless others; he is the chief offender, and it is assumed that all lesser offenders will fare as he does. Thus it is revealed that all those who commit the five or the seven cardinal sins[98] or who slander the Law or who are *icchantika* inherently opposed to taking faith, will become Buddhas like the Tathagata Heavenly King. In the Lotus Sutra, poison turns into sweet dew, the finest of all flavors.

[The second admonition concerns the fact that the Dragon King's daughter attained Buddhahood.] When she attained Buddhahood, this does not mean simply that one person did so. It reveals the fact that all women will attain Buddhahood. In the various Hinayana sutras that were preached before the Lotus Sutra, it is denied that women can ever attain Buddhahood. In the Mahayana sutras other than the Lotus Sutra, it would appear that women can attain Buddhahood or be reborn in the Pure Land. But they may do so only after they have changed into some other form. It is not the kind of immediate attainment of Buddhahood that is encompassed in the doctrine of *ichinen sanzen*. Thus it is an attainment of Buddhahood or rebirth in the Pure Land in name but not in reality. The Dragon King's daughter is, as the phrase has it, "one example that stands for all the rest."[99] When the Dragon King's daughter attained Buddhahood, it opened up the possibility of attaining Buddhahood for all women of later ages.

Confucianism preaches filial piety and care for one's parents, but it is limited to this present life. It provides no way for one to assist one's parents in their future lives, and the Confucian sages and worthies are therefore sages and worthies in name only and not in reality. Brahmanism, though it recognizes the existence of past, present, and future lives, similarly offers no means to assist one's parents to a better life in the future. Buddhism alone can do so, and thus it is the true way of sages and worthies. But in the Hinayana and Mahayana sutras preached before the Lotus Sutra, and in the sects based on these sutras, to gain salvation even for oneself is impossible. One can hardly hope to do anything for one's parents either. Though the texts of these sutras may say [that they can bring about salvation], in reality that is not the case. Only with the preaching of the Lotus Sutra, in which the Dragon King's daughter attained Buddhahood, did it become evident that the attainment of Buddhahood was a possibility for all the mothers of the world. And when it was revealed that even an evil man such as Devadatta could attain Buddhahood, it became evident that Buddhahood was a possibility for all the fathers of the world. [The Confucians have their *Classic of Filial Piety,* but] the Lotus Sutra is the *Classic of Filial Piety* of Buddhism. This ends my discussion of the two admonitions contained in the *Devadatta* chapter.

Awed by the five proclamations of the Buddha [made in the *Hōtō* and *Devadatta* chapters], the countless bodhisattvas promised the Buddha that they would propagate the Lotus Sutra, as described in the *Kanji* chapter. I shall hold up this passage of the sutra like a bright mirror so that all may see how the present-day leaders of the Zen, Ritsu, and Nembutsu sects and their lay followers are guilty of slandering the Law.

On the twelfth day of the ninth month of last year, between the hours of the Rat and the Ox (11:00 P.M. to 3:00 A.M.), this person named Nichiren was beheaded.[100] It is his soul that has come to this island of Sado and, in the second month of the following year, snowbound, is writing this to send to his close followers. [The description of the evil age in the *Kanji* chapter] seems terrifying, but [because I have dedicated myself to the True Law, I, Nichiren,] have nothing to be frightened about. Others reading it will be terrified. This chapter is the bright mirror of Shakyamuni, Tahō, and all the other Buddhas of the ten directions in which contemporary Japan is reflected. At the same time, it may be regarded as a keepsake from me.

In the *Kanji* chapter of the Lotus Sutra, the bodhisattvas, addressing the Buddha, say: "We beg you not to worry. After the Buddha has passed away, in an age of fear and evil we will preach far and wide. There will be many ignorant people who will curse and speak ill of us, and will attack us with swords and staves, but we will endure all these things. There will be monks in that evil age with perverse views and hearts that are fawning and crooked who will say they have attained what they have not attained, being proud and boastful in heart. Or there will be forest-dwelling monks wearing clothing of patched rags and living in retirement who will claim they are practicing the true Way, despising and looking down on the rest of mankind. Greedy for profit and nourishment, they will preach the Dharma to white-robed laymen and will be respected and revered by the world as though they were arhats who possess the six supernatural powers. These men with evil in their hearts, constantly thinking of worldly affairs, will borrow the name of forest-dwelling monks and take delight in proclaiming our faults. . . . Constantly they will go about among the populace, seeking in this way to slander us. They will address the rulers, high ministers, Brahmans, and great patrons of Buddhism as well as the other monks, slandering and speaking evil of us, saying, 'These are men of perverted views who preach non-Buddhist doctrines!' . . . In a muddied kalpa, in an evil age there will be many different things to fear. Demons will take possession of others and through them curse, revile, and heap shame on us. . . . The evil monks of that muddied age, failing to understand the Buddha's expedient means, how he preaches the Dharma in accord with what is appropriate, will confront us with foul language and angry frowns; again and again we will be banished."[101]

Miao-lo, in the eighth volume of his *Hokke Mongu Ki,* comments as follows: "In this passage, three types of arrogance are cited. First there is a section that exposes persons of mistaken views. This represents the arrogance and presumption of the ordinary populace. Next there is a section that exposes the arrogance and presumption of certain members of the Buddhist clergy. Third is a section that exposes the arrogance and presumption of those who pretend to be sages. Of these three types of arrogance, the first can be endured. The second is more formidable than the first, and the third is the most formidable of all. This is because the second is harder to recognize for what it really is, and the third is even harder to recognize."[102]

Priest Chih-tu writes in the *Tōshun:* "First, in the section dealing with the 'ignorant people,' there is a verse telling how the votaries of the Lotus Sutra must endure evils inflicted by the body, mouth, and mind of their opponents. This refers to evil men among the ordinary populace. Next, in the section on the 'monks in that evil age,' there is a verse that deals with arrogant members of the Buddhist clergy. Third, in the section on the 'forest-dwelling monks,' there are three verses dealing with members of the clergy who pretend to be sages and use their positions to act as leaders of all the other evil persons." And the same text goes on to say: "The section that begins 'Constantly they will go about among the populace' describes how these men will appeal to the government authorities, slandering the Law and defaming its supporters."[103]

In the ninth volume of the Nirvana Sutra we read: "Men of devout faith, there are persons called *icchantika,* persons of incorrigible disbelief. They pretend to be arhats, living in deserted places and speaking slanderously of the Mahayana sutras. When ordinary people see them, they suppose that they are all true arhats and speak of them as great bodhisattvas." It also says: "At that time, this sutra will be preached throughout the continent of Jambudvīpa. In that age there will be evil monks who will do violence to this sutra and destroy its unity, losing 'the color, scent, and flavor' of the True Law that it contains. These evil men will read and recite this sutra, but they will ignore and put aside the profound and vital principles that the Buddha has expounded in it and replace them with ornate rhetoric and meaningless talk. They will tear off the first part of the sutra and stick it on at the end, tear off the end and put it at the beginning, put the end and the beginning in the middle and the middle at the beginning or the end. You must understand that these evil monks are the companions of the devil."[104]

The six-volume *Hatsunaion* Sutra states: "There are also *icchantika* who resemble arhats but who commit evil deeds. There are also arhats who resemble *icchantika* but display merciful hearts. The *icchantika* who look like arhats spend their time slandering the Mahayana sutras to the populace. The arhats who look like *icchantika,* on the other hand, are critical of the *shōmon* and go about preaching Mahayana doctrines. They address the populace, saying, 'You and I are all bodhisattvas. Why? Because each and every one of us possesses the Buddha nature.' But the populace will probably call such men *icchantika.*"[105]

In the Nirvana Sutra, the Buddha speaks as follows: "After I have passed away and after the Former Day of the Law has ended and the Middle Day of the Law has begun, there will be monks who will give the appearance of abiding by the rules of monastic discipline. But they will scarcely ever read or recite the sutras, and instead will crave all kinds of food and drink to nourish their bodies. Though they wear the robes of a monk, they will go about searching for alms like so many huntsmen, spying sharply and stalking softly. They will be like a cat on the prowl for mice. And constantly they will reiterate these words: 'I have attained the state of arhat!' Outwardly they will seem to be wise and good, but within they will harbor greed and jealousy. [And when they are asked to preach the Dharma,] they will remain silent, like Brahmans who have taken a vow of silence. They are not true monks—they merely have the appearance of monks.

Consumed by their erroneous views, they slander the True Law."[106]

In the light of the sun and moon that are the Lotus and Nirvana sutras, or in the bright mirrors that are the writings of Miao-lo and Chih-tu, we can discern without a trace of obscurity the ugly faces of the people of Zen, Ritsu, and Nembutsu in present-day Japan. [The *Kanji* chapter of] the Lotus Sutra says: "After the Buddha has passed away, in an age of fear and evil," and the *Anrakugyō* chapter says: "In the evil age hereafter," "in the latter age," and "in the latter age when the Law is on the point of disappearing." The *Fumbetsu Kudoku* chapter says: "In the evil-filled Latter Day of the Law"; the *Yakuō* chapter says, "In the fifth five hundred years," etc. The *Kanzetsu* chapter of the Dharmarakṣa translation of the Lotus Sutra says, "In the latter age" and "in the latter age to come." The same type of language is found in the translation of the Lotus Sutra made by Jñānaguptā and Dharmagupta. T'ien-t'ai states: "In the Middle Day of the Law, the three schools of southern China and the seven schools of northern China are the enemies of the Lotus Sutra."[107] And Dengyō states: "At the end of the Middle Day of the Law, the scholars of the six Nara sects are the enemies of the Lotus Sutra."[108]

In the time of T'ien-t'ai and Dengyō, [the three types of enemies mentioned above] had not yet appeared. But we must recall that when Shakyamuni Buddha and Tahō Buddha sat side by side in the Treasure Tower like the sun and the moon and the Buddhas who were emanations of Shakyamuni had come from the ten directions and were ranged beneath the trees like so many stars, then it was said that, after the thousand years of the Former Day of the Law and the thousand years of the Middle Day of the Law, at the beginning of the Latter Day of the Law, there would be three types of enemies of the Lotus Sutra. How could this pronouncement made by the eighty myriads of millions of nayutas of bodhisattvas have been an empty or a false prediction?

It is now some twenty-two hundred years since the Buddha passed away. Even if it were possible to point straight at the earth and miss it, if the flowers were to cease blooming in spring, still I am certain that these three powerful enemies exist in the land of Japan. If so, then who is to be numbered among the three enemies? And who is to be accounted a votary of the Lotus Sutra? It is a troubling question. Are we—I and my disciples—to be numbered among the three enemies? Or are we to be numbered among the votaries of the Lotus Sutra? It is a troubling question.

In the twenty-fourth year of the reign of King Chao, the fourth ruler of the Chou dynasty in ancient China, on the night of the eighth day of the fourth month, a five-colored light spread across the sky from north to south until all was as bright as noon. The earth shook in six different ways, and though no rain fell, the rivers and streams, wells and ponds brimmed with water. All the trees and grasses bloomed and bore fruit. It was a wondrous happening indeed. King Chao was greatly alarmed, but the Grand Historian Su Yu performed divinations and announced, "A sage has been born in the western region." "What will become of our country?" asked King Chao, to which Su Yu replied, "It will suffer no harm. One thousand years from now, the words of this sage will be brought to this country and will bring benefit to all living beings." Su Yu was a scholar of non-Buddhist texts who had not in the slightest degree freed himself from illusions of thought and desire, and yet he was able to know what would happen a thousand years in the future. And just as he predicted, 1,015 years after the Buddha's passing, in the reign of Emperor Ming, the second ruler of the Later Han dynasty, in the tenth year of the Yung-p'ing era (67 A.D.), the doctrines of Buddhism were introduced to China.[109]

On quite a different level is the prediction I have described above that was made by the various bodhisattvas in the presence of Shakyamuni Buddha, Tahō Buddha, and the Buddhas from the ten directions that were emanations of Shakyamuni Buddha. In view of this prediction, how could the three types of enemies of the Lotus Sutra help but be present in Japan today?

In the *Fuhōzō* Sutra, the Buddha is recorded as saying: "After my passing, during the one thousand years of the Former Day of the Law, there will be twenty-four persons in succession who will spread abroad the True Law as I have taught it."[110] Mahākāśyapa and Ānanda [were contemporaries of the Buddha and so] we will pass them over. But a hundred years later there was the monk Pārśva, six hundred years later the Bodhisattva Aśvaghoṣa, and seven hundred years later the Bodhisattva Nāgārjuna, along with others, all appearing just as the prophecy had said they would.

If so, how could the prophecy in the *Kanji* chapter of the Lotus Sutra be in vain? If this prophecy is at variance with the truth, then the whole Lotus Sutra is at variance with the truth. Then the prediction that Śāriputra will in the future become the Flower Light Buddha and that Mahākāśyapa will become the Light Bright Buddha are all mere lies. In that case, the teachings put forward in the sutras that preceded the Lotus Sutra must be absolutely correct, and Śāriputra and the other *shōmon* are destined never to achieve Buddhahood. If it is true that one should give alms to a dog or a jackal before one gives them to a *shōmon* such as Ānanda, then where do we stand?

[In the passage from the *Kanji* chapter of the Lotus Sutra that I quoted earlier, the text mentioned three groups of people,] saying first that "There will be many ignorant people," referring second to "monks in that evil age," and third to "monks in their clothing of patched rags." The first category of ignorant people are the important lay believers who support monks in the second and third categories. Accordingly, the Great Teacher Miao-lo, commenting on the persons in the first group, says they represent the arrogance and presumption of "the ordinary populace." And the Priest Chih-tu describes how they will "appeal to the government authorities" [in their slanders of the Law and its supporters].

Concerning the second group of enemies of the Lotus Sutra, the sutra says: "There will be monks in that evil age with perverse views and hearts that are fawning and crooked who will say they have attained what they have not attained, being proud and boastful in heart."[111]

Similarly, the Nirvana Sutra says: "In that age there will be evil monks. . . . These evil men will read and recite this sutra, but they will ignore and put aside the profound and vital principles that the Buddha has expounded in it."[112]

The *Maka Shikan* says: "If one lacks faith in the Lotus Sutra, he will object that it pertains to the lofty realm of the sages, something far beyond the capacity of his own wisdom to comprehend. If one lacks wisdom, he will become puffed up with arrogance and will claim to be the equal of the Buddha."[113]

We see an example of this in the statement by the Priest Tao-ch'o: "The second reason [for rejecting the Lotus Sutra] is that its principles are profound but human understanding is slight."[114] In a similar vein, Hōnen says: "Religious practices other than the Nembutsu do not accord with people's capacities. They are not appropriate for the times."[115]

[To combat such views,] Miao-lo states in the tenth volume of his *Hokke Mongu Ki*: "Probably the reason people are mistaken in their understanding of this matter is that they fail to realize how great is the benefit gained even by a beginner in the practice of the Lotus

Sutra. They assume that benefit is reserved for those who are far advanced in practice and disparage the efforts of beginners. Therefore I will now demonstrate that even a little practice will gain profound benefit, and thereby show how great is the power of the Lotus Sutra."[116]

Similarly, the Great Teacher Dengyō declares: "The Former and Middle Days are almost over, and the Latter Day is near at hand. Now indeed is the time when the One Vehicle expounded in the Lotus Sutra will prove how perfectly it fits the capacities of all people. How do we know this is true? Because the *Anrakugyō* chapter of the Lotus Sutra states that, 'In the latter age when the Law is on the point of disappearing,' [the Lotus Sutra will be expounded far and wide]."[117] And Eshin says: "Throughout all Japan, all people share the same capacity to attain Buddhahood through the perfect teaching."[118]

Now which opinion should we believe, that of Tao-ch'o and Hōnen or that of Dengyō and Eshin? The former has not a scrap of evidence in the sutras to support it. The latter is based firmly upon the Lotus Sutra.

Moreover, the Great Teacher Dengyō of Mount Hiei is honored by priests throughout Japan as the master of ordination into the priesthood. How could any priests turn their hearts toward a person like Hōnen, who is possessed by the Devil of the Sixth Heaven, and reject the Great Teacher Dengyō, who established the very ordination ceremonies that these priests themselves underwent? If Hōnen was a truly wise man, why did he not, in his *Senchaku Shū,* mention the passages of explanation by Dengyō and Eshin such as I have quoted above, and resolve the contradiction? He did not do so, because he is the kind of person who hides the teachings of others. When the Lotus Sutra speaks of the second type of enemy, "monks of that evil age," it is referring to men like Hōnen who disregard the precepts and hold perverse views.

The Nirvana Sutra says: "[Until we heard the Lotus Sutra,] we were known as men of perverse views." Miao-lo explains this by saying: "The Buddha is referring to the three types of teachings that preceded the Lotus Sutra and himself, saying that they all may be called perverse views." And the *Maka Shikan* states: "The Nirvana Sutra says, 'Until the time of the Lotus Sutra, we were known as men of perverse views.' Perverseness is bad, is it not?"[119]

In the *Guketsu,* Miao-lo states: "Perverseness is bad. Therefore we must understand that only the perfect teaching [which reveals the truth] is good. But there are two meanings accounted good and that which goes against the truth is to be involved here. First, that which accords with the truth is to be accounted bad. This is the meaning from the relative standpoint. [Second,] attachment is bad and transcending it is good. [This is the meaning from the absolute standpoint.] From both the relative and absolute points of view, we should abandon all that is bad. To be attached to the perfect teaching is bad, and to be attached to the other [three] teachings is of course even worse."[120]

The goods and evils of the non-Buddhist creeds, when compared with the Hinayana sutras, all represent a bad way. Similarly, the good ways expounded in the Hinayana sutras, and the sutras of the four flavors and the three types of teachings, when compared with the Lotus Sutra, are all perverse and bad. The Lotus Sutra alone represents the true good. The perfect teaching of the sutras preached before the Lotus Sutra is so called from the relative viewpoint; from the absolute viewpoint, it must still be counted as bad. Fundamentally it falls into the category of the first three [of the four] types of teachings, and therefore it is bad in that sense as well. To practice the highest principles of the pre-Lotus Sutra teachings is still bad. How much more so, then, is someone who would take a work of insignificant doctrine such as the *Kammuryōju* Sutra, which cannot compare even with the *Kegon* and *Hannya* sutras, as the fundamental teaching? Though such a person borrows ideas from the Lotus, he urges people to "ignore, abandon, close, and discard" the Lotus and devote themselves to the Nembutsu. This is what Hōnen and his disciples and lay supporters do, and they deserve to be called slanderers of the True Law, do they not?

[The *Hōtō* chapter of the Lotus Sutra says] of the assembly of Shakyamuni Buddha, Tahō Buddha, and the various Buddhas of the ten directions, "To make certain that the Law will endure forever, they have come to this place."[121] And yet Hōnen and the other practitioners of the Nembutsu in Japan declare that "In the Latter Day of the Law, the Lotus Sutra will disappear before the Nembutsu." Are such persons not the enemies of Shakyamuni, Tahō, and the other Buddhas?

Concerning the third group of enemies of the Lotus Sutra, the sutra says: "Or there will be forest-dwelling monks wearing clothing of patched rags and living in retirement . . . and they will preach the Dharma to white-robed laymen and will be respected and revered by the world as though they were arhats who possess the six supernatural powers."[122] And the six-volume *Hatsunaion* Sutra states: "There are also *icchantika* who resemble arhats but who commit evil deeds. There are also arhats who resemble *icchantika* but display merciful hearts. The *icchantika* who look like arhats spend their time slandering the Mahayana sutras to the populace. The arhats who look like *icchantika,* on the other hand, are critical of the *shōmon* and go about preaching Mahayana doctrines. They address the populace, saying, 'You and I are all bodhisattvas. Why? Because each and every one of us possesses the Buddha nature.' But the populace will probably call such men *icchantika.*"[123]

The Nirvana Sutra says: "After I have passed away . . . [after the Former Day of the Law has ended and] the Middle Day of the Law has begun, there will be monks who will give the appearance of abiding by the rules of monastic discipline. But they will scarcely ever read or recite the sutras, and instead will crave all kinds of food and drink to nourish their bodies. Though they wear the robes of a monk, they will go about searching for alms like so many huntsmen, spying sharply and stalking softly. They will be like a cat on the prowl for mice. And constantly they will reiterate these words: 'I have attained the state of arhat!' Outwardly they will seem to be wise and good, but within they will harbor greed and jealousy. [And when they are asked to preach the Dharma,] they will remain silent, like Brahmans who have taken a vow of silence. They are not true monks —they merely have the appearance of monks. Consumed by their erroneous views, they slander the True Law."[124]

Miao-lo writes concerning persons of this type: "The third [group] is the most formidable of all. This is because the second is harder to recognize for what it really is, and the third is even harder to recognize." And the *Tōshun* states: "Third, in the section on the 'forest-dwelling monks,' there are three verses dealing with members of the clergy who pretend to be sages and use their positions to act as leaders of all the other evil persons."[125]

As for these "members of the clergy who pretend to be sages and use their positions to act as leaders of all the other evil persons"— where in Japan at the present time should we look for them? On Mount Hiei? In Onjō-ji? In Tō-ji in Kyoto? In the temples of Nara? In the Zen temple Kennin-ji in Kyoto, or the Zen temples Jufuku-ji and Kenchō-ji[126] in Kamakura? We must examine this carefully. Do the words refer to the monks of Enryaku-ji on Mount Hiei who wear helmets on their heads and are dressed in armor? Do they refer to the monks of Onjō-ji who have consecrated their bodies to the Dharma and yet wear suits of mail and carry weapons? But these men do not resemble the forest-dwelling monks "wearing clothing of patched rags and living in retirement" that are described in the sutra, nor do they seem to be the type who are "respected and revered by the world as though they were arhats who possess the six supernatural powers." They are not like the men of the third group who, as Miao-lo said, "are even harder to recognize." It would appear, therefore, that the words refer to men such as Shōitsu of Kyoto and Ryōkan of Kamakura.[127] [Even if they are so denounced,] it does not do to hate others. If one has eyes, one should examine the sutra texts and compare one's behavior with them.

The first volume of the *Maka Shikan* states: "There has never been anything to compare to the brightness and serenity of *shikan* style meditation."[128] In the first volume of the *Guketsu*, Miao-lo writes: "From the time when Emperor Ming of the Han dynasty dreamt of the Buddha down to the Ch'en dynasty, [when the Great Teacher T'ien-t'ai lived,] there were many who participated in the Zen school and received the robe and bowl that were handed down."[129] The *Fuchū* explains this by saying: "The handing down of the robe and bowl refers to the succession of Zen patriarchs from Bodhidharma on down."[130]

In volume five of the *Maka Shikan*, T'ien-t'ai says: "There is a type called Zen men, but their leaders and disciples are blind [to the truth] and lame [in practice], and both leaders and disciples will fall into hell." In the seventh volume, we read: "[I have set forth ten ways of meditation.] But the ninth way has nothing in common with the ordinary priests of the world who concentrate on the written word, nor does it have anything in common with the Zen masters who concentrate on practice. Some Zen masters give all their attention to meditation alone. But their meditation is shallow and false, totally lacking in the rest of the ten ways. This is no empty assertion. Worthy men of later ages who have eyes to see will understand the truth of what I say."[131]

In the seventh volume of the *Guketsu*, Miao-lo comments on this as follows: " 'Priests who concentrate on the written word' refers to men who gain no inner sight or understanding through meditation but concern themselves only with the externals of the Dharma. 'Zen masters [who] give all their attention to meditation' refers to men who do not learn how to attain the true object and wisdom of meditation but fix their minds on the mere techniques of breath control. They are incapable of cutting off the basic delusions. 'Some Zen masters give all their attention to meditation alone,' means that, for the sake of discussion, T'ien-t'ai gives them a certain degree of recognition, but in the end he withdraws it, concluding that their meditation never leads to true understanding. The Zen men in the world today value only empty meditation and have no familiarity with doctrinal teachings. They put together the eight wrong views and the eight worldly desires and talk about the Buddha as being sixteen feet in height. They lump together the five aggregates and the three poisons and call them the eight wrong views. They equate the six sense organs with the six supernatural powers and the four elements with the four noble truths. To interpret the sutras in such an arbitrary manner is to be guilty of the greatest falsehood. Such nonsense is not even worth discussing."[132]

The seventh volume of the *Maka Shikan* states: "In the past, the Zen master of Yeh and Lo became renowned throughout the length and breadth of China. When he arrived, people gathered around him from all directions like clouds, and when he left for another place, they formed a great crowd along the roads. But what profit did they derive from all this bustle and excitement? All of them regretted what they had done when they were on their deathbed."[133]

In the seventh volume of the *Guketsu,* Miao-lo comments: "The text speaks of the 'Zen master of Yeh and Lo.' Yeh is in Hsiang-chou and was the capital of the Ch'i and Wei dynasties. The founder of Zen caused Buddhism to flourish there and converted the people of the region. The Great Teacher T'ien-t'ai, out of deference to the people of his time, refrains from naming anyone specifically. Lo refers to the city of Lo-yang."[134]

The six-volume *Hatsunaion* Sutra says: "The extreme is impossible to see. That is, the extremely evil deeds done by the *icchantika* are all but impossible to perceive."[135] Or, as Miao-lo has said, "The third [group] is the most formidable of all. This is because . . . the third is even harder to recognize."

Those without eyes, those with only one eye, and those with distorted vision cannot see these three types of enemies of the Lotus Sutra who have appeared at the beginning of the Latter Day of the Law. But those who have attained a portion of the Buddha eye can see who they are. "They will address the rulers, high ministers,

Brahmans, and great patrons of Buddhism," [says the *Kanji* chapter].[136] And Priest Chih-tu comments in his *Tōshun*: "These men will appeal to the government authorities, slandering the Law and defaming its supporters."[137]

In the past, when the Middle Day of the Law was coming to an end, Gomyō, Shūen[138] and other monks presented petitions to the throne in which they slandered the Great Teacher Dengyō. Now, at the beginning of the Latter Day of the Law, Ryōkan, Nen'a,[139] and others drew up false documents and presented them to the shogunate. Are they not to be counted among the third group of enemies of the Lotus Sutra?

Nowadays the followers of the Nembutsu address the "rulers, high ministers, Brahmans, and great patrons of Buddhism" who support the Tendai sect, saying, "The doctrines of the Lotus Sutra are so profound that we can barely comprehend them. The Dharma it teaches is extremely deep; our capabilities are extremely shallow." Just as the *Maka Shikan* says, "They object that it pertains to the lofty realm of the sages, something far beyond the capacity of their own wisdom to comprehend."[140]

Again, the men of the Zen sect say: "The Lotus Sutra is a finger pointing at the moon, but the Zen sect is the moon itself. Once one has the moon, of what use is the finger? Zen is the mind of the Buddha. The Lotus Sutra is the word of the Buddha. After the Buddha had finished preaching the Lotus Sutra and all the other sutras, he took a single flower and gave it to Mahākāśyapa alone, [whereby the disciple understood its meaning]. As a symbol of this tacit communication, he also presented Mahākāśyapa with his own robe, which has been handed down from one to another by the twenty-eight patriarchs of Indian Zen and so on to the sixth patriarch of Chinese Zen."[141] For many years now, the whole country has been intoxicated and deceived by this kind of absurd nonsense.

Again, the eminent monks of the Tendai and Shingon sects, though nominally representatives of their respective sects, are in fact quite ignorant of their teachings. In the depths of their greed and out of fear of the courtiers and warriors, they lend their support to the assertions of the Nembutsu and Zen followers and sing their praises. Long ago, Tahō Buddha and the various Buddhas who were emanations of Shakyamuni Buddha acknowledged their allegiance to the Lotus Sutra, saying, "We will make certain that the Law will long endure."[142] But now the eminent leaders of the Tendai sect obsequiously testify that "the doctrines of the Lotus Sutra are profound but human understanding is slight." As a result, the Lotus Sutra exists in Japan today in name only—there is not a single person who actually practices it and attains enlightenment. Who can be called a votary of the Lotus Sutra? We see monks who burn down temples and pagodas and are exiled in numbers too great to count. And we see numerous eminent monks who fawn on the courtiers and warriors and are hated for it by the people. Can men such as these be called the votaries of the Lotus Sutra?

Because the predictions of the Buddha are not false, the country is already full of the three types of enemies of the Lotus Sutra.[143] And yet, as though to belie the golden words of the Buddha, there seems to be no votary of the Lotus Sutra as was predicted would appear. How can this be?

But let us consider. Who is it who is cursed and spoken ill of by the populace? Who is the monk who is attacked with swords and staves? Who is the monk who, because of the Lotus Sutra, is accused in petitions submitted to the courtiers and warriors? Who is the monk who is "again and again banished," as the Lotus Sutra predicted? Who else in Japan besides Nichiren could fit this description?

But I, Nichiren, am not a votary of the Lotus Sutra, because, contrary to the prediction, Heaven has cast me aside. Who, then, in this present age will be the votary of the Lotus Sutra and fulfill the prophecy of the Buddha?

The Buddha and Devadatta are like a form and its shadow — in lifetime after lifetime, they are never separated. Prince Shōtoku and his archenemy Mononobe no Moriya[144] appeared at the same time, like the blossom and the seed pod of the lotus. If there exists a votary of the Lotus Sutra, then the three types of enemies are bound to exist as well. The three types of enemies have already appeared. Who, then, is the votary of the Lotus Sutra? Let us seek him out and make him our teacher. [As the Lotus Sutra says, to find such a person is as rare as for] a one-eyed turtle to chance upon a piece of driftwood [with a hole just the right size to hold him].[145]

Question: It would surely appear that the three types of enemies are present today, but there is no votary of the Lotus Sutra. If I were to say that you are the votary of the Lotus Sutra, then the following serious discrepancies would become apparent. The [Anrakugyō chapter of the] Lotus Sutra says: "The young sons of the heavenly deities will wait on and serve him. Swords and staves will not touch him, and poison will have no power to harm him." And the same passage continues: "If men curse and speak evil of him, their mouths will be closed and stopped up." The *Yakusōyu* chapter says: "They [who have heard the Law] will enjoy peace and security in this life and good circumstances in the next." The *Darani* chapter says that those who do harm to a votary of the Lotus Sutra will "have their heads split into seven pieces like the branches of the *arjaka* tree." Also, the *Kambotsu* chapter states: "[He who honors the Lotus Sutra] will receive his reward of good fortune in his present life." And it adds: "If anyone shall see a person who embraces this sutra and try to expose the faults or evils of that person, he will in his present life be afflicted with white leprosy, whether what he speaks is the truth or not." [How do you explain these discrepancies?][146]

Answer: These doubts of yours are most opportune. I will take the occasion to clear up the points that puzzle you. The *Fukyō* chapter of the Lotus Sutra says: "[Bodhisattva Fukyō] was spoken evil of and cursed." And again: "They would beat him with sticks and staves, and stone him with rocks and tiles."[147] The Nirvana Sutra says: "They will be killed or harmed." The *Hosshi* chapter of the Lotus Sutra states: "Hatred and jealousy toward this sutra abound even during the lifetime of the Buddha. [How much worse will it be in the world after his passing!]"[148]

The Buddha encountered acts of hostility, known as the nine great persecutions, such as being wounded in the foot by Devadatta, and yet he was a votary of the Lotus Sutra, was he not? And Bodhisattva Fukyō, [who, as we have seen above, was cursed and beaten] — was he not a votary of the One Vehicle of the Lotus Sutra? Maudgalyāyana was beaten to death by a Brahman group called Bamboo Staff sometime after the Lotus Sutra predicted that he would attain Buddhahood in a future life. Bodhisattva Kāṇadeva was the fourteenth patriarch in the lineage of Buddhism in India, and Āryasiṁha was the twenty-fifth patriarch,[149] and both men were murdered. Were these men not votaries of the Lotus Sutra? The Chinese monk Chu Tao-sheng was banished to Mount Su, and the monk Fa-tao was branded on the face and exiled south of the Yangtze River.[150] Were these men not upholders of the One Vehicle of the Lotus Sutra? Among scholars of secular learning, both Po Chü-i and Sugawara no Michizane,[151] who was posthumously revered as the god Tenjin of Kitano, were exiled to distant places, and yet were they not worthy men?

If we consider the second part of your question, we must note the following points. Those who did not commit the error of slandering the Lotus Sutra in their previous existences will become votaries of the Lotus Sutra in their present lives. If such persons should be subjected to persecution under a false charge of having committed worldly offenses, then those who persecute them ought to suffer some kind of immediate retribution. It should be like the case of the *asuras* who shoot arrows at Taishaku or the *garuḍa* birds that try to eat the dragon kings of the Icy Lake, but who both invariably suffer injury themselves instead. And yet the Great Teacher T'ien-t'ai says: "The ills and pains I suffer at present are all due to causes in the past, and the meritorious deeds that I do in my present life will be rewarded in the future."[152] Likewise, the *Shinjikan* Sutra states: "If you want to understand the causes that existed in the past, look at the results as they are manifested in the present. And if you want to understand what results will be manifested in the future, look at the causes that exist in the present."[153] The *Fukyō* chapter of the Lotus Sutra says: "After expiating his sins."[154] This indicates that Bodhisattva Fukyō was attacked with tiles and stones because he had in the past committed the offense of slandering the Lotus Sutra.

Second, we should note that, if a person is inevitably destined to fall into hell in his next existence, then even though he commits a grave offense in this life, he will suffer no immediate punishment. The *icchantika,* men of incorrigible disbelief, are examples of this.

The Nirvana Sutra states: "Bodhisattva Kashō said to the Buddha, 'World-Honored One, as you have described, the rays of the Buddha's great nirvana enter the pores of all beings.' " It also states: "Bodhisattva Kashō said to the Buddha, 'World-Honored One, how can those who have not yet set their hearts on enlightenment create the causes that will lead to enlightenment?' " The sutra answered the question this way. "The Buddha said to Kashō, 'There may be persons who listen to the Nirvana Sutra and yet claim that they have no need to set their hearts on enlightenment, and instead slander the True Law. Such persons will immediately dream at night of devils and their hearts will be filled with terror. The devils will say to them, "How foolish you are, my friend! If you do not set your heart on enlightenment now, your life span will be cut short!" These persons quake with fear, and as soon as they wake from the dream, they set their hearts on enlightenment. And you should know that such persons will become great bodhisattvas.' "[155] In other words, although a person might slander the True Law, if he is not an unspeakably evil person, he will be warned at once in a dream and will have a change of heart.

The *icchantika*, on the other hand, are likened to "dead trees or stony mountains" that can never bring forth growth. They are "scorched seeds which, although they encounter the sweet rain," will not grow. They are "bright pearls hidden in mud" which can never shine. They are like "persons with a wound on their hands who nevertheless handle poison." Just as "torrents of rain cannot remain suspended in the sky," [so will they fall into hell]. All these various similes illustrate the fact that *icchantika* of the most evil type will invariably fall into the hell of incessant suffering in their next life. Therefore they do not suffer any immediate punishment in this life. They are like the evil rulers of ancient China, Emperor Chieh of the Hsia dynasty and Emperor Chou of the Yin dynasty. During their reigns, Heaven did not display any unusual manifestations as a warning. That was because their offenses were so grave that their dynasties were already destined to perish.

Third, it would appear that the guardian deities have deserted this country, and this is probably one reason why offenders do not suffer any immediate punishment. In an age that slanders the Law, guardian deities will take their leave and the various heavenly gods will cease to lend their protection. That is why the votaries of the True Law do not receive any sign of divine favor, but on the contrary encounter severe difficulties. The *Konkōmyō* Sutra says: "Those who perform good deeds day by day languish and dwindle in number."[156] We are living in an evil country and an evil age. I have discussed all this in detail in my work entitled *"Risshō Ankoku Ron."*

This I will state. Let the gods forsake me. Let all persecutions assail me. Still I will give my life for the sake of the Law. Śāriputra practiced the way of the bodhisattva for sixty kalpas, but he fell from that high position because he could not endure the ordeal of the Brahman who begged for his eye.[157] Of those who received the seeds of Buddhahood in the time of *gohyaku-jintengō* or in the days of Daitsū Buddha (*sanzen-jintengō*), many in later times abandoned the seeds, fell from their high condition and remained in hell because they followed evil companions.[158]

Whether tempted by good or threatened by evil, if one casts aside the Lotus Sutra, he destines himself for hell. Here I will make a great vow. Though I might be offered the rulership of Japan if I will only abandon the Lotus Sutra, accept the teachings of the *Kammuryōju*

Sutra, and look forward to rebirth in the Western Pure Land, though I might be told that my father and mother will have their heads cut off if I do not recite the Nembutsu—whatever obstacles I might encounter, so long as men of wisdom do not prove my teachings to be false, I will never yield! All other troubles are no more to me than dust before the wind.

I will be the Pillar of Japan. I will be the Eyes of Japan. I will be the Great Ship of Japan. This is my vow, and I will never forsake it!

Question: How can you be certain that the exiles and sentences of death imposed on you are the result of karma created in the past?

Answer: A bronze mirror will reflect color and form. The First Emperor of the Ch'in dynasty had a lie-detecting mirror that would reveal offenses committed in this present life. And the mirror of the Buddha's Law makes clear the causal actions committed in the past. The *Hatsunaion* Sutra states: "Men of devout faith, because you committed countless offenses and accumulated much evil karma in the past, you must expect to suffer retribution for everything you have done. You may be reviled, cursed with an ugly appearance, be poorly clad and poorly fed, seek wealth in vain, be born to an impoverished or heretical family, or be persecuted by your sovereign. It is due to the blessings obtained by protecting the Law that one can diminish in this lifetime his suffering and retribution."[159]

This sutra passage conforms exactly with my own experience. By now all the doubts that I have raised earlier should be dispelled, and thousands of difficulties are nothing to me. But let me show you phrase by phrase how the text applies to me. "You may be reviled," or, as the Lotus Sutra says, "They will despise, hate, envy, and bear grudges" against you—and in exactly that manner I have been treated with contempt and arrogance for over twenty years. "You will be cursed with an ugly appearance," "You will be poorly clad"—these too apply to me. "You will be poorly fed"—that applies to me. "You will seek wealth in vain"—that applies to me. "You will be born to an impoverished family"—that applies to me. "You will be persecuted by your sovereign"—that applies to me. The Lotus Sutra says, "Again and again we will be banished," and the passage from the *Hatsunaion* Sutra speaks of having to suffer various kinds of retribution. [Can there be any doubt that the passage applies to me?]

The passage also says: "It is due to the blessings obtained by protecting the Law that one can diminish in this lifetime his suffering and retribution." The fifth volume of the *Maka Shikan* has this to say on the subject: "The feeble merits produced by a mind only half intent on goodness cannot alter the cycle of birth and death. But if one practices meditation and attains profound insight (*shikan*), so as to control the five aggregates of his life and thus ward off illness and restrain earthly desires, then one can transcend the cycle of birth and death." It also says, "As practice progresses and understanding grows, the three obstacles and four devils emerge, vying with one another to interfere." [160]

From the beginningless past I have been born countless times as an evil ruler who deprived the votaries of the Lotus Sutra of their robes and rations, their fields and crops, much as the people of Japan in the present day go about destroying the temples dedicated to the Lotus Sutra. In addition, I cut off the heads of numberless votaries of the Lotus Sutra. Some of these grave offenses I have already paid for, but there must be some that are not paid for yet. Even if I seem to have paid for them all, there are still ill effects that remain. When the time comes for me to transcend the sufferings of birth and death and attain Buddhahood, it will be only after I have completely freed myself from these grave offenses. My merits are insignificant, but these offenses are grave.

If I practiced the teachings of the provisional sutras [rather than those of the Lotus Sutra], then these retributions for my past grave offenses would not appear. When iron is heated, if it is not strenuously forged, the impurities in it will not become apparent. Only when it is subjected to the tempering process again and again will the flaws appear. When one is pressing hemp seeds, if he does not press very hard, he will not get much oil from them. Likewise, when I vigorously berate those throughout the country who slander the Law, I meet with great difficulties. It must be that my actions in defending the Law in this present life are calling forth retributions for the grave offenses of my past. If iron does not come into contact with fire, it remains black, but if it contacts fire, it turns red. If you place a log across a swift stream, waves will pile up like hills. If you disturb a sleeping lion, it will roar loudly.

The Nirvana Sutra says: "It is like the case of a poor woman. She has no house to live in and no one to aid or protect her, and in addition she is beset by illness, hunger, and thirst, until she decides to take to the road and beg for a living. While staying at an inn, she gives birth to a baby, but the master of the inn drives her away. Though the baby has just been born, she takes it up in her arms and sets out, hoping to journey to another land. But along the way, she encounters fierce wind and rain, and she is troubled by cold and bitten by mosquitoes, hornets, and poisonous insects. Coming at length to the Ganges River, she clasps her child in her arms and begins to cross it. Although the current is very swift, she will not let go of her child, and in the end both mother and child are drowned. But through the merit that the woman gained by her loving tenderness, she is reborn after her death in the Brahma Heaven.

"Monjushiri, if there are men of devout faith who wish to defend the True Law, they should emulate this poor woman crossing the Ganges who sacrificed her life because of her love for her child. Men of devout faith, the bodhisattvas who guard the Law should behave in this way. Do not hesitate to give up your life! Then, although you do not seek enlightenment, enlightenment will come of itself, just as the poor woman, though she did not seek to be reborn in the Brahma Heaven, was nevertheless reborn there."[161]

The Great Teacher Chang-an interprets this story from the Nirvana Sutra in terms of the three obstacles.[162] Observe how he does this. The fact that the woman is called "poor" indicates that the person does not have the treasure of the Law. The fact that she is identified as a woman indicates that the person has a measure of tenderness. The "inn" signifies an impure land. The child she bears is the heart that has faith in the Lotus Sutra, one of the three potentials of the Buddha nature.[163] Being driven out of the inn signifies that the person is exiled. The fact that the baby has just been born means that very little time has passed since the person began to have faith in the Lotus Sutra. The fierce wind the woman encounters is the Imperial decree sentencing the person to exile. The mosquitoes and other insects are the "many ignorant people who curse and speak ill" of the votary of the Lotus Sutra. The fact that both mother and child are drowned indicates that, though in the end the person had his head cut off, he never renounced his faith in the Lotus Sutra. Being reborn in the Brahma Heaven means being reborn in the realm of Buddhahood.

The power of karmic reward extends to all of the Ten Worlds, even to the realm of Buddhahood. Even though one might go around killing people in Japan, China, and other countries, if he does not commit any of the five cardinal sins or does not slander the Law, he will not fall into the hell of incessant suffering. Yet he will be reborn and confined in the other kinds of hell over a period of countless years. Even if one observes a great many rules of discipline and performs a great many good acts, if he performs them with a mind only half intent on goodness, he cannot be reborn in heaven, in the world of form [where beings are free from desires]. To be born a king in the Brahma Heaven, one must add compassion to the karmic reward that leads to rebirth in the threefold world. The poor woman in the sutra passage was reborn in the Brahma Heaven because of her concern for her child. Her case is different from the ordinary law of causality. Chang-an offers two interpretations of it, but in the end it is nothing other than the loving kindness with which the woman cares for her child that makes the difference. Her concern concentrates on one thing, rather like a concentrated meditation of Buddhism. She thinks of nothing but her child, which is similar to the Buddha's profound mercy. That must be why, although she created no other causes to bring it about, she was reborn in the Brahma Heaven.

The path to Buddhahood is not to be found in the Kegon doctrine that the mind is the only reality, in the eightfold negation of the Sanron sect, in the Consciousness-Only doctrine of the Hossō sect, or in the Shingon type of meditation on the five elements of the universe. Only the Tendai doctrine of *ichinen sanzen* is the path to Buddhahood. Even in the case of this doctrine of *ichinen sanzen,* we do not possess the kind of wisdom and understanding to comprehend it fully. Nevertheless, among all the sutras preached by the Buddha during his lifetime, the Lotus Sutra alone contains this jewel which is the doctrine of *ichinen sanzen*. The doctrines of the other sutras are merely yellow stones that appear to be jewels. They are like sand, from which you can extract no oil no matter how hard you squeeze it, or a barren woman who can never bear a child. Even a wise man cannot become a Buddha through the other sutras, but with the Lotus Sutra, even fools can plant the seeds that lead to Buddhahood. As the sutra passage I have quoted earlier puts it, "Although you do not seek enlightenment, enlightenment will come of itself."

Although I and my disciples may encounter various difficulties, if we do not harbor doubts in our hearts, we will as a matter of course attain Buddhahood. Do not have doubts simply because Heaven does not lend you protection. Do not be discouraged because you do not enjoy an easy and secure existence in this life. This is what I have taught my disciples morning and evening, and yet they begin to harbor doubts and abandon their faith.

Foolish men are likely to forget the promises they have made when the crucial moment comes. Some of them feel pity for their wives and children and grieve at the thought of parting from them in this life. In countless births throughout many long kalpas they have had wives and children but parted from them in every existence. They have done so unwillingly and not because of their desire to pursue the way of the Buddha. Since they must part with them in any case, they should remain faithful to their belief in the Lotus Sutra and make their way to Eagle Peak, so that they may lead their wives and children there as well.

Question: You insist that the followers of the Nembutsu and Zen sects will fall into the hell of incessant suffering. This shows that you have a contentious heart. You yourself are in danger of falling into the realm of the *asuras*. Moreover, it is said in the *Anrakugyō* chapter of the Lotus Sutra: "It is undesirable that one should speak of the faults of others or of the other sutras; nor should one regard other monks with contempt."[164] It is because you are going against this passage in the sutra that you have been abandoned by Heaven, is it not?

Answer: The *Maka Shikan* says: "There are two ways to spread the Buddha's teachings. The first is called *shōju* and the second is called *shakubuku*.[165] When the *Anrakugyō* chapter says that one should not speak of the good or bad points of others, it is referring to the *shōju* method. But when the Nirvana Sutra says, 'Carry swords and staves and cut off their heads!' it is referring to the *shakubuku* method. They differ in approach in that one is lenient and the other severe, but they both bring benefit."[166]

In the *Guketsu,* Miao-lo comments on this passage as follows: "With regard to the two ways of spreading the Buddha's teachings, the Nirvana Sutra says, 'Carry swords and staves,' and in the third volume it says that defenders of the True Law need not observe the five precepts or practice the rules of proper behavior. . . . And later on, it tells of how King Sen'yo put to death those who slandered the Law. It also states: 'The new physician, [knowing that the medicine the people had been using was poison,] forbade them to use it, saying, "If anyone takes any more of this medicine, he will have his head cut off!" ' These passages all demonstrate how the method of *shakubuku* should be applied to persons who go against the Law. All the sutras and treatises deal with one or the other of these two methods."[167]

In the *Hokke Mongu,* T'ien-t'ai states: "Question: The Nirvana Sutra clearly states that one should support and follow the ruler, bearing bows and arrows and helping to overthrow evil persons. And yet the *Anrakugyō* chapter of the Lotus Sutra says that one should stay away from persons in power and should behave with humility and loving kindness. There seems to be a major contradiction between the sternness of one approach and the gentleness of the other. Why should they differ so?

"Answer: The Nirvana Sutra speaks mostly about the *shakubuku* approach. But is also mentions dwelling in the state where one looks on all beings as one's own children. Could it say so if it did not have the *shōju* approach? The Lotus Sutra is concerned mainly with the elucidation of the *shōju* approach. But in the *Darani* chapter there is also the curse on anyone who offends the Law which says he will have his head split into seven parts. Could it say so if it did not have the *shakubuku* approach? One should examine both methods and use whichever one accords with the time." [168]

Chang-an, in his commentary on the Nirvana Sutra, writes: "When priests or laymen are defending the Law, the most important thing is for them to adopt the proper basic mental attitude. They should disregard external details, stick to the principles, and in this way spread the teachings of the Nirvana Sutra. Therefore it says that defenders of the True Law need not abide by petty regulations. And that is why it says they need not practice the rules of proper behavior. In past times the age was peaceful and the Law spread throughout the country. At that time it was proper to observe the precepts and not to carry staves. But now the age is perilous and the Law is overshadowed. Therefore it is proper to carry staves and to disregard the precepts. If both past and present were perilous times, then it would be proper to carry staves in both of them. And if both past and present were peaceful times, then it would be proper to observe the precepts in both of them. You should distinguish between the *shōju* and the *shakubuku* methods and never adhere solely to one or the other." [169]

I suppose the learned priests of the time think it is only natural that one should have doubts about this. Therefore, no matter how I explain and try to persuade my own disciples, they still cannot seem to overcome their doubts, but behave like *icchantika* who do not possess the innate nature to become Buddhas. Therefore I have quoted these passages of explanation from T'ien-t'ai, Miao-lo, and others in order to silence their ungrounded criticisms.

These two methods of spreading the Law, *shōju* and *shakubuku,* are like water and fire. Fire hates water, water detests fire. The practitioner of *shōju* laughs with scorn at *shakubuku*. The practitioner of *shakubuku* despairs at the thought of *shōju*. When the country is full of ignorant or evil persons, then *shōju* is the primary method to be applied, as described in the *Anrakugyō* chapter. But at a time when there are many persons of perverse views who slander the Law, then *shakubuku* should come first, as described in the *Fukyō* chapter. It is like using cold water to cool yourself in the hot weather, or longing for a fire when the weather turns cold. Grass and trees are kinsmen of the sun—they suffer in the cold moonlight. Bodies of water are followers of the moon—they lose their true nature when the hot weather comes.

In the Latter Day of the Law, however, both *shōju* and *shakubuku* are to be used. This is because there are two kinds of countries, the country that is passively evil, and the kind that actively seeks to destroy the Law. We must consider carefully to which category Japan at the present time belongs.

Question: If one applies the *shakubuku* method at a time when the *shōju* method would be appropriate, or *shōju* at a time when *shakubuku* would be appropriate, is there any merit to be gained?

Answer: The Nirvana Sutra says: "Bodhisattva Kashō addressed the Buddha, saying, 'The Law body that you possess is as indestructible as a diamond. But I do not yet understand the means by which you acquired it. Would you tell me?'

"The Buddha replied, 'Kashō, it is because I was a defender of the True Law that I am now able to attain this diamond-like body that abides forever and is never destroyed.

" 'Men of devout faith, defenders of the True Law need not observe the five precepts or practice the rules of proper behavior. Rather they should carry knives and swords, bows and arrows [to protect those monks who are pure in upholding the precepts].

" 'There are monks who preach the Dharma in various ways, but still they are not able to utter "the lion's roar" and refute evil persons who go against the Dharma. Monks of this kind can bring no merit either to themselves or to the populace. You should realize that they are in fact shirkers and idlers. Though they are careful in observing the precepts and maintain spotless conduct, you should realize that they are incapable of attaining Buddhahood.

" 'Then at times there may be a monk who raises the lion's roar, and those who break the precepts; as soon as the monk finishes speaking, his listeners are enraged to the point where they attack him. Someone who preaches the Dharma in this way, though he may in the end lose his life, is still worthy of being called a person who observes the precepts and brings merit to both himself and others.' "[170]

Chang-an in the passage quoted earlier says: "You should distinguish between the *shōju* and the *shakubuku* methods and never adhere solely to one or the other." And T'ien-t'ai, as we have seen, declared that one should use whichever method "accords with the time." If you do not, you will be like someone who plants seeds at the end of autumn. Though you may carefully tend the field, you are not likely to harvest any rice or grain.

During the Kennin era (1201–1204), two men came to prominence, Hōnen and Dainichi,[171] who spread the teachings of the Nembutsu and Zen sects respectively. Hōnen denied the worth of the Lotus Sutra now that the world has entered the Latter Day of the Law, saying, "Not a single person has ever attained Buddhahood through that sutra," and "Not one person in a thousand can reach enlightenment through its teachings." Dainichi for his part claimed that the true teachings of Buddhism had been transmitted apart from the sutras. These two doctrines have now spread throughout the entire country. The learned priests of the Tendai and Shingon sects fawn on the Nembutsu and Zen followers or fear them the way a dog wags its tail before its master or a mouse fears a cat. These men enter the service of the ruler and the military leaders, where they preach in such a way as to bring about the destruction of the Buddhist Law and the ruin of the country. These Tendai and Shingon leaders in their present existence will fall into the realm of Hungry Ghosts, and after death will find themselves in the Avīci Hell. Even if they retire to the mountain forests and meditate intensively on *ichinen sanzen,* or retire to a quiet spot and devote themselves to the three mysteries,[172] if they do not understand the times or the people's capacity and perceive which of the two methods, *shōju* or *shakubuku,* is appropriate, then they can never free themselves from the sufferings of birth and death.

Question: When you berate the followers of the Nembutsu and Zen sects and arouse their enmity, what merit does that bring?

Answer: The Nirvana Sutra says, "If even a good priest sees someone slandering the Law and disregards him, failing to reproach him, to oust him, or to punish him for his offense, then that priest is betraying Buddhism. But if he takes the slanderer severely to task, drives him off or punishes him, then he is my disciple and one who truly understands my teachings."[173]

Chang-an comments on this as follows: "He who injures or brings confusion to the Buddhist Law is an enemy of the Law. If one befriends another person but lacks the mercy to correct him, he is in fact his enemy. But he who is willing to reprimand and correct the offender is one who truly understands and defends the Law, a true disciple of the Buddha. He makes it possible for the offender to rid himself of evil, and thus he acts like a parent to the offender. Those who are willing to reproach offenders are disciples of the Buddha. But those who will not oust offenders are enemies of the Buddhist Law."[174]

If we examine the *Hōtō* chapter of the Lotus Sutra, we find Shakyamuni Buddha, Tahō Buddha, and the various Buddhas from the ten directions [who are emanations of Shakyamuni Buddha] gathering together. And why? As the sutra itself says, "To make certain that the Law will long endure, they have come to this place."[175] One may surmise from this that Shakyamuni, Tahō, and the other Buddhas intend to insure the future propagation of the Lotus Sutra so that it can be made available to every single living being in times to come. Their concern and compassion are even greater than that of a father and mother who see their only child inflicted with great suffering. Hōnen, however, shows not the least concern about their compassion, but would tightly shut the gates to the Lotus Sutra so that in the future no one would have access to it. Like a person who tricks a demented child into throwing away his treasure, he tries to induce people to discard the Lotus Sutra, a cruel-hearted thing to do indeed!

If someone is about to kill your father and mother, shouldn't you try to warn them? If a bad son who is insane with drink is threatening to kill his father and mother, shouldn't you try to stop him? If some evil person is about to set fire to the temples and pagodas, shouldn't you try to stop him? If your only child is gravely ill, shouldn't you try to cure him with moxibustion treatment? To fail to do so is to act like those people who do not try to put a stop to the Zen and Nembutsu followers in Japan. As Chang-an says, "If one befriends another person but lacks the mercy to correct him, he is in fact his enemy."

I, Nichiren, am sovereign, teacher, father, and mother to all the people of Japan. But the men of the Tendai sect [who do not refute the heretical sects] are all great enemies of the people. As Chang-an has noted, "He who makes it possible for an offender to rid himself of evil is acting like a parent to him."[176]

He who has not set his heart upon the Way can never free himself from the sufferings of birth and death. Shakyamuni was cursed by all the followers of non-Buddhist teachings and labeled as a man of great evil. The Great Teacher T'ien-t'ai was regarded with intense enmity by the three Buddhist schools of southern China and the seven schools of northern China, and later in Japan the Hossō monk Tokuitsu criticized him for "using his three-inch tongue to try to destroy the five-foot body"[177] of the Buddha. The Great Teacher Dengyō was disparaged by the monks of Nara, who said, "That Saichō has never been to the capital of T'ang China!"[178] But all of these abuses were incurred because of the Lotus Sutra, and they are therefore no shame to the men who suffered them. To be praised by fools—that is the greatest shame. Now that I have been exiled by the authorities, the priests of the Tendai and Shingon sects are no doubt delighted. They are strange and foolish men.

Shakyamuni appeared in the *saha* world, Kumārajīva journeyed to the Ch'in dynasty in China,[179] and Dengyō likewise went to China, [all so that the Lotus Sutra might be preached and propagated]. Bodhisattvas Kānadeva and Āryasimha sacrificed their bodies. Bodhisattva Yakuō burned his arms as an offering, and Prince Shōtoku stripped off the skin on his arms to write the titles of sutras in blood. Shakyamuni, when he was a bodhisattva, sold his flesh to make offerings, and another time, when he was a bodhisattva named Gyōbō, he used his bone as a pen to write down the Dharma.[180]

T'ien-t'ai has said that the practice should "accord with the time." The propagation of the Buddhist Law does indeed follow the times. For what I have done, I have been condemned to exile, but it is a small suffering to undergo in this present life and not one worth lamenting. In future lives I will enjoy immense happiness, a thought that gives me great satisfaction.

THE TRUE OBJECT
OF WORSHIP

Introduction

This work, dated the twenty-fifth day of the fourth month, 1273, was composed during Nichiren's exile at Ichinosawa on the island of Sado, one year after the completion of "The Opening of the Eyes." The full title is *Nyorai no Metsugo Go-gohyakusai ni Hajimu Kanjin no Honzon Shō,* which can be rendered as "Discourse on the Establishment in the Fifth Half-Millennium after the Buddha's Passing of the Object of Worship for Observing One's Own Mind." A cover letter to Toki Jōnin, a senior disciple, instructed that only a small number of the followers be permitted to see it, and never more than a few at a time. The work consists of some thirty questions and answers of varying lengths. Preceding the eighteenth question is a cautionary statement: "The teaching that follows must be kept in strictest secrecy." This further emphasizes the importance Nichiren placed on this work and his concern that it not be misunderstood.

The work is rather obscure in places and difficult to render into English without substantial explanatory amplifications. Thus the translation at times represents a paraphrase rather than a direct translation. The treatise itself is difficult to characterize; it deals largely with the Gohonzon, a mandala or concrete object of worship, depicting the essence of the Lotus Sutra or the Law that Nichiren is transmitting. A specific description of the *honzon* is furnished in a passage in the text that describes the ceremony of transmission: "Nam-myōhō-renge-kyō appears in the center of the Treasure Tower with the Buddhas Shakyamuni and Tahō seated to the right and left, and the Four Bodhisattvas of the Earth, led by Jōgyō, flank them."

The treatise opens with a long explanation of *ichinen sanzen,* the three thousand worlds in an instant of thought, as derived from

T'ien-t-ai's *Maka Shikan*. The questions and answers that follow are devised as a framework within which Nichiren explains the significance of the object of worship. He turns next to *kanjin*, observing the mind, and states that the process of *kanjin* in the Latter Day of the Law is to chant Nam–myoho-renge-kyo with complete faith in the honzon, the object of worship. The implication is that Shakyamuni's practices and the virtues he consequently obtained are all contained within the single phrase Myoho-renge-kyo and that belief in that phrase will enable the believer to obtain the same benefits as had Shakyamuni. Thus, embracing faith in the *honzon* is in itself enlightenment.

This work discusses also in considerable detail the interpenetration and mutual possession of the Ten Worlds, from Hell to the Buddha realm. Further, it goes on to explain that the *saha* world revealed by Shakyamuni in the Lotus Sutra is the eternal Pure Land. There follows an analysis of the purpose of the Buddha's appearance in the world, described in terms of preparation, revelation, and transmission. In terms of Shakyamuni's teachings, preparation is marked by the pre-Lotus teachings, revelation by the threefold Lotus Sutra (the *Muryōgi* Sutra, the Lotus Sutra, and the *Fugen* Sutra), and transmission by the Nirvana Sutra. Considered in terms of the threefold Lotus Sutra, preparation is marked by the *Muryōgi* Sutra and the *Jo* (first) chapter, revelation from the *Hōben* (second) chapter to the first half of the *Fumbetsu Kudoku* (seventeenth) chapter, and transmission, from the second half of the *Fumbetsu Kudoku* chapter to the *Fugen* Sutra. Seen from the viewpoint of the theoretical teaching *(shakumon)*, preparation is again the *Muryōgi* Sutra and the *Jo* chapter, revelation from the *Hōben* chapter to the *Ninki* (ninth) chapter, and transmission from the *Hosshi* (tenth) chapter to the *Anrakugyō* (fourteenth) chapter. Examined from the viewpoint of the essential *(hommon)* teaching, preparation is centered in the first half of the *Yujutsu* (fifteenth) chapter, revelation the second half of the *Yujutsu* chapter, the *Juryō* (sixteenth) chapter and the first half of the *Fumbetsu Kudoku* chapter, and transmission, from the second half of the *Fumbetsu Kudoku* chapter to the end of the Lotus Sutra and the *Fugen* Sutra. In terms of Nichiren's teachings, preparation encompasses all the teachings of all Buddhas throughout space and time, revelation is Nam-myoho-renge-kyo, the ultimate principle hidden in the depths of the *Juryō* chapter, and transmission, the teachings of all Buddhas seen in the light of the Lotus Sutra.

"The True Object of Worship" concludes with numerous citations from various sources relating to the establishment of the true object of worship. The beginning of the Latter Day of the Law, the fifth half-millennium following Shakyamuni's death, is the predicted time in which Nichiren appeared to declare: "Now is when the Bodhisattvas of the Earth will appear and establish in this country the supreme object of worship. . . . They have been waiting for the right time to emerge from the earth and carry out the Lord Buddha's command."

Volume Five of the *Maka Shikan* states: "The mind at each moment is endowed with the Ten Worlds. At the same time, each of the Ten Worlds is endowed with all the others, so that one mind actually possesses one hundred worlds. Each of these worlds in turn possesses thirty realms, which means that in the one hundred worlds there are three thousand realms. The three thousand realms of existence are all possessed by the mind in a single moment. If there is no mind, that is the end of the matter. But if there is the slightest bit of mind, it contains all the three thousand realms. . . . This is what we mean when we speak of the 'region of the unfathomable.' "[1]

Note: "[Three thousand] realms" might also read "[three thousand] factors," but the number is the same. The only difference lies in the method of expansion. Another text of the *Maka Shikan* states: "One world possesses the three realms of existence."[2]

Question: Is the principle of *ichinen sanzen* [the three thousand realms in a single thought-moment] explained in the *Hokke Gengi*?

Answer: Miao-lo states that it is not.

Question: Then is it explained in the *Hokke Mongu*?

Answer: Miao-lo states that it is not.

Question: What are his exact words?

Answer: He says, "Neither of the two mentions *ichinen sanzen*."[3]

Question: Is it explained in any of the first four volumes of the *Maka Shikan*?

Answer: No, it is not.

Question: What proof is there of this?

Answer: Miao-lo says, "When at last he revealed in the *Maka*

Shikan the method of meditation, he at the same time employed the 'three thousand realms' as a way to understand."[4]

Question: Volume Two of the *Hokke Gengi* states: "Each of the Ten Worlds contains the other nine, and in those one hundred worlds are one thousand factors."[5] Volume One of the *Hokke Mongu* states: "Each sense field[6] possesses the Ten Worlds, each of which again includes all of the ten within itself. Since each of those hundred worlds possesses the ten factors, the total becomes one thousand."[7] In the *Kannon Gengi* appears this statement: "The Ten Worlds are all mutually inclusive, thus making one hundred worlds. One thousand factors are inherent within the mind. Even though they are not visible, the mind by its nature possesses all of them."[8]

Question: Is *ichinen sanzen* mentioned in the first four volumes of the *Maka Shikan?*

Answer: Miao-lo says not.

Question: What does he say exactly?

Answer: Volume Five of the *Guketsu* reads: "In comparison with the chapter on Correct Meditation, the preceding chapters do not perfectly describe practice in its totality. But they contain the twenty-five preparatory exercises[9] which lead to understanding, and thus, they provide the way to full practice. The first six chapters, then, are all meant to bring understanding." Also in the same volume: "When at last he revealed in the *Maka Shikan* the method of meditation, he at the same time employed the 'three thousand realms' as a way to understand. This is the ultimate truth of his teachings. That is why Chang-an stated in his introduction: 'The *Maka Shikan* reveals the teaching that T'ien-t'ai himself practiced in the depths of his being.' He had good reason for saying this. I hope that those who read the *Maka Shikan* and seek to understand it will not let their minds be distracted by anything else."[10]

The Great Sage[11] propagated his teachings for thirty years. During the first twenty-nine years he expounded the doctrines contained in the *Hokke Gengi, Hokke Mongu,* and other works. Through them he explained the five periods and the eight teachings as well as the one hundred worlds and the one thousand factors. He not only refuted the erroneous doctrines of the preceding five centuries, but at the same time clarified matters that had not been fully explained by Buddhist scholars of India. The Great Teacher Chang-an states: "Even the great masters of India were not in a class with him, and the

Chinese scholars—well, one need hardly mention them. This is no idle boast—the doctrine he taught was indeed of such excellence."[12] How pitiful that T'ien-t'ai's successors allowed those thieves, the founders of the Kegon and Shingon schools, to steal the priceless gem of *ichinen sanzen* and then, ironically, became their followers! Chang-an was fully aware this would happen when he remarked in sorrow, "If this principle should become lost, it would be a tragedy for the future."[13]

Question: What is the difference between the principle of the one hundred worlds or the one thousand factors, and that of *ichinen sanzen,* the three thousand realms?

Answer: The former concerns only sentient beings, the latter applies to both sentient and insentient beings.

Question: If insentient beings possess the ten factors, is it correct to assume that plants and trees have minds and can attain Buddhahood like sentient beings?

Answer: This is a matter that is difficult to believe and difficult to understand. T'ien-t'ai defined two points that are "difficult to believe" and "difficult to understand." One lies in the realm of doctrinal teachings and the other in the realm of meditative practice. In the sutras preached before the Lotus Sutra we read that adherents of the doctrines of the two vehicles and people of incorrigible disbelief *(icchantika)* are forever barred from attaining Buddhahood, and that Shakyamuni for the first time attained enlightenment in this world. However, we find that the first and second halves of the Lotus Sutra repudiate both these statements. One Buddha who says two things as opposite as fire and water—who could believe him? This is the point "difficult to believe" and "difficult to understand" in the realm of doctrinal teachings. The point "difficult to believe" and "difficult to understand" in the realm of meditative practice concerns the principle of *ichinen sanzen,* which explains that even insentient beings possess the ten factors, and that they possess both material and spiritual aspects.

Both the Buddhist and non-Buddhist scriptures permit wooden or painted images to be used as objects of worship, but T'ien-t'ai and his followers were the first to explain the principle behind this act. If a piece of wood or paper lacked the cause and effect [of Buddhahood] in both material and spiritual aspects, then it would be futile to rely upon it as an object of worship.

Question: What authority do you have for stating that a plant, a tree, or a land manifests cause and effect, or the ten factors?

Answer: Volume Five of the *Maka Shikan* says: "A land of this world also has the ten factors. Thus an evil land has appearance, nature, entity, power and so on."[14] Volume Six of the *Shakusen* states: "Appearance exists only in what is material, nature exists only in what is spiritual. Entity, power, influence, and relation in principle combine both the material and the spiritual. Internal cause and latent effect are purely spiritual; manifest effect exists only in what is material."[15] The *Kongōbei Ron* states: "A plant, a tree, a pebble, a speck of dust—each has the innate Buddha nature, along with the other causes and conditions needed to attain Buddhahood."[16]

Question: You have told us about the sources of this doctrine. Now what is meant by *kanjin?*

Answer: *Kanjin* means to observe one's own mind and to find the Ten Worlds within it. This is what is called *kanjin* ("observing the mind"). For example, though one can see the six sense organs of other people, he cannot see the six sense organs on his own face. Only when he looks into a clear mirror for the first time does he see that he is equipped with all six sense organs. Similarly, various sutras make reference here and there to the six paths and the four noble worlds [that constitute the Ten Worlds], but only in the clear mirror of the Lotus Sutra and the Great Teacher T'ien-t'ai's *Maka Shikan* can one see his own three thousand realms—the Ten Worlds, their mutual possession, and the thousand factors.

Question: What part of the Lotus Sutra do you refer to, and what section of the *Maka Shikan?*

Answer: The *Hōben* chapter of volume one of the Lotus Sutra states that the Buddhas appear in this world "[because] they desire to cause all beings to open the Buddha wisdom."[17] This refers to the realm of Buddhahood inherent in the nine worlds. The *Juryō* chapter states: "Since I attained Buddhahood, an unimaginably long period has passed. The length of my life is infinite kalpas. My life has always existed and shall never end. Men of devout faith, once I also practiced the bodhisattva austerities and the life which I then acquired has yet to be exhausted. My life will last twice as many kalpas from now."[18] Here the sutra refers to the nine worlds inherent in the realm of Buddhahood. The sutra states: "Devadatta shall become a Buddha called Heavenly King Tathagata."[19] This indicates that the world of

Hell also contains the world of Buddhahood. In the sutra it is stated: "[There are ten female demons,] the first named Lambā. . . . [The Buddha says to them:] 'You will receive immeasurable good fortune if only you will protect those who embrace even the title of the Lotus Sutra.' "[20] Thus, the world of Hungry Ghosts contains all the Ten Worlds. When the sutra says: "The Dragon King's daughter . . . attained enlightenment,"[21] it indicates that the world of Animals has the Ten Worlds. The sutra says that the Bhandhi Asura and other *asura* kings will attain supreme enlightenment upon hearing even a single verse or phrase of the sutra.[22] Thus the world of Asura contains the Ten Worlds. The sutra says: "All people who [erect statues to] honor the Buddha . . . have attained the Buddha Way,"[23] meaning that the Human realm contains the Ten Worlds. The sutra states that the heavenly gods, led by Dai-Bonten, declared: "We shall attain enlightenment."[24] Thus the world of Heaven contains the Ten Worlds. The sutra says: "Śāriputra, in one of your lives to come . . . you will become a Buddha called the Flower Light Tathagata."[25] Thus the world of *Shōmon* contains the Ten Worlds. The sutra says: "Those who seek to become *engaku,* monks and nuns, . . . join their hands in reverence, wishing to hear the way to attain the perfect truth."[26] Thus the world of *Engaku* has the Ten Worlds. The sutra describes the multitude of bodhisattvas who appeared from beneath the earth and declared, "We also yearn to receive the pure great law."[27] Thus the world of the Bodhisattva contains the Ten Worlds. The sutra says: "[Men of devout faith, the sutras which the Tathagata expounded are all for the purpose of saving people from their sufferings.] Sometimes I speak of myself, sometimes of others."[28] Thus the world of Buddhahood contains the Ten Worlds.

Question: Although I can see both my own sensory organs and those of others, I cannot see the Ten Worlds in myself or others. How can I believe in them?

Answer: The *Hosshi* chapter of the Lotus Sutra says: "[The Lotus Sutra is] the most difficult to believe and the most difficult to understand."[29] [In describing how difficult it will be to fulfill the teachings of the Lotus Sutra after the Buddha's passing,] the *Hōtō* chapter speaks of the "six difficult and nine easy acts."[30] The Great Teacher T'ien-t'ai states: "Because the theoretical and essential teachings [of the Lotus Sutra] contradict all the earlier sutras, they are extremely difficult to believe and difficult to understand."[31] The Great Teacher Chang-an comments: "The Buddha intended these as his ultimate teachings. How could they ever be easy to understand?"[32] The Great Teacher Dengyō says: "The Lotus Sutra is the most difficult to believe and to understand because in it the Buddha directly revealed what he had attained."[33]

Those who were born in the days of Shakyamuni Buddha and heard his teachings in person had [received the seed of enlightenment from him] and practiced under him in the distant past. In addition, Shakyamuni, as well as Tahō Buddha, the Buddhas in the ten directions of the universe who are Shakyamuni's emanations, the countless Bodhisattvas of the Earth, and the other bodhisattvas such as Monju and Miroku, aided them and encouraged them to have understanding, but even then there were those who failed to believe. Five thousand people left the assembly, [arrogantly thinking that they had understood what they had not]. All gods and men [other than those already present in the assembly] were moved to other worlds [because they were incapable of understanding the Buddha's teachings]. How much more difficult is it to believe in the Lotus Sutra after the Buddha's passing—in the Former and Middle Days of the Law—and even more difficult now at the beginning of the Latter Day of the Law! If it were easy for you to believe in, it would not be the Buddha's true teaching.

Question: The passages from the Lotus Sutra and the explanations by T'ien-t'ai, Chang-an, and others which you have cited are free from obscurities and doubtful points. But you seem to be saying that fire is water, or that black is white. Although they may be the teachings of the Buddha, I find it difficult to accept them. Now I look repeatedly at people's faces, but I see only the human world. I do not see the other worlds. And the same is true when I look at my own face. How am I to believe in the Ten Worlds?[34]

Answer: When we look from time to time at a person's face, we find him sometimes joyful, sometimes enraged, and sometimes calm. At times greed appears in the person's face, at times foolishness, and at times perversity. Rage is the world of Hell, greed is that of Hungry Ghosts, foolishness is that of Animals, perversity is that of Asura, joy is that of Heaven, and calmness is that of Humans. These worlds, the six paths, are all present in the physical appearance of the person's face. The remaining four noble worlds are hidden and dormant and do not appear in the face, but if we search carefully, we can tell that they are there.

Question: Although I am not entirely certain about the six paths, it would appear from what you have said that we possess them. But what about the four noble worlds which cannot be seen at all?

Answer: Earlier you doubted that the six lower worlds exist within the human world, but when I illustrated the point through an analogy, you understood. Perhaps it will be the same with the four noble worlds. I will try to employ reasoning to explain a little bit about the matter. The fact that all things in this world are transient is perfectly clear to us. Is this not because the worlds of the two vehicles are present in the Human world? Even a heartless villain loves his wife and children. He too has a portion of the Bodhisattva world within him. Buddhahood is the most difficult to demonstrate. But since you possess the other nine worlds, you should believe that you have Buddhahood as well. Do not permit yourself to have doubts. The Lotus Sutra, explaining the human world, says that "[the Buddhas appear in this world because] they desire to cause all beings to open the Buddha wisdom."[35] The Nirvana Sutra states: "Those who study the Mahayana teachings, though they have the eyes of ordinary mortals, are said to have 'the eyes of a Buddha.' "[36] That common mortals born in the Latter Day of the Law can believe in the Lotus Sutra is due to the fact that the world of Buddhahood is present in the human realm.

Question: The Buddha clearly explained that each of the Ten Worlds has the same Ten Worlds within itself. Nonetheless, I find it difficult to believe that our base hearts could possess the world of Buddhahood. If I cannot believe it, I will become an *icchantika,* a person of incorrigible disbelief. With your great compassion, please help me to believe and save me from the torture of the Avīci Hell.

Answer: You have already seen and heard the sutra passages concerning "the one great reason" [why the Buddhas appear in this world]. If you still do not believe, then how can anyone from Shakyamuni on down to the four ranks of bodhisattvas[37] or we common mortals of the latter age who have yet to attain Buddhahood, save you from disbelief? Nevertheless, I will try to explain. After all, there were some who could not attain enlightenment through the direct teaching of the Buddha, but were able to do so later through the preaching of Ānanda and the other disciples.

People can attain Buddhahood in two ways: By meeting the Buddha and hearing the Lotus Sutra, or by believing in the sutra even though they do not meet the Buddha. Even before the advent of the Buddha some Brahmans in India came to the correct view of life through the Vedas. In China before the arrival of Buddhism, some had attained the correct view through Taoism and Confucianism. Many wise bodhisattvas and common mortals perceived [even before they heard the Lotus Sutra] that the Buddha had planted the seed of Buddhahood within them in the remote past [of *sanzen-jintengō*], in the days of the Buddha Daitsū. They understood this by hearing the provisional Mahayana sutras of the Kegon, Hōdō, and Hannya periods. They are like *engaku* [who could perceive the impermanence of life in the sight of] scattering blossoms or falling leaves. These, then, are the type of people who came to understand the truth through teachings other than the Lotus Sutra.

But many did not receive the seed of Buddhahood in their past existences and cling to Hinayana or provisional Mahayana teachings, and even if they are fortunate enough to encounter the Lotus Sutra, they cannot advance beyond their Hinayana or provisional Mahayana views. They are convinced that their own views are correct, and as a result they place the Lotus Sutra on the same level with the Hinayana sutras or [provisional Mahayana sutras such as] the *Kegon* and *Daini-chi*. Some even regard the Lotus Sutra as subordinate to these. Such teachers are inferior to the worthy men and sages of Confucianism and Brahmanism. But let us put this question aside for the moment.

The mutual possession of the Ten Worlds is as difficult to believe as fire existing in a stone or flowers within a tree. Yet under the right conditions such phenomena actually occur and can be believed. To believe that Buddhahood exists within the human realm is the most difficult thing of all—as difficult as believing that fire exists in water or water in fire. Nevertheless, the dragon is said to produce fire from water and water from fire, and although people do not understand why, they believe it when they see it occur. Since you now believe that the Human realm contains the other eight worlds from Hell to Bodhisattva, why are you still unable to include Buddhahood? The Chinese sage-kings Yao and Shun were impartial toward all people. They manifested one aspect of Buddhahood within the Human realm. Bodhisattva Fukyō saw the Buddha in everyone he met, and Prince Siddhārtha[38] was a man who became a Buddha. These examples should help you to believe.

Note: The teaching that follows must be kept in strictest secrecy.[39]

Question: Shakyamuni, the lord of teachings, is the Buddha who has destroyed all the three categories of illusion.[40] He is the sovereign of all kings, bodhisattvas, people of the two vehicles, common mortals, and heavenly beings in the ten directions. Whenever the Buddha moves, Bonten attends him on the left and Taishaku on the right. Monks and nuns, laymen and laywomen, as well as the eight kinds of non-human beings who protect Buddhism, follow behind, while the Kongō gods[41] march in the vanguard. With his eighty thousand teachings[42] he leads all people to enlightenment. How could such a great Buddha dwell in the hearts of us common mortals?

Both the teachings before the Lotus Sutra and the first half of the Lotus Sutra itself tell us that Lord Shakyamuni attained his enlightenment for the first time in the world. Searching [into those passages] for the cause of his enlightenment, we find that he practiced bodhisattva austerities in past existences as Prince Nōse, Bodhisattva Judō, King Shibi, and Prince Satta.[43] The Buddha practiced the bodhisattva austerities for three asōgi kalpas or a hundred major kalpas, or for kalpas equal in number to countless dust particles, or for countless asōgi kalpas, or from the time he first aroused the aspiration for enlightenment as a bodhisattva.[44] [The first half of the Lotus Sutra states that] he continued practicing for as long as sanzen-jintengō. During that long period the Buddha served as many as seventy-five, seventy-six, or seventy-seven thousand Buddhas[45] and, finishing his practice, he became Shakyamuni Buddha in this life. Are you saying that each of us has a world of bodhisattva within, which is endowed with all the blessings Shakyamuni attained as a result of his practice?

Again, looking into [these teachings to find] the results of his practice, we see that Shakyamuni Buddha first attained enlightenment in this life. For more than forty years the Buddha revealed himself in four different ways in the four kinds of teachings, and with them he was able to benefit all people by expounding the pre-Lotus Sutra teachings, the theoretical teaching of the Lotus Sutra, and the Nirvana Sutra.[46]

When he preached the *Kegon* Sutra, the Buddha appeared as Vairocana Buddha seated in the center of a lotus flower with one thousand petals. When he expounded the *Agon* sutras, he appeared as a Buddha who had eliminated all illusions by practicing thirty-four kinds of spiritual purification.[47] When he preached the *Hōdō* sutras, he was accompanied by a great multitude of Buddhas. One thousand Buddhas joined him when he expounded the *Hannya* sutras. In the *Dainichi* and *Kongōchō* sutras, he made a dignified appearance with five hundred and seven hundred Buddhas and bodhisattvas, respectively. In the *Hōtō* chapter of the theoretical teaching of the Lotus

Sutra the Buddha manifested himself in four different ways corresponding to the four kinds of lands.[48] When the Buddha expounded the Nirvana Sutra, those assembled saw him variously as a Buddha sixteen feet tall, or as having a body that appears either small or large, or as Vairocana Buddha, or as having a body as vast as space, manifesting four kinds of bodies [according to the *zōkyō, tsūgyō, bekkyō,* or *engyō* teachings].[49] When the Buddha entered nirvana at the age of eighty, he left his relics and teachings to benefit people in the Former, Middle, and Latter Days of the Law.

Now, the essential teaching says that Shakyamuni Buddha attained Buddhahood in the remote past of *gohyaku-jintengō,* and it describes the various austerities that made this possible. Since then he has manifested emanation bodies throughout the ten directions and preached all the teachings of Buddhism to lead infinite numbers of beings to enlightenment. Incomparably more people have been enlightened through the essential teaching than through the theoretical one.[50] The former are like the ocean compared to a drop of water, or like a great mountain compared to a speck of dust. What is more, a bodhisattva of the essential teaching is far superior to any bodhisattva of the theoretical teaching, including Monju, Kannon, or any other in the universe. The difference between them is even greater than that between Taishaku and a monkey. Are you saying that besides these bodhisattvas, the people of the two vehicles who became arhats by destroying their illusions, Bonten, Taishaku, the gods of the sun and moon, the Four Heavenly Kings, the four wheel-turning kings, and the great flames of the great citadel of the hell of incessant suffering are all inherent in the Ten Worlds and three thousand realms of our own mind? Even if you say this is what the Buddha taught, I still cannot believe it.

When we consider it, the teachings that came before the Lotus Sutra must be genuine in both substance and wording. The *Kegon* Sutra describes the Buddha as "perfect and free from all falsehood and defilement like the empty sky."[51] A passage of the *Ninnō* Sutra reads: "One can penetrate the ultimate source of delusion and extirpate his benighted nature until nothing but perfect wisdom remains."[52] In the *Kongō Hannya* Sutra it says: "[When one attains enlightenment,] nothing but pure goodness will remain."[53] Bodhisattva Aśvaghoṣa states in the *Daijō Kishin Ron:* "Only pure merit exists within the matrix of the Tathagata."[54] Bodhisattva Vasubandhu remarks in his *Yuishiki Ron:* "Other remaining defilements and a lesser form of non-defilement, when adamantine meditation is present, will draw forth the ultimate consciousness of perfect clarity and total purity. Then, being no longer depended on, they will be abandoned forever."[55]

The Lotus Sutra is only one, while the sutras taught before it are innumerable. And the older ones have been taught over a longer period than the Lotus Sutra. Therefore, if they contradict the Lotus Sutra, you should accept the older sutras. Bodhisattva Aśvaghoṣa was the Buddha's eleventh successor, whose appearance had been foretold in the sutras. Bodhisattva Vasubandhu was the author of one thousand treatises and was numbered among the four ranks of bodhisattvas. How then can you believe the Great Teacher T'ien-t'ai, a lowly priest living far away from the birthplace of Buddhism who [interpreted the sutras but] did not write a single treatise? Still, I might be able to disregard the pre–Lotus Sutra teachings, which are many, and accept the Lotus Sutra, which is only one, if it said anything to prove this point. But where in the sutra can you find any passages that definitely verify the mutual possession of the Ten Worlds, one thousand factors, and the three thousand realms of life? Even in Chapter Two of the Lotus Sutra we find the following passage: "The Buddha has eliminated all evils."[56] Neither Vasubandhu's *Hokke Ron*[57] nor Bodhisattva Sthiramati's *Hōshō Ron*[58] makes any mention of the mutual possession of the Ten Worlds. Nor are there any writings by the great Buddhists of northern and southern China, or by the priests of the seven temples of Japan, that expound this principle. It is simply T'ien-t'ai's own biased view, and Dengyō made the mistake of transmitting it. That is what the National Teacher Ch'ing-liang[59] meant when he said, "This is an error of T'ien-t'ai's." Priest Hui-yüan said, "By defining Hinayana doctrines as tripitaka or *zōkyō* teachings, T'ien-t'ai has confused Hinayana and Mahayana [for both contain the tripitaka or three divisions of the canon]."[60] Ryōkō criticized him, saying: "T'ien-t'ai is the only one who did not understand the true meaning of the *Kegon* Sutra."[61] Tokuitsu reproached him, saying: "See here, Chih-i, whose disciple are you! With a tongue less than three inches long you slander the teachings that come from the Buddha's long broad tongue!"[62] The Great Teacher Kōbō commented: "Chinese priests of various schools vied with one another to steal the ghee [of the *Kegon* Sutra], calling it their own doctrine."[63] Thus, the doctrine of *ichinen sanzen* is not mentioned in either the provisional or the true teachings. It did not appear in the writings of any of the great

Indian scholars, and no Chinese or Japanese priest has ever espoused it. How then do you dare to believe it?

Answer: Your criticisms are harsh. Nevertheless, the differences between the Lotus Sutra and the other sutras are clear from the text of the sutras themselves. In them we find statements that the Buddha did not reveal the truth in the first forty-two years of his teaching and that he would reveal it in the Lotus Sutra. Tahō and all the other Buddhas throughout the universe presented themselves to testify to the truth of the Lotus Sutra, testimony that they did not give for any other sutra. With the Lotus Sutra Shakyamuni enabled the people of the two vehicles to attain Buddhahood, whereas with the earlier sutras he did not. In the earlier sutras he stated that he attained enlightenment for the first time in this world, but in the Lotus Sutra he revealed that his enlightenment was actually in the remote past of *gohyaku-jintengō*. [64]

I will now explore the problem posed by the scholars you mentioned above. The Great Teacher T'ien-t'ai comments: "Vasubandhu and Nāgārjuna clearly perceived the truth in their hearts, but they did not teach it. Instead, they used the provisional Mahayana teachings, which were suited to their times. However, the Buddhist teachers who came later were biased in their understanding, and the scholars obstinately clung to their own views, until in the end they began to battle with one another. Each defended one small corner of the teachings and thereby completely departed from the true way of the Buddha." [65] The Great Teacher Chang-an says of T'ien-t'ai, "Even the great masters of India were not in a class with him, and the Chinese scholars—well, one need hardly mention them. This is no idle boast —the doctrine he taught was indeed of such excellence." [66]

In their hearts Vasubandhu, Nāgārjuna, Aśvaghoṣa, Sthiramati, and other Buddhist scholars knew [the truth of *ichinen sanzen*], but they did not reveal it to others because the time for it to be expounded had not yet come. As for the Buddhist teachers in China who preceded T'ien-t'ai, some kept this treasure in their hearts and others knew nothing about it. Among those who followed him, some accepted [*ichinen sanzen*] only after first trying to disprove it, and others never accepted it at all.

As regards the passage [in the *Hōben* chapter that you quoted], "The Buddha has eliminated all evils of life," here the Buddha is referring to a teaching from one of the earlier sutras. But when you take a closer look at the sutra, it becomes clear that the mutual possession of the Ten Worlds is being explained. For in the same chapter, this passage occurs: "[The Buddhas appear in this world because] they desire to cause all beings to open the Buddha wisdom." T'ien-t'ai comments on this passage as follows: "If people do not possess innate Buddha wisdom within them, how could the Buddha say he wanted to open it? One must understand that the Buddha wisdom is latent in all human beings."[67] Chang-an [cites a parable to illustrate this and] concludes: "How could people realize their Buddha wisdom if it did not exist within them? How could the poor widow discover her treasure if it had not been in the storehouse?"[68]

It is, however, extremely difficult to convince you that the Lord Buddha exists within us, [as do the nine worlds from Hell to Bodhisattva. In Chapter Ten of the Lotus Sutra] he gives us this admonishment: "Among all the sutras I have preached, now preach, and will preach, this Lotus Sutra is the most difficult to believe and the most difficult to understand."[69] The "six difficult and nine easy acts" he expounded in the next chapter emphasize the difficulty. Hence the Great Teacher T'ien-t'ai states: "Because the theoretical and essential teachings [of the Lotus Sutra] contradict all the earlier sutras, they are extremely difficult to believe and difficult to understand—no less difficult than facing an enemy who is armed with a spear."[70] The Great Teacher Chang-an comments: "The Buddha intended these as his ultimate teachings. How could they ever be easy to understand?"[71] The Great Teacher Dengyō remarks: "The Lotus Sutra is the most difficult to believe and to understand because in it the Buddha directly revealed what he had attained."[72]

In the first eighteen hundred and more years after the Buddha's entry into nirvana, only three persons perceived the True Law. They are Shakyamuni of India, the Great Teacher T'ien-t'ai of China, and the Great Teacher Dengyō of Japan. These three men are all Buddhist sages.

Question: What about Nāgārjuna and Vasubandhu?

Answer: Those sages knew, but did not expound it. They expounded part of the theoretical teaching, but did not teach either the essential teaching or the truth of the Buddha's enlightenment it contains. Perhaps the people in their age were capable of believing it, but the time was not ripe to expound it. Or perhaps neither the people nor the time was appropriate.

After the advent of T'ien-t'ai and Dengyō, many Buddhists learned of *ichinen sanzen* through the wisdom of these two sages. They included Chia-hsiang of the Sanron school; more than one hundred priests of the southern and northern schools of China; Fa-tsang and Ch'ing-liang of the Kegon school; Hsüan-tsang and Tz'u-en of the Hossō school; Shan-wu-wei, Chin-kang-chih, and Pu-k'ung of the Shingon school; and Tao-hsüan of the Ritsu school.[73] At first they all opposed T'ien-t'ai, but later totally accepted his teachings.

Now, to dispel the grave doubts you have about the mutual possession of the Ten Worlds, I refer you to the *Muryōgi* Sutra, which states: "Suppose a prince is born to a king and queen. He may be only a day, two days, or seven days old; a month, two months, or seven months old; a year, two years, or seven years old. He cannot yet administer the affairs of state, but already he is honored and respected by all the nation's ministers and people and has as his companions the sons of other rulers. The royal parents love him without reserve and always talk with him, for he is still very young.

"Men of devout faith, one who embraces this sutra is like the young prince. The various Buddhas can be likened to the king and this sutra to the queen. They give birth to a bodhisattva, their child. Suppose the bodhisattva listens to and accepts the sutra. If he recites even one phrase or verse, or recites it one, two, ten, a hundred, a thousand, ten thousand, or as many times as there are sand grains in a billion Ganges rivers, though he cannot yet grasp the full truth of it, already he will be revered by the four categories of Buddhists and the eight kinds of beings, he will be attended by great bodhisattvas, and continually receive the unreserved protection and compassion of all Buddhas. This is because he is still new to practice."[74]

The *Fugen* Sutra says: "This Mahayana sutra is the repository, the eye and the seed of life for all Buddhas in the ten directions throughout the past, present, and future. . . . You should exert yourself in practice of the Great Vehicle and never let the seed of Buddhahood die out." It also declares: "This all-embracing sutra is the eye of all Buddhas because through its teachings they become endowed with the five types of vision.[75] Since the three bodies of the Buddha's life arise from the sutra, it is the seal of ultimate truth which assures entry into the ocean of nirvana. A Buddha's three pure bodies come from this vast ocean and become the fertile field of good fortune for all human and heavenly beings."[76]

Now we should go on to survey the entire range of the Buddha's teachings, the exoteric and esoteric, as well as Hinayana and Mahayana, specifically the sutras upon which each denomination, Kegon,

Shingon, etc., depends for its doctrine. For example, the *Kegon* Sutra describes Vairocana Buddha seated in the center of a thousand-petaled lotus flower; the *Daijuku* Sutra, a cloud of Buddhas who gathered from all over the universe; the *Hannya* Sutra, the emergence of one thousand Buddhas [teaching the nonduality of] pure and impure; and the *Dainichi* and *Kongōchō* sutras depict more than twelve hundred Buddhas and bodhisattvas. These sutras all reveal the practices of Shakyamuni Buddha and the Buddhahood he attained in this life, but they do not reveal the original cause for his enlightenment in the remote past of *gohyaku-jintengō*.

It is true that the immediate attainment of Buddhahood is revealed in the pre–Lotus Sutra teachings, but they do not mention Shakyamuni Buddha teaching his disciples in the remote past of *sanzen-jintengō* and *gohyaku-jintengō*. Therefore, there is no revelation of when the Buddha started teaching or when he finished.[77] The *Kegon* Sutra seems to belong to the higher two and the *Dainichi* Sutra to all of the four teachings—*zōkyō, tsūgyō, bekkyō,* and *engyō*—but these sutras actually fall into the category of *zōkyō* and *tsūgyō,* the two lower teachings, because they do not expound the three inherent potentials of the Buddha nature: [innate Buddhahood, the wisdom to perceive it, and the cause that makes this wisdom develop]. Then how can we define these sutras as the seed of enlightenment?

The translators of the new versions of the sutras learned about T'ien-t'ai's teaching of *ichinen sanzen* when they returned to China. [When they translated Sanskrit sutras into Chinese,] some put T'ien-t'ai's principle into their translations, and others claimed that the originals they had brought back from India already contained it. Some of the scholars of the T'ien-t'ai school were simply pleased that other schools expounded the same doctrine as theirs, while others praised the Buddhism of India and slighted that of China, or discarded their original doctrines and adopted new ones. These scholars yielded to their devilish nature and stupidity. However, without *ichinen sanzen*, the seed of enlightenment, sentient beings cannot attain enlightenment, and any statue or image would be an object of worship in name alone.

Question: You have not yet fully answered my question about the mutual possession of the Ten Worlds.

Answer: The *Muryōgi* Sutra states: "[If you embrace this sutra,] you will naturally receive the benefits of the six *pāramitās* without having to practice them."[78] The [*Hōben* chapter of the] Lotus Sutra says: "They wish to hear the teaching of perfect endowment."[79] The Nirvana Sutra states: "*Sad* indicates perfect endowment."[80] Bodhisattva Nāgārjuna comments: "*Sad* signifies six."[81] The *Daijō Shiron Gengi Ki* states: "*Sad* connotes six. In India the number six implies perfect endowment."[82] In his annotation of the Lotus Sutra, Chiahsiang writes, "*Sad* is translated as perfect endowment."[83] The Great Teacher T'ien-t'ai remarks: "*Sad* is a Sanskrit word, which is translated as *myō*."[84] A personal interpretation of these quotations may force their meaning some more, but in essence they mean that Shakyamuni's practices and the virtues he consequently attained are all contained within the five characters Myōhō-renge-kyō. If we believe in these five characters, we shall naturally be granted the same benefits as he was.

With full understanding of Shakyamuni's teachings, the four great *shōmon* said: "We have gained the supreme cluster of jewels without expecting it."[85] They represent the world of *Shōmon* that is within ourselves. [The *Hōben* chapter states:] "At the start I pledged to make all people perfectly equal to me, without any distinction between us. By now the original vows that I made have already been fulfilled. I have led all the people onto the path of Buddhahood."[86] Shakyamuni Buddha of supreme enlightenment is our own flesh and blood. His practices and resulting virtues are our bones and marrow. The *Hōtō* chapter of the Lotus Sutra says: "Those who choose to protect this sutra serve Tahō Buddha and me. . . . They also serve all the emanation Buddhas present who dignify and glorify all the worlds."[87] Shakyamuni, Tahō, and all the other Buddhas in the ten directions represent the world of Buddhahood within ourselves. By searching them out within us, we can receive the benefits of Shakyamuni, Tahō, and all the other Buddhas. This is what is meant by [the following passage in Chapter Ten]: "If one hears the Law for even a single moment, he will be able to attain perfect enlightenment."[88]

The *Juryō* chapter reads: "The time is limitless and boundless—a hundred, thousand, ten thousand, hundred thousand nayuta kalpas—since I in fact attained Buddhahood."[89] Present within our lives is the Lord Shakyamuni who obtained the three bodies before *gohyaku-jintengō,* the original Buddha since time without beginning. The *Juryō* chapter states: "Once I also practiced the bodhisattva austerities and the life which I then acquired has yet to be exhausted. My life will last yet twice as many kalpas from now." He was speaking of the world of Bodhisattva within ourselves. The Bodhisattvas of the Earth are the followers of Lord Shakyamuni in our lives. They follow the Buddha just as T'ai-kung and Tan, the Duke of Chou, served as ministers to King Wu of the Chou dynasty and later assisted his son and successor, the infant King Ch'eng[90]; or just as Takeshiuchi served Empress Jingū and later her grandson Crown Prince Nintoku as a highly valued minister.[91] Bodhisattvas Jōgyō, Muhengyō, Jōgyō, and Anryūgyō[92] represent the world of Bodhisattva within ourselves. The Great Teacher Miao-lo declares: "You should realize that our life and its environment are the entity of *ichinen sanzen*. When we attain Buddhahood, according to this principle, our life pervades the entire universe both physically and spiritually."[93]

Shakyamuni revealed in the *Kegon* Sutra the world within the lotus flower [at Buddhagayā] where he attained enlightenment. In the more than fifty years until he died in the grove of sal trees, Shakyamuni Buddha preached the Pure Land of Dainichi Buddha in the *Mitsugon* Sutra,[94] revealed three or four kinds of lands[95] when he three times purified countless lands[96] in the universe in the theoretical teaching of the Lotus Sutra, and revealed the four views[97] in the Nirvana Sutra. All these lands as well as the Pure Land of Amida Buddha and the Emerald Land of Yakushi Buddha are in constant flux—formation, continuance, decline, and disintegration. When the Lord Buddha, Shakyamuni, enters nirvana, all the other Buddhas and their lands also pass away with him.[98]

The *saha* world Shakyamuni revealed in the *Juryō* chapter is the eternal pure land, impervious to the three calamities and the four cycles of change.[99] In this world the Buddha is eternal, transcending birth and death, and his disciples are also eternal. This is the three thousand worlds or the three realms of existence[100] within our own lives. The Buddha did not reveal this truth in the first fourteen chapters of the Lotus Sutra because the time was not right and he found his disciples not yet able to grasp the truth.

Shakyamuni Buddha did not transmit the five characters of Nammyoho-renge-kyo, the heart of the essential teaching of the Lotus Sutra, even to Bodhisattvas Monju and Yakuō, let alone to any lesser bodhisattva. He transferred it only to the Bodhisattvas of the Earth, summoning them and preaching the eight core chapters[—from the fifteenth to the twenty-second chapter—]of the Lotus Sutra.

The true object of worship is described in the ceremony of the transmission as follows:

In the air above the *saha* world [which the Buddha of the essential teaching identified as the pure and eternal land], Myōhō-renge-kyō appears in the center of the Treasure Tower with the Buddhas Sha-kyamuni and Tahō seated to the right and left, and the Four Bodhisatt-vas of the Earth, led by Jōgyō, flank them. Seated below them are Monju, Miroku, and the other bodhisattvas who are followers of the Four Bodhisattvas. All the other greater and lesser bodhisattvas, whether they are disciples of the Buddha of the theoretical teaching or of the Buddhas of the other worlds, are like commoners kneeling on the ground in the presence of nobles and high ministers. The Buddhas who gathered from the other worlds in the ten directions of the universe all remain on the ground, showing that they are only manifestations of the eternal Buddha and that their lands are transient, [not eternal and unchanging].

During the entire fifty years of Shakyamuni's teaching, only in the last eight years did he preach the twenty-eight chapters of the Lotus Sutra. Again, of all these chapters, only in the eight vital chapters did he reveal and transfer the object of worship to the Bodhisattvas of the Earth.[101] During the two millennia of the Former and Middle Days of the Law, statues were made showing Mahākāśyapa and Ānanda flanking Shakyamuni Buddha as he preached Hinayana, and Monju and Fugen flanking Shakyamuni Buddha as he preached the provi-sional Mahayana, the Nirvana Sutra, and the theoretical teaching of the Lotus Sutra.

Even though statues and images were made of Shakyamuni Bud-dha during the two millennia, no image or statue was made of the Buddha of the *Juryō* chapter.[102] Only in the Latter Day of the Law shall the representation of that Buddha appear.

Question: During the two millennia of the Former and Middle Days of the Law, the four ranks of bodhisattvas and teachers con-structed images of Buddhas of the other worlds or of Shakyamuni Buddha preaching Hinayana, provisional Mahayana or the theoretical teaching of the Lotus Sutra and built temples for them. However, no one in India, China, and Japan, neither their kings nor subjects, revered the object of worship revealed in the *Juryō* chapter of the essential teaching or the Four Great Bodhisattvas. Although I think I understand in general what you are saying, I have never heard such a thing before and I therefore find it startling to my ears and perplexing to my mind. Will you explain it to me in greater detail?

Answer: All the teachings Shakyamuni expounded—all the eight volumes and twenty-eight chapters of the Lotus Sutra, the first four flavors of teachings that preceded the sutra and the Nirvana Sutra that came after the Lotus—make an unbroken series of teachings like one perfect sutra. [These can be divided into three parts—preparation, revelation and transmission.] Preparation covers the part from the *Kegon* Sutra, his first preaching at Buddhagayā, to the *Hannya* sutras; revelation includes the *Muryōgi* Sutra, the Lotus Sutra, and the *Fugen* Sutra (ten volumes in all); and transmission indicates the Nirvana Sutra. The ten volumes of the revelation section can also be classified into these three divisions. The *Muryōgi* Sutra and the first chapter of the Lotus Sutra are preparation. Revelation begins with the *Hōben* (second) chapter and ends with the nineteen-line verse of the *Fumbetsu Kudoku* (seventeenth) chapter. Transmission includes the rest of the Lotus Sutra—from the section clarifying the four stages of faith[103]— and the *Fugen* Sutra: one volume, eleven chapters and a half.

We can divide the ten volumes of the *Muryōgi* Sutra, the Lotus Sutra, and the *Fugen* Sutra into two parts: theoretical and essential.[104] Each part has these three divisions. In the theoretical teaching, preparation indicates the *Muryōgi* Sutra and the first chapter of the Lotus Sutra, revelation is the *Hōben* (second) chapter through the *Ninki* (ninth) chapter, and transmission includes the *Hosshi* (tenth) to the *Anrakugyō* (fourteenth) chapters. The Buddha of the theoretical teaching declared that he first attained Buddhahood in this life. He revealed the hundred worlds and the thousand factors inherent in life, though he did not go on to expound their eternal nature. Since the theoretical teaching of the Lotus Sutra thus partially reveals the Buddha's own enlightenment, it excels all the other sutras that the Buddha "had preached, now preached, or would preach," and is difficult to believe and difficult to understand.

Herein the first relationship between Shakyamuni Buddha and his disciples can be traced back to the time when he was the sixteenth son of Daitsū Buddha. At that time he first planted the seed of Buddhahood in their lives. In Shakyamuni's lifetime a few of them could discover the seed when they heard the *Kegon* Sutra and the other teachings of the first four periods. This was not, however, the Buddha's true intention. Their discovery through these teachings was as rare as curing an illness with poison. Common mortals and the people of the two vehicles were led gradually to the Lotus Sutra through the teachings of the first four periods. They then discovered the seed of Buddhahood within themselves and were able to obtain the fruit of enlightenment.

There were people of the human world and of Heaven who took faith in the eight chapters for the first time in Shakyamuni's days. Some took the seed into their lives by listening to a single phrase or verse from among the eight chapters. Others nurtured and harvested the seed they had received, and still others obtained the fruit of enlightenment when they came to the *Fugen* and Nirvana sutras. There were also some for whom the seed received through the Lotus Sutra was brought to fruition by the Hinayana or provisional Mahayana teachings when they were born later in the Former, Middle, and Latter Days of the Law. These last are like the disciples in Shakyamuni's lifetime who discovered the seed of Buddhahood through the teachings of the first four periods.

Preparation, revelation, and transmission are also represented in the fourteen chapters of the essential teaching of the Lotus Sutra. Preparation is the first half of the *Yujutsu* (fifteenth) chapter. Revelation includes the latter half of this chapter, the *Juryō* chapter, and the first half of the *Fumbetsu Kudoku* (seventeenth) chapter—one chapter and two halves. Transmission includes the rest. The Buddha of the essential teaching denied that he first attained Buddhahood in this life. The difference between the theoretical and essential teachings is as great as that between heaven and earth. The latter revealed the eternity of the Ten Worlds and, further, the True Land. The theoretical teaching, the teachings of the first four periods, the *Muryōgi* Sutra and the Nirvana Sutra were all preached according to the capacities of the people. They are, therefore, easy to believe and easy to understand. In contrast, the essential teaching reveals the Buddha's own enlightenment, and therefore, is difficult to believe and difficult to understand. However, even the difference between *ichinen sanzen* of the theoretical and of the essential teachings pales into insignificance before the ultimate principle hidden within the Lotus Sutra.[105]

The essential teaching[106] also has its preparation, revelation, and transmission. Shakyamuni Buddha preached the Lotus Sutra in his life as the sixteenth son of Daitsū Buddha. When he appeared as Shakyamuni he also expounded teachings for fifty years, from the *Kegon* Sutra to the theoretical teaching of the Lotus Sutra and the Nirvana Sutra. All these sutras as well as the innumerable teachings of all the other Buddhas in the universe in the past, present, and future are preparation for revealing the heart of the *Juryō* chapter.

All the teachings other than "one chapter and two halves [of the Lotus Sutra]" are Hinayana in nature and heretical. Not only do they fail to lead to enlightenment, but they also lack the truth. Those who believe in them are of slight virtue, bound by illusion, ignorant, unfortunate, solitary, and like birds and beasts [which do not appreciate their parents' love].

The first half of the Lotus Sutra and the sutras preceding it contain the perfect teaching that one can attain Buddhahood, but even they are not the true cause for Buddhahood. Much less so are teachings of a Hinayana nature such as the *Dainichi* Sutra. It is out of the question to think that the scholars and priests of the seven sects, including Kegon and Shingon, preach the true cause for attaining Buddhahood.

These inferior sutras seem to fall within the *zōkyō, tsūgyō,* and *bekkyō* teachings, but actually they are no better than the lowest two. They may maintain that their doctrines are incomparably profound, but nowhere do they clarify when the Buddha planted the seed of Buddhahood, or when he nurtured and reaped it. These doctrines are no different from Hinayana which demands that one reduce his body to ashes and annihilate his consciousness, for they do not reveal when the Buddha started teaching and when he finished. If a queen should conceive by a slave, her baby would be nothing but an outcast.

Setting aside these lesser teachings, the revelation section that consists of the second through the ninth chapters of the theoretical teaching seems to have been expounded for the sake of the people of the two vehicles rather than for the common people and bodhisattvas in Shakyamuni's lifetime. From a more profound viewpoint, it is intended for the common people after the Buddha's passing—in the Former, Middle, and Latter Days of the Law—and in particular, for the common people in the beginning of the Latter Day.

Question: On what authority do you say so?

Answer: The *Hosshi* chapter of the Lotus Sutra states: "Since hatred and jealousy toward this sutra abound even during the lifetime of the Buddha, how much worse will it be in the world after his passing!"[107] The *Hōtō* chapter states: "The Buddha wishes his teaching to be maintained eternally. . . . The emanation Buddhas assembled here realize the significance of this."[108] Examine what the *Kanji* and *Anrakugyō* chapters state about the future. The theoretical teaching was preached for the people after the Buddha's passing.

As regards the essential teaching, it was addressed exclusively to the people early in the Latter Day of the Law. On the surface the Buddha seems to have preached this teaching for the salvation of the people of his day; he planted the seed of Buddhahood in their lives in the remote past of *gohyaku-jintengō* and nurtured it through his preaching as the sixteenth son of Daitsū Buddha in *sanzen-jintengō* and through the teachings of the first four periods and the theoretical teaching in this life. Then he finally brought his followers to full enlightenment, from *tōgaku* to *myōkaku*,[109] with the essential teaching.

In actuality, however, the essential teaching bears no resemblance whatsoever to the theoretical teaching. Preparation, revelation, and transmission of the essential teaching are intended entirely for the beginning of the Latter Day of the Law. The essential teaching of Shakyamuni's lifetime and that revealed at the beginning of the Latter Day are both pure and perfect [in that both lead directly to Buddhahood]. However, Shakyamuni's is the Buddhism of the harvest, and this is the Buddhism of sowing. The core of his teaching is one chapter and two halves, and for me it is Myōhō-renge-kyō alone.

Question: On what authority do you say that the essential teaching of the Lotus Sutra was meant for the generations of the Latter Day of the Law?

Answer: The *Yujutsu* chapter states: "More numerous than the sands of eight Ganges rivers, bodhisattvas from other worlds arose in the great assembly. Palms pressed together in deep reverence, they bowed and said to the Buddha, 'World-Honored One! Allow us to protect, embrace, read, recite, transcribe, and serve this sutra with diligence and devotion in the *saha* world after your passing. We vow to preach this sutra widely throughout the land.' Thereupon the Buddha said to this multitude of great bodhisattvas, 'Desist, men of devout faith! There is no need for you to protect and embrace this sutra.' "[110] This statement totally contradicts the Buddha's exhortations in the preceding five chapters.[111] Toward the end of the *Hōtō* chapter is the passage: "The Buddha addressed the four categories of Buddhists in a loud voice, saying, 'Who among you will propagate the Lotus Sutra throughout the *saha* world?' "[112] Yakuō and the other great bodhisattvas, Bonten, Taishaku, the gods of the sun and moon, and the Four Heavenly Kings would have followed Shakyamuni's command before anything else even if no other Buddha had supported his exhortations, but Tahō and other Buddhas from throughout the ten directions came to this world to exhort them to propagate the sutra after Shakyamuni's passing. Thus hearing the Buddha's solemn appeal, the bodhisattvas all pledged, saying, "We will not begrudge our lives,"[113] for they desired solely to fulfill the Buddha's will.

However, [in the *Yujutsu* chapter] the Buddha suddenly reversed himself and forbade the bodhisattvas, more numerous than the sands of eight Ganges rivers, from propagating the sutra in this world. We therefore face what appears to be an insoluble contradiction, one that is beyond ordinary understanding.

The Great Teacher T'ien-t'ai gave three reasons for Shakyamuni's action in stopping the bodhisattvas and three more for the summoning of the Bodhisattvas of the Earth. Essentially, the bodhisattvas of the theoretical teaching and the bodhisattvas of the other worlds were not qualified to inherit the *Juryō* chapter of the eternal Buddha's enlightenment. At the dawn of the Latter Day evil people who slander the Law would fill the land, and so the Buddha rejected their pledge and instead summoned the Bodhisattvas of the Earth. He entrusted them with the five characters of Nam-myoho-renge-kyo, the heart of the *Juryō* chapter, for the salvation of all beings. The bodhisattvas of the theoretical teaching were also unqualified because they were not the original disciples of the Buddha. The Great Teacher T'ien-t'ai states: "They are the Buddha's true disciples, destined to propagate the law of his enlightenment."[114] Miao-lo declares: "When the sons disseminate the teachings of their father, they can benefit all people."[115] The *Fushō Ki* states: "Because this is the Law realized by the Buddha at the time of his original enlightenment, it was entrusted to his original disciples."[116]

In the *Yujutsu* chapter Bodhisattva Miroku asked Shakyamuni Buddha: "We believe that none of the Buddha's words, even his teachings given in accordance with the people's capacity, is false, and that his wisdom penetrates all. But when bodhisattvas who have but recently launched their vows hear these words after your passing, they will refuse to believe them and will eventually commit the grave sin of slandering the Buddha's Law. World-Honored One! We sincerely implore you to explain this and remove our doubt, so that men of devout faith who appear after the Buddha's passing, on hearing this matter, will not give rise to doubt."[117] Here Bodhisattva Miroku was imploring the Buddha to preach the *Juryō* chapter for those to come after his passing.

The *Juryō* chapter states: "Some are out of their minds, while others are not. . . . Those children who have not lost their senses can see that the beneficial medicine is good in both color and fragrance, so they take it immediately and are completely cured of their sickness."[118] The sutra explains that all bodhisattvas, people of the two vehicles, and humans and gods received the seed of enlightenment at *gohyaku-jintengō*. It was nurtured by the preaching of the sixteenth son of Daitsū Buddha as well as by Shakyamuni Buddha's four flavors of teachings and the theoretical teaching of the Lotus Sutra. Then they finally attained Buddhahood when they heard the essential teaching of the Lotus Sutra.

The *Juryō* chapter continues: "Those who are out of their minds are equally delighted to see their father return and beg him to cure their sickness, but when they are given the medicine, they refuse to take it. This is because the poison has penetrated deeply, causing them to lose their true minds. Therefore they think that the medicine will not taste good in spite of its fine color and fragrance. [Then the father thinks,] 'Now I must use some means to get them to take it.' [So he tells them this:] 'I leave this good medicine here for you now. You should take it and not worry that it will not cure you.' So instructing them, he again goes off to another land, where he sends a messenger home to announce, . . ." According to the *Fumbetsu Kudoku* chapter, ["the good medicine" of the *Juryō* chapter is left for] "the time of the evil Latter Day of the Law."[119]

Question: Who is the messenger mentioned in the text?

Answer: It means the four ranks of Buddhist sages. They fall into four categories. Most of the leaders of Hinayana appeared in the first five hundred years of the Former Day of the Law, and most of those who taught [provisional] Mahayana came in the second five hundred years. The bearers of the theoretical teaching appeared mainly in the next thousand years, the Middle Day of the Law, and the rest in the beginning of the Latter Day. They are the "messenger" in our time. The bearers of the essential teaching are the countless Bodhisattvas of the Earth who will appear in the beginning of the Latter Day. "This good medicine" is the heart of the *Juryō* chapter, Nam-myoho-renge-kyo—its name, entity, quality, function and influence.[120] The Buddha would not entrust this medicine even to the bodhisattvas of the theoretical teaching, much less to the bodhisattvas of other worlds.

The *Jinriki* chapter states: "Thereupon in the presence of the Buddha the bodhisattvas equal in number to the dust particles of a thousand worlds who had sprung up from the earth, all with a single mind, pressed their palms together, gazed up reverently at his solemn countenance, and said to the Buddha, 'World-Honored One! After your passing we pledge to propagate this sutra throughout every land where your manifestations appear or where you pass into nirvana.' "[121] T'ien-t'ai says: "The great assembly witnessed the Bodhisattvas of the Earth alone making this pledge."[122] Tao-hsien remarks: "The Buddha transmitted this sutra solely to the Bodhisattvas of the Earth. Because this is the Law realized by the Buddha at the time of his original enlightenment, it was entrusted to his original disciples."[123] Bodhisattva Monjushiri is a disciple of Fudō Buddha,[124] who dwells in the golden world to the east. Bodhisattva Kannon is a disciple of Amida Buddha in the west. Bodhisattva Yakuō is a disciple of Nichigatsu Jōmyōtoku Buddha.[125] Bodhisattva Fugen is a disciple of Hōi Buddha.[126] They came to this *saha* world to help Shakyamuni Buddha teach the people of his day. They were bodhisattvas of the provisional and theoretical teachings, and were not entrusted with the supreme Law, so they could not possibly appear and propagate it in the Latter Day.

The *Jinriki* chapter states: "At that time the World-Honored One demonstrated his great mystic powers to the entire assembly, extending his long, broad tongue till it reached upward to the Brahma Heaven. All the other Buddhas from the worlds throughout the ten directions seated on lion king thrones under jewel trees did the same, extending their long, broad tongues."[127] In no other sutra, whether Hinayana or Mahayana, exoteric or esoteric, is there a passage that describes Shakyamuni Buddha and all the other Buddhas extending their tongues to the Brahma Heaven. The *Amida* Sutra states that Buddhas covered a major world system with their broad, long tongues, but lacks the truth that such a gesture would substantiate. The *Hannya* Sutra tells how the Buddha's tongue covered the major world system and radiated infinite light when he expounded the *Hannya*. Yet this cannot be a proof [comparable to that of the *Jinriki* chapter]. Since these two sutras are mere provisional teachings, they obscured the Buddha's enlightenment in the remotest past.

After the Buddha displayed his ten great mystic powers described in the *Jinriki* chapter,[128] he transferred the five characters of the Mystic Law to the Bodhisattvas of the Earth: "At that time the Buddha addressed Jōgyō and the host of other bodhisattvas, saying, 'The mystic powers of a Buddha are boundless, beyond imagination. Even if I were to exert all these powers for infinite kalpas in explaining the great benefit of this sutra to ensure its propagation, I could never explain them fully. In essence, I have described in this sutra all the laws of the Buddha, all the invincible mystic powers of the Buddha, all the secret storehouses of the Buddha, and all the profound practices of the Buddha.' "[129] T'ien-t'ai says: "This paragraph begins the third stage of the chapter, where the Buddha transfers the essence of his teachings to the Bodhisattvas of the Earth."[130] Dengyō states: "The *Jinriki* chapter says, 'In essence, I have described in this sutra all the laws of the Buddha.' In the Lotus Sutra the Buddha revealed all the laws, invincible mystic powers, secret storehouses, and profound practices of his enlightenment."[131] Demonstrating ten great mystic powers, the Buddha transferred the five characters Myōhō-renge-kyō to the Four Great Bodhisattvas, Jōgyō, Anryūgyō, Jōgyō, and Muhengyō.

[Miao-lo states that] the first five of the ten great mystic powers are meant for those living in Shakyamuni's lifetime, and the last five for the generations after his passing.[132] But in a deeper sense all are intended for future generations. The Buddha confirms this later in the same chapter: "Because they [the Bodhisattvas of the Earth] will faithfully uphold this sutra after the Buddha's passing, all the Buddhas rejoice and display their limitless mystic powers."[133]

The following *Zokurui* chapter states: "At this time Shakyamuni Buddha rose from his place of preaching, and displaying his great mystic powers, stroked with his right hand the heads of the infinite numbers of bodhisattvas, saying, 'I now transfer [the Lotus Sutra] to you.' "[134] The Buddha first transferred the Law to the Bodhisattvas of the Earth, and then to the bodhisattvas of the theoretical teaching, bodhisattvas of other worlds, Bonten, Taishaku, the Four Heavenly Kings, and others. Then "all the emanation Buddhas, who had gathered from the ten directions of the universe, returned to their respective lands . . . and the Buddha ordered that the Treasure Tower of Tahō Buddha return to its original place." After the Bodhisattvas of the Earth had departed, the Buddha transferred the sutra to the people of the theoretical teaching and the bodhisattvas from other worlds, picking up, as it were, the gleanings left over from the *Jinriki* and *Zokurui* chapters, as he preached the last six chapters of the Lotus Sutra, the *Fugen* Sutra, and the Nirvana Sutra.

Question: Did the Bodhisattvas of the Earth then appear in this world during the two millennia of the Former and Middle Days of the Law to spread the Lotus Sutra?

Answer: No, they did not.

Question: Your answer comes as a surprise. If the Lotus Sutra, especially the essential teaching, is intended primarily for those people living after the Buddha's demise, and the Buddha entrusted the sutra to the Bodhisattvas of the Earth, why did they not appear during the first two millennia to spread the sutra?

Answer: I will not say.

Question: I am asking you again, what was the reason?

Answer: I will not disclose it.

Question: Once more, what was the reason?

Answer: If I disclose it, all will refuse to believe and, what is worse, will slander the sutra, as in the Latter Day of Ionnō Buddha.[135] Even my own disciples would slander the sutra if I tried to explain, so I can only keep silent.

Question: Nonetheless, I urge you to answer. Unless you do, you will be violating the Buddha's precept against concealing the truth.

Answer: Then since I have no choice, I will try to give you a brief explanation. The *Hosshi* chapter states: "[Since hatred and jealousy toward this sutra abound even during the lifetime of the Buddha,] how much worse will it be in the world after his passing?"[136] The *Juryō* chapter states: "I leave this good medicine here for you now."[137] The *Fumbetsu Kudoku* chapter speaks of "the time of the evil Latter Day of the Law."[138] The *Yakuō* chapter says: "During the last half-millennium after my death the Lotus Sutra will spread widely throughout the world."[139] In the Nirvana Sutra occurs a passage which reads: "Suppose that a couple has seven children, one of whom falls ill. Although the parents love all their children equally, they worry most about the sick child."[140]

These passages are a crystal mirror of the Buddha's will. They show that the Buddha did not appear for the sake of those present during the eight years when he revealed the Lotus Sutra at Eagle Peak, but for those who would come after him in the Former, Middle, and Latter Days. His advent was specifically for people like us, those living in the beginning of the Latter Day, not for those who lived in the two thousand years of the Former and Middle Days of the Law. "The sick child" mentioned in the Nirvana Sutra represents the slanderers of the Lotus Sutra in the Latter Day. The Buddha will now "leave this good medicine here" especially for those who "think that the medicine will not taste good in spite of its fine color and fragrance."

The Bodhisattvas of the Earth did not appear in the Former and Middle Days of the Law for good reason.

Hinayana and provisional Mahayana were spread in the first millennium because the time was not ripe for the true teaching and the people were not ready to embrace it. The four ranks of bodhisattvas in the Former Day led those who had received the seed of Buddhahood by hearing the Lotus Sutra during Shakyamuni's lifetime to attain enlightenment through Hinayana and provisional Mahayana teachings. [If the Bodhisattvas of the Earth had spread the Lotus Sutra at that time instead of later,] the people would have reviled it and thereby destroyed all the merit of the maturing of that seed they had accumulated in Shakyamuni's lifetime. [Therefore the bodhisattvas did not emerge then.] People of the first millennium are like those in the Buddha's lifetime who gradually matured and attained enlightenment through the four flavors of provisional teachings.

In the middle of and late in the second millennium, Bodhisattva Kannon was reborn as Nan-yüeh and Bodhisattva Yakuō as T'ien-t'ai. They openly preached the theoretical teaching and kept the essential teaching to themselves. T'ien-t'ai fully revealed the hundred worlds, the thousand factors, and the three thousand realms. They expounded in principle that all beings embody [*ichinen sanzen*], but they did not establish the actual practice of the five characters of Nam-myoho-renge-kyo or the true object of worship of the essential teaching. The time was not right for propagation, although even then some people had the proper capacity.

Now, in the beginning of the Latter Day of the Law, Hinayana adherents attack the doctrines of Mahayana, and provisional Mahayana believers denounce the true Mahayana teachings. East is mistaken for west, and heaven and earth are turned upside down. The four ranks of bodhisattvas of the theoretical teaching are gone, and all the gods have deserted the country and no longer lend it protection. At this very time the Bodhisattvas of the Earth appear in the world for the first time to give the medicine of the five characters Myōhō-renge-kyō to the ignorant people of the Latter Day. This is what is meant by: "Even if they revile the true teaching and fall into the evil paths, they thereby create the causes for eventual attainment of Buddhahood."[141]

You who are my disciples, take this to heart! The Bodhisattvas of the Earth were the first disciples of Lord Shakyamuni when he settled his heart on enlightenment in the remotest past, yet they were not faithful to him [in India]. They did not come to Buddhagayā after he attained enlightenment, nor did they come to the grove of sal trees when he entered nirvana. They also failed to appear when the Buddha preached the first fourteen chapters of the Lotus Sutra, and they left the assembly when he preached the last six chapters. They only attended the Buddha when he expounded the first eight chapters of the essential teaching. Since such noble bodhisattvas received the Mystic Law and made a solemn oath to Shakyamuni Buddha, Tahō Buddha, and all the other Buddhas, is it possible that they will not appear now at the beginning of the Latter Day of the Law? Know this: in the time for *shakubuku* the Four Bodhisattvas appear as wise kings who rebuke and convert evil kings, and in the time for *shōju* they appear as priests to embrace and spread true Buddhism.

Question: Does the Buddha predict their coming in the Latter Day?

Answer: [The *Yakuō* chapter of the Lotus Sutra states that] during the last half-millennium after the Buddha's death the Lotus Sutra will spread widely throughout the world. T'ien-t'ai predicts: "In the fifth five hundred years, the Mystic Way shall spread and benefit mankind far into the future."[142] Miao-lo states: "The beginning of the Latter Day of the Law the Mystic Law will not be without inconspicuous benefit."[143] The Great Teacher Dengyō declares, "The Former and Middle Days are almost over, and the Latter Day is near at hand."[144] This declaration conveys that his was not the right time for propagation. Born in Japan, he foresaw the beginning of the Latter Day of the Law, saying, "The propagation of the true teaching will begin in the age when the Middle Day of the Law ends and the Latter Day opens, in a land to the east of T'ang and to the west of Katsu, among people stained by the five impurities who live in a time of conflict. The sutra says: 'Since hatred and jealousy abound even during the lifetime of the Buddha, how much worse will it be in the world after his passing!' There is good reason for this statement."[145]

"Conflict" refers to the present internal strife and imminent invasion from the western sea. Now is when the Bodhisattvas of the Earth will appear and establish in this country the supreme object of worship on the earth which depicts Shakyamuni Buddha of the essential teaching attending [the original Buddha]. This object of worship has never appeared in India or China. Its time had not come when Prince Shōtoku in Japan constructed the Shitennō-ji,[146] so he could only make a statue of Amida, a Buddha in another world, as the object of worship. When Emperor Shōmu[147] erected Tōdai-ji, he made a statue of the Buddha of the *Kegon* Sutra [Vairocana Buddha] as the object of worship but could not manifest the true meaning of the Lotus Sutra. The Great Teacher Dengyō almost revealed the truth of the sutra, but because the time had not yet come, he constructed a statue of Yakushi Buddha who dwells in an eastern realm of the universe, but he did not represent the Four Bodhisattvas of the Earth in any form.

Thus, the revelation of the true object of worship has been entrusted only to the Bodhisattvas of the Earth. They have been waiting for the right time to emerge from the earth and carry out the Lord Buddha's command. They did not appear in the Former or Middle Day. But if they did not appear in the Latter Day of the Law, their vows would be outright lies, and the prophecies of Shakyamuni, Tahō, and the other Buddhas would be no more than froth on the waters.

We have recently experienced earthquakes, comets, and other calamities such as never occurred in the Former or Middle Day. These signs could not be caused by *garuḍas, asuras,* or dragons; they must foretell the appearance of the Four Great Bodhisattvas. T'ien-t'ai states: "By observing the fury of the rain we can tell the greatness of the dragon that caused it, and by observing the flourishing of the lotus flowers we can tell the depth of the pond in which they grow."[148] Miao-lo says: "Wise men can see omens and what they foretell, as snakes know the way of snakes."[149] When the skies are clear, the ground is illuminated. Similarly, when one knows the Lotus Sutra, he understands the meaning of all worldly affairs.

Showing profound compassion for those ignorant of the gem of *ichinen sanzen,* the Buddha wrapped it within the five-character phrase [Myōhō-renge-kyō], with which he then adorned the necks of those living in the Latter Day. The Four Great Bodhisattvas will protect anyone who embraces the Mystic Law as faithfully as T'ai-kung and the Duke of Chou protected King Wen, and as devotedly as the four white-haired elders served Emperor Hui.[150]

Nichiren

The twenty-fifth day of the fourth month in the tenth year of Bun'ei (1273)

Cover Letter

Lord Toki[151]

I have received the summer kimono, three *sumi* inksticks, and five writing brushes.

I have written down some of my thoughts concerning the doctrine of observing the mind. I am sending the treatise to you, Ōta, Kyōshin Gobō,[152] and the others. It concerns the most important matter concerning me, Nichiren. Only those of single-minded faith should be allowed to read it.

The treatise contains many difficult points and few answers. What it reveals, however, has never been heard of before, and is bound to startle those who read or hear of it. Even if you show it to others, never let three or four persons read it together at a time.

In the twenty-two hundred and twenty odd years since the Buddha's passing, the heart of this treatise has never been revealed before. Despite the official persecution facing me, I expound it now at the beginning of the fifth half-millennium, when the time is ripe for its propagation. I hope those who read it will remain firm in their faith so that both master and disciples can together reach the pure land of Eagle Peak and behold with reverence the faces of Shakyamuni, Tahō, and all the other Buddhas in the universe.

With my deep respect,
Nichiren

The twenty-sixth day of the fourth month in the tenth year of Bun'ei (1273)

THE SELECTION OF THE TIME

Introduction

"The Selection of the Time" *(Senji Shō)* is dated the tenth day of the sixth month, 1275 and was written after Nichiren had retired to Mount Minobu. It is addressed to a follower by the name of Yui who lived in Nishiyama in Suruga.

In the third month of the previous year, 1274, a government official arrived in Sado Island where Nichiren was living in exile, with a pardon for him. Nichiren returned to Kamakura at once and then retired to Mount Minobu in the fifth month. In the tenth month Mongol forces attacked Japan, fulfilling Nichiren's earlier prediction of a foreign invasion. In the fourth month of 1275 emissaries from the Mongols arrived in Japan bearing a letter from Kublai Khan threatening to invade Japan again. The Japanese government officials executed the envoys, reinforced their defenses, and waited nervously for the expected invasion.

This work is arranged in the question-and-answer form often used in Buddhist works. Nichiren made frequent use of this format; here he uses a total of thirty-seven questions and answers of varying lengths. Nichiren opens with the passage: "One who wishes to study the teachings of Buddhism must first learn to understand the time." Nichiren then proceeds to discuss the importance of the concept of time in the history of the development of Buddhist teachings. Basing his remarks on the five five-hundred-year periods that cover the 2,500 years that followed Shakyamuni's death, as described in the *Daijuku* Sutra, Nichiren proceeds to trace the spread of Buddhism through the three countries of India, China, and Japan, relating these teachings to the concept of the Former, Middle, and Latter Days of the Law. In the first five hundred years of the Former Day, Mahākāśyapa, Ānanda, and others propagated the Hinayana teachings in India. The second five hundred years of the Former Day witnessed the appearance of Nāgārjuna, Vasubandhu, and others, who propagated provisional Mahayana teachings.

Nichiren then describes the first five hundred years of the Middle Day, when the Great Teacher T'ien-t'ai made his appearance in China and propagated the theoretical teaching of the Lotus Sutra, in other words, the first half of this sutra. Toward the end of the Middle Day, the Great Teacher Dengyō propagated this same teaching in Japan.

But now time, and the world with it, had entered into the Latter Day of the Law, when Shakyamuni's teaching had become obscured and lost. Nichiren saw himself as the votary of the Lotus Sutra destined to propagate this scripture, particularly the second half of the sutra, or the essential teaching, and as the sovereign, teacher, and parent to all.

The latter half of the text details what Nichiren found to be the errors and transgressions of the other schools of Buddhism, the Pure Land, Shingon, and Zen. These errors and their failure to reverence the Lotus Sutra above all other works he found to be the cause of the many disasters that were afflicting Japan. In the *"Rissho Ankoku Ron"* Nichiren found the Pure Land sect of Nembutsu followers to be the principal source of these disasters. In the present work he found priests of the Shingon sect to be responsible for the evils that had befallen the country. Not only does he take them to task for stealing T'ien-t'ai's doctrines and subverting them, but also for asserting the superiority of their own *Dainichi* Sutra over the Lotus.

Nichiren criticized severely those Tendai priests who succeeded Dengyō and mixed Shingon teachings into the doctrines based on the Lotus Sutra. He says: "In China and Japan in the past, sages of outstanding wisdom and ability have from time to time appeared. But none, as an ally of the Lotus Sutra, has faced such powerful enemies within the country as have I, Nichiren. From the facts present before your very eyes, it should be apparent that Nichiren is the foremost person in the entire world."

Nichiren goes on to explain that the various disasters that have occurred, the great earthquake of the Shōka era and the frightening comet that appeared in the Bun'ei period, were brought about by the failure of the rulers to honor the supremacy of the Lotus Sutra. He explains that without begrudging his life and despite persecution by powerful enemies, he has struggled unremittingly to reveal the true teaching of the Lotus Sutra.

One who wishes to study the teachings of Buddhism must first learn to understand the time. In the past, when the Buddha Daitsūchi-shō appeared in the world, he remained for a period of ten small kalpas without preaching a single sutra. Thus the Lotus Sutra says, "He sat for ten small kalpas."[1] And later, "Because the Buddha knew that the time had not yet come, though entreated by others, he sat in silence."[2]

Likewise Lord Shakyamuni of the present world spent the first forty years and more of his preaching life without expounding the Lotus Sutra, because, as the sutra says, "the time to expound it had not yet come."[3]

Lao Tzu remained in his mother's womb for eighty years, waiting to be born,[4] and Bodhisattva Miroku abides in the inner court of the Tuṣita Heaven[5] for a period of 5,670 million years, awaiting the time for his advent in the world. The cuckoo sings when spring is waning, the cock waits until the break of day to crow. If even these lowly creatures have such an understanding of time, then how can a person who wishes to practice the teachings of Buddhism fail to make certain what time it is?

When Shakyamuni Buddha prepared to preach at the place where he had gained enlightenment, the various Buddhas made their appearance in the ten directions and all the great bodhisattvas gathered around. Bonten, Taishaku, and the Four Heavenly Kings came with their robes fluttering. The dragons and others of the eight kinds of lowly beings[6] pressed their palms together, the common mortals of superior capacity bent their ears to listen, and the bodhisattvas who in their present bodies have attained the stage where they perceive the non-birth and non-extinction of the phenomenal world, along with Bodhisattva Gedatsugatsu, all begged the Buddha to preach. But the World-Honored One did not reveal a single word concerning the doctrines that hold that persons in the two realms of *shōmon* and *engaku* can attain Buddhahood, or that he himself had attained enlightenment countless ages in the past, nor did he set forth the most vital teachings of all, those concerning *ichinen sanzen* and the fact that one can attain Buddhahood in his present form. There was only one reason for this: the fact that, although his listeners possessed the capacity to understand such doctrines, the proper time had not yet come. Or, as the Lotus Sutra says, "because the time to expound it had not yet come."

But when Shakyamuni Buddha preached the Lotus Sutra to the

gathering on Eagle Peak, the great king Ajātaśatru, the most unfilial person in the entire world, was allowed to sit among the listeners. Devadatta, who had spent his whole life slandering the Law, was told that in the future he would become a Buddha called Heavenly King, and the dragon king's daughter, though impeded by the five obstacles,[7] became a Buddha without changing her dragon form. Those predestined for the realms of shōmon and engaku were told that they would in fact become Buddhas, like scorched seeds that unexpectedly sprout and put forth flowers and fruit. The Buddha revealed that he had attained enlightenment countless ages in the past, which puzzled his listeners as greatly as if he had asserted that an old man of a hundred was the son of a man of twenty-five.[8] And he also expounded the doctrine of ichinen sanzen, explaining that the nine worlds have the potential for Buddhahood, and that Buddhahood retains the nine worlds.[9]

Thus a single word of this Lotus Sutra that he preached is as precious as a wish-granting jewel,[10] and a single phrase is the seed of all Buddhas. We may leave aside the question of whether Shakyamuni's listeners at that point possessed the capacity to understand such doctrines or not. The fact is that the time had come for him to preach them. As the Lotus Sutra says, "Now this is the very time when I must decisively preach the teaching of the great vehicle."[11]

Question: If one preaches the great Law to persons who do not have the capacity to understand it, then the foolish ones among them will surely slander it and will fall into the evil paths of existence. Is the person who does the preaching not to blame for this?

Answer: If a man builds a road for others and someone loses his way on it, is that the fault of the road-builder? If a skilled physician gives medicine to a sick person but the sick person, repelled by the medicine, refuses to take it and dies, should one blame the physician?

Question: The second volume of the Lotus Sutra says, "When you are among ignorant men, do not preach this sutra!"[12] The fourth volume says, "[This scripture] must not be distributed or recklessly transmitted to others."[13] And the fifth volume states, "This Lotus Sutra is the secret storehouse of Buddhas. Among the sutras, it holds the highest place. It should be guarded through the long night and never recklessly expounded."[14] These passages from the sutra would seem to indicate that one should not expound the Law to those who do not have the capacity to understand it.

Answer: I refer you to the passage in the Fukyō chapter that states,

"He would say to people, 'I deeply respect you.' " The chapter also says, "But among the four categories of Buddhists he addressed, there were some who flared up in anger, whose minds were possessed by foul thoughts, and they cursed and abused him, saying, 'This stupid monk!' " It also says, "Some among the people would beat him with sticks and staves, and stone him with rocks and tiles."[15] And in the *Kanji* chapter it says, "There will be many ignorant people who will curse and speak ill of us, and will attack us with swords and staves."[16] These passages imply that one should preach the Law even though he may be reviled and cursed and even beaten for it. Since the sutra so teaches, is the one who preaches to blame?

Question: Now these two views appear to be as incompatible as fire and water. May I ask how one is to resolve this dilemma?

Answer: T'ien-t'ai says that one should use whatever method "accords with the time."[17] And Chang-an says, "You should distinguish between the *shōju* and *shakubuku* methods and never adhere solely to one or the other."[18] What these remarks mean is that at times, the Buddha's teaching will be met with slander and one therefore refrains from expounding it for the present, and at other times, even though one encounters slander, one nevertheless makes a point of preaching anyway. There are times when, although a few persons may have the capacity to believe, the great majority will only slander the Buddha's teaching, and one therefore refrains from expounding it for the present. And there are other times when, although the great majority of persons are bound to slander the Buddha's teaching, one nevertheless makes a point of preaching anyway.

When Shakyamuni Buddha first attained enlightenment and prepared to preach, the great bodhisattvas Hōe, Kudokurin, Kongōdō, Kongōzō, Monju, Fugen, Miroku, and Gedatsugatsu, as well as Bonten, Taishaku, the Four Heavenly Kings, and countless numbers of common mortals of superior capacity came to hear him.[19] When he preached at the Deer Park, Ājñāta Kauṇḍinya and the others of the five ascetics, along with Mahākāśyapa and his two hundred fifty followers, Śāriputra and his two hundred fifty followers, and eighty thousand heavenly beings all gathered to listen.[20]

At the ceremony of the great assembly for the *Hōdō* sutras, Shakyamuni's father, King Śuddhodana, displayed a sincere desire for Buddhism, and Shakyamuni therefore entered the palace and preached the *Kambutsu Zammai* Sutra for him. And for the sake of his deceased mother, Queen Māyā, he secluded himself in the Trayastriṃśā Heaven for a period of ninety days and there preached the Māyā Sutra. Where his father and mother were concerned, one would think he could not possibly withhold even the most secret teaching of the Law. And yet he did not preach the Lotus Sutra for them. In the final analysis, the Buddha's preaching of the Lotus Sutra has nothing to do with the capacities of his listeners. As long as the proper time had not yet come, he would on no account expound it.[21]

Question: When is the time for the preaching of the Hinayana sutras and the provisional sutras, and when is the time for the preaching of the Lotus Sutra?

Answer: Even bodhisattvas, from those in the ten stages of faith to those on the verge of full enlightenment,[22] find it difficult to judge matters concerning time and capacity. How then can ordinary beings such as ourselves be able to judge such matters?

Question: Is there no way to determine them?

Answer: Let us borrow the eye of the Buddha[23] to consider this question of time and capacity. Let us use the sun of the Buddha[24] to illuminate the nation.

Question: What do you mean by that?

Answer: In the *Daijuku* Sutra, Shakyamuni Buddha, the World-Honored One, addresses Bodhisattva Gatsuzō and predicts the future. Thus he says that the first five hundred years after his passing will be the age of attaining liberation,[25] and the next five hundred years, the age of meditation[26] (making one thousand years). The next five hundred years will be the age of reading, reciting, and listening,[27] and the next five hundred years, the age of building temples and stupas[28] (making two thousand years). Concerning the next five hundred years after that, he says, "Quarrels and disputes will arise among the adherents to my teachings, and the Pure Law will become obscured and lost."[29]

These five five-hundred-year periods, which total twenty-five hundred years, are delineated in different ways by different people. The Meditation Master Tao-ch'o of China declares that during the first four of the five five-hundred-year periods, which constitute the Former and Middle Days of the Law, the Pure Law of the Hinayana and Mahayana teachings will flourish, but that after the beginning of the Latter Day of the Law, these teachings will all perish. At that time, only those who practice the Pure Land teaching, the Pure Law of the Nembutsu, will be able to escape the sufferings of birth and death.[30]

The Japanese priest Hōnen defines the situation in this way.[31] According to him, the Lotus, *Kegon, Dainichi,* and various Hinayana sutras which have spread in Japan, along with the teachings of the Tendai, Shingon, Ritsu, and other sects, constitute the Pure Law of the two thousand years of the Former and Middle Days of the Law referred to in the passage from the *Daijuku* Sutra cited above. But once the world enters the Latter Day of the Law, all these teachings will be completely obliterated. Even though men should continue to practice such teachings, not a single one of them will succeed in escaping from the sufferings of birth and death. Thus Nāgārjuna in his *Jūjūbibasha Ron* and the priest T'an-luan refer to such teachings as the "difficult-to-practice way";[32] Tao-ch'o declares that not a single person has ever attained enlightenment through them;[33] and Shan-tao says that not one person in a thousand can be saved by them.[34] After the Pure Law of these teachings has become obscured and lost, then the Great Pure Law—namely, the three Pure Land sutras[35] and the single practice of calling upon the name of Amida Buddha—will make its appearance, and when people devote themselves to this practice, even though they may be evil or ignorant persons, "If there are ten of them, then all ten will be reborn in the Pure Land, and if there are a hundred of them, then all hundred will be reborn there."[36] This is the meaning of the passage: "Only the single doctrine of the Pure Land constitutes the road that leads to salvation."[37]

Hōnen therefore declares that if men desire happiness in the next life, they should withdraw their support from Mount Hiei, Tō-ji, Onjō-ji, and the seven major temples of Nara,[38] as well as from all the various temples and monasteries throughout the islands of Japan, and should seize all the fields and land holdings that have been donated to these temples and devote these resources to the building of Nembutsu halls. If they do so, they will be certain to be reborn in the Pure Land. Thus he urges them to recite the words Namu Amida Butsu.

It has now been more than fifty years since these teachings spread throughout our country. My refutation of these evil doctrines is now a thing of the past. There is no doubt that our present age corresponds to the fifth five-hundred-year period described in the *Daijuku* Sutra, when "the Pure Law will become obscured and lost."[39] But that which is to come after "the Pure Law has become obscured and lost" is the Great Pure Law of Nam-myoho-renge-kyo, and the heart and core of the Lotus Sutra. This is what should be propagated and spread throughout the continent of Jambudvīpa—with its eighty thousand kingdoms, their eighty thousand rulers, and the ministers and countless subjects in the domain of each ruler—so that it may be chanted by all persons, just as the name of Amida is now chanted by the mouths of the monks, nuns, laymen, and laywomen throughout Japan.

Question: What passages can you cite to prove this?

Answer: The seventh volume of the Lotus Sutra says, "In the fifth five hundred years after my death, widely declare and spread [the Lotus Sutra] and never allow its flow to cease."[40] This indicates that "widely declaring and spreading [the Lotus Sutra]" will be accomplished in the time after "the Pure Law becomes obscured and lost," as the *Daijuku* Sutra puts it.

Again, the sixth volume speaks of "one who is able to uphold this sutra in the evil age of the Latter Day of the Law,"[41] and the fifth volume talks of "the latter age when the Law is on the point of disappearing."[42] The fourth volume states, "Since hatred and jealousy toward this sutra abound even during the lifetime of the Buddha, how much worse will it be in the world after his passing?"[43] And the fifth volume says, "The people will be full of hostility, and find it extremely difficult to believe."[44] And the seventh volume, speaking of the fifth five-hundred-year period which is the age of conflict, says, "Do not allow the devil, the devil's people, or the deities, dragons, *yakṣas, kumbhāṇḍas,*[45] or their kind to seize the advantage."[46]

The *Daijuku* Sutra says, "Quarrels and disputes will arise among the adherents to my teachings."[47] And the fifth volume of the Lotus Sutra similarly says, "There will be monks in that evil age," "Or there will be forest-dwelling monks," and, "Demons will take possession of others."[48]

These passages describe the following situation. During the fifth five-hundred-year period, eminent priests who are possessed by demons will be found everywhere throughout the country. At that time, a single wise man[49] will appear. The eminent priests who are possessed by demons[50] will deceive the ruler, his ministers, and the common people into slandering and abusing this man, attacking him with sticks, staves, tiles, and stones, and condemning him to exile or death. At that time, Shakyamuni, Tahō, and the Buddhas of the ten directions will speak to the great bodhisattvas who sprang up from the earth, and the great bodhisattvas will in turn report to Bonten,

Taishaku, the gods of the sun and the moon, and the Four Heavenly Kings. As a result, strange occurrences and omens will appear in abundance in the heavens and on earth.

If the rulers of a country fail to heed this warning, then the Buddhas and the great bodhisattvas will order neighboring countries to censure those evil rulers and the evil priests of their countries. Then great struggles and disputes such as have never been known in the past will break out in the world.

At that time, all the people living in the four continents illuminated by the sun and moon, fearing the destruction of their nation or the loss of their lives, will pray to the Buddhas and bodhisattvas for help. And if there is no sign that their prayers will be answered, they will put their faith in this single humble priest whom they earlier despised. Then all the countless eminent priests, the great rulers of the eighty thousand countries and the numberless common people will all bow their heads to the ground, press their palms together, and in one voice will chant Nam-myoho-renge-kyo. It will be like that occasion during the Buddha's demonstration of his ten mystic powers,[51] described in the *Jinriki* chapter of the Lotus Sutra, when all the beings in the worlds of the ten directions, without a single exception, turned toward the *saha* world and cried out together in a loud voice, Namu Shakyamuni Buddha, Namu Shakyamuni Buddha, Nam-myoho-renge-kyo, Nam-myoho-renge-kyo![52]

Question: The sutra passages you have cited clearly prove your point. But are there any prophecies in the writings of T'ien-t'ai, Miao-lo, or Dengyō that would support your argument?

Answer: Your process of questioning is backwards! If I had cited passages from the commentaries of men such as T'ien-t'ai and the others and you had then asked whether there were sutra passages to support them, that I could understand. But since I have already cited passages from the sutras that clearly prove the argument, it is hardly necessary to ask if there are similar passages in the commentaries. If by chance you found that the sutras and the commentaries disagreed, would you then discard the sutras and follow the commentaries?

Question: What you say is perfectly true. Nevertheless, we ordinary persons have only a very remote idea of what the sutras mean, while the commentaries are more accessible and easier to understand. If there are clear passages of proof in such relatively understandable commentaries, then citing them might help us have greater faith in your argument.

Answer: I can see that you are very sincere and earnest in your questioning, so I will cite a few passages from the commentaries. The Great Teacher T'ien-t'ai states, "In the fifth five hundred years, the Mystic Way shall spread and benefit mankind far into the future."[53] The Great Teacher Miao-lo says, "The beginning of the Latter Day of the Law will not be without inconspicuous benefit."[54]

The Great Teacher Dengyō declares, "The Former and Middle Days are almost over, and the Latter Day is near at hand. Now indeed is the time when the One Vehicle expounded in the Lotus Sutra will prove how perfectly it fits the capacities of all people. How do we know this is true? Because the *Anrakugyō* chapter of the Lotus Sutra states, 'In the latter age when the Law is on the point of disappearing, [the Lotus Sutra will be expounded far and wide].' "[55] And Dengyō further states, "The propagation of the true teaching will begin in the age when the Middle Day of the Law ends and the Latter Day opens, in a land to the east of T'ang and to the west of Katsu,[56] among people stained by the five impurities[57] who live in a time of conflict. The sutra says, 'Since hatred and jealousy toward this sutra abound even during the lifetime of the Buddha, how much worse will it be in the world after his passing?' There is good reason for this statement."[58]

Shakyamuni Buddha was born in the Kalpa of Continuance,[59] in the ninth kalpa of decrease, when the span of human life was diminishing and measured a hundred years. The period when the span of human life diminishes from a hundred years to ten years accordingly falls within the period represented by the fifty years of the Buddha's preaching life, the two thousand years of the Former and Middle Days of the Law that follow his passing, and the ten thousand years of the Latter Day of the Law that follow that. During this period, the Lotus Sutra was destined to be propagated and spread widely on two occasions. The first was the last eight years of the Buddha's life [when he preached the Lotus Sutra], and the second is the five hundred years at the beginning of the Latter Day of the Law.

T'ien-t'ai, Miao-lo, and Dengyō were not born early enough to be present when the Buddha was in the world and preached the Lotus Sutra, nor were they born late enough to be present in the Latter Day of the Law. To their regret, they were born in the interval between these two times, and it is clear from their writings that they looked forward with longing to the beginning of the Latter Day of the Law.

Theirs was like the case of the hermit-sage Asita who, when he viewed the newborn Prince Siddhartha, the future Shakyamuni Buddha, remarked in sorrow, "I am already over ninety, so I will not live to see this prince attain enlightenment. After my death, I will be reborn in the world of formlessness,[60] so I cannot be present during the fifty years when he preaches the Law, nor can I be reborn in this world during the Former, Middle, or Latter Day of the Law!"[61] Such was his lament.

All those who are determined to attain the Way should take note of these examples and rejoice! Those concerned about their next life would do better to be common people in this, the Latter Day of the Law, than be mighty rulers during the two thousand years of the Former and Middle Days of the Law. Why won't people believe this? Rather than be the chief priest of the Tendai sect, it is better to be a leper who chants Nam-myoho-renge-kyo! As Emperor Wu of the Liang dynasty said in his vow, "I would rather be Devadatta and sink into the hell of incessant suffering than be the non-Buddhist sage Udraka Rāmaputra!"[62]

Question: Do the scholars Nāgārjuna and Vasubandhu say anything about it [Nam-myoho-renge-kyo]?

Answer: Nāgārjuna and Vasubandhu knew about it in their hearts, but they did not expound it in words.

Question: Why did they not expound it?

Answer: There are many reasons. For one, the people of their day did not have the capacity to understand it. Second, it was not the proper time. Third, these men were bodhisattavs of the theoretical teaching[63] and hence had not been entrusted with the task of expounding it.

Question: Could you explain the matter in greater detail?

Answer: The Former Day of the Law began on the sixteenth day of the second month, the day after the Buddha's passing. The Venerable Mahākāśyapa received the transmission of the Buddha's teachings and propagated them for the first twenty years. For the next twenty years, this task fell to the Venerable Ānanda, for the next twenty years to Śāṇavāsa, for the next twenty years to Upagupta, and for the next twenty years to Dhṛtaka. By that time a hundred years had passed. But the only teachings that were spread abroad during this period were those of the Hinayana sutras. Even the titles of the Mahayana sutras failed to receive mention, so the Lotus Sutra, needless to say, was not propagated at this time.

Men such as Mikkaka, Buddhanandi, Buddhamitra, Pārśva, and

Puṇyayaśas then inherited the teachings, and, during the remainder of the first five hundred years after the Buddha's passing, the doctrines of the Mahayana sutras began little by little to come to light, although no particular effort was made to propagate them. Attention was concentrated on the Hinayana sutras alone. All this transpired during the period mentioned in the *Daijuku* Sutra as the first five hundred years, which constitute the age of attaining liberation.

During the latter part of the Former Day of the Law, six hundred to a thousand years after the Buddha's passing, there appeared such men as Aśvaghoṣa, Kapimala, Nāgārjuna, Āryadeva, Rāhulata, Saṃghanandi, Saṃghayaśas, Kumārata, Jayata, Vasubandhu, Manorhita, Haklenayaśas, and Aryasiṃha.[64] These ten or more teachers started out as adherents of non-Buddhist doctrines. Following that, they made a thorough study of the Hinayana sutras, and still later, they turned to the Mahayana sutras and used them to disprove and demolish the doctrines of the Hinayana sutras.

But although these great men used the Mahayana sutras to refute the Hinayana, they did not fully clarify the superiority of the Lotus Sutra in comparison to the other Mahayana sutras. Even though they did touch somewhat on this question, they did not make clear such vitally important doctrines as the ten mystic principles[65] of the theoretical and the essential teachings, the fact that persons in the two realms of *shōmon* and *engaku* can attain Buddhahood, the fact that the Buddha attained enlightenment countless kalpas in the past, the fact that the Lotus Sutra is the most difficult of all the sutras preached in the past, present or future, or the doctrines of the hundred worlds and thousand factors and of *ichinen sanzen*.

They did no more than point a finger at the moon, as it were, or touch on some parts of the Lotus Sutra. But they said nothing at all about whether or not the process of instruction is revealed from beginning to end, whether or not the original relationship between master and disciple is clarified, or which teachings would lead to enlightenment and which would not.[66] Such, then, were the developments in the latter five hundred years of the Former Day of the Law, the time noted in the *Daijuku* Sutra as the age of meditation.

By some time after the thousand years of the Former Day of the Law, Buddhist teachings had spread throughout the entire land of India. But in many cases, Hinayana doctrines prevailed over those of the Mahayana, or provisional sutras were permitted to overshadow and efface the sutra of the true teaching. In a number of respects,

Buddhism was in a chaotic condition. Gradually, the number of persons attaining enlightenment declined, while countless others, though adhering to Buddhist doctrines, fell into the evil paths of existence.

Fifteen years after the beginning of the Middle Day of the Law[67] which followed the thousand years of the Former Day, Buddhism spread eastward and was introduced into the land of China. During the first hundred years or more of the first half of the Middle Day of the Law, the Buddhist doctrines introduced from India were vigorously disputed by the Taoist teachers of China, and neither side could win a clear victory. Though it appeared at times as though the issue had been decided, those who embraced Buddhism were as yet lacking in deep faith. Therefore, if it had become apparent that the sacred teachings of Buddhism were not a unified doctrine but were divided into Hinayana and Mahayana, provisional and true, and exoteric and esoteric teachings,[68] then some of the believers might have had doubts and turned instead to the non-Buddhist teachings. It was perhaps because the Buddhist monks Kāśyapa Mātaṅga and Chu-fa-lan[69] feared such a result that they made no mention of such divisions as Mahayana and Hinayana or provisional and true teachings when they brought Buddhism to China, though they were perfectly aware of them.

During the five dynasties that followed, the Wei, Chin, Sung, Ch'i, and Liang, disputes took place within Buddhism over the differences between the Mahayana and Hinayana, provisional and true, and exoteric and esoteric teachings, and it was impossible to determine which was correct. As a result, from the ruler on down to the common people, there were many people who had doubts about the doctrine.

Buddhism thus became split into ten different schools, the three schools of the south and seven schools of the north. In the south there were the schools that divided the Buddha's teachings into three periods, into four periods, and into five periods, while in the north there were the five-period school, the school that recognized incomplete-word and complete-word teachings, the four-doctrine school, five-doctrine school, six-doctrine school, the two-Mahayana-doctrine school, and the "one-voice" school.[70]

Each of these schools clung fiercely to its own doctrines and clashed with the others like fire encountering water. Yet in general they shared a common view. Namely, among the various sutras preached during the Buddha's lifetime, they put the *Kegon* Sutra in first place, the Nirvana Sutra in second place, and the Lotus Sutra in third place. They admitted that, in comparison to such sutras as the *Agon, Hannya,* Vimalakirti, and *Shiyaku,* the Lotus Sutra represents the truth, a "complete-teaching" sutra that sets forth correct views. But they held that, in comparison to the Nirvana Sutra, it represents a doctrine of non–eternity, an "incomplete-teaching" sutra that puts forth heretical views.

From the end of the fourth through the beginning of the fifth hundred years following the introduction of Buddhism in the Later Han dynasty, in the time of the Ch'en and Sui dynasties, there lived a humble priest named Chih-i, the man who would later be known as the Great Teacher T'ien-t'ai Chih-che.[71] He refuted the mistaken doctrines of the northern and southern schools and declared that among the teachings of the Buddha's lifetime, the Lotus Sutra ranks first, the Nirvana Sutra second, and the *Kegon* Sutra third. This is what occurred in the first five hundred years of the Middle Day of the Law, the period corresponding to that described in the *Daijuku* Sutra as the age of reading, reciting, and listening.

During the latter five hundred years of the Middle Day of the Law, in the reign of Emperor T'ai-tsung[72] at the beginning of the T'ang dynasty, the Tripitaka Master Hsüan-tsang journeyed to India, spending nineteen years visiting temples and stupas in the one hundred and thirty states of India and meeting with numerous Buddhist scholars. He investigated all the profound doctrines contained in the twelve divisions of the scriptures and the eighty thousand sacred teachings of Buddhism[73] and encountered therein the two schools of the Hossō and the Sanron.

Of these two, the Mahayana Hossō doctrine was said to have been taught long ago by Miroku and Asaṅga and in more recent times by the scholar Śīlabhadra. The latter transmitted it to Hsüan-tsang, who brought it to China and taught it to Emperor T'ai-tsung.

The heart of the Hossō doctrine lies in its assertion that Buddhist teachings should accord with the capacities of the listeners. If people have the capacity to understand the doctrine of the one vehicle, then the doctrine of the three vehicles can be no more than an expedient to instruct them, and the doctrine of the one vehicle, the only true way of enlightening them. For people such as these, the Lotus Sutra should be taught. On the other hand, if they have the capacity to understand the three vehicles, then the one vehicle can be no more than an expedient to instruct them, and the three vehicles, the only true way of enlightening them. For people such as these, the *Jimmitsu* and *Shōman* sutras should be taught. This, say the proponents of the Hossō school, is a principle that T'ien-t'ai failed to understand.

Emperor T'ai-tsung was a very wise ruler whose name was known throughout the world and who was said to have surpassed in virtue the Three Rulers and Five Emperors[74] of antiquity. He not only reigned over the entire land of China, but also extended his influence to more than eighteen hundred foreign countries ranging from Kao-ch'ang in the west to Koguryŏ[75] in the east. He was regarded as a ruler who had mastered both Buddhist and non-Buddhist teachings. And since Hsüan-tsang was first in the favor and devotion of this wise ruler, there was none among the leaders of the Tendai school who ventured to risk losing his head by challenging him, and the true teachings of the Lotus Sutra were neglected and forgotten throughout the country.

During the reigns of T'ai-tsung's heir, Emperor Kao-tsung, and Kao-tsung's stepmother, Empress Wu, there lived a priest called Fa-tsang.[76] He observed that the Tendai school was under attack from the Hossō school and took this opportunity to champion the *Kegon* Sutra, which T'ien-t'ai had relegated to a lower place, declaring that the *Kegon* Sutra should rank first, the Lotus Sutra second, and the Nirvana Sutra third among the sutras preached during the Buddha's lifetime.

In the reign of Emperor Hsüan-tsung, the fourth ruler following T'ai-tsung, in the fourth year of the K'ai-yüan era (716), the Tripitaka Master Shan-wu-wei came to China from the western land of India, and in the eighth year of the same era (720), the Tripitaka masters Chin-kang-chih and Pu-k'ung also came to China from India. These men brought with them the *Dainichi, Kongōchō,* and *Soshitsuji* sutras and founded the Shingon school. This school declares that there are two types of Buddhist teachings: the exoteric teachings of Shakyamuni Buddha, which are expounded in the *Kegon,* Lotus, and similar sutras, and the esoteric teachings of Dainichi or Mahavairocana Buddha, which are expounded in the *Dainichi* and similar sutras. The Lotus Sutra holds first place among the exoteric teachings. But although its fundamental principles somewhat resemble those of the esoteric teachings expounded by Dainichi Buddha, it contains no description whatsoever of the mudras and mantras to be used in religious rituals. It fails to include any reference to the three mysteries of body, speech, and mind[77] and hence is to be regarded as an "incomplete teaching."

Thus all of these three schools mentioned above, the Hossō, Kegon, and Shingon, attacked the Tendai school and the teachings of the Lotus Sutra. Perhaps because none of the members of the Tendai school could measure up to the stature of the Great Teacher T'ien-t'ai, though they were aware of the falsity of these other teachings, they did not attempt to speak out against them in public as T'ien-t'ai had. As a result, everyone throughout the country, from the ruler and high ministers on down to the common people, was led astray from the true teachings of Buddhism, and no one any longer came to attain enlightenment. Such were the events of the first two hundred years or more of the latter five-hundred-year period of the Middle Day of the Law.

Some four hundred years or more after the beginning of the Middle Day of the Law,[78] the sacred scriptures of Buddhism were brought to Japan from the kingdom of Paekche in Korea, along with a wooden statue of the Buddha Shakyamuni, and also priests and nuns. At this time the Liang dynasty in China was coming to an end, to be replaced by the Ch'en dynasty, while in Japan, Emperor Kimmei, the thirtieth sovereign[79] since Emperor Jimmu, was on the throne.

Emperor Kimmei's son, Emperor Yōmei, had a son named Prince Jōgū[80] who not only worked to spread the teachings of Buddhism but also designated the Lotus Sutra, Vimalakirti Sutra, and Śrīmālā Sutra as texts that would insure the protection of the nation.

Later, in the time of the thirty-seventh sovereign, Emperor Kōtoku,[81] the teachings of the Sanron and Jōjitsu schools were introduced to Japan by Kanroku,[82] a priest from Paekche. During the same period, the priest Dōshō,[83] who had been to China, introduced the teachings of the Hossō and Kusha schools.

In the reign of Empress Genshō, the forty-fourth sovereign, a monk from India named Shan-wu-wei, already mentioned earlier, brought the *Dainichi* Sutra to Japan, but he returned to China, where he had been residing, without spreading its teachings abroad in Japan.[84]

In the reign of Emperor Shōmu,[85] the forty-fifth sovereign, the Kegon school was introduced from the Korean kingdom of Silla by a priest of that state called the Preceptor Shinjō.[86] The Administrator of Monks Rōben[87] inherited its teachings and in turn introduced them to Emperor Shōmu. He also helped to construct the great image of the Buddha at Tōdai-ji.

During the time of the same emperor, the priest Chien-chen[88] came from China, bringing with him the teachings of the Tendai and Ritsu schools. But although he spread the Ritsu teachings and built a Hinayana ordination platform at Tōdai-ji, he died without even so much as mentioning the name of the Hokke sect.[89]

Eight hundred years after the beginning of the Middle Day of the Law, in the reign of the fiftieth sovereign, Emperor Kammu, there appeared a young priest without reputation named Saichō, who was later to be known as the Great Teacher Dengyō. At first he studied the doctrines of the six sects—Sanron, Hossō, Kegon, Kusha, Jōjitsu, and Ritsu—as well as the Zen teaching, under the Administrator of Monks Gyōhyō,[90] and others. Later he founded a temple called Kokushō-ji, which in time came to be known as Hiei-zan or Mount Hiei.[91] There he pored over the sutras and treatises of the six sects, as well as the commentaries written by their leaders. But he found that these commentaries often contradicted the sutras and treatises upon which these sects relied and were replete with one-sided opinions. It became apparent to him that if people were to accept such teachings, they would all fall into the evil paths of existence. In addition, though the leaders of each of the different sects proclaimed that they had understood the true meaning of the Lotus Sutra and praised their own particular interpretation, none of them had in fact understood its teachings correctly. Saichō felt that, if he were to state this opinion openly, it would surely lead to quarrels and disputes. But if he remained silent, he would be going against the spirit of the Buddha's vow.[92] He agonized over what course to take, but in the end, fearful of violating the Buddha's admonition, made known his views to Emperor Kammu.

Emperor Kammu, startled at his declaration, summoned the leading authorities of the six sects to engage in debate.[93] At first these scholars in their pride were similar to banners raised aloft like mountains, and their evil minds worked like poisonous snakes, but in the end they were forced to bow in defeat in the presence of the ruler, and each and every person of the six sects and the seven major temples of Nara acknowledged himself a disciple of Saichō.

It was like that earlier occasion when the Buddhist scholars of northern and southern China gathered in the palace of the Ch'en dynasty and, having been bested in debate by the Great Teacher T'ien-t'ai, became his disciples. But [of the three types of learning] T'ien-t'ai had employed only perfect meditation and perfect wisdom.[94] The Great Teacher Dengyō, by contrast, attacked the Hinayana specific ordination for administering the precepts, which T'ien-t'ai had failed to controvert, and administered the Mahayana specific ordination[95] described in the *Bommō* Sutra to eight eminent priests of the six sects.[96] In addition, he established on Mount Hiei a specific ordination platform for administering the precepts of the perfect and immediate enlightenment of the Lotus Sutra. Thus the specific ordination in the precepts of perfect and immediate enlightenment at Enryaku-ji on Mount Hiei was not only the foremost ordination ceremony in Japan, but a great ordination in the precepts of Eagle Peak such as had never been known either in India or China or anywhere else in the world during the eighteen hundred or more years since the Buddha's passing. This ceremony of ordination had its beginning in Japan.

If we examine the merit achieved by the Great Teacher Dengyō, we would have to say that he is a sage who surpasses Nāgārjuna and Vasubandhu and who excels both T'ien-t'ai and Miao-lo. If so, then what priest in Japan today could turn his back on the perfect precepts of the Great Teacher Dengyō, whether he belongs to Tō-ji, Onjō-ji, or the seven major temples of Nara, whether he is a follower of one of the eight sects[97] or of the Jōdo, Zen, or Ritsu sect in whatever corner of the land? The priests of the nine regions of China became the disciples of the Great Teacher T'ien-t'ai with respect to the perfect meditation and perfect wisdom that he taught. But since no ordination platform for universally administering the precepts of perfect and immediate enlightenment was ever established in China, some of them might not have become his disciples with regard to the precepts. In Japan, however, [because Dengyō in fact established such an ordination platform] any priests who fail to become disciples of the Great Teacher Dengyō can only be regarded as heretics and men of evil.

As to the question of which of the two newer sects brought from China is superior, the Tendai or the Shingon, the Great Teacher Dengyō was perfectly clear in his mind. But he did not demonstrate which was superior in public debate, as he had done previously with regard to the relative merit of the Tendai sect in comparison to the six older sects. Perhaps on that account, after the death of Dengyō, Tō-ji, the seven major temples of Nara, Onjō-ji, and other temples throughout the provinces of Japan all began proclaiming that the Shingon sect is superior to the Tendai sect, until everyone from the ruler on down to the common people believed that such was the case.

Thus the true spirit of the Tendai-Hokke sect really flourished only during the lifetime of the Great Teacher Dengyō. Dengyō lived at the end of the Middle Day of the Law, during the period described in the *Daijuku* Sutra as the age of building temples and stupas. The time had not yet arrived when, as the *Daijuku* Sutra says, "Quarrels and disputes will arise among the adherents to my teachings, and the Pure Law will become obscured and lost."[98]

Now more than two hundred years have passed since we entered the Latter Day of the Law, a time of which, as the *Daijuku* Sutra records, the Buddha predicted that "quarrels and disputes will arise among the adherents to my teachings, and the Pure Law will become obscured and lost." If these words of the Buddha are true, it is a time when the whole world will without doubt be embroiled in quarrels and disputes.

Reports reaching us say that the entire land of China, with its 360 states and 260 or more provinces, has already been conquered by the kingdom of the Mongols. The Chinese capital was conquered some time ago, and the two rulers Emperor Hui-tsung and Emperor Ch'in-tsung[99] were taken captive by the northern barbarians and ended their days in the region of Tartary. Meanwhile, Hui-tsung's grandson, Emperor Kao-tsung,[100] driven out of the northern capital, established his residence in the countryside at the temporary palace at Lin-an, and for many years he did not see the capital.

In addition, the six hundred or more states of Koryŏ and the states of Silla and Paekche on the Korean Peninsula have all been conquered by the great kingdom of the Mongols, and in like manner the Mongols have even attacked the Japanese territories of Iki, Tsushima, and Kyushu.[101] Thus the Buddha's prediction concerning the occurrence of quarrels and disputes has proved anything but false. It is like the tides of the ocean that never fail to come when the time arrives.

In view of the accuracy of his prediction, can there be any doubt that, after this period described in the *Daijuku* Sutra when "the Pure Law will become obscured and lost," the Great Pure Law of the Lotus Sutra will be spread far and wide throughout Japan and all the other countries of the world?

Among the Buddha's various teachings, the *Daijuku* Sutra represents no more than an exposition of provisional Mahayana doctrine.

In terms of teaching the way to escape from the sufferings of birth and death, it belongs to the period when the Buddha had "not yet revealed the truth,"[102] and so cannot lead to enlightenment those who have not yet formed any connection with the Lotus Sutra. And yet in what it states concerning the six paths, the four forms of birth,[103] and the three existences of life, it does not display the slightest error.

How, then, could there be any error in the Lotus Sutra, of which the Buddha said that he "now must reveal the truth"?[104] Tahō Buddha likewise testified to its truth, and the Buddhas from the ten directions put forth their long, broad tongues until they reached the Brahma Heaven as a sign of testimony. And Shakyamuni Buddha also extended his tongue, which is incapable of telling falsehoods, until it reached the Akaniṣṭha Heaven,[105] saying that in the fifth five-hundred-year period after his passing, when the entire body of Buddhist doctrine would be about to disappear, Bodhisattva Jōgyō would come forward with the five characters of Myōhō-renge-kyō and administer them as good medicine to those afflicted with white leprosy—those persons of incorrigible disbelief (*icchantika*) and those who slander the Law. And he charged Bonten, Taishaku, the gods of the sun and moon, the Four Heavenly Kings, and the dragon deities to act as that bodhisattva's protectors. How could these golden words of his be false? Even if the great earth were to turn upside down, a high mountain crumble and fall, summer not follow spring, the sun move eastward, or the moon fall to earth, this prediction could never fail to come true!

If that is so, then, in this time of "quarrels and disputes," how can the ruler, the ministers, and the common people of Japan hope to escape harm when they vilify and abuse the envoy of the Buddha[106] who is attempting to spread the teaching of Nam-myoho-renge-kyo, send him into exile and attack and beat him, or inflict all kinds of trouble upon his disciples and followers? And stupid and ignorant persons must surely think when I say this that I am merely calling down curses upon the people.

A person who spreads the teaching of the Lotus Sutra is father and mother to all the living beings in Japan. For, as the Great Teacher Chang-an says, "He who makes it possible for the offender to rid himself of evil, is acting like a parent to him."[107] If so, then I, Nichiren, am the father and mother of the present emperor of Japan, and the teacher and lord of the Nembutsu believers, the Zen followers, and the Shingon priests.

And yet, from the ruler on down to the common people, all treat me with enmity. How, then, can the sun and moon go on shining down on their heads, and how can the gods of the earth continue to bear up their feet? When Devadatta attacked the Buddha, the earth shook and trembled and flames shot out of it. When King Dammira cut off the head of the Venerable Āryasiṁha, his own right hand that held the sword dropped off and fell to the ground.[108] Emperor Hui-tsung branded the face of the priest Fa-tao and exiled him south of the Yangtze, but before half a year had passed, the emperor was taken prisoner and carried off by the barbarians.[109] And these attacks of the Mongols are occurring for the same reason. Though one may gather together as many soldiers as there are in the five regions of India and build one's fortress in the Iron-wheel Mountain,[110] it will do no good. The people of Japan are certain to encounter the calamity of war.

From this situation one should understand that I am in fact the votary of the Lotus Sutra. Shakyamuni Buddha stated that, if anyone should abuse or curse someone who is spreading the teaching of the Lotus Sutra in the evil times of the later age, that person would be guilty of a crime that is a hundred, a thousand, ten thousand, a hundred thousand times greater than if he had been an enemy of the Buddha for the space of an entire kalpa. And yet nowadays the ruler and the people of Japan, following their personal whims, seem to hate me even more intensely than they would an enemy of their own parents or one who had been a foe from their previous lifetime, or upbraid me even more severely than they would a traitor or a murderer. I wonder that the earth does not open up and swallow them alive, or that thunder does not come down from heaven and tear them apart!

Or am I perhaps not the votary of the Lotus Sutra after all? If not, then I am wretched indeed! What a miserable fate, in this present life to be hounded by everyone and never know so much as a moment of peace, and in the next life to fall into the evil paths of existence! If in fact I am not the votary of the Lotus Sutra, then who will uphold the one vehicle, the teaching of the Lotus Sutra?

Hōnen ordered people to discard the Lotus Sutra, Shan-tao said, "Not one person in a thousand can reach enlightenment through its teachings!" and Tao-ch'o said, "Not a single person has ever attained Buddhahood through that sutra!" Are these men, then, the votaries of the Lotus Sutra? The Great Teacher Kōbō said that one who practices the teaching of the Lotus Sutra is following "a childish theory." Is he perhaps the votary of the Lotus Sutra?[111]

The Lotus Sutra speaks of a person who "is able to uphold this sutra"[112] or who "is able to preach this sutra."[113] What does it mean when it speaks of someone who "is able to preach" this sutra? Does it not mean someone who will proclaim, in the words of the Lotus Sutra itself, that "among the sutras, it holds the highest place,"[114] and who will maintain its superiority over the *Dainichi, Kegon,* Nirvana, *Hannya,* and other sutras? Is this not the kind of person the sutra means when it speaks of "the votary of the Lotus Sutra"? If these passages from the sutra are to be believed, then in the seven hundred years and more since Buddhism was introduced to Japan, there has never been a single votary of the Lotus Sutra other than the Great Teacher Dengyō and I, Nichiren.

Again and again I wonder that the persons who attack me do not, as the Lotus Sutra says, suffer the punishment of having their "heads split into seven pieces"[115] or their "mouths closed and stopped up,"[116] but I realize there are reasons. Such punishments are no more than trivial penalties fit to be inflicted where there are only one or two offenders. But I, Nichiren, am the foremost votary of the Lotus Sutra for the entire world. Therefore, people who ally themselves with those who slander me or treat me with malice deserve to meet with the greatest difficulties in the world, such as the great earthquake[117] that rocked Japan in the Shōka era, or the great comet[118] that appeared as a punishment upon the entire world in the Bun'ei era. Just look at these happenings! Though in the centuries since the Buddha's passing there have been other practitioners of Buddhism who were treated with malice, great disasters such as these have never been known before. That is because there has never before been anyone who taught the people at large to chant Nam-myoho-renge-kyo! With respect to this virtue, is there anyone in the whole world who dares to face me and say he is my equal, anyone within the four seas who dares to claim he can stand side by side with me!

Question: During the Former Day of the Law, the capacities of the people may have been somewhat inferior to those of the people who lived when the Buddha was in the world. And yet they were surely much superior to those of the people in the Middle and Latter Days of the Law. How then can you say that in the early years of the Former Day of the Law, the Lotus Sutra was ignored? It was during the thousand years of the Former Day of the Law that such men as Aśvaghoṣa, Nāgārjuna, Āryadeva, and Asaṅga appeared. Bodhisattva Vasubandhu, who is known as the "scholar of a thousand works," wrote the *Hokke Ron* or Treatise on the Lotus Sutra, in which he declared that the Lotus is first among all the sutras. The Tripitaka Master Paramārtha, in describing the transmission of the Lotus Sutra, says that in India there were more than fifty scholars who spread the teachings of the Lotus Sutra and that Vasubandhu[119] was one of them. Such was the situation in the Former Day of the Law.

Turning to the Middle Day of the Law that followed, we find that the Great Teacher T'ien-t'ai appeared in China around the middle of the period and wrote the *Hokke Gengi, Hokke Mongu,* and *Maka Shikan* in thirty volumes, in which he explored all the depths of meaning in the Lotus Sutra. At the end of the Middle Day of the Law, the Great Teacher Dengyō appeared in Japan. He not only transmitted to our country the two doctrines of perfect wisdom and perfect meditation expounded by the Great Teacher T'ien-t'ai, but also established a great ordination platform of the perfect and immediate enlightenment on Mount Hiei. Thus the perfect precepts were acknowledged throughout Japan, and everyone from the ruler on down to the common people looked up to Enryaku-ji on Mount Hiei as his guide and teacher. How then can you say that in the Middle Day of the Law, the teachings of the Lotus Sutra were not widely disseminated and spread abroad?

Answer: It is a commonly accepted assertion among the scholars of our times that the Buddha invariably preached his teachings in accordance with the capacities of his listeners. But in fact this is not how the Buddha truly taught. If it were true that the greatest doctrines were always preached for the persons with the most superior capacities and understanding, then why, when the Buddha first achieved enlightenment, did he not preach the Lotus Sutra? Why, during the first five hundred years of the Former Day of the Law, were the teachings of the Mahayana sutras not spread abroad? And if it were true that the finest doctrines are revealed to those who have a particular connection with the Buddha, then why did Shakyamuni Buddha preach the *Kambutsu Zammai* Sutra for his father, King Śuddhodana, and the *Māyā* Sutra for his mother, Queen Māyā, [rather than the Lotus Sutra]? And if the reverse were true, namely, that secret doctrines should never be revealed to evil persons having no connection with the Buddha nor to slanderers of Buddhism, then why did the monk Kakutoku teach the Nirvana Sutra to all the countless monks who were guilty of breaking the precepts?[120] Or why did Bodhisattva Fukyō address the four kinds of people, who were slanderers of the Law, and propagate to them the teachings of the Lotus Sutra?

Thus we can see that it is a great mistake to assert that the teachings are invariably expounded according to the listeners' capacities.

Question: Do you mean to say that Nāgārjuna, Vasubandhu, and the others did not teach the true doctrines of the Lotus Sutra?

Answer: That is correct. They did not teach them.

Question: Then what doctrines did they teach?

Answer: They taught the doctrines of provisional Mahayana, the various exoteric and esoteric teachings such as the *Kegon, Hōdō, Hannya, Dainichi,* and other sutras, but they did not teach the doctrines of the Lotus Sutra.

Question: How do you know that this is so?

Answer: The treatises written by Bodhisattva Nāgārjuna run to some three hundred thousand verses. Not all of them have been transmitted to China and Japan, so it is difficult to make statements about their true nature. However, examining the ones that have been transmitted to China such as the *Jūjūbibasha Ron, Chū Ron,* and *Daichido Ron,* we may surmise that the treatises remaining in India are of a similar nature.

Question: Among the treatises remaining in India, are there any that are superior to the ones transmitted to China?

Answer: There is no need for me to make pronouncements of my own on the subject of Bodhisattva Nāgārjuna. For the Buddha himself predicted that after he had passed away, a man called Bodhisattva Nāgārjuna would appear in southern India, and that his most important teachings would be found in a treatise called the *Chū Ron.*[121]

Such was the Buddha's prediction. And accordingly we find that there were some seventy scholars in India who followed in the wake of Nāgārjuna, all of them major scholars. And all of these seventy scholars took the *Chū Ron* as the basis of their teachings. The *Chū Ron* is a work in four volumes and twenty-seven chapters, and the core of its teachings is expressed in a four-phrase verse[122] that describes the nature of phenomena arising from dependent origination. This four-phrase verse sums up the four teachings and three truths contained in the *Kegon, Hannya,* and other sutras.[123] It does not express the three truths as revealed and unified in the Lotus Sutra.

Question: Is there anyone else who thinks the way you do in this matter?

Answer: The Great Teacher T'ien-t'ai says, "Do not presume to compare the *Chū Ron* [to the teachings of the Lotus Sutra]."[124] And elsewhere he ways, "Vasubandhu and Nāgārjuna clearly perceived the truth in their hearts, but they did not teach it. Instead, they preached the provisional Mahayana teachings, which were suited to their times."[125] Miao-lo remarks, "For demolishing false opinions and establishing the truth, nothing can compare to the Lotus Sutra."[126] And Ts'ung-i states, "Nāgārjuna and Vasubandhu cannot compare with T'ien-t'ai."[127]

Question: In the latter part of the T'ang dynasty, the Tripitaka Master Pu-k'ung introduced to China a treatise in one volume entitled *Bodaishin Ron,* whose authorship he ascribed to Bodhisattva Nāgārjuna. The Great Teacher Kōbō says of it, "This treatise represents the heart and core of all the one thousand treatises of Nāgārjuna."[128] What is your opinion on this?

Answer: This treatise consists of seven leaves. There are numerous places in it that could not be the words of Nāgārjuna. Therefore in the catalog of Buddhist texts it is sometimes listed as a work of Nāgārjuna and sometimes as a work of Pu-k'ung. The matter of its authorship has never been resolved. In addition, it is not a summation of the lifetime teachings of the Buddha, and contains many loose statements. To begin with, a vital passage, the one asserting that the Shingon teachings constitute the only way to Buddhahood, is in error, since it denies the fact that the Lotus Sutra enables one to attain Buddhahood in one's present form, a fact well attested by both scriptural passages and actual events.[129] Instead it asserts that the Shingon sutras enable one to attain Buddahood in one's present form, an assertion for which there is not the slightest proof in scriptural passages or actual events. And that one word "only" in the assertion that the Shingon teachings constitute the only way to Buddhahood is the greatest error of all.

In view of the facts, it seems likely that the work was written by Pu-k'ung himself who, in order to ensure that the people of the time would regard it with sufficient gravity, attributed it to Nāgārjuna.

Pu-k'ung makes a number of other errors as well. Thus, in his translation *Kanchi Giki*,[130] which deals with the Lotus Sutra, he defines the Buddha of the *Juryō* chapter as the Buddha Amida, an obvious and glaring mistake. He also claims that the *Darani* chapter of the Lotus Sutra should follow immediately after the *Jinriki* chapter and that the *Zokurui* chapter should come at the very end, views that are not even worth discussing.

And that is not all. He stole the Mahayana precepts from the Tendai school and, obtaining support in the form of a command from Emperor Tai-tsung, established them in the five temples on Mount Wu-t'ai. And he decreed that the classification of doctrinal tenets used by the Tendai school should be adopted for the Shingon school as well. On the whole, he did many things to confuse and mislead the world. It is acceptable to use translations of sacred texts by other persons, but translations of sutras or treatises from the hand of Pu-k'ung are not to be trusted.

When both old and new translations [131] are taken into consideration, we find that there are 186 persons who have brought sutras and treatises from India and introduced them to China in translation. With the exception of one man, the Tripitaka Master Kumārajīva, all of these translators have made errors of some kind. But among them, Pu-k'ung is remarkable for the large number of his errors. It is clear that he deliberately set out to confuse and mislead others.

Question: How do you know that the translators other than Kumārajīva made errors? Do you mean not only to destroy the Zen, Nembutsu, Shingon, and the others of the seven major sects, but to discredit all the works of the translators that have been introduced to China and Japan?

Answer: This is a highly confidential matter and I should discuss it in detail only when I am face to face with the inquirer. However, I will make a few comments here. Kumārajīva himself said, "When I examine the various sutras in use in China, I find that all of them differ from the Sanskrit originals. How can I make people understand this? I have only one great wish. My body is unclean, for I have taken a wife. But my tongue alone is pure and could never speak false words concerning the teachings of Buddhism. After I die, make certain that I am cremated. If at that time my tongue is consumed by the flames, then you may discard all the sutras that I have translated." Such were the words that he spoke again and again from his lecture platform. As a result, everyone from the ruler on down to the common people hoped they would not die before Kumārajīva, so that they might see what happened.

Eventually Kumārajīva died and was cremated, and his impure body was completely reduced to ashes. Only his tongue remained, resting atop a blue lotus that had sprung up in the midst of the flames. It sent out shining rays of five-colored light that made the night as bright as day and in the daytime outshone the rays of the sun. This, then, is why the sutras translated by all the other scholars came to be held in little esteem, while those translated by Kumārajīva, particularly his translation of the Lotus Sutra, spread rapidly throughout China.[132]

Question: That tells us about the translators who lived at the time of Kumārajīva or before. But what about later translators such as Shan-wu-wei or Pu-k'ung?

Answer: Even in the case of translators who lived after Kumārajīva, if their tongues burned up when they were cremated, it means that there are errors in their work. The Hossō sect in earlier times enjoyed a great popularity in Japan. But the Great Teacher Dengyō attacked it, pointing out that, though the tongue of Kumārajīva was not consumed by the flames, those of Hsüan-tsang and Tz'u-en burned along with their bodies. Emperor Kammu, impressed by his argument, transferred his allegiance to the Tendai-Hokke sect.

In the third and ninth volumes of the Nirvana Sutra, we find the Buddha predicting that, when his teachings were transmitted from India to other countries, many errors would be introduced into them, and the chances for people to gain enlightenment through them would be reduced. Therefore the Great Teacher Miao-lo remarks, "Whether or not the teachings are grasped correctly depends upon the persons who transmit them. It is not determined by the sage's original pronouncements."[133]

He is saying that, no matter how the people of today may follow the teachings of the sutras in hopes of a better life in the hereafter, if the sutras they follow are in error, then they can never attain enlightenment. But that is not to be attributed to any fault of the Buddha.

In studying the teachings of Buddhism, apart from the distinctions between Hinayana and Mahayana, provisional and true, and exoteric and esoteric teachings, this question of the reliability of the sutra translation is the most important of all.

Question: You say that during the thousand years of the Former

Day of the Law, scholars knew in their hearts that the truth of the Lotus Sutra far surpassed the teachings of the other exoteric and esoteric sutras, but that they did not proclaim this fact to others, merely teaching the doctrines of the provisional Mahayana. This may be the case, but I find it difficult to agree.

Around the middle of the thousand years of the Middle Day of the Law, the Great Teacher T'ien-t'ai Chih-che appeared. In the ten volumes or thousand leaves of his *Hokke Gengi,* he discussed in detail the meaning of the five characters composing the title of the Lotus Sutra, *Myōhō-renge-kyō.* In the ten volumes of his *Hokke Mongu,* he discussed each word and phrase of the sutra, from the opening words, "Thus I heard," through the very last words, ". . . they bowed and departed." He interpreted them in the light of four guidelines, namely, causes and circumstances, correlated teachings, the theoretical and essential teachings, and the observation of the mind,[134] once more devoting a thousand leaves to the discussion.

In the twenty volumes composing these two works, the *Hokke Gengi* and *Hokke Mongu,* he likened the teachings of all the other sutras to streams and rivers and the Lotus Sutra to the great ocean. He demonstrated that the waters that make up the Buddhist teachings of all the worlds of the ten directions flow, without the loss of a single drop, into that great ocean of the *Myōhō-renge-kyō.* In addition, he examined all the doctrines of the great scholars of India, not overlooking a single point, as well as the doctrines of the ten teachers of northern and southern China, refuting those that deserved to be refuted and adopting those that were worthy of acceptance. In addition to the works just mentioned, he also expounded the *Maka Shikan* in ten volumes, in which he summed up the Buddha's lifetime teachings on meditation in the concept of *ichinen,* and encompassed all the living entities and their environments of the Ten Worlds in the concept of *sanzen.*

The pronouncements found in this work of T'ien-t'ai surpass those of all the scholars who lived in India during the thousand years of the Former Day of the Law, and are superior to the commentaries of the teachers who lived in China during the five hundred years preceding T'ien-t'ai. Therefore the Great Teacher Chi-tsang[135] of the Sanron school wrote a letter urging a hundred or more of the leaders and elders of the schools of northern and southern China to attend the Great Teacher T'ien-t'ai's lectures on the sutras. "That which happens only once in a thousand years, that which takes place only once in five hundred years,[136] has happened today," he wrote. "Nan-yüeh with his superior sageness, T'ien-t'ai with his clear wisdom—long ago they received and upheld the Lotus Sutra with body, mouth and mind, and now they have appeared once again as these two honored teachers. Not only have they caused the sweet dew of *amṛta*[137] to fall in the land of China, but indeed, they have made the drums of the Law thunder even as far away as India. They possess the mystic enlightenment that comes with inborn understanding, and their expositions of the sacred texts truly are unparalleled since the time of the Wei and Chin dynasties. Therefore I wish to go with a hundred or more priests of the meditational practice and beg to receive the lectures of the Great Teacher Chih-che."[138]

The Discipline Master Tao-hsüan of Mount Chung-nan praised the Great Teacher T'ien-t'ai by saying, "His thorough understanding of the Lotus Sutra is like the noonday sun shining down into the darkest valley; his exposition of the Mahayana teachings is like a powerful wind roaring at will through the great sky. Though the teachers of words and phrases might gather by the thousands and attempt to inquire into his wondrous arguments, they could never understand them all. . . . His teachings are as clear as a finger pointing at the moon, . . . and their essence returns to the ultimate truth."[139]

The Great Teacher Fa-tsang of the Kegon school praised T'ien-t'ai in these words: "Men like Nan-yüeh and T'ien-t'ai can understand the truth through intuition, and in practice have already ascended to the first stage of security. They recall the teachings of the Law as they heard them on Eagle Peak and present them that way today."[140]

There is an account of how the Tripitaka Master Pu-k'ung of the Shingon school and his disciple Han-kuang both abandoned the Shingon school and became followers of the Great Teacher T'ien-t'ai. "The *Kōsō Den* states, 'When Han-kuang together with Pu-k'ung was traveling in India, a monk said to him, "In the land of China there are the teachings of T'ien-t'ai, which are most suitable in helping to distinguish truth from falsehood and illuminating what is partial and what is perfect. Would it not be well to translate these writings and bring them here to this country?" ' "[141]

This story was related by Han-kuang to the Great Teacher Miao-lo. When he heard the story, Miao-lo exclaimed, "Does this not mean that Buddhism has been lost in India, the country of its origin, and must now be sought in the surrounding regions? But even in China there are few people who recognize the greatness of T'ien-t'ai's teachings. They are like the people of Lu."[142]

Now if there had been any major treatises in India that could compare to these three works in thirty volumes by T'ien-t'ai, then why would the Indian monk have asked that T'ien-t'ai's commentaries be brought from China? In view of all this, how can you deny that during the Middle Day of the Law, the true meaning of the Lotus Sutra was made clear and that the widespread proclamation and propagation of its teachings (kōsen-rufu) was accomplished throughout the entire world?

Answer: The Great Teacher T'ien-t'ai preached and spread throughout China a perfect meditation and perfect wisdom surpassing the lifetime teachings of the Buddha that had never been preached previously by any of the scholars in the fourteen hundred or more years since the Buddha's death, that is, in the thousand years of the Former Day of the Law and the first four hundred years of the Middle Day. His fame even reached as far as India. This would seem to resemble the widespread proclaiming and propagating of the Lotus Sutra that we have talked about earlier. But at this time an ordination platform of the perfect and immediate enlightenment had not yet been established. Instead, men followed the Hinayana precepts, which were grafted onto the perfect wisdom and perfect meditation—a rather ineffectual combination. It was like the sun in eclipse or the moon when it is less than full.

Whatever you may say, the time of the Great Teacher T'ien-t'ai corresponds to the period described in the *Daijuku* Sutra as the age of reading, reciting, and listening. The time had not yet come for *kōsen-rufu,* or broadly proclaiming and propagating the Lotus Sutra.

Question: The Great Teacher Dengyō was born in Japan in the time of Emperor Kammu. He refuted the mistaken beliefs that had held sway in Japan for the two hundred or more years since the time of Emperor Kimmei and declared his support for the perfect wisdom and perfect meditation taught by the Great Teacher T'ien-t'ai. In addition, he repudiated as invalid the ordination platforms that had been established at three places in Japan[143] to confer the Hinayana precepts brought over by the priest Chien-chen and instead set up a Mahayana specific ordination platform of the perfect and immediate enlightenment on Mount Hiei. This was the most momentous event that had ever taken place in India, China, Japan, or anywhere else in the world during the eighteen hundred years following the Buddha's death.

I do not know whether the Great Teacher Dengyō's inner enlightenment was inferior or equal to that of Nāgārjuna and T'ien-t'ai, but I am convinced that in calling upon all Buddhist believers to adhere to a single doctrine, he showed himself to be superior to Nāgārjuna and Vasubandhu and surpassed even Nan-yüeh and T'ien-t'ai.

In general, we may say that during the eighteen hundred years following the death of the Buddha, these two men, T'ien-t'ai and Dengyō, were the true votaries of the Lotus Sutra. Thus Dengyō writes in his work *Hokke Shūku:* "The Lotus Sutra says, 'To seize Mount Sumeru and fling it far off to the measureless Buddha lands— that is not difficult. . . . But in the evil times after the Buddha's passing to be able to preach this sutra—that is difficult indeed!' In commenting on this passage, I have this to say: Shakyamuni taught that the shallow is easy to embrace, but the profound is difficult. To discard the shallow and seek the profound requires courage. The Great Teacher T'ien-t'ai trusted and obeyed Shakyamuni Buddha and worked to uphold the Hokke school, spreading its teachings throughout China. We of Mount Hiei inherited the doctrines from T'ien-t'ai and work to uphold the Hokke sect and to disseminate its teachings throughout Japan."[144]

The meaning of this passage of commentary is as follows: From the time of the Buddha's advent in the Wise Kalpa[145] in the ninth kalpa of decrease, when the human life span was diminishing and had shrunk to a hundred years, through the fifty years of his preaching life as well as during the eighteen hundred or more years after his death, there might actually have been a small person only five feet in height who could nevertheless lift a gold mountain 168,000 *yojana* or 6,620,000 *ri* in height and hurl it over the Iron-wheel Mountain faster than a sparrow flies, just as he might take a one- or two-inch tile and toss it a distance of one or two *chō*.[146] But even if there should have been such a person, it would be rarer still for someone to appear in the Latter Day of the Law who could expound the Lotus Sutra as the Buddha did. Yet the Great Teacher T'ien-t'ai and the Great Teacher Dengyō were just such persons, able to teach it in a manner similar to the Buddha.

The scholars in India never attained the truth of the Lotus Sutra. In China in the period before T'ien-t'ai, some of the teachers realized the truth but did not go so far as to announce that it is revealed in the

Lotus Sutra, and others did not even realize it. As for later men such as Tz'u-en, Fa-tsang, or Shan-wu-wei, they were the kind who say that east is west or declare that heaven is earth. And these are not opinions that the Great Teacher Dengyō put forward merely to enhance his own worth.

On the nineteenth day of the first month of the twenty-first year of the Enryaku era (802), Emperor Kammu paid a visit to the temple at Mount Takao. He summoned more than ten eminent priests from the six sects and seven major temples of Nara, including Zengi, Shōyū, Hōki, Chōnin, Kengyoku, Ampuku, Gonsō, Shūen, Jikō, Gen'yō, Saikō, Dōshō, Kōshō, and Kambin,[147] to come to the temple to debate with the Dharma Master Saichō. But they became tongue-tied after their first words and could not speak a second or third time. Instead, all bowed their heads as one and pressed their palms together in a gesture of awe. The Sanron teachings concerning the two types of teachings, the teachings of the three periods, and the thrice-turned wheel of the Law;[148] the Hossō doctrines concerning the teachings of the three periods and the five natures;[149] and the Kegon doctrines of the four teachings, the five teachings, the root teaching, and the branch teachings, the six forms, and the ten mysteries[150]—all their frameworks were utterly refuted. It was as though the beams and rafters of a great edifice had broken and collapsed, and the ten and more eminent priests were like once-proud banners dipped in token of defeat.

At that time the emperor was greatly amazed at the proceedings, and on the twenty-ninth day of the same month he dispatched Hiroyo and Kunimichi[151] as imperial envoys to question the men of the seven temples and six sects at greater length. All of them in turn submitted a memorial acknowledging that they had been defeated in the debate and won over by Dengyō's arguments. "When we privately examine the *Hokke Gengi* and other commentaries by T'ien-t'ai, we find that they sum up all the teachings expounded by Shakyamuni Buddha in his lifetime. The full purport of the Buddha's doctrines is made clear, without a single point being left unexplained. The Tendai sect surpasses all other sects, and is unique in pointing out the single way for all to follow. The doctrines that it expounds represent the most profound mystic truth and are something that we students of the seven major temples and six sects have never before heard of, and never before seen. Now at last the dispute that has continued so long between the Sanron and Hossō sects has been resolved as dramatically as though ice had melted. The truth has been made abundantly clear, as though clouds and mist had parted to reveal the light of the sun, moon, and stars. In the two hundred or more years since Crown Prince Shōtoku spread the Buddhist teachings in this country, a great many sutras and treatises have been lectured upon and their principles have been widely argued, but until now, many doubts still remained to be settled. Moreover, the lofty and perfect doctrine of the Lotus Sutra had not yet been properly explained and made known. Was it that the persons who lived during this period were not yet qualified to taste its perfect flavor?

"In our humble view, the ruler of our sacred dynasty[152] has received the charge given long ago by Shakyamuni Buddha and has undergone profound instruction in the pure and perfect teaching of the Lotus Sutra, so that the doctrines of the unique and wonderful truth that it expounds have for the first time been explained and made clear. Thus we, the scholars of the six sects, have for the first time understood the ultimate truth. From now on, all the beings in this world who are endowed with life will be able to embark on the ship of the wonderful and perfect truth and quickly reach the opposite shore. Zengi and the others of our group have met with great good fortune because of karmic bonds and have been privileged to hear these extraordinary words. Were it not for some profound karmic tie, how could we have been born in this sacred age?"

In China in past times Chia-hsiang[153] assembled some hundred other priests and, together with them, acknowledged the Great Teacher T'ien-t'ai to be a true sage. And later in Japan, the two hundred or more priests of the seven temples of Nara proclaimed the Great Teacher Dengyō to be worthy of the title of sage. Thus, during the two thousand years and more after the passing of the Buddha, these two sages appeared in the two countries of China and Japan respectively. In addition, the Great Teacher Dengyō established on Mount Hiei an ordination platform for conferring the great precepts of perfect and immediate enlightenment, precepts which even the Great Teacher T'ien-t'ai had never propagated. How then can you deny that in the latter part of the Middle Day of the Law, the "wide proclamation and propagation" (kōsen-rufu) of the Lotus Sutra was achieved?

Answer: As I have explained in my earlier discussion, a great truth that was not spread abroad by Mahākāśyapa or Ānanda was in time propagated by Aśvaghoṣa, Nāgārjuna, Āryadeva, and Vasubandhu. And as I have also explained in my discussion, there was a great truth that was not fully made known by Nāgārjuna, Vasubandhu, and the others but was propagated by the Great Teacher T'ien-t'ai. And, as I have further explained, it remained for the Great Teacher Dengyō to establish an ordination platform of the great precepts of perfect and immediate enlightenment which were not spread abroad by the Great Teacher T'ien-t'ai Chih-che.

And, unbelievable as it may seem, there clearly appears in the text of the Lotus Sutra a True Law that is supremely profound and secret,[154] one which, though expounded in full by the Buddha, in the time since his passing has never yet been propagated by Mahākāśyapa, Ānanda, Aśvaghoṣa, Nāgārjuna, Asaṅga, or Vasubandhu, nor even by T'ien-t'ai or Dengyō. And the most difficult and perplexing question is whether or not this profound Law can be broadly proclaimed and propagated throughout the world now at the beginning of the Latter Day of the Law, the fifth of the five five-hundred-year periods following the Buddha's death.

Question: What is this secret Law? First, tell me its name, and then I want to hear its meaning. If what you say is true, then perhaps Shakyamuni Buddha will appear in the world once more, or Bodhisattva Jōgyō will once again emerge from the earth. Speak quickly, for pity's sake!

They say that the Tripitaka Master Hsüan-tsang, after dying and being reborn six times,[155] was finally able to reach India, where he spent nineteen years. But he claimed that the one-vehicle doctrine of the Lotus Sutra was a mere "expedient teaching" and that the *Agon* sutras of Hinayana Buddhism represent the true doctrine. And the Tripitaka Master Pu-k'ung, when he paid a return visit to India, his homeland, announced that the Buddha of the *Juryō* chapter of the Lotus Sutra is Amida! This is like saying that east is west or calling the sun the moon. They drove their bodies in vain, and exerted their minds to no avail.

But we have been fortunate enough to be born in the Latter Day of the Law and can advance in our faith without making a single false step. We need not spend three asōgi kalpas in practice or feed our heads to tigresses in order to obtain the invisible crown of the Buddha's head.[156]

Answer: This Law is revealed in the text of the Lotus Sutra, so it is an easy matter for me to explain it to you. But first, before clarifying this Law, there are three important concerns[157] that I must mention. It is said that, no matter how vast the ocean, it will not hold within it the body of a dead person,[158] and no matter how thick the crust of the earth, it will not support one who is undutiful to his parents.[159] According to the Buddhist teaching, however, even those who commit the five cardinal sins may be saved, and even those who are unfilial may gain salvation. It is only the *icchantika* or men of incorrigible disbelief, those who slander the Law and those who pretend to uphold the precepts, ranking themselves above all others, who cannot be forgiven.

The three sources of difficulty mentioned above are the Nembutsu sect, the Zen sect, and the Shingon sect. The first, the Nembutsu sect, has spread throughout Japan, and the Nembutsu is on the lips of the four categories of Buddhists.[160] The second, the Zen sect, has produced arrogant monks who talk of their "three robes and one begging bowl" and who fill the area within the four seas, regarding themselves as the enlightened leaders of the whole world. The third, the Shingon sect, is in a class by itself. It receives support from Mount Hiei, Tō-ji, the seven temples of Nara, and Onjō-ji as well as from the high priestly officials including the chief priest of Mount Hiei, Omuro,[161] the chief official of Onjō-ji, and supervisors of the various temples and shrines.[162] Since the sacred mirror kept in the imperial palace was destroyed by fire,[163] the precious mudra of the Shingon Buddha Dainichi has been regarded as a mirror of the Buddha to take its place; and since the precious sword was lost in the western sea,[164] the five great deities of Shingon[165] have been looked upon as capable of cutting down the enemies of the Japanese nation. So firmly entrenched are these beliefs that, though the stone that marks the duration of a kalpa might be worn completely away,[166] it would seem that they would never be overthrown, and though the great earth itself might turn upside down, people would never question them.

When the Great Teacher T'ien-t'ai defeated in debate the leaders of the other schools of northern and southern China, the Shingon teachings had not yet been introduced to that country, and when the Great Teacher Dengyō won victory over the six sects of Japan, the Shingon doctrines escaped refutation. On several occasions they have managed to evade their powerful enemies, and on the contrary have succeeded in overshadowing and imperiling the great Law of the Lotus Sutra. In addition, the Great Teacher Jikaku,[167] who was a disciple of the Great Teacher Dengyō, went so far as to adopt the doctrines of the Shingon sect and introduce them to Mount Hiei, the headquarters of the Tendai sect, thus obscuring Tendai doctrines and turning the entire sect into a sphere of Shingon influence. But who could effectively oppose a person of such authority as Jikaku?

Thus, helped on by prejudiced views, the false doctrines of the Great Teacher Kōbō continued to escape condemnation. It is true that the priest Annen[168] did voice a certain opposition to Kōbō. But all he did was to demote the *Kegon* Sutra from second place and substitute the Lotus Sutra for it; he still ranked the Lotus Sutra as inferior to the *Dainichi* Sutra. He was nothing more than an arranger of worldly compromises.

Question: In what way are these three sects in error?

Answer: Let us first consider the Jōdo or Nembutsu sect. In China in the time of the Ch'i dynasty there was a priest named T'an-luan. He was originally a follower of the Sanron school, but when he read the treatise by Nāgārjuna entitled *Jūjūbibasha Ron,* he espoused the two categories of the difficult-to-practice way and the easy-to-practice way. Later there was a man called the Meditation Master Tao-ch'o, who lived during the T'ang dynasty. Originally he had given lectures on the Nirvana Sutra, but when he read T'an-luan's account of his conversion to faith in the Jōdo or Pure Land teachings, Tao-ch'o abandoned the Nirvana Sutra and likewise changed over to the Pure Land faith, establishing the two categories of the Sacred Way teachings and the Pure Land teachings.[169] In addition, Tao-ch'o had a disciple named Shan-tao who posited two types of religious practice which he called sundry practices and correct practices.[170]

In Japan some two hundred years after the beginning of the Latter Day of the Law, in the reign of Emperor Gotoba, there lived a man named Hōnen. Addressing his words to all priests and lay believers, he stated: "Buddhist teachings are based upon the capacities of the people of the period. The Lotus Sutra and the *Dainichi* Sutra, the doctrines of the eight or nine sects including the Tendai and Shingon, the teachings of the Buddha's lifetime—the Mahayana and Hinayana, the exoteric and esoteric, provisional and true teachings—as well as the sects based on them, were all intended for people of superior capacities and superior wisdom who lived during the two thousand years of the Former and Middle Days of the Law. Now that we have entered the Latter Day of the Law, no matter how diligently one may practice such teachings, they will bring no benefit. Moreover, if one mixes such practices with the practice of the Nembutsu addressed to the Buddha Amida, then the Nembutsu will be rendered ineffective and will not lead the believer to rebirth in the Pure Land.

"This is not something that I have taken it upon myself to declare. Bodhisattva Nāgārjuna and the Dharma Master T'an-luan both designate such practices as the difficult-to-practice way. Tao-ch'o says that not a single person ever attained enlightenment through them, and Shan-tao affirms that not one person in a thousand can be saved by them.

"These persons whom I have quoted were all leaders of the Jōdo sect, and so you may be inclined to question their word. But there is the late eminent priest Eshin,[171] unsurpassed by any wise priests of the Tendai or Shingon sect in the Latter Day of the Law. He stated in his work entitled *Ōjō Yōshū* that the doctrines of exoteric and esoteric Buddhism are not the kind of Law that can free us from the sufferings of birth and death. Moreover, the work entitled *Ōjō Jūin* by Yōkan[172] of the Sanron sect states the same opinion. Therefore, if people will abandon the Lotus Sutra, Shingon, and other teachings, and devote themselves entirely to the Nembutsu, then ten persons out of ten and a hundred persons out of a hundred will be reborn in the Pure Land."[173]

These pronouncements of Hōnen precipitated debates and disputes with the priests of Mount Hiei, Tō-ji, Onjō-ji, and the seven major temples of Nara. But Eshin's words in the preface to his *Ōjō Yōshū* appeared to be so compelling that in the end Kenshin,[174] the chief priest of the temple on Mount Hiei, surrendered to the Nembutsu doctrine and became a disciple of Hōnen.

In addition to that, even persons who were not disciples of Hōnen began to recite the Nembutsu to Amida Buddha far more often than they paid reverence to any other Buddha, their mouths continually murmuring it, their minds constantly occupied with it, until it seemed that everyone throughout the country of Japan had become a follower of Hōnen.

In the past fifty years, every person within the four borders of the nation has become a follower of Hōnen. And if everyone has become a follower of Hōnen, then every person in the country of Japan is a slanderer of the Law. Now, if a thousand sons or daughters should band together to murder one parent, then all one thousand of them would be guilty of committing one of the five cardinal sins. And if one of them as a result should fall into the hell of incessant suffering, then how could the others escape the same fate?

In the end, it would seem as though Hōnen, angry at having been condemned to exile, turned into an evil spirit and took possession of the ruler and the priests of Mount Hiei and Onjō-ji who had earlier persecuted him and his followers, causing these persons to plot rebellion or to commit other evil acts.[175] As a result, they were almost all destroyed by the Kamakura authorities in eastern Japan. The few priests of Mount Hiei or Tō-ji who managed to survive are treated with contempt by ordinary men and women. They are like performing monkeys that are laughed at by the crowd or subjugated barbarians who are despised even by children.

The men of the Zen sect, taking advantage of this situation, pronounced themselves "observers of the precepts," deceiving the eyes of the people and putting on such lofty airs that, no matter what false doctrines they presumed in their madness to put forward, these doctrines were not recognized as erroneous.

This sect called Zen claims to represent a "special transmission outside the sutras," which was not revealed by the Buddha in the numerous sutras preached during his lifetime but was whispered in secret to the Venerable Mahākāśyapa. Thus the proponents of this sect maintain that, if one studies the various sutras without understanding the teachings of the Zen sect, he will be like a dog trying to bite at a clap of thunder or a monkey trying to grasp the moon's reflection in the water.

Zen is a false doctrine that appeals to the kind of persons in Japan who have been abandoned by their fathers and mothers because of their lack of filial devotion or dismissed from service by their lords and masters because of their outrageous conduct, to young priests who are too lazy to apply themselves to their studies, and to the disreputable nature of prostitutes. Even though its followers have all embraced the precepts, they are no more than swarming locusts feeding upon the people of the nation. That is why Heaven glares down in anger and the gods of the earth shudder.

The Shingon sect is a far greater source of trouble than the other two sects I have discussed above, a major form of heresy, and I would therefore like to discuss it in outline here.

In the reign of Emperor Hsüan-tsung of the T'ang dynasty, Shan-wu-wei, Chin-kang-chih, and Pu-k'ung brought the *Dainichi, Kon-*

gōchō, and *Soshitsuji* sutras from India and introduced them to China. The teachings of these three sutras are very clearly set forth. If we look for the basic principle, we find that it consists in unifying the two vehicles of *shōmon* and *engaku* in the one vehicle of Bodhisattva and repudiating the two vehicles to reveal the one vehicle. As far as practices go, the school employs mudras and mantras.

Such a doctrine cannot compare even with the one vehicle of Buddhahood which is one as opposed to three,[176] as set forth in the *Kegon* and *Hannya* sutras, nor is it even as profound as the specific teaching or the perfect teaching that preceded the Lotus Sutra, as clarified by the Tendai school. In its basic meaning at least, it corresponds merely to the two lower types of teachings, the Tripitaka teaching (*zōkyō*) and the connecting teaching (*tsūgyō*).

Shan-wu-wei no doubt realized that, if he were to expound the teachings set forth in these sutras, he would be ridiculed by the men of the Kegon and Hossō schools and laughed at by those of the Tendai school. And yet, since he had gone to all the trouble of bringing these works from India, probably he did not feel inclined simply to remain silent on the matter.

At this time there was a priest of the Tendai school called the Meditation Master I-hsing,[177] a perverse man. Shan-wu-wei went to him and questioned him on the Buddhist doctrines taught in China. The Ācārya[178] I-hsing, deceived as to his motives, not only revealed to Shan-wu-wei the main principles of the Sanron, Hossō, and Kegon doctrines, but even explained the teachings of the Tendai school to him.

Shan-wu-wei realized that the Tendai teachings were even finer than he had supposed when he had heard of them in India, and that the doctrines of the three sutras he had brought could never compete with them. But he set about to deceive I-hsing, saying, "My good priest, you are one of the cleverest men of China, and the Tendai school has a truly profound and wonderful teaching. But the Shingon school whose teachings I have brought to China excels it in the fact that it employs mudras and mantras."

I-hsing appeared to find this reasonable, and Shan-wu-wei then said to him, "Just as the Great Teacher T'ien-t'ai wrote commentaries on the Lotus Sutra, so I would like to compose a commentary on the *Dainichi* Sutra in order to propagate the Shingon teachings. Could you write it down for me?" I-hsing replied, "That would be easy enough."

But in what way should I-hsing write? The Tendai school was unassailable, and though each of the other schools of Buddhism had competed in trying to refute its doctrines, none had gained the slightest success because of a single point. That point was the fact that in the *Muryōgi* Sutra, an introductory teaching to the Lotus Sutra, the Buddha had declared that in the various sutras that he had preached during the previous forty years or more, he had not yet revealed the truth, thus invalidating the doctrines based upon those various sutras. And in the *Hosshi* and *Jinriki* chapters of the Lotus Sutra, the Buddha stated that no sutras that would be preached in later times could ever equal the Lotus Sutra. In the passage of the *Hosshi* chapter concerning the comparison of the Lotus Sutra and others preached at the same time, he also made clear the superiority of the Lotus Sutra. Therefore I-hsing asked Shan-wu-wei to which of these three categories—the sutras preached before the Lotus Sutra, those preached contemporaneously with it, or those preached later—the *Dainichi* Sutra should be assigned.

At that point, Shan-wu-wei hit upon an exceedingly cunning idea. "The *Dainichi* Sutra," he explained to I-hsing, "begins with a chapter called the *Jūshin* chapter. Just as in the case of the *Muryōgi* Sutra, which refutes all the sutras that had been preached in the previous forty or more years, this *Jūshin* chapter invalidates all other sutras. The remaining chapters of the *Dainichi* Sutra, from the *Nyūmandara* chapter through the end, became known in China in two versions, the Lotus Sutra and the *Dainichi* Sutra, though in India they constituted a single sutra. Shakyamuni Buddha, addressing Śāriputra and Miroku, preached the *Dainichi* Sutra, which he called the Lotus Sutra, but he omitted the explanations of the mudras and mantras and expounded only the doctrines. This is the work that Kumārajīva introduced to China and which the Great Teacher T'ien-t'ai employed. At the same time, however, Mahavairocana or Dainichi Buddha, addressing Vajrasattva,[179] preached the Lotus Sutra, which he called the *Dainichi* Sutra. This is the work now called the *Dainichi* Sutra, a work that I often saw when I was in India. Therefore I want you to explain that the *Dainichi* Sutra and Lotus Sutra are to be savored as works that are essentially the same in flavor, like water and milk. If you do so, then the *Dainichi* Sutra can stand superior to all the other sutras preached in the past, present and future in the same way that the Lotus Sutra does.

"As to the mudras and mantras, if they are used to adorn the doctrine of the mind which is expressed in the term *ichinen sanzen,* this will constitute a secret teaching in which the three mysteries are provided.[180] And with this doctrine containing the three mysteries, the Shingon will prove superior to the Tendai school, which speaks only of the mystery of the mind. Shingon is like a general of the first rank who dons armor, slings his bow and arrows over his shoulder, and fastens a sword at his waist. But the Tendai school, with nothing but the mystery of the mind, is like a general of the first rank who is stark naked."[181]

The Ācārya I-hsing wrote all this down just as Shan-wu-wei dictated it.

Throughout the 360 states of China, there was no one who knew about this ruse. At first there were some disputes over the relative merits of the Tendai and Shingon teachings. But Shan-wu-wei was the kind of person who was able to command a great deal of respect,[182] whereas the men of the Tendai school were regarded lightly. Moreover, at this time there were no men of wisdom such as the Great Teacher T'ien-t'ai had been. Thus day by day the Tendai school lost more ground to the Shingon, and finally all debate ceased.

As more and more years have gone by, these fraudulent beginnings of the Shingon school have become completely obscured and forgotten. When the Great Teacher Dengyō of Japan went to China and returned with the teachings of the Tendai school, he also brought back the Shingon teachings. The Tendai school he recommended to the emperor of Japan, but the Shingon teachings he turned over to the eminent priests of the six sects to study. Dengyō had already established the superiority of the Tendai teachings over those of the six sects before he went to China. After he came back from China, he attempted to establish an ordination platform for conferring the precepts of perfect and immediate enlightenment, but this involved him in a great deal of controversy.[183] He had many enemies and probably felt that establishing the ordination platform would be difficult enough to accomplish even if he devoted all his efforts to it. Or perhaps he felt that the refutation of the Shingon teachings should be left until the Latter Day of the Law. In any event, he did not discuss the Shingon teachings in the presence of the emperor, nor make any clear pronouncement on the matter to his disciples. However, he did leave a one-volume secret work entitled *Ebyō Shū,*[184] in which he describes how various priests of the seven sects were won over to the Tendai teachings. In the preface to that work, he mentions the fraudulence of the Shingon teachings.

The Great Teacher Kōbō went to China during the Enryaku era,[185] when the Great Teacher Dengyō went. There he studied the teachings of the Shingon school under Hui-kuo[186] of the temple called Ch'ing-lung-ssu. After returning to Japan, he pronounced judgment on the relative merits of the doctrines preached by Shakyamuni in the course of his life, declaring that the Shingon teachings ranked first, the Kegon second, and those of the Lotus Sutra third.

The Great Teacher Kōbō enjoys a quite unusual amount of respect among the people of our time. However, although I hesitate to touch on such matters, in questions of the Buddhist teaching, he committed a rather unusual number of errors. If we stop to consider the matter in general, it would appear that when he went to China, he merely learned the ritual mudras and mantras that are used by the Shingon school and introduced these to Japan. But he does not seem to have delved into the doctrines of the school to any great extent. After he returned to Japan and observed the situation at the time, he saw that the Tendai sect was flourishing to an unusual degree, and he concluded that it would be difficult to propagate the Shingon doctrines that he himself adhered to. Therefore, he adopted the viewpoint of the Kegon sect, whose doctrines he had studied earlier in Japan, declaring [as the Kegon sect does of its own teachings] that the Shingon doctrines were superior to the Lotus Sutra. But he realized that if he simply asserted the supremacy of his own sect's teachings over the Lotus Sutra in the same manner as the Kegon sect, people would not be likely to pay much heed to his words. He consequently gave a new twist to the Kegon doctrine,[187] declaring that his argument represented the true intent of the *Dainichi* Sutra, the *Bodaishin Ron* by Bodhisattva Nāgārjuna, and the Shingon authority Shan-wu-wei, thus bolstering his position with absurd falsehoods. And yet the followers of the Tendai sect failed to speak out strongly against him.

Question: In his *Jūjūshin Ron, Hizō Hōyaku*, and *Ben Kemmitsu Nikyō Ron*, the Great Teacher Kōbō makes such statements as "Each vehicle that is put forward is claimed to be the true vehicle, but when examined from a later stage, they are all seen to be mere childish theory";[188] [Shakyamuni Buddha] is in the region of ignorance, not in the position of enlightenment";[189] [The various exoteric Mahayana sutras such as the Lotus Sutra] are comparable to the fourth flavor, that of butter";[190] and, "The Buddhist scholars of China have vied with one another to steal the ghee of the Shingon and claim that it is the possession of their own sect."[191] What are we to make of such statements put forth in these commentaries?

Answer: I have been greatly astonished at the statements in these commentaries and have accordingly searched through the various sutras, including the three attributed to the Buddha Dainichi. But I do not find a single word or phrase in the sutras to indicate that, in comparison to the *Kegon* and *Dainichi* sutras, the Lotus Sutra is mere "childish theory," that with regard to the *Rokuharamitsu* Sutra T'ien-t'ai acted as a thief, or that the *Shugo* Sutra describes Shakyamuni Buddha as being "in the region of ignorance." These are all utterly ridiculous assertions. And yet for the past three or four hundred years, a sufficiently large number of intelligent persons in Japan accepted them, so that they have now come to be looked upon as perfectly reasonable and well founded. I would like for a moment therefore to discuss some of the more patently false opinions put forth by Kōbō and point out other absurdities in his thinking.

It was during the period of the Ch'en and Sui dynasties that the Great Teacher T'ien-t'ai likened the Lotus Sutra to ghee, the finest of the five flavors. It was some two centuries later, in the middle years of the T'ang dynasty, that the Tripitaka Master Prajñā[192] translated the *Rokuharamitsu* Sutra and introduced it to China. Only if the *Rokuharamitsu* Sutra—which places the *dharani* teachings in the fifth or highest category, comparing them to ghee—had existed in China during the Ch'en and Sui dynasties would it make any sense to claim that the Great Teacher T'ien-t'ai "stole the ghee of the Shingon."

A similar example exists in the case of the priest Tokuitsu[193] of Japan. He bitterly criticized the Great Teacher T'ien-t'ai for rejecting the doctrine of the teachings of the three periods[194] that is set forth in the *Jimmitsu* Sutra, declaring that T'ien-t'ai had used his three-inch tongue to destroy the Buddha's five-foot body.[195] The Great Teacher Dengyō in turn attacked Tokuitsu, pointing out that the *Jimmitsu* Sutra was first introduced to China by Hsüan-tsang in the early decades of the T'ang dynasty. In other words, it was brought to the country a number of years after T'ien-t'ai, who lived during the Ch'en and Sui, had already passed away. How then could he have rejected a doctrine that was not introduced to China until the period after his death? Faced with such an argument, Tokuitsu was not only reduced to silence, but his tongue broke into eight pieces, and he died.

But this is nothing compared to the evil accusations made by Kōbō. In his writings he labels as thieves Fa-tsang of the Kegon school, Chia-hsiang of the Sanron, Hsüan-tsang of the Hossō, and T'ien-t'ai, as well as other various Buddhist leaders of northern and southern China, and in fact all the Tripitaka masters and teachers who have lived since the time when Buddhism was first introduced to China in the Later Han.

In addition, it should be noted that likening the Lotus Sutra to ghee was by no means a comparison invented by T'ien-t'ai on his own initiative. The Buddha himself said in the Nirvana Sutra that the Lotus Sutra was like ghee, and later Bodhisattva Vasubandhu wrote that the Lotus Sutra and Nirvana Sutra were comparable to ghee.[196] And Bodhisattva Nāgārjuna terms the Lotus Sutra a "wonderful medicine."[197] If anyone who compares the Lotus Sutra to ghee is to be labeled a thief, then are Shakyamuni, Tahō, and the other Buddhas of the ten directions, along with Bodhisattvas Nāgārjuna and Vasubandhu, all to be branded as thieves?

Though Kōbō's disciples and the Shingon priests of Tō-ji in Japan may be so poor-sighted that they cannot distinguish black from white with their own eyes, they should trust the sight of others[198] and recognize the misfortunes invited by their own faults! Moreover, where are the precise passages in the *Dainichi* and *Kongōchō* sutras that refer to the Lotus Sutra as a "childish theory"? Let them produce them! Even if these sutras should perhaps refer to the Lotus Sutra in those terms, it may quite possibly be an error in translation. Such matters should be examined with great care and attention before they are put forward.

We are told that Confucius thought nine times before saying one word, and that Tan, the Duke of Chou, would bind up his hair three times in the course of washing it and spit out his food three times in the course of a meal in order not to keep callers waiting.[199] Thus we see that even among the men depicted in the non-Buddhist writings who study ephemeral worldly affairs, those who are wise proceeded with great caution. How then can men like Kōbō be so careless and shallow in judgment in matters pertaining to the Law?

Such erroneous views of Kōbō's were handed down until they reached Shōkaku-bō,[200] the founder of the temple called Dembō-in, who stated in his *Shari Kōshiki:* "The figure worthy of true respect is the Buddha of the Nondual Mahayana. The three-bodied donkey- or ox-Buddha is not even fit to draw his carriage. The Truly profound doctrines are the teachings of the twofold mandala. The teachers of the four doctrines of the exoteric vehicles are not worthy even to tend the shoes of those who teach the mandala!"

By the teachers of the "four doctrines of the exoteric vehicles," he means those who teach the Hossō, Sanron, Kegon, and Lotus Sutra doctrines, and by the "three-bodied donkey- or ox-Buddha," he means the Buddha of the four sutras of the Lotus, *Kegon, Hannya,* and *Jimmitsu.* He is saying that this Buddha and these monks are not even worthy to act as ox-drivers or sandal-bearers for the teachers of Shingon doctrine such as Kōbō or Shōkaku-bō himself.

There was a man in India known as the Great Arrogant Brahman who was born with innate wisdom and was widely read.[201] Both the exoteric and the esoteric teachings of Buddhism were stored up in his breast, and he had both the Buddhist and the non–Buddhist writings in the palm of his hand. Even the king and his ministers bowed their heads before him, and the common people looked up to him as a teacher and guide. But in the excess of his arrogance, he went so far as to make himself a dais supported by four legs representing the deities Maheśvara, Viṣṇu, and Nārāyaṇa, along with Shakyamuni Buddha, four sages whom the world holds in great honor, seating himself on it when he expounded his doctrines. He was like the Shingon priests of our time when they spread their mandala with its representations of Shakyamuni and the other various Buddhas and perform their *abhiṣeka* ceremony,[202] or like the Zen priests when they declare that the teachings of their sect represent a great Law that steps upon the head of the Buddha.[203]

At this time there was a humble monk called the scholar Bhadraruci who declared that the Brahman should be corrected, but neither the ruler and high ministers nor the common people would listen to such a suggestion. In the end, the Brahman charged his disciples and lay followers to go about spreading countless falsehoods and abusing and beating Bhadraruci. But Bhadraruci, disregarding the danger to his life, continued to denounce the Brahman until the ruler, coming to hate Bhadraruci, arranged for him to debate with the Brahman in hopes of silencing him. Contrary to his expectations, however, the Brahman was the one defeated in the debate.

The king looked up to heaven, then threw himself upon the ground lamenting, and said, "I have been privileged to hear your words on this matter firsthand and to free myself from my erroneous views. But my father, the former king, was completely deceived by this man and by now has probably fallen into the hell of incessant suffering!" So saying, he clung to the knees of the scholar Bhadraruci and wept in sorrow.

At Bhadraruci's suggestion, the Brahman was placed on the back of a donkey so that he might be led in disgrace throughout the five regions of India and shown to all. But the evil in his heart only grew stronger than ever, and in his living form he fell into the hell of incessant suffering. Was he any different from the men of the Shingon and Zen sects in the world today?

The Chinese Meditation Master San-chieh[204] stated that the Lotus Sutra, which represents the teachings of the Buddha Shakyamuni, is a doctrine suited for the first and second stages of Buddhism, which correspond to the Former and Middle Days of the Law. For the Latter Day of the Law, however, he asserted that one should adopt the "universal teaching" that he himself had set forth. He declared that if one should try to practice the Lotus Sutra in these present times of the Latter Day of the Law, he would surely fall into the great Avīci Hell of the ten directions, because its teachings do not accord with the nature and capabilities of the people of the Latter Day.

He carried out prostrations and penances at the proper hours six times each day and observed the four daily meditation periods, conducting himself like a living Buddha. Many people paid him honor and his disciples numbered more than ten thousand. But one young woman dared to recite the Lotus Sutra and to censure him for his doctrines.[205] As a result, he lost his voice on the spot and was reborn as a huge snake that devoured a number of his disciples and lay supporters, as well as girls and young women. And now Shan-tao and Hōnen, with their pernicious doctrine that not one person in a thousand can be saved by the Lotus Sutra, are just like this man San-chieh.

Many years have passed now since these great sources of trouble, the Nembutsu, Zen, and Shingon teachings, came into existence, and one should not underestimate their influence. But I feel that if I speak out against them in this way, there will perhaps be those who will heed my words.

And yet there is something that is more evil than these three teachings, so evil that it is countless times more difficult to believe.

Though the Great Teacher Jikaku was the third disciple of the Great Teacher Dengyō, everyone from the ruler on down to the common people believed him to be a more outstanding person than Dengyō himself. He made an exhaustive study of the teachings of the Shingon sect and of the Hokke sect, and stated in his writings that the Shingon teachings are superior to those of the Lotus Sutra. As a result, the community of priests on Mount Hiei, which numbered three thousand, as well as the Buddhist scholars in every province throughout Japan, all came to accept his opinion on this matter.

The followers of Kōbō had thought that, although he was their teacher, he had perhaps gone too far when he declared the Lotus Sutra inferior to the *Kegon* Sutra. But when they saw that the Great Teacher Jikaku put forth a similar opinion in his exegetical writings, they took it as an accepted fact that the Shingon teachings were indeed superior to the Lotus Sutra.

Mount Hiei, the headquarters of the Tendai sect, ought to have been the staunchest opponent to this opinion established in Japan that the Shingon teachings are superior to the Lotus Sutra. Yet Jikaku silenced the mouths of the three thousand priests of Mount Hiei and prevented them from speaking out, and as a result, the Shingon sect was able to have its way. In effect, the Great Teacher Jikaku was the foremost ally of Tō-ji, the leading Shingon temple in the Kyoto area!

Though the Jōdo and Zen sects may have flourished in other countries, they would never have been able to spread throughout Japan in countless kalpas if Enryaku-ji on Mount Hiei had not given its assent. But the priest Annen, known as the first worthy of Mount Hiei, wrote a work called the *Kyōjijō Ron* in which he ranked the nine sects of Buddhism in the order of their superiority, placing the Shingon sect in the first place, the Zen sect in the second, the Tendai-Hokke sect in the third, the Kegon sect in the fourth, etc.[206] Because of this egregious error in interpretation, the Zen sect has been able to spread its teachings throughout Japan, bringing the country to the brink of ruin. And Hōnen was able to propagate the teachings of the Jōdo or Nembutsu sect and similarly imperil the nation as a result of the opinions first put forth by Eshin in the preface to his *Ōjō Yōshū*. The Buddha tells us that the lion's flesh will be consumed by worms within the body of the lion himself. How true are those words!

The Great Teacher Dengyō spent a period of fifteen years in Japan studying the Tendai and Shingon doctrines on his own. He was endowed by nature with a wonderful degree of understanding, and without the aid of a teacher realized the truth. But in order to dispel the doubts of the world, he journeyed to China, where he received instruction in the teachings of the Tendai and Shingon schools. The scholars in China held various opinions, but Dengyō believed in his heart that the Lotus Sutra was superior to the Shingon teachings. Therefore he did not use the word "sect" when referring to the teachings of Shingon, but simply spoke of the Shikan and Shingon practices of the Tendai sect.[207] He decreed that two monks should be ordained each year and should spend a period of twelve years in study on Mount Hiei. In addition, he received an imperial edict designating the Lotus, *Konkōmyō,* and *Ninnō* sutras as the three scriptures for the protection of the nation and decreeing that they be read and recited in the Shikan-in.[208] It went on to liken these three sutras to the three treasures of the imperial household, the eternal and foremost treasures of the Japanese nation, which are the sacred jewel, the sacred sword, and the sacred mirror. After Dengyō's death, the first chief priest of the Tendai sect on Mount Hiei, the priest Gishin,[209] and the second chief priest, the Great Teacher Enchō,[210] carried on Dengyō's intentions without any deviation.

The third chief priest, the Great Teacher Jikaku, also went to China, where he spent ten years studying the relative merits of the exoteric and esoteric teachings under eight distinguished priests.[211] He also studied under priests of the Tendai school such as Kuang-hsiu and Wei-chüan.[212] But in his heart he believed that the Shingon school was superior to the Tendai school. He felt that his teacher, the Great Teacher Dengyō, had not gone into the matter in sufficient detail, that he had not remained for an extended period in China and hence had acquired only a rough understanding of the Shingon doctrines.

After Jikaku returned to Japan, he founded a great lecture hall called Sōji-in west of the Shikan-in in the Tōdō area[213] on Mount Hiei, in which he established Dainichi Buddha of the Diamond Realm as an object of worship. In front of this image, he composed, on the basis of Shan-wu-wei's commentary on the *Dainichi* Sutra, a seven-volume commentary on the *Kongōchō* Sutra and a seven-volume commentary on the *Soshitsuji* Sutra, making a total of fourteen volumes.[214]

The essence of these commentaries is as follows: "There are two types of teachings. One is called the exoteric, which corresponds to the doctrine of the three vehicles; in this, worldly truth and the superior truth of Buddhism are not completely fused. The other is called the esoteric, which corresponds to the doctrine of the one vehicle; in this, worldly truth and the superior truth of Buddhism are fused together into a single entity. In turn, there are two types of esoteric teachings. One is called the esoteric teachings of theory; these are the doctrines found in works such as the *Kegon, Hannya,* Vimalakirti, Lotus, and Nirvana sutras. But these, though they teach the nondualism of worldly truth and the superior truth, say nothing about mantras and mudras. The second is called the esoteric teachings of both theory and practice; these are the doctrines found in the *Dainichi, Kongōchō,* and *Soshitsuji* sutras. These teach the nondualism of worldly truth and the superior truth, and also explain mantras and mudras."

This essentially means that, in regard to the relative superiority of the Lotus Sutra and the three Shingon sutras just mentioned, they agree in principle, both teaching the doctrine of *ichinen sanzen,* but mudras and mantras are not mentioned in the Lotus Sutra. The Lotus Sutra thus represents the esoteric teachings of theory, while the three Shingon sutras represent the esoteric teachings of both theory and practice. They are hence as far apart as heaven and earth, or clouds and mud, say the commentaries. Moreover, Jikaku insists that this is no private interpretation of his own, but represents the essential view put forward by the Tripitaka Master Shan-wu-wei in his commentary on the *Dainichi* Sutra.

But perhaps he felt that the relative worth of the Tendai and Shingon sects was still a matter of doubt, or perhaps he hoped to dispel the misgivings of others. In any event, the biography of the Great Teacher Jikaku states as follows: "After the great teacher had completed writing his commentaries on the two sutras and thus accomplished his aim, he wondered to himself whether or not his commentaries conformed to the will of the Buddha, for he believed that if they did not conform to the Buddha's will, they should never be widely circulated in the world. He therefore placed the commentaries before the image of the Buddha and determined to spend seven days and seven nights earnestly praying and endeavoring to make clear the validity of his purpose. On the fifth day, early in the morning at the time of the fifth watch, he dreamt that it was high noon and the sun was shining in the sky. Looking up, he took a bow and shot an arrow at it. The arrow struck the sun, which immediately began to roll over and over. After he woke from his dream, he realized that his views were profoundly in accord with the will of the Buddha, and he determined to transmit his commentaries to future ages." [215]

While the Great Teacher Jikaku was in Japan, he made a thorough study of the teachings of both Dengyō and Kōbō, and he spent a period of ten years in China studying under the eight distinguished priests mentioned earlier, including the Tripitaka Master Pao-yüeh of southern India, studying all the loftiest and most secret doctrines. On this basis, he completed his commentaries on the two sutras. In addition, he prayed to the image of the Buddha, and awoke from dreaming that he had seen the arrow of wisdom strike the sun of the Middle Way. So great was his joy that he requested Emperor Nimmyō to issue an edict acknowledging Mount Hiei as a center of Shingon practice.

Though he was the chief priest of the Tendai sect, he virtually became a Shingon prelate, declaring that the three Shingon sutras were the works that would ensure peace and protection of the nation. It has now been more than four hundred years since he spread these doctrines. The eminent leaders who have accepted them are as numerous as rice and hemp seedlings, and the fervent believers who have embraced them are as plentiful as bamboo plants and rushes.

As a result, of all the temples established throughout Japan by Emperor Kammu and the Great Teacher Dengyō, there is not one that has not become a propagator of the Shingon doctrine. Both courtiers and warriors alike invite Shingon priests to attend to their religious needs, look up to them as their teachers, confer offices upon them and place them in charge of temples. And in the ceremony carried out at the consecration of Buddhist images or paintings, the "opening of the eyes," the priests of all the eight sects of Buddhism now use the mudras and mantras associated with the eyes of the Buddha Dainichi!

Question: When it comes to those who maintain that the Lotus Sutra is superior to the Shingon teachings, should they try to make use of these commentaries by Jikaku, or should they reject them?

Answer: Shakyamuni Buddha laid down a rule for future conduct when he said that we should "rely on the Law and not upon persons." [216] Bodhisattva Nāgārjuna says, "Do not rely on treatises that distort the sutras; rely only on those that are faithful to the sutras." [217] The Great Teacher T'ien-t'ai states, "That which accords with the sutras is to be accepted and heeded. But put no faith in anything that in word or meaning fails to do so." [218] And the Great Teacher Dengyō says, "Depend upon the preachings of the Buddha and do not put faith in traditions handed down orally." [219]

If one attends to such statements in the sutras, treatises, and commentaries, then he should not make dreams a basis for evaluating the Buddhist teachings. Rather, he should pay particular attention to those sutras and treatises that make clear the relative superiority of the Lotus Sutra and the *Dainichi* Sutra.

As for the assertion that the "opening of the eyes" ceremony for Buddhist paintings and statues cannot be carried out without the use of Shingon mudras and mantras, this is the sheerest nonsense! Are we to suppose that, before Shingon appeared on the scene, Buddhist paintings and statues could not be consecrated? In the period before the appearance of Shingon, there were paintings and statues in India, China, and Japan that walked about or preached the Law or spoke aloud. [220] It would rather appear that since people have begun to use Shingon mudras and mantras in consecrating the Buddha images, the effectiveness of the ceremony has been completely lost!

This is a generally acknowledged point. I would merely like to say that, when it comes to determining the truth of Jikaku's assertions, there is no need for me, Nichiren, to cite any outside evidence to refute them. We have only to examine Jikaku's own interpretations to understand the truth of the matter.

Question: How do we come to understand it?

Answer: We understand it when we realize that the source of Jikaku's delusion was the dream that he had after he had written his commentaries asserting that the Shingon teachings are superior to the Lotus Sutra. If his dream had been an auspicious one, then we would have to conclude that Jikaku was correct in claiming that Shingon is superior. But can a dream of shooting the sun be called auspicious? Just try to find, anywhere in all the five thousand or seven thousand volumes of Buddhist scriptures or in the three thousand and more volumes of non-Buddhist literature, any evidence suggesting that to dream of shooting the sun is an auspicious occurrence!

Let us look at a few pieces of evidence. King Ājātaśatru dreamt that the moon was falling out of the sky. [221] When he consulted his high minister Jīvaka, the latter said, "This is a sign of the Buddha's passing." And when Subhadra [222] also dreamt that the sun was falling from the sky, he said to himself, "This is a sign of the Buddha's passing!" When the *asura* demons fought with the deity Taishaku, they first of all shot arrows at the sun and moon.[223] The evil rulers Emperor Chieh of the Hsia dynasty and Emperor Chou of the Yin dynasty in ancient China are both said to have repeatedly shot arrows at the sun, and both destroyed themselves and brought an end to their dynasties.

Queen Māyā dreamt that she conceived the sun, and thereafter gave birth to Prince Siddhārtha, who in time became the Buddha Shakyamuni. For this reason, the Buddha's name as a child was Sun Seed.[224] Japan or Nihon is so called because it is the land of Tenshō Daijin, the Sun Goddess. In light of these examples, Jikaku's dream must mean that he used his two commentaries as arrows to shoot at the Sun Goddess Tenshō Daijin, the Great Teacher Dengyō, Shakyamuni Buddha, and the Lotus Sutra. I, Nichiren, am an ignorant man and I know nothing about the sutras and treatises. But I do know this much: any man who would conclude from such a dream that the Shingon teachings are superior to the Lotus Sutra will surely in this present life destroy his nation and ruin his family, and after his death will fall into the Avīci Hell.

We in fact have a piece of evidence to settle the matter. If, when Japan and the Mongol forces engaged in combat,[225] the prayers of the Shingon priests had proved effective and Japan had won victory on that account, then we might be persuaded that Shingon is worthy of respect. But at the time of the hostilities in the Jōkyū era,[226] though a considerable number of Shingon priests prayed for the victory of the imperial forces and invoked curses on the forces of the Kamakura shogunate, the leader of the latter, the Gon no Tayū,[227] emerged victorious. As a result, the Retired Emperor Gotoba was exiled to the island of Oki, and his sons were exiled to the island of Sado and to another province.[228] Such was the effect of the Shingon prayers for victory. In the end, the Shingon prayers were like the cries of the fox that give him away, and the curses, as the Lotus Sutra says, "returned to the originators."[229] The three thousand priests of Mount Hiei were also attacked by the Kamakura troops and forced to submit.[230]

Now the Kamakura government is at the height of power. Therefore, the Shingon priests of Tō-ji, Mount Hiei, Onjō-ji, and the seven major temples of Nara, along with those priests of the Hokke sect who have forgotten the teachings of their own sect and instead slander the Law, have all made their way east to the Kanto region, where they bow their heads, bend their knees, and seek in various ways to win over the hearts of the warriors. They are in turn assigned positions as superintendents or chief officials of various temples and mountain monasteries, where they proceed to follow the same evil doctrines that earlier brought about the downfall of the imperial forces, using them to pray for the peace and safety of the nation!

The shogun and his family, along with the samurai who are in their service, very likely believe that as a result of such prayers, the nation will actually become peaceful and secure. But so long as they employ the services of priests who invite grave disaster by ignoring the Lotus Sutra, the nation will in fact face certain destruction.

When I think how pitiful it would be if the nation were to be destroyed, and how lamentable would be the loss of life involved, I feel that I must risk my own life in order to make the truth of the situation clear. If the ruler desires the security of the nation, he should question the manner in which things are proceeding and try to discern the truth. But instead, all he does is listen to the calumnies of others and in one way or another treat me with animosity.

In past ages, when there were those who slandered the Law, Bonten, Taishaku, the gods of the sun and moon, the Four Heavenly Kings, and the deities of the earth, all of whom have sworn to defend the Lotus Sutra, would look on with disapproval. But because there was no one to proclaim the matter aloud, they would be forgiving, as one would be with an only child who misbehaves, at times pretending not to notice such slander, at times administering a mild reproof. Now that I am present to make clear the matter, however, I can only be amazed that the ruler should continue to listen to persons who slander the Law. Yet he does so, and on the contrary even goes so far as to persecute the rare individual who attempts to enlighten him and rescue him from error. Not for just one or two days, one or two months, or even one or two years, but for a number of years on end now, I have met with greater difficulties than the sticks and staves that Bodhisattva Fukyō was obliged to face, and have encountered more fearful opposition than the murderous attacks inflicted on the monk Kakutoku.[231]

During this period, the two great deities Bonten and Taishaku, the gods of the sun and moon, the Four Heavenly Kings, the gods of stars, and the deities of the earth have manifested their anger in various ways and again and again have delivered reprimands.[232] And yet the attacks on me have only worsened. Finally, Heaven in its wisdom has made the situation known to the sages of neighboring countries, enlisting them to add to the reprimands,[233] and has caused the great demon spirits to invade the nation and deceive the people's hearts, inciting them to rebel against their own rulers.[234]

It is only reasonable to assume that, whether good or evil, the greater the portents, the greater will be the occurrences to follow. Now we have seen huge comets of a magnitude never known before in the 2,230 or more years since the Buddha's passing, and have experienced earthquakes such as were never encountered before during that time. In China and Japan in the past, sages of outstanding wisdom and ability have from time to time appeared. But none, as an ally of the Lotus Sutra, has faced such powerful enemies within his country as have I, Nichiren. From the facts present before your very eyes, it should be apparent that Nichiren is the foremost person in the entire world.

In the seven hundred and more years since Buddhism was first introduced to Japan, there have been five thousand or seven thousand volumes of sutras read, and eight or ten sects[235] propounded. The men of wisdom who have appeared have been as numerous as rice and hemp seedlings, and those who have spread the teachings abroad have been as plentiful as bamboo plants and rushes. And yet of all the various Buddhas, there is none more highly revered, and none whose name is more widely called upon, than the Buddha Amida.

This practice of invoking the name of the Buddha Amida was advocated by Eshin in his work *Ōjō Yōshū,* and, as a result, one third of the people of Japan became believers in the Nembutsu, the calling on the name of Amida. When Yōkan wrote the *Ōjō Jūin* and the *Ōjō Kōshiki,*[236] two thirds of all the people of this country became followers of the Nembutsu. And when Hōnen wrote his *Senchaku Shū,* then everyone alike in this nation of ours became a Nembutsu devotee. Thus those people who chant the name of the Buddha Amida these days are by no means disciples of only one person.

This thing called the Nembutsu is a daimoku or chant based on the *Muryōju, Kammuryōju,* and *Amida* sutras, which are provisional Mahayana sutras. If the daimoku of provisional Mahayana sutras is widely propagated and spread abroad, it must be a prelude to the propagation of the daimoku of the true Mahayana sutra, must it not? People who have a mind for such concerns should consider this matter carefully. If the provisional sutras are spread abroad, then the true sutra will surely be spread abroad. If the daimoku of the provisional sutras is spread abroad, then the daimoku of the true sutra will also surely be spread abroad.

In all the seven hundred and more years from the time of Emperor Kimmei to the present emperor,[237] such a thing has never been seen or heard of, namely, a wise man who says let us chant Nam-myoho-renge-kyo, who urges others to chant it and chants it himself.

When the sun rises, the stars go into hiding. When a wise king appears, foolish kings perish. When the true sutra is spread abroad, the provisional sutras will cease to circulate, and when a man of wisdom chants Nam-myoho-renge-kyo, those ignorant of it will follow after him as shadows follow a form and echoes follow a sound.

There can be no room to doubt that I, Nichiren, am the foremost votary of the Lotus Sutra in all of Japan. Indeed, from this we may assume that, even in China and India and throughout the entire world, there is no one who can stand side by side with me.

Question: The great earthquake of the Shōka era, the huge comet of the Bun'ei era—what caused these to appear?

Answer: In the Tendai teachings it is said, "Wise men can see omens and what they foretell, as snakes know the way of snakes."[238]

Question: What do you mean by that?

Answer: When Bodhisattva Jōgyō appeared from beneath the earth, the other bodhisattvas such as Miroku, Monjushiri, Kanzeon, and Yakuō, though they had severed themselves from the first forty-one of the forty-two levels of ignorance,[239] had not yet severed themselves from the last one, or basic ignorance. Hence they were in effect ignorant persons, and consequently failed to understand that this bodhisattva, Jōgyō, had been summoned so that he might widely propagate Nam-myoho-renge-kyo of the *Juryō* chapter in the Latter Day of the Law.

Question: Is there anyone in Japan, China, or India who understands this matter?

Answer: Even the great bodhisattvas who have eradicated the illusions of thought and desire[240] and severed themselves from the forty-one levels of ignorance cannot understand such a thing. How then could persons who have not rid themselves of even one iota of delusion be expected to do so?

Question: But if there is no wise man who understands why these calamities have arisen, then how can proper steps be taken to deal with them? If one does not understand the origin of an illness, though he may try to treat the sick person, the treatment will surely fail and the patient will die. Now if the people resort to prayers without understanding the basic cause of these disasters, can there be any doubt that the nation will in time face ruin? Ah, how dreadful to think of it!

Answer: They say that snakes know seven days in advance when a heavy rain is going to occur, and that crows know what lucky or unlucky events are going to take place in the course of a whole year. This must be because snakes are followers of the great dragons who make the rains fall, and crows have for a long time studied such matters of divination. Now I, Nichiren, am only a common mortal, and therefore have no understanding of the cause of these disasters. Nevertheless, I believe I can generally instruct you concerning this matter.

In the time of King P'ing of the Chou dynasty, persons appeared who let their hair hang down and went about naked. A court official named Hsin Yu divined on the basis of this and said, "Within a hundred years, this dynasty will come to an end." In the time of King Yu of the Chou, the mountains and rivers collapsed and were destroyed and the earth shook. A courtier named Po Yang, observing this, said, "Within twelve years our great ruler will meet with some dire happening."[241]

Now the great earthquake and the huge comet that have appeared are calamities brought about by Heaven, which is enraged because the ruler of our country hates Nichiren and sides with the Zen, Nembutsu, and Shingon priests who preach doctrines that will destroy the nation!

Question: How can I believe that?

Answer: The *Saishōō* Sutra says, "Because evil men are respected and favored and good men are subjected to punishment, the stars and constellations, along with the winds and rains, all fail to move in their proper seasons."[242]

If this passage from the sutra is correct, then there can be no doubt that there are evil men in this country of ours and that the ruler and his ministers put their trust in such men. Moreover, there can be no doubt that there is a wise man in this country, and that the ruler of the nation hates and treats him as an enemy.

The same sutra also says, "The deities of the Heaven of the Thirty-three Gods will all feel rage in their hearts, and strange and unusual shooting stars will fall to earth, two suns will come out at the same time, marauders will appear from other regions and the people of the country will meet with death and disorder."[243]

Already in this country we have had strange happenings in the heavens as well as earthly prodigies, and the men of a foreign country have come to attack us. Can there be any doubt that the thirty-three heavenly gods are angry?

The *Ninnō* Sutra states, "Evil monks, hoping to gain fame and profit, in many cases appear before the ruler, the heir apparent or the other princes and take it upon themselves to preach doctrines that lead to the violation of the Buddhist Law and the destruction of the nation. The ruler, failing to perceive the truth of the situation, listens to and puts faith in such doctrines."

The same work also refers to a time "when the sun and moon depart from their regular courses, when the seasons come in the wrong order, when a red sun or a black sun appears, when two, three, four, or five suns appear at the same time, when the sun is eclipsed and loses its light, or when one, two, three, four, or five coronas appear around the sun."[244]

These passages mean that if evil monks fill the nation and deceive the ruler, the heir apparent and the other princes, preaching doctrines that lead to the violation of the Buddhist Law and the downfall of the nation, and if the ruler and the other men in high positions allow themselves to be deceived by these monks and come to believe that such doctrines will in fact ensure the protection of the Buddhist Law and the nation, and act accordingly, then the sun and the moon will behave strangely, and great winds, rains, and fires will make their appearance. Next will come internal disorder, relatives and kin turning against each other and bringing about armed revolt. Many allies and supporters of the ruler and other men in high positions will be struck down, and then invaders will come from other nations to attack them, until they are forced to commit suicide or are captured alive or obliged to surrender. This will come about entirely because they heed doctrines that lead to the destruction of the Buddhist Law and cause the downfall of the nation.

The *Shugo* Sutra says, "The Law taught by Shakyamuni Buddha cannot be in the least bit harmed by the various devils of heaven, or by the non-Buddhists, or by evil men, or by hermit-sages who have attained the five supernatural powers.[245] And yet it can be so thoroughly destroyed by those evil monks who are monks in name and appearance only that nothing whatsoever remains of it. In this respect it is like Mount Sumeru. Though one might gather all the grass and wood from the major world system and pile it up as fuel and burn it for a long period of time, Mount Sumeru would not suffer the least degree of injury. But when the conflagration that marks the end of the world breaks out and fire appears from within the mountain itself, then in an instant the whole mountain will be consumed by the flames and not even ashes will remain."[246]

The *Rengemen* Sutra says, "The Buddha said to Ānanda, 'It is like the case of a lion who has died. No creature that lives in the air, in the soil, in water or on land will venture to eat the flesh of the dead lion. Only the worms that are born from the body of the lion itself will feed on the lion's flesh. In the same way, Ānanda, the Buddha's Law cannot be destroyed by outside forces. But the evil monks who exist within the body of my Law—they are the ones who will destroy this Law that the Buddha has labored over and worked to establish for a period of three great asōgi kalpas!"[247]

What do these passages from the sutras mean? In the past, the Buddha Kāśyapa described to King Kŗki the Latter Day of the Law of the Buddha Shakyamuni and revealed what sort of people would destroy Shakyamuni's teachings.[248] Evil men might appear such as King Mihirakula, who burned all the Buddhist halls and monasteries of the five regions of India and murdered all the monks and nuns of the sixteen major states,[249] or Emperor Wu-tsung[250] of China, who destroyed more than 4,600 temples and pagodas in the nine provinces of China and forced 260,500 priests and nuns to return to lay life. But such men could not destroy the Law preached by Shakyamuni Buddha. It is the priests themselves, who wrap their bodies in the three robes permitted to them, hang a single begging bowl about their necks, store up in their minds the eighty thousand teachings, and with their mouths recite the twelve divisions of the sutras—they are the ones who will destroy the Buddha's Law.

It is like the case of Mount Sumeru, the golden mountain. Though one might gather all the grass and wood in the major world system and pile it up until it completely filled the Heaven of the Four Heavenly Kings as well as the others of the six heavens of the world of desire, and burn it for one year, two years, or ten thousand billion years, the mountain would not suffer the slightest injury. But when the time comes for the great fire that ends the world, a tiny flame no bigger than a bean will break out at the base of the mountain, and not only will Mount Sumeru be consumed, but the entire major world system will likewise be destroyed.

If the Buddha's predictions are to be believed, then it would appear that the Buddhist priests of the ten sects or the eight sects of our country will be the ones to burn up the Mount Sumeru of the Buddha's teaching. The priests of the Hinayana sects of Kusha, Jō-jitsu, and Ritsu will be the flames of anger that burn with jealous hatred of the Mahayana sects. And priests such as Shan-wu-wei of the Shingon school, San-chieh of the Zen school,[251] and Shan-tao of the Jōdo school are the worms that are born from the flesh of the lion that is the Buddha's teaching.

The Great Teacher Dengyō in his writings described the eminent scholars of the Sanron, Hossō, Kegon, and other sects of Japanese Buddhism as six kinds of worms.[252] I, Nichiren, would dub the founders of the Shingon, Zen, and Jōdo sects the three kinds of worms, and Jikaku, Annen, and Eshin of the Tendai sect the three worms who devoured the lion-body of the Lotus Sutra and the Great Teacher Dengyō!

So long as Nichiren, who is working to expose the root of these great slanders against the Law, is treated with animosity, the heavenly deities will withhold their light, the gods of the earth will be angered, and omens and calamities will appear in great numbers. You must understand that, because I speak concerning the most important matter in the entire world, my words are accompanied by portents of the first magnitude. How tragic, how pitiful, that all the people of this nation of Japan should fall into the great citadel of the hell of incessant suffering! But how fortunate, how joyous, to think that, with this unworthy body, I have received in my heart the seed of Buddhahood!

Just see how it will be! When tens of thousands of armed ships from the great kingdom of the Mongols come over the sea to attack Japan, everyone from the ruler on down to the multitudes of common people will turn their backs on all the Buddhist temples and all the shrines of the gods and will raise their voices in chorus, crying Nam-myoho-renge-kyo, Nam-myoho-renge-kyo! They will press their palms together and say, "Priest Nichiren, Priest Nichiren, save us!"

In India King Mihirakula was obliged to press his palms together in submission before King Bālāditya, and in Japan Taira no Mune-mori was forced to pay reverence to Kajiwara Kagetoki.[253] This is in accord with the principle that men of great arrogance should end by bowing before their enemies.

Those vicious and arrogant monks described in the Lotus Sutra in the beginning armed themselves with sticks and staves and used them to belabor Bodhisattva Fukyō. But later they pressed their palms together and repented of their error. Devadatta inflicted an injury on Shakyamuni Buddha that drew blood, but when he was on his death-bed, he cried out, "Namu [Devotion]!" If only he had been able to cry, "Namu Buddha [Devotion to the Buddha]!" he would have been spared the fate of falling into hell. But so grave were the deeds he had committed that he could only utter the word "Namu" and could not pronounce the word "Buddha" before he died.

And soon the eminent priests of Japan will no doubt be trying to cry out, "Namu Nichiren Shonin [Devotion to the sage Nichiren]!" But most likely they will only have time enough to utter the one word, "Namu!" How pitiful, how pitiful!

In the secular texts it is said, "A sage is one who knows those things that have not yet made their appearance." And in the Buddhist texts it says, "A sage is one who knows the three existences of life— past, present, and future."

Three times now I have gained distinction by having such knowl-edge. The first time was the first year of the Bunnō era (1260), when the reverse marker of Jupiter was in the sector of the sky with the cyclical sign *kanoe-saru,* on the sixteenth day of the seventh month, when I presented my *"Risshō Ankoku Ron"* to His Lordship, the lay priest of Saimyō-ji, by way of Yadoya Nyūdō.[254] At that time, I said to Yadoya Nyūdō, "Please advise His Lordship that devotion to the Zen sect and the Nembutsu sect should be abandoned. If this advice is not heeded, trouble will break out within the Hōjō family, and the nation will be attacked by a foreign power."

The second time was the twelfth day of the ninth month of the eighth year of the Bun'ei era (1271), at the hour of the Monkey (3:00– 5:00 P.M.), when I said to the magistrate Hei no Saemon, "Nichiren is the pillar and beam of Japan. If you lose me, you will be toppling the pillar of Japan! Immediately we will face the disaster of 'internal strife,' or conflict within the realm, and also 'foreign invasion.' Not only will the people of our nation be put to death by foreign invaders, but many of them will also be taken prisoner. All the Nembutsu and Zen temples such as Kenchō-ji, Jufuku-ji, Gokuraku-ji, Daibutsu-den and Chōraku-ji should be burned to the ground and their priests taken to Yui beach to have their heads cut off! If this is not done, then Japan is certain to be destroyed!"

The third time was the eighth day of the fourth month of last year, or the eleventh year of the Bun'ei era (1274), when I said to Hei no Saemon,[255] "Since I have been born in the ruler's domain, I must follow him in my actions. But I need not follow him in the beliefs of my heart. There can be no doubt that the Nembutsu leads to the hell of incessant suffering, and that the Zen sect is the work of devils. And the Shingon sect in particular is a great plague to this nation of ours. The task of praying for victory over the Mongols should not be entrusted to the Shingon priests! If so grave a matter is entrusted to them, then the situation will only worsen rapidly and our country will face destruction!"

Hei no Saemon then asked, "When do you think the Mongols will attack?"

I replied, "The sacred scriptures do not indicate the time. But the signs show that Heaven is more than a little angry. It would appear that the attack is imminent and will probably occur before this year has ended!"

Yet it was not I, Nichiren, who made these three important pronouncements. Rather it was in all cases the spirit of Shakyamuni Buddha that had entered into my body. And at having personally experienced this, I am beside myself with joy!

This is the all-important doctrine of *ichinen sanzen* taught in the Lotus Sutra. What does the Lotus Sutra mean when it says, "This reality consists of appearance"?[256] "Appearance," the first of the ten factors of life, is the most important of them all; this is why the Buddha appeared in the world. Wise men can see omens and what they foretell, just as snakes know the way of snakes.

Little streams come together to form the great ocean, and tiny particles of dust accumulate to form Mount Sumeru. When I, Nichiren, first took faith in the Lotus Sutra, I was like a single drop of water or a single particle of dust in all the country of Japan. But later, when two people, three people, ten people, and eventually ten thousand billion people, come to recite the Lotus Sutra and transmit it to others, then they will form a Mount Sumeru of wonderful enlightenment,[257] a great ocean of nirvana! Seek no other path by which to attain Buddhahood!

Question: At the time of your second pronouncement on the twelfth day of the ninth month of the eighth year of the Bun'ei era, when you incurred the displeasure of the authorities, how did you know that if harm was done to you, rebellion would break out and the country would also be attacked by armies from abroad?

Answer: The fiftieth volume of the *Daijuku* Sutra states: "There may perhaps be various kings of the *kṣatriya* class who act in a way contrary to the Dharma, causing anguish to the *shōmon* disciples of the World-Honored One. Perhaps they may curse and revile them or beat and injure them with swords and staves, or deprive them of their robes and begging bowls and the other things they need. Or perhaps they may arrest or persecute those who give alms to the disciples. If there should be those who do such things, then we will see to it that their enemies in foreign lands rise up suddenly of their own accord and march against them, and we will cause uprisings to break out within their states. We will bring about pestilence and famine, unseasonable winds and rains, and contention, wrangling, and slander. And we will make certain that those rulers do not last for long, but that their nations are brought to destruction."[258]

There are many passages such as this in the sutras, but I have chosen this one because it is particularly pertinent to the times and to my own position. In this passage, the persons who are speaking are all the deities of the threefold world, including Bonten, Taishaku, the Devil of the Sixth Heaven, the gods of the sun and moon, the Four Heavenly Kings, and all the dragons. These eminent beings appeared before the Buddha and took a vow, declaring that, after the Buddha's death, in the Former, Middle, and Latter Days of the Law, if there should be monks of heretical belief who complain to the ruler concerning one who practices the True Law, and if those who are close to the ruler or who are loyal to him should simply accept the word of these monks because of respect for them and, without inquiring into the truth of the matter, heap abuse and slander on this wise man, then they, the deities, would see to it that, though there may have been no reason for such an occurrence, major revolt would suddenly break out within that country, and in time the nation would also be attacked by enemies from abroad, so that both the ruler and his state would be destroyed.

On the one hand, I am delighted to think that my prophecies shall come true, yet on the other hand, it pains me deeply. I have not committed any fault in my present existence. All I have done is try to repay the debt I owe to the country of my birth by endeavoring to save it from disaster. That my advice was not heeded was certainly a cause of great regret to me.

Not only was it not heeded, but I was summoned before the authorities, and the scroll of the fifth volume of the Lotus Sutra was snatched from the breast of my robe and I was harshly beaten with it.[259] In the end, I was arrested and paraded through the streets of the city. At that time, I called out, "You gods of the sun and moon up in the sky, here is Nichiren meeting with this great persecution. If you are not ready to risk your lives to aid me, does this mean, then, that I am not the true votary of the Lotus Sutra? If that is so, then I should correct my mistaken belief at once. If, on the other hand, Nichiren is the true votary of the Lotus Sutra, then you should send some sign of that fact to this country at once! If you do not do so, then you, the gods of the sun and moon and all the other deities, will be no more than great liars who have deceived Shakyamuni, Tahō, and all the other Buddhas of the ten directions. Devadatta was guilty of falsehood and deception and Kokālika was a great liar,[260] but you deities are guilty of telling lies that are ten thousand billion times greater!"

I had no sooner uttered these words than the nation was suddenly faced with internal revolt. Since the country has fallen into grave disorder, then, although I may be a mere common mortal of no social standing, so long as I uphold the Lotus Sutra, I deserve to be called the foremost Great Man[261] in all Japan at this time.

Question: In the delusion that is arrogance, there are different types of arrogance such as the seven types, the nine types, and the eight types.[262] But your arrogance is ten thousand billion times greater than the greatest degree of arrogance defined in the Buddhist teachings.

The scholar Guṇaprabha refused to bow before Bodhisattva Miroku,[263] and the Great Arrogant Brahman made himself a dais supported by four legs representing the sages Maheśvara, Viṣṇu and Nārāyaṇa, along with Shakyamuni Buddha.[264] Mahādeva, though only a common mortal, declared that he was an arhat, and the scholar Vimalamitra[265] proclaimed himself foremost within all the five regions of India. These men were all guilty of faults that condemned them to the hell of incessant suffering. How, then, do you dare to claim that you are the wisest man in the entire world? Will you not fall into hell like the others? What a frightful thing to do!

Answer: Have you really understood the meaning of the seven

types of arrogance, or of the nine types or the eight types? Shakya-muni Buddha, the World-Honored One, declared, "I am the fore-most throughout the threefold world!" All the non-Buddhist leaders predicted that Heaven would surely punish him immediately, or that the earth would open up and swallow him. [But no such thing happened.]

The three hundred or more priests of the seven major temples of Nara asserted that the priest Saichō [the Great Teacher Dengyō] was an incarnation of Mahādeva or of the Iron Belly Brahman.[266] Never-theless, Heaven did not punish him, but on the contrary protected him in various ways, and the earth did not open up and swallow him but remained as hard as a diamond. The Great Teacher Dengyō founded a temple on Mount Hiei and became the eyes of all people. In the end, the priests of the seven major temples acknowledged their fault and became his disciples, and the people of the various provinces throughout the country became his lay supporters. Thus, when someone who is superior declares that he is superior, it may sound like arrogance, but that person will in fact receive great benefits [because he is actually praising the Law which he embraces].

The Great Teacher Dengyō said, "The Tendai-Hokke sect is supe-rior to the other sects because of the sutra that it is founded on. Therefore, in declaring its superiority, it is not simply praising itself and disparaging others."[267]

The seventh volume of the Lotus Sutra states, "Just as Mount Sumeru is the highest among the various mountains, so this Lotus Sutra holds the highest position among all the sutras."[268] The sutras which the Buddha preached earlier such as the *Kegon, Hannya,* and *Dainichi* sutras, the *Muryōgi* Sutra which he preached at the same time as the Lotus Sutra, and the Nirvana Sutra which he was to preach later, altogether amounting to the five thousand or seven thousand volumes, as well as the sutras of the land of India, the dragon king's palace, the Heaven of the Four Heavenly Kings, the Trāyastriṃśa Heaven and the sun and the moon, and those of all the worlds in the ten directions, are lesser mountains such as the Earth Mountain, the Black Mountain, the lesser Iron-wheel Mountain, or the greater Iron-wheel Mountain in comparison to this Lotus Sutra which has been brought to Japan, for it is comparable to Mount Sumeru.

The seventh volume also says, "He who can accept and uphold this sutra will be like this too—he will be the first among all the multitude of living beings."[269]

Let us consider what this passage means. The other sutras have their supporters. Thus, the *Kegon* Sutra is upheld by the bodhisattvas Fugen, Gedatsugatsu, Nāgārjuna, and Aśvaghoṣa, the Great Teacher Fa-tsang, the Teacher of the Nation Ch'ing-liang, Empress Tse-t'ien, the Preceptor Shinjō, the Administrator of Monks Rōben, and Emperor Shōmu.[270] The *Jimmitsu* and *Hannya* sutras have as their supporters Bodhisattva Shōgishō, the Venerable Subhūti, the Great Teacher Chia-hsiang, the Tripitaka Master Hsüan-tsang, the emperors T'ai-tsung and Kao-tsung, the priests Kanroku and Dōshō, and Emperor Kōtoku.[271] Upholding the *Dainichi* Sutra of the Shingon sect are the bodhisattvas Vajrasattva, Nāgārjuna, and Nāgabodhi, King Sātavāhana, the Tripitaka masters Shan-wu-wei, Chin-kang-chih, and Pu-k'ung, the emperors Hsüan-tsung and Tai-tsung, Hui-kuo, the Great Teacher Kōbō, and the Great Teacher Jikaku.[272] And upholding the Nirvana Sutra are Bodhisattva Kashō Dōji, the fifty-two types of beings, and the Tripitaka Master Dharmakṣema. Fa-yün of Kuang-che-ssu temple and the ten eminent priests, three from southern China and seven from northern China, also embraced sutras other than the Lotus Sutra.[273]

But if, in contrast to all these, the common mortals of the evil age that is the Latter Day of the Law, persons who do not observe a single one of the precepts and who appear to others to be *icchantika* or persons of incorrigible disbelief, firmly believe, as the sutra states, that there is no path to Buddhahood outside of the Lotus Sutra, which surpasses all other sutras preached before, at the same time, or after it —then such persons, though they may not have a particle of understanding, are ten thousand billion times superior to those great sages who uphold the other sutras. That is what this passage from the Lotus Sutra is saying.

Among the supporters of the other sutras, there are some who encourage other people to uphold such sutras temporarily as a step toward leading them to the Lotus Sutra. There are others who continue to cling to the other sutras and never move on to the Lotus Sutra. And there are still others who not only continue to uphold the other sutras, but are so intensely attached to them that they even declare the Lotus Sutra to be inferior to such sutras.

But the votary of the Lotus Sutra should now keep the following in mind. The Lotus Sutra says, "Just as the ocean is foremost among all bodies of water such as rivers and streams, so one who upholds the Lotus Sutra will likewise be foremost."[274] It also says, "Just as the god of the moon is foremost among all the heavenly bodies [shining in the night sky], so one who upholds the Lotus Sutra will likewise be foremost."[275] Keep these passages in mind. All of the wise men of Japan at the present time are like the host of stars, and I, Nichiren, am like the full moon.

Question: Is there anyone from times past who has spoken the way you have just done?

Answer: The Great Teacher Dengyō states, "One should understand that the sutras on which the other sects base their teachings are not the first among the sutras, and those persons who uphold such sutras are not the first among the multitude. But the Lotus Sutra, which is upheld by the Tendai-Hokke sect, is the foremost of all the sutras, and therefore those who embrace the Lotus Sutra are first among the multitude. This is borne out by the words of the Buddha himself. How could it be mere self-praise?"[276]

A tick that attaches itself to the tail of a *ch'i-lin*[277] can race a thousand *ri* in one day, and a worthless mortal who accompanies a wheel-turning king can circle in an instant about the four continents of the world. Who would question the truth of such matters? Dengyō's words, "How could it be mere self-praise?" should be kept in mind.

If what he says is correct, then a person who upholds the Lotus Sutra just as it teaches must be superior to the deity Bonten and more worthy than the deity Taishaku. If you have the *asura* demons to help you, you can lift and carry even Mount Sumeru. If you have dragons in your employ, you can drain all the water in the ocean until it runs dry.

The Great Teacher Dengyō says, "Those who praise him [the Great Teacher T'ien-t'ai] will receive blessings that will pile up as high as Mount Sumeru, while those who slander him will be committing a fault that will condemn them to the hell of incessant suffering."[278] And the Lotus Sutra states, "They will despise, hate, envy, and bear grudges against those who read, recite, transcribe, and embrace this sutra. . . . After they die, they will fall into the hell of incessant suffering."[279]

If these golden words of Shakyamuni Buddha are true, if the testimony to their truth given by Tahō Buddha is not false, and if the sign of assent given by the Buddhas of the ten directions when they extended their tongues is to be trusted, then there can be no doubt that all the persons in Japan at the present time are destined to fall into the hell of incessant suffering.

The eighth volume of the Lotus Sutra says, "If in future ages there should be one who accepts and upholds, reads and recites this sutra, . . . his wishes shall not be in vain, and he will receive his reward of good fortune in his present life."[280] And it also says, "If there should be someone who makes offerings to a votary of this sutra and praises him, then he will have manifest reward for it in his present life."[281]

In these two passages are the words "he will receive his reward of good fortune in his present life" and "he will have manifest reward for it in his present life." If these words, which comprise sixteen characters in the original, are meaningless, and if Nichiren does not receive some great reward in this present life, then these golden words of the Buddha will be in the same category as the empty lies of Devadatta, and the testimony of Tahō Buddha which guaranteed their truth will be no different from the baseless assertions of Kokā-lika. Then none of the persons who slander the True Law will ever be condemned to the hell of incessant suffering, and the Buddhas of the three existences of life do not exist! But could such a thing be possible?

Therefore I say to you, my disciples, try practicing as the Lotus Sutra teaches, exerting yourselves without begrudging your lives! Test the truth of Buddhism! Nam-myoho-renge-kyo, Nam-myoho-renge-kyo!

Question: In the Lotus Sutra we find this passage: "We do not hold our own lives dear. We value only the supreme Way."[282] And the Nirvana Sutra says, "For example, if an envoy who is skilled in discussion and knows how to employ clever expedients should be sent to a foreign country to carry out a mission for his sovereign, it is proper that he should relate the words of his ruler without holding back any of them, even though it may cost him his life. And a wise man should do the same in teaching Buddhism, going out among the common run of people, willing to give up his life, and proclaim without fail the Buddha's secret teaching as it is contained in the Mahayana sutras, namely, that all beings possess the Buddha nature."[283] But under what circumstances should one be prepared to sacrifice one's life and safety? I would like you to explain the matter to me in detail.

Answer: When I first embarked upon the Buddhist practice, I

supposed that the statement, "We do not hold our own lives dear," meant receiving the imperial command and traveling to China the way men like Dengyō, Kōbō, Jikaku, and Chishō did, or that it meant setting out from China as Hsüan-tsang did, traveling all the way to India, dying six times in the attempt, and striving again with each rebirth. Or I thought that it meant throwing away one's life the way Sessen Dōji did in order to learn the second half of a verse, or burning one's arms as an offering for seventy-two thousand years the way Bodhisattva Yakuō did.[284] But if we go by the passage of scripture that you have quoted, these are not the kind of thing that is meant.

As to this passage in the sutra, "We do not hold our own lives dear," the sutra earlier describes the three powerful enemies who will vilify and attack one with swords and staves and in all likelihood deprive one of life and safety. And to understand the passage in the Nirvana Sutra that speaks of carrying out one's duty "even though it may cost him his life," we should look at the passage later on in the same sutra that says, "There are persons called *icchantika*, persons of incorrigible disbelief. They pretend to be arhats, living in deserted places and speaking slanderously of the Mahayana sutras. When ordinary people see them, they suppose that they are all true arhats and speak of them as great bodhisattvas."[285]

Speaking of the third of the three powerful enemies, the Lotus Sutra says, "Or there will be forest-dwelling monks wearing clothing of patched rags and living in retirement. . . . They will be respected and revered by the world as though they were arhats who possess the six supernatural powers."[286] And the *Hatsunaion* Sutra says, "There are also *icchantika* who resemble arhats but who commit evil deeds."[287]

These passages from the sutras speak of powerful enemies of the True Law. And such enemies are to be found not so much among evil rulers and evil ministers, or among non-Buddhists and devil kings, or among monks who disobey the precepts. Rather they are those great slanderers of the Law who are to be found among the eminent monks who appear to be upholders of the precepts and men of wisdom.

The Great Teacher Miao-lo, speaking of such men, says, "the third is the most formidable of all. This is because the second is harder to recognize for what it really is, and the third is even harder to recognize."[288]

The fifth volume of the Lotus Sutra says, "This Lotus Sutra is the secret storehouse of Buddhas. Among the sutras, it holds the highest place."[289] In this passage we should note the words "holds the highest place." If we are to believe this passage, then we must say that the true votary of the Lotus Sutra is one who proclaims the Lotus Sutra to be foremost among all the sutras.

Let us suppose now that there are many persons who are held in great respect throughout the nation, and that these persons claim that there are other sutras superior to the Lotus Sutra, disputing with the votary of the Lotus Sutra on this point. These persons enjoy the trust and support of the ruler and his ministers, while the votary of the Lotus Sutra has no influential supporters and has few believers; therefore the whole nation joins in heaping abuse on him. If at that time he conducts himself in the manner of Bodhisattva Fukyō or the scholar Bhadraruci and continues to assert the superiority of the Lotus Sutra, he will almost certainly lose his life. To practice with such resolve in the face of this threat is the most important thing of all.

Now I, Nichiren, am confronting just such a situation. Though I am an ordinary and humble man, I have proclaimed that the Great Teacher Kōbō, the Great Teacher Jikaku, the Tripitaka masters Shan-wu-wei, Chin-kang-chih, Pu-k'ung, and others of their kind are potent enemies of the Lotus Sutra and that, if the words of the sutra are to be trusted, they have without doubt fallen into the hell of incessant suffering. To proclaim such a thing as this is a very grave step. It would be easier to walk naked into a raging fire, easier to take up Mount Sumeru in one's hands and toss it away, easier to hoist a great stone on one's back and walk across the ocean, than to do what I have done. To establish the True Law in this country of Japan is indeed a difficult thing.

If Shakyamuni Buddha of the pure land of Eagle Peak, Tahō Buddha of the land of Treasure Purity, the Buddhas of the ten directions who are Shakyamuni Buddha's emanations, the innumerable bodhisattvas who sprang up out of the earth, Bonten and Taishaku, the gods of the sun and moon, and the Four Heavenly Kings do not, conspicuously or inconspicuously, give me their protection and lend me aid, then they will never know a single day or a single hour of peace and safety!

REPAYING DEBTS OF GRATITUDE

Introduction

Hōon Shō, or "Repaying Debts of Gratitude," is chronologically the last of the five major writings of Nichiren. It is dated the twenty-first day of the seventh month of 1276, a little more than two years after Nichiren had retired to Mount Minobu. It was occasioned by news of the death of Nichiren's first teacher, Dōzen-bō, who had been the chief priest of the Seichō-ji in Awa when Nichiren first entered the temple at the age of twelve. Nichiren wrote this lengthy treatise to express his gratitude toward his first teacher and sent it to Jōken-bō and Gijō-bō, senior monks at the time he entered the temple. Nichiren entrusted this text to one of his disciples and requested that it be read aloud at the Seichō-ji, both at Kasagamori on the summit of Mount Kiyosumi and in front of the tomb of his late teacher.

In 1233 Nichiren had first entered the temple to study Buddhism. At that time temples served as centers of learning as well as religion, and it was at the Seichō-ji that Nichiren gained the basis of his extraordinary literary skills that were to become so much a part of his own teaching technique. At the time the Seichō-ji belonged to the Tendai sect which had long since been infused with the mystic rituals of the esoteric Shingon sect. Dōzen-bō had also become a devotee of Jōdo or Pure Land Buddhism that revered Amida Buddha and his Western Paradise.

At the age of eighteen Nichiren journeyed to Kamakura for study, returning briefly to the Seichō-ji three years later, before setting out for the Tendai center on Mount Hiei near Kyoto. He stayed here and at other temples in Kyoto and Nara, continuing his studies. In 1253 after ten years' absence he returned once again to the Seichō-ji. Arrangements had been made for him to give a sermon on the fruits of his studies at this temple and it was here that he first chanted Nam-myoho-renge-kyo and championed the primacy of the Lotus Sutra. He took the opportunity to denounce the teachings of Pure Land Buddhism, enraging Tōjō Kagenobu, the steward of the area. Troops were sent to arrest Nichiren, but Dōzen-bō, although he could not defend him openly, instructed the senior priests to guide his disciple to safety. It was not until 1264 when Nichiren visited his home in Awa that they met again. Despite his failure to convince his teacher to abandon his belief in Amida, Nichiren felt a genuine gratitude toward him, which the present treatise served to express.

Nichiren begins his treatise by emphasizing the need to repay one's obligations to one's parents, teachers, and one's ruler. To these basic Confucian duties Nichiren adds the need to repay one's obligations to the three treasures of Buddhism. In order to discharge this last obligation one must dedicate oneself single-mindedly to the practice of Buddhism and the attainment of enlightenment. To this end Nichiren traces the development of the various sects of Buddhism in India, China, and Japan, centering on the various sutras that each sect emphasizes. He concludes that only the Lotus Sutra contains the ultimate truth and that this is the teaching that must be propagated in the Latter Day of the Law.

In the concluding portion of this work Nichiren establishes that the Buddhism that he teaches comprises the Three Great Secret Laws *(sandai hihō)*—the invocation or *daimoku (hommon no daimoku)*, the object of worship *(hommon no honzon)*, and the sanctuary or place of worship *(hommon no kaidan)*. These Nichiren found hidden in the text of the *Juryō* (sixteenth) chapter of the Lotus Sutra. The present treatise does not describe the Three Great Secret Laws in detail, but this is the earliest instance in which Nichiren specifies each of the three by name, declaring that this teaching will save people throughout the ten thousand years of the Latter Day of the Law.

The old fox never forgets the hillock where he was born;[1] the white turtle repaid the kindness he had received from Mao Pao.[2] If even lowly creatures know enough to do this, then how much more should human beings! Thus Yü Jang, a worthy man of old, fell on his sword in order to repay the debt he owed his lord Chih Po,[3] and the minister Hung Yen for similar reasons cut open his stomach and inserted the liver of his dead lord, Duke Yi of Wei.[4] What can we say, then, of persons who are devoting themselves to Buddhism? Surely they should not forget the debts of gratitude they owe to their parents, their teachers, and their country.

But if one intends to repay these great debts of gratitude, he can hope to do so only if he studies and masters the Buddhist teachings, becoming a person of wisdom. If he does not, he will be like a man who attempts to lead a company of the blind over bridges and across rivers when he himself has sightless eyes. Can a ship steered by someone who cannot even tell the direction of the wind ever carry the traveling merchants to the mountains where treasure lies?

If one hopes to study and master the Buddhist teachings, then he cannot do so without devoting time to the task. And if he wants to have time to spend on the undertaking, he cannot continue to wait on his parents, his teachers, and his sovereign. Until he attains the road that leads to emancipation, he should not defer to the wishes and feelings of his parents and teachers, no matter how reasonable they may be.

Many people may think that counsel such as this runs counter to secular virtues and also fails to accord with the spirit of Buddhism. But in fact secular texts such as the *Classic of Filial Piety* make clear that there are times when one can be a loyal minister or a filial child only by refusing to obey the wishes of one's sovereign or parents. And in the sacred scriptures of Buddhism it is said, "By renouncing one's obligations and entering nirvana one can truly repay those obligations in full."[5] Pi Kan refused to go along with his sovereign's wishes and thereby came to be known as a worthy man.[6] Crown Prince Siddhārtha disobeyed his father King Śuddhodana and yet became the most outstanding filial son in all the threefold world.[7] These are examples of what I mean.

Once I had understood this and prepared to cease deferring to my parents and teachers and instead to delve into the truths of Buddhism, I found that there are ten bright mirrors that reflect the sacred doctrines of the Buddha's lifetime of teachings. These are the ten sects of Buddhism known as the Kusha, Jōjitsu, Ritsu, Hossō, Sanron, Shingon, Kegon, Jōdo, Zen, and Tendai-Hokke sects.[8] Scholars today believe that, with these ten sects as enlightened teachers, one should understand the heart of all the sacred scriptures, and claim that these ten mirrors all in an accurate manner reflect the path of the Buddha's teachings. However, we may set aside for now the three Hinayana sects [Kusha, Jōjitsu, and Ritsu]. They are like a message that is somehow sent to a foreign country by a private citizen and therefore lacks authority.

But the seven Mahayana sects are a great ship that can carry us across the vast sea of suffering and take us to the shore of the pure land. By studying and understanding them, we can save ourselves and at the same time lead others to salvation. When, with this thought in mind, I began to examine them, I found that each of the seven Mahayana sects sings its own praises, saying, "Our sect and our sect alone represents the very heart of the Buddha's lifetime of teaching!"

There are men such as Tu-shun, Chih-yen, Fa-tsang, and Ch'eng-kuan⁹ of the Kegon school, Hsüan-tsang, Tz'u-en, Chih-chou, and Chishō¹⁰ of the Hossō sect; Hsing-huang and Chia-hsiang¹¹ of the Sanron school; Shan-wu-wei, Chin-kang-chih, Pu-k'ung, Kōbō, Ji-kaku, and Chishō¹² of the Shingon sect; Bodhidharma, Hui-k'o, and Hui-neng¹³ of the Zen sect; and Tao-ch'o, Shan-tao, Huai-kan, and Genkū [Hōnen]¹⁴ of the Jōdo sect. Basing themselves on the particular sutras and treatises favored by their respective sects, these leaders of the various sects all claim that "our sect" understands all of the myriad sutras, that "our sect" has grasped the innermost meaning of the Buddha's teachings.

Thus, some of these men claim, "The *Kegon* Sutra is first among all the sutras; other sutras such as the Lotus and the *Dainichi* are its underlings." Again, the leaders of the Shingon sect claim, "The *Dainichi* or Great Sun Sutra is first among all the sutras; the other sutras are like crowds of little stars." The men of the Zen sect say, "The *Ryōga* Sutra is first among all the sutras." And so forth for the men of the various other sects. The many Buddhist teachers whose names I have listed above are honored by the people of our time, who pay reverence to them in the way that all the heavenly deities pay reverence to the god Taishaku and follow them in the way the hosts of stars follow the sun and the moon.

For ordinary people like us, whomever we may take as our teacher, if we have faith in him, then we will not think him inadequate in any way. But though others may still revere and believe [in the teachers of their respective sects], I, Nichiren, have found it difficult to dispel my doubts.

When we look at the world, we find each of the various sects saying, "We are the one, we are the one!" But within a nation, there can be only one man who is sovereign. If two men try to be sovereign, the country will know no peace. Likewise, if one house has two masters, it will surely face destruction. Must it not be the same with the sutras?

Among the various sutras, there must be one that is the monarch of all. Yet the ten sects and seven sects I have mentioned all argue with each other over which of the sutras it is and can reach no consensus. It is as though seven men or ten men were all trying to be the monarch of a single nation, thus keeping the populace in constant turmoil.

Wondering how to resolve this dilemma, I made a vow. I decided that I would not heed the claims of these eight or ten sects, but would do as the Great Teacher T'ien-t'ai did and let the sutras themselves be my sole teacher, in this way determining which of the various teachings of the Buddha's lifetime are superior and which are inferior. With this in mind, I began to read through all the sutras.

In a scripture called the Nirvana Sutra, the Buddha says, "Rely on the Law and not upon persons."[15] Relying on the Law here means relying on the various sutras. Not relying upon persons means not relying on persons other than the Buddha, such as Bodhisattvas Fugen and Monjushiri or the various Buddhist teachers I have enumerated earlier.

In the same sutra, the Buddha also says, "Rely on the sutras that are complete and final and not on those which are not complete and final."[16] When he speaks of the "sutras that are complete and final," he is referring to the Lotus Sutra, and when he speaks of "those which are not complete and final," he means the *Kegon, Dainichi,* Nirvana, and other sutras preached before, during, and after the preaching of the Lotus Sutra.

If we are to believe these dying words of the Buddha, we must conclude that the Lotus Sutra is the only bright mirror we should have, and that through it we can understand the heart of all the sutras.

Accordingly, let us turn to the text of the Lotus Sutra itself. There we find it stated that "This Lotus Sutra [is the secret storehouse of Buddhas]. Among the sutras, it holds the highest place."[17] If we accept these words of the sutra, then, like Taishaku dwelling on the peak of Mount Sumeru, like the wish-granting jewel that crowns the wheel-turning kings,[18] like the moon that dwells above the forest of trees, like the fleshy protuberance that tops the head of a Buddha[19] so the Lotus Sutra stands like a wish-granting jewel crowning the *Kegon, Dainichi,* Nirvana, and all the other sutras.

If we set aside the pronouncements of the scholars and teachers and rely upon the text of the sutra, then we can see that the Lotus Sutra is superior to the *Dainichi, Kegon,* and all the other sutras as plainly and as easily as a sighted person can distinguish heaven from earth when the sun is shining in a clear blue sky.

And if we examine the texts of the *Dainichi, Kegon,* and the other sutras, we will find that there is not a word or even a dot in them that resembles the above-cited passage of the Lotus Sutra. True, at times they speak about the superiority of the Mahayana sutras as compared to the Hinayana sutras, or of the Buddhist truth as opposed to secular truth, or they praise the truth of the Middle Way as opposed to the various views that phenomena are non-substantial or that they have only provisional existence. But in fact they are like the rulers of petty kingdoms who, when addressing their subjects, speak of themselves as great kings. It is the Lotus Sutra that, in comparison to these various rulers, is the true Great King.

The Nirvana Sutra alone of all the sutras has passages that resemble those of the Lotus Sutra. For this reason, the Buddhist scholars who preceded T'ien-t'ai in both northern and southern China were led astray into declaring that the Lotus Sutra is inferior to the Nirvana Sutra. But if we examine the text of the Nirvana Sutra itself, we will find that, as in the *Muryōgi* Sutra, the comparison is being made between the Nirvana Sutra and the sutras of the Kegon, Agon, Hōdō, and Hannya periods that were expounded during the first forty or more years of the Buddha's preaching life. It is in comparison to these earlier sutras that the Nirvana Sutra declares itself to be superior.

Moreover, the Nirvana Sutra, comparing itself with the Lotus Sutra, says, "When this [Nirvana] sutra was preached . . . the prediction had already been made in the Lotus Sutra that the eight thousand *shōmon* disciples would attain Buddhahood,[20] a prediction which was like a great harvest. Thus, the autumn harvest was over and the crop had been stored away for winter [when this Nirvana Sutra was expounded], and there was nothing left for it [but a few gleanings]."[21] This passage from the Nirvana is saying that the Nirvana is inferior to the Lotus Sutra.

The above passages [from the Lotus and Nirvana sutras] are perfectly clear on this point. Nevertheless, even the great scholars of northern and southern China went astray, so students of later ages should take care to examine them very thoroughly. For the passage [from the Lotus Sutra] not only establishes the superiority of the Lotus Sutra over the Nirvana Sutra, but indicates its superiority over all other sutras in the worlds of the ten directions.

Earlier, there were those who were misled concerning these passages, but after such great teachers as T'ien-t'ai, Miao-lo, and Dengyō had clearly indicated their meaning, one would suppose that any person with eyes would understand them. Nevertheless, even such men as Jikaku and Chishō of the Tendai sect failed to understand these passages correctly, so what can one expect from the members of the other sects?

Someone might doubt my words, saying that, although the Lotus Sutra is the finest among all the sutras that have been brought to China and Japan, in India and in the realms of the dragon kings, the Four Heavenly Kings, the sun and the moon, the Trayastriṁśā Heaven, or the Tuṣita Heaven,[22] there are as many sutras as there are sands in the Ganges. Among these, may there not be one that is superior to the Lotus Sutra?

I would reply that by looking at one thing, you can surmise ten thousand. This is what is meant by the statement that you can come to know all under heaven without ever going out of your garden gate. But a fool will have doubts, saying, "I have seen the sky in the south, but I have not seen the sky in the east or west or north. Perhaps the sky in those other three directions has a different sun in it from the one I know." Or he will see a column of smoke rising up beyond the hills, and, although the smoke is in plain sight, because he cannot see the fire itself, he will conclude that the fire may not really exist. Such a person is my questioner, an *icchantika* or man of incorrigible disbelief, no different from a man with sightless eyes!

In the *Hosshi* chapter of the Lotus Sutra, Shakyamuni Buddha, uttering words of absolute sincerity from his golden mouth, establishes the relative superiority of the various sutras he expounded during the fifty or more years of his preaching life, saying, "The scriptures I preach number in the countless millions. Among all those I have preached, now preach, and will preach, this Lotus Sutra is the most difficult to believe and the most difficult to understand."[23]

Though this scripture, the Lotus Sutra, was preached by a single Buddha, Shakyamuni, all the bodhisattvas from the stage of *tōgaku*[24] on down should honor it and have faith in it. For the Buddha Tahō came from the east and testified to the truth of the sutra, and all other Buddhas assembled from the ten directions and stretched their long, broad tongues up to the Brahma Heaven just as Shakyamuni did.[25] Afterward, they all returned to their respective lands.

The words "have preached, now preach, and will preach" include not only the sutras preached by Shakyamuni in his fifty years of teaching, but all the sutras preached by all the Buddhas of the ten directions and three existences without setting aside a single character or even a single dot. It is in comparison to all of these that the Lotus Sutra is proclaimed to be superior. At that time all the Buddhas of the ten directions indicated their agreement. If, after they had returned to their respective lands, they had told their disciples that there was in fact a sutra that is superior to the Lotus Sutra, do you suppose their disciples would ever have believed them?

If there are those who, though they have not seen it with their own eyes, nevertheless suspect that there may be a sutra superior to the Lotus Sutra somewhere in India or in the palaces of the dragon kings, the Four Heavenly Kings, or the gods of the sun and moon, I would say this. Were not Bonten and Taishaku, the gods of the sun and moon, the Four Heavenly Kings, and the dragon kings present when Shakyamuni preached the Lotus Sutra? If the sun and the moon and the other deities should say, "There is a sutra superior to the Lotus Sutra; you merely do not know about it," then they would be a sun and moon who speak great falsehoods!

In that case, I would berate them, saying, "Sun and moon, you dwell up in the sky rather than on the ground as we do, and yet you never fall down—this is because of the power you gain by observing most strictly the precept of never telling a lie. But now if you tell this great lie by saying there is a sutra superior to the Lotus Sutra, I am certain that, even before the Kalpa of Decline[26] arrives, you will come plummeting down to earth. What is more, you will not stop falling until you have reached the depths of the great citadel of the hell of incessant suffering which is surrounded by solid iron! Beings who tell such great lies should not be allowed to remain a moment longer in the sky, circling above the four continents of the earth!" That is how I would berate them.

Yet such men of great wisdom, such great teachers and Tripitaka masters as Ch'eng-kuan of the Kegon school or Shan-wu-wei, Chin-kang-chih, Pu-k'ung, Kōbō, Jikaku, and Chishō of the Shingon sect, proclaim that the *Kegon* and *Dainichi* sutras are superior to the Lotus

Sutra. Though it is not for me to judge in such matters, I would say that, in the light of the higher principles of Buddhism, such men would appear to be archenemies of the Buddhas, would they not? Beside them, evil men such as Devadatta and Kokālika[27] are as nothing. In fact they are in a class with Mahādeva and the Great Arrogant Brahman.[28] And those who put faith in the teachings of such men—they too are a fearful lot indeed.

Question: Do you really proclaim that Ch'eng-kuan of the Kegon school, Chia-hsiang of the Sanron school, Tz'u-en of the Hossō school, and Shan-wu-wei and the others of the Shingon school on down to Kōbō, Jikaku, and Chishō are the enemies of the Buddha?

Answer: This is a very important question, a matter of the gravest concern to the Buddhist Law. Yet, on examining the text of the sutra, I find that if someone should declare that there is a sutra superior to the Lotus Sutra, then, regardless of who that person may be, he cannot escape the charge of slandering the Law. Therefore, if we go by what the sutra says, then persons such as this must be regarded as enemies of the Buddha. And if out of fear I fail to point out this fact, then the distinctions of relative merit made among the various sutras will all have been made in vain.

If, out of awe of these great teachers of the past, I should simply point at their latter-day followers and call them enemies of the Buddha, then these latter-day followers of the various sects would say, "The assertion that the *Dainichi* Sutra is superior to the Lotus Sutra is not something that we ourselves invented on our own. It is the doctrine taught by the patriarchs of our sect. Though we may be no match for them in observing the precepts, in wisdom and understanding, or in status, when it comes to the doctrines that they taught, we never diverge from them in the slightest." And in that case, one would have to admit that they are guilty of no fault.

Nevertheless, if I know that this assertion is false and yet, out of fear of others, I fail to say so, then I will be ignoring the stern warning of the Buddha, who said, "He should never hold back any of the teachings, even though it may cost him his life."[29]

What am I to do? If I speak up, I face fearful opposition from the world at large. But if I am silent, I can hardly escape the condemnation of failing to heed the Buddha's stern warning. Forward or backward, my way is blocked.

Yet perhaps it is only to be expected. For, as the Lotus Sutra states, "Since hatred and jealousy toward this sutra abound even during the lifetime of the Buddha, how much worse will it be in the world after his passing?"[30] Again elsewhere, "The people will resent [the Lotus Sutra] and find it extremely difficult to believe."[31]

When Shakyamuni Buddha had been conceived by his mother Queen Māyā, the Devil of the Sixth Heaven gazed down into Queen Māyā's womb and said, "My archenemy, the sharp sword of the Lotus Sutra, has been conceived. Before the birth can take place, I must do something to destroy it!" Then the devil transformed himself into a learned physician, entered the palace of King Śuddhodana and said, "I am a learned physician and I have brought some excellent medicine that will insure the safe delivery of the child." In this way he attempted to poison the queen.[32]

When the Buddha was born, the devil caused stones to rain down on him and mixed poison in his milk. Later, when the Buddha left the palace to enter the religious life, the devil changed himself into a black venomous serpent and tried to block his way. In addition, he entered the bodies of such evil men as Devadatta, Kokālika, King Virūḍhaka and King Ajātaśatru, inciting them to hurl a great stone at the Buddha which injured him and drew blood, or to kill many of the Shakyas, the Buddha's clansmen, or murder his disciples.[33]

These great persecutions were planned long ago, schemes that were designed to prevent the Buddha, the World-Honored One, from preaching the Lotus Sutra. It is persecutions such as these that the sutra means when it says, "Hatred and jealousy . . . abound even during the lifetime of the Buddha."

In addition to these troubles arising long before the Buddha preached the Lotus Sutra, there were others that occurred later when he expounded the sutra itself. [These were the doubts that arose when Shakyamuni revealed that] for forty-some years, Śāriputra, Maudgalyāyana, and the great bodhisattvas had in fact been among the archenemies of the Lotus Sutra.[34]

But the sutra says, "How much worse will it be in the world after his passing!"[35] By this we know that, in a latter age after the death of the Buddha, there are bound to be persecutions and difficulties even greater and more fearful than those that occurred during his lifetime. If even the Buddha had difficulty bearing up under such persecutions, how can ordinary human beings be expected to bear them, particularly when these troubles are destined to be even greater than those that occurred during the Buddha's lifetime?

Though one might wonder what great persecutions could possibly be more terrible than the huge rock thirty feet long and sixteen feet wide that Devadatta rolled down on the Buddha or the drunken elephant that King Ajātaśatru sent charging after him,[36] if persecutions greater than those that arose during the Buddha's lifetime keep occurring again and again to someone who is not guilty of the slightest fault, then one should realize that that person is a true votary of the Lotus Sutra in the age after the Buddha's passing.

The successors of the Buddha were among the four ranks of bodhisattvas; they were messengers of the Buddha. Yet Bodhisattva Āryadeva was killed by a Brahman, the Venerable Āryasiṃha had his head cut off by King Dammira, Buddhamitra had to stand for twelve years under a red flag before he could attract the notice of the ruler, and Bodhisattva Nāgārjuna had to stand seven years under a similar flag. Bodhisattva Aśvaghoṣa was sold to an enemy country for the sum of three hundred thousand coins, and the scholar Manoratha died of chagrin. These are examples of troubles that took place in the thousand years of the Former Day of the Law.[37]

We come now to a time five hundred years after the beginning of the Middle Day of the Law or one thousand five hundred years after the death of the Buddha. At that time in China there was a wise man who was at first known as Chih-i and later as the Great Teacher T'ien-t'ai Chih-che. He determined to spread the teachings of the Lotus Sutra in their true form. There had been thousands and thousands of wise men who preceded T'ien-t'ai, and they had held various opinions concerning the teachings set forth by the Buddha in his lifetime, but in general, they were grouped into ten schools or traditions, the so-called three schools of the south and seven schools of the north. Of these, one school emerged as foremost among them. This was the third of the three southern schools, the school of the Dharma Teacher Fa-yün of the temple called Kuang-che-ssu.[38]

Fa-yün divided the teachings of the Buddha's lifetime into five periods. From among the teachings of these five periods, he selected three sutras, the *Kegon,* the Nirvana, and the Lotus. He declared that, among all the sutras, the *Kegon* Sutra ranks first and is comparable to the monarch of a kingdom. The Nirvana Sutra ranks second and is like the regent or prime minister, while the Lotus Sutra ranks third and is like one of the court nobles. All the other sutras are inferior to these and are comparable to the common people.

Fa-yün was by nature a man of outstanding wisdom. Not only did he study under such great teachers as Hui-kuan, Hui-yen, Seng-jou and Hui-tz'u,[39] but he refuted the doctrines of various teachers of the northern and southern schools, and retired to the seclusion of the mountain forest, where he devoted himself to the study of the Lotus, Nirvana, and *Kegon* sutras.

As a result, Emperor Wu of the Liang dynasty summoned him to court and had a temple called Kuang-che-ssu built for him within the palace grounds, paying him great honor. When Fa-yün lectured on the Lotus Sutra, flowers fell down from the heavens just as they had done when Shakyamuni Buddha first preached it.

In the fifth year of the T'ien-chien era (506 A.D.), there was a great drought. The emperor had the Dharma Teacher Fa-yün lecture on the Lotus Sutra, and when he reached the verses in the *Yakusōyu* chapter that read, "The rain, spread equally,/in all four directions comes down,"[40] soft rain began to fall from the sky. The emperor was so overwhelmed with admiration that he appointed Fa-yün on the spot to the rank of Administrator of Monks (*sōjō*), and he served him in person as the various deities served the god Taishaku and as the common people look up in awe to their sovereign. In addition, it was revealed to someone in a dream that Fa-yün had been lecturing on the Lotus Sutra ever since the time of the Buddha named Tōmyō[41] in the distant past.

Fa-yün wrote a commentary in four volumes on the Lotus Sutra. In this commentary he stated, "This sutra is not truly eminent," and spoke of it as "an unusual expedient."[42] By this he meant that the Lotus Sutra does not fully reveal the truth of Buddhism.

Was it because Fa-yün's teachings met with the approval of the Buddha that the flowers and the rain came down on him from the sky? In any event, as a result of the wonderful and unusual things that happened to him, the people of China came to believe that the Lotus Sutra was in fact perhaps inferior to the *Kegon* and Nirvana sutras. This commentary by Fa-yün was in time disseminated to the kingdoms of Silla, Paekche, and Koguryŏ in Korea and to Japan, where people in general came to hold the same opinion as that prevalent in China.

Shortly after the death of Fa-yün, in the latter years of the Liang dynasty and the early years of the Ch'en, there appeared a young priest known as the Dharma Teacher Chih-i. He was a disciple of the Great Teacher Nan-yüeh, but perhaps because he wished to clarify his understanding of his teacher's doctrines, he entered the storehouse where the scriptures were kept and examined the texts again and again. He singled out the *Kegon,* Nirvana, and Lotus sutras as worthy of special attention, and of these three, he lectured on the *Kegon* Sutra in particular. In addition, he compiled a book of devotional exercises[43] in honor of the Buddha Vairocana of the *Kegon* Sutra and day after day furthered his understanding of this sutra. The people of his time supposed that he did this because he considered the *Kegon* Sutra to be the foremost of all sutras. In fact, however, he did it because he had grave doubts about Fa-yün's assertion that the *Kegon* Sutra was to be ranked first, the Nirvana Sutra second, and the Lotus Sutra third, and he therefore wished to make a particularly close examination of the *Kegon* Sutra.

After he had done so, he concluded that, among all the sutras, the Lotus Sutra was to be ranked first, the Nirvana Sutra second, and the *Kegon* Sutra third. He also announced in sorrow that, although the sacred teachings of the Buddha had spread throughout the land of China, they had failed to bring benefit to its inhabitants but on the contrary caused people to stray into the evil states of existence. This, he concluded, was due to the errors of their teachers.

It was as though the leaders of the nation had told the people that east is west, or that heaven is earth, and the common people had accepted their assertions and believed accordingly. Later, if some person of humble stature should come forward and tell them that what they called west was really east, or that what they called heaven was really earth, they would not only refuse to believe him, but they would curse and attack him in order to ingratiate themselves with their leaders.

Chih-i pondered what to do about the situation. He felt that he could not remain silent, and he therefore spoke out in severe condemnation of Fa-yün of Kuang-che temple, asserting that, because of his slanders against the True Law, he had fallen into hell. With that, the Buddhist teachers of the north and south rose up like angry hornets and descended on him like a flock of crows.

Some proposed that Chih-i should have his head smashed; others, that he should be driven out of the country. The ruler of the Ch'en dynasty, hearing of what was going on, summoned a number of Buddhist leaders from north and south and had them appear in his presence along with Chih-i so that he could listen to the proceedings. There were such monks as Hui-yung, a disciple of Fa-yün, and Fa-sui, Hui-k'uang, and Hui-heng,[44] over a hundred men, all of the rank of Supervisor of Monks (*sōzu*), Administrator of Monks, or higher.

They struggled to outdo each other in speaking ill of Chih-i, raising their eyebrows and glaring angrily, or clapping their hands in an impatient rhythm.

Chih-i, though he was seated in a humble position far below the others, showed no sign of emotion and made no slip of speech. Instead, with quiet dignity he took notes on each of the charges and assertions made by the other monks and succeeded in refuting them. Then he began to attack his opponents, saying, "According to the teachings of Fa-yün, the *Kegon* Sutra ranks first, the Nirvana Sutra second, and the Lotus Sutra third. In what sutra is the proof of this to be found? Please produce a passage that gives clear and certain proof of this!" Pressed in this way, the other monks all lowered their heads and turned pale, unable to say a word in reply.

He continued to press them, saying, "In the *Muryōgi* Sutra, the Buddha mentions how he 'then preached the twelve divisions of the *Hōdō* sutras, the *Makahannya* Sutra, and the *Kegon* Sutra deriving from the [Buddha's] ocean-imprint meditation.'[45] Thus the Buddha himself mentions the *Kegon* Sutra by name and denies its worth, saying that in these sutras preached before the *Muryōgi* Sutra, 'I have not yet revealed the truth.' If in the *Muryōgi* Sutra, which is inferior to the Lotus Sutra, the *Kegon* Sutra is attacked in this way, then what grounds could there be for asserting that the *Kegon* Sutra represents the highest achievement of the Buddha's preaching life? Gentlemen, if you wish to show your loyalty to your teacher, then please produce some scriptural passage that will refute and override this passage I have cited from the *Muryōgi* Sutra and vindicate your teacher's doctrines!

"And on what passage of scripture do you base your assertion that the Nirvana Sutra is superior to the Lotus Sutra? In the fourteenth volume of the Nirvana Sutra, there is a discussion of the relative merit of the Nirvana Sutra in comparison to the sutras of the Kegon, Agon, Hōdō, and Hannya periods, but no mention whatsoever of its merit in comparison to the Lotus Sutra.

"Earlier in the same sutra, however, in the ninth volume, the relative merits of the Nirvana and Lotus sutras are made abundantly clear. The passage states, 'When this [Nirvana] sutra was preached, . . . the prediction had already been made in the Lotus Sutra that the eight thousand *shōmon* disciples would attain Buddhahood, a prediction which was like a great harvest. Thus, the autumn harvest was over and the crop had been stored away for winter [when this Nirvana Sutra was expounded], and there was nothing left for it [but a few gleanings].'

"This passage makes clear that the other sutras were the work of spring and summer, while the Nirvana and Lotus sutras were like a ripening or fruition. But while the Lotus Sutra was like a great fruition in which the harvest is gathered in autumn and stored away for winter, the Nirvana Sutra was like the gleaning of the fallen grain that takes place at the end of autumn and the beginning of winter.

"In this passage, the Nirvana Sutra is in effect acknowledging that it is inferior to the Lotus Sutra. And the Lotus Sutra speaks about the sutras that have already been preached, are presently being preached, and are to be preached in the future. By this, the Buddha is indicating that the Lotus Sutra is not only superior to the sutras preached before it as well as those preached at the same time, but is also superior to those he will preach afterward.

"If the Lord Shakyamuni laid it down so clearly, what room could there be for doubt? Nevertheless, because he was concerned about what might happen after his passing, he determined to have Tahō Buddha of the land of Treasure Purity in the east act as a witness to the truth of his words. Therefore, Tahō Buddha sprang forth from out of the earth and testified to the verity of the Lotus Sutra, saying, 'All that you [Shakyamuni Buddha] have expounded is the truth.'[46] In addition, various Buddhas from the ten directions who were emanations of Shakyamuni Buddha gathered around and put forth their long, broad tongues until the tips reached to the Brahma Heaven, as did Shakyamuni's, in witness to the truth of the teachings.

"After that, Tahō Buddha returned to the land of Treasure Purity, and the various Buddhas who were emanations of Shakyamuni returned to their respective lands in the ten directions. Then, when neither Tahō Buddha nor the emanations were present, Lord Shakyamuni preached the Nirvana Sutra. If he claimed that the Nirvana Sutra is superior to the Lotus Sutra, would his disciples in fact have believed such a thing?"[47]

This was the way Chih-i, the Great Teacher T'ien-t'ai, chided them. He was like the brilliant light of the sun and moon striking the eyes of the *asuras,* or the sword of the King of Han[48] pressing against the necks of his barons, and his opponents accordingly closed their eyes tightly and let their heads droop. In his appearance and manner, T'ien-t'ai was like the lion king roaring at foxes and rabbits, or like a hawk or an eagle swooping down on doves and pheasants.

As a result, the fact that the Lotus Sutra is superior to the *Kegon* and Nirvana sutras became known not only throughout the whole of China, but word of it also spread to the five regions of India.[49] There the Indian treatises of both the Mahayana and Hinayana divisions of Buddhism were inferior to T'ien-t'ai's doctrine, and the people there praised him, wondering if the Lord Shakyamuni had appeared in the world once again, or whether Buddhism would now have a second beginning.

In time the Great Teacher T'ien-t'ai passed away, and the Ch'en and Sui dynasties came to an end and were replaced by the T'ang dynasty. T'ien-t'ai's successor, the Great Teacher Chang-an, also passed away, and there were few who continued to study the type of Buddhism taught by T'ien-t'ai.

Then, in the reign of Emperor T'ai-tsung,[50] there appeared a monk named the Tripitaka Master Hsüan-tsang. He journeyed to India in the third year of the Chen-kuan era (629) and returned in the nineteenth year of the same era (645). During his journey, he conducted a thorough investigation of Buddhism in India and on his return introduced to China the school known as Hossō.

This school is to the T'ien-t'ai or Tendai sect as fire is to water. Hsüan-tsang brought with him works such as the *Jimmitsu* Sutra, the *Yuga Ron,* and the *Yuishiki Ron*[51] that were unknown to T'ien-t'ai, and claimed that, although the Lotus Sutra is superior to the other sutras, it is inferior to the *Jimmitsu* Sutra. Since this was a text that T'ien-t'ai had never seen, his followers in these later times, shallow as they were in wisdom and understanding, seemed inclined to accept this allegation.

Moreover, Emperor T'ai-tsung was a wise ruler, but he placed extraordinary faith in the teachings of Hsüan-tsang. As a result, though there were those who might have wished to speak out in protest, they were, as is too often the case, awed by the authority of the throne and held their peace. Thus, regrettable as it is to relate, the Lotus Sutra was thrust aside. Hsüan-tsang taught that if people have the capacity to understand the three vehicles, then the one vehicle[52] can be no more than an expedient to instruct them, and the three vehicles, the only true way of enlightening them, along with the theory of the five natures[53] into which all beings are inherently divided.

Though these new teachings came from India, the home of Buddhism, it was as though the non-Buddhist teachings of India had invaded the land of China. The Lotus Sutra was declared to be a mere expedient teaching, and the *Jimmitsu* Sutra, the embodiment of the truth. Thus the testimony given by Shakyamuni, Tahō, and the other Buddhas of the ten directions was totally ignored, and instead Hsüan-tsang and his disciple Tz'u-en were looked upon as living Buddhas.

Later, during the reign of Empress Wu,[54] a monk called the Dharma Teacher Fa-tsang[55] appeared who, in order to vent his anger over the attacks that had been made earlier by the Great Teacher T'ien-t'ai on the *Kegon* Sutra, founded a new school called the Kegon school. In doing so, he utilized a new translation of the *Kegon* Sutra[56] that had recently been completed, using it to supplement the older translation of the *Kegon* Sutra that had been the target of T'ien-t'ai's attack. This school proclaimed that the *Kegon* Sutra represents the "root teaching" of the Buddha, while the Lotus Sutra represents the "branch teachings."

To sum up, the teachers in northern and southern China ranked the *Kegon* Sutra first, the Nirvana Sutra second, and the Lotus Sutra third. T'ien-t'ai ranked the Lotus first, the Nirvana second, and the *Kegon* third. And the newly founded Kegon school ranked the *Kegon* first, the Lotus second, and the Nirvana third.

Later, in the reign of Emperor Hsüan-tsung, the Tripitaka Master Shan-wu-wei journeyed to China from India, bringing with him the *Dainichi* and *Soshitsuji* sutras. In addition, the Tripitaka Master Chin-kang-chih appeared with the *Kongōchō* Sutra.[57] Moreover, Chin-kang-chih had a disciple named the Tripitaka Master Pu-k'ung.

These three men were all Indians who not only came from very distinguished families but who were in character quite different from the priests of China. The doctrines that they taught appeared highly impressive in that they included mudras and mantras, something that had never been known in China since the introduction of Buddhism in the Later Han. In the presence of this new Buddhism, the emperor bowed his head and the common people pressed their palms together in reverence.

These men taught that, whatever the relative merits of the *Kegon, Jimmitsu, Hannya,* Nirvana, and Lotus sutras might be, they were all exoteric teachings, the various preachings of Shakyamuni Buddha. The *Dainichi* Sutra which they had newly introduced, on the other hand, represented the royal pronouncements of Dainichi or Mahā-vairocana, the Dharma King. The other sutras were the multiple sayings of the common people; this sutra was the unique pronouncement of the Son of Heaven. Works such as the *Kegon* and Nirvana sutras could never hope to reach as high as the *Dainichi* Sutra even with the help of a ladder. Only the Lotus Sutra bears some resemblance to the *Dainichi* Sutra.

Nevertheless, the Lotus Sutra was preached by Shakyamuni Buddha and thus represents merely the truth as spoken by a commoner, where the *Dainichi* Sutra represents the truth as spoken by the Son of Heaven. Hence, although the words resemble each other, the persons who spoke them are as far apart as the clouds in the sky and the mud on the earth. The difference between them is like the moon that is reflected in muddy water on the one hand and in clear water on the other. Both alike are reflections of the moon, yet the nature of the water that catches the reflection is vastly different.

Such were the assertions put forth by these men, and no one attempted to examine them carefully or make clear their true nature. Instead, the other schools of Buddhism all bowed down and acknowledged themselves subservient to this new school called the Shingon.

After Shan-wu-wei and Chin-kang-chih died, Pu-k'ung made a trip to India and brought back to China a treatise entitled *Bodaishin Ron*,[58] and the Shingon school grew all the more influential.

In the Tendai school, however, there appeared a priest known as the Great Teacher Miao-lo. Though he lived more than two hundred years after the time of the Great Teacher T'ien-t'ai, he was extremely wise and had a clear understanding of the teachings of T'ien-t'ai. Thus he perceived, from the heart of T'ien-t'ai's interpretations, that the Lotus Sutra is superior to the *Jimmitsu* Sutra and the Hossō school —which had been introduced to China after T'ien-t'ai's time—as well as to the Kegon school and the Shingon school with its *Dainichi* Sutra, both schools which had first been established in China.

Up until then, either because T'ien-t'ai's followers lacked the wisdom to see what was wrong, or because they feared others or were in awe of the ruler's power, no one had spoken out. It was clear that a correct understanding of the teachings of T'ien-t'ai was about to be lost, and that the errors and heresies that were rife surpassed even those that had prevailed in northern and southern China in the period before the Ch'en and Sui dynasties. Therefore Miao-lo compiled commentaries on T'ien-t'ai's works in thirty volumes, the writings known as *Guketsu, Shakusen,* and *Shoki*.[59] These thirty volumes of commentary served not only to eliminate passages of repetition in

T'ien-t'ai's works and to elucidate points that were unclear, but at the same time in one stroke they refuted the Hossō, Kegon, and Shingon schools, which had escaped T'ien-t'ai's censures because they did not exist in China during his lifetime.

Turning now to Japan, we find that in the reign of the thirtieth sovereign Emperor Kimmei, on the thirteenth day of the tenth month in the thirteenth year of his reign (552), cyclical sign *mizunoe-saru,* a copy of the Buddhist scriptures and a statue of Shakyamuni Buddha were brought to Japan from the Korean kingdom of Paekche. And in the reign of Emperor Yōmei, Crown Prince Shōtoku began the study of Buddhism. He dispatched a court official named Wake no Imoko to go to China and bring back the copy of the Lotus Sutra in one volume that had belonged to him in a previous life,[60] and expressed his determination to honor and protect the sutra.

Later, by the reign of the thirty-seventh sovereign Emperor Kōtoku, the Sanron, Kegon, Hossō, Kusha, and Jōjitsu sects were introduced to Japan, and in the time of the forty-fifth sovereign Emperor Shōmu, the Ritsu sect was introduced, thus making a total of six sects. But during the time from Emperor Kōtoku to the reign of the fiftieth sovereign Emperor Kammu, a period of over 120 years during which fourteen sovereigns reigned, the Tendai and Shingon sects had not yet been introduced.

During the reign of Emperor Kammu, there was a young priest named Saichō who was a disciple of the Administrator of Monks Gyōhyō[61] of Yamashina-dera. He made a thorough study of Hossō and the others of the six sect mentioned above, but he felt that he had yet to reach a true understanding of Buddhism. Then he came upon a commentary which the Dharma Teacher Fa-tsang of the Kegon school had written on the *Kishin Ron,*[62] and in it were quotations from the works of the Great Teacher T'ien-t'ai.

These works of T'ien-t'ai seemed to be worthy of special attention, but Saichō did not even know whether they had yet been brought to Japan or not. When he questioned someone about this, the person replied that there had been a priest named Chien-chen[63] of the temple called Lung-hsing-ssu in Yang-chou in China who had studied the T'ien-t'ai teachings and had been a disciple of the Discipline Master Tao-hsien.[64] In the latter part of the Tempyō-Shōhō era (753), he came to Japan, where he worked to spread a knowledge of the Hinayana rules of monastic discipline. He had brought with him copies of the works of T'ien-t'ai, but had not attempted to disseminate them. All this took place, Saichō was told, during the time of the forty-fifth sovereign Emperor Shōmu.

When Saichō asked if he could see these writings, they were brought out and shown to him. On his first perusal of them, he felt as though he had been awakened from all the delusions of birth and death. And when he began to consider the basic doctrines of the six sects of earlier Buddhism in the light of what he found in these writings, it became apparent that each of the sects was guilty of doctrinal error.

Immediately he vowed to do something about the situation, saying, "Because the people of Japan are all patrons of those who are slandering the True Law, the nation will surely fall into chaos!" He thereupon expressed his criticisms of the six sects, but when he did so, the great scholars of the six sects and the seven major temples of Nara rose up in anger and flocked to the capital, until the nation was in an uproar.

These men of the six sects and seven major temples were filled with the most intense animosity toward Saichō. But as it happened, on the nineteenth day of the first month of the twenty-first year of the Enryaku era (802), Emperor Kammu paid a visit to the temple called Takao-dera, and he summoned fourteen eminent priests— namely, Zengi, Shōyū, Hōki, Chōnin, Kengyoku, Ampuku, Gonsō, Shūen, Jikō, Gen'yō, Saikō, Dōshō, Kōshō, and Kambin[65]—to come to the temple and debate with Saichō.

These various men of the Kegon, Sanron, Hossō, and other sects expounded the teachings of the founders of their respective sects just as they had learned them. But Saichō took notes on each point put forward by the men of the six sects and criticized it in the light of the Lotus Sutra, the works of T'ien-t'ai, or other sutras and treatises. His opponents were unable to say a word in reply, their mouths as incapable of speech as if they were noses.

The emperor was astounded and questioned Saichō in detail on various points. Thereafter he handed down an edict criticizing the fourteen men who had opposed Saichō.

They in turn submitted a memorial acknowledging their defeat and apologizing, in which they said, "We, students of the seven major temples and six sects, . . . have for the first time understood the ultimate truth."

They also said, "In the two hundred or more years since Crown Prince Shōtoku spread the Buddhist teachings in this country, a great many sutras and treatises have been lectured upon and their principles have been widely argued, but until now, many doubts still remained to be settled. Moreover, the lofty and perfect doctrine of the Lotus Sutra had not yet been properly explained and made known."

They also said, "Now at last the dispute that has continued so long between the Sanron and Hossō sects has been resolved as dramatically as though ice had melted. The truth has been made abundantly clear, as though clouds and mist had parted to reveal the light of the sun, moon, and stars."

Saichō, in his appraisal of the teachings of his fourteen opponents, wrote as follows: "You each lecture upon the single scripture [of your own sect], and though you sound the drums of the Dharma within the deep valleys, both lecturer and hearers continue to go astray on the paths of the three vehicles. Though you fly the banners of doctrine from lofty peaks and both teachers and disciples have broken free from the bonds of the threefold world, you still persist on the road of the enlightenment that takes countless kalpas to achieve, and confuse the three kinds of carts with the great white ox cart outside the gate.[66] How could you possibly attain the first stage of security[67] and reach enlightenment in this world that is like a house on fire?"[68]

The two officials [Wake no] Hiroyo and [his younger brother] Matsuna[69] [who were present at the debate] commented as follows: "Through Nan-yüeh, the Mystic Law of Eagle Peak was made known, and through T'ien-t'ai, the wonderful enlightenment of Mount Ta-su[70] was opened up. But one regrets that the single vehicle of the Lotus is impeded by provisional teachings, and one grieves that the unification of the three truths[71] has yet to be made manifest."

The fourteen priests commented as follows: "Zengi and the others of our group have met with great good fortune because of karmic bonds and have been privileged to hear these extraordinary words. Were it not for some profound karmic tie, how could we have been born in this sacred age?"

These fourteen men had in the past transmitted the teachings of the various Chinese and Japanese patriarchs of their respective schools such as Fa-tsang and Shinjō[72] of the Kegon school, Chia-hsiang and the Kanroku[73] of the Sanron school, Tz'u-en and Dōshō[74] of the Hossō school, or Tao-hsüan and Chien-chen of the Ritsu school. Thus, although the vessel in which the water of the doctrine was contained had changed from generation to generation, the water remained the same.

But now these fourteen men abandoned the erroneous doctrines that they had previously held and embraced the teachings of the Lotus Sutra as expounded by Saichō, the Great Teacher Dengyō. Therefore, how could anyone in later times assert that the *Kegon, Hannya,* or *Jimmitsu* Sutra surpasses the Lotus Sutra?

These fourteen men had of course studied the doctrines of the three Hinayana sects, [Jōjitsu, Kusha, and Ritsu]. But since the three Mahayana sects [of Kegon, Sanron, and Hossō] had suffered a doctrinal defeat, we need hardly mention the Hinayana sects. However, there are some persons today who, being unaware of what actually happened, believe that one or another of the six sects did not suffer a doctrinal defeat. They are like blind men who cannot see the sun and moon, or deaf men who cannot hear the sound of thunder, and who therefore conclude that there are no sun and moon in the heavens, or that the skies emit no sound.

With regard to the Shingon sect, during the reign of the forty-fourth sovereign Empress Genshō, Shan-wu-wei brought the *Dainichi* Sutra to Japan, but returned to China without spreading a knowledge of it.[75] Moreover, Gembō brought back from China a commentary on the *Dainichi* Sutra, the *Dainichikyō Gishaku* in fourteen volumes, as did the Preceptor Tokusei of Tōdai-ji.[76]

These works were studied by the Great Teacher Dengyō, but he had doubts about what they said concerning the relative worth of the *Dainichi* and Lotus sutras. Therefore, in the seventh month of the twenty-third year of the Enryaku era (804), he went to China, where he met the priests Tao-sui of the Hsi-ming-ssu and Hsing-man of Fo-lung-ssu, and received the Shikan teachings and the great precepts for perfect and immediate enlightenment. He also met the priest Shun-hsiao of Ling-kan-ssu and received instruction in the Shingon teachings.[77] He returned to Japan in the sixth month of the twenty-fourth year of Enryaku (805). He was granted an audience with Emperor Kammu, and the emperor thereupon issued an edict instructing the students of the six sects to study the Shikan and Shingon teachings and to preserve them in the seven major temples of Nara.

In China there were various theories concerning the relative superiority of these two teachings, the Shikan and the Shingon. Moreover, the *Dainichikyō Gishaku* claims that, though they are equal in terms of principle, the Shingon is superior in terms of practice.

The Great Teacher Dengyō, however, realized that this was an error on the part of Shan-wu-wei and understood that the *Dainichi* Sutra is inferior to the Lotus Sutra. Therefore he did not establish the

Shingon teachings as an eighth sect, but instead incorporated them into the teachings of the seventh sect, the Hokke sect,[78] after removing from them the label "Shingon sect." He declared that the *Dainichi* Sutra is to be regarded as a supplementary sutra of the Hokke-Tendai sect and ranked it along with the *Kegon, Daibon Hannya*,[79] and Nirvana sutras. However, at the time there was much dispute over whether or not a vitally important Mahayana specific ordination platform of perfect and immediate enlightenment should be established in Japan. Perhaps because of the trouble that arose on this account, it seems that the Great Teacher Dengyō did not give his disciples clear instructions concerning the relative superiority of the Shingon and Tendai teachings.

In a work called the *Ebyō Shū*, however, he clearly states that the Shingon school stole the correct doctrines of the Hokke-Tendai school and incorporated them into its interpretation of the *Dainichi* Sutra, thereafter declaring that the two schools were equal in terms of principle.[80] Thus the Shingon school had in effect surrendered to the Tendai school.

This is even more evident when we consider that, after the death of Shan-wu-wei and Chin-kang-chih, the Shingon patriarch Pu-k'ung went to India, where he met Bodhisattva Nāgabodhi.[81] Nāgabodhi informed him that there were no treatises or commentaries in India that made clear the Buddha's intent, but that in China there was a commentary by a man named T'ien-t'ai that enabled one to distinguish correct from incorrect teachings and to understand the difference between partial doctrines and those that are complete. He exclaimed this in admiration and repeatedly begged that a copy of the work be brought to India.

This incident was reported to the Great Teacher Miao-lo by Pu-k'ung's disciple Han-kuang[82] as is recorded at the end of the tenth volume of Miao-lo's *Hokke Mongu Ki*.[83] It is also recorded in Dengyō's *Ebyō Shū*. From this it is perfectly evident that the Great Teacher Dengyō believed the *Dainichi* Sutra to be inferior to the Lotus Sutra.

Thus it becomes apparent that Shakyamuni Buddha, the Great Teacher T'ien-t'ai, the Great Teacher Miao-lo, and the Great Teacher Dengyō were of one mind in regarding the Lotus Sutra as the greatest of all the sutras, including the *Dainichi* Sutra. Moreover, Bodhisattva Nāgārjuna, who is regarded as the founder of the Shingon sect, held the same opinion, as becomes obvious if we carefully examine his

Daichido Ron. Unfortunately, however, the *Bodaishin Ron* produced by Pu-k'ung is full of errors and has led everyone astray, bringing about the present confusion.

We come now to the disciple of the Administrator of Monks Gonsō[84] of Iwabuchi named Kūkai, known in later ages as Kōbō Daishi or the Great Teacher Kōbō. On the twelfth day of the fifth month in the twenty-third year of Enryaku (804), he set out for China. After arriving there, he met the priest Hui-kuo,[85] whose teacher belonged to the third generation of the Shingon lineage beginning with Shan-wu-wei and Chin-kang-chih. From Hui-kuo he received the transmission of the two Shingon mandalas. He returned to Japan on the twenty-second day of the tenth month in the second year of Daidō (807).

It was then the reign of Emperor Heizei, Emperor Kammu having passed away a short time before. Kūkai was granted an audience with Emperor Heizei, who placed great confidence in him and embraced his teachings, valuing them above all. Not long after (809), Emperor Heizei ceded the throne to Emperor Saga, with whom Kūkai likewise ingratiated himself. The Great Teacher Dengyō passed away on the fourth day of the sixth month of the thirteenth year of Kōnin (822), during the reign of Emperor Saga. From the fourteenth year of the same era (823), Kūkai served as teacher to the sovereign. He established the Shingon sect, was given supervision of the temple known as Tō-ji,[86] and was referred to as the Shingon Priest. Thus Shingon, the eighth sect of Buddhism in Japan, had its start.

Kūkai commented as follows on the relative merit of the teachings of the Buddha's lifetime: "First is the *Dainichi* Sutra of the Shingon sect, second is the *Kegon* Sutra, and third are the Lotus and Nirvana sutras.

"In comparison to the *Agon, Hōdō,* and *Hannya* sutras, the Lotus is a true sutra, but from the point of view of the *Kegon* and *Dainichi* sutras, it is a doctrine of childish theory.

"Though the Lord Shakyamuni was a Buddha, in comparison to the Buddha Dainichi or Mahāvairocana, he was still in the region of ignorance. The latter is as exalted as an emperor; the former, by comparison, is as lowly as a subjugated barbarian.

"The Great Teacher T'ien-t'ai is a thief. He stole the ghee of the Shingon and claimed that the Lotus Sutra is ghee."[87]

This is the sort of thing that Kūkai, or the Great Teacher Kōbō, wrote. As a result, though people may previously have believed that the Lotus is the greatest of all sutras, after hearing of the Great Teacher Kōbō, they no longer regarded it as worthy of notice.

I will set aside the heresies propounded by Brahmans in India. But these pronouncements of Kūkai are certainly worse than those put forward by the priests of northern and southern China who declared that, in comparison to the Nirvana Sutra, the Lotus Sutra is a work of heretical views. They go even farther than the assertions of those members of the Kegon school who stated that, in comparison to the *Kegon* Sutra, the Lotus Sutra represents the "branch teachings." One is reminded of that Great Arrogant Brahman of India who fashioned a tall dais with the deities Maheśvara, Nārāyaṇa, and Viṣṇu, along with Shakyamuni Buddha, as the four legs to support it, and then climbed up on it and preached his fallacious doctrines.

If only the Great Teacher Dengyō had still been alive, he would surely have had a word to say on the subject. But how could his disciples Gishin,[88] Enchō,[89] Jikaku, and Chishō have failed to question the matter more closely? That was a great misfortune to the world!

The Great Teacher Jikaku went to China in the fifth year of Jōwa (838) and spent ten years there studying the doctrines of the Tendai and Shingon schools. With regard to the relative merit of the Lotus and *Dainichi* sutras, he studied under Fa-ch'üan, Yüan-cheng, and others, eight Shingon teachers[90] in all, and was taught by them that, although the Lotus and *Dainichi* sutras are equal in principle, the latter is superior in terms of practice. He also studied under Chih-yüan, Kuang-hsiu, and Wei-chüan[91] of the Tendai school, and was taught that the *Dainichi* Sutra belongs to the Hōdō group of sutras [which are inferior to the Lotus Sutra].

On the tenth day of the ninth month in the thirteenth year of Jōwa (846), he returned to Japan, and on the fourteenth day of the sixth month of the first year of Kajō (848), an imperial edict was handed down [permitting him to conduct the Shingon initiation ceremonies]. Perhaps because he had had difficulty determining the relative merit of the Lotus and *Dainichi* sutras when he was studying in China, he proceeded to write a seven-volume commentary on the *Kongōchō* Sutra and a seven-volume commentary on the *Soshitsuji* Sutra,[92] making a total of fourteen volumes. The gist of these commentaries is that the doctrines set forth in the *Dainichi, Kongōchō,* and *Soshitsuji* sutras and the doctrines expounded in the Lotus Sutra ultimately indicate the same principle, but because of the ritual use of mudras and mantras associated with the former, the three Shingon sutras just mentioned are superior to the Lotus Sutra.

In essence, this agrees exactly with the view of Shan-wu-wei, Chin-kang-chih, and Pu-k'ung set forth in their commentary on the *Dainichi* Sutra.[93] But perhaps Jikaku still had doubts in his mind, or perhaps, having resolved his own doubts, he wished to clear up the doubts of others. In any event, he placed his fourteen volumes of commentary before the object of worship in the temple where he resided and made this appeal in prayer: "Though I have written these works, the Buddha's intention is very difficult to determine. Are the *Dainichi* Sutra and the other two Shingon sutras associated with it superior? Or are the Lotus Sutra and the two sutras[94] associated with it to be ranked higher?"

While he was earnestly praying in this manner, on the fifth day, early in the morning at the time of the fifth watch,[95] a sign suddenly came to him in a dream. He dreamed that the sun was up in the blue sky, and that he took an arrow and shot at it. The arrow flew up into the sky and struck the sun. The sun began to roll over and over, and when it had almost fallen to the earth, Jikaku woke from his dream.

Delighted, he said, "I have had a very auspicious dream. These writings, in which I have declared that Shingon is superior to the Lotus Sutra, are in accord with the Buddha's will!" He then requested that an imperial edict be issued to this effect, and he disseminated his teaching throughout the country of Japan.

But the edict that was handed down as a result of this request says in effect, "It has at last become known that the Shikan doctrines of the Tendai sect and the doctrines of the Shingon sect are in principle in perfect agreement." Jikaku had prayed to confirm that the Lotus Sutra is inferior to the *Dainichi* Sutra, but the edict that was issued says that the Lotus Sutra and the *Dainichi* Sutra are the same!

The Great Teacher Chishō in his youth in Japan was a disciple of the priest Gishin, the Great Teacher Enchō, the Superintendent [Kōjō],[96] and Jikaku. Thus he received instruction in both the exoteric and esoteric doctrines as they were taught in Japan at the time. But presumably because he was in doubt as to the relative superiority of the Tendai and Shingon sects, he journeyed to China. He arrived in China in the second year of Ninju (852),[97] where he studied under the Shingon priests Fa-ch'üan and Yüan-cheng. In general, their teachings accorded with the view held by Jikaku, namely that the *Dainichi* Sutra and the Lotus Sutra are equal in terms of principle but that the former is superior in terms of practice.

Chishō also studied under the priest Liang-hsü of the Tendai school, who taught him that, with regard to the relative merit of the Shingon and Tendai schools, the *Dainichi* Sutra of the Shingon school cannot compare with the *Kegon* and Lotus sutras.

After spending seven years in China, Chishō returned to Japan on the seventeenth day of the fifth month in the first year of Jōgan (859).[98]

In his commentary on the *Dainichi* Sutra entitled the *Dainichikyō Shiki,* Chishō states: "Even the Lotus Sutra cannot compare [to the *Dainichi* Sutra], much less the other doctrines."[99] In this commentary, therefore, he argues that the Lotus Sutra is inferior to the *Dainichi* Sutra. On the other hand, in another work, the *Juketsu Shū,* he states: "The doctrines of Shingon and Zen . . . can at best serve as a kind of introduction to the *Kegon,* Lotus and Nirvana sutras."[100] And he repeats this same view in his *Fugenkyō Ki* and *Hokke Ron Ki.*[101]

On the twenty-ninth day, the day of the cyclical sign *mizunoe-saru,* of the fourth month of the eighth year of Jōgan, the year *hinoe-inu* (866), an imperial edict was handed down which stated: "We have heard that the two sects, Shingon and Tendai, and their teachings are both worthy to be called the ghee of Buddhism, and to be described as profound and recondite."

Again, on the third day of the sixth month, an edict proclaimed: "Ever since the Great Teacher Dengyō in former times established the two disciplines[102] as the proper way for the Tendai sect, the successive heads of the sect in generation after generation have all followed this practice and transmitted both types of doctrines. Why then should their successors in later times depart from this old and established tradition?

"And yet we hear that the priests of Mount Hiei do nothing but turn against the teachings of the patriarch Dengyō and instead follow the prejudices and inclinations of their own hearts. It would appear that they give themselves almost entirely to promulgating the doctrines of other sects and make no attempt to restore the old disciplines of the Tendai sect.

"On the path inherited from the master, one cannot neglect either the Shikan or the Shingon teachings. In diligently transmitting and spreading the doctrine, must not one be proficient in both types of teachings? From now on, only a person who is thoroughly familiar with both teachings shall be appointed as head of the Tendai sect at Enryaku-ji, and this shall become a regular practice for future times."

These two men, Jikaku and Chishō, as we have seen, were disciples of Dengyō and Gishin, and in addition they journeyed to China and met eminent teachers of the Tendai and Shingon schools there. And yet it appears that they could not make up their minds as to the relative merits of these two sects. Sometimes they declared that the Shingon is superior, sometimes that the Lotus Sutra is superior, and sometimes they said that the two are equal in terms of principle but that the Shingon is superior in terms of practice. Meanwhile, an edict warned that anyone attempting to argue the relative merit of the two sects would be judged guilty of violating the imperial decree.

These pronouncements of Jikaku and Chishō were clearly inconsistent, and it would appear that the followers of the other sects placed no trust in them whatsoever. Nevertheless, an imperial edict, as we have seen, states that the two sects are equal, putting this forward as the doctrine of the Tendai patriarch, the Great Teacher Dengyō. But in what work of the Great Teacher Dengyō is this view to be found? This is something that must be looked into carefully.

For me, Nichiren, to be challenging Jikaku and Chishō because of doubts over a matter pertaining to the Great Teacher Dengyō is like a person confronting his parents and arguing with them over who is older, or a person confronting the god of the sun and claiming that his own eyes shine more brilliantly. Nevertheless, those who would defend the views of Jikaku and Chishō must produce some sort of clear spiritual evidence to support their case. Only if they do so can they hope to gain credence for such views.

The Tripitaka Master Hsüan-tsang had been to India and seen a copy of the *Daibibasha Ron*[103] there, but that did not prevent him from being criticized by the Dharma Teacher Fa-pao,[104] who had never been to India. The Tripitaka Master Dharmarakṣa saw a copy of the Lotus Sutra in India, but that did not prevent a man of China from pointing out that the *Zokurui* chapter was out of place in the translation he made of it, though that man had never seen the original text.[105]

In like manner, though Jikaku may have studied under the Great Teacher Dengyō and received instruction from him, and though Chishō may have obtained the oral transmission from the priest

Gishin, if they go against the teachings recorded in the authentic writings of Dengyō and Gishin, then how can they help but incur suspicion?

The work entitled *Ebyō Shū* by Dengyō is the most secret of his writings. In the preface to that work, he writes: "The school of Shingon Buddhism that has recently been brought to Japan deliberately obscures how its transmission was falsified in the recording [by I-hsing, who was deceived by Shan-wu-wei], while the Kegon school that was introduced earlier attempts to disguise the fact that it was influenced by the doctrines of T'ien-t'ai. The Sanron school, which is so infatuated with the concept of Emptiness, has forgotten Chia-hsiang's humiliation, and conceals the fact that he was completely won over to the T'ien-t'ai teachings by Chang-an. The Hossō school, which clings to the concept of being, denies that its leader Chih-chou was converted to the teachings of the Tendai school, and that Liang-p'i used those teachings in interpreting the *Ninnō* Sutra. . . . Now with all due circumspection I have written this work entitled *Ebyō Shū* in one volume to present to wise men of later times who share my convictions. The time is the reign of the fifty-second sovereign of Japan, the seventh year of the Kōnin era, the year *hinoe-saru* (816)."[106]

Farther on, in the main text of the same work, he writes: "There was an eminent monk in India who had heard that the teachings of the T'ang priest T'ien-t'ai were most suitable for distinguishing correct from incorrect doctrines, and expressed a longing to become better acquainted with them."

He continues: "Does this not mean that Buddhism has been lost in India, the country of its origin, and must now be sought in the surrounding regions? But even in China there are few people who recognize the greatness of T'ien-t'ai's teachings. They are like the people of Lu."[107]

This work, as may be seen from these quotations, criticizes the Hossō, Sanron, Kegon, and Shingon sects. Now if the Great Teacher Dengyō believed that the Tendai and Shingon sects are of equal worth, then why would he criticize the latter? Furthermore, he compares the Shingon patriarch Pu-k'ung and others to the ignorant people of the state of Lu. If he really approved of the Shingon teachings as formulated by Shan-wu-wei, Chin-kang-chih, and Pu-k'ung, then why would he speak ill of these men by comparing them to the people of Lu? And if the Shingon teachings of India were identical with or superior to the teachings of the Tendai sect, then why did the eminent monk of India question Pu-k'ung about them and say that the True Law had been lost in India?

Be that as it may, these two men, Jikaku and Chishō, in words claimed to be the disciples of the Great Teacher Dengyō, but at heart they were not. That is why Dengyō wrote in the preface to his work, "Now with all due circumspection I have written this work entitled *Ebyō Shū* in one volume to present to wise men of later times who share my convictions."[108] The words "who share my convictions" mean in effect "those who share my conviction that the Shingon sect is inferior to the Tendai sect."

In the edict quoted earlier, which Jikaku himself had requested, it says that they "do nothing but turn against the teachings of the patriarch Dengyō and instead follow the prejudices and inclinations of their own hearts." It also states, "On the path inherited from the master, one cannot neglect either the Shikan or the Shingon teachings." But if we are to accept the words of the edict, we would have to say that Jikaku and Chishō themselves are the ones who have turned against their teacher Dengyō. It may be impertinent that I make charges of this kind, but if I do not do so, then the relative merit of the *Dainichi* and Lotus sutras will continue to be misunderstood as it is at present. That is why I risk my life to bring these charges.

[Since they themselves were mistaken,] it is altogether natural that these two men, Jikaku and Chishō, did not venture to accuse the Great Teacher Kōbō of doctrinal error. Instead of wasting all those supplies and making work for other people by insisting upon traveling all the way to China, they should have made a more careful and thorough study of the doctrines of the Great Teacher Dengyō, who was their own teacher!

It was only in the time of the first three leaders of the Tendai sect, the Great Teacher Dengyō, the priest Gishin, and the Great Teacher Enchō, that the True Law was taught on Mount Hiei. Thereafter the chief priests of the Tendai sect were transformed into Shingon leaders. The area continued to be called Mount Tendai, but was presided over by a Shingon master.

Jikaku and Chishō, as we have seen, contradict the passage in the Lotus Sutra concerning all the sutras that the Buddha "has preached, now preaches, and will preach."[109] And having contradicted that passage of the scripture, are they not to be regarded as the archenemies of Shakyamuni, Tahō, and the other Buddhas of the ten directions? One might have thought that Kōbō was the foremost slanderer of the Law, but Jikaku and Chishō taught errors that far surpass those of Kōbō.

When an error is as far from the truth as water is from fire or the earth from the sky, people will refuse to believe it, and such errors will have no chance of acceptance. Thus, for example, the doctrines of the Great Teacher Kōbō are so full of such errors that even his own disciples would not accept them. As for the practices and ceremonies of the sect, they accepted his instructions, but they could not bring themselves to accept his doctrines concerning the relative merits of the sutras. Therefore, they substituted for them the doctrines of Shan-wu-wei, Chin-kang-chih, Pu-k'ung, Jikaku, and Chishō. It is the doctrine of Jikaku and Chishō that declares the Shingon and Tendai sects to be identical in principle, and all the people have accepted that declaration.

Recognizing this situation, even followers of the Tendai sect, hoping to be asked to perform the "opening of the eyes" ceremony for the dedication of Buddhist paintings or statues, adopt the mudras and mantras in which the Shingon sect is believed to excel. Thus in effect the whole of Japan goes over to the Shingon sect, and the Tendai sect is left without a single follower.

A monk and a nun, a black object and a dark blue object, are so easily confused that a person with poor eyesight might well mistake one for the other. But a priest and a layman, or a white object and a red object, even a person with poor eyesight would never confuse, much less someone with good eyes. Now the doctrines of Jikaku and Chishō are as easy to mistake for the truth as a monk is for a nun, or a black object for a dark blue one. Therefore, even wise men are led astray, and the ignorant fall into error. As a result, for the past four hundred years and more, on Mount Hiei, in Onjō-ji[110] and Tō-ji, in Nara, the five provinces surrounding the capital, the seven outlying regions,[111] and indeed throughout the whole land of Japan, all the people have been turned into slanderers of the Law.

In the fifth volume of the Lotus Sutra, the Buddha states: "Monjushiri, this Lotus Sutra is the secret storehouse of Buddhas. Among the sutras, it holds the highest place."[112]

If this passage of the scripture is to be believed, then the Lotus Sutra must represent the True Law that dwells supreme above the

Dainichi and all the numerous other sutras. How then, one wonders, would Shan-wu-wei, Chin-kang-chih, Pu-k'ung, Kōbō, Jikaku, and Chishō interpret this passage in the sutra and reconcile it with their beliefs?

Again, the seventh volume of the Lotus Sutra states: "He who can accept and uphold this sutra will be like this too—he will be the first among all the multitude of living beings."[113] If this passage of the sutra is to be believed, then the votary of the Lotus Sutra must be like the great sea as compared to the various rivers and streams, like Mount Sumeru among the host of mountains, like the god of the moon amid the multitude of stars, like the great god of the sun amid the other shining lights, like the wheel-turning kings [among all minor kings], like the god Taishaku [among the thirty-three gods], and the great god king Bonten among all various kings.

The Great Teacher Dengyō in his work entitled *Hokke Shūku* writes: "This sutra is like this too . . . it is first among all the sutras. He who can accept and uphold this sutra will be like this too—he will be the first among all the multitude of living beings."[114]

After quoting this passage from the Lotus Sutra, Dengyo notes a passage from the work entitled *Hokke Gengi* by T'ien-t'ai [which interprets] the same passage of scripture, and explains its meaning as follows: "One should understand that the sutras on which the other sects base their teachings are not the first among the sutras, and those persons who uphold such sutras are not the first among the multitude. But the Lotus Sutra, which is upheld by the Tendai-Hokke sect, is the foremost of all the sutras, and therefore those who embrace the Lotus Sutra are first among the multitude. This is borne out by the words of the Buddha himself. How could it be mere self-praise?"[115]

Later in the work just mentioned, Dengyō says, "Detailed explanations concerning the texts on which the various sects base their teachings are given in a separate work."[116] The separate work he is referring to, the *Ebyō Shū,* states: "Now the founder of our sect, the Great Teacher T'ien-t'ai, preached the Lotus Sutra and interpreted the Lotus Sutra in a way that placed him far above the crowd; in all of China, he stood alone. One should clearly understand that he was a messenger of the Buddha. Those who praise him will receive blessings that will pile up as high as Mount Sumeru, while those who slander him will be committing a fault that will condemn them to the hell of incessant suffering."[117]

If we go by the Lotus Sutra and the interpretations of it put forward by T'ien-t'ai, Miao-lo, and Dengyō, then, in Japan at the present time, there is not a single votary of the Lotus Sutra!

In India, when Shakyamuni Buddha was preaching the Lotus Sutra as described in the *Hōtō* chapter, he summoned all the various Buddhas and had them take their seats upon the ground. Only Dainichi Buddha was seated within the Treasure Tower, on the lower seat to the south, while Shakyamuni Buddha was seated on the upper seat to the north.[118]

This Dainichi Buddha is the master of the Dainichi of the Womb Realm described in the *Dainichi* Sutra, and of the Dainichi of the Diamond Realm described in the *Kongōchō* Sutra. This Dainichi or Tahō Buddha, who has as his vassals the Dainichi Buddhas of the two worlds just mentioned, is in turn surpassed by Shakyamuni Buddha, who sits in the seat above him. This Shakyamuni Buddha is a true votary of the Lotus Sutra. Such was the situation in India.

In China, in the time of the Ch'en emperor [Shu-pao], the Great Teacher T'ien-t'ai defeated in debate the Buddhist leaders of northern and southern China, and was honored with the title of Great Teacher while still alive. As Dengyō says of him, he was "far above the crowd; in all of China, he stood alone."

In Japan, the Great Teacher Dengyō defeated in debate the leaders of the six sects and became the founder and first leader of the Tendai sect in Japan.

In India, China, and Japan, these three persons alone—Shakyamuni, T'ien-t'ai, and Dengyō—were what the Lotus Sutra calls "the first among all the multitude of living beings."

Thus the *Hokke Shūku* by Dengyō states: "Shakyamuni taught that the shallow is easy to embrace, but the profound is difficult. To discard the shallow and seek the profound requires courage. The Great Teacher T'ien-t'ai trusted and obeyed Shakyamuni Buddha and worked to uphold the Hokke school, spreading its teachings throughout China. We of Mount Hiei inherited the doctrine from T'ien-t'ai and work to uphold the Hokke school and to disseminate its teachings throughout Japan."[119]

In the eighteen hundred years or more since the passing of the Buddha, there has been only one votary of the Lotus Sutra in China and one in Japan. If Shakyamuni himself is added to the number, that makes a total of three persons.

The secular classics of China claim that a sage will appear once every thousand years, and a worthy man once every five hundred. In the Yellow River where the Ching and Wei rivers[120] flow into it, the flow of the two tributary rivers remains separate. But it is said that once every five hundred years, one side of the river will flow clear, and once every thousand years, both sides of the river will flow clear. [In the same way, sages and worthy men appear at fixed intervals.]

In Japan, as we have seen, only on Mount Hiei in the time of the Great Teacher Dengyō was there a votary of the Lotus Sutra. Dengyō was succeeded by Gishin and Enchō, the first and second chief priests of the sect, respectively. But only the first chief priest Gishin followed the ways of the Great Teacher Dengyō. The second chief priest Enchō was half a disciple of Dengyō and half a disciple of Kōbō.

The third chief priest, Jikaku, at first acted like a disciple of the Great Teacher Dengyō. But after he went to China at the age of forty, though he continued to call himself a disciple of Dengyō and went through the motions of carrying on Dengyō's line, he taught a kind of Buddhism that was wholly unworthy of a true disciple of Dengyō. Only in the matter of the precepts for perfect and immediate enlightenment established by Dengyō did he conduct himself like a true disciple.

He was like a bat, for a bat resembles a bird yet is not a bird, and resembles a mouse yet is not a mouse. Or he was like an owl or a *hakei* beast.[121] He ate his father, the Lotus Sutra, and devoured his mother, those who embrace the Lotus Sutra. When he dreamed that he shot down the sun, it must have been a portent of these crimes. And it must be because of these acts that, after his death, no grave was set aside for him.

The temple Onjō-ji, representing Chishō's branch of the Tendai sect, fought incessantly with the temple Enryaku-ji on Mount Hiei, which represented Jikaku's branch of the sect,[122] the two going at each other like so many *asuras* and evil dragons. First Onjō-ji would be burned down, then the buildings on Mount Hiei. As a result, the image of Bodhisattva Miroku that had been the special object of worship of Chishō was burned, and the special object of worship of Jikaku, as well as the great lecture hall on Mount Hiei, were likewise burned. The monks of the two temples must have felt as though they had fallen into the hell of incessant suffering while they were still in this world. Only the Main Hall on Mount Hiei remained standing.

The lineage of the Great Teacher Kōbō has likewise ceased to be what it should have been. Kōbō left written instructions that no one who had not received the precepts at the ordination platform [established by Chien-chen] at Tōdai-ji should be allowed to become head of Tō-ji. The Retired Emperor Kampyō,[123] however, founded a temple [in Kyoto] called Ninna-ji and moved a number of monks from Tō-ji to staff it, and he also issued a decree clearly stating that no one should be allowed to reside in Ninna-ji unless he had received the precepts for perfect and immediate enlightenment at the ordination platform on Mount Hiei. As a result, the monks of Tō-ji are neither disciples of Chien-chen, nor are they disciples of Kōbō. In terms of the precepts, they are Dengyō's disciples. However, they do not behave like true disciples of Dengyō. They turn their backs on the Lotus Sutra, which Dengyō considered to be supreme.

Kōbō died on the twenty-first day of the third month in the second year of the Jōwa era (835), and the imperial court sent a representative to offer prayers at his funeral. Later, however, his disciples gathered together and, bent on deception, announced that he [had not died at all but] had entered a state of deep meditation, and some of them even claimed that they had had to shave his head [because his hair had grown long]. Others asserted that while he was in China, he had hurled a three-pronged *vajra* implement[124] all the way across the ocean to Japan; that in answer to his prayers, the sun had come out in the middle of the night; that he was an incarnation of Dainichi Buddha; or that he had instructed the Great Teacher Dengyō in the eighteen paths[125] of esoteric Buddhism. Thus by enumerating their teacher's supposed virtues and powers, they hoped to make him appear wise, in this way lending support to his false doctrines and deluding the ruler and his ministers.

In addition, on Mount Kōya there are two main temples, the original temple[126] and the Dembō-in. The original temple, which includes the great pagoda, was founded by Kōbō and is dedicated to the Buddha Dainichi [of the Womb Realm]. The temple called Dembō-in was founded by Shōkaku-bō[127] and is dedicated to the Dainichi of the Diamond Realm. These two temples fight with each other day and night, in the same way as Onjō-ji at the foot of Mount Hiei and Enryaku-ji on top of Mount Hiei. Was it the accumulation of deceit that brought about the appearance in Japan of these calamities?[128]

You may pile up dung and call it sandalwood, but when you burn it, it will give off only the odor of dung. You may pile up a lot of great lies and call them the teachings of the Buddha, but they will never be anything but a gateway to the great citadel of the hell of incessant suffering.

The stupa built by the non-Buddhist leader Nirgranthajñatiputra over a period of several years conferred great benefit upon living beings, but when Bodhisattva Aśvaghoṣa bowed to it, it suddenly collapsed.[129] The Brahman Devil Eloquence taught from behind a curtain and for a number of years succeeded in fooling others, but Bodhisattva Aśvaghoṣa attacked him and exposed his falsehoods.[130] The Brahman leader Ulūka turned himself into a stone and remained in that form for eight hundred years, but when Bodhisattva Dignāga berated him, he turned into water.[131] The Taoist priests for several hundred years deceived the people of China, but when they were rebuked by the Buddhist monks Kāśyapa Mātaṅga and Chu-fa-lan, they burned their own scriptures that purported to teach the way of the immortals.[132]

Just as Chao Kao[133] seized control of the country and Wang Mang[134] usurped the position of emperor, so the leaders of the Shingon sect deprived the Lotus Sutra of the rank it deserves and declared that its domain belongs instead to the *Dainichi* Sutra. If the monarch of the Law has been deprived of his kingdom in this manner, can the monarch of men hope to remain peaceful and unharmed?

Japan today is filled with followers of Jikaku, Chishō, and Kōbō —there is not a single person who does not slander the Law!

If we stop to consider the situation, it is very much like that which prevailed in the Latter Day of the Buddha Daishōgon or the Latter Day of the Law of the Buddha Issai Myōō.[135] In the Latter Day of the Law of the Buddha Ionnō, even though people repented of their wrongdoings, they still had to suffer for a thousand kalpas in the Avīci Hell.[136] What, then, of the situation today? The Shingon priests, the people of the Zen sect, and the followers of the Nembutsu show not the slightest sign of repentance in their hearts. Can there be any doubt that, as the Lotus Sutra says, "In this way they will be reborn again and again [in hell] for kalpas without number"?[137]

Because Japan is a country where the Law is slandered, Heaven has abandoned it. And because Heaven has abandoned it, the various benevolent deities that in the past guarded and protected the nation have burned their shrines and returned to the City of Tranquil Light.[138]

Now there is only Nichiren who remains behind, announcing and giving warning of these things. But when I do so, the rulers of the nation treat me like an enemy. People by the hundreds curse me and speak ill of me, attack me with staves and sticks, swords and knives. Door after door is closed to me, house after house drives me away. And when the authorities find that even such treatment does not stop me, they intervene in the matter. Twice they sent me into exile,[139] and once, on the twelfth day of the ninth month in the eighth year of Bun'ei (1271), they very nearly cut off my head.[140]

The *Saishoo* Sutra says, "Because evil men are respected and favored and good men are subjected to punishment, . . . marauders will appear from other regions and the people of the country will meet with death and disorder."[141]

The *Daijuku* Sutra states, "There may perhaps be various kings of the *kṣatriya* class who act in a way contrary to the Dharma, causing anguish to the *shōmon* disciples of the World-Honored One. Perhaps they may curse and revile them or beat and injure them with swords and staves, or deprive them of their robes and begging bowls and the other things they need. Or perhaps they may restrain and persecute those who give alms to the disciples. If there should be those who do such things, then we [the benevolent deities] will see to it that their enemies in foreign lands rise up suddenly of their own accord and march against them, and we will cause uprisings to break out within their states. We will bring about pestilence and famine, unseasonable winds and rains, and contention, wrangling, [and slander]. And we will make certain that those rulers do not last for long, but that their nations are brought to destruction."[142]

As these passages from the sutras indicate, if I, Nichiren, were not here in Japan, then one might suppose that the Buddha was a teller of great lies for making such predictions and that he could not escape falling into the Avīci Hell.

On the twelfth day of the ninth month in the eighth year of Bun'ei (1271), I stood in the presence of Hei no Saemon[143] and several hundred others and declared, "Nichiren is the pillar of Japan! If you lose Nichiren, you will be toppling the pillar that supports Japan!"

The passages of scripture I have quoted indicate that if the rulers, heeding the slanders of evil monks or the vicious talk of others, should inflict punishment on men of wisdom, then warfare will immediately break out, great winds will blow, and attackers will appear from foreign lands. In the second month of the ninth year of Bun'ei (1272), fighting did in fact break out between two factions of the Hōjō family;[144] in the fourth month of the eleventh year of Bun'ei (1274), there were violent winds;[145] and in the tenth month of the same year, the Mongol forces attacked Japan. Has not all of this come about because of the treatment that has been given to me, Nichiren? This is exactly what I have been predicting from times past. Can anyone be in doubt about the matter?

The errors preached by Kōbō, Jikaku, and Chishō have for many long years been spread about the country, and then on top of them have come the confusions propagated by the Zen and Nembutsu sects. It is as though, in addition to adverse winds, one should be visited by huge waves and earthquakes as well. With all this, the nation has been brought to the verge of destruction.

In the past the grand minister of state and lay priest Taira no Kiyomori usurped the power of government, and after the Jōkyū Disturbance the imperial court ceased to exercise its rule and the seat of authority shifted east to Kamakura.[146] But these were no more than internal disturbances; the nation as yet had not faced invasion from abroad.

Moreover, though at that time there were those who slandered the Dharma, there were also a few persons who continued to uphold the True Law of the Tendai sect. And in addition, at that time no wise man had appeared who would attempt to remedy the situation. As a result, things were relatively peaceful.

If the lion is sleeping and you do not wake him, he will not roar. If the current is swift but you do not pull against it with your oar, no waves will rise up. If you do not accuse the thief to his face, he will remain unruffled; if you do not add fuel to the fire, it will not blaze up. In the same way, though there may be those who slander the Law, if no one comes forward to expose their error, then the government will continue for the time being on its regular course and the nation will remain undisturbed.

For example, when the Buddhist Law was first introduced to Japan, nothing out of the ordinary occurred. But later, when Mononobe no Moriya[147] began burning Buddhist statues, seizing monks, and putting the torch to Buddhist halls and pagodas, then fire rained down from heaven, smallpox broke out in the nation, and there were repeated military clashes.

But the situation now is far worse. Today those who slander the Law fill the entire country, and I, Nichiren, attack them, strong in my determination to uphold what is right and just. We battle no less fiercely than the *asura* demons and the god Taishaku, or the Buddha and the Devil King.

The *Konkōmyō* Sutra states, "There will be times when enemies among the neighboring states will begin to have thoughts as follows: 'We must call out all our four types of troops and destroy that country [where the slanderers of the Law live].' "[148]

The same sutra also says, "There will be times when the rulers of neighboring states, observing the situation and mobilizing their four types of troops, will make ready to set out for the country [where the slanderers of the Law live], determined to subdue it. At that time we [the great deities] will instruct all the countless, limitless numbers of *yakṣas*[149] and other deities who are our followers to assume disguises and protect these rulers, causing their enemies to surrender to them without difficulty."[150]

The *Saishōō* Sutra states the same thing, as do the *Daijuku* and *Ninnō* sutras. According to the statements of these various sutras, if the ruler of a state persecutes those who practice the True Law and instead sides with those who practice erroneous teachings, then the heavenly kings Bonten and Taishaku, the gods of the sun and the moon, and the Four Heavenly Kings will enter the bodies of the wise rulers of neighboring states and will attack his state. For example, King Kṛta[151] was attacked by King Himatala, and King Mihirakula[152] was overthrown by King Bālāditya. Kings Kṛta and Mihirakula were rulers in India who attempted to eradicate Buddhism. In China, too, all those rulers who tried to destroy Buddhism were attacked by worthy rulers.

But the situation in Japan today is much worse. For here the rulers appear to be supporters of the Buddhist Law, but they assist the priests who are destroying Buddhism and persecute the votary of the True Law. As a result, ignorant people all fail to realize what is happening, and even wise persons, if they are no more than moderately wise, have difficulty grasping the situation. Even the lesser deities of heaven, I suspect, do not understand. For this reason, the confusion and depravity in Japan today are even greater than those in India or China in the past.

In the *Hōmetsujin* Sutra the Buddha speaks as follows: "After I have entered nirvana, in the troubled times when the five cardinal sins prevail, the way of the Devil will flourish. The Devil will appear in the form of Buddhist monks and attempt to confuse and destroy my teachings. . . . Those who do evil will become as numerous as the sands of the ocean, while the good will be extremely few, perhaps no more than one or two persons."[153]

And the Nirvana Sutra says, "In this way, those who believe in the Nirvana Sutra will take up no more land than can be placed on top of a fingernail. . . . Those who do not believe in the sutra will occupy all the lands in the ten directions."[154]

These passages from the scriptures are extremely apt, considering the times we live in, and they are deeply etched in my mind. Nowadays in Japan one hears people everywhere declaring, "I believe in the Lotus Sutra," and "I, too, believe in the Lotus Sutra." If we took them at their word, we would have to conclude that there is not a soul who slanders the Law. But the passage from the sutra which I have just quoted says that in the Latter Day, the slanderers of the Law will occupy all the lands in the ten directions, while those who uphold the True Law will take up no more land than can be placed on top of a fingernail. What the sutra says and what the people of the world today say are as different as fire is from water. People these days say that in Japan, Nichiren is the only one who slanders the Law. But the sutra says that there will be more slanderers of the Law than the great earth itself can hold.

The *Hōmetsujin* Sutra says that there will be only one or two good persons, and the Nirvana Sutra says that the believers can fit into the space of a fingernail. If we accept what the sutras say, then in Japan Nichiren is the only good person, the one who fits into the space of a fingernail. Therefore I hope that people who are seriously concerned about the matter will consider carefully whether they want to accept what the sutras say, or what the world says.

Someone might object that the passage in the Nirvana Sutra speaks about the votaries of the Nirvana Sutra being so few that they can fit into the space of a fingernail, while I am talking about the Lotus Sutra. I would reply to this as follows.

The Nirvana Sutra defines itself as being contained in the Lotus Sutra. The Great Teacher Miao-lo says, "The great sutra is itself pointing to the Lotus Sutra and saying that it is the ultimate."[155] The words "the great sutra" here refer to the Nirvana Sutra. The Nirvana Sutra is calling the Lotus Sutra the ultimate. Therefore, when followers of the Nirvana school state that the Nirvana Sutra is superior to the Lotus Sutra, it is the same as calling a retainer a lord or a servant a master.

To read the Nirvana Sutra means to read the Lotus Sutra. For the Nirvana Sutra is like a worthy man who rejoices to see another holding his sovereign in esteem even when he himself is treated with contempt. Thus the Nirvana Sutra would despise and regard as its enemy anyone who tried to demote the Lotus Sutra and praise the Nirvana Sutra instead.

With this example in mind, one must understand the following point. If there are likewise those who read the *Kegon* Sutra, the *Kammuryōju* Sutra, the *Dainichi* Sutra, or some other sutra, and they do so thinking that the Lotus Sutra is inferior to those sutras, then they are doing violence to the very heart of those sutras! One must also understand the following point. Even though one reads the Lotus Sutra and appears to believe in it, if he thinks that he may also attain enlightenment through any other sutra as well, then he is not really reading the Lotus Sutra!

For example, the Great Teacher Chia-hsiang wrote a work in ten volumes entitled the *Hokke Genron*[156] in which he praised the Lotus Sutra. But Miao-lo criticized the work, saying, "There are slanders in it—how can it be regarded as true propagation and praise?"[157]

Chia-hsiang was in fact an offender against the Lotus Sutra. Thus, when he was defeated by the Great Teacher T'ien-t'ai and served him, he no longer lectured on the Lotus Sutra. "If I were to lecture on it," he said, "I could not avoid falling back into the paths of evil." And for seven years, he made his own body a bridge for T'ien-t'ai to walk on.[158]

Similarly, the Great Teacher Tz'u-en wrote a work in ten volumes entitled the *Hokke Genzan*[159] in which he praised the Lotus Sutra, but the Great Teacher Dengyō criticized it, saying, "Even though he praises the Lotus Sutra, he destroys its heart."[160]

If we consider these examples carefully, we will realize that, among those who read the Lotus Sutra and sing its praises, there are many who are destined for the hell of incessant suffering. Even men like Chia-hsiang and Tz'u-en were actually slanderers of the one vehicle of the Lotus Sutra. And if such can be said of them, it applies even more to men like Kōbō, Jikaku, and Chishō, who displayed open contempt for the Lotus Sutra.

There are those like Chia-hsiang, who ceased giving lectures, dispersed the group of disciples that had gathered around him, and became a disciple of T'ien-t'ai, even making his body into a bridge for his teacher. But in spite of these actions, the offense of his earlier slanders of the Lotus Sutra was not, I expect, so easily wiped out. The crowd of people who despised and attacked Bodhisattva Fukyō, although they later came to believe in his teachings and became his followers, still carried the burden of their former actions and had to spend a thousand kalpas in the Avīci Hell as a result.

Accordingly, if men like Kōbō, Jikaku, and Chishō had lectured on the Lotus Sutra, even if they had repented of their errors, they would still have had difficulty making up for their former grave offenses. And of course, as we know, they never had any such change of heart. On the contrary, they completely ignored the Lotus Sutra and spent day and night carrying out Shingon practices and morning and evening preaching Shingon doctrine.

The bodhisattvas Vasubandhu and Aśvaghoṣa were both on the point of cutting out their tongues because of the offense they had committed [in their younger days] by adhering to Hinayana doctrines and criticizing Mahayana. Vasubandhu declared that, although the *Agon* sutras of the Hinayana were the words of the Buddha, he would not let his tongue utter them even in jest. And Aśvaghoṣa, as an act of penance, wrote the *Kishin Ron* in which he refuted the Hinayana teachings.

Chia-hsiang in time went to the Great Teacher T'ien-t'ai and begged for his lectures. In the presence of a hundred or more distinguished Buddhists, he threw himself on the ground, and, with sweat pouring from every part of his body and tears of blood streaming from his eyes, he declared that from then on he would not see his disciples any more and would no longer lecture on the Lotus Sutra. For, as he said, "If I were to go on facing my disciples and lecturing on the Lotus Sutra, they might suppose that I have the ability to understand the sutra correctly, when in fact I do not."

Chia-hsiang was both older and more eminent than T'ien-t'ai, and yet, in the presence of others, he deliberately put his teacher T'ien-t'ai on his back and carried him across a river. Whenever T'ien-t'ai was about to ascend the lecture platform, Chia-hsiang would take him on his back and carry him up to the platform. After T'ien-t'ai's death, when Chia-hsiang was summoned into the presence of the emperor of the Sui dynasty,[161] he is said to have wept and dragged his feet like a little child whose mother has just died.

When one examines the work entitled *Hokke Genron* by Chia-hsiang, one finds that it is not the kind of commentary that speaks slanderously of the Lotus Sutra. It merely says that, although the Lotus Sutra and the other Mahayana sutras differ in the profundity of their teachings, they are at heart one and the same. Is this statement perhaps the source of the charge that the work slanders the Law?

Both Ch'eng-kuan of the Kegon school and Shan-wu-wei of the Shingon school declared that the Lotus Sutra and the *Dainichi* Sutra reveal the same principle. Therefore, if Chia-hsiang is to be blamed for the statement I have just referred to, then Shan-wu-wei can hardly escape being blamed as well.

Shan-wu-wei in his youth was the ruler of a kingdom in central India. But he abdicated the throne and traveled to other lands, where he met two men named Shushō and Shōdai from whom he received instruction in the Lotus Sutra.[162] He built a hundred thousand stone stupas, and appeared to be a votary of the Lotus Sutra. Later, however, after he had received instruction in the *Dainichi* Sutra, he seems to have concluded that the Lotus Sutra is inferior to the *Dainichi* Sutra. He did not insist on this opinion at first, but came to do so later when he went to China and became a teacher to Emperor Hsüan-tsung of the T'ang dynasty.

Perhaps because he was consumed by jealousy of the Tendai school, he died very suddenly and found himself bound with seven cords of iron and dragged by two guardians of hell to the court of Emma, the king of hell. But he was told that his life span had not reached its conclusion and therefore was sent back to the world of men.

While in hell, he suspected that he had been brought before Emma because he had slandered the Lotus Sutra, and he therefore quickly set aside all his Shingon mudras, mantras, and methods of concentration and instead chanted the passage from the Lotus Sutra that begins, "Now this threefold world is all my [the Buddha's] domain,"[163] whereupon the cords that bound him fell away and he was returned to life.

On another occasion, he was ordered by the imperial court to recite prayers for rain and rain did in fact suddenly begin to fall, but a huge wind also rose up and did great damage to the country.

Later, when he really did die, his disciples gathered around his deathbed and praised the remarkable way in which he died, but in fact he fell into the great citadel of the hell of incessant suffering. You may ask how I know that this is so. I would reply that, if you examine his biography, you will find it stated, "Looking now at Shan-wu-wei's remains, one can see that they are gradually shrinking, the skin is turning blackish and the bones are exposed."[164]

Shan-wu-wei's disciples perhaps did not realize that this was a sign that after his death he had been reborn in hell, but supposed that it was a manifestation of his virtue. Yet in describing it, the author of the biography exposed Shan-wu-wei's guilt, recording that after his death his body gradually shrank, the skin turned black, and the bones began to show.

We have the Buddha's own golden word for it that, if a person's skin turns black after he dies, it is a sign that he has done something that destined him for hell. What was it, then, that Shan-wu-wei did that would destine him for hell? In his youth he gave up the position of ruler, showing that he had an incomparable determination to seek the Way. He traveled about to more than fifty different lands in India in the course of his religious practice, and his unbounded compassion even led him to visit China. The fact that the Shingon teachings have been transmitted through India, China, Japan, and the other lands of the world and numerous practitioners ring bells in prayer is due to the merit of this man, is it not? Those who are concerned about their own destiny after death should inquire carefully as to the reason why Shan-wu-wei fell into hell.

Then there was Chin-kang-chih, who was a son of the ruler of a kingdom in southern India. He introduced the *Kongōchō* Sutra to China, and his virtue was similar to that of Shan-wu-wei. He and Shan-wu-wei acted as teachers to one another.

Chin-kang-chih received an imperial order to conduct prayers for rain. Within the space of seven days, rain did in fact fall, and the Son of Heaven was very pleased. Suddenly, however, a violent wind arose, and the ruler and his ministers, much disillusioned, sent men to drive Chin-kang-chih out of the country, though in the end he managed to remain in China under one pretext or another.

Sometime later, when one of the emperor's favorite daughters lay dying, he was ordered to pray for her recovery. He selected two seven-year-old girls who served at the court to be substitutes for the dying lady and had piles of firewood lighted all around them, so that they burned to death. It was indeed a cruel thing to do. Moreover, the emperor's daughter failed to return to life.

Pu-k'ung came to China together with Chin-kang-chih.[165] But, perhaps because his suspicions were aroused by the happenings I have just mentioned, after Shan-wu-wei and Chin-kang-chih died, he returned to India and studied Shingon doctrine all over again, this time under Nāgabodhi. In the end, he became a convert to the teachings of the T'ien-t'ai school. But although he acknowledged allegiance to these teachings in his heart, he would never do so in his outward actions.

Pu-k'ung, too, was ordered by the emperor to pray for rain, and within three days, rain did in fact fall. The emperor was pleased and dispensed rewards with his own hand. But shortly after, a huge wind descended from the sky, buffeting and damaging the imperial palace and toppling the quarters of the upper noblemen and high ministers until it seemed that not a building would be left standing. The emperor, astounded, issued an imperial command for prayers that the wind be stopped. But though it would stop for a little, it would start blowing again and again, until in the end it blew uninterrupted for a space of several days. Eventually, messengers were dispatched to drive Pu-k'ung out of the country, and then at last the wind subsided.

The evil winds of these three men have become the huge wind of the Shingon leaders that blows throughout all of China and Japan! And if that is so, then the great gale that arose on the twelfth day of the fourth month in the eleventh year of Bun'ei (1274) must have been an adverse wind brought about by Kaga Hōin[166] of the Amida Hall, one of the most eminent monks of Tō-ji, when he was praying for rain. We must conclude that the evil teachings of Shan-wu-wei, Chin-kang-chih, and Pu-k'ung have been transmitted without the slightest alteration. What a strange coincidence indeed!

Let us turn now to the Great Teacher Kōbō. At the time of the great drought in the second month of the first year of Tenchō (824), the emperor first ordered Shubin[167] to pray for rain, and within seven days Shubin was able to make rain fall. But the rain fell only in the capital and did not extend to the countryside.

Kōbō was then ordered to take over the prayers for rain, but seven days passed and there was no sign of it. Another seven days passed and there still were no clouds. After seven more days had passed, the emperor ordered Wake no Matsuna to go and present offerings in the Shinsen-en garden, whereupon rain fell from the sky for a period of three days.[168] Kōbō and his disciples thereupon proceeded to appropriate this rain and claim it as their own, and for more than four hundred years now, it has been known as "Kōbō's rain."

Jikaku said he had a dream in which he shot down the sun. And Kōbō told a great falsehood, claiming that, in the spring of the ninth year of the Kōnin era (818), when he was praying for an end to the great epidemic, the sun came out in the middle of the night.

Since the Kalpa of Formation,[169] when the earth took shape, down to the ninth kalpa of decrease in the Kalpa of Continuance,[170] twenty-nine kalpas have passed by, but in all that time, the sun has never been known to come out at night! And as to Jikaku's dream of the sun, where in all the five thousand or seven thousand volumes of the Buddhist scriptures or the three thousand or more volumes of the secular classics is it recorded that to dream of shooting the sun is auspicious? The king of the *asuras,* angered at the deity Taishaku, shot an arrow at the sun god, but the arrow came back and struck the king himself in the eye. Chou,[171] the last ruler of the Yin dynasty, used the sun as a target for his arrows, and in the end he was destroyed.

In Japan, in the reign of Emperor Jimmu, the emperor's elder brother Itsuse no Mikoto engaged in battle with the chieftain of Tomi, Nagasunebiko,[172] and Itsuse no Mikoto was wounded in the hand by an arrow. He said, "I am a descendant of the sun deity. But because I have drawn my bow while facing the sun, I have incurred this punishment from the sun deity."

In India, King Ajātaśatru renounced his earlier mistaken views and became a follower of the Buddha. He returned to his palace and lay down to sleep, but later rose up in alarm and said to his ministers, "I have dreamed that the sun has left the sky and fallen to the earth!" His ministers said, "Perhaps this means the passing away of the Buddha."[173] Subhadra also had the same kind of dream just before the Buddha passed away.[174]

It would be particularly inauspicious to dream, [as Jikaku claims he did,] of shooting the sun in Japan, since the supreme deity in Japan is Amaterasu, the Sun Goddess, and the name of the country, Japan, means "the Land of the Rising Sun." In addition, Shakyamuni Buddha is called the "Sun Seed" because his mother Queen Māyā dreamed that she conceived the sun and in time gave birth to this child, the crown prince, [who later became the Buddha].[175]

The Great Teacher Jikaku established Dainichi Buddha as the object of worship on Mount Hiei and rejected Shakyamuni Buddha. He paid honor to the three Shingon sutras and acted as an enemy to the Lotus Sutra and its two companion sutras. That was no doubt the reason why he dreamed this dream of shooting the sun.

On the subject of dreams, there is also the case of the priest Shantao in China. In his youth he met a priest named Ming-sheng[176] of Mi-chou and received instruction in the Lotus Sutra. Later, however, when he met Tao-ch'o, he threw aside the Lotus Sutra and put all his trust in the *Kammuryōju* Sutra. He even wrote a commentary on the sutra,[177] which asserted that with the Lotus Sutra, not one person in a thousand can be saved, whereas the Nembutsu practice insures that ten persons out of ten or a hundred persons out of a hundred will be reborn in the Pure Land. In order to prove his point, he prayed before Amida Buddha to confirm whether or not his views accorded with the Buddha's intent. His commentary says, "Every night in a dream a priest would appear and tell me what to write," and, "Therefore this commentary should be regarded with the same respect as the sutra itself." It also says, "The *Kannen Hōmon* should also be revered as though it were a sutra."[178]

The Lotus Sutra says, "Among those who hear of this Law, there is not one who shall not attain Buddhahood."[179] But Shan-tao says that not one in a thousand will be saved.[180] The Lotus Sutra and Shan-tao are as different as fire is from water. Shan-tao says that the *Kammuryōju* Sutra can save ten persons out of ten, or a hundred persons out of a hundred. But in the *Muryōgi* Sutra the Buddha says that in the *Kammuryōju* Sutra, "I have not yet revealed the truth."[181] The *Muryōgi* Sutra and this priest of the Willow Cloister[182] are as far apart as heaven and earth.

In view of this, can we really believe that Amida Buddha took the form of a priest and appeared to Shan-tao in dreams to assure him that his commentary represented the truth? Was not Amida among those present when the Lotus Sutra was preached, and did he not extend his tongue along with the others and testify to the truth of the sutra? Were his attendants, the bodhisattvas Kannon and Seishi,[183] not also present when the Lotus Sutra was preached? The answers to these questions are obvious, and in like manner, if we stop to think of it, we can see that Jikaku's dream was a portent of evil.

Question: The Great Teacher Kōbō in his *Shingyō Hiken* or Secret Key to the Heart Sutra writes: "In the spring of the ninth year of Kōnin (818), the empire was troubled by a great plague. Thereupon the emperor in person dipped his writing brush in gold, took a piece of dark blue paper in his hand, and wrote out a copy of the *Hannya Shingyō,* or Heart Sutra in one roll. I had been appointed by the ruler to lecture on the Heart Sutra. Having compiled my explanations of its meaning, I [was delivering the lecture but] had not yet reached my concluding remarks, when those who had recovered from the plague began to fill the streets of the capital. Moreover, when night came, the sun continued to shine bright and red.

"This was certainly not the result of any virtuous observance of the precepts on the part of an ignorant person like myself, but was due rather to the power of faith manifested by the sovereign as the gold-wheel-turning king.[184] Nevertheless, those who go to pray at the shrines of the gods should recite this commentary of mine. For I was present long ago at Eagle Peak when the Buddha preached the Heart Sutra, and I personally heard him expound its profound doctrines. How, then, could I fail to understand its meaning?"[185]

Again in the work entitled *Kujakkyō Ongi,* or Annotations on the Peacock Sutra, we read: "After the Great Teacher Kōbō returned from China, he desired to establish the Shingon sect in Japan, and representatives of all the various sects were summoned to the imperial court. But many of them had doubts about the Shingon doctrine of the attaining of Buddhahood in one's present form. The Great Teacher Kōbō thereupon formed his hands in the wisdom mudra and faced south. Suddenly his mouth opened and he turned into the golden-colored Buddha Mahavairocana—that is, he reverted to his original form. In this way he demonstrated that the Buddha is present in the individual and that the individual is present in the Buddha, and that one can immediately attain Buddhahood in this very existence. On that day, all doubts concerning the matter were completely resolved, and from that time the Shingon or Yuga[186] sect with its doctrines of secret mandalas was established."

The same work also says, "At this time the leaders of the other sects all bowed to the opinion of the Great Teacher Kōbō and for the first time received instruction in Shingon, sought its benefit and practiced it. Dōshō of the Sanron sect, Gennin of the Hossō sect, Dōō[187] of the Kegon set, and Enchō of the Tendai sect were all among those who did so."[188]

In addition, the biography of the Great Teacher Kōbō states: "On the day when he set out by ship from China, he voiced a prayer, saying, 'If there is a spot that is particularly suitable for the teaching of these doctrines that I have learned, may this three-pronged *vajra* implement land there!' Then he faced in the direction of Japan and threw the implement up into the air. It sailed far away and disappeared among the clouds. In the tenth month, he returned to Japan.

The same work states, "He journeyed to the foot of Mount Kōya and determined to establish his place of meditation there . . . and later it was discovered that the three-pronged *vajra* implement which he had thrown out over the sea was there on the mountain."[189]

It is clear from these two or three incidents that the Great Teacher Kōbō was a person of inestimable power and virtue. Since he was a person of such great power, why do you say that one should not believe in his teachings, and that anyone who does so will fall into the Avīci hell?

Answer: I, too, admire and believe in these various accomplishments of his. There are other men of old who possessed such uncanny powers. But the possession of such power does not indicate whether that person's understanding of the Buddhist Law is correct or not. Among the Brahman believers of India there have been men who could pour the water of the Ganges River into their ear and keep it there for twelve years, who could drink the ocean dry, grasp the sun and moon in their hands, or change the disciples of Shakyamuni Buddha into oxen or sheep.[190] But such powers only made them more arrogant than ever and caused them to create further karma to suffer in the realm of birth and death. It is men like these whom T'ien-t'ai is referring to when he says, "They seek after fame and profit and increase their illusions of thought and desire."[191]

The Chinese priest Fa-yün of Kuang-che-ssu could make it rain suddenly or cause flowers to bloom immediately, but Miao-lo writes of him, "Though he could bring about a response in this way, his understanding still did not accord with the truth [of the Lotus Sutra]."[192] When the Great Teacher T'ien-t'ai read the Lotus Sutra, soft rain began to fall in an instant, and the Great Teacher Dengyō caused the rain of amṛta[193] to fall within the space of three days. However, they did not say that because of such powers their understanding of the truth coincided with that of the Buddha.

Regardless of what unusual powers Kōbō may have had, he described the Lotus Sutra as a doctrine of childish theory, and wrote that Shakyamuni Buddha was still in the region of darkness. Men of wisdom and understanding should have nothing to do with such writings!

Say what you may, there are surely doubtful points in the accounts of Kōbō's powers you have just cited. The text says, "In the spring of the ninth year of Kōnin (818), the empire was troubled by a great plague." But spring is ninety days long.[194] On which day of which month of spring did this happen? This is the first doubtful point.

Secondly, was there in fact an outbreak of plague in the ninth year of Kōnin?

Thirdly, the text says, "When night came, the sun continued to shine bright and red." If it really did so, then this is an occurrence of major importance. During the ninth year of Kōnin, Emperor Saga reigned. But did the court historians of the left and right[195] record any such event?

Even if they had, it would be difficult to believe. During the twenty kalpas of the Kalpa of Formation, as well as nine kalpas of the Kalpa of Continuance, a total of twenty-nine kalpas, never once has such a thing occurred. What then is this about the sun appearing in the middle of the night? In all the teachings expounded by Shakyamuni Buddha during his lifetime, there is no mention of any such thing. And in the *Three Records* and *Five Canons*[196] of China which describe the three sovereigns and five emperors of antiquity, there is no prediction that at some future date the sun will come out in the middle of the night. In the scriptures of Buddhism, we are told that in the Kalpa of Decline, two suns, three suns, or even seven suns will appear, but these will appear in the daytime, not at night. And if the sun should appear at night in our own region, the continent of Jambudvīpa in the south, then what about the other three regions of the east, west, and north?

Regardless of what the Buddhist scriptures or the secular works may have to say about such an event, if in fact there were some entry in the diaries of the courtiers, the other families of the capital, or the priests of Mount Hiei saying that in the spring of the ninth year of Kōnin, in such and such a month, on such and such a day, at such an hour of the night the sun appeared, then we might perhaps believe it. [But no such record exists.]

Later, the text says, "I was present long ago at Eagle Peak when the Buddha preached the Heart Sutra, and I personally heard him expound its profound doctrines." This is surely a wild falsehood that is intended to make people have faith in his commentary. If not, are we to believe that at Eagle Peak the Buddha announced that the Lotus Sutra was a piece of "childish theory" and that the *Dainichi* Sutra represented the truth, and that Ānanda and Monju were simply mistaken in saying that the Lotus Sutra represents the truth?

As for making it rain, even a promiscuous woman and a breaker of the precepts[197] were able by their poems to cause rain to fall. Yet Kōbō prayed for twenty-one days and still it did not rain, so what sort of powers could he have possessed? This is the fourth doubtful point.

The *Kujakkyō Ongi* states, "The Great Teacher Kōbō thereupon formed his hands in the wisdom mudra and faced south. Suddenly his mouth opened and he turned into the golden-colored Buddha

Mahāvairocana." Now in what year of the reign of what ruler did this happen?

In China from the time of the Chien-yüan era (140–134 B.C.), and in Japan from the time of the Taihō era (701–704), among the records of events kept by priests and the laity, those of important occurrences have always been accompanied by the name of the era in which they took place. With an event as important as that described, why then is there no mention of who the ruler was, who his high ministers were, what the name of the era was, or what day and hour the event took place?

The passage goes on to list "Dōshō of the Sanron sect, Gennin of the Hossō sect, Dōō of the Kegon sect, and Enchō of the Tendai sect" [as those who learned the Shingon doctrines from Kōbō]. Enchō is known posthumously as the Great Teacher Jakkō and was the second chief priest of the Tendai sect. Now at that time, why were Gishin, the first chief priest, or the Great Teacher Dengyō, the founder of the sect, not invited to be present? Enchō, the second chief priest of the Tendai sect, was a disciple of the Great Teacher Dengyō and also became a disciple of Kōbō. Rather than inviting a disciple or rather than inviting men of the Sanron, Hossō, and Kegon sects, why did Kōbō not invite the two most important men of the Tendai sect, Dengyō and Gishin?

Speaking of the time when these men were invited, the *Kujakkyō Ongi* states, "From that time the Shingon or Yuga sect with its doctrines of secret mandalas was established." This would seem to refer to a time when both Dengyō and Gishin were still alive. From the second year of Daidō (807), in the reign of Emperor Heizei, until the thirteenth year of Kōnin (822) [when Dengyō died], Kōbō was very active in spreading the Shingon doctrines, and during this period both Dengyō and Gishin were still alive. Moreover, Gishin lived on until the tenth year of Tenchō (833). Is it possible that Kōbō waited until after then before trying to introduce his Shingon teachings to a leader of the Tendai sect? The whole matter is very strange.

The *Kujakukyō no Ongi* was written by Shinzei,[198] a disciple of Kōbō, and therefore it is difficult to trust what it says. Is it likely that a person of such deluded views would have troubled to read the writings of the courtiers, the other important families, or Enchō on which to base his account? One should also check the writings of Dōshō, Gennin, and Dōō to see if they have anything to say on the matter.

The text says, "Suddenly his mouth opened and he turned into the golden-colored Buddha Mahāvairocana." What does it mean by the expression "his mouth opened"? The writer probably intended to write *miken*, meaning the "area between the eyebrows,"[199] but he mistakenly wrote "mouth" instead. Because he wrote a book of fabrications, he quite likely made mistakes of this kind.

The whole passage says, "The Great Teacher Kōbō thereupon formed his hands in the wisdom mudra and faced south. Suddenly his mouth opened and he turned into the golden-colored Buddha Mahāvairocana."

Now in the fifth volume of the Nirvana Sutra we read: "Mahākāśyapa spoke to the Buddha, saying, 'World-Honored One, I will no longer depend upon the four ranks of saints.[200] Why is this? Because in the Ghoṣira Sutra that the Buddha preached for the sake of Ghoṣira,[201] it is said that the devil king in heaven, because he is determined to try to destroy the Buddhist Law, will turn himself into the likeness of a Buddha. He will have all the thirty-two marks and eighty characteristics[202] of a Buddha, will be solemn and imposing in appearance, and a round halo of light will radiate from him ten feet in all directions. His face will be round and full like the moon at its fullest and brightest, and the white curl in the area between his eyebrows will be whiter than snow. . . . From his left side will come water, and from his right side will come fire.' "[203]

Again, in the sixth volume of the Nirvana Sutra, it is recorded, "The Buddha announced to Mahākāśyapa, 'After I have passed into nirvana, . . . this Devil of the Sixth Heaven and other devils will in time try to destroy this True Law of mine. . . . He will change himself into the form of an arhat or of a Buddha. The devil king, though still subject to illusion, will assume the form of one who has been freed from illusion, and will try to destroy this True Law of mine.' "[204]

The Great Teacher Kōbō declared that, in comparison to the *Kegon* and *Dainichi* sutras, the Lotus Sutra was a piece of "childish theory." And this same man, we are told, appeared in the form of a Buddha. He must be the devil who, as the Nirvana Sutra states, will change his shape, that is still subject to illusion, into that of a Buddha and attempt to destroy the True Law of Shakyamuni.

This "True Law" referred to in the Nirvana Sutra is the Lotus Sutra. Therefore we find later on in the Nirvana Sutra the statement, "It has already been a long time since I attained Buddhahood."[205]

The text also says that the sutra itself is contained in the Lotus Sutra.

Shakyamuni, Tahō, and the other Buddhas of the ten directions declared with regard to the various sutras that the Lotus Sutra represents the truth; the *Dainichi* and all the other sutras do not represent the truth. Yet Kōbō appeared in the form of a Buddha and announced that, compared to the *Kegon* and *Dainichi* sutras, the Lotus Sutra is a piece of "childish theory." If the words of the Buddha are true, then Kōbō must be none other than the Devil of the Sixth Heaven, must he not?

Again, this matter of the three-pronged *vajra* implement appears to be particularly suspicious. It would be difficult to believe even if a Chinese [who had not known the circumstances] had come to Japan and happened to dig up the *vajra* implement. Surely someone must have been sent earlier to bury it in that particular spot. Since Kōbō was a Japanese, he could have arranged such a thing. There are many such wild and absurd stories associated with his name. Such incidents hardly lend support to the assertion that his teachings accord with the will of the Buddha.

Thus the doctrines of the Shingon, Zen, and Nembutsu sects spread and prospered in Japan. Eventually, Takanari, the Retired Emperor of Oki, began making efforts to overthrow the Gon no Tayū.[206] Since he was the sovereign, the leader of the nation, people supposed that, even without assistance, it would be as easy as a lion pouncing on a rabbit or a hawk seizing a pheasant. Moreover, for a period of several years appeals had been made at Mount Hiei, the temples of Tō-ji, Onjō-ji, and the seven major temples of Nara, as well as to the Sun Goddess, the Great Bodhisattva Hachiman, and the deities of the Sannō, Kamo, and Kasuga shrines,[207] asking that the emperor's enemies be subdued and that the gods lend their aid. Yet, when war broke out, the imperial forces were not able to hold out for more than two or three days. In the end, the three retired emperors were exiled to the islands of Sado and Oki and the province of Awa, respectively,[208] where they ended their lives.

Moreover, Omuro,[209] who was leading the prayers to subdue the enemies of the court, was not only driven out of Tō-ji temple, but his favorite, the page Setaka,[210] who was as dear to him as his very eyes, was beheaded. Thus, as the Lotus Sutra says, the curses in the end "returned to the originators."[211]

But this is a trifling matter compared to what is to come. Hereafter, I have no doubt that the officials and the countless common people of Japan will without exception suffer a fate like that of heaps of dry grass to which a torch has been set, like huge mountains crumbling and valleys being filled up, for our country will be attacked by enemies from abroad.

I, Nichiren, am the only one in the whole country of Japan who understands why these things will happen. But if I speak out, I will be treated as King Chou of the Yin dynasty treated Pi Kan, tearing open his chest; as King Chieh of the Hsia dynasty treated Lung-feng, cutting off his head, or as King Dammira treated Āryasiṁha, beheading him. I will be banished like the priest Chu Tao-sheng, or branded on the face like the Tripitaka Master Fa-tao.[212]

In the Lotus Sutra, however, it is written, "We do not hold our own lives dear. We value only the supreme Way."[213] And the Nirvana Sutra warns, "He should never hold back any of the teachings, even though it may cost him his life."[214]

If in this present existence I am so fearful for my life that I fail to speak out, then in what future existence will I ever attain Buddhahood? Or in what future existence will I ever be able to bring salvation to my parents and my teacher? With thoughts such as these uppermost in my mind, I decided that I must begin to speak out. And, just as I had expected, I was ousted, I was vilified, I was attacked, and I suffered wounds. Finally, on the twelfth day of the fifth month in the first year of the Kōchō era (1261), the year with the cyclical sign kanoto-tori, having incurred the displeasure of the authorities, I was banished to Itō in the province of Izu. Eventually, on the twenty-second day of the second month of the third year of Kōchō (1263), the year with the cyclical sign mizunoto-i, I was pardoned and allowed to return.

After that, I became more determined than ever to attain enlightenment and continued to speak out. Accordingly, the difficulties I encountered became increasingly severe, like great waves that rise up in a gale. I experienced with my own body the kind of attacks with sticks and staves that Bodhisattva Fukyō suffered in ancient times. It would seem that even the persecutions suffered by the monk Kakutoku[215] in the latter age after the death of the Buddha Kangi Zōyaku could not compare to my trials. Nowhere in all the sixty-six provinces and the two offshore islands of Japan, not for a day, not for an hour, could I find a place to rest in safety.

Even sages who persevere in their practice as earnestly as did Rāhula in ancient times, strictly observing all the two hundred and fifty precepts, or men who are as wise as Pūrṇa,[216] speak evil of Nichiren when they encounter him. Even worthy men who are as honest and upright as the court officials Wei Cheng[217] or Fujiwara no Yoshifusa,[218] when they see Nichiren, forsake reason and treat him unjustly.

How much more so is this the case with the ordinary people of the day! They behave like dogs who have seen a monkey, or hunters in pursuit of a deer. Throughout the whole of Japan, there is not a single person who says, "Perhaps this man has some reason for his behavior."

But that is only to be expected. For whenever I come upon a person who recites the Nembutsu, I tell him that those who put their faith in the Nembutsu will fall into the hell of incessant suffering. Whenever I come upon a person who honors the Shingon teachings, I tell him that Shingon is an evil doctrine that will destroy the nation. And to [Hōjō Tokimune,] the ruler of the nation, who honors the Zen sect, I, Nichiren, declare that Zen is the creation of devils.

Since I willingly bring these troubles upon myself, when others vilify me, I do not rebuke them. Even if I wanted to rebuke them, there are too many of them. And even when they strike me, I feel no pain, for I have been prepared for their blows from the very beginning.

And so I went about with ever increasing vigor and ever less concern for my safety, trying to persuade others to change their ways. As a result, several hundred Zen priests, several thousand Nembutsu believers, and even more Shingon teachers went to the magistrate or the men of powerful families, or to their wives or their widows who had taken holy orders, and filled their ears with endless slanders concerning me.

Finally, all were convinced that I was the gravest offender in the entire nation, for it was said that in my capacity as a priest, I was saying prayers and spells for the destruction of Japan, and that I had reported that the deceased officials Hōjō Tokiyori and Hōjō Shigetoki[219] had fallen into the hell of incessant suffering. Their widows insisted that investigation was unnecessary; rather, I should have my head cut off, and my disciples should likewise be beheaded or exiled to distant lands or placed in confinement. So infuriated were they that their demands for punishment were immediately carried out.

On the night of the twelfth day of the ninth month in the eighth year of Bun'ei (1271), the year with the cyclical sign *kanoto-hitsuji,* I

was to have been beheaded at Tatsunokuchi in the province of Sagami. But for some reason the execution was postponed and that
night I was taken to a place called Echi. On the night of the thirteenth
day, people made a great uproar, saying I had been pardoned. But,
again for reasons that are unclear, I was ordered into exile on the
island of Sado.

While people speculated from one day to the next if I would be
beheaded, I passed four years on Sado.[220] Then, on the fourteenth
day of the second month in the eleventh year of Bun'ei (1274), the
year with the cyclical sign *kinoe-inu,* I was pardoned. On the twenty-
sixth day of the third month of the same year, I returned to Kamakura, and on the eighth day of the fourth month I had an interview
with Hei no Saemon. I reported on various matters and informed
him that the Mongols would certainly invade Japan within that year.
Then on the twelfth day of the fifth month, I left Kamakura and came
to this mountain where I am now living.

All these things I have done solely in order to repay the debt I owe
to my parents, the debt I owe to my teacher, the debt I owe to the
three treasures of Buddhism, and the debt I owe to my country. For
their sake I have been willing to destroy my body and to give up my
life, though as it turns out, I have not been put to death after all.

If a wise man makes three attempts to warn the leaders of the
nation and they still refuse to heed his advice, then he should retire to
a mountain forest. This has been the custom from ages past, and I
have accordingly followed it.

I am quite certain that the merit I have acquired through my efforts
is recognized by everyone from the three treasures of Buddhism on
down to Bonten, Taishaku, and the gods of the sun and moon.
Through this merit I will surely lead to enlightenment my parents
and my teacher, the late Dōzen-bō.[221]

But there are certain doubts that trouble me. Maudgalyāyana, a
disciple of the Buddha, attempted to save his mother Shōdai-nyo, but
he could not do so, and she remained in the realm of Hungry Ghosts.[222]
The monk Sunakṣatra[223] was a son of the World-Honored One, and
yet he fell into the Avīci Hell. Thus, although one may exert one's
full effort to save others, it is very difficult to save them from the
karmic retribution that they have brought upon themselves.

The late Dōzen-bō treated me as one of his favorite disciples, so I
cannot believe that he bore any hatred toward me. But he was a timid
man, and he could never bring himself to give up his position at the

temple where he lived, Seichō-ji. Moreover, he was fearful of what Tōjō Kagenobu,[224] the steward of the region, might do if he gave ear to my teachings. And at Seichō-ji he had to live in the midst of priests like Enchi and Jitsujō,[225] who were as evil as Devadatta or Kokālika, and to put up with their intimidations, so that he became more fearful than ever. As a result, he turned a deaf ear to the disciple he had been fondest of, one who had followed him for many years. One wonders what will become of such a man in the next life.

There is one thing to be thankful for. Kagenobu, Enchi, and Jitsujō all died before Dōzen-bō did, and that was something of a help. These men all met an untimely death because of the chastisement of the Ten Goddesses who protect the Lotus Sutra. After they died, Dōzen-bō began to have some faith in the Lotus Sutra. But it was rather like obtaining a stick after the fight is over, or lighting a lamp at midday—the proper time had already passed.

In addition, I cannot keep from thinking that, whatever happens, one ought to feel pity and concern for one's own children or disciples. Dōzen-bō was not an entirely helpless man, and yet, though I was exiled all the way to the island of Sado, he never once tried to visit me. This is hardly the behavior of one who believes in the Lotus Sutra.

In spite of all that, I thought a great deal of him, and when I heard the news of his death, I felt as though, whether I had to walk through fire or wade through water, I must rush to his grave, pound on it, and recite a volume of the Lotus Sutra for his sake.

However, it often happens with worthy men that, although they do not think of themselves as having retired from the world, other people assume that they have, and therefore, if they were to come rushing out of retreat for no good reason, people would suppose that they had failed to accomplish their purpose. For this reason, no matter how much I might wish to visit his grave, I feel that I cannot do so.

Now you two, Jōken-bō and Gijō-bō,[226] were my teachers in my youth. You are like the Administrators of Monks Gonsō and Gyōhyō who were the teachers of the Great Teacher Dengyō, but later, on the contrary, became his disciples. When Tōjō Kagenobu was bent on harming me and I decided that I must leave Mount Kiyosumi [on which Seichō-ji is located], you helped me escape in secret. You have performed an unrivaled service for the Lotus Sutra. There can be no doubt about the reward that awaits you in your next rebirth.

Question: Within the eight volumes and twenty-eight chapters that constitute the entirety of the Lotus Sutra, what part represents the true heart of the work?

Answer: The heart of the *Kegon* Sutra is the title *Daihōkōbutsu Kegon* Sutra. The heart of the *Agon* sutras is the title *Bussetsu Chū-agon* Sutra. The heart of the *Daijuku* Sutra is the title *Daihōdō Daijuku* Sutra. The heart of the *Hannya* Sutra is the title *Makahannya Haramitsu* Sutra. The heart of the *Muryōju* Sutra is the title *Bussetsu Muryōju* Sutra. The heart of the *Kammuryōju* Sutra is the title *Bussetsu Kammuryōju* Sutra. The heart of the *Amida* Sutra is the title *Bussetsu Amida* Sutra. The heart of the Nirvana Sutra is the title *Daihatsunehan* Sutra. It is the same with all the sutras. The daimoku or title of the sutra, which appears before the opening words *nyoze gamon* or "Thus have I heard,"[227] is in all cases the true heart of the sutra. This is true whether it is a Mahayana sutra or a Hinayana sutra. As for the *Dainichi* Sutra, the *Kongōchō* Sutra, the *Soshitsuji* Sutra, and so forth —in all cases the title constitutes the heart.

The same is true of the Buddhas. Dainichi Nyorai, Nichigatsu Tōmyō Buddha, Nentō Buddha,[228] Daitsūchishō Buddha, Unraionnō Buddha[229]—in the case of all these Buddhas, the name itself contains within it all the various virtues that pertain to that particular Buddha.

The same, then, applies to the Lotus Sutra. The five characters *Myō-hō-ren-ge-kyō* that appear before the opening words "Thus have I heard" comprise the true heart of the eight volumes of the work. Moreover, they are the heart of all the sutras, as well as the True Law that stands above all the Buddhas and bodhisattvas, the people of the two vehicles, and all the heavenly deities and human beings, *asuras* and dragon gods.

Question: If one person should chant Nam-myoho-renge-kyo without understanding its meaning, and another person should chant the words *Namu Daihōkōbutsu Kegonkyō* without understanding their meaning, would the merit acquired by the two persons be equal, or would one acquire greater merit than the other?

Answer: One would acquire greater merit than the other.

Question: Why do you say so?

Answer: A small river can accommodate the water flowing into it from dew, brooks, wells, ditches, and little streams, but it cannot accommodate the water from a big river. A big river can accommodate the water from a small river with its dew, brooks, and so forth, but it cannot accommodate the water from the great ocean. Now the *Agon* sutras are like the small river with its wells, streams, brooks, and dew, while the *Hōdō* sutras, the *Amida* Sutra, the *Dainichi* Sutra, and the *Kegon* Sutra are like the big river that accommodates the small river. But the Lotus Sutra is like the great ocean that can hold all the water from dew, brooks, wells, streams, small rivers, big rivers, and the rains from heaven, without losing a single drop.

Suppose that a person is burning with fever. If he sits down beside a large body of cold water and stays there for a while, his fever will abate, but if he lies down beside a little body of water, he will continue to suffer as before. In the same way, if an *icchantika* or person of incorrigible disbelief, who has committed the five cardinal sins and has slandered the Law, should try to cool himself beside the little bodies of water that are the *Agon, Kegon, Kammuryōju,* and *Dainichi* sutras, the raging fever caused by his great offenses would never be dispelled. But if he should lie down on the great snowy mountain that is the Lotus Sutra, then the raging fever caused by the five offenses, his slander of the Law, and his incorrigible disbelief, would be dispelled instantly.

Therefore, ignorant people should by all means have faith in the Lotus Sutra. For although one may think that all the titles of the sutras are the same in effect and that it is as easy to chant one as another, in fact the merit acquired even by an ignorant person who chants the title of the Lotus Sutra is as far superior to that acquired by a wise man who chants some other title as heaven is to earth!

To illustrate, even a person with great strength cannot break a strong rope with his bare hands. But if one has a little knife, then even a person of meager strength can sever the rope with ease. Even a person with great strength cannot cut through a piece of hard stone with a dull sword. But if one has a sharp sword, then even a person of meager strength can cut the stone in two.

Or, to give another example, even though one may not know what is in the medicine, if one takes a dose of it, he can cure his illness. But if he takes only ordinary food, his illness will never be cured. Or to give yet another example, a medicine with supernatural properties can actually increase one's life span, whereas ordinary medicine, though it can cure illness, can never prolong one's life.

Question: Of the twenty-eight chapters of the Lotus Sutra, which is the heart, which is the most essential?

Answer: Some would say that each chapter is essential to the matter that it deals with. Some would contend that the *Hōben* and *Juryō* chapters are the heart, others that the *Hōben* alone is the heart, or that the *Juryō* alone is the heart. Some would say that the passage, "to cause all beings to awaken to the Buddha wisdom, to reveal it, to let all beings know it and enter into it,"[230] is the heart, others that the "true aspect"[231] is the heart.

Question: What is your opinion?

Answer: I believe that the words Nam-myoho-renge-kyo constitute the heart.

Question: What is your proof?

Answer: The fact that Ānanda, Monju, and the others wrote, "Thus have I heard."

Question: What do you mean by that?

Answer: Over a period of eight years, Ānanda, Monju, and the others listened to the innumerable principles of the Lotus Sutra, never missing a single sentence, a single verse, a single word. Yet, after the Buddha had passed away, at the time of the compilation of his teachings, when the 999 arhats took up their writing brushes and dipped them in ink, they first of all wrote the words *Myōhō-renge-kyō,* and after that they intoned the words, "Thus have I heard." Therefore these five words *Myō-hō-ren-ge-kyō* must be the heart of the eight volumes and twenty-eight chapters that compose the work, must they not?

Therefore the Dharma Teacher Fa-yün of Kuang-che-ssu, who is said to have lectured on the Lotus Sutra ever since the distant age of Nichigatsu Tōmyō Buddha, states: "The words 'Thus have I heard' indicate that one is going to transmit the doctrines he has heard preached. The title, which precedes these words, sums up the sutra as a whole."[232]

The Great Teacher T'ien-t'ai, who was present on Eagle Peak when the Lotus Sutra was preached and heard it in person, writes, "The word 'thus' indicates the essence of a doctrine heard from the Buddha."[233] And the Great Teacher Chang-an writes, "The transcriber [Chang-an] comments on [T'ien-t'ai's explanation of the title of the Lotus Sutra], saying, 'Hence [his explanation of the title in] the preface conveys the profound meaning of the sutra as a whole, and the profound meaning indicates the heart of the work.' "[234]

In this passage, the words "heart of the work" signify that the daimoku or title of the work is the heart of the Lotus Sutra. As the Great Teacher Miao-lo states, "It is the heart of the Lotus Sutra that encompasses all the doctrines preached by the Buddha in the course of his lifetime."[235]

India comprises seventy states,[236] but they are known collectively by the name Gasshi [the Land of the Moon], or India. Japan comprises sixty provinces,[237] but they are known collectively by the name Ni-hon [the Land of the Sun], or Japan. Within the name India are contained all the seventy states, as well as all their people, animals, treasures, and so forth. Within the name Japan are contained all the sixty-six provinces. The feathers sent as tribute from Dewa, the gold of Ōshū[238] and all the other treasures of the nation, as well as the people and animals, temples and shrines, are all contained within the two characters that form the name Ni-hon or Japan.

One who possesses the Heavenly Eye[239] can look at the two characters of the name Japan and see all the sixty-six provinces along with their people and animals. One who possesses the Dharma Eye[240] can see all the people and animals now dying in one place, now being born in another place.

It is like hearing someone's voice and knowing what the person must look like, or seeing someone's footprints and judging whether the person is large or small. Or it is like estimating the size of a pond by looking at the lotuses that grow in it, or imagining the size of the dragons by observing the rain that they cause to fall. Each of these examples illustrates the principle that all things are expressed in one.

It might appear from this that the daimoku or title of any *Agon* sutra must contain all the teachings of the Buddhas, but in fact it contains only one Buddha, the Shakyamuni of the Hinayana teachings. It might also appear that the titles of the *Kegon, Kammuryōju,* and *Dainichi* sutras must contain all the teachings of the Buddhas, but in fact they do not include the doctrine concerning the attainment of Buddhahood by people in the two realms of *shōmon* and *engaku,* or the Shakyamuni Buddha who gained enlightenment in the far distant past. They are like flowers that bloom but are followed by no fruit, thunder that rolls but brings no rain, a drum that has no sound, eyes that cannot see, a woman who bears no child, or a person who has no life or spirit in him.

The mantras associated with the Buddhas Dainichi, Yakushi, and Amida and Bodhisattva Kannon are of the same nature. Though in the various sutras containing these mantras they are said to be like a great king, Mount Sumeru, the sun and moon, good medicine, a wish-granting jewel or a sharp sword, they are as far beneath the daimoku of the Lotus Sutra as mud is beneath the clouds.

Not only are they vastly inferior, but all of them have lost their respective inherent functions. When the sun comes up, the light of the crowds of stars is completely eclipsed; when bits of iron are placed near a magnet, they lose their property. When a great sword is exposed to even a small fire, it ceases to be of any use; when cow's milk or donkey's milk comes into the presence of lion king's milk, it turns to water. A pack of foxes will forget all their tricks if they meet up with a dog; a band of dogs will all quake with fright if they encounter a small tiger.

In the same way, if one chants Nam-myoho-renge-kyo, then the power of the words Namu Amida Butsu, the power of the mantras invoking Dainichi, the power of Bodhisattva Kannon, and the power of all the Buddhas, all the sutras, and all the bodhisattvas will without exception vanish before the power of Myōhō-renge-kyō.

Unless these other sutras manage to borrow the power of Myōhō-renge-kyō, they will all become worthless things. This is a fact that stands before our very eyes in the present age.

Because I, Nichiren, chant and spread Nam-myoho-renge-kyo, the power of Namu Amida Butsu will be like a moon waning, a tide running out, grass withering in autumn and winter, or ice melting in the sun. Watch and see!

Question: If this Law that you have been describing is in fact so wonderful, why is it not better known? Why have not Mahākāśyapa, Ānanda, Aśvaghoṣa, Nāgārjuna, Asaṅga,[241] Vasubandhu, Nan-yüeh, T'ien-t'ai, Miao-lo, and Dengyō spread it abroad the way Shan-tao spread the practice of Namu Amida Butsu throughout China or the way Eshin, Yōkan,[242] and Hōnen spread it in Japan, turning the whole country into worshipers of Amida Buddha?

Answer: This is an old criticism, not by any means one that is raised here for the first time.

Bodhisattvas Aśvaghoṣa and Nāgārjuna were great scholars who lived, respectively, six hundred and seven hundred years after the death of the Buddha. When these men appeared in the world and began spreading the doctrines of the Mahayana sutras, the various followers of the Hinayana raised objections.

"Mahākāśyapa and Ānanda," they said, "lived on for twenty or forty years after the death of the Buddha, preaching the True Law.

Presumably they conveyed the heart of all the teachings that the Buddha had propounded during his lifetime. Now we find that what these two men emphasized were simply the concepts of suffering, emptiness, impermanence, and non-self. Aśvaghoṣa and Nāgārjuna may be very wise, but are we to suppose that they are superior to Mahākāśyapa and Ānanda? This is our first objection.

"Mahākāśyapa obtained his enlightenment through direct encounters with the Buddha. But these two men, Aśvaghosa and Nāgārjuna, have never encountered the Buddha. This is our second objection.

"The Brahman philosophers who preceded the Buddha taught that life is permanent, joyful, endowed with self, and pure. Later, when the Buddha appeared in the world, he declared that life is marked by suffering, emptiness, impermanence, and non-self. Now Aśvaghoṣa and Nāgārjuna insist that it is permanent, joyful, endowed with self, and pure. This being so, we must suppose that, since both the Buddha and Mahākāśyapa have passed away from the world, the Devil of the Sixth Heaven has taken possession of these two men and is trying to overthrow the teachings of Buddhism and replace them with the teachings of the Brahman heretics.

"If that is so, then these men are the enemies of Buddhism! We must smash their skulls, cut off their heads, put an end to their lives, see that they get no more to eat! Let us drive them from the country!"

Such were the declarations of the Hinayana believers. And Aśvaghoṣa and Nāgārjuna, being two men alone, were forced day and night to listen to these shouts of calumny, and morning and evening to bear the attacks of sticks and staves.

But these two men were in fact messengers of the Buddha. For in the *Māyā* Sutra, it is predicted that Aśvaghoṣa will appear six hundred years, and Nāgārjuna, seven hundred years, after the Buddha's death. The same prediction is also recorded in the *Ryōga* Sutra, and of course in the *Fuhōzō* Sutra as well.[243]

But the Hinayana believers would not heed these predictions, and instead attacked the Mahayanists blindly and without reason. "Since hatred and jealousy abound even during the lifetime of the Buddha, how much worse will it be in the world after his passing?"[244] says the Lotus Sutra. Looking at the time of Aśvaghoṣa and Nāgārjuna, one begins to have a little understanding of what these words of the sutra really mean. Moreover, Bodhisattva Āryadeva was killed by a Brahman, and the Venerable Āryasiṁha had his head cut off. These events, too, give one cause for thought.

Then, some fifteen hundred years or more after the death of the Buddha, in the country of China, which lies east of India, the Great Teacher T'ien-t'ai appeared in the world during the years of the Ch'en and Sui dynasties. He declared that among the sacred teachings put forth by the Buddha, there were the Mahayana and the Hinayana, the exoteric and the esoteric, the provisional and the true. Mahākāśyapa and Ānanda had concentrated on spreading the Hinayana teachings, he explained. Aśvaghoṣa, Nāgārjuna, Asaṅga, and Vasubandhu had spread the provisional Mahayana teachings. But with regard to the true Mahayana teaching of the Lotus Sutra, they had merely touched on it briefly but concealed its meaning, or had described the surface meaning of the sutra but failed to discuss the differences that mark the Buddha's teachings expounded throughout his lifetime. Or they had described the theoretical teaching but not the essential teaching, or they had understood the theoretical and essential teachings but not *kanjin,* or the method for observing the mind.[245]

When the Great Teacher T'ien-t'ai expounded these views, the millions of followers of the ten schools of Buddhhism, three in southern China and seven in northern China, all with one accord gave a great laugh of derision.

"Here in these latter days, a truly amazing priest has made his appearance among us!" they exclaimed. "Though there have at times been persons who adhered to biased views and opposed us, never has there been anyone who maintained that all the 260 or more Tripitaka masters and teachers of Buddhism who have lived since the introduction of Buddhism in the tenth year of the Yung-p'ing era (67 A.D.) of the Later Han, the year with the cyclical sign *hinoto-u,* down to these present years of the Ch'en and Sui, were ignorant. And on top of that, he says that they are slanderers of the Law who are destined to fall into the evil states of existence. Such is the kind of person that has appeared!

"He is so insane that he even maintains that the Tripitaka Master Kumārajīva, the man who introduced the Lotus Sutra to China, was an ignorant fool! Whatever he may say about the men of China, imagine his saying that the great scholars of India such as Nāgārjuna and Vasubandhu and the several hundred others, all of them bodhisattvas of the four ranks, did not teach the true doctrine! Anyone who killed this man would be doing no more than killing a hawk! In fact he would be more praiseworthy than someone who kills a demon!"

This was the way they railed at the Great Teacher T'ien-t'ai. And later, in the time of the Great Teacher Miao-lo, when the Hossō and Shingon doctrines were introduced from India, and the Kegon school was first established in China, Miao-lo spoke out against these teachings and was met with a similar uproar.

In Japan, the Great Teacher Dengyō made his appearance 1,800 years after the Buddha had passed away. After examining the commentaries of T'ien-t'ai, he began to criticize the six sects of Buddhism that had flourished in Japan in the 260 or more years since the time of Emperor Kimmei. People in turn slandered him, saying that the Brahmans who lived in the time of the Buddha or the Taoists of China must have been reborn in Japan.

Dengyō also proposed to set up an ordination platform for administering the great precepts of perfect and immediate enlightenment, such as had never existed in India, China, or Japan in the 1,800 years since the Buddha's death. Indeed he went farther than this, declaring that the ordination platform at Kannon-ji in the western region of Tsukushi, the ordination platform at Ono-dera in the eastern province of Shimotsuke, and the ordination platform at Tōdai-ji in the central province of Yamato[246] all stank with the foul odor of the Hinayana precepts and were as worthless as broken tile and rubble. And the priests who upheld such precepts, he said, were no better than foxes and monkeys.

In reply, his critics exclaimed, "Ah, how amazing! This thing that looks like a priest must in fact be a great swarm of locusts that has appeared in Japan and is about to gobble up the tender shoots of Buddhism in one swoop. Or perhaps the tyrant Chou of the Yin dynasty or Chieh of the Hsia has been reborn in Japan in the shape of this priest. Perchance Emperor Wu of the Later Chou and Emperor Wu-tsung[247] of the T'ang have reappeared in the world. At any moment now, Buddhism may be wiped out and the nation overthrown!"

As for the ordinary people, they clapped their hands in alarm and waggled their tongues, saying, "Whenever the priests of these two types of Buddhism, Mahayana and Hinayana, appear together, they fight like Taishaku and the asuras, or like Hsiang Yü and Kao-tsu[248] disputing possession of the kingdom!"

Dengyō's opponents continued to revile him, saying, "In the time of the Buddha, there were two ordination platforms, one belonging to the Buddha and the other to Devadatta, and a number of people were killed in the dispute over them.[249] This man may well defy the other sects, but he declares that he must set up an ordination platform for administering the precepts of perfect and immediate enlightenment such as even his master, the Great Teacher T'ien-t'ai, was unable to establish. How strange! And how frightening, how frightening!"

But Dengyō had his passages of scripture to support him, and as you know, the Mahayana ordination platform was eventually set up and has been in existence for some time now on Mount Hiei.

Thus, although their enlightenment may have been the same, from the point of view of the teaching which they propagated, Aśvaghoṣa and Nāgārjuna were superior to Mahākāśyapa and Ānanda, T'ien-t'ai was superior to Aśvaghoṣa and Nāgārjuna, and Dengyō surpassed T'ien-t'ai. In these latter times, people's wisdom becomes shallow, while Buddhism becomes more profound. To give an analogy, a mild illness can be cured with ordinary medicine, but a severe illness requires a medicine with supernatural properties. A man who is weak must have strong allies to help him.

Question: Is there a True Law that was not propagated even by T'ien-t'ai and Dengyō?

Answer: Yes, there is.

Question: What sort of teaching is it?

Answer: It consists of three things. It was left behind by the Buddha for the sake of those who live in the Latter Day of the Law. It is the True Law that was never propagated by Mahākāśyapa or Ānanda, Aśvaghoṣa or Nāgārjuna, T'ien-t'ai or Dengyō.

Question: What form does it take?

Answer: First, in Japan and all the other countries throughout the world, the object of worship should in all cases be the Lord Shakyamuni of the essential teaching.[250] The Shakyamuni Buddha and Tahō Buddha who appear in the Treasure Tower, as well as all other Buddhas, along with the four bodhisattvas including Jōgyō, shall act as attendants to this Buddha. Second, there is the high sanctuary of the essential teaching. Third, in Japan, China, India, and all the other countries of the world, every person, regardless of whether he is wise or foolish, shall set aside other practices and join in the chanting of Nam-myoho-renge-kyo. This teaching has never been taught before. Here in the world, in all the 2,225 years since the passing of the Buddha, not a single person chanted it. Nichiren alone, without sparing his voice, now chants Nam-myoho-renge-kyo, Nam-myoho-renge-kyo.

The size of the waves depends upon the wind that raises them, the height of the flames depends upon how much firewood is piled on, the size of the lotuses depends upon the pond in which they grow, and the volume of rain depends upon the dragons that make it fall. The deeper the roots, the more prolific the branches. The farther the source, the longer the stream.

The Chou dynasty lasted for seven hundred years because of the propriety and filial devotion of its founder, King Wen. The Ch'in dynasty, on the other hand, lasted hardly any time at all, because of the perverse ways of its founder, the First Emperor of the Ch'in. If Nichiren's compassion is truly great and encompassing, Nam-myoho-renge-kyo will spread for ten thousand years and more, for all eternity, for it has the beneficial power to open the blind eyes of every living being in the country of Japan, and it blocks off the road that leads to the hell of incessant suffering. Its benefit surpasses that of Dengyō and T'ien-t'ai, and is superior to that of Nāgārjuna and Mahākāśyapa.

A hundred years of practice in the land of Perfect Bliss cannot compare to the benefit gained from one day's practice in this impure world. Two thousand years of propagating Buddhism during the Former and Middle Days of the Law are inferior to an hour of propagation in this, the Latter Day of the Law. This is in no way because of Nichiren's wisdom, but simply because the time makes it so. In spring the blossoms open, in autumn the fruit appears. Summer is hot, winter is cold. The season makes it so, does it not?

"In the fifth five hundred years after my death, widely declare and spread [the Lotus Sutra] and never allow its flow to cease. And do not allow the devil, the devil's people, or the deities, dragons, yakṣas, kumbhāṇḍas, or their kind to seize the advantage."251

If [the Buddha's prophecy expressed in] this passage of the Lotus Sutra should prove to be in vain, then Śāriputra will never become the Flower Light Tathagata, the Venerable Mahākāśyapa will never become the Light Bright Tathagata, Maudgalyāyana will never become the Tamalapattra Sandalwood Fragrance Buddha, Ānanda will never become the Mountain Sea Wisdom Unrestricted Power King Buddha, the nun Mahāprajāpatī252 will never become the Beheld with Joy by All Sentient Beings Buddha, and the nun Yaśodharā253 will never become the Form Resplendent with Ten Million Lights Buddha. All the talk of sanzen-jintengō is then likewise mere nonsense, and gohyaku-jintengō, too, is a lie. Very likely the Lord Shakyamuni has fallen into the hell of incessant suffering, Tahō Buddha is gasping amid the flames of the Avīci Hell, the Buddhas of the ten directions have their home now in the eight major hells, and all the various bodhisattvas are being forced to suffer in the 136 hells.[254]

But how could such a thing ever be? Since the sutra's prediction was not made in vain, then it is certain that all the people of Japan will chant Nam-myoho-renge-kyo!

Thus the flower will return to the root, and the essence of the plant will remain in the earth. The benefit that I have been speaking of will surely accumulate in the life of the late Dōzen-bō. Nam-myoho-renge-kyo, Nam-myoho-renge-kyo.

Written on the twenty-first day, seventh month of the second year of Kenji (1276), cyclical sign *hinoe-ne*.

Respectfully sent from Mount Minobu, Hakiri Village, in Kōshū, to Jōken-bō and Gijō-bō of Mount Kiyosumi, district of Tōjō, province of Awa.

Cover Letter

I have received your letter. One should never speak of matters pertaining to the Buddhist doctrine to someone who has no faith, regardless of whether the person is a close friend or relation or a stranger. This is something you should keep in mind.

I have inscribed the Gohonzon for you. Even more in the years after the passing of the Buddha than during his lifetime, even more during the Middle Day of the Law than during the Former Day, and even more now in the beginning of the Latter Day of the Law than during the Middle Day, the enemies of this Lotus Sutra are bound to grow in power. If you understand this, you as well as anyone else will realize that there is no one in Japan other than myself who is a true votary of the Lotus Sutra.

A sketchy report of the death of Dōzen-bō reached me last month. I felt that I should go in person as quickly as possible, as well as sending the priest who bears this letter, Nikō. However, though I do not think of myself as one who has retired from the world, other people seem to look at me in that way, and so I make it a rule not to leave this mountain.

This priest Nikō informed me of private reports from various people that there are likely to be doctrinal debates with the other sects in the near future. I have therefore been sending people to a number of temples in the different provinces in order to search out sutras and doctrinal writings from all over the country. I had sent this priest Nikō on such a mission to the province of Suruga, and he has just now returned [so I am sending him with this letter].

In the enclosed treatise I have written matters of the utmost gravity. It would be wrong, therefore, to make the contents known to persons who do not understand the essence of Buddhism. And even if they are made known only to persons who do, if there are too many people involved, then word of the contents is likely to reach the ears of outsiders. That would not be conducive to your welfare, nor to mine.

Therefore, I ask that just the two of you, you and Gijō-bō, have the work read aloud two or three times at the summit of Kasagamori, with this priest Nikō to do the reading. Please have him read it once before the grave of the late Dōzen-bō as well. After that, leave it in the possession of Nikō and have him read it to you repeatedly. If you listen to it again and again, I believe you will come to understand and appreciate its meaning.

With my deep respect,
Nichiren

The twenty-sixth day of the seventh month
To the priest of Kiyosumi[255]

ON *VARIOUS ACTIONS OF THE PRIEST NICHIREN*

Introduction

The title usually given to this work, *Shuju Onfurumai Gosho*, means simply "The Letter on Various Actions," but the honorific particle *on* prefixed to the word *furumai,* "actions" or "behavior," makes it clear that the actions referred to are those of Nichiren and suggests that the title was appended by someone other than the author. The work is also known as *Sado Shō,* or "Concerning Sado," though it covers a great deal more than Nichiren's two and a half years of exile on the island of Sado.

Written in the third month of 1276, the work is in the form of a letter addressed to a widow known as Kōnichi-ama who lived in Amatsu in Awa, Nichiren's native province. Her son had earlier converted to Nichiren's teachings, and through him she herself became a convert. Sometime thereafter her son died. At that time, Nichiren wrote to thank her for a letter she had sent him and to encourage her in her faith.

The present writing gives a vivid account of the preceding eight years of his life, beginning in 1268 when the Mongol Empire sent an envoy to Japan to demand that it acknowledge fealty to the Mongols. Nichiren, in his *"Risshō Ankoku Ron"* had earlier predicted trouble of this kind from abroad, and, as he explains, he took this opportunity to remonstrate once more with the government authorities in Kamakura. He then goes on to describe the so-called Tatsunokuchi Persecution in 1271, when he was arrested by the authorities and very nearly put to death, and continues with an account of his years of exile in Sado, his return to Kamakura in 1274, and his eventual retirement to Mount Minobu, where this letter was written. It constitutes a crucial source for Nichiren's life and is one of the most dramatic and powerful works of autobiographical writing in all of Japanese literature.

On the eighteenth day of the first intercalary month of the fifth year of Bun'ei (1268), an official announcement arrived from the great Mongol Empire in which those barbarians of the west declared their intention to attack Japan. My prediction in the *"Rishō Ankoku Ron,"* which I wrote in the first year of Bun'ō (1260), cyclical sign *kanoe-saru,* had been fulfilled to the letter. My admonitions have surpassed even those set forth in the *yüeh-fu* poems of Po Chü-i,[1] or the prophecies of Shakyamuni Buddha. Can there be anything more wondrous in this latter age? If our land were governed by a wise king or sage ruler, then the highest honors in Japan would be bestowed upon me and I would be awarded the title of Great Teacher[2] while still alive. I had expected to be consulted [about the Mongols], invited to the war council, and asked to defeat them through the power of prayer. Since that did not happen, however, I sent letters of warning to eleven of our country's leaders in the tenth month of the same year.

If there were a wise leader in this country, he would immediately think, "What a wonder! This is surely no ordinary matter. The deities Tenshō Daijin and Hachiman must intend to enter into this priest as a means to save Japan." In actuality, however, the government officials slandered and deceived my messengers. They ignored or refused to reply to my letters, and even when they did reply, they deliberately neglected to report the content of my letters to the Regent. Their behavior was highly irregular. Even if the letters concerned only some personal matter of mine, the ruler should nevertheless pay them due attention were they reported to him, this being the proper way of government. But in this case, the letters were a warning of dire things to come that would affect the destiny of not only the Regent's government but of every other official as well. Even if the officials did not heed my warning, to slander my messengers was going too far. This came about because all Japanese, high and low, have for a long time now shown hostility toward the Lotus Sutra. Thus they have piled up great offenses and become possessed by devils. The ultimatum from the Mongols has deprived them of the last remnants of sanity. In ancient China, Emperor Chou of the Yin dynasty refused to heed the admonitions of his loyal minister Pi Kan and instead had Pi Kan's heart cut out.[3] Later his dynasty was overthrown by kings Wen and Wu of the Chou. King Fu-ch'a of the state of Wu, instead of listening to the remonstrances of his minister Wu Tzu-hsü, forced the latter to commit suicide.[4] Eventually Fa-ch'a was killed by King Kou-chien of the state of Yüeh.

Thinking how tragic it would be if our country were to meet with a similar fate, I risked my reputation and life to remonstrate with the authorities. But, just as a high wind creates waves or a powerful dragon brings forth torrential rains, so my admonitions called forth increasing animosity. The Regent's Supreme Council met to discuss whether to behead me or banish me from Kamakura and whether to confiscate the estates of my disciples and lay supporters, or to imprison, execute, or exile them to distant places.

[Hearing this,] I rejoiced, saying that I had long expected it to come to this. In the past Sessen Dōji offered his life for the sake of half a verse, Bodhisattva Jōtai sold his body, Zenzai Dōji threw himself into a fire, Gyōbō Bonji tore off a piece of his own skin, and Bodhisattva Yakuō burned his own arm. Bodhisattva Fukyō was beaten with staves, Āryasiṁha was beheaded, and Bodhisattva Kāṇadeva was killed by a Brahman, [all because of their devotion to Buddhism].[5]

These events should be considered in terms of the times in which they occurred. The Great Teacher T'ien-t'ai declared that practice should "accord with the times."[6] His disciple the Great Teacher Chang-an interpreted this to mean, "You should distinguish between shōju and shakubuku and never adhere solely to one or the other."[7] The Lotus Sutra represents a single truth, but the way of its practice varies greatly according to the people's capacity and the time.

Shakyamuni Buddha made a prophecy, saying: "After my death, during the beginning of the Latter Day of the Law that follows the two millennia of the Former and Middle Days, a person will appear who will propagate only the heart of the Lotus Sutra, the five characters of the daimoku. At that time an evil king will be in power and evil priests, more numerous than the particles of dust comprising the great earth, will argue with one another over the various Mahayana and Hinayana sutras. When the votary of the daimoku challenges the priests, they will incite their lay believers to abuse, beat, or imprison him, to confiscate his lands, to exile or behead him. In spite of such persecutions, he will continue his propagation without ceasing. Meanwhile the ruler who persecutes him will be beset by rebellion and his subjects will devour each other like hungry ghosts. Finally the land will be attacked by a foreign country, for the Buddhist gods Bonten and Taishaku, the gods of the sun and the moon, and the Four Heavenly Kings have ordained that other countries shall assault a land that is hostile to the Lotus Sutra."[8]

None of you who declare yourselves to be my disciples should ever give way to cowardice. Neither should you allow concern for your parents, wives, or children to hold you back, or be worried about your property. Since countless kalpas past you have thrown away your life more times than the number of dust particles on earth in order to save your parents, your children, or your lands. But not once have you given up your life for the Lotus Sutra. You may have tried to practice its teachings to some extent, but whenever you were persecuted, you backslid and ceased to live by the sutra. That is like boiling water only to pour it into cold water, or like trying to strike fire but giving up halfway. Each and every one of you should be certain deep in your hearts that sacrificing your life for the Lotus Sutra is like exchanging rocks for gold or dung for rice.

Now at the beginning of the Latter Day of the Law, I, Nichiren, am the first to embark on propagating, throughout the continent of Jambudvīpa, the five characters of Myōhō-renge-kyō, which are the heart of the Lotus Sutra and the eyes of all Buddhas. During the more than twenty-two hundred years that have passed since Shakyamuni entered nirvana, not even Mahākāśyapa, Ānanda, Aśvaghoṣa, Nāgārjuna, Nan-yüeh, T'ien-t'ai, Miao-lo, or Dengyō has propagated them. My disciples, form your ranks and follow me, and you will surpass even Mahākāśyapa or Ānanda, T'ien-t'ai or Dengyō! If you quail before the threats of the rulers of this little island country [and abandon your faith], how will you face the even more terrible anger of Emma, the King of Hell? If, while calling yourselves the Buddha's messengers, you give way to fear, you will be the most despicable of persons!

[While the Regent's government could not come to any conclusion,] priests of the Jōdo, Ritsu, Shingon, and other sects, who realized they could not rival me in wisdom, sent petitions to the government. Finding that their petitions were not accepted, they approached the wives and widows of high-ranking officials and slandered me in various ways. [The women reported the slander to the officials,] saying, "According to what some priests told us, Nichiren declared that the late Hōjō Tokiyori and Hōjō Shigetoki[9] have fallen into the hell of incessant suffering. He said that the temples Kenchō-ji, Jufuku-ji, Gokuraku-ji, Chōraku-ji, and Daibutsu-ji[10] should be burned down and the high priests Tao-lung and Ryōkan beheaded." Even though the Regent's Supreme Council was unable to reach a decision, my guilt could scarcely be denied. To confirm whether I had or had not made those statements, I was summoned to the court. At the court the magistrate said, "You have heard what the Regent stated. Did you say these things or not?" I answered. "Every word is mine. Only the statement that the late officials Hōjō Tokiyori and Hōjō Shigetoki had fallen into hell is a fabrication. Yet I have most certainly been declaring this doctrine [that the sects they belonged to lead to hell] even while they were alive.

"Everything I said was with the future of our country in mind. If you wish to maintain this land in peace and security, it is imperative that you summon the priests of the other sects for a debate in your presence. If you ignore this advice and punish me unreasonably on their behalf, the entire country will have cause to regret your decision. If you condemn me, you will be rejecting the Buddha's envoy. Then you will have to face the punishment of Bonten and Taishaku, of the gods of the sun and the moon, and of the Four Heavenly Kings. Within one hundred days after my exile or execution, or within one, three, or seven years, there will occur what the sutras call 'internal strife,' rebellion within your clan. This will be followed by foreign invasion from all sides, particularly from the west. Then you will regret what you have done!" Hearing this, the magistrate Hei no Saemon, forgetting all the dignity of his rank, became wild with rage like Taira no Kiyomori.[11]

On the night of the twelfth day of the ninth month in the eighth year of Bun'ei (1271), cyclical sign *kanoto-hitsuji*, I was arrested in a manner which was extraordinary and unlawful, even more outrageous than the arrest of the priests Ryōkō, who was actually guilty of treason, and Ryōken, who sought to destroy the government.[12] Hei no Saemon led several hundred armor-clad warriors to take me. Wearing the headgear of a court noble, he glared in anger and spoke in a rough voice. These actions were in essence no different from those of the Prime Minister Taira no Kiyomori, who seized power only to lead the country to destruction.

Observing this, I realized it was no ordinary event and thought to myself, "I expected something like this to happen sooner or later. How fortunate that I can give my life for the Lotus Sutra! If I am to lose this worthless head for Buddhahood, it will be like trading sand for gold or rocks for jewels!"

Shōu-bō, Hei no Saemon's chief retainer, rushed up, snatched the fifth scroll of the Lotus Sutra from inside my robes, and struck me in the face with it three times.[13] Then he threw it on the floor. Warriors seized the nine other scrolls of the sutra, unrolled them and trampled on them or wound them about their bodies, scattering the scrolls all over the matting and wooden floors until every corner of the house was strewn with them.

I said in a loud voice, "See how Hei no Saemon has gone mad! You gentlemen have just toppled the pillar of Japan!" Hearing this, the assembled troops were taken aback. When they saw me standing before the fierce arm of the law unafraid, they must have realized that they were in the wrong, for the color drained from their faces.

Both on the tenth, [when I was summoned,] and on this night, the twelfth, I fully described to Hei no Saemon the heresies of the Shingon, Zen, and Jōdo sects, as well as Ryōkan's failure in his prayers for rain.[14] [As his warriors listened,] they would burst into laughter, and at other times become furious. However, I will not go into the details here.

Ryōkan prayed for rain from the eighteenth day of the sixth month to the fourth day of the following month, but I blocked his prayers so that no rain came. Ryōkan prayed himself into a sweat, but nothing fell except his own tears. There was no rain in Kamakura, but on the contrary, strong gales blew continually.

At this news I sent a messenger to him three times, saying, "If a person cannot manage to cross a moat ten feet wide, how can he cross one that is a hundred or two hundred feet? Izumi Shikibu, a licentious woman, violated one of the eightfold precepts by writing poetry, but still she made the rain fall with a poem.[15] The priest Nōin, although he broke the precepts, was successful in bringing rainfall with a poem.[16] How is it possible then that hundreds and thousands of priests, all of whom observe the two hundred and fifty precepts, gather to pray for rain and can do no more than raise a gale, even after one or two weeks of prayer? It should be clear from this that none of you will be able to attain rebirth in the Pure Land." The priest Ryōkan read the message and wept with vexation, and to others he reviled me.

When I reported what had happened with Ryōkan, Hei no Saemon attempted to defend him, but it was hopeless. In the end he was unable to utter a word. I will not record all of our conversation as it was too detailed.

That night of the twelfth, I was placed under the custody of Hōjō Nobutoki, lord of the province of Musashi, and around midnight was taken out of Kamakura to be executed. As we set out on Waka-miya Avenue,[17] I looked at the crowd of warriors surrounding me and said, "Don't make a fuss. I won't cause any trouble. I merely wish to say my last words to Bodhisattva Hachiman." I got down from my horse and called out in a loud voice, "Bodhisattva Hachi-man, are you truly a god? When Wake no Kiyomaro was about to be beheaded, you appeared as a moon ten feet wide.[18] When the Great Teacher Dengyō lectured on the Lotus Sutra, you bestowed upon him a purple surplice.[19] I, Nichiren, am the foremost votary of the Lotus Sutra in Japan, and am entirely without guilt. I have expounded the Law to save all the people of Japan from falling into the great citadel of the hell of incessant suffering for slandering the Lotus Sutra. Moreover, if the forces of the great Mongol empire attack this country, can even Tenshō Daijin and Hachiman remain safe and un-harmed? When Shakyamuni Buddha expounded the Lotus Sutra, Tahō Buddha and the other Buddhas and bodhisattvas of the ten directions gathered, shining like so many suns and moons, stars and mirrors. In the presence of the countless heavenly gods as well as the benevolent deities and sages of India, China, and Japan, the Lord Buddha urged each one to pledge to protect the votary of the Lotus Sutra at all times. Each and every one of you gods made this pledge. I should not have to remind you. Why do you not appear at once to fulfill your oath?" Finally I called out, "If I am executed tonight and go to the pure land of Eagle Peak, I will immediately report to Shakyamuni Buddha that Tenshō Daijin and Hachiman have broken their oath to him. If you feel this will go hard with you, you had better do something about it right away!" Then I remounted my horse.

As the party passed the shrine on Yui beach,[20] I spoke again. "Stop a minute, gentlemen, I have a message for someone living near here," I said. I sent a boy called Kumaō to Shijō Kingo,[21] who rushed to meet me. I told him, "Tonight I will be beheaded. This is something I have wished for many years. In this *saha* world, I have been born as a pheasant only to be caught by hawks, born a mouse only to be eaten by cats, and born human only to be killed attempting to defend my wife and children from enemies. Such things have befallen me more times than there are specks of dust on the earth. But until now, I have never given up my life for the sake of the Lotus Sutra. [In this life,] I was born to become a poor priest, unable fully to repay the debt of gratitude I owe to my parents and to my country. Now I will present my severed head to the Lotus Sutra and share the blessings therefrom with my parents, and with my disciples and believers, just as I have promised you." Then the four Shijō brothers, holding on to my horse's reins, went with me to Tatsunokuchi at Koshigoe.

Finally we came to a place that I knew must be the site of my execution. Indeed, the soldiers stopped and began to mill around in excitement. Shijō Kingo, in tears, said, "These are your last moments!" I replied, "You don't understand! What greater joy could there be? Don't you remember what you have promised?" I had no sooner said this when a brilliant orb as bright as the moon burst forth from the direction of Enoshima, shooting across the sky from southeast to northwest. It was shortly before dawn and still too dark to see anyone's face, but the radiant object clearly illumined everyone like bright moonlight. The executioner fell on his face, his eyes blinded. The soldiers were filled with panic. Some ran off into the distance, some jumped down from their horses and huddled on the ground, while others crouched in their saddles. I called out, "Here, why do you shrink from this vile prisoner? Come closer! Come closer!" But no one would approach me. "What if the dawn should break? You must hurry up and execute me—once the day breaks it will be too ugly a job!" I urged them on, but they made no response.

They waited a short while, and then I was told to proceed to Echi in the same province of Sagami. I replied that since none of us knew the way, someone would have to guide us there. No one was willing to take the lead, but after we had waited for some time, one soldier finally said, "That's the road you should take."

Setting off, we followed the road and around noon reached Echi. We then proceeded to the residence of Homma Rokurōzaemon. There I ordered saké for the soldiers. When the time came for them to leave, some bowed their heads, joined their palms, and said in a most respectful manner, "We did not realize what kind of a man you are.

We hated you because we had been told that you slandered Amida Buddha, the one we worship. But now that we have seen with our own eyes what has happened to you, we have realized how worthy a person you are, and will discard the Nembutsu that we have practiced for so long." Some of them even took their Nembutsu rosaries out of their tinder bags and flung them away. Others pledged that they would never again chant the Nembutsu. After they left, Rokurōzaemon's retainers took over the guard. Then Shijō Kingo and his brothers took their leave.

That evening, at the hour of the Dog (7:00–9:00 P.M.), a messenger from Kamakura arrived with an order form the Regent. The soldiers were sure that it would be a command to behead me, but Umanojō, Homma's magistrate, came running with the letter, knelt and said, "We were afraid that you would be executed tonight, but now the letter has brought wonderful news. The messenger said that since the lord of Musashi has left for a spa in Atami this morning at the hour of the Hare (5:00–7:00 A.M.), he set off at once and rode for four hours to get here because he feared that something might happen to you. The messenger will leave immediately to take news to the lord in Atami tonight." The accompanying letter read, "This person is not really guilty. He will shortly be pardoned. If you execute him you will have cause to regret."

Now it was the night of the thirteenth. There were scores of warriors stationed around my lodging and in the main garden. Because it was the middle of the ninth month, the moon was very round and full. I went out into the garden and there, turning toward the moon, recited the verse portion of the *Juryō* chapter of the Lotus Sutra. Then I spoke briefly about the relative merits of the various sects and about the teachings of the Lotus Sutra. I said, "You, the god of the moon, participated in the ceremony of the Lotus Sutra. When the Buddha expounded the *Hōtō* chapter, you received his order, and in the *Zokurui* chapter, when the Buddha laid his hand on your head, you vowed to fulfill the World-Honored One's command [to transmit and protect the Lotus Sutra]. You are that very god. Would you have an opportunity to fulfill the vow you made in the Buddha's presence if it were not for me? Now that you see me in this situation, you should rush forward joyfully to receive the sufferings of the votary of the Lotus Sutra in his stead, thereby carrying out the Buddha's command and also fulfilling your vow. It is strange indeed that you have not yet done anything. If nothing is done to set this country to rights, I will never return to Kamakura. Even if you do not intend to do anything for me, how can you go on shining with such a complacent face? The *Daijuku* Sutra says, 'The sun and moon will not show their brightness.' The *Ninnō* Sutra says, 'Both the sun and the moon shall act discordantly.' The *Saishōō* Sutra says, 'The thirty-three heavenly gods will be enraged.'[22] What about these passages, moon god? What is your answer?"

Then, as though in reply, a large star, bright as the Morning Star, fell from the sky and hung in a branch of the plum tree in front of me. The soldiers, astounded, jumped down from the veranda, fell on their faces in the garden, or ran behind the house. Immediately the sky clouded over and a fierce wind started up, raging so violently that the whole island of Enoshima seemed to roar. The sky shook, echoing with a sound like pounding drums.

At dawn on the fourteenth day, around the hour of the Hare (5:00–7:00 A.M.), a man called Jūrō Nyūdō came and said to me, "Last night there was a huge commotion in the Regent's residence at the hour of the Dog (7:00–9:00 P.M.). They summoned a diviner, who said, 'The country is going to erupt in turmoil because you punished that priest. If you do not call him back to Kamakura immediately, there is no telling what will happen to this land.' At that someone said, 'Let's pardon him!' Others said, 'Since he predicted that war would break out within a hundred days, why don't we wait and see what happens.' "

I was kept at Echi for more than twenty days. During that period seven or eight cases of arson and an endless succession of murders took place in Kamakura. Slanderers went around saying that my disciples were setting the fires. The government officials thought this might be true and made up a list of over 260 of my followers who they believed should be expelled from Kamakura. Word spread that these persons were all to be exiled to remote islands and that those disciples already in prison would be beheaded. It turned out, however, that the fires were set by the Nembutsu and Ritsu believers in an attempt to implicate my disciples. There were other things that happened, but they are too numerous to mention here.

I left Echi on the tenth day of the tenth month (1271) and arrived on Sado Island on the twenty-eighth day of the same month. On the first day of the eleventh month, I was taken to a small hut that stood in a field called Tsukahara behind Homma Rokurōzaemon's residence in Sado. One room with four posts, it stood on some land where corpses were abandoned, a place like Rendaino in Kyoto.[23] Not a single statue of the Buddha was enshrined there; the boards of the roof did not meet and the walls were full of holes. The snow fell and piled up, never melting away. I spent my days there, sitting in a straw raincoat or lying on a deerskin. At night it hailed and snowed and there were continual flashes of lightning. Even in the daytime the sun hardly shone. It was a wretched place to live.

I felt like Li Ling in China, who was imprisoned in a rocky cave in the land of the northern barbarians, or the Tripitaka Master Fa-tao, who was branded on the forehead and exiled to the area south of the Yangtze by Emperor Hui-tsung of the Sung.[24] Nevertheless, King Suzudan received severe training under the hermit sage Ashi to obtain the blessings of the Lotus Sutra, and even though Bodhisattva Fukyō was beaten by the staves of arrogant monks, he achieved honor as votary of the one vehicle.[25] Therefore, nothing is more joyful to me than to have been born in the Latter Day of the Law and to suffer persecutions because I propagate the five characters of Myōhō-renge-kyō. For more than twenty-two hundred years after the death of Shakyamuni, no one, not even the Great Teacher T'ien-t'ai, experienced the truth of the passage in the sutra that says, "The people will resent [the Lotus Sutra] and find it extremely difficult to believe."[26] Only I have fulfilled the prophecy in the sutra, "We will be banished again and again."[27] The Buddha conferred a prediction of Buddha-hood upon all who embrace even a single phrase or verse from the sutra; thus there can be no doubt that I will reach supreme enlightenment. It is Regent Hōjō Tokimune above all who has been of greatest aid to me. Hei no Saemon is to me what Devadatta was to Shakyamuni. The Nembutsu priests are comparable to Kokālika and the Ritsu followers to Sunakṣatra.[28] Shakyamuni lives today; this is the age of the Buddha. This is what the Lotus Sutra describes as the true aspect of all phenomena, or more precisely, consistency from beginning to end.[29]

The fifth volume of the *Maka Shikan* states: "As practice progresses and understanding grows, the three obstacles and four devils emerge, vying with one another to interfere." It also states: "A wild boar scraping up against a gold mountain only makes it glitter, rivers flowing into an ocean increase its volume, fuel added to the fire only makes it burn higher, and the wind inflates the body of the *gura* insect."[30] These passages mean that if one understands and practices the Lotus Sutra just as it teaches in accordance with the people's capacity and at the right time, then these seven obstacles and devils will confront him. Among them, the Devil of the Sixth Heaven[31] [is the most powerful. He] will possess one's sovereign, parents, wife or children, lay believers or evil men, and through them will attempt in a friendly manner to divert him from his practice of the Lotus Sutra, or will oppose him outright. The practice of Buddhism is always accompanied by persecutions and difficulties corresponding in severity to whichever sutra one may uphold. To practice the Lotus Sutra, the highest sutra of all, will provoke particularly harsh persecutions. To practice as it teaches, and in accordance with the time and the people's capacity, will incite truly agonizing ordeals.

The eighth volume of the *Guketsu* states: "So long as a person does not try to depart from the cycle of birth and death and aspire to the Buddha vehicle, the devil will watch over him like a parent."[32] This passage means that even though one may cultivate roots of goodness, so long as he practices Nembutsu, Shingon, Zen, Ritsu, or any teaching other than the Lotus Sutra, he will have the devil for a parent. The devil will cause other persons to respect that man and give him alms, and people will be deluded into believing that he is a truly enlightened priest. If he is honored by the sovereign, for instance, the people are sure to offer him alms. On the other hand, a priest who incurs the enmity of the ruler and others [because of the Lotus Sutra] is surely practicing the True Law.

Devadatta more than anyone else proved the validity of Shakyamuni's teachings. In this age as well, it is not one's friends but one's enemies who assist his progress. We find examples before our very eyes. The Hōjō clan in Kamakura could not have firmly established itself as the ruler of Japan had it not been for the challenges posed by Wada Yoshimori and the Retired Emperor Gotoba.[33] In this sense these men were the best allies the Hōjō clan could have. For me, my best allies in attaining Buddhahood are Tōjō Kagenobu, the priests Ryōkan, Tao-lung, and Dōamidabutsu, and Hei no Saemon and Regent Hōjō Tokimune. I am grateful when I think that without them I could not have proved myself to be the votary of the Lotus Sutra.

In the yard around the hut the snow piled deeper and deeper. No one came to see me; my only visitor was the piercing wind. The *Maka Shikan* and the Lotus Sutra lay open before my eyes and Nammyoho-renge-kyo flowed from my lips. My evenings passed in discourse to the moon and stars on the differences among the various sects and the profound meaning of the Lotus Sutra. Thus, one year gave way to the next.

One finds people of mean spirit wherever one goes. The rumor reached me that the Ritsu and Nembutsu priests on the island of Sado, including Yuiamidabutsu, Shōyu-bō, Inshō-bō, and Jidō-bō and hundreds of their followers, had met to decide what to do about me. One of them is reported to have said, "Nichiren, the notorious enemy of Amida Buddha and an evil teacher to all people, has been exiled to our province. As we all know, exiles to this island seldom manage to survive. Even if they do, they never return home. So no one is going to be punished for killing an exile. Nichiren lives all alone at a place called Tsukahara. No matter how strong and powerful he is, if there's no one around, what can he do? Let's go together and shoot him with arrows!" Another said, "He was supposed to be beheaded, but his execution has been postponed for a while because the Regent's wife is about to have a child. The postponement is merely temporary, though. I hear he is eventually going to be executed." A third said, "Let's ask Lord Homma to behead him. If he refuses, we can plan something ourselves." There were many proposals about what to do with me, and eventually several hundred people gathered at the constable's office.[34]

Homma Rokurōzaemon addressed them, saying, "An official letter has arrived from the Regent directing that the priest shall not be executed. This is no ordinary, contemptible criminal, and if anything happens to him, I will be guilty of grave dereliction. Instead of killing him, why don't you confront him in religious debate?" Following this suggestion, the Nembutsu and other priests, accompanied by apprentice priests carrying the three Jōdo sutras,[35] the *Maka Shikan,* the Shingon sutras, and other literature under their arms or hanging from their necks, gathered at Tsukahara on the sixteenth day of the first month (1272). They came not only from the province of Sado but also from the nearby provinces of Echigo, Etchū, Dewa, Mutsu, and Shinano. Several hundred priests and others gathered in the spacious yard of the hut and in the adjacent field. Homma Rokurōzaemon, his brothers, and his entire clan came, as well as lay priest farmers,[36] all in great numbers. The Nembutsu priests uttered streams of abuse, the Shingon masters turned pale with rage, and the Tendai monks vowed to vanquish the opponent. The lay believers cried out in hatred, "There he is—the notorious enemy of our Amida Buddha!" The uproar and the jeering resounded like thunder and seemed to shake the earth. I let them clamor for a while and then said, "Silence, all of you! You are here for a religious debate. This is no time for abuse." At this, Homma and several others voiced their accord, and some of them grabbed the abusive Nembutsu priests by the neck and pushed them back.

The priests proceeded to cite the doctrines of the *Maka Shikan* and the Shingon and the Nembutsu teachings. I responded to each point, establishing the exact meaning of what had been said, then coming back with questions. However, I needed to ask only one or two at most before they were completely silenced. They were far inferior even to the Shingon, Zen, Nembutsu, and Tendai priests in Kamakura, so you can imagine how the debate went. I overturned them as easily as a sharp sword cutting through a melon or a gale bending the grass. They were not only poorly versed in Buddhism but contradicted themselves. They confused sutras with treatises or commentaries with treatises. I discredited the Nembutsu by telling how Shantao fell out of the willow tree, and refuted the story about the Great Teacher Kōbō's three-pronged *vajra* implement and of how he transformed himself into Dainichi Buddha.[37] As I demonstrated each falsity and aberration, some of the priests swore, some were struck dumb, while others turned pale. There were Nembutsu adherents who admitted the error of their sect; some threw away their robes and beads on the spot and pledged never to chant the Nembutsu again.

The members of the group all began to leave, as did Rokurōzaemon and his men. As they were walking across the yard, I called the lord back to make a prophecy. I first asked him when he was departing for Kamakura, and he answered that it would be around the seventh month, after his farmers had finished their work in his fields. Then I said, "For a warrior, the 'work in the fields' means assisting his lord in times of peril and receiving lands in recognition of his service. Fighting is about to break out in Kamakura. You should hasten there to distinguish yourself in battle, and then you will be rewarded with fiefs. Since your warriors are renowned throughout the province of Sagami, if you remain here in the countryside tending to your farms and arrive too late for the battle, your name will be disgraced." I do not know what he thought of this, but Homma, dumbfounded, did not utter a word. The Nembutsu and Ritsu priests and lay believers looked bewildered, not comprehending what I had said.

After everyone had gone, I began to put into shape a work in two volumes called *Kaimoku Shō* or "The Opening of the Eyes," which I had been working on since the eleventh month of the previous year. I wanted to record the wonder [of my enlightenment], in case I should be beheaded. The essential message in this work is that the destiny of Japan depends solely upon me. A house without pillars collapses and a person without a soul is dead. I am the soul of the people of Japan. Hei no Saemon has already toppled the pillar, and the country grows turbulent as unfounded rumors and speculation rise up like phantoms to cause dissension in the Hōjō clan. Further, Japan is about to be attacked by a foreign country, as I described in my *"Risshō Ankoku Ron."* Having written to this effect, I entrusted the manuscript to Shijō Kingo's messenger. The disciples around me thought that what I had written was too provocative, but they could not do anything about it.

Just then a ship arrived at the island on the eighteenth day of the second month. It carried the news that fighting had broken out in Kamakura and then in Kyoto, causing indescribable suffering. Homma Rokurōzaemon, leading his men, left on fast ships that night for Kamakura. Before departing, he humbly begged for my assistance with palms joined.

He said, "I doubted the truth of the words you spoke on the sixteenth day of last month, but they have come true in less than thirty days. I see now that the Mongols will surely attack us, and it is equally certain that believers in the Nembutsu are doomed to the hell of incessant suffering. I will never chant the Nembutsu again."

To this I replied, "Whatever I may say, unless Regent Hōjō Tokimune heeds my words, the people of Japan will not heed them either, and in that case our country will surely be ruined. Although I myself may be insignificant, I propagate the Lotus Sutra and therefore am the envoy of Shakyamuni Buddha. Tenshō Daijin and Hachiman are respected as tutelary gods of this country, but they are only minor gods as compared with Bonten, Taishaku, the gods of the sun and moon, and the Four Heavenly Kings. It is said, however, that to kill someone who serves these two gods is equal to the sin of killing seven and a half ordinary persons. The Prime Minister Taira no Kiyomori and the Retired Emperor Gotoba perished because they did so. Thus, persecuting me is incomparably worse than molesting the servants of those two gods. As I am the envoy of Shakyamuni Buddha, Tenshō Daijin and Hachiman should prostrate themselves before me with their palms pressed together. The votary of the Lotus Sutra is attended by Bonten and Taishaku on either side, and the gods of the sun and moon light his path before and behind. Even if my counsel is heeded, if I am not given due respect [as the votary of the Lotus Sutra], then the country will perish. How ominous that the authorities have turned hundreds of persons against me and have even banished me twice! This country is surely doomed, but since I have asked the Buddhist gods to withhold their punishment on our land, it has survived until now. However, that punishment has finally descended because these unreasonable actions continued. And if my counsel is not heeded on this occasion, Japan will undoubtedly be destroyed by the attacks of the Mongol forces. That would seem to be the kind of disaster that Hei no Saemon is intent upon calling forth. When it happens, I doubt that you and your followers can find any safety even on this island!" After I had finished speaking, Homma, looking deeply perplexed, set off on his way.

The lay believers, hearing of this, said to one another, "Perhaps this priest has some kind of spiritual powers. How terrifying! From now on, we had better cease giving any alms and support to the Nembutsu and Ritsu priests!" The Ritsu priests, who were followers of Ryōkan, and the Nembutsu priests said, "[Since this priest predicted the outbreak of rebellion in Kamakura,] perhaps he is one of the conspirators himself." After this things grew somewhat quieter.

Then the Nembutsu priests gathered again in council. "If things go on this way," they said, "we will die of starvation. By all means, let us rid ourselves of this priest! Already more than half the people in the province have gone over to his side. What are we to do?"

Yuiamidabutsu, the leader of the Nembutsu priests, along with Dōkan, a disciple of Ryōkan, and Shōyu-bō,[38] who were leaders of the Ritsu priests, journeyed in haste to Kamakura. There they reported to Hōjō Nobutoki, lord of the province of Musashi, "If this priest remains on the island of Sado, there will soon be not a single Buddhist hall left standing or a single monk remaining! He takes the statues of Amida Buddha and throws them in the fire or casts them into the river. Day and night he climbs the high mountains, bellows to the sun and moon, and curses the Regent. The sound of his voice can be heard throughout the entire province."

When Hōjō Nobutoki heard this, he decided there was no need to report it to the Regent. Instead he sent private orders that any followers of Nichiren in the province of Sado should be driven out of the province or imprisoned. He also sent official letters containing similar instructions. He did so three times. I will not attempt to describe what happened thereafter—you can probably imagine. Some people were thrown into prison because they were said to have walked past my hut, others were exiled because they were reported to have given me donations, or their wives and children were taken into custody. Hōjō Nobutoki then reported what he had done to the Regent. But quite contrary to his expectations, the Regent issued a letter of pardon on the fourteenth day, the second month, of the eleventh year of Bun'ei (1274), which reached Sado on the eighth day of the third month.

The Nembutsu priests held another council. "This man, the arch-enemy of the Buddha Amida and slanderer of Priest Shan-tao and Saint Hōnen, has incurred the displeasure of the authorities and hap-pened to be banished to this island. How can we bear to see him pardoned and allowed to return home alive!"

While they were engaged in various plots, for some reason there was an unexpected change in the weather. A favorable wind began to blow and I was able to leave the island. The strait can be crossed in three days with a favorable wind, but not even in fifty or a hundred days when the weather is bad. I crossed over in no time at all.

Thereupon the Nembutsu, Ritsu, and Shingon priests of the pro-vincial capital of Echigo and the Zenkō-ji in Shinano gathered from all directions to hold a meeting. "What a shame that the Sado priests should have allowed Nichiren to return alive! Whatever we do, we must not let this priest make his way past the living body of the Buddha Amida!"[39]

But in spite of their machinations, a number of warriors from the provincial government office in Echigo were dispatched to escort me. Thus I was able to pass safely by Zenkō-ji, and the Nembutsu priests were powerless to stop me. I left the island of Sado on the thirteenth day of the third month, and arrived in Kamakura on the twenty-sixth day of the same month.

On the eighth day of the fourth month, I had an interview with Hei no Saemon. In contrast to his behavior on previous occasions, his manner was quite mild and he treated me with courtesy. An accom-panying lay priest asked me about the Nembutsu, a layman asked about the Shingon sect, and another person asked about Zen, while Hei no Saemon himself inquired whether it was possible to attain enlightenment through any of the sutras preached before the Lotus

Sutra. I replied to each of these questions by citing passages from the sutras.

Then Hei no Saemon, apparently acting on behalf of the Regent, asked when the Mongol forces would invade Japan. I replied, "They will surely come within this year. I have already expressed my opinion on this matter, but it has not been heeded. If you try to treat someone's illness without knowing its cause, you will only make the person sicker than before. In the same way, if the Shingon priests are permitted to try to overcome the Mongols with their prayers and imprecations, they will only bring about the country's military defeat. Under no circumstances whatever should the Shingon priests, or the priests of any other sects for that matter, be allowed to offer up prayers. If each of you has a real understanding of Buddhism, you will understand this matter on hearing me explain it to you.

"Also, I notice that, although advice from others is heeded, when I offer advice, it is for some strange reason invariably ignored. Nevertheless, I would like to state certain facts here so that you may think them over later. Emperor Gotoba was the sovereign of the nation and Hōjō Yoshitoki was his subject, [and yet the latter attacked and defeated the emperor]. Why would the Sun Goddess Tenshō Daijin permit a subject to attack an emperor, who should be like a father to him? Why would Bodhisattva Hachiman allow a vassal to attack the lord with impunity? And yet, as we know, the emperor and the courtiers supporting him were defeated by Hōjō Yoshitoki. That defeat was no mere accident. It came about because they put their faith in the misleading teachings of the Great Teacher Kōbō and the biased views of the Great Teachers Jikaku and Chishō, and because the monks of the monasteries of Mount Hiei, Tō-ji, and Onjō-ji, in their opposition to the Kamakura shogunate, offered prayers for its defeat. Thus their curses 'returned to the originators,'[40] as the Lotus Sutra says, and as a consequence the emperor and his courtiers were forced to suffer defeat. The military leaders in Kamakura knew nothing of such rituals, so no prayers to subdue the enemy were offered; thus they were able to win. But if they now offer such prayers, they will meet with the same fate as the courtiers.

The Ezo people of northern Japan have no understanding of the principles of birth and death. Andō Gorō was a pious man who knew the laws of cause and effect and erected many Buddhist halls and pagodas.[41] Why is it, then, that the Ezo cut off his head? In view of these events, I have no doubt that if these priests are allowed to go on offering prayers for victory, Your Lordship will meet with some untoward event. And when that happens, you must not under any circumstances say that I failed to warn you!" Such was the stern manner in which I addressed him.

When I returned home, I heard that the priest Hōin of the Amida Hall had been asked to pray for rain from the tenth day of the fourth month. This Hōin is the most learned priest of Tō-ji and the teacher of Dōjo of Ninna-ji.[42] He has mastered the esoteric teachings of the Great Teachers Kōbō, Jikaku, and Chishō and has memorized all the doctrines of the various sects such as Tendai and Kegon. He began praying for rain on the tenth day, and on the eleventh a heavy rain fell. There was no wind, but only a gentle rain that fell for a day and a night. Hōjō Tokimune, the lord of the province of Sagami, was said to have been so deeply impressed that he presented Hōin with thirty *ryō* in gold, a horse, and other gifts as a reward.[43]

When the people of Kamakura heard this, eminent and humble alike clapped their hands, pursed their lips, and laughed with derision, saying, "That Nichiren preached a false kind of Buddhism and came near to getting his head cut off. He was finally pardoned in the end, but instead of learning his lesson, he goes on slandering the Nembutsu and Zen sects, and even dares to speak ill of the esoteric teachings of Shingon. How fortunate that we have had this rain to serve as proof of the power of Shingon prayers!"

Faced with such criticism, my disciples became quite downcast and complained that I had been too provocative in my attacks on the Shingon sect. But I said to them, "Just wait a while. If the evil teachings of the Great Teacher Kōbō could in fact produce effective prayers for the welfare of the nation, then the Retired Emperor Gotoba would surely have been victorious in his struggle with the Kamakura shogunate, and Setaka, the favorite boy attendant of Dōjo of Ninna-ji, would not have had his head cut off.[44] Kōbō in his *Jūjūshin Ron* states that the Lotus Sutra is inferior to the *Kegon* Sutra. In his *Hizō Hōyaku* he claims that the Shakyamuni Buddha of the *Juryō* chapter of the Lotus Sutra is an ordinary mortal, and in his *Ben Kemmitsu Nikyō Ron* he calls the Great Teacher T'ien-t'ai a thief.[45] Moreover, Shōkaku-bō, in his *Shari Kōshiki* states that the Buddha who preached the one vehicle of the Lotus Sutra is not even worthy to tend the shoes of a Shingon master.[46] Hōin of the Amida Hall is a follower of the men who taught these perverse doctrines. If such a man could show himself superior to me, then the Dragon Kings who send down the rain must be the enemies of the Lotus Sutra, and they will surely be chastised by the gods Bonten and Taishaku and the Four Heavenly Kings. There must be more to this than meets the eye!"

"What do you mean by 'more than meets the eye'?" my disciples asked with scornful smiles.

I replied, "Shan-wu-wei and Pu-k'ung both caused rain to fall in answer to their prayers, but it appears that they also brought about high winds. When Kōbō prayed for rain, it fell after twenty-one days had passed. But under such circumstances, it is the same as though he had not caused it to rain at all, since some rain is naturally bound to fall in the course of a twenty-one day interval. The fact that it happened to rain while he was praying for it is in no way remarkable. What is really impressive is to cause it to fall through a single ceremony, the way T'ien-t'ai and Senkan did.[47] That is why I say there must be something peculiar about this rain."

I had not even finished speaking when a great gale began to blow. Houses of every size, temples and shrines, old trees, and government buildings all were swept up into the air or toppled to the ground. A huge shining object flew through the sky, and the earth was strewn with beams and rafters. Men and women were blown to their death, and many cattle and horses were struck down. One might have excused such an evil wind if it had come in autumn, the typhoon season, but this was only the fourth month, the beginning of summer. Moreover, this wind did not blow throughout the country but struck only the eight provinces of the Kanto region, and in fact only the two provinces of Musashi and Sagami. It blew strongest in Sagami; and within Sagami, it blew strongest in Kamakura; and within Kamakura, it blew strongest at the government headquarters, Wakamiya, and the temples Kenchō-ji and Gokuraku-ji. It was apparent that it was no ordinary wind, but rather the result of Hōin's prayers alone. The people who had earlier pursed their lips and laughed at me suddenly turned sober, and my disciples too were astonished.

As I had expected all along, my warnings had gone unheeded. If after three attempts to warn the rulers of the nation one's advice is still unheeded, one should leave the country.[48] With that thought in mind, I accordingly left Kamakura on the twelfth day of the fifth month and came here to Mount Minobu.

In the tenth month of the same year (1274), the Mongols launched their attack. Not only were the islands of Iki and Tsushima assaulted and captured, but the forces of the Dazaifu government office in Kyushu were defeated as well. When the military leaders Shōni Nyūdō and Ōtomo[49] received word of this, they fled from the scene, and the remaining warriors were struck down without difficulty. [Though the Mongol forces withdrew,] it was apparent just how weak Japan's defenses would be if they should launch another attack in the future.

The *Ninnō* Sutra says, "When the sage departs, the seven types of calamity will invariably arise."[50] The *Saishōō* Sutra states, "Because evil men are respected and favored and good men are subjected to punishment, marauders will appear from other regions and the people of the country will meet with death and disorder."[51] If these pronouncements of the Buddha are true, then evil men certainly exist in our country and the ruler favors and respects such men while treating good men with enmity.

The *Daijuku* Sutra states, "The sun and moon do not show their brightness and there is drought on every side. Thus do evil kings and evil monks who commit unrighteous acts bring destruction upon my True Law."[52] In the *Ninnō* Sutra we read, "The evil monks, seeking for all the fame and gain they can get, will appear in the presence of the ruler, the heir apparent, and the princes and expound doctrines that lead to the destruction of Buddhism and the destruction of the state. The ruler, unable to discern the true nature of the monks' words, listens to them with trust, and thus they become the cause for the destruction of Buddhism and the destruction of the state."[53] And the Lotus Sutra speaks of the "evil monks of a defiled age."[54] If these passages in the sutras are true, then there must unquestionably be evil monks in this country. The crooked trees should be cut down on the treasure-filled mountains, and dead bodies should not be consigned to the great sea. Though the Great Sea of the Buddhist Law and the Treasure Mountain of the One Vehicle may admit the rubble and trash of the five cardinal sins or the dirty water of the four major offenses,[55] they have no room for the "dead bodies" of those who slander the Lotus Sutra, or for the "crooked trees" who are *icchantika,* men of incorrigible disbelief. Therefore those who endeavor to practice the Buddhist Law and who care about what happens to them in future lives should know what a fearful thing it is to slander the Lotus Sutra.

Many people wonder why anyone should pay heed to a person like myself who speaks ill of Kōbō, Jikaku, and others of their group. I do not know about other regions, but I know that the people of

Tōjō and Saijō in the province of Awa have good reason to believe what I say. They have seen the proof right before their eyes. Endon-bō of Inomori, Saigyō-bō and Dōgi-bō of Kiyosumi, and Jitchi-bō of Kataumi were all eminent monks; but one should inquire what kind of death they met with. However, I will say no more of them.[56] Enchi-bō spent three years in the great hall of Seichō-ji copying the text of the Lotus Sutra in laborious fashion, bowing three times as he copied each character. He had memorized all ten volumes, and every day and night recited the entire sutra twice for a period of fifty years. Everyone predicted that he would surely become a Buddha. But I alone said that he, along with Dōgi-bō, was even more certain to fall into the depths of the hell of incessant suffering than were the Nembutsu priests. You would do well to inquire carefully just how these men met death. If it had not been for me, people would have believed that these monks had attained Buddhahood.

You should realize from this that the manner of the death of Kōbō, Jikaku, and the others indicated that a truly miserable fate was in store for them. But their disciples contrived to keep the matter secret, so that even the members of the imperial court never learned of it. Hence these men have been looked up to with increasing reverence in later ages. And if there had been no one like me to reveal the truth, they would have gone on being honored in that manner for endless ages to come. The heretical teacher Ulūka [turned to stone at his death,] but eight hundred years later [his errors were brought to light and] the stone melted and turned to water.[57] And in the case of another heretical teacher, Kapila, a thousand years passed before his faults were brought to light.[58]

A person is able to be born in human form because he or she has observed the five precepts in a previous existence.[59] And if he continues to observe the five precepts in this life, then the twenty-five benevolent deities will protect him, and Dōshō and Dōmyō, the two heavenly messengers who have been with him since birth on his left and right shoulders respectively, will guard him.[60] So long as he commits no fault, the demons will have no chance to do him harm. And yet in this country of Japan, there are countless people who cry out in misery. We know, too, that the people of the islands of Iki and Tsushima had to suffer at the hands of the Mongols, and what befell the defenders of the Dazaifu in Kyushu. What fault were the people of this country guilty of that they should meet with such a fate? One would surely like to know the answer. One or two of the persons there may have been guilty of evil, but is it possible that all of them could have been?

The blame lies entirely in the fact that this country is filled with Shingon priests who follow the doctrines handed down from Kōbō, Jikaku, and Chishō; with Nembutsu priests who are later-day disciples of Shan-tao and Hōnen; and with the followers of Bodhidharma and the other patriarchs of the Zen sect. That is why the gods Bonten and Taishaku, the Four Heavenly Kings, and the other deities, true to the vow they took when the Lotus Sutra was expounded to split into seven pieces the head [of anyone who troubles a preacher of the sutra],[61] have sent down this punishment.

Some people may be perplexed at this point and object that, although those who do harm to the votary of the Lotus Sutra are supposed to have their heads split into seven pieces, there are men who slander Nichiren and yet do not have broken heads. Are we to conclude, they may ask, that Nichiren is not a true votary of the Lotus Sutra?

I would reply by saying that, if Nichiren is not a votary of the Lotus Sutra, then who is? Is Hōnen a votary, who in his writings ordered people to throw the Lotus Sutra away? Is the Great Teacher Kōbō a votary, who said that Shakyamuni was still in the region of ignorance?[62] Or are Shan-wu-wei or Jikaku votaries, who taught that although the Lotus Sutra and Shingon are equal in theory, the latter is superior in practice?

Again, this matter of the head being split into seven pieces—one need not imagine the kind of split made by a sharp sword. On the contrary, the Lotus Sutra says that the split is like that of the "branches of the *arjaka* tree." In a person's head there are seven drops of liquid and outside there are seven demons [who try to drink them].[63] If the demons drink one drop, the person's head begins to ache. If they drink three drops, his life will be endangered, and if they drink all seven drops, he will die. People in the world today all have heads that have split apart like the branches of the *arjaka* tree, but they are so steeped in evil karma that they are not even aware of the fact. They are like persons who have been injured while they were asleep or in a state of drunkenness and have not yet become conscious of their injury.

Rather than saying that the head is split into seven pieces, we sometimes say that the mind is split into seven pieces. The skull bone under the scalp breaks apart at the time of death. Many people of our own period had their heads split open in the great earthquake of the Shōka era (1257) or at the time of the appearance of the great comet in the Bun'ei era (1264). At the time their heads split open, they had a coughing condition, and when their five major internal organs[64] failed to function correctly, they suffered from dysentery. How could they have failed to realize that they were being punished because they slandered the votary of the Lotus Sutra!

Because venison is tasty, the deer is hunted and killed; because oil can be obtained from the turtle, the turtle loses his life. If a woman is attractive, there will be many who envy her. The ruler of a nation has much to fear from other nations, and the life of a man with great wealth is constantly in danger. He who abides by the Lotus Sutra will inevitably attain Buddhahood. Therefore the Devil of the Sixth Heaven, the lord of this threefold world, will become intensely jealous of anyone who abides by the sutra. This devil king, we are told, attaches himself like a plague demon to people in a way that cannot be detected by the eye. Thereafter, like persons who gradually become drunk on fine old wine, rulers, fathers and mothers, wives and children gradually become possessed by him and are filled with envy toward the votary of the Lotus Sutra. And that is precisely the situation we face today in the world around us. Because I chant Nam-myoho-renge-kyo I have for over twenty years been driven from place to place. Twice I have incurred the wrath of the authorities, and in the end I have retired to this mountain.

Here I am surrounded by four mountains, Shichimen to the west, Tenshi-no-take to the east, Minobu to the north, and Takatori to the south. Each is high enough to touch the sky, and so steep that even flying birds have trouble crossing them. In their midst are four rivers called Fujigawa, Hayakawa, Ōshirakawa, and Minobugawa. In the middle, in a ravine some hundred yards or so across, I have built my hut. I cannot see the sun in the daytime or the moon at night. In winter there is deep snow, and in summer the grass grows thick. Because so few people come to see me, the trail is very hard to travel. This year, especially, the snow is so deep that I have no visitors at all. Knowing that my life may end at any time, I put all my trust in the Lotus Sutra. In these circumstances, your letter was particularly welcome. It seemed almost like a message from Shakyamuni Buddha or from my departed parents, and I cannot tell you how grateful I was.

Nam-myoho-renge-kyo
Nam-myoho-renge-kyo

Miscellaneous Letters

EARTHLY DESIRES ARE ENLIGHTENMENT

Introduction

This letter was sent by Nichiren from his exile on Sado on the second day of the fifth month, 1272, to Shijō Kingo (c. 1230–1300), a samurai who served the Ema family, a branch of the Hōjō clan. It was written in gratitude for a visit that Shijō had paid in the fourth month. The trip to Sado was an arduous one, involving a crossing of the Japan Sea, and required that Shijō absent himself from his duties in Kamakura for more than a month. The subject of the letter, "earthly desires are enlightenment," is sometimes rendered "the very passions are enlightenment," and is a basic concept of Mahayana Buddhism. Nichiren urges Shijō to maintain his faith in and devotion to the Lotus Sutra.

I deeply appreciate your recent visit here and your constant concern over the numerous persecutions which have befallen me. I have met these great persecutions as the votary of the Lotus Sutra and do not regret them in the slightest. No life could be more fortunate than mine, no matter how many times one might repeat the cycle of birth and death. [Were it not for these troubles,] I might have remained in the three or four evil paths. But now, to my great joy, I am sure to sever the cycle of sufferings and attain the fruit of Buddhahood.

T'ien-t'ai and Dengyō suffered persecutions arising out of hate and jealousy merely because they propagated theoretical *ichinen sanzen* of *shakumon* (the theoretical teaching). In Japan this teaching was propagated and handed down successively by Dengyō, Gishin,[1] Enchō,[2] Jikaku, and others. Among the many disciples who followed the Great Teacher Jie,[3] the eighteenth chief priest of the Tendai sect, were Danna, Eshin, Sōga, and Zen'yu.[4] At that time the sect's teachings were divided in two: Danna, the Administrator of Monks, transmitted the doctrinal teachings while Eshin, the Supervisor of Monks, devoted himself to the meditative practices. Doctrine is comparable to the moon and practice to the sun. Doctrinal practices are shallow, while meditative practices are deep. The teachings expounded by Danna were therefore broad but shallow, while Eshin's teachings were deep but limited.

The teaching that I, Nichiren, am now propagating may seem limited, but it is actually most profound. This is because it goes deeper than the teachings expounded by T'ien-t'ai and Dengyō. It reveals the three important matters contained in the *Juryō* chapter of the essential teaching.[5] To practice only the seven characters of Nam-myoho-renge-kyo may appear limited, yet since this Law is the master of all Buddhas of the past, present, and future, the teacher of all bodhisattvas in the ten directions, and the guide that enables all beings to attain Buddhahood, its practice is incomparably profound.

The sutra states, "The wisdom of all Buddhas is infinitely profound and immeasurable."[6] "All Buddhas" means every Buddha throughout the ten directions in every age of the past, present, and future. It represents every single Buddha and bodhisattva of any sutra or sect whatsoever, including both Dainichi Buddha of the Shingon sect and Amida Buddha of the Jōdo sect, every Buddha of the past, the future, or the present, including even Shakyamuni Buddha himself.

Next, what is meant by the "wisdom" of all Buddhas? It is the true aspect of all phenomena, the Dharma entity of the ten factors that leads all beings to Buddhahood. What then is the dharma entity? It is nothing other than Nam-myoho-renge-kyo. T'ien-t'ai states, "The profound principle of the 'true aspect' is the originally inherent Law of Myōhō-renge-kyō."[7] The true aspect of all phenomena indicates the two Buddhas Shakyamuni and Tahō [seated together in the Treasure Tower]. Tahō represents all phenomena and Shakyamuni, the true aspect. The two Buddhas also indicate the two principles of truth as object *(kyō)* and the subjective wisdom to grasp it *(chi)*. Tahō Buddha signifies the truth as object and Shakyamuni the subjective wisdom. Although these are two, they are fused into one in the Buddha's enlightenment.[8]

These teachings are of prime importance. They mean that earthly desires are enlightenment and that the sufferings of birth and death are nirvana. When one chants Nam-myoho-renge-kyo even during the sexual union of man and woman, then earthly desires are enlightenment and the sufferings of birth and death are nirvana. Sufferings are nirvana only when one realizes that life throughout its cycle of birth and death is neither born nor destroyed. The *Fugen* Sutra states, "Even without extinguishing earthly desires or denying the five desires, they can purify all of their senses and eradicate all of their misdeeds."[9] It is stated in the *Maka Shikan* that "the ignorance and dust of desires are enlightenment and the sufferings of birth and death are nirvana."[10] The *Juryō* chapter of the Lotus Sutra says, "This is my constant thought: how can I cause all living beings to gain entry to the highest Way and quickly attain Buddhahood?"[11] And the *Hōben* chapter states, "The aspect of this world [as it manifests the Law,] abides eternally."[12] The Dharma body is none other than Nam-myoho-renge-kyo.

It was this most august and precious Lotus Sutra which in the past I trampled underfoot, scowled upon in disgust and refused to believe in. In one way or another, I maliciously ridiculed people who studied the Lotus Sutra and who taught it to at least one other person, thereby passing on the Law for the future. In addition, I did everything I could to hinder them from embracing the sutra by asserting that they could practice it in the next life but it would not benefit them in this life. Countless slanderous acts such as these have now brought on the many severe persecutions I have suffered in my lifetime. Because I once disparaged the highest of all sutras, I am now looked down upon and my words go unheeded. The *Hiyu* chapter states that [because one slandered the Lotus Sutra in the past] other people will have no sympathy with him even though he sincerely tries to be friendly with them.

As a votary of the Lotus Sutra, you suffered severe persecutions, yet still you came to my assistance. In the *Hosshi* chapter the Buddha states, "I will send monks and nuns and laymen and laywomen [to make offerings to the teacher of the Lotus Sutra and hear his preaching of the Law]."[13] If you are not one of these laymen, then to whom else could the passage possibly refer? You have not only heard the

Law, but have taken faith in it and since then have followed it without turning aside. How wondrous! How extraordinary! Then how can there be any doubt that I, Nichiren, am the teacher of the Lotus Sutra? I have fulfilled the words of the Buddha: "He is the envoy of the Buddha, sent to carry out the Buddha's work."[14] I have propagated the five characters of the daimoku which were entrusted to Bodhisattva Jōgyō when the two Buddhas sat together within the Treasure Tower. Does this not indicate that I am an envoy of Bodhisattva Jōgyō? Moreover, following me as a votary of the Lotus Sutra, you also tell others of this Law. What else could this be but the transmission of the Mystic Law?

Carry through with your faith in the Lotus Sutra. You cannot strike fire from flint if you stop halfway. Bring forth the great power of faith and establish your reputation among all the people of Kamakura and the rest of Japan as "Shijō Kingo of the Hokke sect."[15] Even a bad reputation will spread far and wide. A good reputation will spread even farther, particularly if it is a reputation for devotion to the Lotus Sutra.

Explain all this to your wife, and work together like the sun and moon, a pair of eyes, or the two wings of a bird. With the sun and the moon, how can you fall into the paths of darkness? With a pair of eyes, how can you fail to behold the faces of Shakyamuni, Tahō, and all the other Buddhas of the ten directions? With a pair of wings, you will surely be able to fly in an instant to the treasure land of Tranquil Light. I will write in more detail on an other occasion.

With my deep respect,
Nichiren

The second day of the fifth month (1272).

WINTER ALWAYS TURNS TO SPRING

Introduction

This letter, dated the fifth month of 1275, is one of several that Nichiren wrote to Myōichi-ama, a woman believer related to Nis-shō (1221–1323), one of his six elder priest-disciples. Myōichi-ama was an educated woman who had lost her husband and was having a difficult time raising her two children. Nichiren wrote to encourage her with the frequently cited passage explaining that those with faith in the Lotus Sutra are as though in the midst of winter, which will, without fail, turn into spring.

If the sun and the moon were not in the heavens, how could plants grow? Children usually have both father and mother, and it is diffi-cult for them when one parent is dead. Your husband had to leave behind both a daughter and a son who is ill, and you, their mother, who suffer from a poor constitution. To whom could he entrust his family before leaving the world?

At the end of his life the Buddha, the World-Honored One, la-mented, "Now I am about to enter nirvana. The only thing troubling my heart is King Ajātaśatru."[1] Bodhisattva Kāśyapa[2] then asked him, "Since the Buddha's mercy is impartial, your regret in dying should stem from compassion for all mankind. Why do you single out King Ajātaśatru?" The Buddha replied, "Suppose that a couple has seven children, one of whom falls ill. Although the parents love all their children equally, they worry most about the sick child."[3] T'ien-t'ai cited this passage in his *Maka Shikan*.[4] To the Buddha, all people are his children. Just like parents who worry most about their sick child, among all people, the Buddha is most concerned about a man evil enough to slay his own parents and become an enemy of the Buddha's teachings. King Ajātaśatru was the ruler of Magadha. He murdered his father, King Bimbisāra, a powerful patron of Shakyamuni, and became an enemy of the Buddha. In consequence, the heavens forsook him, the sun and the moon rose out of rhythm, and the earth shook violently to cast him off. All his subjects came to oppose Buddhism, and the neighboring kingdoms started to attack Magadha. All this happened because King Ajātaśatru took the wicked Devadatta for his teacher. Finally, on the fifteenth day of the second month leprous sores broke out all over his body, and it was foretold that he would die and fall into the hell of incessant suffering on the seventh day of the third month. Saddened by this, the Buddha was reluctant to enter nirvana. He lamented, "If I can but save King Ajātaśatru, all other wicked people can also be saved."

Your late husband had to leave behind his daughter and ailing son. It must have troubled him deeply that his aged wife, as feeble as a withered tree, would be left alone to worry about her children. The persecutions which befell Nichiren must have weighed heavily on his heart. Since the Buddha's words are in no way false, the Lotus Sutra is certain to spread. Knowing this, your husband must have felt that something wonderful would happen and this priest would one day be highly respected. When I was exiled, he must have wondered how the Lotus Sutra and the ten demon daughters[5] could possibly have allowed it to happen. Were he still living, how joyful he would be to see Nichiren pardoned! How glad he would be to see my prediction fulfilled, now that the Mongol Empire has attacked Japan and the country is in crisis. Such are the feelings of common mortals.

Those who believe in the Lotus Sutra are as if in winter, which never fails to turn into spring. Since ancient times never has anyone seen or heard of winter turning into autumn. Nor have we ever heard of any believer in the Lotus Sutra who remained a common mortal. A passage from the sutra reads, "Among those who hear of this Law, there is not one who shall not attain Buddhahood."[6]

Your husband gave his life for the Lotus Sutra. His entire livelihood depended on a small fief, and that was confiscated because of [his faith in] the Lotus Sutra. Surely that equaled giving his life for the Lotus Sutra. Sessen Dōji offered his life for but half a stanza of a Buddhist teaching,[7] and Bodhisattva Yakuō burned his arms in offering to the Buddha. They were both saints, so they could endure these austerities as easily as water pours on fire. But your husband was a common mortal, so he was [at the mercy of his sufferings,] like paper placed in fire.[8] Therefore, he will certainly receive blessing as great as theirs. He may be watching his wife and children in the mirrors of the sun and moon every moment of the day and night. Since you and your children are common mortals, you cannot see or hear him, just as neither can the deaf hear thunder nor the blind see the sun. But do not doubt that he is close at hand protecting you.

Just when I was thinking that if at all possible I must somehow go and see you, you had a robe sent here to me. Your thoughtfulness was totally unexpected. Since the Lotus Sutra is the noblest of all sutras, I may yet gain influence in this lifetime. If so, rest assured that I will watch over your children whether you are living then or not. When I was in Sado and during my stay here, you sent your servant to help me. Neither in this nor future lifetimes shall I ever forget what you have done for me. I will not fail to repay my debt of gratitude to you. Nam-myoho-renge-kyo, Nam-myoho-renge-kyo.

With my deep respect,
Nichiren

The fifth month in the first year of Kenji (1275)

THE EMBANKMENTS OF FAITH

Introduction

This letter is dated the third day of the ninth month, 1275, two years after Nichiren's return from exile in Sado. It is addressed to Sennichi-ama, the wife of Abutsu-bō (d. 1279), a native of Sado who was converted by Nichiren during his stay there.

Here Nichiren is replying to questions concerning the results of different degrees of slander against Buddhism. He is not so much concerned with specific slanders against the Lotus Sutra as with slanders that diminish the dignity of human life. He encourages Sennichi-ama to strengthen her faith and aspirations toward enlightenment.

In your letter you asked how the retribution varies according to the degree of slander against Buddhism. To begin with, the Lotus Sutra was taught to lead all people to Buddhahood. However, only those who have faith in it attain Buddhahood. Those who slander it fall into the great citadel of the hell of incessant suffering. As the sutra states, "One who refuses to take faith in this sutra and instead slanders it immediately destroys the seeds for becoming a Buddha in this world. . . . After he dies, he will fall into the Avīci Hell."[1]

There are many degrees of slander: shallow and profound, slight and heavy. Even among those who embrace the Lotus Sutra, very few uphold it steadfastly both in mind and in deed. Few are the practitioners who can uphold this sutra. But those who do will not suffer serious retribution even if they have committed minor offenses against Buddhism. Their strong faith expiates their sins as surely as a flood extinguishes tiny fires.

In the Nirvana Sutra Shakyamuni states, "If even a good monk sees someone slandering the Law and disregards him, failing to reproach him, to oust him, or to punish him for his offense, then that monk is betraying Buddhism. But if he takes the slanderer severely to task, drives him off or punishes him, then he is my disciple and one who truly understands my teachings."[2] This admonition forces me to speak out against slander in spite of the persecutions I face, for fear that I might become an enemy of Buddhism if I did not.

However, slander can be either minor or serious, and there are times when we should overlook it rather than attack it. The adherents of the Tendai and Shingon sects slander the Lotus Sutra and should be refuted. But without great wisdom it is very difficult to differentiate correctly between their doctrines and the teachings which Nichiren expounds. Therefore, at times you might be well advised to refrain from attacking them, just as I did in the *"Rissho Ankoku Ron."*[3]

Whether or not we reproach another for his slander, the retribution for grave offenses is difficult to avoid. If we see or hear a person commit slander and make no attempt to stop him even though he could be saved, we betray our great gifts of sight and hearing and so commit an act of utter mercilessness.

Chang-an wrote, "If you befriend another person but lack the mercy to correct him, you are in fact his enemy."[4] The consequences of this offense are extremely difficult to erase. The most important thing is to continually strengthen your compassion to benefit others.

When a person's slanders are minor, he may sometimes need to be admonished, but at other times this is unnecessary, for he may be able to correct his faults without being told. Reprove a person [for acting against Buddhism] when necessary, so that both of you can forestall the consequences of slander. Then, you should forgive him. The point is that even minor slanders can lead to serious ones, and then the effects he must suffer would be far worse. This is what Chang-an meant when he wrote. "He who makes it possible for an offender to rid himself of evil is acting like a parent to him."[5]

There are examples of slander even among Nichiren's disciples and believers. I am sure that you have heard about Ichinosawa Nyūdō.[6] In his heart he is one of Nichiren's disciples, but outwardly he still remains in the Nembutsu sect. Therefore, I am very concerned about his next life but have nevertheless presented him with the ten volumes of the Lotus Sutra.[7]

Strengthen your faith now more than ever. Anyone who teaches the truths of Buddhism to others is bound to incur hatred from men and women, priests and nuns. Let them say what they will. The most important thing is for you to entrust your life to the golden teachings of the Lotus Sutra, Shakyamuni Buddha, T'ien-t'ai, Miao-lo, Dengyō, and Chang-an. This is the way to practice correctly according to the Buddha's teachings. The Lotus Sutra reads, "If one teaches this sutra for even a moment in the dreaded age, [he will receive offerings from all the deities and people.]"[8] This passage explains that in the Latter Day of the Law when evil persons stained by the three poisons will prevail, anyone who embraces the true teaching for even a short time will receive offerings from heavenly gods and human beings.

Now you should make a great vow and aspire for [Buddhahood] in your next life. If you refuse to believe or slander the True Law even in the slightest, you will fall into the great citadel of the hell of incessant suffering. Suppose there is a ship that sails on the open sea. Even if the ship is stoutly built, should it leak even a bit, the passengers are certain to drown together. Even though the embankment between rice fields is firm, if there is only one tiny crack in it, the water will never be contained. You must bail the sea water of slander and disbelief [out of the ship of your life] and solidify the embankments of your faith. If a believer's offense is slight, forgive him and lead him to obtain benefits. If it is serious, admonish him to strengthen his faith so that he can expiate the sin.

You are a very unusual woman since you asked me to explain the effects of various degrees of slander. You are every bit as praiseworthy as the Dragon King's daughter when she said, "I will reveal the Mahayana doctrine to save people from suffering."[9] The Lotus Sutra reads, "To ask about the meaning of this sutra will indeed be difficult."[10] There are very few people who inquire about the meaning of the Lotus Sutra. Always be determined to denounce slander against Buddhism to the best of your ability. It is indeed remarkable that you should be helping me to reveal my teachings.

Respectfully,
Nichiren

The third day of the ninth month in the first year of Kenji (1275)

ON ITAI DŌSHIN

Introduction

"On Itai Dōshin" was presented to Takahashi Nyūdō, a lay follower in the Fuji district of Suruga. The letter is dated the sixth day of the eighth month, but no year is given. Because of the reference to the "recent incident at Atsuhara," we may presume that it was written between 1275, when the difficulties there began, and 1280, some time after the first Mongol invasion of that year, when the Atsuhara difficulties had been resolved.

This letter stresses the importance of unity in the face of "numerous evils" arrayed against the followers of Nichiren, and predicts the imminence of a second Mongol invasion, that will, in the end, serve to excise the slanders against Buddhism.

I have received the white winter robe and the thick-quilted one, as well as one *kan*[1] of coins, through the offices of Hōki-bō.[2] Hōki-bō and Sado-bō[3] and the believers in Atsuhara,[4] united in their resolve, proved the true strength of *itai dōshin*.[5]

If *itai dōshin* [many or varied in body, one in mind] prevails among the people, they will achieve all their goals, whereas in *dōtai ishin* [one in body, different in mind], they can achieve nothing remarkable. The more than three thousand volumes of Confucian and Taoist literature are filled with examples. King Chou of Yin led 700,000 soldiers into battle against King Wu of Chou and his 800 men.[6] Yet King Chou's army lost because of disunity while King Wu's men defeated him because of perfect unity. Even an individual at cross purposes with himself is certain to end in failure. Yet a hundred or even a thousand people can definitely attain their goal if they are of one mind. Though numerous, the Japanese will find it difficult to accomplish anything, because they are divided in spirit. On the contrary, I believe that although Nichiren and his followers are few in number, because they act in *itai dōshin,* they will accomplish their great mission of propagating the Lotus Sutra. Though evils may be numerous, they cannot prevail over a single great truth, just as many raging fires will be quenched by a single shower of rain. This principle also holds true with Nichiren and his followers.

You have served the Lotus Sutra with devotion for many years and in addition, you demonstrated remarkable resolve during the recent incident at [Atsuhara]. Many people including Hōki-bō and Sado-bō have told me so. I have listened carefully and reported everything to the god of the sun and to Tenshō Daijin.

I should have replied to you earlier, but there was no one who could bring this letter to you. Ben Ajari[7] left here so quickly that I had no time to finish writing before his departure.

Some people may be wondering whether the Mongols will really attack again, but I believe that invasion is now imminent. The ruin of our country would be deplorable, but if the invasion does not happen, the Japanese people will slander the Lotus Sutra more than ever and all of them will fall into the hell of incessant suffering.

The nation may be devastated by the superior strength of the Mongols, but slander of Buddhism will cease almost entirely. Defeat would be like moxa cautery which cures disease or acupuncture which relieves pain. Both are painful at the moment but bring happiness later.

I, Nichiren, am the emissary of the Lotus Sutra, while the Japanese are like King Mihirakula[8] who eliminated Buddhism throughout India. The Mongol Empire may be like King Himatala[9] of the Himalaya, a messenger from heaven sent to punish those hostile to the votary of the Lotus Sutra. If the Japanese repent, they will be like King Ajātaśatru who became a devout follower of Buddhism, thereby curing his own leprosy and prolonging his life by forty years.[10] Like Ajātaśatru, they will profess faith in spite of their earlier disbelief, and in their present life gain the realization that no phenomenon is either born or perishes.

With my deep respect,
Nichiren

The sixth day of the eighth month

HAPPINESS IN THIS WORLD

Introduction

This letter was written at Minobu on the twenty-seventh day of the sixth month, 1276. It is addressed to Shijō Kingo, who also received the letter "Earthly Desires are Enlightenment" (see above). Shijō was a loyal retainer, well versed in medicine and the martial arts. He was an early convert to Nichiren's teachings, much to the displeasure of his lord and the military men who surrounded him. Nichiren wrote him this brief letter in an effort to encourage him to withstand the difficulties he faced.

There is no true happiness for human beings other than chanting Nam-myoho-renge-kyo. The sutra says, "The people there [in my land] are happy and at ease."[1] "Happy and at ease" here means the joy derived from the Law. You are obviously included among the "people," and "there" indicates the entire world, which includes Japan. "Happy and at ease" means to know that our lives—both our bodies and our minds, ourselves and our surroundings—are the entity of *ichinen sanzen* and the Buddha of absolute freedom. There is no true happiness apart from having faith in the Lotus Sutra. It promises us "peace and security in this life and good circumstances in the next."[2] Never let life's hardships disturb you. After all, no one can avoid problems, not even saints and sages.

Just chant Nam-myoho-renge-kyo, and when you drink saké, stay at home with your wife. Suffer what there is to suffer, enjoy what there is to enjoy. Regard both suffering and joy as facts of life and continue chanting Nam-myoho-renge-kyo, no matter what happens.

Then you will experience boundless joy from the Law. Strengthen your faith more than ever.

With my deep respect,
Nichiren

The twenty-seventh day of the sixth month in the second year of Kenji (1276), cyclical sign hinoe-ne

LETTER TO JAKUNICHI-BŌ

Introduction

Jakunichi-bō Nikke (n.d.) was a young disciple, the son of the local lord, Sakuma, of Okitsu, Isumi district, Kazusa Province (present-day Chiba Prefecture). In the Bun'ei era (1264–1275) his family had been converted by Nichiren during a pilgrimage of propagation he had made at the time. Jakunichi-bō became a priest and later built a temple known as Tanjō-ji in Kominato in honor of the place of Nichiren's birth.

I deeply appreciate your sending a letter to this distant place. It is extremely rare to be born as a human being. Not only are you endowed with human life, but you have the rare fortune to encounter Buddhism. Moreover, out of the Buddha's many teachings you have found the daimoku of the Lotus Sutra and become its votary. Truly you have served ten billions of Buddhas in your past existences!

Nichiren is the supreme votary of the Lotus Sutra in Japan. In this land only he has lived the twenty-line verse of the *Kanji* chapter.[1] Eighty myriads of millions of bodhisattvas pledged with this verse to propagate the Lotus Sutra but not one of them fulfilled it. The parents who gave life to this extraordinary person, Nichiren, are the most blessed of all people in Japan. It is destiny that they should have been my parents, and I, their child. Since Nichiren propagates the Lotus Sutra as the envoy of Shakyamuni, then his parents must also share this relationship. They are like King Myōshōgon and Lady Jōtoku [who followed their sons] Jōzō and Jōgen, [in the practice of Buddhism].[2] Could the two Buddhas Shakyamuni and Tahō have been reborn as Nichiren's parents? Or if not, could his parents have been among the eighty myriads of millions of bodhisattvas or the Four

Bodhisattvas led by Bodhisattva Jōgyō? It is beyond comprehension.

Names are important for all things. That is why the Great Teacher T'ien-t'ai placed "designation" first among the five major principles.[3] Giving myself the name Nichiren signifies that I have understood the Buddha vehicle by myself. This may sound boastful, but there are specific reasons for what I say. The sutra reads, "Just as the light of the sun and moon illuminates all obscurity, this person will practice among the people and dispel the darkness of all beings."[4] Consider exactly what this passage means. "This person will practice among the people" means that the first five hundred years of the Latter Day of the Law will witness the advent of Bodhisattva Jōgyō, who will illuminate the darkness of human ignorance and earthly desires with the light of Nam-myoho-renge-kyo. Nichiren's endeavors, as this bodhisattva's envoy, to have all Japanese embrace the Lotus Sutra embody the meaning of this passage. His efforts never slacken, even here on this mountain.

The passage continues, "After I have passed into extinction, one must accept and uphold this sutra. Such a person, with respect to the Buddha Way, is assured, and there can be no doubt."[5] Therefore, those who become Nichiren's disciples and followers should realize the profound karmic relationship they share with him and spread the Lotus Sutra in the same spirit. Being a votary of the Lotus Sutra is a bitter and unavoidable destiny.

Fan K'uai, Chang Liang,[6] Masakado, and Sumitomo[7] never acted cowardly because they cared so deeply about their honor and abhorred disgrace. But disgrace in this life is nothing. What counts is disgrace which appears in the next life. Proceed to the Lotus Sutra's place of enlightenment, bearing in mind the time when [you must face] the guards of hell and demons will strip you of your garments on the bank of the river of three crossings. The Lotus Sutra is the robe that will keep you from disgrace after this life. The Lotus Sutra reads, "like the naked who obtain clothing."[8] Believe in the Gohonzon with all your heart, for it is the robe to protect you in the next life. No wife would ever leave her husband unclothed, nor could any parents fail to feel compassion for their child shivering in the cold. Shakyamuni Buddha and the Lotus Sutra are like one's wife and parents. You have helped Nichiren and saved him from disgrace in this life; in return, he will protect you from disgrace in the next. Death came to someone yesterday, it may come to us today. Blossoms turn into fruit and brides become mothers-in-law. Chant Nam-myoho-renge-kyo and be always diligent in your faith.

I cannot thank you enough for your frequent letters. Jakunichi-bō, please convey all these teachings in detail to the other disciples.

Nichiren

The sixteenth day of the ninth month (1279)

APPENDIX 1

SANSKRIT PERSONAL NAMES

Sanskrit Names	Japanese Names
Agastya	Akada 阿竭多
Ajātaśatru	Ajase 阿闍世
Ajita	Agita 阿耆多; Aitta 阿逸多
Ājñāta Kauṇḍinya	Anyakyōjinnyo 阿若憍陳如 or Kurin 俱隣
Ānanda	Anan 阿難
Āryadeva	Daiba 提婆
Āryasiṃha	Shishi Sonja 師子尊者
Asaṅga	Mujaku 無著
Asita	Ashida 阿私陀
Aśoka	Aiku; Asoka 阿育
Aśvaghoṣa	Memyō 馬鳴 or Asubakusha 阿溼縛婁沙
Aśvajit	Asetsuji 阿説示
Bālāditya	Gennichi-ō 幻日王
Bhadrapāla	Baddabara 跋陀婆羅
Bhadraruci	Ken'ai Ronji 賢愛論師
Bhadrika	Batsudairika 跋提梨迦
Bhandhi asura	Bachi ashura 婆稚阿修羅
Bimbisāra	Bimbashara 頻婆舍羅
Bodhidharma	Daruma 達磨
Buddhamitra	Buddamitta 仏陀密多
Buddhananda	Buddanandai 仏陀難提
Chandraprabhā	Gakkō 月光
Ciñcāmāṇavika	Senshanyo 栴遮女
Cunda	Junda 純陀
Daśabala Kāśyapa	Jūriki Kashō 十力迦葉
Devadatta	Daibadatta 提婆達多 or Chōdatsu 調達
Dharmagupta	Darumakikuta 達摩掬多
Dharmakṣema	Dommushin 曇無讖
Dharmapāla	Gohō 護法
Dharmarakṣa	Hōgo 法護
Dhṛtaka	Daitaka 提多迦
Dignāga	Jinna 陳那

Sanskrit Names	Japanese Names
Droṇodana	Kokubon-ō 斛飯王
Ghoṣira	Kushira 瞿師羅
Guṇaprabha	Tokukō Ronji 徳光論師
Haklenayaśas	Kakurokuyasha 鶴勒夜奢
Himatala	Sessenge-ō 雪山下王
Jayata	Jayana 闍夜那
Jinu	Gito 耆菟
Jīvaka	Giba 耆婆
Jñānagupta	Janakutta 闍那崛多
Kālodāyin	Karudai 迦留陀夷
Kāṇadeva	Kanadaiba 迦那提婆
Kapila	Kabira 迦毘羅
Kapimala	Kabimara 迦毘摩羅
Kāśyapa	Kashō 迦葉
Kāśyapa Mātaṅga	Kashōmatō 迦葉摩騰
Kātyāyana	Kasennen 迦旃延
Kokālika	Kugyari 瞿伽利
Kṛki	Kiriki 訖利季
Kṛta	Kirita 訖利多
Kumārajīva	Kumarajū 鳩摩羅什
Kumārata	Kumarada 鳩摩羅馱
Kumārāyaṇa	Kumaraen 鳩摩羅炎
Lambā	Ramba 藍婆
Mādhava	Matō 摩沓
Madhyāntika	Madenchi 末田地
Mahādeva	Daiten 大天
Mahākāśyapa	Kashō 迦葉
Mahānāma	Shakumanan 釈摩男
Mahāprajāpatī	Makahajahadai 摩訶波闍波提
Maheśvara	Makeishura 摩醯首羅 or Daijizai-ten 大自在天
Manoratha	Nyoi ronji 如意論師
Manorhita	Manura 摩奴羅
Maudgalyāyana	Mokuren 目連
Māyā	Maya 摩耶
Mihirakula	Daizoku-ō 大族王
Mikkaka	Mishaka 弥遮迦
Nāgabodhi	Ryūchi 竜智
Nāgārjuna	Ryūju 竜樹
Nanda	Nanda 難陀
Nārāyaṇa	Naraen-ten 那羅延天
Nirgranthajñātiputra	Niken 尼犍
Padmaprabha	Kekō 華光

Sanskrit Names	Japanese Names
Paramārtha	Shindai 真諦
Pārśva	Kyō-biku 脇比丘
Pilindavatsa	Hitsuryō 畢陵
Prajñā	Hannya 般若
Prasenajit	Hashinoku-ō 波斯匿王
Puṇyayaśas	Funasha 富那奢
Pūrṇa	Furuna 富楼那
Puṣyamitra	Hosshamittara-ō 弗沙弥多羅王
Rāhula	Ragora 羅睺羅 or Raun 羅云
Rāhulata	Rago 羅睺
Rṣabha	Rokushaba 勒沙婆
Saṃghanandi	Sōgyanandai 僧伽難提
Saṃghayaśas	Sōgyayasha 僧伽耶奢
Śāṇavāsa	Shōnawashu 商那和修
Śāriputra	Sharihotsu 舍利弗 or Shinshi 身子
Sātavāhana	Inshō-ō 印生王
Shakyamuni (Śākyamuni)	Shakuson 釈尊
Siddhārtha	Shitta 悉達
Śīlabhadra	Kaigen 戒賢
Śīlāditya	Kainichi-ō 戒日王
Siṃhahanu	Shishikyō-ō 師子頬王
Sthiramati	Kenne 賢慧
Subhadra	Shubaddara 須跋陀羅
Subhūti	Shubodai 須菩提
Sudāya	Shuda 須陀
Śuddhodana	Jōbon-ō 浄飯王
Sunakṣatra	Zenshō 善星 or Shizen 四禅
Udayana	Uden 優塡
Udraka Rāmaputra	Uzuranhotsu 欝頭羅弗
Ulūka	Kuru 拘留 or Urusōgya 漚楼僧伽
Upagupta	Ubakikuta 優婆毱多
Utpalavarṇā	Renge 蓮華 or Keshiki 華色
Vaidehī	Idaike 韋提希
Vaipulya	Hōkō 方広
Vairocana	Birushana 毘盧遮那
Vasubandhu	Seshin 世親 or Tenjin 天親
Vatsa	Tokushi 犢子
Vimalakīrti	Yuimakitsu 維摩詰
Vimalamitra	Muku Ronji 無垢論師
Virūḍhaka	Haruri-ō 波瑠璃王
Viṣṇu	Bichū-ten 毘紐天
Yaśodharā	Yashutara nyo 耶輸多羅女

APPENDIX 2

CHINESE PERSONAL NAMES

Chinese Names	Japanese Names
Chang-an	Shōan 章安
Chang Liang	Chō Ryō 張良
Chao, King	Shō-ō 昭王
Chao Kao	Chō Kō 趙高
Ch'en Ch'en	Chin Shin 陳臣
Ch'eng, King	Sei-ō 成王
Ch'eng-kuan	Chōkan 澄観
Chia-hsiang	Kajō 嘉祥
Chia-shang	Kashō 嘉尚
Chi-cha	Kisatsu 季札
Chieh, King	Ketsu-ō 桀王
Chih-chou	Chishū 智周
Chih-i	Chigi 智顗
Chih Po	Chi Haku 智伯
Chih-tu	Chido 智度
Chih-yen	Chigon 智儼
Chih-yüan	Shion 志遠
Ch'ing-liang	Shōryō 清涼
Ching-shuang	Kyōsō 鏡霜
Chin-kang-chih	Kongōchi 金剛智
Ch'in-tsung, Emperor	Kinsō-tei 欽宗帝
Chi-tsang	Kichizō 吉蔵
Chou, King	Chū-ō 紂王
Chuang Tzu	Sōshi 荘子
Chu-fa-lan	Jikuhōran 竺法蘭
Ch'ung Hua	Chō Ka 重華
Ch'u Shan-hsin	Cho Zenshin 褚善信
Chu Tao-sheng	Jiku Dōshō 竺道生
Confucius	Kōshi 孔子
Fa-ch'üan	Hassen 法全

Chinese Names	Japanese Names
Fan K'uai	Han Kai 樊噲
Fa-tao	Hōdō 法道
Fa-tsang	Hōzō 法蔵
Fa-yün	Hōun 法雲
Fei Shu-ts'ai	Hi Shukusai 費叔才
Fu-ch'a	Fusa 夫差
Fu Hsi	Fuku Gi 伏義
Han-kuang	Gankō 含光
Hsiang Yü	Kō U 頂羽
Hsin Yu	Shin Yū 辛有
Hsüan-tsang	Genjō 玄奘
Hsüan-tsung, Emperor	Gensō-tei 玄宗帝
Huai-kan	Ekan 懷感
Huang Ti	Kō Tei 黄帝
Hua T'o	Ka Da 華陀
Hu Hai	Ko Gai 胡亥
Hui, Emperor	Kei Tei 恵帝
Hui-heng	Egō 慧胆
Hui-k'o	Eka 慧可
Hui-kuan	Ekan 慧観
Hui-kuang	Ekō 慧曠
Hui-kuo	Keika 恵果
Hui-neng	Enō 慧能
Hui-tsung, Emperor	Kisō-tei 徽宗帝
Hui-tz'u	Eji 慧次
Hui-yen	Egon 慧厳
Hui-yüan	Eon 慧遠
Hui-yüan	Eon 慧苑
Hui-yung	Eei 慧栄
Hung Yen	Kō En 弘演
I-hsing	Ichigyō 一行
I-lung	Iryō 遺竜
Juan Chi	Gen Seki 阮籍
Kan-chiang	Kanshō 干将
Kao-tsung, Emperor	Kōsō-tei 高宗帝
Kou-chien	Kōsen 勾践
Kuang-hsiu	Kōju 広修
Kuang-wu, Emperor	Kōbu-tei 光武帝
K'uei-chi	Kiki 窺基
Kung Yen	Kō In 公胤
Lao Tzu	Rōshi 老子
Liang-hsü	Ryōsho 良諝

Chinese Names	Japanese Names
Liang-p'i	Ryōfun 良賁
Li Kuang	Ri Kō 李広
Li Ling	Ri Ryō 李陵
Li Lou	Ri Rō 離婁
Li Ssu	Ri Shi 李斯
Liu Pang	Ryū Hō 劉邦
Lung-feng	Ryūhō 竜蓬
Lü Hui-t'ung	Ryo Keitsū 呂慧通
Mao Pao	Mō Hō 毛宝
Ma-tzu	Mashi 麻子
Miao-lo	Myōraku 妙楽
Ming, Emperor	Mei-tei 明帝
Ming-sheng	Myōshō 明勝
Mo-yeh	Bakuya 莫耶
Nan-yüeh	Nangaku 南岳
Pao-yüeh	Hōgatsu 宝月
Pien Ch'üeh	Hen Jaku 扁鵲
Pien Ho	Ben Ka 卞和
Pi Kan	Hi Kan 比干
P'ing, King	Hei-ō 平王
Po-ch'i	Hakuki 伯奇
Po Chü-i (Po Lo-tien)	Haku Kyoi 白居易 (Haku Rakuten 白楽天)
Po I	Haku I 伯夷
Po Yang	Haku Yō 白陽
P'u-kuang	Fukō 普光
Pu-k'ung	Fukū 不空
San-chieh	Sangai 三階
Seng-chao	Sōjō 僧肇
Seng-ch'üan	Sōsen 僧詮
Seng-jou	Sōnyū 僧柔
Shang Chün	Shō Kin 商均
Shan-tao	Zendō 善導
Shan-wu-wei	Zemmui 善無畏
Shen-fang	Shimbō 神肪
Shen Nung	Shin Nō 神農
Shen Yao, Emperor	Shingyō-tei 神堯帝
Shih K'uang	Shi Kō 師曠
Shu Ch'i	Shuku Sei 叔斉
Shun	Shun 舜
Shun-hsiao	Jungyō 順暁
Ssu-ma	Shiba 司馬

Chinese Names	Japanese Names
Su Wu	So Bu 蘇武
Su Yu	So Yū 蘇由
T'ai-kung Wang	Taikō Bō 太公望
Tai-tsung, Emperor	Daisō-tei 代宗帝
T'ai-tsung, Emperor	Taisō-tei 太宗帝
Tan, Duke of Chou	Shūkō Tan 周公旦
Tan Chu	Tan Shu 丹朱
T'an-luan	Donran 曇鸞
Tao-an	Dōan 道安
Tao-ch'o	Dōshaku 道綽
Tao-hsien	Dōsen 道暹
Tao-hsüan	Dōsen 道宣
Tao-sui	Dōsui 道邃
T'ien-t'ai	Tendai 天台
Ting Lan	Tei Ran 丁蘭
Ts'ai Yin	Sai In 蔡愔
Tse-t'ien, Empress	Sokuten-kōgō 則天皇后
Ts'ung-i	Jūgi 従義
Tu-shun	Tojun 杜順
Tz'u-en	Jion 慈恩
Wang Chao-chün	Ō Shōkun 王昭君
Wang Ling	Ō Ryō 王陵
Wang Mang	Ō Mō 王莽
Wang Shou	Ō Ju 王寿
Wang Tsun	Ō Jun 王遵
Wei Cheng	Gi Chō 魏徴
Wei-chüan	Yuiken 惟蠲
Wei Yüan-sung	Ei Gensū 衛元嵩
Wen, King	Bun-ō 文王
Wu, King	Bu-ō 武王
Wu Ch'eng	Mu Sei 務成
Wu-lung	Oryō 烏竜
Wu-tsung, Emperor	Busō-tei 武宗帝
Wu Tzu-hsü	Go Shisho 伍子胥
Yang Kuei-fei	Yō Kihi 楊貴妃
Yao	Gyō 堯
Yen Hui	Gan Kai 顔回 or Gan En 顔淵
Yi, Duke	I Kō 懿公
Yin Chi-fu	In Kippo 尹吉甫
Yin Shou	In Ju 尹寿
Yu, King	Yō-ō 幽王

Chinese Names	Japanese Names
Yü	U 禹
Yüan-cheng	Genjō 元政
Yü Jang	Yo Jō 予讓

NOTES

Risshō Ankoku Ron

1. Reference is to a passage in Shan-tao's *Hanju-san* (T47, 448c) in which he says that calling on the name of Amida Buddha serves as a sword to cut off earthly desires, karma, and suffering.

2. One of the twelve vows of Yakushi Buddha, which appear in the *Yakushi Hongan* Sutra (T14, 405 ff). This sutra also says that if one hears the name of Yakushi Buddha, he can become free from all desires.

3. T9, 54c. Here this is a reference to a practice of the Tendai sect.

4. Another reference to the Tendai sect, which held a ritual of prayer based on this passage (T8, 832b–c).

5. According to the *Ninnō* Sutra, a type of ceremony originally held by the god Taishaku to defeat the evil king Chosho (T8, 830a).

6. Ritual in which priests of the Shingon sect placed five jars, colored white, blue, red, yellow, and black, on a platform and put into them, respectively, gold, silver, lapis lazuli, pearls, and crystal. In addition, they placed in these jars the five grains, five herbs, and five types of incense and then filled them with water and set flowers in them. The ritual of filling jars in this manner was believed to drive away disasters.

7. Spirits referred to in the *Kyakuon Jinshu* Sutra (ZZ1, 3, 5, 388–389). Jap *shichi kijin*.

8. The *Go dairiki bosatsu* enumerated in the *Ninnō* Sutra (T8, 833a). According to this sutra, if a ruler embraces the correct teachings of Buddhism, these five powerful bodhisattvas will protect him and the people of his country.

9. Ritual for protecting the country. The four corners of the capital mean the northeast, southeast, southwest, and northwest. In these four corners of the capital, the god who eliminates epidemics and the god of medicine were enshrined to protect against the invasion of demons and evil spirits. These gods were enshrined at the four boundaries of the country for similar reasons. This ritual was often held when an emperor became ill. In the Kamakura period the gods were enshrined at the four corners of the site of government buildings and the four boundaries of the city of Kamakura.

10. Jupiter, Mars, Venus, Mercury, and Saturn. The more distant planets were unknown in Japan at this time.

11. The Buddha, the Law, and the Order or Priesthood.

12. This refers to an oracle said to have been received from Bodhisattva Hachiman in the reign of the fifty-first sovereign, Emperor Heizei (774–824). The *"Risshō Ankoku Ron"* was written in the reign of the ninetieth sovereign, Emperor Kameyama (1249–1305).

13. Also called the four kinds of believers, namely, priests, nuns, laymen, and laywomen. Jap *shishu*.

14. One of the eight kinds of non-human beings who protect Buddhism. Originally Hindu demons, they were later incorporated into Buddhism as protectors of the True Law, under the command of Bishamonten, one of the Four Heavenly Kings. Jap *yasha*.

15. T16, 429c–430a. The full title of the sutra is *Konkōmyō Saishōō Kyō*.

16. The first two divisions of the threefold world of unenlightened beings who transmigrate among the six paths. According to Vasubandhu's *Kusha Ron,* this world is divided into three: 1) the world of desire, 2) the world of form, where the inhabitants are free from desires but are still bound by some material restrictions, and 3) the world of formlessness, where one is free both from desire and the restrictions of matter. *See* Six paths in glossary. Jap *sangai*.

17. Sweet, pungent, sour, bitter, salty, astringent, and faint flavors. Jap *shichimi*.

18. The three essences that nourish human life and society: 1) the five grains, the essence of earth; 2) the strength of man, nourished by the five grains; and 3) the Law of Buddhism. Jap *sanshōke*.

19. Killing, stealing, committing adultery, lying, deceiving, defaming, engaging in duplicity, greed, anger, and stupidity.

20. From a verse in chapter 56 of the *Daijuku* Sutra (also called *Daijikkyō* or *Daishūkyō*). T13, 379b.

21. Celestial houses, divided into four houses of seven major heavenly bodies each, corresponding respectively to the directions and seasons of east/ spring, south/summer, west/autumn, and north/winter. Also referred to as the twenty-eight lunar mansions.

22. The first quotation is from T8, 830a; the second from T8, 833a.

23. Second of the four classes or castes of ancient India, the priestly class, the military and ruling class (Skt *kṣatriya*), farmers and traders, serfs.

24. Rulers of major kingdoms. In ancient India, when the ruler of a powerful kingdom ascended the throne, the ruler of smaller kingdoms and their ministers poured water on his head.

25. T14, 407c.

26. King of the country of Kośala. He converted to Buddhism at the urging of his wife and through instruction from Shakyamuni and worked to protect and support the Buddhist Order.

27. According to ancient Indian cosmology, each world has a sun, a moon, and a great Mt. Sumeru at its center, surrounded by four continents. The southern continent Jambudvīpa was considered to be the land where Buddhism spread.

28. Reference to an unusual phenomenon where the sun is seen as a multiple image. Such illusions involving the sun have appeared in the form

of many bright discs arcing outward from the sun. Scientists say that they are caused by reflection or refraction of light by ice crystals floating in the stratosphere.

29. The Metal Star is Venus. The Broom Star, the Fire Star, and the Water Star refer to comets, Mars, and Mercury respectively. Most of the other stars mentioned make up parts of the twenty-eight celestial houses.

30. Demon fire refers to fires of unknown origin attributed to the anger of demons. Dragon fire means fires ascribed to the wrath of dragons, who were thought to be able to change water into fire at will. It may also indicate fires caused by lightning. Heavenly fire is said to be caused by the wrath of Heaven, and mountain god fire—possibly a reference to volcanic eruptions —by the wrath of mountain gods. Human fire refers to fires caused by human error or negligence. Tree fire probably indicates forest fires caused by spontaneous combustion, and bandit fire means fires set by invaders.

31. Wheat, rice, beans, and two types of millet. Also a generic term for all grains, which is the meaning here.

32. Bandits who do evil amid the confusion of disasters caused by fire, water, and wind respectively. Demon bandits are said to be abductors.

33. T8, 832b–c.

34. T13, 173a.

35. Reference is to the tradition that Emperor Ming (27–75) dreamt of a golden man levitating above the garden. He awakened and asked his ministers about the dream. One of them said that he had once heard of the birth of a sage in the western region during the reign of King Chao of the Chou dynasty and that this sage had been called the Buddha. The emperor sent eighteen envoys to the western region in order to obtain the Buddha's teachings. They reached India, where they loaded Buddhist images and scriptures on white horses and brought them back to China in A.D. 67. The story appears in *Kōsō Den* (T50, 322a–323b).

36. Prince Shōtoku (574–622), second son of the thirty-first emperor, Yōmei, is famous for his application of the spirit of Buddhism to government. As regent for Empress Suiko, he carried out various reforms. He revered the Lotus Sutra, *Shōman* Sutra, and Vimalakirti Sutra; commentaries on them are attributed to him. In 587, while still a youth, he is said to have joined with Soga no Umako in attacking and killing Mononobe no Moriya, a powerful minister who opposed Buddhism and the Soga clan.

37. Site of Enryaku-ji, head temple of the Sammon school of the Tendai sect. This school derives from Jikaku Daishi (Ennin, 794–864), the third chief priest of Japanese Tendai.

38. Onjō-ji, also called Mii-dera, is the head temple of the Jimon school of the Tendai sect and is located in Ōtsu. This school derives from Chishō Daishi (Enchin, 814–891), the fifth chief priest of the Tendai sect, Tō-ji, or Eastern Temple, more properly known as Kyōō-gokoku-ji, located in Kyoto, is one of the most important temples of the Shingon sect.

39. Areas under the direct control of the emperor.

40. A mountain located to the northeast of Rājagṛha, the capital of Magadha in ancient India, where Shakyamuni is said to have expounded the

Lotus Sutra. It is often referred to as Vulture Peak, following the Sanskrit, but Kumārajīva's translation calls it Eagle Peak and this has been followed here. Jap Ryōju-sen; Skt Gṛdhrakūṭa.

41. Haklenayaśas was the twenty-third of Shakyamuni's twenty-four successors or descendants, according to Tendai tradition. Kukkuṭapāda is near Rājagṛha, the capital of Magadha. Mahākāśyapa is said to have transmitted the teachings to Ānanda and to have died on this mountain.

42. T8, 833c.

43. T12, 497c.

44. The power of being anywhere at will; the power of seeing anything anywhere; the power of hearing any sound anywhere; the power of knowing the thoughts of all other minds; the power of knowing past lives; and the power of eradicating illusions.

45. T9, 36b–c.

46. The four stages attainable by people of the *shōmon* realm: 1) those who have entered the way to enlightenment; 2) those destined to return once more to the human world; 3) those who have no further need to return there; and 4) the arhat who has attained enlightenment.

47. Condensed from a passage in the Nirvana Sutra, chapter 4, *Nyoraishō-bon* (T12, 386b).

48. *Senchaku Shū* (or *Senjaku Shū*) is the abbreviated title of *Senchaku Hongan Nembutsu Shū* (Selection of the Nembutsu of the Original Vow), a work in two volumes written in 1198 at the request of Kujō Kanezane, which constitutes the basic text of the Jōdo (Pure Land) sect. In it Hōnen (1133–1212), basing himself on the three major sutras of the Jōdo sect, exhorts people to discard all teachings other than the Nembutsu teachings. The following quotations are from *Senchaku Shū*, T83, 1–4, 9–12, 15–19.

49. Tao-ch'o (562–645) is traditionally held to be the second patriarch of the Pure Land school in China.

50. The Sacred Way teachings are those that assert that one should practice in this present *saha* world and attain enlightenment through one's own efforts. By contrast, the Pure Land teachings define the *saha* world as a defiled world and assert that, relying on the power of Amida Buddha, one should aspire to rebirth in the Pure Land to the west, where one can practice and attain enlightenment by hearing the teachings of Amida Buddha.

51. T'an-luan (476–542) is traditionally held to be the founder of the Pure Land school in China. His *Ōjō Ron Chū* is in 2v. T40, no. 1819.

52. Shan-tao (613–681) was a priest of the Pure Land school in China. In his *Ōjō Raisan* (Praise of Rebirth in the Pure Land, T47, no. 1980), he classified Buddhist practices into the categories of correct and sundry. According to him, the correct practices were those directed toward Amida Buddha. The correct practices are further divided into five: 1) reading and reciting, 2) meditating, 3) worshipping, 4) calling the name, and 5) praising and giving offerings. These five practices are directed toward Amida Buddha, the Pure Land sutras, and the Pure Land. The sundry practices are also divided into five in a similar manner; the latter part of the text discusses these sundry practices.

53. A list of the sutras that the priest Yüan-chao compiled at the command of Emperor Te-tsung during the Cheng-yüan era (785–804) (T55, no. 2157).

54. The Great Wisdom Sutra (Skt *Mahāprajñāpāramitā-sūtra*), a very long sutra that expounds the doctrine of emptiness (T5–7, no. 220).

55. A one-volume Mahayana work expounding the eternity of the Law (T17, no. 819).

56. In the *Kammuryōju* Sutra, sixteen types of meditation and three kinds of practices are described, which lead people to rebirth in the Pure Land. In the first thirteen types of meditation, one concentrates his mind on the splendor of the Pure Land and the features of the Buddhas and bodhisattvas. These types of meditation are regarded as "concentrated meditation." The other three types of meditation and the three kinds of practices can be carried out even if one's mind is not focused. Therefore they are called "unconcentrated practice." Hōnen regarded both concentrated and unconcentrated practices as practices that the Buddha expounded in accordance with people's capacities. He asserted that only the practice of the Nembutsu was the Buddha's true teaching as well as the sole teaching appropriate for the Latter Day of the Law. The term Nembutsu is interpreted in various ways, though it literally means to concentrate on and bring to mind a Buddha. Shan-tao and Hōnen took the Nembutsu to mean calling on the name of Amida Buddha and emphasized this practice.

57. Three requisites for reaching the Pure Land: a sincere mind, a mind of deep faith, and a mind resolved to attain the Pure Land.

58. Excerpted translation from a passage in Shan-tao's *Kammuryōju-kyō Shō* (T37, 272b–273a).

59. Those who propagated Buddhism correctly, i.e., men such as Nāgārjuna and Vasubandhu in India, T'ien-t'ai, Chang-an and Miao-lo in China, Dengyō and Gishin in Japan, etc.

60. The basic sutras of the Japanese Jōdo or Pure Land sect, the *Muryōju* Sutra in two volumes (T12, no. 366), the *Kammuryōju* Sutra (T12, no. 365) and the *Amida* Sutra (T12, no. 364).

61. This refers to the eighteenth of the forty-eight vows, described in the *Muryōju* Sutra, that Bodhisattva Hōzō, the name of Amida Buddha before his enlightenment, made to bring all people to the Pure Land.

62. *See* Five periods in the glossary.

63. T9, 15b.

64. Bodhisattvas Kannon and Seishi.

65. Gishin (781–833), Dengyō's successor, was the first *zasu* or chief priest of Enryaku-ji, the head temple of the Sammon branch of the Tendai sect. On Jikaku and Chishō *see* glossary.

66. Buddhas whose images were enshrined in the head temple of the Tendai sect on Mt. Hiei. It is said that the image of Yakushi is enshrined as well as that of Shakyamuni because Yakushi Buddha, having vowed to "heal all ills" (*see* n. 2 above), represents the parable of the excellent physician in the *Juryō* (sixteenth) chapter of the Lotus Sutra.

67. Kokūzō is a bodhisattva said to possess immeasurable wisdom and

blessings. An image of Bodhisattva Kokūzō was enshrined on Mt. Hiei. Jizō is a bodhisattva entrusted by Shakyamuni Buddha with the mission of saving people. It is said that he will appear during the period from the death of Shakyamuni Buddha until the appearance of Miroku Buddha in order to instruct the people of the six paths. This bodhisattva's image was also installed on Mt. Hiei.

68. At the ceremony of the Lotus Sutra, Shakyamuni Buddha transferred his teachings to the bodhisattvas of the theoretical teaching such as Yakuō and entrusted them with the mission of propagating them in the Middle Day of the Law. It is said that Bodhisattva Yakuō was later born as the Great Teacher T'ien-t'ai in China and the Great Teacher Dengyō in Japan. On the basis of the parable of the excellent physician in the *Juryō* chapter of the Lotus Sutra, T'ien-t'ai and Dengyō used Yakushi Buddha, the Buddha of Healing, lord of the Emerald World in the eastern part of the universe, as an object of worship for their sect. In this sense, to neglect the Buddha Yakushi and revere the Buddha Amida is to ignore the Lord Buddha's transmission.

69. Nāgārjuna's *Chū Ron* (T39, no. 1564) and *Jūnimon Ron* (T30, no. 1568), and the *Daichido Ron* (T25, no. 1509) also attributed to Nāgārjuna, as well as the *Hyaku Ron* (T30, no. 1569) attributed to Āryadeva.

70. The Nirvana Sutra describes five types of practices for bodhisattvas, as contrasted to the single practice advocated by the Pure Land sect.

71. Eshin Sōzu (942–1017), also known as Genshin, a Tendai monk of Mt. Hiei, in 985 compiled the *Ōjō Yōshū* or "Essentials of Salvation" (T84, no. 2682), a work in three chapters that describes the tortures of hell, the delights of the Pure Land, and the advantages of the Nembutsu. The work exerted great influence in Japan and even gained recognition in China.

72. The three major works of T'ien-t'ai: the *Maka Shikan*, the *Hokke Mongu*, and the *Hokke Gengi*, consisting of thirty volumes and the three commentaries on them by Miao-lo: the *Maka Shikan Bugyōden Guketsu*, the *Hokke Mongu Ki*, and the *Hokke Gengi Shakusen*.

73. The eight major sects of Buddhism well established in Japan before the Kamakura period. Historically they fall into two groups: the Kusha, Jōjitsu, Ritsu, Hossō, Sanron and Kegon sects which prospered in the Nara period, and the Tendai and Shingon sects which appeared in the Heian period.

74. According to Hōnen's biography, in a dream he received permission from Shan-tao to spread the practice of calling on the name of Amida and was entrusted with the Pure Land teaching.

75. T'an-luan, Tao-ch'o, and Shan-tao.

76. The period in which Hōnen propagated the Pure Land teaching.

77. T46, 19a. The *Shih Chi* was written by Ssu-ma Ch'ien (145?–c. 90 B.C.), recording the history of China from the time of the legendary Yellow Emperor to the historian's own time. Efforts to locate the passage quoted here in the *Shih Chi* have not been successful.

78. T46, 210b. The *Tso Chuan* is attributed to Tso Ch'iu-ming of the Spring and Autumn period (c. 770–403 B.C.) It is a commentary on the

Ch'un-ch'iu or *Spring and Autumn Annals,* a chronicle (722–481 B.C.) of twelve dukes of the state of Lu. The passage quoted is from Duke Hsi, twenty-second year.

79. Juan Chi (210–263) was a noted Chinese poet. The quotation continues the passage noted in n. 78 above.

80. *See* the English translation by Edwin O. Reischauer, *Ennin's Diary.* New York: The Ronald Press, 1955, p. 300.

81. In 1221 the retired Emperor Gotoba played a leading role in a struggle for power between the imperial court in Kyoto and the Hōjō clan in Kamakura, an incident known as the Jōkyū disturbance. The imperial forces were defeated and two other retired emperors were sent into exile.

82. From the thirty-six-chapter version (Southern Edition) of the Nirvana Sutra (T12, 381a).

83. Ryūkan (1148–1227), Shōkō (1162–1238), Jōkaku (1163–1247), and Sasshō (dates unknown) were priests of the Jōdo sect. Ryūkan is the founder of the Chōraku-ji school and is also called Kaikū or Muga. He studied the Tendai doctrine under Kōen at Enryaku-ji and later lived at Chōraku-ji in Kyoto. Shōkō is the founder of the Chinzei school and second patriarch of the Jōdo sect. At first he studied the Tendai doctrine on Mt. Hiei, but later became Hōnen's disciple. Jōkaku first studied the Tendai doctrine, but converted to Hōnen's teaching and advocated the doctrine of one-time recitation, which teaches that if one once invokes the name of Amida Buddha he can be reborn in the Pure Land. For this reason he was expelled by Hōnen. Sasshō, also known as Zembō, studied the Tendai doctrine but later followed Jōkaku's teaching. Still later he went on to establish his own independent teaching.

84. A blacksmith in Pāvā village who was deeply moved by Shakyamuni's preaching and reverently prepared a meal for him on the last night before his nirvana.

85. Those particularly grave among the ten evil offenses: killing, stealing, committing adultery, and lying.

86. T12, 425a–b.

87. T12, 434c.

88. An *anāgāmin* (Jap *anagon*) or "non-returner" is one who has reached the third of the four stages which persons in the realm of *shōmon* can attain. The fourth and highest stage is that of arhat. *See* n. 46.

89. The above quotations are also from the Nirvana Sutra (T12, 459a, 460b).

90. T8, 832b.

91. T12, 381a–b.

92. Figure in the Nirvana Sutra who put thirty-six questions to the Buddha and heard the Buddha's teachings. He is different from Mahākāśyapa (Jap Kashō), one of the Buddha's ten major disciples.

93. A reference to the state of Buddhahood that can neither decline nor be destroyed.

94. A basic code of Buddhism that prohibits killing, theft, adultery, lying, and intoxicating drink.

95. This and the following quotations are all from the Nirvana Sutra (T12, 383b–384b).

96. One of the seven ancient Buddhas or Buddhas of the Past. Of these seven, the Buddha Kashō was the sixth to appear and Shakyamuni Buddha was the seventh.

97. T9, 15b.

98. Japan. The phrase originally referred to China.

99. Lectures held on the anniversary of T'ien-t'ai's death on the twenty-fourth day of the eleventh month of each year.

100. T13, 379c.

101. The Avīci Hell is elsewhere called the hell of incessant suffering. Devadatta committed three of the five cardinal sins, disrupting the peace of the Order, injuring the Buddha, and, as stated here, killing a person who had reached the stage of an arhat. Immediately the ground opened and he fell into this, the nethermost of the eight hot hells.

102. A Chinese term referring to rebels and outlaws. Here "white waves" indicates Hōnen and other priests of the Pure Land sect, as well as the followers of other sects that Nichiren views as heretical. "The Ocean of the Buddha" signifies Shakyamuni's teachings. The phrases "green groves" and "Mountain of the Law" in the next sentence likewise refer to evil men and Shakyamuni's teachings respectively.

103. Fu Hsi, Shen Nung, Yao, and Shun are legendary sage rulers of ancient China.

104. Expressions taken from early Chinese literature that indicate dramatic change.

105. All the above quotations concerning disasters have appeared earlier.

106. Contraction of a passage previously cited (T13, 173c).

107. T8, 833c.

108. The first quotation has been previously cited (T9, 15b); the quotation from the *Fukyō* (twentieth) chapter can be found at T9, 51a.

109. T12, 575a.

110. T'an-luan, Tao-ch'o, Shan-tao, Eshin, and Hōnen.

Rationale for Writing

1. Yadoya Zemmon, or Mitsunori (n.d.), was majordomo to Hōjō To-kiyori (1227–1263), the retired regent, who was known as the lay priest of Saimyō-ji.

2. An ancient state on the Korean Peninsula.

3. Sanron, Jōjitsu, Hossō, Kusha, Ritsu, and Kegon, the six major sects of Buddhism that flourished in the ancient Japanese capital of Nara.

4. Gyōhyō (722–797) studied Kegon, Zen, Ritsu, and Hossō doctrines, but was celebrated for his concentration on meditation techniques. Originally from the Daian-ji, a Sanron temple in Nara, he served at the Sōfuku-ji in Ōmi, where Saichō became his disciple. The Yamashina Temple is an old name for the Kōfuku-ji in Nara.

5. This note is in the original text. Saichō (767–822) is usually referred to by Nichiren by his posthumous title Dengyō Daishi, or the Great Teacher Dengyō. He was the founder of the Tendai sect in Japan and was greatly admired by Nichiren.

6. Chien-chen (Jap Ganjin, 688–763) was a celebrated Chinese monk who was invited to Japan to perform orthodox ordination ceremonies. After five failed attempts he finally arrived in Japan in 754, where he conducted ceremonies conferring the precepts on the emperor, high court officials, and numerous Buddhist priests.

7. Enryaku-ji, the head temple of the Tendai sect and site of the ordination platform of Mahayana Buddhism.

8. The ancient name of Kyoto. Earlier the capital had been moved from Nara to Nagaoka.

9. Gonsō (758–827) was a priest and scholar of the Sanron sect at Daian-ji in Nara. Kōbō Daishi, founder of the Japanese Shingon sect, was his disciple. Details concerning Chōyō are not known.

10. This debate is frequently referred to by Nichiren. Apparently it was a retreat and study session of Tendai texts that lasted for several months. Dengyō distinguished himself with his knowledge of Tendai doctrine.

11. These are systems by which these sects sought to classify the body of Buddhist scriptures. The "Five Teachings" of Kegon divides the sutras into Hinayana, early Mahayana, advanced Mahayana, abrupt teachings, and perfect teachings. The "Three Periods" of the Hossō sect divides the sutras into: 1) the teaching that all is existence; 2) the teaching that all is void; and 3) the doctrine of the Middle Way. The Sanron's "Two Storehouses" are teachings for *shōmon* and teachings for bodhisattvas, and the "Three Periods" of that school are 1) the doctrine that both the subjective mind and its object exist; 2) the doctrine that only the mind exists; and 3) the doctrine that both the mind and object are empty.

12. Emperor Seiwa (850–880), in youth known as Prince Korehito, was the fourth son of Emperor Montoku. According to tradition, Emperor Montoku was unable to decide whether to name Prince Korehito or another of his sons as successor, and had the two princes engage in a *sumō* wrestling match to settle the matter. It is said that Prince Korehito won because of the prayers offered on his behalf by the Tendai priest Eryō (801–859).

13. Dainichi Nōnin (d. 1196?) was a self-enlightened Zen priest who established temples in Settsu and Kyoto. Because he was criticized for not having received his teachings from a master, in 1189 he sent two disciples to China to have his teachings authenticated by a prominent Lin-chi (Jap Rinzai) Zen master, Cho-an Te-kuang (1121–1203). His school, known as the Nihon Daruma-shū, or Japanese Bodhidharma school, flourished for some time during the early Kamakura period. Details of Nōnin's biography are not known; he may well have died before the Kennin era.

14. Dengyō Daishi.

The Opening of the Eyes, Part I

1. The Three Rulers are Fu Hsi, Shen Nung, and Huang Ti, legendary rulers of ancient China said to have realized model governments. They were followed by the Five Emperors Shao Hao, Chuan Hsü, Ti Kao, T'ang Yao, and Yü Shun. They, in turn, were followed by King (or Emperor) Yü of the Hsia, King T'ang of the Yin, and King Wen of the Chou dynasties.

2. When King Wu decided to revolt against Emperor Chou of the Yin dynasty, he carved a wooden figure of his father, who had cherished the same desire, before setting out on his campaign.

3. During the Later Han dynasty, Ting Lan, who had lost his mother at the age of fifteen, made a statue of her and served it as if she were still alive.

4. Emperor Chou was so absorbed in his affection for his consort, Ta Chi, that he totally neglected the government. When Pi Kan remonstrated with him, Emperor Chou flew into a rage and had him killed.

5. Duke Yi of the state of Wei loved cranes and lived extravagantly, losing the support of the public. While his minister Hung Yen was away on a journey, enemies attacked Wei and killed Duke Yi. They ate the duke's flesh except for his liver, and then left the land. Returning, Hung Yen saw the disastrous scene and wept. He cut open his own stomach and inserted the duke's liver in it to save him from shame and dishonor.

6. Yin Shou and Wu Ch'eng are legendary figures. T'ai-kung Wang was a general who served King Wen and, after the king's death, served King Wu, Wen's son. He fought valorously in the battle against Emperor Chou of the Yin dynasty and contributed to the prosperity of the Chou dynasty.

7. This assertion is found in the *Chuang Tzu* and the *Shih Chi* (Records of the Historian).

8. The *Three Records* are said to record the deeds of the Three Rulers. The *Five Canons* are the writings of the Five Emperors. The *Three Histories* are the works of the Three Kings. None of these works is extant.

9. First two of the five constant virtues taught by Confucius.

10. Their names are unknown.

11. Celestial houses, divided into four houses of seven major heavenly bodies each, corresponding respectively to the four directions and four seasons of east, or spring; south, summer; west, autumn; and north, winter. They are also known as the twenty-eight lunar mansions.

12. This is found in the *Lieh Tzu,* an early Taoist text.

13. Propriety and music were regarded as requisite for enhancing one's sense of morality, to maintain social order, and for cultivating one's aesthetic sense.

14. Three types of learning or disciplines essential for the Buddhist practitioner. Jap *sangaku.*

15. *Maka Shikan Bugyōden Guketsu,* T46, 343c.

16. *Maka Shikan,* T46, 77b.

17. T46, 78c. The three sages are Confucius, his disciple Yen Hui, and Lao Tzu.

18. T46, 343c. The *Shōjōhōgyō* Sutra is an apocryphal work composed in China, and no longer extant.

19. Kapila was a founder of the Sankhya school, one of the six philosophical schools in ancient India. Ulūka was also called Kanada, a founder of the Vaiśeṣika school, one of the above six schools. Ṛṣabha's teachings are said to have prepared the way for Jainism.

20. These men are identified as Purāṇa-kāśyapa, Maskari-gośālīputra, Sañjaya-Vairāṭīputra, Ajita-keśakambala, Kakuda Kātyāyana, and Nirgran-thajñātiputra. Their names are variously given.

21. The whole of India.

22. The basic code of Buddhism that prohibits killing, theft, adultery, lying, and intoxicating drink.

23. Prohibitions against the ten evils of killing, theft, adultery, lying, flattery, defaming, duplicity, greed, anger, and ignorant views.

24. The two highest worlds of the threefold world. *See* glossary under Threefold world.

25. Source unknown.

26. Source unknown.

27. Quoted in the *Maka Shikan*, T46, 77a–b.

28. T9, 28a. The three poisons are greed, anger, and stupidity. Jap *sandoku*.

29. Epithets of the Buddha from various sutras.

30. 1) Illusions of thought and desire possessed by persons in the six paths; 2) illusions preventing bodhisattvas from saving others; and 3) the forty-two basic illusions that prevent a bodhisattva from attaining enlightenment (Jap *sanwaku*). They are described in the *Maka Shikan*, T46, 37c.

31. The births and deaths of those in the realms of *shōmon, engaku,* and bodhisattva that they undergo as they advance in their practice. This is apart from the cycle of birth and death in the six paths.

32. Also referred to as fundamental darkness. That which gives rise to desires and illusions. Jap *gampon no mumyō*.

33. Not an exact number. The figure is frequently given as 84,000 and is used to indicate a vast number.

34. A passage from the *Muryōgi* Sutra that reads: "In these more than forty years I have not yet revealed the truth." T9, 386b.

35. A passage from the *Hōben* (second) chapter of the Lotus Sutra that reads: "The World-Honored One has long expounded his doctrines and now must reveal the truth." T9, 6a.

36. A passage from the *Hōtō* (eleventh) chapter of the Lotus Sutra. T9, 32c.

37. This is described in the *Jinriki* (twenty-first) chapter of the Lotus Sutra. T9, 51c.

38. This refers to the theory of *ichinen sanzen* as found in the "theoretical" teachings of the Lotus (*shakumon,* chapters 1–14) and the "actual" teachings as found in the "essential" (*hommon,* chapters 15–28) chapters.

39. They do not recognize that *shōmon* and *engaku* can become Buddhas.

40. Nirvana Sutra, T12, 522c and elsewhere.

41. *Fubukkyō* indicates those who incorporate the Hinayana teachings into their own school and claim that it is their own doctrine. *Gakubuppōjō* indicates those who plagiarize Buddhist ideas and set forth the Mahayana teaching as the doctrine of their own school. They seem to learn Buddhism but later end in error. They are described in *Maka Shikan,* T46, 132b.

42. T46, 68c.

43. A sixth-century Buddhist monk in China. Out of a desire for fame and profit he began to associate with a group of Taoists and eventually returned to lay life. His memorial to the throne was instrumental in influencing Emperor Wu of the Chou to put into effect a strenuous persecution of Buddhism.

44. A classification of the Buddhist teachings according to the form of exposition.

45. T46, 324b.

46. T'ien-t'ai's designation in the *Hokke Gengi,* chapter 10, of the major systems of classification of the Buddhist sutras used during the Northern and Southern dynasties period. T33, 801a.

47. Hsüan-tsang (602–664) is famed for his trip to India to bring back copies of Buddhist texts. On his return he translated some seventy-five scriptures into Chinese. Tz'u-en (632–682), also known as K'uei-chi, was Hsüan-tsang's major disciple.

48. Shan-wu-wei (Skt Śubhakarasiṃha; Jap Zemmui, 637–735) first introduced the esoteric teachings to China in 716. He was closely associated with the court and translated several scriptures into Chinese. Chin-kang-chih (Skt Vajrabodhi; Jap Kongōchi, 671–741) arrived in China in 720. He also was well received by the court and engaged in translation activities.

49. Ch'eng-kuan (738–839) is regarded as the fourth patriarch of the Kegon (Chin Hua-yen) school. He served at the courts of seven emperors, wrote numerous treatises, and gained many titles and honors. He was awarded the title National Teacher Ch'ing-liang.

50. T10, 465c.

51. Dengyō took part in a series of lectures on the Lotus Sutra in 802, in which he distinguished himself. Nichiren frequently mentions the occasion; precise details are unclear.

52. The eight persons mentioned in the text, from Śāriputra to Rāhula, are counted among the ten major disciples of Shakyamuni Buddha. Śāriputra was known as the foremost in wisdom among all the *shōmon* disciples of the Buddha. It was prophesied in the *Hiyu* (third) chapter that he would attain Buddhahood. Mahākāśyapa was known as the foremost in ascetic practice to purify the mind and body, Subhūti as the foremost in understanding the doctrine of emptiness, Kātyāyana as the foremost in debating, and Maudgalyāyana as the foremost in occult powers. The *Juki* (sixth) chapter predicted that these four disciples would attain Buddhahood. Pūrṇa, noted as the foremost in eloquence, was given a prediction of Buddhahood in the *Gohyaku-Deshi Juki* (eighth) chapter. Ānanda heard more of the Buddha's teach-

ings than any other disciple and it was predicted in the *Ninki* (ninth) chapter that he would attain Buddhahood. Rāhula, known as the foremost in inconspicuous observance of the precepts, also received a prophecy of Buddhahood in the same chapter.

53. The prophecy of Buddhahood for the five hundred and seven hundred *shōmon* disciples appears in the eighth chapter, and for the two thousand *shōmon* in the ninth chapter. Mahāprajāpatī and Yaśodharā were, respectively, Shakyamuni's aunt and wife. The *Kanji* (thirteenth) chapter predicts that both of them will attain Buddhahood.

54. T9, 7a.

55. This quotation is from the *Muryōgi* Sutra, generally regarded as an introduction to the Lotus Sutra. T9, 386b.

56. The above two quotations are from the Lotus Sutra, T9, 6a, 10a.

57. T10, 182a.

58. One of the four continents that, according to ancient Indian cosmology, surround Mt. Sumeru, the highest of all mountains. It represents the human world as then known. People on this continent are of bad karma; thus Buddhism spreads there in order that they may be saved.

59. A unit of distance, said to be the distance an army could cover in a day. Approximately twenty-four kilometers.

60. According to ancient Indian cosmology, one of four circles, made respectively of gold, water, wind, and emptiness, that supported Mt. Sumeru and the surrounding continents.

61. T13, 88a.

62. One's debt of gratitude toward one's parents, teacher, sovereign, and the three treasures of Buddhism.

63. Precepts for the monks of Hinayana Buddhism.

64. Rules for Hinayana monks, based on the two hundred and fifty precepts.

65. Three types of meditation taught in the *Kusha Ron*. The first is a meditation for lay people who have not yet extinguished delusions; the second is for lay people who carry out a definite practice, but whose meditation is still not free from delusions and earthly desires; and the third enables one to obtain wisdom completely free from delusions, designed for those who have become monks.

66. The highest state of Hinayana enlightenment that the *shōmon* can achieve.

67. All three of the above quotations are from the Vimalakirti Sutra. T14, 549b.

68. T21, 649c.

69. T8, 273b–c.

70. T15, 643a. The resolute meditation described here is an approximate translation of the title of this sutra. Its full title is *Shuryōgon Zammai-kyō*.

71. T14, 5400.

72. The threefold world (Jap *sangai*) comprises the world of desire, the world of form, and the world of formlessness. All beings here are unenlight-

ened and transmigrate within the six paths. The world of desire includes Hell, Hungry Ghosts, Animals, Fighting Demons (Asuras), Humans, and Heaven. The six heavens of the world of desire are the Heaven of the Four Heavenly Kings (halfway up Mt. Sumeru), the Heaven of the Thirty-three Gods (atop Mt. Sumeru), the Yāma, Tuṣita, Nirmāṇarati, and Māra Heavens (located in the air above Mt. Sumeru). The beings in the world of form have physical form but are free of desires. This world comprises four meditation (Skt *dhyāna*) heavens. The world of formlessness consists of four realms attained by progressively deeper meditation.

73. They vary with the sutras. The *Hōtō* (eleventh) chapter of the Lotus Sutra describes them as gold, silver, lapis lazuli, shell of the giant clam, coral, pearl, and carnelian.

74. T9, 32b–c.

75. The ten mystic powers described in the *Jinriki* (twenty-first) chapter of the Lotus Sutra. The first two are described below.

76. T9, 51b.

77. The *Zokurui* (twenty-second) chapter. T9, 52c.

78. This indicates the preaching of the *Kegon* Sutra.

79. A world in Indian cosmology consists of Mt. Sumeru, its surrounding continents, seas, and mountain ranges, a sun, a moon, and other heavenly bodies, extending upward to the first meditation heaven and downward to the circle of wind on which the earth rests. A thousand worlds make a minor world system, one thousand minor world systems form an intermediate world system, and one thousand intermediate world systems form a major world system, which then contains a billion worlds. The universe was believed to contain countless major world systems.

80. Ashuku (east), Hōsō (south), Muryōju (west), Mimyōshō (north).

81. East, west, north, south, up, and down.

82. T9, 11a. In the context of the Lotus Sutra, these are Śāriputra's words.

83. According to the *Nihon Shoki* (Chronicles of Japan), Buddhism was introduced to Japan in 552 A.D.

84. T9, 34a.

85. T12, 925a.

86. The revelation that Shakyamuni Buddha attained enlightenment countless kalpas in the past. This appears in the *Juryō* (sixteenth) chapter of the essential (Jap *hommon*) teaching of the Lotus Sutra. The first important teaching is that persons of the two realms of *shōmon* and *engaku* can attain Buddhahood. This is explained in the theoretical *(shakumon)* teaching.

87. The Kalpa of Continuance is the second of the four stages of formation, continuance, decline, and disintegration which a world is said to go through. Each of these stages lasts for twenty small kalpas. A small kalpa is approximately sixteen million years long. According to the *Kusha Ron,* during the kalpa of continuance, the human life span is said to undergo a repeated cycle of increase and decrease. In the first hundred years of the kalpa it numbers eighty thousand years. Each hundred years it decreases by a factor of one year, until it finally measures ten years. Thereafter it increases by one

year every hundred years until it again measures eighty thousand years. In the kalpa of continuance this decrease and increase (consisting of one small kalpa) is repeated twenty times. Shakyamuni Buddha is said to have appeared in the ninth period of decrease.

88. Doctrines of the *Kegon* Sutra. The ten mysteries represent the ten characteristics of the interdependency of all things and phenomena. They are described in *Kegon Ichijō Jūgenmon* (T45, 514b). The six forms represent the six aspects of everything: the whole containing the parts, the interdependency of the parts making the whole, the unity of the parts in the whole, the variety of the parts, the variety making the whole, and the identity of the parts. These are discussed in *Kegon Gokyō Shō,* T45, 507c.

89. T10, 747c.

90. T2, 826c.

91. The exact location of this passage has not been determined.

92. T14, 537c.

93. T18, 94a.

94. T8, 825b.

95. The *Daijuku* Sutra says that during this *samādhi* the spiritual and physical functions of all beings are reflected within the mind of the bodhisattva, just as all things are reflected in the ocean. T13, 106c.

96. T9, 386a.

97. In the *Hōben* (second) chapter of the Lotus Sutra Shakyamuni expounded the ten factors or suchnesses to indicate that all people are endowed with the Buddha nature; this provided a theoretical basis for the assertion that all people can become Buddhas. Later in the same chapter Shakyamuni declares that the goal of Buddhist practice is not the three realms of *shōmon, engaku,* and bodhisattva, but the supreme state of Buddhahood. These are the sections which "discuss the three realms of *shōmon, engaku,* and bodhisattva as provisional goals."

98. T9, 5c.

99. T9, 5a.

100. T9, 10a.

101. The eight chapters from the *Hōben* (second) chapter to the *Ninki* (ninth) chapter.

102. T9, 9c.

103. T9, 41b.

104. T9, 41c.

105. T9, 42b.

106. Ibid. Nayuta is a numeral variously given as ten million or one hundred billion.

107. The four teachings here refer to the classification of the four teachings of doctrine (Jap *kehō no shikyō*) formulated by Chegwan on the basis of T'ien-t'ai's writings. They are: 1) the tripitaka teaching (Jap *zōkyō*), consisting of sutras, *vinaya,* and *abhidharma,* corresponding to Hinayana teachings; 2) the connecting or shared teaching (Jap *tsūgyō*) which include the *Hōdō* or *Vaipulya,* early Mahayana teachings; 3) the specific or distinctive teaching (Jap *bekkyō*) which includes the *Hannya* or Wisdom sutras; and 4) the com-

plete or perfect teaching (Jap *engyō*), which includes the Nirvana and Lotus sutras. See *Tendai Shikyo Gi*, T46, 774c ff.

108. The practice of the four teachings leading to the attainment of enlightenment.

109. *Hokke Gengi*, T33, 766b.

110. Also śāla or sāla tree. The Buddha passed away in a grove of sal trees in Kuśinagara. The sal tree grows to some thirty meters in height and bears light yellow blossoms.

111. The three bodies (Skt *trikāya;* Jap *sanjin*) of a Buddha are: 1) the Dharma body, or Law body (Skt *dharmakāya;* Jap *hosshin*), the Law to which the Buddha is enlightened; 2) the Bliss or Reward body (Skt *sambhogakāya;* Jap *hōshin*), the body obtained by those who have completed bodhisattva practice and are awakened to the Buddha wisdom; and 3) the Manifested body (Skt *nirmāṇakāya;* Jap *ōjin*), the physical form in which the Buddha appears in the world.

112. Asaṅga and his brother Vasubandhu were establishers and systematizers of the Yogācāra (Consciousness-Only) school in India. Their dates are not known.

113. Fourth of the six heavens in the world of desire, the lowest division of the threefold world.

114. A state in northeast India. Asaṅga was a native of Gandhara but lived most of his life in Ayodhyā.

115. Dharmapāla, Nanda, and Śīlabhadra were scholars of the Yogāchāra school, associated with the Nālandā monastery in India.

116. Ruler in India during the first half of the seventh century. He was known also as Harṣa. He had faith in Buddhism and built many stupas, and is said to have shown special favor to Śīlabhadra and Hsüan-tsang.

117. Hsüan-tsang (602–664) has appeared before and is frequently mentioned by Nichiren. He spent seventeen years visiting the holy places of India, studying at the Nālānda monastery under Śīlabhadra. When he returned to China he was received with the highest of honors. He is often regarded as the founder of the Fa-hsiang (Hossō) school. *See also* n. 47.

118. Shen-fang (no dates) is mentioned in the biography of K'uei-chi in the *Sō Kōsō Den* (T50, 725c). Chia-shang and P'u-kuang have biographies in the same work (728b, 727a) but no dates are given. K'uei-chi (632–682), known also as Tz'u-en after the temple in which he lived, was Hsüan-tsang's foremost disciple and the organizer of the Fa-hsiang (Hossō) teachings. He, too, is frequently mentioned by Nichiren.

119. Dōji (675–744) was the third patriarch of the Sanron sect in Japan. He was well versed in the Hossō as well as the Sanron doctrines. He visited China in 701. Dōshō was the founder of the Hossō sect in Japan. In 653 he went to China where he studied the Hossō doctrines under Hsüan-tsang.

120. An old name of the Kōfuku-ji in Nara.

121. Tu-shun (557–640) was the founder of the Kegon (Hua-yen) school. His disciple, Chih-yen (602–668), is regarded as the second patriarch and Fa-tsang (643–712) the third. Fa-tsang systematized the teachings and is con-

sidered by many to be the real founder of the school. Ch'eng-kuan (also known as Ch'ing-liang, 738–839) is counted as the fourth patriarch.

122. Pu-k'ung (Skt Amoghavajra; Jap Fukū, 705–774) is considered the sixth patriarch in the Shingon tradition. A native of India, he arrived in China in 720 and was active in the translation of esoteric texts. He was greatly honored by Hsüan-tsung and other T'ang emperors. The other figures mentioned have appeared before.

123. T10, 443c.

124. T18, 94a. The "I" refers to Mahāvairocana Buddha.

125. Ancient states in the Korean peninsula.

126. Vatsa was the founder of the Hinayana Vātsīputrīya school that broke away from the Sarvāstivāda school. Vaipulya added Mahayana to non-Buddhist teachings.

127. The former is said to have opposed Vasubandhu and died insane. The latter was a Sāṅkhya scholar whose teachings were refuted, causing him to vomit blood and die. They are mentioned in *Daitō Saiiki Ki,* T51, 892c, 913c.

128. The human life span was diminishing. *See* n. 87.

129. An adaptation of a passage in the Nirvana Sutra, T12, 925a.

130. This sutra describes how the Buddha's teachings disappear after his death. It also explains that in the Latter Day of the Law devils appear in the form of priests and carry out slanderous acts against the Law. T12, 1119c.

131. Reference is to the story of Daitsū Buddha and his sixteen sons which appears in the *Kejōyu* (seventh) chapter of the Lotus Sutra. In the remote past of *sanzen-jintengō,* Daitsū preached the Lotus Sutra to his sixteen sons. These sons then preached the sutra to the people, some of whom attained enlightenment. These people belong to the first group. The second group comprises those who took faith in the sutra at that time but later discarded their faith, accepting lower teachings of Hinayana Buddhism. However, these people heard the Lotus Sutra again and attained enlightenment when the sixteenth son appeared in India as Shakyamuni Buddha. The third group comprises those who heard the Lotus Sutra in *sanzen-jintengō* but did not take faith in it and could not attain enlightenment even when reborn in the lifetime of Shakyamuni Buddha.

132. An immensely long period of time as described in the *Juryō* (sixteenth) chapter of the Lotus Sutra. It exceeds in duration the *sanzen-jintengō* described in the *Kejōyu* (seventh) chapter of the sutra.

133. Tao-ch'o (562–645) is regarded as the second patriarch of the Pure Land school in China and Shan-tao (613–681) as the third. Hōnen (1133–1212) is the founder of the Pure Land sect in Japan.

134. Tao-ch'o's *Anraku Shū,* T47, 13c. The quotation that follows is from the same passage.

135. Shan-tao's *Ōjō Raisan,* T47, 439c.

136. The six difficult and nine easy acts are frequently mentioned by Nichiren. The six difficult acts are: 1) to propagate the Lotus Sutra widely, 2) to copy it or cause someone else to copy it, 3) to recite it even for a short

while, 4) to teach it even to one person, 5) to hear of and accept the Lotus Sutra and inquire of its meaning, and 6) to maintain faith in it. The nine easy acts are: 1) to teach innumerable sutras other than the Lotus Sutra, 2) to lift up Mt. Sumeru and hurl it across the universe over countless Buddha lands, 3) to kick a major world system into a different quarter with one's toe, 4) to stand in the highest heaven and to preach innumerable sutras other than the Lotus Sutra, 5) to grasp the sky with one's hand and to travel about with it, 6) to place the earth on one's toenail and ascend to the Brahma Heaven, 7) to walk across a burning prairie carrying a bundle of hay on one's back without being burned, 8) to preach the eighty-four thousand teachings and thus enable one's listeners to obtain the six supernatural powers, and 9) to enable innumerable people to reach the stage of arhat and acquire the six supernatural powers.

137. A world was said to go through a continuous cycle of formation, continuance, decline, and disintegration, each of these four phases lasting one medium kalpa. The end of the kalpa of decline is marked by a great fire that consumes the world.

138. These persecutions refer to the exiles to the Izu Peninsula and Sado Island.

139. T9, 31b.

140. T9, 15b.

141. T9, 39a.

142. These quotations from the *Kanji* (thirteenth) chapter are at T9, 36b–c.

143. T9, 50c.

144. T12, 591c. Gautama is the surname of Shakyamuni Buddha.

145. *Hokke Mongu,* T34, 110b.

146. *Hokke Mongu Ki,* T34, 306c.

147. *See* n. 46.

148. Tokuitsu (780?–842?) was a famous Hossō priest who carried on a long-standing controversy with Dengyō. The *Shugo Kokkai Shō* contains details of this controversy, including many quotations (of which this is one) from Tokuitsu's *Chūhen Gikyō* (Mirror on Orthodox and Heterodox Doctrine), the original of which is no longer extant. Chih-i is another name for T'ien-t'ai. The quotation is from *Shugo Kokkai Shō,* DDZ 2, 349.

149. Chih-tu (no dates) was a disciple of Miao-lo. The full title of the work referred to as *Tōshun,* named after the place where the author lived, is *Hokekyō Shogisan,* ZZ 1, 45, 3, 273a.

150. Hui-kuang (468–537) was a specialist in the *vinaya* (precepts) and is considered the founder of the Ti-lun (Jiron) school. He wrote numerous commentaries and was officially appointed superintendent of monks. The six superintendents of the Nara temples who opposed Dengyō in 819 were: Jōe (d. 826) of Kōfuku-ji, Buan (764–840) of Tōshōdai-ji, Shūen (771–835) of Kōfuku-ji, Taien (no dates) of Saidai-ji, Sebyō (d. 832) of Gangō-ji, and Chief Superintendent Gomyō (750–834) of Gangō-ji. DDZ 1, 195–196.

151. DDZ 3, 251.

152. In the twenty-line verse in the *Kanji* (thirteenth) chapter of the Lotus Sutra the countless assembled bodhisattvas vow to brave various hardships in propagating the Lotus Sutra in the Latter Day of the Law. These hardships were later categorized by Miao-lo as the work of the three powerful enemies. This passage refers to the first of the three powerful enemies. This and the following passages from the verse are found at T9, 36b–c. The *Kanji* chapter itself refers only to "swords and staves." "Rocks and tiles" is an interpolation from the *Fukyō* (twentieth) chapter, T9, 50c.

153. This passage refers to the second of the three powerful enemies.

154. This passage refers to the third of the three powerful enemies: monks who enjoy the respect of the general public but, in fear of losing fame and profit, induce the authorities to persecute the votaries.

155. Not a direct quote. The *Fu Hōzō Innen Den* (T50, 307b) refers to a story in which the Buddha predicts to Ānanda that a certain child would in a hundred years be reborn as a great wheel-turning king. This is interpreted to refer to Aśoka.

156. T12, 1013c.

157. T12, 954c. Madhyāntika is the third of the twenty-four successors of Shakyamuni Buddha.

158. Two of the three extant Chinese versions of the Lotus Sutra are mentioned here. The three are: *Shō-hokke Kyō,* translated by Dharmarakṣa. *Myōhō-renge-kyō* by Kumārajīva, and *Tembon-hoke-kyō* by Jñānagupta and Dharmagupta. Among these versions, Kumārajīva's is by far the most widely used.

159. The son of Shou-meng, king of Wu. In 544 B.C. he was ordered to visit other countries as an envoy. At that time he was given a valuable sword. When he happened to be passing through the country of Hsü, the lord of the state saw Chi-cha's sword and wanted it, though he did not dare to say so. Chi-cha, however, understood the lord's desire and in his heart promised to give him the sword after he had fulfilled his mission and returned to Hsü. But when he returned he found that the lord had already died. True to his promise, he offered the sword at the lord's grave.

160. The details of the following story are unknown.

161. First of the three categories of illusion established by T'ien-t'ai. *See* n. 30.

162. The eight phases of a Buddha's existence are: 1) descending from Heaven, 2) entering the mother's body, 3) emerging from the mother's body, 4) renouncing secular life, 5) conquering devils, 6) attaining enlightenment, 7) turning the wheel of the Law, and 8) entering nirvana.

163. When Mao Pao was walking along the Yangtze River he saw a fisherman catch a turtle and prepare to kill it. He bought the turtle and put it back in the water. Later, Mao Pao was defeated by a powerful general called Stone Tiger. When he fled in retreat to the Yangtze River, the turtle that he had saved appeared and carried him on its back to the opposite shore.

164. A pond constructed by Emperor Wu of the Former Han dynasty. One day he saw a fish in the pond suffering because of a hook caught in its

throat. The emperor felt pity for the fish and removed the hook, putting the fish back in the water. Later, to repay his obligation, the fish offered a bright pearl to the emperor.

165. Younger brother of King Śuddhodana, the father of Shakyamuni.

166. Evil rulers of antiquity. Because Emperor Chieh, the seventeenth ruler of the Hsia dynasty, perpetrated every possible atrocity, he was overthrown by his enemies and the Hsia dynasty perished. Emperor Chou, the last ruler of the Yin dynasty, was a slave to his consort Ta Chi, and totally misgoverned the country. He was defeated by King Wu of the Chou dynasty.

167. *Shōmon* disciples who received a prophecy of attaining Buddhahood in the *Gohyaku Deshi Juki* (eighth) chapter of the Lotus Sutra. Each of them was given the title of Universal Brightness Tathagata.

168. The disciples who gathered after the Buddha's death at the first great assembly to compile his teachings.

169. Four of the five types of vision are given here. The five are: 1) the physical eye of common mortals that can distinguish color and form, 2) the heavenly eye that can see things in darkness and the distance, 3) the wisdom eye that permits *shōmon* and *engaku* to perceive that all phenomena are without substance, 4) the eye of the Law (Dharma) by which bodhisattvas penetrate all teachings, and 5) the Buddha eye that perceives the true nature of things in the past, present, and future.

170. A fabulous beast that is said to eat its own father.

171. Maudgalyāyana, Mahākāśyapa, Kātyāyana, and Subhūti.

172. *Shōmon* literally means to hear *(mon)* the voice *(shō)* of the Buddha. In this passage a true *shōmon* is described as one who engages in altruistic practice, that is, causing the voice *(shō)* of the Buddha to be heard *(mon)*.

173. The Lotus Sutra.

174. I.e., to serve the Buddha and practice his teachings.

175. T9, 18c–19a.

176. The first four of the five flavors: milk, cream, curdled milk, butter, and ghee mentioned in the Nirvana Sutra (T12, 531a). These five are equated with the five teachings: the *Kegon, Agon, Hōdō (Vaipulya), Hannya,* and Nirvana-Lotus in T'ien-t'ai's *Hokke Gengi* (T33, 808a) and elsewhere in Tendai texts.

177. This story appears in the Vimalakīrti Sutra. When Mahākāśyapa heard Vimalakīrti speak about enlightenment, he could not understand it at all and wept over the fact that he did not inherently possess the seed of Buddhahood. The sutra relates that the sound of his weeping echoed throughout the major world system. T14, 547a.

178. This story is also found in the Vimalakīrti Sutra. One day Subhūti came to Vimalakīrti asking for alms. Vimalakīrti filled Subhūti's bowl but told him that he did not deserve to receive alms and that those who offered alms to him would invariably fall into the three evil paths. At that time Subhūti was so shocked that he almost went off without his alms bowl. T14, 540c.

179. This story is found in the *Daichido Ron*. When Shakyamuni Buddha

reproached Śāriputra for eating impure food, Śāriputra was so surprised that he spat it out. Impure food is so called because it is not an offering made from the offerer's heart. T25, 70c.

180. This story appears in the Vimalakirti Sutra. When Shakyamuni Buddha saw Pūrṇa preaching the Hinayana teachings to the people, he told Pūrṇa that he should not put impure things in a precious vessel. T14, 540c.

181. In the period before Shakyamuni renounced the secular life, he married Yaśodharā, a beautiful woman whom Devadatta had wished to marry. As a result Devadatta nurtured a grudge against Shakyamuni.

182. Based on a passage in the Nirvana Sutra. T12, 459a.

183. The above stories are included among the nine great ordeals or persecutions (Jap kuō no dainan) suffered by Shakyamuni Buddha. They are described in the Daichido Ron (T25, 121c). These stories are also found in other texts.

184. The story of King Virūḍhaka appears in the Binaya Zōji (T24, 240a) and elsewhere; it is also included in the nine ordeals mentioned above. The story of the nun Utpalavarṇā is found in the Daichido Ron (T25, 165a). Kālodāyin's disaster is described in the Jūju Ritsu (T23, 121c ff.). The fate of Maudgalyāyana is found in the Binaya Zōji (T24, 287c). All of these stories appear also in the various Agon texts.

185. Adapted from a passage in the Nirvana Sutra, T12, 592c.

186. T14, 540c.

187. These passages from the Muryōgi and Lotus sutras have appeared previously.

188. The Fu Hōzō Innen Den (T50, 300c) states that when Mahākāśyapa felt that death was approaching, he went to Mt. Kukkuṭapāda in Magadha, Central India, where he entered into meditation. It is said that Mahākāśyapa will reappear when Bodhisattva Miroku appears in the world, 5,670 million years after the Buddha's death.

189. Reference is to a passage in the Yakuō (twenty-third) chapter of the Lotus Sutra (T9, 54c) that reads: "In the fifth five hundred years after my nirvana, widely declare and spread it [the Lotus Sutra] throughout Jambud-vīpa and never allow its flow to cease."

190. Reference is to kyōge betsuden furyū monji, a special transmission outside the scriptures, not dependent on words and phrases, an expression commonly used in Zen.

191. Drawn from passages in Hōnen's Senchaku Shū, T83, 2, 17–19.

192. Accounts of the sixty bodhisattvas mentioned here are found in the Kegon Sutra. T10, 81a, 99c, 121a, 178c, 72a, 179a. The Japanese readings of their names are: Hōe, Kudokurin, Kongōdō, Kongōzō, Kenshu, and Gedatsugatsu, repectively.

193. These four types of ten stages are divisions of the fifty-two stages through which a bodhisattva advances from his first resolve to his attainment of Buddhahood, as described in the Bosatsu Yōraku Hongō Sutra, T24, 1011–1016.

194. Awakening to the profound and subtle principle of Mahayana. Described in the Vimalakirti Sutra, T14, 546b.

195. The four types of teachings, previously mentioned, are the *zōkyō* (tripitaka), *tsūgyō* (connecting or shared), *bekkyō* (specific or distinctive), and *engyō* (perfect or complete) teachings. *See* n. 107.

196. *Zenchishiki* is also used in Buddhism in the sense of a good friend or good teacher.

197. The two deities are Śiva and Viṣṇu and the three ascetics Kapila, Ulūka, and Ṛṣabha.

198. After he renounced secular life, Shakyamuni engaged in various practices for twelve years until he attained enlightenment. It is said that for the first six years he engaged in ascetic practices (painful) and for the second six years he engaged in the practice of meditation (comfortable).

199. This story appears in the *Jo* (first) chapter of the Lotus Sutra. In the distant past Monju appeared as Bodhisattva Myōkō, a disciple of Nichigatsu Tōmyō Buddha. After the Buddha's death Myōkō continued to embrace the Lotus Sutra which his teacher had expounded. The Buddha had fathered eight sons before renouncing the world. These sons of the departed Buddha practiced under Myōkō until they attained Buddhahood. The last of them to attain Buddhahood was Nentō Buddha, under whom Shakyamuni practiced the sutra for enlightenment in a previous existence.

200. Kings who rule the world by turning the wheel of the Law. These wheels are of four kinds: gold, silver, copper, and iron. The gold-wheel-turning king rules the lands in all directions; the silver-wheel-turning king the eastern, western, and southern lands; the copper-wheel-turning king the eastern and southern lands; and the iron-wheel-turning king the southern land. They are described in the *Kusha Ron,* T29, 64b–c.

201. T9, 6c.

202. T12, 414a, 654c. A passage similar to the following appears in "The True Object of Worship."

203. This treatise is associated with the Sanron school. Only three of the original ten *chüan* are extant. The passage cited is not included.

204. Chi-tsang (549–623) is a priest of the Sanron school in China; he is also known as Chia-hsiang. The quotation has not been identified.

205. T33, 775a.

206. T25, 408b.

207. Cited in the *Kakuzenshō: Hokke Hiketsu,* DBZ 46, 666.

208. The Shingon tradition holds that Nāgārjuna received the *Dainichi Sutra* from Bodhisattva Kongōsatta along with other esoteric teachings preserved in an iron tower in southern India.

209. The exact transliteration is Namu-myōhō-renge-kyō, but it is pronounced Nam-myōhō-renge-kyō.

210. Reference is to the six *pāramitās* (perfections), the six practices required of bodhisattvas that lead to Buddhahood. They are: almsgiving, maintaining the precepts, patience or forbearance, assiduousness or persistence, meditation, and the obtaining of wisdom.

211. The thirty-two remarkable physical characteristics and eighty extraordinary features possessed by Buddhas and bodhisattvas.

212. *Maka Shikan Bugyōden Guketsu,* T46, 289c.

213. T9, 7a.

214. One of the four universal vows of a Buddha or bodhisattva. The others are to remove all earthly desires, to master all the Buddhist teachings, and to obtain supreme enlightenment. They are used by all schools of Buddhism.

215. T9, 8c.

216. T9, 12a.

217. *Shugo Kokkai Shō*, DDZ 2, 622.

218. Reference is to the *Gejimmitsu* Sutra (T16, no. 676) used in the Hossō school.

The Opening of the Eyes, Part II

1. T9, 34a. The following quotation is from the same passage.

2. A kind of lily used in religious ceremonies.

3. A Buddha's throne or seat. A Buddha is likened to the lion, king of beasts.

4. Bodhisattvas Hōe, Kudokurin, Kongōdō, and Kongōzō who appear in the *Kegon* Sutra.

5. Symbolism found in the Shingon sutras. On four of the eight petals four Buddhas are seated with four bodhisattvas on the other four petals. Dainichi Buddha is seated in the center of the lotus; this scene is described in the *Dainichi* Sutra. The *Kongōchō* Sutra depicts thirty-seven Buddhas and bodhisattvas including Dainichi Buddha.

6. Ashuku (east), Hōshō (south), Muryōju (west), Mimyōshō (north).

7. "Transformation bodies" refers to the manifold forms which a Buddha himself assumes.

8. *Hokke Gengi*, T33, 798b.

9. *See* n. 4.

10. Monju, Fugen, Miroku, and Kannon.

11. The sixteen bodhisattvas who attend on the Buddhas of the four quarters of the universe.

12. T'ai-kung Wang is the title of a popular general who served Kings Wen and Wu of the Chou dynasty. The other three sages are Yin Shou, Wu Ch'eng, and Lao Tzu. They are all mentioned in the first chapter of this work.

13. Emperor Kao-tsu (256–195 B.C.), founder of the Han dynasty, tried to disown his son, the future Emperor Hui. Hui's mother, Empress Lü, persuaded four eminent recluses who lived on Mt. Shang to become his advisors. They were known as Master Tung-yüan, Scholar Lu-li, Ch'i Li-chi, and Master Hsia-huang. On seeing these four recluses, the emperor was impressed by their dignity and accepted Hui as his successor.

14. This sentence is found in the *Hokke Mongu Ki*, T34, 325a.

15. This entire passage is not drawn directly from a canonical work, but represents Nichiren's elaboration on events described in the Lotus Sutra.

16. Lotus Sutra, T9, 40b–c.

17. *Hokke Mongu*, T34, 125c–126a.

18. *Hokke Mongu Ki,* T34, 326b.

19. An epithet of Miroku, meaning "invincible."

20. Lotus Sutra, T9, 41b. The following quotation is a continuation of this passage.

21. A city in Magadha, ninety-six kilometers southwest of Pāṭaliputra. It is near to Buddhagayā where Shakyamuni Buddha was enlightened.

22. A treasure chamber said to stand on the border between the worlds of form and desire.

23. A lake that existed in the Bamboo Grove Monastery in Rājagṛha, Magadha.

24. Lotus Sutra, T9, 41b.

25. Prince Shōtoku (574–622) is frequently referred to by Nichiren. Emperor Yōmei is the thirty-first sovereign by current reckoning.

26. The source of these stories has not been identified. Nichiren mentions them elsewhere.

27. Lotus Sutra, T9, 41c.

28. T9, 325c.

29. T12, 341b.

30. The *Devadatta* (twelfth) chapter describes the master-disciple relationship between Devadatta and Shakyamuni in their previous existence. In a previous existence Shakyamuni was a king. In order to learn the Mahayana teachings, he served a hermit named Asita for one thousand years. After relating this story, he identifies the king as himself and Asita as Devadatta. He is now the teacher of the man who once taught him. The *Devadatta* chapter thus provides an answer to the question posed in the *Kammuryōju* Sutra.

31. Both quotations are from the *Juryō* (sixteenth) chapter (T9, 42b). In the *Anrakugyō* (fourteenth) chapter the Buddha had yet to recount his enlightenment in the remote past.

32. This quotation has not been located. It is said to be from the *Kegonkyō Gōron.*

33. *Hizō Hōyaku,* T77, 371a.

34. The eight phases are 1) descending from Heaven, 2) entering his mother's body, 3) emerging from her body, 4) renouncing the world, 5) conquering devils, 6) attaining enlightenment, 7) turning the wheel of the Law, and 8) entering nirvana.

35. The first of the ten stages of security and the first of the ten stages of development that comprise part of the fifty-two stages of bodhisattva practice. *See* Fifty-two stages in glossary.

36. These are practices designed to eradicate delusions of thought and desire. There are sixteen in the first category and eighteen in the second. They are described in *Daibibasha Ron,* T27, 780a, and *Maka Shikan,* T46, 27c.

37. The *Kegongyō Sho* divides the manifested body into superior and inferior. T34, 933.

38. This quotation is said to be from the *Hokke Gohyakumon Ron,* chapter 2 (ZZ 2, 5, 4). The exact quotation has not been identified.

39. When Dengyō Daishi went to China he studied chiefly T'ien-t'ai's

teachings based on the Lotus Sutra. When he returned to Japan, however, he also brought some esoteric teachings with him. For this reason Nichiren refers to him as the patriarch of esoteric and exoteric Buddhism, since his introduction of esoteric texts preceded that of Kōbō Daishi.

40. DDZ 3, 257.

41. That is, they do not reveal the Buddha's attainment of enlightenment in the distant past as explained in the Lotus Sutra.

42. The eunuch Chao Kao (d. 207 B.C.) was minister to Shih-huang-ti (259–210 B.C.), first emperor of the Ch'in dynasty. When Shih-huang-ti died, Chao Kao issued a false edict setting the emperor's youngest son on the throne. He brought about the death of the emperor's eldest son, as well as many generals and high-ranking ministers, and finally the second emperor. He wielded great power and attempted to control the throne. He was finally killed by the third emperor, Shih-huang-ti's grandson. Dōkyō (d. 772) was a Hossō priest at the Tōdai-ji, whose prayers were found effective in restoring the retired Empress Kōken to health. When she resumed the throne as the Empress Shōtoku, he acquired considerable power and was accused of trying to usurp the throne. On the empress' death in 770 he was sent into exile.

43. Hokke Ron, full title: Myōhō-renge-kyō Upadaisha, T26, 9b.

44. T10, 465c.

45. T18, 94a. The "I" refers to Mahavairocana Buddha.

46. The Taizōkai, or Womb Realm mandala, described in the Dainichi Sutra and the Kongōkai, or Diamond Realm mandala, described in the Kongōchō Sutra.

47. From the preface to Ebyō Tendai Shū, DDZ3, 344.

48. A poem by an anonymous poet from the ninth volume of the Kokin Waka Shū. Only the first part of the poem is quoted here. See Nihon Koten Bungaku Taikei, v. 9, p. 410.

49. Liang-hsü's dates are unknown. He was in the ninth generation after T'ien-t'ai and the teacher of Chishō Daishi (Enchin, 814–891), the fifth Tendai patriarch in Japan, when the latter visited China.

50. A rephrasing of a passage in Chishō's Juketsu Shū, DNBZ 26, 389.

51. In the Jūjūshin Ron Kōbō Daishi, in his classification of the various Buddhist teachings, ranked the Lotus Sutra eighth, the Kegon Sutra ninth, and the esoteric teachings tenth.

52. Jitte or Jitsue (786–847), Shinga (801–879), Enchō (771–837), and Kōjō (779–858). Among these Enchō had perhaps no direct connection with Kōbō Daishi.

53. The translation has been expanded in explanation of technical terms used. Chia-hsiang is more commonly known as Chi-tsang (549–623). The Hokke Genron is in T34, no. 1720.

54. This work appears in both seven- and fourteen-volume versions. Tz'u-en is more commonly referred to as K'uei-chi (632–682). The quotation appears to be an adaptation of a passage at T45, 266b.

55. ZZ1, 53, 3. The passage cited has not been identified.

56. Ch'eng-kuan (738–839), fourth patriarch of the Hua-yen (Kegon) school wrote the Kegongyō Sho in 60 chapters (T35, no. 1735). This reference

has not been located. The subsequent quotation probably refers to *Kegon Kyō Shoshō Gendan,* ZZ1, 8, 3–4, but here again, it has not been located.

57. T9, 8b.

58. The Buddhas are Ashuku (east), Nichigatsu Tōmyō (south), Amida (west), Enken (north), Shishi (below), and Bon'on (above). The twenty-five bodhisattvas protect all who worship Amida Buddha.

59. Venerable Buddhas, bodhisattvas, and other beings represented on the two Shingon mandalas.

60. The six Nara sects and the Shingon sect.

61. The scene where Shakyamuni preached the Lotus Sutra. The two places are atop Eagle Peak and in the air. The three assemblies are: the first assembly at Eagle Peak, the assembly in the air, and the second assembly at Eagle Peak. The first assembly at Eagle Peak continues from the first chapter through the first half of the *Hōtō* (eleventh) chapter. The assembly in the air lasts from the latter half of the *Hōtō* chapter to the *Zokurui* (twenty-second) chapter, and the second assembly at Eagle Peak from the *Yakuō* (twenty-third) to the *Fugen* (twenty-eighth) chapter.

62. This and the following quotations are found at T9, 33c ff.

63. The Queen Mother of the West is a legendary goddess in China. The peaches in her garden are said to bear fruit every three thousand years. The udumbara flower is said to bloom once every three thousand years to herald the appearance of a gold-wheel-turning monarch in the world.

64. Liu Pang and Hsiang Yü took advantage of the confusion following the death of Shih-huang-ti, the first emperor of the Ch'in dynasty, to raise an army and overthrow the dynasty. Thereafter the two engaged in a protracted struggle for power. This ended in the victory of Liu Pang, who founded the Han dynasty in 206 B.C.

65. The Minamoto clan, led by Minamoto no Yoritomo (1147–1199), waged a long campaign to wrest political power from the Taira clan. The Tairas were finally defeated at Dannoura and Taira no Munemori (1147–1185), the last head of his clan, died in the battle. Minamoto no Yoritomo subsequently established the Kamakura shogunate.

66. The garuḍa are gigantic birds in Indian mythology that are said to feed on dragons. The Icy Lake, located in the Himalaya, contains cool, clear water that removes all sufferings. The lake is said to be inhabited by a dragon king.

67. *See* glossary under "six difficult and nine easy acts."

68. *Maka Shikan,* T46, 74a.

69. The Hossō (Fa-hsiang) school divides all of Shakyamuni's teachings into three periods. The first period contains the doctrines of the Four Truths, which corresponds to the Hinayana teachings. The second period includes the teachings that assert that the essential nature of all things is empty. The *Hannya* Sutra belongs to this period. The teachings in the third period reveal the Consciousness-Only doctrine and refute extreme attachment to the doctrine of emptiness. Included in the third period are the *Jimmitsu,* Lotus, *Kegon,* and Nirvana sutras.

70. Nirvana Sutra, T12, 401b.

71. Reference is to Buddhist teachers on whom one can rely, as explained in the Nirvana Sutra and elsewhere. They are the four ranks of *shōmon*, the last of which is the most advanced stage of arhat. T'ien-t'ai, in his *Hokke Gengi*, related the four ranks to the fifty-two stages of bodhisattva practice.

72. Nirvana Sutra, T12, 401b. Continuation of previous passage.

73. T25, 53c.

74. *Hokke Gengi*, T33, 800a.

75. *Hokke Shūku*, DDZ3, 245.

76. *Juketsu Shū*, T74, 295b.

77. T9, 33b. The expression used here, *ikontō*, past, present, and future, refers specifically to this passage in the Lotus Sutra. The translation has been enlarged to include the meaning of the original passage.

78. *Hokke Mongu Ki*, T34, 280b.

79. *Hokke Gengi Shakusen*, T33, 858a.

80. T16, 754b. The *Jūji* is a separate translation of the *Jūji* chapter of the *Kegon* Sutra.

81. T12, 1083b.

82. The four grave offenses are killing, stealing, carnal behavior, and lying. These apply to monks. The eight grave offenses apply to nuns and include the above four, plus touching a male, meeting a male in secret, concealing the misbehavior of another, and following a monk whose offenses have been exposed. The five cardinal sins are killing one's father, killing one's mother, killing an arhat, shedding the blood of a Buddha, and causing disunity among the community of monks.

83. T8, 868b–c.

84. Basic teachings of Buddhism. The first is that all existence is suffering. The second is that suffering is caused by selfish craving, the third is that selfish craving can be eliminated, and the fourth is that it can be eliminated by following the noble eightfold path.

85. Reference is to the bodhisattva way.

86. T16, 697a–b.

87. T6, 666c.

88. The deepest of the eight consciousnesses. It is regarded as giving rise to all phenomena, knowledge, and experience.

89. T18, 3b ff. The Master of Secrets is Vajrasattva (Jap Kongōsatta), to whom Dainichi Buddha transmitted the Law.

90. T10, 441a. The passage relating to the offerings of musical instruments is repeated in the text. "This chapter" at the close of the quotation refers to the *Kenshu* chapter of the *Kegon* Sutra.

91. T12, 449a.

92. Mt. Sumeru is highest among the nine mountains described in Indian cosmology. The text has been somewhat expanded in the interest of clarity.

93. *Ben Kemmitsu Nikyō Ron*, T77, 379a.

94. Ibid., T77, 375b.

95. This refers to the Chinese monk Fa-hsien's journey to India. Deploring the lack of Buddhist scriptures in China, he left Ch'ang-an in 399 in search of them. He traveled overland to India and there learned Sanskrit and

studied the sutras, writings on discipline *(vinaya),* and other Buddhist treatises. He returned to China by sea in 414, bringing numerous scriptures and Buddhist images with him.

96. Asanga is said to have ascended to the Tuṣita Heaven and there inherited the teachings from Bodhisattva Miroku. *Daitō Saiiki Ki,* T51, 896b.

97. Sunakṣatra was a monk who devoted himself to Buddhist austerities and attained a limited form of enlightenment. He was arrogant, however, and believed he had mastered Buddhism; later he turned to non-Buddhist teachings and discarded his faith in Buddhism. He is said to have fallen into hell alive. T12, 560b. Ajātaśatru was a king of Magadha in Shakyamuni's time. He is said to have murdered his father so that he might ascend the throne. Later he converted to Buddhism. T12, 480b.

98. To the standard five cardinal sins are added killing a monk of high virtue and killing a teacher.

99. *Hokke Mongu Ki,* T34, 274b.

100. This refers to the Tatsunokuchi Persecution of 1271.

101. T9, 36c ff.

102. T34, 315a.

103. *Hoke Kyō Shogisan,* ZZ1, 45, 3, 277a–b.

104. T12, 419a, 421c–422a.

105. *Bussetsu Hatsunaion* Sutra translated by Fa-hsien. T12, 892c.

106. T12, 386b.

107. Source unknown, possibly a rephrasing of a passage in the *Hokke Gengi,* chapter 10.

108. Source unknown, possibly a rephrasing of a passage in the *Hokke Shūku* or *Kenkai Ron.*

109. The story of King Chao and Su Yu appears in *Busso Tōki* (T49, 325c). The traditional date for the introduction of Buddhism to China is 67 A.D.

110. The exact location of this quotation has not been identified. The *Fuhōzō* Sutra *(Fu Hōzō Innen Den)* lists twenty-three successors (T50, 297–322). The *Maka Shikan* (T46, 1a–b) gives twenty-four, which is the figure accepted by the Tendai sect. They are: 1) Mahākāśyapa, 2) Ānanda, 3) Madhyāntika (omitted in the *Fu Hōzō Innen Den),* 4) Śāṇavāsa, 5) Upagupta, 6) Dhṛtaka, 7) Miccaka, 8) Buddhanandi, 9) Buddhamitra, 10) Pārśva, 11) Puṇyayaśas, 12) Aśvaghoṣa, 13) Kapimala, 14) Nāgārjuna, 15) Āryadeva, 16) Rāhulata, 17) Saṅghānandi, 18) Gayaśāta, 19) Kumārata, 20) Jayata, 21) Vasubandhu, 22) Manorhita, 23) Haklenayaśas, 24) Siṁha-bhikṣu (Āryasiṁha). Siṁha-bhikṣu, who lived in India during the sixth century is said to have been beheaded by a king who was the enemy of Buddhism, thus bringing to an end the line of succession.

111. T9, 36b.

112. T12, 419a.

113. T46, 10b.

114. *Anraku Shū,* T47, 13c.

115. *Senchaku Shū,* T83, 17a.

116. T34, 344c.

117. *Shugo Kokkai Shō.* The precise citation has not been identified.

118. *Ichijō Yōketsu,* T74, 351a. Eshin Sōzu, otherwise known as Genshin (942–1017), is famed as the compiler of the *Ōjō Yōshū,* the "Essentials of Salvation," a work that had great influence on the development of Jōdo (Pure Land) Buddhism. Here he is referring to the Lotus Sutra.

119. The first quotation is at T12, 407b. The quotation from Miao-lo is a rephrasing of a passage in the *Hokke Gengi Shakusen* (T33, 393c). The three types of teachings are the *zōkyō, tsūgyō,* and the *bekkyō.* The quotation from *Maka Shikan* is at T46, 17b.

120. T46, 203b.

121. T9, 33c.

122. T9, 36b.

123. T12, 892c.

124. T12, 386b.

125. These quotations have all been previously cited.

126. Mt. Hiei refers to the headquarters of the Sammon branch of Tendai at Enryaku-ji. Onjō-ji, also called Mii-dera, is the headquarters of the Jimon branch of Tendai, and is located in Ōtsu. The Tō-ji (Kyōō gokoku-ji) is an important Shingon temple in Kyoto; all these temples have been previously mentioned. The Kennin-ji, Jufuku-ji, and Kenchō-ji are all important Rinzai Zen temples.

127. Shōitsu (commonly read Shōichi) is the Kokushi (National Teacher) title of Enni Ben'en (1202–1280), founder of the major Rinzai Zen temple Tōfuku-ji in Kyoto. Ryōkan (1217–1303) was a noted Ritsu leader in Kamakura, whom Nichiren regarded as an archenemy.

128. T46, 1a.

129. T46, 142b.

130. *Hokke Sandaibu Fuchū,* ZZ1, 44, 3, 168b. An annotation by Shen-chih Ts'ung-i (1042–1091) of T'ien-t'ai's three major works *(Maka Shikan, Hokke Gengi,* and *Hokke Mongu),* as well as Miao-lo's commentaries on them.

131. T46, 49a, 78a.

132. T46, 382a–b. The eight wrong views (Jap *hachija*) are the opposite of the eightfold path. They are: wrong beliefs, wrong thinking, wrong speech, wrong conduct, wrong way of life, wrong encouragement, wrong thoughts, wrong and meditation. The eight wordly desires refer to the eight winds (Jap *hachifū*): prosperity, decline, disgrace, honor, praise, censure, suffering, and pleasure. The Buddha in his manifested body (Jap *ōjin*) is said to be sixteen feet high. The five aggregates (Jap *go'on*) are the *skandhas,* the constituent elements of form, perception, conception, volition, and consciousness that unite temporarily to form an individual living being. The six sense organs are eyes, ears, nose, tongue, body, and mind. The six supernatural powers of a Buddha are the ability to see anything anywhere, to hear anything anywhere, to know the thoughts of others, to know past lives, to be anywhere at will, and to eradicate the passions.

133. T46, 99b. Later commentators identify the "master of Yeh and Lo" with Bodhidharma, the founder of Zen in China. T'ien-t'ai, however, does not mention him or any other contemporary figure by name.

134. T46, 385c.

135. T12, 892b. The following quotation has been previously cited.

136. T9, 36c.

137. This quotation has previously been cited.

138. Gomyō (750–834) was a priest of the Hossō sect. He entered Kon-kōmyō-ji and first studied under Dōkō. In 819 he petitioned the throne to protest Dengyō Daishi's attempt to construct a Mahayana ordination plat-form. Shūen (771–835) was a learned Hossō priest from Kōfuku-ji, who also protested Dengyō Daishi's request to construct an ordination platform. Both priests are frequently mentioned by Nichiren.

139. Nen'a (1199–1287) was the founder of the Chinzei school of Jōdo (Pure Land) Buddhism. Also known as Ryōchū, he is regarded as the third patriarch after Hōnen and Benchō.

140. T46, 10b.

141. Standard Zen histories hold that when Shakyamuni held up a flower before the assembly at Eagle Peak, no one could fathom his meaning. Mahā-kāśyapa alone understood and smiled and the Buddha transferred his teaching to him. Mahākāśyapa in turn handed the teaching on to Ānanda, from whom it was transferred eventually to Bodhidharma, the twenty-eighth patriarch, who had come to China from India. Where T'ien-t'ai held that the teaching had been cut off with the death of Siṁha-bhikṣu (Āryasiṁha), the twenty-fourth successor or patriarch, Zen maintained that the teaching had indeed been handed down to a twenty-fifth patriarch before Siṁha-bhikṣu's death. Bodhidharma is considered the founder of Zen in China. He, in turn, handed down the teaching to Hui-k'o. Hui-neng (638–713) is the sixth patriarch of Chinese Zen.

142. T9, 33c–34a.

143. The three types of enemies are described in the *Kanji* (thirteenth) chapter of the Lotus Sutra (T9, 36b). Miao-lo in his *Hokke Mongu Ki* (T34, 315a) enumerates them as: 1) laymen who curse the Lotus votary and beat him with staves, 2) monks, filled with heretical wisdom, who pride them-selves in their knowledge, and 3) seemingly sage-like people who receive the respect of society but who, for fame and profit, persecute and harm the votaries of the Lotus.

144. When Buddhism was introduced to Japan Mononobe no Moriya, a powerful minister, opposed it. Prince Shōtoku (574–622) and another minis-ter, Soga no Umako (d. 626), supported the new religion. The Soga faction won; Mononobe no Moriya was killed in 587.

145. This simile appears in the Lotus Sutra, T9, 60c.

146. These quotations from the Lotus Sutra appear at T9, 39c, 19b, 59b, and 62a respectively.

147. T9, 36b.

148. T12, 384b and T9, 31b.

149. Āryasiṁha (Siṁha-bhikṣu) is usually listed as the twenty-fourth suc-cessor or patriarch.

150. Chu Tao-sheng (d. 434) maintained that even an *icchantika* possessed the Buddha nature; for this assertion he was banished. He was vindicated

when the translation into Chinese of the Nirvana Sutra verified his assertion. His biography is in *Kōsō Den* (T50, 366b–367a). Fa-tao (1086–1147) was a Sung dynasty monk who opposed the emperor's change of allegiance from Buddhism to Taoism. He wrote a memorial in protest, enraging the emperor, who had his face branded and sent him into exile. His story is in *Busso Tōki*, T49, 420c–421b.

151. Po Ch'ü-i (772–846) is the famed T'ang poet. Sugawara no Michizane (845–903) is the celebrated statesman, scholar, and poet, who was demoted to a lowly position in Kyushu on the basis of groundless accusations. He is revered as the god Tenjin at the Kitano Shrine in Kyoto.

152. *Hokke Gengi*, T33, 748b.

153. This passage is not in the *Shinjikan* Sutra. It appears in the *Shokyō yōshū* (T54, 129c) as a quotation from an unidentified sutra.

154. T9, 51b. In the context of the sutra itself, this passage refers to the retribution incurred by those who slandered Fukyō. Here and in other writings, Nichiren interprets it so as to refer to Bodhisattva Fukyō himself.

155. T12, 417c.

156. T16, 347b.

157. This story appears in the *Daichido Ron* (T25, 145a) and elsewhere. Śāriputra was practicing the bodhisattva way when a Brahman begged for his eye. Śāriputra gave it to him, but the Brahman was so revolted by its smell that he dropped and crushed it. Seeing this, Śāriputra withdrew from his practice and fell into the Avīci Hell for countless kalpas.

158. The text has been expanded somewhat for the sake of clarity.

159. T12, 877c.

160. T46, 49b, 49a.

161. T12, 613c.

162. This passage is discussed in the *Nehangyō Sho*, T38, 47c ff. The three obstacles (Jap *sanshō*) are earthly passions, karma, and retribution.

163. This passage has been expanded for clarity. The three inherent potentials of the Buddha nature (Jap *san'in busshō*) are: 1) inherent Buddha nature (Jap *shōin busshō*), 2) the wisdom to perceive it (Jap *ryōin busshō*), and 3) the actions to practice and develop this wisdom (Jap *en'in busshō*). The text has *ryōin no ko,* i.e., the "child" that is *ryōin busshō*. Nichiren here has equated faith with wisdom.

164. T9, 38a.

165. *Shōju* is to propagate Buddhism by gradually leading a person, without refuting his attachment to another teaching. *Shakubuku* is to propagate the teaching by strictly refuting this attachment. Both terms are mentioned in the *Shōman* Sutra (T12, 217c), as well as in the *Maka Shikan*.

166. T46, 137c.

167. T46, 444a–b. King Sen'yo is a previous incarnation of Shakyamuni Buddha. According to the Nirvana Sutra (T12, 434c), King Sen'yo was the ruler in Jambudvīpa, who believed in the Mahayana sutras. When Brahmans slandered these sutras he had them put to death. The sutra says that because of this he was never thereafter in danger of falling into hell. According to the Nirvana Sutra (T12, 378a), the medicine that the old physician prescribed did

harm to the people. To save their lives the new physician persuaded the king to use stringent measures to prohibit the use of the medicine.

168. T34, 118c.

169. *Nehangyō Sho,* T38, 84c.

170. T12, 383b.

171. Dainichi Nōnin is a Zen priest frequently mentioned by Nichiren. He was probably dead, however, before the Kennin era.

172. The mysteries of body, speech, and mind; also the practices performed with these three.

173. T12, 381a.

174. *Nehangyō Sho,* T38, 80b.

175. T9, 33c.

176. This and the previous quotation are from *Nehan-gyō Sho,* T38, 80b.

177. This episode concerning Tokuitsu is frequently mentioned by Nichiren. Portions of his lost work, *Chūhen Gikyō,* are cited in Dengyō's *Shugo Kokkai Shō.*

178. The source of this quotation has not been identified. Saichō is another name for Dengyō.

179. Kumārajīva accepted an invitation from Yao Hsing, king of the Later Ch'in dynasty, and came to the capital, Ch'ang-an, in 401. There he participated in the translation of numerous Buddhist scriptures from Sanskrit into Chinese.

180. This story appears in the *Daichido Ron* (T25, 412a). A devil disguised as a Brahman appeared to Gyōbō Bonji and said, "I will reveal to you the Buddha's teaching if you are prepared to inscribe it by using your skin as paper, your bone as a pen, and your blood as ink." When Gyōbō indicated his willingness to comply, the devil disappeared and a real Buddha appeared to teach him the Law.

The True Object of Worship

1. T46, 54a. Each of the Ten Worlds (*see* glossary) has ten factors (*see* glossary, Jap *jūnyoze*), each of which possesses the three realms of existence (*see* glossary, *sanseken*). The thirty realms refer to the ten factors multiplied by the three realms. The three thousand realms are the realms of *ichinen sanzen* (*see* glossary).

2. The original text contains two parenthetical notes, both by Nichiren, one directly following "Volume Five of the *Maka Shikan* states," and the other at the end of the passage. They are placed together here in the translation. The *Maka Shikan* gives two ways to derive the *sanzen* of *ichinen sanzen.* One begins with the hundred worlds, multiplies them by the three realms and then by the ten factors to arrive at the three thousand factors. The other begins with the hundred worlds, multiplies them by the ten factors and then by the three realms to form the three thousand realms. Although the explanation differs, the principle is the same.

3. *Maka Shikan Bugyōden Guketsu,* T46, 296a.

4. T46, 296a.

5. T33, 693c.

6. (Jap *ichinyū*). Each of the six sense organs and the objects that stimulate them.

7. T34, 7b.

8. T34, 888c. The *Kannon Gengi* is T'ien-t'ai's annotation of the *Fumon* (twenty-fifth) chapter of the Lotus Sutra.

9. T46, 277b. "Correct Meditation" is the name of the seventh chapter in the *Maka Shikan*. The twenty-five preparatory exercises (Jap *nijūgo hōben*) are to be undertaken prior to entering T'ien-t'ai meditation. Detailed in the *Maka Shikan* and elsewhere, they are: 1) observation of the precepts and purification of one's life; 2) acquiring appropriate food and clothing; 3) maintaining quiet surroundings; 4) ridding one's self of miscellaneous affairs; 5) acquiring a good teacher; 6–10) restraining desires for things seen, heard, smelled, tasted, or touched; 11–15) overcoming the five obstacles of greed, anger, sleep, excitement, and depression; 16–20) regulating eating, sleeping, posture, breathing, and mind; 21) gaining the aspiration for enlightenment; 22) perseverance; 23) concentration; 24) skilled use of wisdom; and 25) single-mindedness.

10. T46, 296a.

11. The Great Sage is T'ien-t'ai Chih-i.

12. *Hokke Gengi,* T33, 704c.

13. *Hokke Gengi,* Preface, T33, 681a.

14. T46, 54a.

15. T33, 918b.

16. T46, 784b. The *Kongōbei Ron* by Miao-lo maintains that even insentient beings possess the potential for Buddhahood.

17. T9, 7a.

18. T9, 42c.

19. T9, 35a.

20. T9, 59a.

21. T9, 35c.

22. T9, 30c.

23. T9, 8c.

24. T9, 12a.

25. T9, 11c.

26. T9, 6a.

27. T9, 51c.

28. T9, 42c.

29. T9, 31b.

30. *See* glossary under Six difficult and nine easy acts.

31. *Hokke Mongu,* T34, 110a.

32. *Kanjin Ron Sho,* T46, 609c.

33. *Hokke Shūku,* DDZ3, 251.

34. The standard interpretation of the Ten Worlds or realms, is that these are distinct realms or categories of beings from the lowest to the highest: 1) Hell; 2) Hungry Ghosts; 3) Animals; 4) Asura or Fighting Demons; 5) Humans; 6) Heavenly Beings. These are the Six Paths (worlds, realms), all still

in the world of transmigration. Above these are the Four Noble Worlds: 7) the *Shōmon* (Skt śrāvaka), those who seek enlightenment for themselves through study and practice; 8) the *Engaku* (Skt pratyekabuddha), those who gain enlightenment through their own efforts; 9) Bodhisattvas, who seek enlightenment, but postpone their attainment of Buddhahood out of compassion for all other sentient beings; and 10) Buddhas, the enlightened ones. Here Nichiren interprets them as potential states of life inherent in human beings. *See also* glossary, under Six paths, Ten worlds.

35. T9, 7a.

36. T12, 638a.

37. As described in chapter eight *(Shie-bon)* of the thirty-six-chapter Nirvana Sutra (T12, 637 ff.).

38. Shakyamuni's given name.

39. This note appears in the original text.

40. The three categories of illusion (Jap *sanwaku*) are described in the *Maka Shikan* (T46, 62 ff.). They are: 1) illusions of thought and desire, 2) illusions as numerous as particles of dust or sand, and 3) illusions that obstruct awakening to the ultimate reality.

41. The eight kinds of non-human beings (Jap *hachibu shu*) enumerated in various Buddhist texts. They are: 1) gods, 2) dragons, 3) *yasha* (Skt *yakṣa*), beings, sometimes described as fierce demons, who are followers of Bishamonten, one of the Four Heavenly Kings, 4) *kendatsuba* (Skt *gandharva*), gods of music, 5) *ashura* (Skt *asura*), fighting demons, said to live at the bottom of the ocean surrounding Mt. Sumeru and who inhabit the fourth of the Ten Worlds, 6) *karura* (Skt *garuḍa*), birds that devour dragons, 7) *kinnara* (Skt *kinnara*), gods with beautiful voices, and 8) *magoraka* (Skt *mahoraga*), gods in the form of snakes. The Kongō gods are deities who wield weapons to protect Buddhism.

42. All of Shakyamuni's teachings.

43. The story of Prince Nōse appears in the *Kengu* Sutra (T4, 405a–c), of Bodhisattva Judō in the *Zuiō Hongi* Sutra (T3, 472c), of King Shibi in the *Bosatsu Honjō Manron* (T3, 333b), and of Prince Satta in the *Konkōmyō* Sutra (T16, 354c).

44. The translation has been substantially augmented here.

45. A bodhisattva is supposed to serve seventy-five thousand Buddhas for one million kalpas, seventy-six thousand Buddhas for another million kalpas, and seventy-seven thousand Buddhas for a third million kalpas.

46. The text has been augmented here. The four different ways refer to the four different aspects Shakyamuni assumed when he preached the four doctrines (*zōkyō, tsūgyō, bekkyō,* and *engyō*). *See* glossary under eight teachings.

47. The thirty-four methods of cutting off illusions of thought and desire. They are described in the *Maka Shikan,* T46, 27c.

48. The *Hōtō* (eleventh) chapter of the Lotus Sutra states that before opening the Treasure Tower, and in order to make room for the Buddhas of the ten directions who were his emanations, Shakyamuni "transformed the land three times," purifying first the mundane world, then innumerable lands

in space, and then innumerable other lands further away in space, so that they all became like one Buddha land. These three transformations and the resulting pure Buddha land are interpreted respectively in terms of the four kinds of lands mentioned in the sutras: 1) the Land of Enlightened and Unenlightened Beings, where beings of the six paths (Hell to Heaven) dwell together with beings of the four higher worlds (*shōmon* to Buddhahood); 2) the Land of Transition, where *shōmon* and *engaku* live; 3) the Land of Actual Reward, inhabited by bodhisattvas; and 4) the Land of Eternal Light, Buddha land. The Buddha is further said to display four aspects corresponding respectively to these four kinds of lands: the inferior manifested body, the superior manifested body, the reward body, and the Dharma body.

49. These four kinds of Buddha bodies correspond to the four aspects just enumerated in the above note.

50. The theoretical teaching (*shakumon*) comprises the first half of the Lotus Sutra, chapters one through fourteen. The essential teaching (*hommon*) comprises chapters fifteen through twenty-eight. This division was established by T'ien-t'ai in his *Hokke Mongu* (T34, 2ff.). The theoretical teaching was expounded by the historical Shakyamuni Buddha, who attained enlightenment in India; the essential teaching was expounded by the Buddha who explains that the historical Buddha is but a transient role, and that his true identity is the Buddha who gained enlightenment in the remote past of *gohyaku-jintengō*.

51. T10. Quotation not identified.

52. T8, 827c.

53. T8. Quotation not identified.

54. T32, 584b.

55. T31, 55a.

56. T9, 8a.

57. T26, no. 1519.

58. T31, no. 1611. Full title is *Kukyō Ichijō Hōshō Ron*.

59. The National Teacher Ch'ing-liang is the honorary title of the fourth Kegon patriarch, Ch'eng-kuan (738–839). The source of the quotation has not been traced.

60. Hui-yüan's dates are unknown. An eighth-century Kegon priest, he studied under Fa-tsang and later advanced his own distinctive interpretation of the Kegon teachings. The quotation is a paraphrase of a passage in the *Zoku Kegon Kyō Ryakusho Kanjoki*, ZZ1, 5, 1, 9a.

61. No information is available on Ryōkō or the source of this quotation.

62. Tokuitsu's (also read Tokuichi) remark appears frequently in Nichiren's writings. He was a celebrated Hossō priest who disputed frequently with Dengyō Daishi on doctrinal matters. The quotation appears in the *Shugo Kokkai Shō*, T73, 143a, 145a. The long broad tongue is one of the thirty-two distinguishing marks of a Buddha.

63. *Ben Kemmitsu Nikyō Ron*, T77, 379a.

64. This passage has been greatly expanded in translation for the sake of clarity.

65. *Maka Shikan*, T46, 55a.

66. *Hokke Gengi,* T33, 704c. Note here that the *Hokke Gengi* is narrated by T'ien-t'ai and recorded by Chang-an. The present quotation is attributed to Chang-an; the one in the following paragraph to T'ien-t'ai.

67. *Hokke Gengi,* T33, 693a.

68. *Kanjin Ron Sho,* T46, 609b.

69. T9, 31b.

70. *Hokke Mongu,* T34, 110a–b.

71. *Kanjin Ron Sho,* T46, 609c.

72. Drawn from a passage in the *Hokke Shūku,* DDZ3, 251.

73. All of these priests are mentioned frequently by Nichiren. *See* glossary under individual names.

74. T9, 388a.

75. The five types of vision are: 1) the eye of ordinary humans; 2) the divine eye of heavenly beings that can see everywhere without regard to distance or degree of illumination; 3) the eye of wisdom that perceives the principle that all things are empty; 4) the Dharma eye by which bodhisattvas penetrate all teachings in order to save people; and 5) the Buddha eye that is awakened to the true nature of all things.

76. T9, 391a.

77. The language of the original here and in the preceding paragraph is highly condensed and technical and has been amplified considerably in translation.

78. T9, 388b.

79. T9, 6c. A passage similar to the following appears in "The Opening of the Eyes I."

80. T12, 414a, 654c.

81. *Daichido Ron,* T25, 408b.

82. This treatise is associated with the Sanron school. Only three of the original *chüan* are extant. The passage cited is not included among them.

83. Chia-hsiang has appeared previously. The quotation has not been identified.

84. *Hokke Gengi,* T33, 775a.

85. T9, 17c. The four great *shōmon* are: Maudgālyayāna, Mahākāśyapa, Kātyāyana, and Subhūti. Their attainment of Buddhahood is predicted in the *Juki* (sixth) chapter of the Lotus Sutra.

86. T9, 8c.

87. T9, 34a.

88. T9, 31a.

89. T9, 42b. The following quotation is from the same chapter. T9, 42c.

90. When Emperor Wu of the Chou dynasty battled with Emperor Chou of the Yin dynasty, T'ai-kung, as supreme commander, defeated the armies of Yin. Tan, the Duke of Chou, was the younger brother of Emperor Wu. After Wu's death, Ch'eng, Emperor Wu's son, was still a child, so Tan administered the affairs of state for him.

91. Takeshiuchi was a legendary general and statesman who appears in the ancient chronicles of Japan. He is said to have served five emperors, but no documentary evidence concerning him exists.

92. Bodhisattvas who emerged from the earth, as described in the *Jūji Yujutsu* (fifteenth) chapter of the Lotus Sutra. The names of the two Jōgyō are written with different characters.

93. *Maka Shikan Bugyōden Guketsu*, T46, 295c.

94. T16, no. 682.

95. The three kinds of lands are the Land of Enlightened and Unenlightened Beings, the Land of Transition, and the Land of Actual Reward, which are expounded in the pre-Lotus Sutra teachings. The four kinds of lands are these three plus the Land of Eternal Light expounded in the theoretical teaching of the Lotus Sutra and in the Nirvana Sutra. *See also* n. 48.

96. As described in the *Hōtō* (eleventh) chapter of the Lotus Sutra.

97. According to the *Zōbō Ketsugi* Sutra, the conclusion to the Nirvana Sutra, those present in the grove of sal trees at the time of the Buddha's entry into nirvana perceived the scene in four different ways according to their capacity and level of development. Some saw it as a place of earth, plants, trees, and stone walls; some saw it as pure and adorned with the seven kinds of precious substances such as gold and silver; others saw it as the place where all Buddhas of the past, present, and future carry out their practices; and still others saw it as the inconceivable truth which all Buddhas attain. These four views of the sal grove are interpreted as corresponding to the four kinds of lands. T85, 1337a.

98. The technical language of this passage in the original has been considerably expanded here for clarity.

99. The three calamities are those that occur at the end of a kalpa. They are variously described. The four cycles of change are formation, continuance, decline, and disintegration of a kalpa, as mentioned in the preceding paragraph.

100. The three realms of existence (Jap *sanseken*) are: 1) the realm of the five aggregates, or *skandhas;* 2) the realm of living beings; and 3) the realm of the environment. Originally described in the *Daichido Ron* (T25, 546c), the concept was developed as an integral part of the concept of *ichinen sanzen*. The living being is an individual that at any time manifests one or another of the Ten Worlds. The five aggregates are the elements temporarily brought together to form a living being, and the environment is the place where the living being functions.

101. Here again the wording of the original has been expanded for the sake of clarity.

102. In other words, the eternal Buddha.

103. The four stages of faith were formulated by T'ien-t'ai in relation to the Lotus Sutra and described in the *Hokke Mongu* (T34, 137b). They are: 1) to arouse even a moment's faith and understanding with respect to the Lotus Sutra; 2) to understand the general purport of the sutra's words; 3) to preach its teachings widely for the sake of others; and 4) to realize with deep faith the ultimate wisdom.

104. The terms "theoretical teaching" and "essential teaching" are generally used to mean respectively the first and second halves of the twenty-eight chapters of the Lotus Sutra. Here Nichiren includes the *Muryōgi* Sutra and the

Fugen Sutra with the Lotus Sutra to form the ten volumes of the threefold Lotus Sutra (Jap *Hokke sambu-kyō*). The "theoretical teaching," as described here, indicates the *Muryōgi* Sutra and the first fourteen chapters of the Lotus Sutra; the "essential teaching" is the last fourteen chapters and the *Fugen* Sutra.

105. In the original this sentence appears slightly earlier, after the sentence reading, "The latter revealed the eternity of the Ten Worlds and, further, the True Land." It has been transposed here in the translation for clarity's sake.

106. In the text of the original, Nichiren uses the same term "essential teaching" *(hommon)* in two senses. At the beginning of the preceding paragraph, it indicates the text of the latter fourteen chapters of the Lotus Sutra. Here, it indicates the ultimate truth contained within the essential teaching, the enlightenment of the eternal Buddha.

107. T9, 31b.

108. T9, 34a.

109. Based on the *Bosatsu Yōraku Hongō* Sutra (T24, 1011–1016), these are the last two stages in T'ien-t'ai's classification of the fifty-two stages of bodhisattva practice; *tōgaku* is the fifty-first stage, the highest stage of the bodhisattva, and *myōkaku* is the last stage, Buddhahood. The stages are discussed in the *Hokke Gengi* (T33, 731c). The highly technical language of the original has been expanded here for clarity.

110. T9, 40a.

111. Chapters ten through fourteen.

112. T9, 33c. The four categories of Buddhists are monks, nuns, laymen, and laywomen.

113. T9, 36c.

114. *Hokke Mongu,* T34, 124c.

115. *Hokke Mongu Ki,* T34, 324a.

116. *Hoke Kyō Mongu Fushō Ki,* by Tao-hsien, a T'ang dynasty T'ien-t'ai school priest of whom little is known. The *Fushō Ki* is a commentary on Miao-lo's *Hokke Mongu Ki.* ZZ1, 45, 2, 105b. The above paragraph has been augmented for the sake of clarity.

117. T9, 41c. "These words" in the quoted passage refers to Shakyamuni's declaration that the Bodhisattvas of the Earth are his original disciples.

118. This and the following quotation are at T9, 43a.

119. T9, 46a.

120. These are the five categories used by T'ien-t'ai to explain the title of the Lotus Sutra. *Hokke Gengi,* T33, 681c–682a.

121. T9, 51c.

122. *Hokke Mongu,* T34, 142a.

123. *Hoke-kyō Mongu Fushō Ki,* ZZ1, 45, 2, 105b.

124. Fudō (or Fudōchi) Buddha, described in the *Kegon* Sutra, T10, 58a.

125. A Buddha described in the *Yakuō* (twenty-third) chapter of the Lotus Sutra. When Bodhisattva Yakuō practiced austerities in a previous existence, this Buddha expounded the Lotus Sutra.

126. A Buddha described in the *Fugen* (twenty-eighth) chapter of the Lotus Sutra. According to the sutra, Bodhisattva Fugen came to the cere-

mony of the Lotus Sutra from Hōi Buddha's land in the eastern part of the universe.

127. T9, 51c.

128. These ten mystic powers are described in this chapter of the Lotus Sutra and are explained by T'ien-t'ai in the *Hokke Mongu*, T34, 141 ff.

129. T9, 52a.

130. *Hokke Mongu*, T34, 142a.

131. *Hokke Shūku*, DDZ3, 244.

132. *Hokke Mongu Ki*, T34, 349c.

133. T9, 52b.

134. This and the following quotations are from T9, 52c. Described is the conclusion of the "ceremony in the air," which began in the *Hōtō* (eleventh) chapter.

135. Ionnō Buddha appears in the *Fukyō* (twentieth) chapter of the Lotus Sutra. He is the first of two billion Buddhas, one after the other, each with the same name. Bodhisattva Fukyō appeared in the world after the death of Ionnō Buddha in the remote past, and propagated a teaching that showed respect for all beings because of their innate Buddha nature. He was slandered and beaten, and those who reviled him fell into hell. Later, however, after expiating their sins, they were reborn with Fukyō and saved by following his teaching.

136. T9, 31b.

137. T9, 43a.

138. T9, 46a.

139. T9, 54c.

140. T12, 481a, 724a.

141. *Hokke Mongu Ki*, T34, 349c.

142. *Hokke Mongu*, T34, 2c.

143. *Hokke Mongu Ki*, T34, 157b.

144. *Shugo Kokkai Shō*, T74, 177b.

145. *Hokke Shūku*, DDZ3, 251. T'ang refers to China, Katsu to a Tungusic nation in northeastern China that flourished for about a hundred years from the mid-sixth century. Thus, east of T'ang and west of Katsu refers to Japan.

146. The Shitennō-ji was founded in 587 and is located in present-day Osaka.

147. Emperor Shōmu (701–756) was the forty-fifth emperor of Japan. He established Kokubun-ji (state-established provincial temples) in each province as well as the Tōdai-ji in Nara.

148. *Hokke Mongu*, T34, 125b.

149. *Hokke Mongu Ki*, T34, 326b.

150. This story is frequently mentioned by Nichiren. When Emperor Kao-tsu (256–195 B.C.), founder of the Han dynasty, tried to disown his own son, the future Emperor Hui, Hui's mother persuaded four elderly recluses to become his advisors. On seeing these four elders, Emperor Kao-tsu was so impressed by their dignity that he finally accepted Emperor Hui as his successor.

151. Toki Jōnin (1216–1299?), a prominent lay disciple.

152. Ōta refers to Ōta Jōmyō, a lay follower, also known as Ōta Gorō-zaemon (1222–1283). Kyōshin Gobō is known also as Soya Nyūdō (1224–1291), a lay follower who later became a lay priest *(nyūdō)*.

The Selection of the Time

1. T9, 22c. Daitsūchishō (often abbreviated Daitsū) appears in the *Kejōyu* (seventh) chapter of the Lotus Sutra. He taught this sutra in the distant past.

2. T9, 26b.

3. T9, 8a.

4. The preface of the *Rōshi Keko* Sutra states that Lao Tzu was white-haired at birth and had the appearance of an old man (T54, 1266b). This is a spurious sutra of which only the first and tenth chapters are extant.

5. The fourth of the six heavens in the world of desire. Bodhisattvas are said to be reborn here just before their last rebirth in the world, where they will attain Buddhahood.

6. Non-human beings that protect Buddhism. They are: gods, dragons, a kind of demon called *yakṣa,* gods of music called *gandharva,* demons called *asura* that live at the bottom of the sea, birds called *garuḍa* that prey on dragons, gods with beautiful voices called *kinnara,* and *mahoraga,* gods shaped like snakes.

7. According to some texts a woman cannot become a Bonten, a Tai-shaku, a devil king, a wheel-turning king, or a Buddha.

8. In the *Yujutsu* (fifteenth) chapter of the Lotus Sutra Shakyamuni explains to Miroku and others in the assembly that he has been guiding since the distant past the bodhisattvas who emerged from the earth. Miroku and the others are puzzled: how, they wonder, is it possible that he taught so many bodhisattvas in the mere forty years since his enlightenment? It was as though he had asserted that a youth of twenty-five had pointed to a hundred-year old man and said: "This is my son." T9, 42a.

9. All the worlds except for the tenth, Buddhahood.

10. A jewel that will grant whatever one desires. It is described in various texts. The *Daichido Ron* says it can be obtained from the head of a dragon king (T25, 478a) and elsewhere, from the relics of a Buddha (T25, 134a).

11. T9, 8a.

12. T9, 16a.

13. T9, 31b.

14. T9, 39a.

15. T9, 50a. The four categories of Buddhists are monks, nuns, laymen, and laywomen.

16. T9, 36b.

17. *Hokke Mongu,* T34, 118c.

18. *Nehangyō Sho,* T38, 84c. For *shōju* and *shakubuku,* see glossary.

19. Those to whom Shakyamuni preached the *Kegon* Sutra, directly after his enlightenment.

20. The Deer Park (Skt Mṛgadāva) was located at Vārāṇaśī, present-day

Benares. Here Shakyamuni preached the *Agon* sutras. The five ascetics were Ājñāta Kauṇḍinya, Aśvajit, Bhadrika, Daśabala Kāśyapa, and Mahānāma. They engaged in ascetic practices with Shakyamuni before his enlightenment, but when Shakyamuni gave up asceticism they left him. After his enlightenment he returned to the Deer Park and expounded to these five ascetics the teachings that became the *Agon* sutras.

21. The *Hōdō* (Vaipulya) sutras are those preached in the Hōdō period, the third of the five periods of preaching whose classification is ascribed to T'ien-t'ai (*Tendai Shikyō Gi*, T46, 774c). Included are the Vimalakirti Sutra, the Sūraṅgama Sutra, etc. The *Kambutsu Zammai* Sutra is in T15, no. 643; the Māyā Sutra in T12, no. 383. The Trayastriṁśā Heaven is the Heaven of the Thirty-three Gods. It is the second of the six heavens in the world of desire. Located on a plateau atop Mount Sumeru, it is ruled over by Taishaku from a palace in the center. Eight gods reside on each of the four peaks that stand at the corners of the plateau. Māyā, the mother of Shakyamuni, died shortly after his birth and is said to have been reborn in this heaven.

22. The ten stages of faith are the first ten of the fifty-two stages of bodhisattva practice. Those on the verge of full enlightenment are in the fifty-first stage *(tōgaku)*, the last before attaining Buddhahood.

23. The highest of the five types of vision. They are: 1) the eye of the common people or man; 2) the divine eye, that of heaven; 3) the eye of wisdom, that of *shōmon* and *engaku;* 4) the eye of the Law, that of the bodhisattva; and 5) the Buddha eye that perceives all things in the past, present, and future.

24. An epithet for the Buddha because he dispels darkness and illusions. The term is found in the Nirvana Sutra (T12, 480a).

25. The period when people are sure to attain enlightenment by practicing the Buddha's teachings (Jap *gedatsu kengo*).

26. The period in which people will practice meditation in order to perceive the truth (Jap *zenjō kengo*). The above two five-hundred-year periods represent the *shōbō,* the period of the True Law, or the Former Day of the Law.

27. The period when people will concentrate on reading and copying the sutras and listening to lectures on them (Jap *dokuju tamon kengo*).

28. The period when numerous temples and stupas are built (Jap *tazō tōji kengo*). The above two five-hundred-year periods represent the *zōhō* (or *zōbō*), the period of the Simulated Law, or the Middle Day of the Law.

29. The last five hundred years refers to the last of the five-hundred-year periods, the beginning of *mappō,* the Degenerate Age, or the Latter Day of the Law. The quotation and the descriptions of the various periods are drawn from the *Daijuku* Sutra (T13, 363a).

30. *Anraku Shū,* T47, 13c.

31. The following passage is based on the *Senchaku Shū,* T83, 17a.

32. The *Jūjūbibasha Ron* discusses the "difficult-to-practice" and the "easy-to-practice ways" (T26, 41a). The difficult way is the exertion of strenuous effort over countless kalpas in order to achieve enlightenment. The easy way, as practiced by the Pure Land school, is to rely on the power of Amida

Buddha for salvation. T'an-luan follows this classification in his *Ōjō Ron Chū*, T40, 826a.

33. *Anraku Shū*, T47, 13c.

34. *Ōjō Raisan*, T47, 439c.

35. The *Muryōju, Kammuryōju,* and *Amida* sutras.

36. *Ōjō Raisan*, T47, 439c.

37. *Anraku Shū*, T47, 13c.

38. The seven major Nara temples are Tōdai-ji, Kōfuku-ji, Gangō-ji, Daian-ji, Yakushi-ji, Saidai-ji, and Hōryū-ji.

39. T13, 363b.

40. T9, 54c. *See* glossary under *Kōsen rufu.*

41. T9, 46a.

42. T9, 38c.

43. T9, 31b.

44. T9, 39a.

45. Demons that drain human vitality.

46. T9, 54c.

47. T13, 363b.

48. All three of these quotations appear in a verse in the *Kanji* (thirteenth) chapter; it details the three powerful enemies who will attack the votaries of the Lotus Sutra in the evil latter age. The first quote comes from the passage: "There will be monks in that evil age with perverse views and hearts that are fawning and crooked who will say they have attained what they have not attained, being proud and boastful at heart." The second comes from the passage: "Or there will be forest-dwelling monks wearing clothing of patched rags and living in retirement who will claim they are practicing the true Way, despising and looking down on the rest of mankind." The third comes from the passage: "In a muddied kalpa, in an evil age there will be many different things to fear. Demons will take possession of others and through them curse, revile, and heap shame on us." (T9, 36b–c).

49. Nichiren.

50. Reference is probably to the Ritsu priest Ryōkan Ninshō (1217–1303) and the Chinese Zen priest Lan-ch'i Tao-lung (Rankei Dōrru, 1213–1278), among others.

51. They include extending the long, broad tongue to the Brahma Heaven, emitting light from the pores, etc.

52. T9, 52a. The text reads only: "Namu Shakyamuni Buddha, Namu Shakyamuni Buddha." Nichiren has added the "Nam-myoho-renge-kyo."

53. *Hokke Mongu*, T34, 2c.

54. *Hokke Mongu Ki*, T34, 157b.

55. *Shugo Kokkai Shō*, T74, 177b–c.

56. In other words, Japan.

57. The five impurities or defilements are: impurity of the kalpa or age; of desire or agony; of beings; of thought or views; and of the life span itself. They are listed in the *Hōben* (second) chapter of the Lotus Sutra.

58. *Hokke Shūku*, DDZ 3, 251.

59. One of the four kalpas set forth in ancient Indian cosmology: the

Kalpa of Formation, the Kalpa of Continuance, the Kalpa of Decline, and the Kalpa of Disintegration. During the Kalpa of Continuance, a cyclical increase and decrease in the human life span repeats itself nineteen times. The "ninth kalpa of decrease" means the ninth period of decrease.

60. The third division of the threefold world. A purely spiritual realm, the world of formlessness is free from the restrictions of matter.

61. This story appears in the *Kako Genzai Inga* Sutra (T3, 626c ff.)

62. Emperor Wu (464–549) of the Liang strongly supported Buddhism and was himself an active practitioner. The story appears in Miao-lo's *Maka Shikan Bugyoden Guketsu* (T46, 214b). Udraka Rāmaputra was a hermit and the second teacher under whom Shakyamuni practiced. He is said to have been reborn in the highest of the four realms in the world of formlessness.

63. Nichiren's argument is as follows: The point is that Devadatta, though destined to incur retribution for his evil deeds, had at least formed a connection with Buddhism. In the pre-Lotus sutras and in the theoretical teaching or first fourteen chapters of the Lotus Sutra, Shakyamuni did not reveal his identity as one who had gained enlightenment in the remote past. Nāgārjuna and Vasubandhu appeared in the Former and Middle Days of the Law, when the pre-Lotus Sutra and theoretical teachings spread. The Bodhisattvas of the Earth, appearing in the *Yujutsu* (fifteenth) chapter of the Lotus Sutra, are alone considered capable of being entrusted with the propagation in the Latter Day of the Law.

64. All the men in this and the two preceding paragraphs comprise the twenty-four successors who are said to have inherited Shakyamuni's lineage.

65. The ten mystic principles (Jap *jūmyō*) are set forth by T'ien-t'ai in the *Hokke Gengi* (T33, 697–717) in explanation of the character *myō* of *Myōhōrenge kyō*, the title of the Lotus Sutra. There are two categories of these ten mystical principles, ten for the theoretical teaching and ten for the essential teaching.

66. This passage refers to the "three standards of comparison" (Jap *sanshu no kyōsō*) enumerated by T'ien-t'ai in his *Hokke Gengi* (T33, 683b) to assert the superiority of the Lotus Sutra over other sutras. The first standard is whether or not a particular sutra can lead people of all capacities to enlightenment (sutras other than the Lotus Sutra do not say that all can attain enlightenment). The second standard is whether or not the process of teaching is revealed from beginning to end (this is revealed in the Lotus Sutra, where in the *Kejōyu* [seventh] chapter it is explained that the Buddha implanted the seed of Buddhahood in the distant past and will lead individuals to Buddhahood through this sutra). The third standard is whether or not the relationship between master (the Buddha) and disciple is clarified (sutras other than the Lotus Sutra explain that Shakyamuni attained Buddhahood in this present life; the Lotus Sutra explains in the *Juryō* [sixteenth] chapter that he attained it in the distant past of *gohyaku jintengo* and that he has been instructing his disciples since that time). In this passage "whether or not the process of instruction is revealed from beginning to end" corresponds to the second standard; "whether or not the original relationship between master and disciple is clarified" corresponds to the third standard; and "which teach-

ing would lead to enlightenment and which would not" corresponds to the first standard.

67. Reference is to the year 67 A.D., the traditional date for the introduction of Buddhism to China during the reign of Emperor Ming of the Later Han.

68. Here, "exoteric and esoteric teachings" refers to the classification of the four teachings of method (Jap *kegi no shikyō*) discussed by T'ien-t'ai in the *Hokke Mongu* (T34, 3b). This is a classification of Shakyamuni's teachings according to the manner in which they were expounded: sudden, gradual, secret, and indeterminate or variable. The secret teaching is here termed "esoteric," while the other three categories correspond to "exoteric."

69. Two Indian monks said to have introduced Buddhism into China. The Sanskrit for Chu-fa-lan is unknown. Legend has it that in 67 A.D. they traveled from India to Lo-yang at the request of Emperor Ming of the Later Han dynasty and translated the *Shijūnishō* Sutra at the Pai-ma-ssu in Lo-yang.

70. A designation by T'ien-t'ai of the different systems of classification used by different schools during the Northern and Southern dynasties period. They are discussed in the *Hokke Gengi* (T33, 801a–b).

71. Chih-i is the name by which "the Great Teacher T'ien-t'ai" is usually called, although Nichiren almost invariably refers to him by this posthumous title. Chih-che is another title awarded him. He lived from 538 to 597 or approximately five hundred years after 67 A.D., the traditional date for the introduction of Buddhism into China.

72. T'ai-tsung (598–649) was the second emperor of the T'ang dynasty.

73. The twelve divisions of the scriptures is a classification of all the Buddhist canonical writings in accordance with their presentation, style, and content. The eighty thousand sacred teachings indicate the totality of the Buddha's teachings.

74. The Three Rulers (Fu Hsi, Shen Nung, and Huang Ti) and Five Emperors (Shao Hao, Chuan Hsü, Ti Kao, T'ang Yao, and Yü Shun) are legendary figures of Chinese antiquity.

75. Kao-ch'ang was a kingdom in the southern foothills of the T'ien-shan mountains. It was conquered by Emperor T'ai-tsung in 640. Koguryŏ was an ancient kingdom in what is now North Korea. It was conquered by Emperor Kao-tsung in 668.

76. Fa-tsang (643–712) was the third patriarch of the Kegon school in China and was a systematizer of the doctrine of the school. He lectured on the *Kegon* Sutra at the request of Empress Wu.

77. The three mysteries of body, speech, and mind is a doctrine of Shingon Buddhism. In terms of practice, the mystery of the body refers to mudras, the mystery of speech to mantras, and the mystery of the mind to Shingon meditation practices. By practicing these three mysteries, the body, speech, and mind of the practitioner are identified as they are with the body, speech, and mind of Dainichi Buddha, thus enabling one to gain enlightenment in his present form.

78. The traditional date for the introduction of Buddhism to Japan is in the thirteenth year of the reign of Emperor Kimmei (552).

79. Emperor Kimmei is now regarded as the twenty-ninth emperor because the administration of the fifteenth ruler, Empress Jingū, is no longer considered a formal reign. In Nichiren's time, however, she was included in the lineage, thus accounting for the designation of Emperor Kimmei as the thirtieth emperor.

80. Another name for Prince Shōtoku (574–622).

81. Emperor Kōtoku (596–654) reigned from 645 to 654. He is currently counted as the thirty-sixth emperor.

82. Kanroku (Kor Kwalluk, dates unknown) was a seventh-century priest from Paekche in Korea, who, according to the *Honchō Kōsō Den* (DBZ 102, 27) is said to have brought the Sanron and Jōjitsu teachings to Japan, as well as works relating to astronomy, the calendar, and geography in 602. The accuracy of this account is in doubt.

83. Dōshō (629–700) was the founder of the Hossō sect in Japan. In 653 he went to China where he studied under Hsüan-tsang for eight years.

84. Empress Genshō reigned 715–723. Mention of Shan-wu-wei's stay in Japan appears in the *Genkō Shakusho* (DBZ 101, 12). The story is quite apocryphal but was widely held as true in Nichiren's time.

85. Emperor Shōmu (701–756), reigned 724–749, was a staunch supporter of Buddhism. He established temples in each province in the country, that came to be known as Kokubun-ji, and founded the Tōdai-ji in Nara as well.

86. Shinjō (Kor Simsang, d. 742) was the founder of the Japanese Kegon sect. He studied in China under Fa-tsang before coming to Japan. His biography is in *Honchō Kōsō Den* (DBZ 102, 30).

87. Rōben, also read Ryōben (689–773), was the successor to Shinjō and devoted himself to the construction of the Tōdai-ji. In 752 he was appointed its first chief priest.

88. Better known by the Japanese reading of his name, Ganjin (688–763). He made several attempts to reach Japan but failed five times because of shipwrecks or pirate attacks. He finally arrived in 754 and founded the Ritsu sect. Ganjin brought to Japan many of T'ien-t'ai's writings, although he did not spread his teachings.

89. Reference is to the Tendai sect which is based on the Lotus Sutra.

90. Gyōhyō (722–797) was a disciple of the Chinese Discipline Master Tao-hsüan (702–760) who came to Japan in 736. Gyōhyō studied Kegon, Zen, Ritsu, and Hossō, but concentrated on meditation techniques. Saichō (Dengyō Daishi) studied under him for six years at the Kokubun-ji in Ōmi.

91. The Kokubun-ji in Ōmi where Saichō first became a monk was known as Kokushō-ji. The name also refers to the Hieizan-ji, or Mount Hiei temple, founded by Saichō, later to become the Enryaku-ji.

92. The vow to spread the teachings of Buddhism and lead the people to salvation.

93. Reference is to the so-called debate of 802 at Takaosan-ji, frequently alluded to in Nichiren's writings.

94. With "perfect meditation and wisdom" Nichiren refers to the three types of learning or disciplines (Jap *sangaku*): precepts, meditation, and wis-

dom, as interpreted by T'ien-t'ai. Where T'ien-t'ai concerned himself with meditation and wisdom in terms of the Lotus Sutra, he continued to make use of Hinayana precepts and ordination.

95. The ordination ceremony in which one receives ten major precepts and forty-eight minor precepts, as set forth in the *Bommō* Sutra (T24, 1005a).

96. On the first day of the ninth month, 805, Dengyō administered a set of precepts and *kanjō,* the symbolic sprinkling of water, on the eight eminent priests of the six sects. They were Dōshō (756–816), Shūen (771–835), Gonsō (758–827), Enchō (771–837), Shōnō (n.d.), Shōshū (n.d.), Kōen (n.d.), and Kōi (737–814). *Eizan Daishi Den, DDZ* 5, Furoku, 24.

97. The Sanron, Hossō, Kegon, Kusha, Jōjitsu, Ritsu, Tendai, and Shingon sects.

98. T13, 363b.

99. Hui-tsung (1081–1135) and Ch'in-tsung (1100–1161) were the eighth and ninth emperors of the Northern Sung dynasty. The "northern barbarians" were Jurchen, a nomadic people of Manchuria, who established the Chin dynasty in northern China. They captured the Sung capital of K'ai-feng in 1126.

100. Kao-tsung (1107–1187) was the first emperor of the Southern Sung dynasty. Lin-an is the present-day city of Hang-chou.

101. This refers to the Mongol invasion of 1274.

102. A passage from the *Muryōgi* Sutra (T9, 386b), which is here considered as introductory to the Lotus Sutra. In the text Shakyamuni states: "In these more than forty years I have not yet revealed the truth." This is interpreted to mean that all his prior teachings were provisional or expedient.

103. A classification of the four ways of coming into existence: 1) birth from the womb; 2) birth from eggs; 3) birth from moisture, as worms were believed to be born; and 4) birth by transformation, as in the case of beings in heavens or hells. It was held that such beings, after the end of their previous lifetimes, suddenly appear in these realms due to their karma, without the help of parents or other intermediary agencies.

104. T9, 6a.

105. The highest heaven in the world of form.

106. Nichiren himself.

107. *Nehangyō Sho,* T38, 80b.

108. Dammira (Skt unknown) was a king of Kashmir in northern India who destroyed the Buddhist temples and stupas in his kingdom. It is said that when he killed the Buddhist teacher Āryasiṁha, he lost his right hand and died seven days later. *Fu Hōzō Innen Den,* T50, 321c.

109. Fa-tao (1086–1147) was a priest of Sung China. When Emperor Hui-tsung, a Taoist follower, acted to suppress Buddhism, Fa-tao remonstrated with him, for which he was branded on the face and exiled to Tao-chou. He was later pardoned, but Hui-tsung was captured by the invading Chin forces and taken to Manchuria, where he lived until his death in 1135. *Busso Tōki,* T49, 421a.

110. The outermost of eight circular mountains said to surround Mt. Sumeru. Here it is mentioned to suggest impregnability.

111. These condemnations of the Lotus Sutra by Pure Land and Shingon practitioners have appeared previously. Shan-tao's remark is found in the *Ōjō Raisan*, T47, 439c; Tao-ch'o's in the *Anraku Shū*, T47, 13c. Kōbō Daishi's comment is from the *Hizō Hōyaku*, T77, 374c.

112. T9, 46a.

113. T9, 34a.

114. T9, 39a.

115. T9, 59b.

116. T9, 39b.

117. This refers to the earthquake of the twenty-third day of the eighth month of Shōka 1 (1257).

118. This refers to a comet (an evil omen) that appeared on the fifth day of the seventh month of Bun'ei 1 (1264).

119. This statement, attributed to Paramārtha (499–569), is found in the *Hokke Denki* (T51, 52c), compiled by the T'ang dynasty priest Seng-hsiang (n.d.).

120. Kakutoku is a monk mentioned in the Nirvana Sutra. At the end of the Former Day of the Law following the death of the Buddha Kangi Zō-yaku, Kakutoku appeared and remonstrated with the monks who were guilty of breaking the precepts. They attacked him with swords and staves. At that time the king, Utoku, fought against the monks to protect the orthodox Buddhist teachings. Kakutoku escaped, but Utoku died of the wounds he had sustained. It is said that King Utoku was reborn as Shakyamuni Buddha and Kakutoku as Kashō Buddha. T12, 383c–384a.

121. These "predictions" are found in the Māyā Sutra (T12, 1013c) and the *Daijō Nyū Ryōga* Sutra (T16, 627c). The text of the passage in this sutra suggests concepts expressed by Nāgārjuna in the *Chū Ron*. For this reason Nichiren apparently felt that the passage predicted the teachings found in that treatise.

122. The four-phrase verse (T30, 33b) referred to is: "We speak of all things as empty / which are dependent in origination / They are no more than existence in name only / This is the Middle Way."

123. The four teachings are the tripitaka teaching, the connecting or shared teaching, the specific or differentiated teaching, and the perfect teaching. The three truths (Jap *santai*) are the truth of emptiness *(kūtai)*, the truth of temporary existence *(ketai)*, and the truth of the Middle Way *(chūtai)*.

124. *Hokke Gengi*, T33, 713c.

125. *Maka Shikan*, T46, 55a.

126. *Hokke Gengi Shakusen*, T33. 868b.

127. Ts'ung-i (1042–1091) was a Sung Tendai scholar. His *Hokke San-daibu Fuchū* in fourteen volumes (ZZ1, 43, 5–44, 3) contains a passage to this effect, although the exact quotation has not been found.

128. *Ben Kemmitsu Nikyō Ron*, T77, 378b. The *Bodaishin Ron* is found in T32, no. 1665.

129. "Actual events" refer to predictions and events contained in the Lotus Sutra, such as the dragon king's daughter attaining Buddhahood in the space of a moment.

130. T19 (no. 1000), 596b. The work contains esoteric rituals based on the Lotus Sutra.

131. Translations made before the time of Hsüan-tsang are referred to as "old translations." His and subsequent translations are known as "new translations."

132. The biography of Kumārajīva appears in the *Kōsō Den*, T50, 330a–333a.

133. *Hokke Mongu Ki*, T34, 341a. The "sage" referred to here is Vasubandhu. Miao-lo attributed an error in Vasubandhu's commentary on the Lotus Sutra, the *Hokke Ron*, to the translator. Nichiren, in the following statement: "that is not to be attributed to any fault of the Buddha," uses Miao-lo's statement to refer to the Buddha.

134. These four guidelines are: 1) "causes and circumstances," to interpret the words and phrases of the sutra in terms of the causes and circumstances that prompted the Buddha to expound them; 2) "correlated teachings," to interpret the sutra's words and phrases in terms of the four teachings and five periods; 3) "the theoretical and essential teachings," to interpret them in light of the theoretical and essential teachings of the Lotus Sutra; and 4) "the observation of the mind," to perceive the truth within one's own mind through the practice of meditation.

135. Chi-tsang (549–623) is also known as Chia-hsiang and is sometimes regarded as the founder of the Sanron school. He wrote commentaries on the three treatises *Chū Ron*, *Hyaku Ron*, and *Jūnimon Ron*, asserting that among the various sutras, the *Hannya* sutras expounded the supreme teaching.

136. This passage refers to the Chinese maxim that a sage appears only once in a thousand years, and a worthy man only once in five hundred years.

137. The sweet-smelling beverage of the gods that is said to remove one's sufferings and make one immortal.

138. This statement appears in the *Kokusei Hyakuroku*, compiled by Chang-an, T'ien-t'ai's successor. T46, 822a.

139. Cited from the *Zui Tendai Chisha Daishi Betsuden*, T50, 191c–192a. Tao-hsüan (596–667) is the founder of the Nan-shan branch of the Ritsu school. He is the compiler of a large number of works, including the *Zoku Kōsō Den*.

140. *Kegon Gokyō Shō* (full title: *Kegon Ichijō Kyōgi Bunzai Shō*, T45, 481a). The first stage of security is the eleventh of the fifty-two stages of bodhisattva practice. *See* Fifty-two stages in glossary.

141. The story of Han-kuang and Pu-k'ung and the Indian monk appears in the *Sō Kōsō Den* (T50, 879b) under the biography of Han-kuang (n.d.). Han-kuang is counted among the six major disciples of Pu-k'ung.

142. The *Hokke Mongu Ki* (T34, 359c) repeats the above story and remarks that just as the people of Lu failed to recognize the greatness of Confucius, so the people of China failed to recognize the greatness of T'ien-t'ai's teachings.

143. The ordination platforms at Tōdai-ji in Nara, Yakushi-ji in Shimotsuke, and Kanzeon-ji in Tsukushi.

144. This is not a precise quotation. Dengyō Daishi discusses the six difficult and nine easy acts in the *Hokke Shūku*, DDZ 3, 273.

145. The present major kalpa (Jap *kengō*) in which a thousand Buddhas of great wisdom are said to appear to save the people.

146. *Yojana* is the distance an army can march in a day; a *ri* is given as six *chō* (0.65 km.); in the Heian period it was understood as 36 *chō* (3.93 km.). One *chō* is about 300 feet. All these figures are approximate and differ with the time and source.

147. Of the fourteen priests of the seven major Nara temples listed here, information is available only for Zengi (729–812), a Sanron priest from Daian-ji, Gonsō (758–827), a Sanron priest connected with Saidai-ji, Shūen (771–835), a Hossō priest from Kōfuku-ji, and Dōshō (756–816), a celebrated Hossō scholar.

148. The two teachings are: 1) those for *shōmon* and *engaku* and 2) those expounded for bodhisattvas. The three periods is a classification by the Sanron school of the Buddhist teachings into three periods: 1) the teaching that both mind and objective reality are real; 2) the teaching that objective reality is without substance and that mind alone is real; and 3) the teaching that both mind and objective reality are without substance. Both concepts are discussed in the *Hokke Gisho* (T34, 484a). The thrice-turned wheel refers to three categories of the Buddha's teachings as expounded by Chi-tsang in his *Hokke Yūi* (T34, 634a ff.). They are: 1) the basic teachings designed for bodhisattvas, as first preached by Shakyamuni Buddha (in other words, the *Kegon* Sutra); 2) the teachings of the *Agon, Hōdō*, and *Hannya* sutras, designed for those of inferior capacity; and 3) the teaching that unites the three vehicles into one: the Lotus Sutra.

149. The Hossō school classifies the Buddhist teachings into three periods on the basis of order of preaching and content. The first period comprises the *Agon* sutras, in which the Buddha taught that the self was without substance but that the elements of existence (dharmas) were real. In the second period, characterized by the *Hannya* sutras, he taught that all things were empty. In the third period, represented by the *Kegon, Gejimmitsu*, and Lotus sutras, attachment to the idea that dharmas are either real or non-substantial is refuted. The five natures are a classification of human beings in terms of capacity. They are: 1) those predestined to become *shōmon*; 2) those predestined to become *engaku*; 3) those predestined to become bodhisattvas; 4) an indeterminate group comprising those who possess two or more of the *shōmon, engaku*, and bodhisattva natures; and 5) those who do not have the nature of enlightenment and thus can never escape from the six paths. These concepts are described in the *Gejimmitsu* Sutra, T16, 693a ff.

150. The four teachings is a classification devised by Fa-tsang's disciple Hui-yüan (n.d.) in his *Zoku Kegongyō Ryakusho Kanjō Ki* (ZZ1, 5, 1–3) that differs from Fa-tsang's classification (Hinayana, early Mahayana, late Mahayana, sudden, and complete [*Kegon Gokyō Shō*, T45, 481b]). The root and branch teachings are described in the *Kegon Yui* (T34, 634a). The *Kegon* Sutra represents the root and the Lotus Sutra the branch. The six forms (Jap *rokusō*)

are described in Fa-tsang's *Kegon Gokyō Shō* (T45, 507c) and represent the analysis of the phenomenal world on the basis of both diversity and identity. The ten mysteries (Jap *jūgen*) are described in Chih-yen's *Kegon Ichijō Jūgen-mon* (T45, 515b ff.) and appear in a somewhat altered form in the *Kegon Gokyō Shō* (T45, 499a). The ten mysteries represent the different aspects of the interrelationship of all phenomena.

151. Wake no Hiroyo (d. 809) and Ōtomo no Kunimichi (768–828).

152. Emperor Kammu.

153. *See* n. 135.

154. Reference is to the Three Great Secret Laws (Jap *sandai hihō*), referred to indirectly in the "Repaying Debts of Gratitude" and elsewhere. They represent the *honzon* (object of worship), *daimoku* (invocation), and *kaidan* (sanctuary) that Nichiren identifies as hidden in the *Juryō* (sixteenth) chapter of the Lotus Sutra.

155. Hsüan-tsang is said to have died and been reborn six times on his perilous journey to India.

156. An asōgi (Skt *asamkhya*) kalpa is one of immense length, one asōgi representing ten to the fifty-ninth power. Prince Satta, Shakyamuni in a previous incarnation, offered his body to a starving tigress that had given birth to seven cubs (*Konkōmyō* Sutra, T16, 354b). The invisible crown on a Buddha's head is one of the eighty minor marks of a Buddha.

157. The refutation of Nembutsu, Zen, and Shingon, mentioned in the following paragraph.

158. One of the eight wonders of the ocean, described in the Nirvana Sutra (T12, 558c).

159. Reference is to a passage in the forty-volume *Kegon* Sutra in which the god of the earth refuses to protect three kinds of people: those who cause the death of their king, those who are unfilial towards their parents, and those who deny the law of cause and effect or slander the three treasures (T19, 715a).

160. Monks, nuns, laymen, and laywomen.

161. Omuro is another name for the Ninna-ji, a Shingon temple in Kyoto. It is also the title of a retired emperor or prince who entered the priesthood and lived at this temple. Here reference is to Prince Dōjo (1196–1249), the second son of Emperor Gotoba.

162. Reference is to the supervisors at Mt. Kōya, the Kumano shrines, and elsewhere.

163. The sacred mirror is one of the three imperial regalia, the others being the sword and the jewel. The mirror was lost in a fire in 960.

164. The sword was lost in the battle of Dannoura in 1185 in which the Minamoto clan defeated the Taira forces.

165. The five fierce deities, Fudō Myōō, Gōsanze, Gundari, Daiitoku, and Kongōyasha, that destroy demons at the behest of the five Buddhas of the Diamond Realm.

166. According to the *Daichido Ron,* a kalpa is longer than the time required to wear away a cube of stone forty *ri* on each side, if a heavenly

nymph alights on it and brushes it with a piece of cloth once every hundred years (T25, 100c).

167. Jikaku Daishi is the posthumous title of Ennin (794–866), the third chief priest of Enryaku-ji. He went to China in 838 where he studied both T'ien-t'ai and esoteric teachings, returning in 847. *See also* glossary.

168. Annen (841–889?) was a Tendai priest, the disciple of Jikaku Daishi. He was chief priest of Genkyō-ji in Kyoto and was the author of a large number of works on Tendai esoteric teachings.

169. Tao-ch'o in the *Anraku Shū* (T47, 13c) divided Buddhist teachings into the Sacred Way, those teachings that required practice in this world through one's own efforts, and those that advocated rebirth in the Pure Land, relying on the power of Amida Buddha (Jap *Shōdō Jōdo Nimon*).

170. Shan-tao, in his *Kammuryōjubutsu Kyō Sho* (T37, 272a) spoke of sundry practices and correct practices. The sundry practices were all those other than the correct, or Pure Land teaching (Jap *zōgyō shōgyō*).

171. Eshin Sōzu or Genshin (942–1017) was a celebrated Tendai priest who compiled the *Ōjō Yōshū*, or "Essentials of Salvation" (T84, no. 2682), that advocated Pure Land teachings.

172. Yōkan (1032–1111), also known as Eikan, studied Kegon, Hossō, and esoteric doctrines and was associated with the Tōdai-ji in Nara. He later converted to Pure Land teachings. His *Ōjō Jūin*, or "Ten Conditions for Rebirth in the Pure Land" (T84, no. 2683), was written in 1104.

173. *Senchaku Shū*, T83, 17a.

174. Kenshin (1130–1192) was the sixty-first chief priest of Enryaku-ji, but converted to the Pure Land teachings while still the chief priest of a Tendai temple.

175. Hōnen was exiled to Tosa in 1207 by Emperor Gotoba, who was later unsuccessful in his attempt to rebel against the Kamakura shogunate, an incident known as the Jōkyū Disturbance.

176. The vehicles of *shōmon*, *engaku*, and bodhisattva.

177. I-hsing (683–727), a disciple of Shan-wu-wei, translated numerous esoteric works and was responsible for compiling his teacher's commentary on the *Dainichi* Sutra. He was famed also as a mathematician and astronomer.

178. An honorific title for a teacher or eminent priest (Jap *ajari*).

179. Kongōsatta in Japanese, the second of the first eight patriarchs of Shingon. He is said to have received the teaching directly from Dainichi Buddha.

180. The mysteries of body, speech, and mind.

181. Some of the material in the above quotation may derive from the *Dai Birushana Jōbutsu Kyō Sho* (T39, no. 1796) compiled by I-hsing.

182. He is said to have been a descendant of an Indian royal family and was greatly favored by Emperor Hsüan-tsung.

183. Dengyō Daishi sought permission to establish an ordination center for the Mahayana precepts in 819. This attempt was strongly opposed by the priests of the six sects of Nara. Permission was finally granted in 827, a week after his death.

184. The *Ebyō Tendai Shū* (DDZ3, 334 ff.) was written by Dengyō Daishi in 813. It contains thirteen sections designed to demonstrate how Buddhist scholars of various schools in China based their teachings on the doctrines of T'ien-t'ai.

185. Kōbō Daishi went to China in 804; Dengyō Daishi sailed in the same fleet but on a different ship.

186. Hui-kuo (746–805) was a disciple of Pu-k'ung and is counted as the seventh patriarch of Shingon in China. He was Kōbō Daishi's teacher.

187. Where Kegon ranked its teachings as the tenth and highest, Kōbō Daishi, in his *Jūjūshin Ron* placed Shingon tenth, Kegon ninth, and the Lotus Sutra eighth.

188. *Hizō Hōyaku,* T77, 374c.

189. Ibid., T77, 371a, 373a.

190. *Ben Kemmitsu Nikyō Ron,* T77, 378c. Following the frequently-used classification of the Buddhist teachings into five categories, likening them to the five flavors of fresh milk, cream, curdled milk, butter, and ghee, Kōbō Daishi classified Mahayana sutras, including the Lotus Sutra under butter, and the Shingon teachings under ghee.

191. Ibid., T77, 379a.

192. Prajñā (Chin Pan-jo; Jap Hannya, 744–810?) was a native of Kashmir who arrived in Canton in 781 and in Ch'ang-an in 790. He translated a large number of works, including the *Rokuharamitsu* Sutra.

193. A famous Hossō priest, frequently mentioned by Nichiren. Also known as Tokuichi.

194. *See* n. 149.

195. This statement, attributed to Tokuitsu, is found in the *Shugo Kokkai Shō,* T74, 145a.

196. *Hokke Ron* T26, 7b.

197. *Daichido Ron* T25, 107a.

198. Those, mentioned above, who compared the Lotus Sutra to ghee.

199. These anecdotes are mentioned in the *Shih Chi.* Tan, the Duke of Chou, was a younger brother of Emperor Wu of the Chou dynasty. He implemented a number of reforms in state affairs and established a firm foundation for the dynasty. He was so eager to find able persons and anxious not to overlook anyone that he would receive visitors even while washing his hair or during the course of a meal. The reference to Confucius is to a passage in the *Analects,* 16:10.

200. Shōkaku-bō is the temple name of Kakuban (1095–1143), the precursor of the Shingi, or New Doctrine school of Shingon. The Dembō-in was the temple he established on Mt. Kōya. After it was moved to Negoro it became the head temple of the Shingi school. The *Shari Kōshiki* is a compilation of lectures on the occasion of ceremonies in honor of the Buddha's relics. The following quotation (*Kōgyō Daishi Zenshū,* v. 2, 1283) refers to the Buddha of the Nondual Mahayana, in other words Dainichi Buddha, who represents the basic oneness of the Womb and Diamond Realms. The three-bodied donkey- or ox-Buddha signifies the Buddha who expounded the exoteric teachings, including the Lotus Sutra, that is Shakyamuni. The three

bodies of a Buddha are the Dharma body, the Reward body, and the Manifested body. The donkey or ox may also be interpreted as the exposed ox or the ox on bare ground, also indicative of the exoteric teachings. The twofold mandala refers to the Diamond and Womb Realm mandalas used in the esoteric teachings.

201. The following story, including the details concerning Bhadraruci (Jap Kenai Ronshi), is based on a passage in *Daitō Saiiki Ki*, T51, 935c–936a.

202. The consecration ceremony in which water is poured on the head of the person to be initiated (Jap *kanjō*).

203. Possibly a reference to the *Busso Rekidai Tsūsai* (T49, 598c), which relates how, when Emperor Su-tsung of the T'ang asked the priest Hui-chung about the meditation in which there is no distinction between self and others, Hui-chung replied that the emperor should step on the head of the Buddha.

204. San-chieh, more commonly known as Hsin-hsing (540–594), was the founder of the San-chieh, or Three Stages school, that flourished during the Sui dynasty. Hsin-hsing, basing his calculations on one of many theories, claimed that the Latter Day of the Law had arrived in 550 A.D. and that, in this degenerate world, there was no alternative other than to practice a universal teaching that did not distinguish the efficacy of various sutras. He held that the Buddha nature was inherent in all sentient beings. The school acquired enormous wealth that was eventually confiscated; it was banned in 713.

205. This story appears in the *Hokke Denki* (T51, 92b) and in the *Shakumon Jikyō Roku* (T51, 806c).

206. Annen has two works of similar title but differing content: *Kyōji Jō* and *Kyōji Jōron*. The passage cited is from *Kyōji Jō* (T75, 362a–b). Annen ranked the Sanron sect fifth, the Hossō sect sixth, the Ritsu sect seventh, the Jōjitsu sect eighth, and the Kusha sect ninth.

207. "Shikan" (meditation and insight) here refers to the entire Tendai meditation system and "Shingon" to the esoteric practices added to it.

208. *Sange Gakushō Shiki*, DDZ 1, 6. The Shikan-in, also called the Ichijō shikan-in, is another name for the Kompon Chūdō, the main temple building on Mt. Hiei.

209. Gishin (781–833) was Dengyō Daishi's disciple and accompanied him to China in 804. He was the first head priest of the Enryaku-ji and in 827 established an ordination platform on Mt. Hiei, fulfilling his teacher's wishes.

210. Enchō (772–837) was the second head priest of Enryaku-ji. He studied under Dengyō Daishi and was appointed head priest by imperial decree in 833.

211. These eight distinguished priests are variously given. Annen, in his *Taizōkai Daihō Taijuki* (T75, 54a) lists eight priests, the *Genkō Shakusho* (DBZ 101, 170 ff.) eleven. They are generally listed as the Shingon priests: Tsung-jui, Ch'üan-ya, Yüan-cheng, I-chen, Fa-ch'üan, Pao-yüeh, K'an, and Wei-chin.

212. Kuang-hsiu (771–843) is eighth in the Tendai lineage in China. He

was a disciple of Tao-sui, one of the Chinese teachers of Dengyō Daishi. Wei-chüan (n.d.) is Kuang-hsiu's disciple.

213. One of the three areas *(santō)* into which Mt. Hiei is divided. The Tōdō, the principal area, encompasses the Kompon Chūdō and other large buildings. Other areas were the Saitō, established by Enchō, and Yokawa, established by Ennin.

214. The *Kongōchō Daikyōōgyō Sho* (T61, no. 2223) and the *Soshitsuji Karakyō Ryakusho* (T61, no. 2227).

215. *Jikaku Daishi Den (Zoku Gunsho Ruiju,* v. 8, pt. 2, 692–693).

216. Nirvana Sutra, T12, 401b, 642a.

217. A rephrasing of a passage in the *Jūjūbibasha Ron,* T26, 53c.

218. *Hokke Gengi,* T33, 800a.

219. *Hokke Shūku,* DDZ 3, 245.

220. Nichiren is referring to a variety of stories of the miraculous powers of paintings and statues. Such stories appear in the *Āgamas* and elsewhere. In Japan the *Genkō Shakusho* (DBZ 101, 480) relates how a statue of the Bodhisattva Miroku at a nunnery in Katsuragi in Yamato alerted a guard that it was about to be stolen, and how a statue of Yakushi at the Teiden-ji in Tōtōmi called out to be rescued from the bottom of a river, and thus was saved.

221. This story appears in the *Daihatsu Nehangyō Gobun,* T12, 911b.

222. The *Daichido Ron* (T25, 80c) states that Subhadra had a dream in which all people were deprived of their eyesight, the sun fell from the sky, the seas ran dry, and Mt. Sumeru was toppled by a great wind. Awaking, he was seized with fear. When Subhadra could not determine the meaning of the dream, a heavenly being appeared and told him that the Buddha would enter nirvana that night. Subhadra accordingly went to Shakyamuni to receive instruction in the teachings.

223. This story appears in the *Jō-agon, Zōichi-agon,* and elsewhere.

224. This story appears in *Buppon Gyōjikkyō* (T3, 674b) and in *Shakushi Fu* (T50, 85a).

225. A reference to the Mongol invasion of 1274, a year before "The Selection of the Time" was written. The invasion was thwarted by a storm that heavily damaged the Mongol fleet, forcing it to withdraw.

226. A reference to the Jōkyū Disturbance, the Retired Emperor Gotoba's unsuccessful attempt to overthrow the Kamakura government.

227. Hōjō Yoshitoki (1163–1224), the second regent of the Kamakura government.

228. The retired emperors Juntoku and Tsuchimikado, the sons of Gotoba, were exiled to the island of Sado and Tosa Province, respectively.

229. T9, 58a.

230. The priests of Mt. Hiei were said to have performed esoteric prayer rituals for the defeat of the Kamakura shogunate.

231. The story of Bodhisattva Fukyō appears in the Lotus Sutra (T9, 50c). The monk Kakutoku is described in the Nirvana Sutra (T12, 383c). *See also* n. 120.

232. Nichiren refers to the natural disasters that ravaged Japan at this time. They are enumerated in the "Rationale for Writing the *Risshō Ankoku Ron.*"

233. This refers to the Mongol invasion.

234. This may refer to the unsuccessful coup staged by Hōjō Tokisuke (1247–1272) against his half brother, Regent Hōjō Tokimune (1251–1284) in 1272.

235. Sanron, Hossō, Kegon, Kusha, Jōjitsu, Ritsu, Tendai, Shingon, plus Zen and Jōdo.

236. *Ōjō Jūin* (T84, no. 2863) and *Ōjō Kōshiki* (T84, no. 2725).

237. The ninety-first emperor, Gouda.

238. *Hokke Mongu Ki,* T34, 326b.

239. The forty-two levels of ignorance that the bodhisattva must overcome. They are described in the *Ninnōkyō Sho* (T33, 284b).

240. The first of the three categories of illusion formulated by T'ien-t'ai in the *Maka Shikan* (T46, 37b). *See* Three illusions in the glossary.

241. The story of King P'ing derives from the *Tso Chuan;* the story of King Yu from the *Shih Chi.*

242. T16, 443a.

243. T16, 442c.

244. The above quotations from the *Ninnō* Sutra are at T8, 833c and 832a.

245. The powers of 1) seeing anything anywhere, 2) hearing any sound anywhere, 3) knowing the thoughts of all other minds, 4) knowing past lives, and 5) being anywhere at will.

246. T19, 573b.

247. T12, 1072c.

248. This story appears in the *Shugo Kokkaishu Darani* Sutra (T19, 572b).

249. King Mihirakula (Daizoku ō), according to the *Daitō Saiiki Ki* (T51, 888b–889a), attacked Bālāditya, a king of Magadha, who was a Buddhist, but was instead captured by him. Released through the intercession of Bālāditya's merciful mother, Mihirakula fled to Kashmir and later killed its king. He went on to attack Gandhāra where he destroyed temples and stupas. As a result, when he was about to die, the earth trembled and a storm arose, and he fell into the hell of incessant suffering.

250. Wu-tsung (814–846) was the fifteenth T'ang emperor. He initiated a persecution of Buddhism in 845 during the Hui-ch'ang era.

251. San-chieh or Hsin-hsing of the San-chich school was not a member of the Zen school.

252. *Kenkai Ron,* T74, 615c.

253. Taira no Munemori (1147–1185) was the leader of the Taira clan who held a high position at court. When the Taira fought with the Minamoto clan at Dannoura, he was captured and had to humble himself before Kajiwara Kagetoki (d. 1200), a Minamoto warrior who was originally from the Taira clan.

254. The lay priest Saimyōji was the name adopted by Hōjō Tokiyori (1227–1263) on his retirement, Saimyō-ji being the temple where he took

religious vows. As former regent, he still wielded great influence in the Hōjō clan. Yadoya Nyūdō is Yadoya Mitsunori (n.d.), an official influential in the Kamakura government.

255. Hei no Saemon or Taira no Yoritsuna (d. 1293) was an important official in the Hōjō regency, who strongly opposed Nichiren.

256. T9, 5c.

257. Wonderful enlightenment refers to *myōkahu*, the last of the fifty-two stages of bodhisattva practice, in other words, the state of Buddhahood.

258. T13, 355c.

259. The incident involving the scroll of the fifth volume of the Lotus Sutra occurred when Hei no Saemon came with his men to arrest Nichiren at Matsubagayatsu on the afternoon of the twelfth day of the ninth month of 1271. The fifth volume contains the *Kanji* (thirteenth) chapter, which predicts that votaries of the Lotus Sutra will be attacked with swords and staves, and will face the three powerful enemies.

260. While continuing to slander the Buddha's teaching, Devadatta falsely asserted that he had attained Buddhahood. In this way he deceived King Ajātaśatru and led him toward the evil paths. Kokālika, a disciple of Devadatta, falsely accused Śāriputra and Maudgalyāyana of having committed great evil acts and finally fell into hell for his slander. These stories are to be found in several works; the exact source Nichiren used cannot be identified.

261. An epithet of the Buddha.

262. The seven types of arrogance are described in the *Jōjitsu Ron* (T32, 314b–c); the eight types in *Abidatsuma Honruisoku Ron* (T26, 693a–b); and the nine types in *Abidatsuma Hotchi Ron* (T26, 1028b–c).

263. This story is related in the *Daitō Saiiki Ki* (T51, 891b–c). Guṇaprabha (Tokukō Ronshi) first learned the Mahayana teachings, but later regressed to the Hinayana teachings. When he met with Miroku in the Tuṣita heaven, he was so arrogant that he refused to receive instruction from him.

264. This story has appeared previously. It is found in *Daitō Saiiki Ki* (T51, 935c–936a). The translation has been amplified to provide the names of the four sages.

265. Mahādeva was a monk who appeared about one hundred years after Shakyamuni's death. He set forth "five new opinions" concerning the state of arhatship, precipitating the first schism in the Buddhist community (*Daibibasha Ron*, T27, 510c). Vimalamitra (Muku Ronji) was an Indian monk, a native of Kashmir, who vowed to destroy the reputation of Vasubandhu and of Mahayana Buddhism. He is described in *Daitō Saiiki Ki*, T51, 892b.

266. The Iron Belly Brahman was an arrogant Brahman in southern India who asserted that he possessed all types of wisdom within his belly. Fearful that it would burst, he tied iron sheet metal around it. The story is found in *Daichido Ron*, T25, 137b.

267. *Hokke Shūku*, DDZ3, 257.

268. T9, 54a.

269. T9, 54b.

270. Fa-tsang (643–712) is the third patriarch of the Kegon school; Ch'ingliang is the honorary title of Ch'eng-kuan (738–839), the fourth patriarch.

Empress Tse-t'ien is Empress Wu (623–705), Shinjō (Kor Simsang, d. 742) is a Korean monk, the founder of Japanese Kegon. Rōben (689–773) is the founder of the Tōdai-ji and second Japanese Kegon patriarch, and Emperor Shōmu (701–756) was a firm supporter of Buddhism.

271. Shōgishō is the bodhisattva to whom Shakyamuni addressed his preaching in the *Gejimmitsu* Sutra; Subhūti was one of Shakyamuni's ten major disciples; Chia-hsiang, more commonly known as Chi-tsang (549–623), was a Sanron school patriarch; Hsüan-tsang (602–664) is famed for his visit to India and his translation of the sutras; T'ai-tsung (598–649) and Kao-tsung (628–683) were the second and third T'ang emperors; Kanroku (Kor Kwallŭk, n.d.) was a Korean priest who arrived in Japan in 602; Dōshō (629–700) was the founder of the Hossō sect in Japan; and Emperor Kōtoku (597–654) was an emperor under whom many reforms were initiated.

272. Vajrasattva, Nāgārjuna, and Nāgabodhi are considered the second, third, and fourth patriarchs of the Shingon school. Sātavāhana was a king of southern India who appeared about seven centuries after Shakyamuni's death. Shan-wu-wei (Śubhākarasiṃha, 637–735), Chin-kang-chih (Vajrabodhi, 671–741), and Pu-k'ung (Amoghavajra, 705–774) were important Indians who brought the esoteric teachings to China and translated numerous texts. Hsüan-tsung (685–762) and Tai-tsung (726–779) were the sixth and eighth T'ang emperors. Hui-kuo (746–805) was the teacher of Kōbō Daishi (Kūkai, 774–835), the founder of the Shingon sect in Japan, and Jikaku Daishi (Ennin, 794–866) incorporated esoteric doctrines into the Tendai teachings.

273. Kashō Dōji is the bodhisattva addressed by Shakyamuni in the *Kashō Bosatsu* chapter of the Nirvana Sutra. The fifty-two types of beings are those who gathered at the assembly of the Nirvana Sutra. They are described in *Nehangyō Sho* (T38, 42b). Dharmaksema (385–433) was a central Indian monk who was converted to Mahayana on reading the Nirvana Sutra. Fa-yün (467–529) was a famed Liang dynasty priest who attained the highest administrative rank. The ten eminent priests are the representatives of the three schools from south China and the seven from north China, described by T'ien-t'ai in the *Hokke Gengi* (T33, 801a).

274. T9, 54a.

275. T9, 54a.

276. *Hokke Shūku*, DDZ3, 257.

277. An imaginary beast that appears in Chinese legend. It was believed to appear to herald the advent of a sage and to look something like a fiery horse.

278. *Tendai Ebyō Shū*, DDZ3, 364.

279. T9, 15b.

280. T9, 62a.

281. T9, 62a.

282. T9, 36c.

283. T12, 419a, 660a.

284. The story of Sessen Dōji appears in the Nirvana Sutra (T12, 449a); the story of Bodhisattva Yakuō is found in the Lotus Sutra (T9, 53c).

285. T12, 419a, 660a.

286. T9, 36b.

287. T12, 292c.

288. Said to derive from the *Hokke Mongu Ki*. The precise reference has not been found.

289. T9, 39a.

Repaying Debts of Gratitude

1. This appears in the "Nine Pieces" of the *Ch'u-tz'u* (Elegies of Ch'u) and other Chinese works. A commentary on the *Ch'u-tz'u* by Chu Hsi of the Sung dynasty states, "The old fox dies, invariably turning its head toward the hillock. This is because he never forgets the place of his birth."

2. This story appears in the *Shih-wen Lei-chü* (Collection of Stories and Poems) and elsewhere. When the young Mao Pao, who later became a general of the Chin dynasty, was walking along the banks of the Yangtze, he saw a fisherman about to kill a turtle he had caught. Moved to pity, he gave the fisherman his clothing in exchange for the turtle, thus saving its life. Later, pursued by enemies, he reached the banks of the Yangtze. There the turtle he had saved in his youth appeared to carry him to safety.

3. According to the *Shih Chi* (Records of the Historian), Yü Jang of Chin first served the Fan and Chung-hang families but was not given an important position. Later, Yü Jang served under Chih Po, who treated him with great favor. In time Chih Po was killed by Hsiang-tzu, the lord of Chao. To avenge his lord, Yü Jang disguised himself as a leper by lacquering his body, made himself a mute by drinking lye, and in this way attempted to approach Hsiang-tzu. But his attempt at assassination failed and he was caught. Hsiang-tzu, understanding his feeling of loyalty, gave Yü Jang his robe. Yü stabbed it three times to show his enmity for the man who killed his lord, and then turned his sword upon himself.

4. This story also appears in the *Shih Chi*. While Hung Yen was away on a journey, enemies attacked the state of Wei and killed his lord, Duke Yi, and devoured his body, leaving only the duke's liver. Then they left the land. When Hung Yen returned, he saw the disastrous scene and wept. He slit open his own stomach and inserted the liver to save his lord from dishonor, and so died.

5. This passage is from a verse in the *Shōshinji Donin* Sutra. The full text is no longer extant, but this passage is cited in the *Hōon Jūrin* (T53, 448b).

6. This story is found in the *Shih Chi*. Emperor Chou of the Yin dynasty was so absorbed in his affection for his consort Ta Chi, that he totally neglected affairs of state. When his minister Pi Kan remonstrated with him, Emperor Chou flew into a rage and had him killed.

7. Siddhārtha is Shakyamuni's given name. While young he renounced his right to succeed to the throne in order to live the life of a religious mendicant.

8. A more elaborate name for the Tendai sect.

9. Tu-shun (557–640), Chih-yen (602–668), Fa-tsang (643–712), and

Ch'eng-kuan (738–839) are the first four patriarchs of the Kegon (Chin Hua-yen) school in China.

10. Hsüan-tsang (602–664), Tz'u-en (632–682), Chih-chou (678–733), and Chishō were scholars of the Hossō (Chin Fa-hsiang) school. Hsüan-tsang is generally regarded as the founder and Tz'u-en who formally established the school is considered his successor. Chih-chou is the fourth patriarch counting from Hsüan-tsang. Chishō is thought to refer either to Chihō (Kor Chipong, n.d.), who studied the Hossō doctrines under Chih-chou or to Dōshō (629–700), who studied under Hsüan-tsang and founded the Hossō sect in Japan.

11. Hsing-huang, more commonly known as Fa-lang (507–581), and Chia-hsiang, known also as Chi-tsang (549–623), are establishers of the Sanron (Chin San-lun) school.

12. Shan-wu-wei (Śubhakarasiṁha, 637–735), Chin-kang-chih (Vajra-bodhi, 671–741), and Pu-k'ung (Amoghavajra, 705–744) are establishers of the Shingon (Chin Chen-yen) school in China. Kōbō Daishi (Kūkai, 774–835) is the founder of Shingon in Japan. Jikaku Daishi (Ennin, 794–866) and Chishō Daishi (Enchin, 814–891) are Tendai priests who incorporated Shingon concepts into their teachings.

13. Bodhidharma (n.d.), Hui-k'o (n.d.), and Hui-neng (638–713) are the first, second, and sixth patriarchs of Zen (Chin Ch'an) in China.

14. Tao-ch'o (562–645) and Shan-tao (613–681) are listed as the second and third patriarchs of Jōdo or the Pure Land school in China. Huai-kan (seventh century) studied under Shan-tao's guidance. Genkū is another name for Hōnen (1133–1212), the founder of the Jōdo sect in Japan.

15. T12, 401b, 642a.

16. T12, 401b, 642a.

17. T9, 39a.

18. The wheel-turning kings are ideal rulers in Indian mythology. In Buddhism they rule the world by justice rather than force. As are Buddhas and bodhisattvas, they are endowed with the thirty-two distinctive marks. They rule the four continents surrounding Mt. Sumeru by turning wheels of gold, silver, copper, and iron. They are described in the *Daichido Ron* (T25, 87b) and elsewhere. The wish-granting jewel is said to have the power of producing whatever one wishes. It is described in *Daichido Ron* (T25, 134a).

19. One of the thirty-two marks of a Buddha.

20. T9, 36a.

21. T12, 420a, 661b. The translation has been amplified in the above quotations.

22. The Trāyastriṁśa Heaven is the Heaven of the Thirty-three Gods, the second heaven of the six heavens in the world of desire. It is located on a plateau atop Mt. Sumeru, where thirty-three gods, including Taishaku, are said to live. Taishaku rules from a palace at the center and the other thirty-two gods live on four peaks, eight gods to a peak, on the four corners of the plateau. The Tuṣita Heaven is the fourth of the six heavens in the world of desire. Bodhisattva Miroku is said to dwell in the inner court of this heaven.

23. T9, 25c.

24. *Tōgaku* is the fifty-first of the fifty-two stages of bodhisattva practice, the stage just before the attainment of Buddhahood.

25. One of the ten mystical powers displayed by Shakyamuni in the *Jinriki* (twenty-first) chapter of the Lotus Sutra (T9, 51c). Here it represents the truth of the Lotus Sutra.

26. The period in which a world decays. One of the four kalpas of formation, continuance, decline, and disintegration which a world repeatedly undergoes. The Kalpa of Decline lasts for twenty medium kalpas, in the first nineteen of which sentient beings in the six lower worlds from Hell through Heaven gradually disappear. In the last medium kalpa, the world is destroyed by fire, water, or wind.

27. Devadatta slandered Shakyamuni Buddha's teachings; Kokālika, his disciple, falsely accused the Buddha's disciples and fell into hell. The stories appear in various sources.

28. Mahādeva was a monk who lived one hundred years after Shakyamuni Buddha and was responsible for bringing about the first schism in Buddhism. He is described in the *Daibibasha Ron* (T27, 510c). The Great Arrogant Brahman is frequently mentioned by Nichiren. His story appears in the *Daitō Saiiki Ki* (T51, 935c–936a).

29. An abbreviation of a passage from the Nirvana Sutra that states: "For example, if an envoy who is skilled in discussion and knows how to employ clever expedients should be sent to a foreign country to carry out a mission for his sovereign, it is proper that he should relate the words of his ruler without holding back any of them, even though it may cost him his life. And a wise man should do the same in teaching Buddhism, going out among the common run of people, willing to give up his life, and proclaim without fail the Buddha's secret teaching as it is contained in the Mahayana sutras, namely, that all beings possess the Buddha nature." T12, 419a.

30. T9, 31b.

31. T9, 39a.

32. The source of this story has not been traced. King Śuddhodana was the father of Shakyamuni. The Devil of the Sixth Heaven is described in the *Daichido Ron* (T25, 123a).

33. The first two of these villains have appeared before. Virūdhaka was a king of Kośala in the days of Shakyamuni Buddha. His father was Prasenajit. His mother was originally the servant of a lord of the Shakya tribe. Virūdhaka was humiliated by the Shakyas because of his lowly birth and vowed to take revenge. After he seized the throne, he led an army against the Shakya kingdom, killing about five hundred people. It is said that seven days later, in accordance with Shakyamuni's prediction, he burned to death and fell into hell. His story is given in the *Binaya Zōji* (T24, 240a). Ajātaśatru was a king of Magadha who eventually was converted to Buddhism by Shakyamuni. His story appears in the Nirvana Sutra (T12, 480b–c) and elsewhere.

34. The translation has been expanded here for the sake of clarity. The two major revelations of the Lotus Sutra, that people of the two vehicles can attain Buddhahood and that Shakyamuni has been the Buddha since the

remote past, awoke great doubts on the part of the *shōmon* disciples (represented by Śāriputra and Maudgalyāyana) and the great bodhisattvas, respectively. Because the two groups had been unaware of these crucial teachings before the Lotus Sutra was revealed, Nichiren says they were its "archenemies."

35. T9, 31b.

36. The huge rock is described in the *Hokke Mongu Ki* (T34, 313b); stories of drunken and evil elephants appear in *Zōichi Agon,* Nirvana Sutra, and elsewhere.

37. In the above paragraph the successors of Shakyamuni Buddha are the twenty-four successors, or patriarchs who followed after the Buddha. The *Fu Hōzō Innen Den* (T50, no. 1719) lists twenty-three successors. T'ien-t'ai, in the *Maka Shikan* (T46, 1a–b), inserts Madhyāntika as the third successor, making a total of twenty-four. The four ranks of bodhisattvas are teachers who propagate Buddhism. They are described in the *Nehangyō Sho* (T38, 94a). Āryadeva or Kāṇadeva, given in the text as Daiba Bosatsu, is fifteenth of the twenty-four successors. He studied under Nāgārjuna and was killed by an antagonist during a religious debate. He is described in *Fu Hōzō Innen Den* (T50, 318c–319b). Āryasiṁha (Shishi Sonja) was the twenty-fourth successor and lived in central India during the sixth century. While propagating Buddhism in Kashmir, he was beheaded by King Dammira, an enemy of Buddhism. The story has it that instead of blood, pure white milk flowed from his wound (*Fu Hōzō Innen Den,* T50, 321c). Buddhamitra was the ninth of the twenty-four successors. The king of the country in which he lived was attached to Brahmanism and sought to purge his country of Buddhist influences. Buddhamitra is said to have walked back and forth in front of the palace for twelve years, bearing a red flag. The king finally relented and permitted a debate with a Brahman teacher; Buddhamitra won and converted the king (*Fu Hōzō Innen Den,* T50, 314a). Nāgārjuna was the fourteenth successor. The source of the story concerning the flag has not been traced. The story of Aśvaghoṣa, the twelfth successor, appears in *Daitō Saiiki Ki* (T51, 913b) and *Memyō Bosatsu Den* (T50, 183c). When Aśvaghoṣa was preaching Buddhism in Pāṭaliputra in Magadha, King Kaniṣka led his army against Pāṭaliputra and demanded a huge sum in tribute; the defeated king offered Aśvaghoṣa in place of the money. The story of Manoratha appears in *Daitō Saiiki Ki* (T51, 880c). The king of Śrāvastī resented Manoratha and sought to humiliate him. He assembled one hundred scholars from various schools to debate with him. Ninety-nine yielded, but the last, in collusion with the king, refused to yield to Manoratha, who is said to have bitten off his tongue and died. Manoratha is the only one of the figures mentioned here who is not counted among the successors; it is possible that Nichiren confused him with Manorhita, the twenty-second successor.

38. Fa-yün (467–529) was a famed lecturer on the Lotus Sutra and the Vimalakirti Sutra. He was appointed chief priest of the Kuang-che-ssu by Emperor Wu of the Liang. In 525 he became General Administrator of Monks.

39. Hui-kuan (368–438), Hui-yen (363–443), Seng-jou (431–494), and Hui-tz'u (434–490) were all celebrated priests during the Northern and Southern dynasties period.

40. T9, 19c.

41. Reference is to Nichigatsu Tōmyō, a Buddha said to have appeared in the distant past to preach the Law. The *Jo* (first) chapter of the Lotus Sutra refers to twenty thousand Buddhas who appeared one after another in the past, all bearing the same name, Nichigatsu Tōmyō. The last Nichigatsu Tōmyō Buddha expounded the Lotus Sutra to Bodhisattva Myōkō, a previous incarnation of Bodhisattva Monju.

42. This presumably refers to Fa-yün's *Hokekyō Giki* (T33, no. 1715), although the above two quotations are not found in this commentary.

43. Reference is to the section of the *Kokusei Hyakuroku* (T46, 795a–c) that sets forth forms of daily and nightly worship of the Buddha Vairocana and all the other Buddhas. The *Kokusei Hyakuroku* is a compilation of discourses and materials relating to T'ien-t'ai, edited by his disciple. Kokusei refers to the Kuo-ch'ing-ssu, a temple where T'ien-t'ai resided.

44. Hui-yung (d. 586), Fa-sui (n.d.), Hui-k'uang (534–613), and Hui-heng (515–589) were, as indicated, all prominent monks of the period.

45. T9, 386b. According to T'ien-t'ai's classification, the *Hōdō* is the third of the five periods of Shakyamuni's teaching and includes the *Konkōmyō* Sutra, the Vimalakirti Sutra, and the three Pure Land sutras. The *Makahannya* is the *Makahannya Haramitsu* Sutra (T8, no. 223). The ocean-imprint meditation, or *samādhi*, is mentioned frequently in the *Kegon* Sutra. The term used here is *Kegon kaikū*, or Kegon ocean-emptiness. All phenomena of the three existences appear clearly in the mind, just as all things are reflected on the ocean's surface when the waves are at rest.

46. T9, 42c.

47. This lengthy quotation cannot be traced, and may in fact be Nichiren's summary of T'ien-t'ai's views.

48. The *asura* king, in his battle with Taishaku, is said to have been blinded by the light of the sun and moon. Liu Pang (247–195 B.C.), the founder of the Han, is said to have controlled the other lords by wielding his three-foot sword.

49. All of India.

50. T'ai-tsung (598–649) was the second emperor of the T'ang.

51. *Gejimmitsu* Sutra (T16, no. 676), *Yugashiji Ron* (T30, no. 1579), and the *Jōyuishiki Ron* (T31, no. 1585).

52. The teaching of the Lotus Sutra.

53. A doctrine of the Hossō school that divides human beings into five groups on the basis of their inborn religious capacities: *shōmon, engaku,* bodhisattvas, an indeterminate group that possesses two of the previous three natures, but leaves the future development undetermined, and a fifth group, destined to transmigrate through the six paths for all time. Described in the *Daijō Nyū Ryōga* Sutra (T16, 597a–b).

54. Empress Wu (624–705), also known as Tse-t'ien, was originally the concubine of T'ai-tsung, the second T'ang emperor, and later consort of

Kao-tsung, the third emperor. She ascended the throne in 690 and was a staunch supporter of Buddhism.

55. Fa-tsang (643–712) was the third patriarch of the Kegon school in China. He is often regarded as the founder of the school because he contributed greatly to the systematization of the doctrine. He is said to have lectured to Empress Wu on the *Kegon* Sutra.

56. The eighty-fascicle *Kegon* Sutra, translated by Śikṣānanda in the T'ang dynasty (T10, no. 279).

57. The *Dainichi* Sutra (T18, no. 848), *Soshitsuji* Sutra (T18, no. 894), and *Kongōchō* Sutra (T18, no. 866) are the basic scriptures of esoteric Buddhism.

58. The abbreviated title of a work said to have been translated by Pu-k'ung, but probably written by Pu-k'ung himself (T32, no. 1665).

59. The *Maka Shikan Bugyōden Guketsu* (T46, no. 1912), *Hokke Gengi Shakusen* (T33, no. 1717), and *Hokke Mongu Ki* (T34, no. 1719).

60. This story is found in the *Genkō Shakusho* (DBZ 101, 176).

61. Gyōhyō (722–797) was a priest of the Sanron sect. He was ordained a priest at Yamashina-dera. Later, he became the chief priest of Sōfuku-ji in Ōmi Province and was appointed as provincial teacher by the imperial court. In 778 he performed the ceremony in which Dengyō Daishi (Saichō) was ordained a priest.

62. *Daijō Kishin Ron Giki*, T44, no. 1846.

63. Chien-chen (Jap Ganjin, 688–763) was a founder of the Ritsu sect in Japan. He studied both T'ien-t'ai and Lü (Ritsu) teachings and was invited to Japan to instruct monks and nuns in the precepts. He made several attempts to reach Japan, eventually arriving in 754, by which time he was blind. He established an ordination platform at the Tōdai-ji and conferred the precepts on Emperor Shōmu and some four hundred others.

64. Tao-hsien (n.d.) was a Tendai school monk who was active in Ch'ang-an between 766 and 779. Some texts identify the monk as the famous Ritsu master Tao-hsüan (596–667). Tao-hsüan's disciple, Tao-an (654–717) was Chien-chen's teacher.

65. Of the fourteen priests listed here we know the dates for only Zengi (729–812), Gonsō (758–827), Shūen (771–835), and Dōshō (756–816). Hōki may also be read Buki.

66. Reference is to the parable of the burning house in the *Hiyu* (third) chapter of the Lotus Sutra.

67. The eleventh of the fifty-two stages of bodhisattva practice.

68. *Eizan Daishi Den*, DDZ5, 8.

69. Wake no Hiroyo (n.d.) and Matsuna (783–846) were sons of Wake no Kiyomaro (733–799), a court official of the early Heian period.

70. The text has been slightly expanded for clarity. Nan-yüeh is another name for Hui-ssu (515–577), T'ien-t'ai's teacher. Ta-su is the place where T'ien-t'ai studied under Hui-ssu.

71. The three truths (Jap *santai*) are: non-substantiality (Jap *kūtai*), temporary existence (Jap *ketai*), and the Middle Way (Jap *chūtai*). They indicate the three phases of one truth and are discussed in the *Hokke Gengi* (T33, 704c) and *Maka Shikan* (T46, 25b).

72. Shinjō (Kor Simsang, d. 742) was the founder of the Japanese Kegon sect. A native of Silla, he went to Japan, where he lived at the Daian-ji in Nara. In 740 he gave the first lecture on the *Kegon* Sutra in Japan.

73. Kanroku (Kor Kwallŭk, n.d.) was a seventh-century priest from Paekche. He went to Japan in 602, lived at the Gangō-ji in Nara and introduced the teachings of Sanron and Jōjitsu as well as works relating to the calendar, astronomy, and geography.

74. Dōshō (629–700) was the founder of the Hossō sect in Japan. In 653 he went to China and studied under Hsüan-tsang. After an eight-year period in China he returned to Japan and propagated the Hossō doctrines.

75. The legend that Shan-wu-wei went to Japan is found in the *Genkō Shakusho* (DBZ 101, 12).

76. Gembō (d. 746) was a priest of the Hossō sect. After twenty years of study in China, he returned to Japan, bringing images of the Buddha as well as sutras, treatises, and commentaries totaling more than five thousand volumes. The *Dainichikyō Gishaku* is a commentary by I-hsing (ZZ1, 36, 3–5). It is also known as the *Dainichikyō Sho* (T39, no. 1796). No information on Tokusei is available.

77. Little is known of these three priests under whom Dengyō Daishi studied.

78. Here another name for the Tendai sect.

79. *Daibon Hannya* refers to the *Dai Hannya* Sutra (T8), no. 223).

80. *Ebyō Tendai Shū* DDZ3, 344.

81. Nāgabodhi is considered the fourth patriarch of the Shingon school and the teacher of Chin-kang-chih (Vajrabodhi).

82. Han-kuang (n.d.) is listed as one of the six great disciples of Pu-k'ung.

83. T34, 359c.

84. Gonsō (758–827) was one of the fourteen priests who were involved in the meeting at Takao-dera in 802. He ordained Kōbō Daishi when the latter was twenty.

85. Hui-kuo (741–805) was the seventh patriarch of the Shingon school and Kōbō Daishi's teacher.

86. Tō-ji, or Kyōō-gokoku-ji is the head temple of the Tōji branch of Shingon. Originally built in 796, it was given to Kōbō Daishi by Emperor Saga in 823.

87. Kūkai's *Jūjūshin Ron* ranks the Shingon teachings highest, the Kegon teachings in second place, and the Lotus Sutra in third. The reference to the Lotus Sutra as "childish theory" appears in his *Hizō Hōyaku* (T77, 374c). The statement that Shakyamuni is still in the region of ignorance is based on the same text (T77, 371a). Reference to "stealing the ghee of Shingon" appears in the *Ben Kemmitsu Nikyō Ron* (T77, 378c).

88. Gishin (781–833) was Dengyō Daishi's immediate successor and the first chief priest of Enryaku-ji, the head temple of the Sammon branch of the Tendai sect. When Dengyō traveled to China in 804, Gishin accompanied him as his interpreter. In 827 he established a Mahayana ordination center on Mt. Hiei in fulfillment of Dengyō's wishes.

89. Enchō (772–837) was the second chief priest of Enryaku-ji. He took

the tonsure under Dengyō, and after Gishin's death was appointed chief priest by the imperial court.

90. In addition to the two priests given in the text, these Shingon teachers are given in Annen's *Taizōkai Daihō Taijuki* (T75, 54a) as: Tsung-jui, Ch'üan-ya, I-chen, Pao-yüeh, K'an, and Wei-chin.

91. Chih-yüan (768–844) was a Tendai priest who lived at a temple on Mt. Wu-t'ai known as the Hua-yen-ssu. Kuang-hsiu (771–843) was the eighth patriarch in the Tendai lineage, counting from T'ien-t'ai. He was also a disciple of Tao-sui, who taught the Tendai doctrine to Dengyō Daishi. Wei-chüan (n.d.) was a leading disciple of Kuang-hsiu.

92. *Kongōchō Kyō Sho* (T61, no. 2223) and *Soshitsuji Kyō Ryakusho* (T61, no. 2227).

93. *Dainichikyō Sho* (T39, no. 1796) compiled by I-hsing. Chin-kang-chih and Pu-k'ung did not compile commentaries on this sutra.

94. The *Muryōgi* Sutra and the *Fugen* Sutra are regarded as the introduction and the epilogue to the Lotus Sutra.

95. The hour of the Tiger (3:00–5:00 A.M.).

96. Gishin and Enchō have been mentioned previously. Kōjō (779–858), here given only by his position, *bettō,* was a disciple of Dengyō Daishi and also studied the esoteric doctrines under Kōbō Daishi.

97. The third year of Ninju (853) is generally accepted as the date of Chishō's journey to China.

98. The sixth month of the second year of Ten'an (858) is the generally accepted date.

99. T58, 19b.

100. T74, 309a. The *Juketsu Shū* records the oral teachings entrusted to Chishō during his stay in China by Liang-hsü on Mt. T'ien-t'ai.

101. The *Fugenkyō Ki* is found in T56, no. 2194; the *Hokke Ron Ki* in DBZ25.

102. Tendai Shikan (meditations and insight) and the esoteric practices.

103. The *Abidatsuma Daibibasha Ron* (T27, no. 1545) is an exhaustive commentary on the Hinayana doctrines in two hundred fascicles compiled in Kashmir in the second century. It was translated into Chinese by Hsüan-tsang.

104. Fa-pao (n.d.) was a T'ang dynasty priest who contributed to the translation of Buddhist scriptures as one of Hsüan-tsang's major disciples.

105. Dharmarakṣa (231–308?) was a monk from Tun-huang who went to China during the Western Chin dynasty and translated Buddhist scriptures into Chinese. The oldest extant Chinese version of the Lotus Sutra, entitled *Shō-hokke-kyō,* is his work. The *Zokurui* is the twenty-second chapter of Kumārajīva's translation of the Lotus Sutra, but Dharmarakṣa put this chapter at the end of his version. The man of China is a reference to Miao-lo, who stated in his *Hokke Mongu Ki* (T34, 350c) that Kumārajīva's placement of the *Zokurui* chapter was correct.

106. The above passage drawn from the *Ebyō Tendai Shū* (DDZ3, 344) has been greatly expanded to render the quotation intelligible in translation, and represents the standard interpretation. The purport, of course, is to

demonstrate T'ien-t'ai's influence on other schools of Buddhism. Chia-hsiang (Chi-tsang, 549–623), often regarded as the first patriarch of the Sanron school, is said to have been embarrassed while giving a lecture by the criticism of a seventeen-year-old Tendai monk. Chih-chou (678–733) was the third patriarch of the Hossō school. Liang-p'i (n.d.) is said to have followed T'ien-t'ai's annotations of the *Ninnō* Sutra.

107. DDZ3, 361. This passage is drawn from the *Hokke Mongu Ki* (T34, 359c).

108. DDZ3, 344.

109. T9, 31b.

110. The head temple of the Jimon school of the Tendai sect, located in Ōtsu. It is also known as Mii-dera.

111. The five provinces are Yamashiro, Yamato, Kawachi, Izumi, and Settsu. The seven outlying regions are: Tōkaidō, Tōsandō, Hokurikudō, San'indō, San'yōdō, Nankaidō, and Saikaidō.

112. T9, 39a.

113. T9, 54b.

114. DDZ3, 257.

115. Ibid.

116. DDZ3, 279.

117. DDZ3, 364.

118. Dainichi here indicates Tahō Buddha, who is referred to in this way in Pu-k'ung's *Hokke Giki,* to show Tahō's superiority over the Dainichi Buddha of Shingon. Also, the *Hōtō* (eleventh) chapter describes Tahō Buddha seated to the south or left, which, according to Indian custom, is inferior to the north or right, the position Shakyamuni occupies.

119. DDZ3, 273.

120. The Ching and Wei are rivers in Shansi Province. The Ching is always turbid and the Wei clear.

121. The owl was said to eat its mother, and the legendary *hakei,* a beast like a tiger, to eat its father.

122. Some time after Chishō's death, friction over doctrinal differences arose between his followers and those in the line of Jikaku. It culminated in a violent dispute over succession to the chief priesthood after the death of Ryōgen, the eighteenth chief priest of Enryaku-ji. In 993 the followers of Chishō left Enryaku-ji and established themselves at Onjō-ji (Mii-dera). The priests of the two temples attacked one another repeatedly.

123. Emperor Uda (867–931), the fifty-ninth emperor. After his abdication in 897 he took Buddhist vows and was known as the Retired Emperor Kampyō.

124. An implement used in Shingon ritual, representing the power of divine weapons made of an indestructible substance identified with the diamond. There are also single-pronged and five-pronged *vajra.*

125. Esoteric practices employing eighteen different mudras, nine for the Diamond Realm and nine for the Womb Realm.

126. Kongōbu-ji, the head temple of the Shingon sect, located at Mt. Kōya.

127. Shōkaku-bō is another name for Kakuban (1095–1143), a Shingon priest frequently mentioned by Nichiren. In 1134 he became *zasu,* or head of Mt. Kōya, but his attempts at rapid reform won him the enmity of the priests of Mt. Kōya. He and his followers were forced to flee to Mt. Negoro, where he took over the Emmyō-ji. His followers founded the Shingi (New Doctrine) school of Shingon in opposition to the traditional teachings of Mt. Kōya and Tō-ji, which were referred to as Kogi (Old Doctrine).

128. The internecine quarrels between two factions on both Mt. Hiei and Mt. Kōya.

129. This story appears in the *Fu Hōzō Innen Den* (T50, 315b). King Kaniṣka happened to pass by the stupa adorned with seven kinds of gems that Nirgranthajñātiputra, one of the six non-Buddhist teachers and the founder of Jainism, had built. He mistook it for a Buddhist stupa and worshipped it, whereupon it collapsed. Nichiren says that Aśvaghoṣa was the one who caused this stupa to collapse, probably because King Kaniṣka was converted to Buddhism by Aśvaghoṣa.

130. This story appears in the *Daitō Saiiki Ki* (T51, 913a–b). In India there was a conceited Brahman named Devil Eloquence who amused himself with paradoxical theories and worshipped demons. He lived in a forest secluded from people. Because he conducted debates from behind a curtain, nobody had seen his true form. One day Aśvaghoṣa, together with the ruler, went to confront him in debate and argued him into silence. Then Aśvaghoṣa lifted the curtain, exposing his demonic appearance.

131. Ulūka is frequently referred to by Nichiren. He was the founder of the Vaiśeṣika school, one of the six main schools of Brahmanism in India. This story appears in the *Maka Shikan Bugyōden Guketsu* (T46, 435c), although the account there differs slightly from Nichiren's version.

132. Kāśyapa Mātaṅga and Chu-fa-lan (Sanskrit unknown) were Indian monks traditionally believed to have introduced Buddhism to China. They are said to have come to China in 67 A.D. at the request of Emperor Ming of the Later Han dynasty. Emperor Ming is said to have dreamed about the Buddha and to have sent emissaries to bring back his teachings. The story appears in the *Kōsō Den* (T50, 322a–323b).

133. Chao Kao (d. 207 B.C.) was a minister to Shih Huang-ti, ruler of the state of Ch'in and the first unifier of China. When the emperor died, the eunuch official Chao Kao forged an edict putting the emperor's youngest son on the throne. He brought about the death of the emperor's eldest son, as well as that of many generals and high ministers and eventually the second emperor. In this way he manipulated power and attempted to control the throne, but was finally killed by the third ruler, Shih Huang-ti's grandson.

134. Wang Mang (45 B.C.–23 A.D.) was a high official who lived toward the end of the Former Han dynasty and controlled the throne by appointing nine-year-old Emperor P'ing to succeed. Eventually he poisoned P'ing, usurped the throne, and established a short-lived dynasty called the Hsin.

135. According to the *Butsuzō* Sutra (T15, 794c–795a), in the remote past after the death of Daishōgon Buddha, his followers split into five sects, and only the monk Fuji correctly upheld what the Buddha had taught. The

leaders of the four other sects held heretical views and persecuted Fuji. For this reason, they and their followers fell into hell, where they suffered for a long time. Later they were able to encounter and practice the True Law of the Buddha Issai Myōō. However, because of their grave offenses in the past, not one of them was able to attain nirvana at that time but had to endure again the sufferings of hell. The *Butsuzō* Sutra does not specifically mention that they were reborn in the Latter Day of the Law of the Buddha Issai Myōō.

136. This refers to the people who persecuted Bodhisattva Fukyō after the death of the Buddha Ionnō, as described in the *Fukyō* (twentieth) chapter of the Lotus Sutra. Fukyō revered all the people he met for their inherent Buddha nature, but they ridiculed and attacked him with sticks and rocks. While the sutra itself says that Fukyō appeared in the Middle Day of the Law of Ionnō Buddha, both here and in other writings Nichiren changes this to read "the Latter Day of the Law of Ionnō Buddha," probably to stress that the decline of Buddhism and the persecution of the votary of the True Law as described in the *Fukyō* chapter paralleled, he felt, the situation in his own time.

137. T9, 15c.

138. The Land of Tranquil Light or the Buddha land, one of the four kinds of land described by T'ien-t'ai in the *Kammuryōju Butsu Kyō Sho* (T37, 188c).

139. The Izu exile from the fifth month, 1261, to the second month, 1263, and the Sado exile from the tenth month, 1271, to the third month, 1274.

140. A reference to the Tatsunokuchi persecution.

141. T16, 443a.

142. T13, 355c.

143. Hei no Saemon (d. 1293), known also as Taira no Yoritsuna. A senior official of the Hōjō regency, he served both Hōjō Tokimune (1251–1284) and Hōjō Sadatoki (1270–1311). He ignored Nichiren's petition.

144. The translation is expanded somewhat for clarity. Reference is to the insurrection of Hōjō Tokisuke (1247–1272), elder half brother of Hōjō Tokimune, who failed in an attempt to seize power.

145. A reference to prayers for rain conducted by the Shingon priest Hōin, which produced not only rain but a destructive gale as well. The incident is described in detail in "On Various Actions of the Priest Nichiren."

146. This passage has been paraphrased for clarity. Taira no Kiyomori (1118–1181), here given as Daijō Nyūdō, was the leader of the Taira clan. From 1160 on he held military control in Kyoto and dominated the court. Nichiren frequently refers to the Jōkyū Disturbance of 1221 in which the Retired Emperor Gotoba attempted unsuccessfully to break free from the dominance of the Hōjō regency.

147. Mononobe no Moriya (d. 587) was an official of the Yamato court who opposed the spread of Buddhism. He burned monasteries and is said to have cast Buddhist statues into a canal in Naniwa (Osaka).

148. T16, 341b. The four types of troops are those that travel by foot, horse, chariot, and elephant.

149. Indian mythological beings incorporated into Buddhism. They are one of the eight kinds of non-human beings that protect Buddhism.

150. T16, 341b.

151. A king of Kashmir in India who opposed Buddhism. After he became king he was conquered by Kaniṣka, king of Gandhāra. But upon Kaniṣka's death, he regained the throne and banished the Buddhist monks, destroying Buddhism in the area. Because of this he was killed by Himatala (Jap Sessenge-ō), king of Tukhāra and a patron of Buddhism. The story appears in *Daitō Saiiki Ki* (T51, 886a).

152. Mihirakula (Daizoku-ō) was a king of the ancient kingdom of Ceka in India. He turned against Buddhism and banished the Buddhist monks. He later attempted to conquer Magadha, but was captured by King Bālāditya (Gennichiō), a Buddhist. The story appears in the *Daitō Saiiki Ki* (T51, 888c).

153. T12, 1118c.

154. T12, 563b, 809c.

155. *Hokke Mongu Ki,* T34, 212c.

156. T34, no. 1720. Chia-hsiang is also known as Chi-tsang.

157. *Hokke Mongu Ki,* T34, 306b.

158. Chia-hsiang (Chi-tsang) is said to have carried T'ien-t'ai on his back and lifted him up when T'ien-t'ai mounted an elevated seat for preaching.

159. T34, no. 1723. Tz'u-en is also known as K'uei-ch'i.

160. *Hokke Shūku,* DDZ3, 252.

161. The second ruler, Emperor Yang (569–618).

162. This story appears in the *Sō Kōsō Den* (T50, 714b). Shushō and Shōdai were men of India, but their Sanskrit names are not known.

163. T9, 14c. The line following in the verse reads: "The living beings in it are all my children."

164. *Sō Kōsō Den,* T50, 716a.

165. A comparison of dates would indicate that Pu-k'ung did not meet Chin-kang-chih and become his disciple until after he had arrived in China, but this may not have been known in Nichiren's time.

166. Kaga Hōin, sometimes referred to as simply Hōin, is also known as Jōshō (n.d.). The Amida Hall was located in Kamakura. Nichiren has mentioned him previously and deals with him in detail in "Various Actions of the Priest Nichiren."

167. Shubin (n.d.) was a Shingon priest who studied Hossō and Sanron teachings as well. In 823 he was given Sai-ji (West Temple) by Emperor Saga, while Kōbō Daishi was given Tō-ji (East Temple).

168. Shinsen-en was a garden established by Emperor Kammu within the imperial palace. It was the site of a large pond where prayers for rain were performed. According to the *Genkō Shakusho* (DBZ101, 20), a dragon lived in this pond and when it made an appearance rain would fall. Matsuna's offerings were made to this dragon.

169. The Kalpa of Formation is the first stage of the four-stage cycle of formation, continuance, decline, and disintegration which a world is said to undergo repeatedly. This kalpa lasts for twenty medium kalpas, during which time a world takes shape and living beings appear on it.

170. The period corresponding to the second stage of the four-stage cycle, during which a world and its inhabitants continue to exist. In this kalpa the life span of human beings is said to repeat a cycle of change, decreasing by a factor of one year every hundred years until it reaches ten years, and then increasing at the same rate until it reaches eighty thousand years. It then decreases again until it reaches ten years and then proceeds to increase again. A period when the human life span is lengthening is called a kalpa of increase, while a period when it is diminishing is called a kalpa of decrease. "The ninth kalpa of decrease" corresponds to the present age.

171. King Chou was the dissolute ruler of the Yin dynasty who was conquered by King Wu of the Chou dynasty. According to the *Shih Chi*, he had a human figure made and called it a heavenly god and caused people to treat it with contempt. Furthermore, it is said that he shot arrows at a leather bag filled with blood, claiming that he had shot the god of the sun.

172. A powerful local leader in Yamato. According to the *Nihon Shoki*, Jimmu, the legendary first emperor, proceeded southward to invade the Yamato region, where he was engaged in battle by Nagasunebiko and driven back. The name Nagasunebiko does not appear in the original text.

173. The story of Ajātaśatru's dream appears in *Daihatsu Nehangyō Gobun* (T12, 911b).

174. Subhadra was the last convert of Shakyamuni Buddha. According to the *Daichido Ron* (T25, 80c), he had a dream in which all people were deprived of their eyesight and left standing naked in the darkness, whereupon the sun fell from the sky, the earth cracked, the seas ran dry, and Mt. Sumeru was toppled by a great wind. In the morning, being told that the Buddha would enter nirvana before the next day, he went to Shakyamuni and joined the Order, and that night attained the state of arhat.

175. This story appears in the *Shaka Shi Fu* (T50, 85b).

176. Ming-sheng (n.d.) was a priest of the Sanron school during the T'ang dynasty. He was a disciple of Fa-lang and Chia-hsiang was one of his fellow priests.

177. Presumably the *Kammuryōju Kyō Sho* (T37, no. 1753). The quotation has not been traced.

178. The *Kannen Hōmon* is the *Kannen Amida Butsu Sōkai Zammai Kudoku Hōmon* (T47, no. 1959), a work by Shan-tao setting forth the practices for and benefits of worshipping Amida Buddha.

179. T9, 9b.

180. *Ōjō Raisan*, T47, 439c.

181. T9, 386b.

182. A reference to Shan-tao. One story has it that Shan-tao attempted to commit suicide by hanging himself from a branch of a willow tree in front of the temple where he lived in hopes of going to the Pure Land. However, either the rope or the willow branch broke and he fell to the ground. He died a week later in torment from his injuries. Nichiren frequently cites this story. The *Zoku Kōsō Den* (T50, 684b) attributes the suicide to a follower of Shan-tao.

183. Two attendants of Amida Buddha. Kannon and Seishi represent compassion and wisdom, respectively.

184. One of the four types of wheel-turning kings. *See* p. 390, n.200.

185. *Hannya Shingyō Hiken* (T57, 12c). The passage appears in a postface to the text and was in all likelihood not written by Kōbō Daishi.

186. Yuga (Skt Yoga) or "union" is another name for the Shingon sect. Esoteric Buddhism stresses the union of body, voice, and mind of common mortals with those of Dainichi Buddha. In terms of practice, mudras represent the body, mantras the voice, and meditation on the mandalas, the mind.

187. Dōshō (799–875) first studied the Sanron doctrines but later became a follower of Kōbō Daishi. Gennin (818–887) first studied the Hossō doctrines but later studied the esoteric teachings under Shinga. In 885 he became the chief priest of Tō-ji. Dōō (d. 851) first studied Hossō but later turned to the Kegon teachings.

188. T61, 756c. The *Kujakkyō Ongi* was compiled in 953 by Kanjō (901–979). The authorship is in dispute and Nichiren, later in the text, attributes the work to Shinzei.

189. *Kōbō Daishi Goden* (*Zoku Gunsho Ruijū*, v. 8, pt. 2, 534).

190. Reference is to Agastya, Jinu, Sechi (Skt unknown), and Kudon (Skt Gautama) whose stories appear in the Nirvana Sutra (T12, 590a ff.).

191. *Hokke Gengi* (T33, 707b). Illusions of thought and desire represent the first of the three categories of illusion (Jap *sanwaku*) described by T'ien-t'ai in the *Maka Shikan* (T46, 37c).

192. *Hokke Gengi Shakusen*, T33, 836a.

193. Ambrosia (Jap *kanro*). In ancient India it was regarded as the sweet-tasting beverage of the gods. In China it was thought to rain down from the heavens when the world became peaceful. The word *amṛta* means immortal.

194. The ninety-day period from the beginning of the first month through the end of the third. In the lunar calendar, the first day of the first month was regarded as the beginning of spring.

195. "Court historian" was an official position of the Grand Council of State. There were eight altogether: four of the left and four of the right. A historian of the left recorded events; a historian of the right recorded the words of the emperor.

196. The *Three Records* were works said to record the deeds of the three legendary rulers: Fu Hsi, Shen Nung, and Huang Ti. The *Five Canons* were the writings concerning the five emperors (Shao Hao, Chuan Hsü, Ti Kao, T'ang Yao, and Yü Shun) who followed the legendary rulers. These works no longer exist.

197. A reference to the poet and court lady-in-waiting Izumi Shikibu (b. 976?) and the priest Nōin (998–1050) whose works include poems praying for rain.

198. Shinzei (800–860) was probably not the compiler of the *Kujakkyō Ongi*. *See* n. 188.

199. Implying one of the thirty-two marks of a Buddha, a tuft of white hair between the eyebrows.

200. The four ranks are: 1) *shōmon* who have yet to attain any of the four stages of Hinayana enlightenment; 2) those who have reached the first stage, at which one enters the stream leading to nirvana, or the second stage, at which one must undergo only one more rebirth before attaining nirvana; 3) those who have attained the third stage at which one will never be reborn in this world; and 4) those who have eliminated the illusions of thought and desire and attained the fourth stage, that of arhat.

201. Ghoṣira was a wealthy householder of Kauśāmbī, who built the Ghoṣiravāna Monastery to invite Shakyamuni to preach. The Ghoṣira Sutra does not appear in the present collection of sutras but is referred to in the Nirvana Sutra (T12, 397a; 637c).

202. The thirty-two marks and eighty (lesser) characteristics of a Buddha. The thirty-two marks, a few enumerated here, are possessed not only by Buddhas and bodhisattvas, but also by the gods Bonten and Taishaku and the wheel-turning kings. The eighty (lesser) characteristics are found only in Buddhas and bodhisattvas.

203. T12, 397a, 637c.

204. T12, 402c, 643b.

205. T12, 403a.

206. Reference is again to the Jōkyū Disturbance of 1221. Takanari, the Retired Emperor of Oki, refers to Emperor Gotoba; Gon no Tayū is Hōjō Yoshitoki (1163–1224).

207. Sannō refers to the Mountain King, enshrined at the Hie Jinja, a shrine located in Sakamoto at the eastern foot of Mt. Hiei, who serves as its guardian god. The Kamo shrine served to guard the imperial court after Emperor Kammu moved the capital to Kyoto. The Kasuga shrine was dedicated to the ancestor-god of the Fujiwara family in Nara and was also revered by the imperial court.

208. Gotoba was exiled to the island of Oki and Juntoku to the island of Sado. Tsuchimikado was exiled to Tosa Province in Shikoku and later was moved to the neighboring province of Awa (different from the Awa Province in eastern Japan where Nichiren was born).

209. Omuro refers here to the Prince Dōjō, a figure frequently mentioned by Nichiren.

210. Setaka (d. 1221) was a young boy who was a favorite of Dōjō.

211. T9, 58a.

212. For King Chou and Pi Kan, *see* n. 6. King Chieh abandoned himself to a dissolute life and beheaded his loyal retainer Lung-feng when the latter remonstrated with him. For the Indian figures mentioned here, *see* n. 37. Chu Tao-sheng (d. 434) was a disciple of Kumārajīva who insisted, on the basis of his study of the *Daihatsunaion* Sutra, Fa-hsien's Chinese version of the Nirvana Sutra, that even *icchantika,* or persons of incorrigible disbelief, have the potential to attain Buddhahood. For this he was banished from the community of monks to a mountain in Su-chou. Later, when the Nirvana Sutra was translated by Dharmakṣema into Chinese under the title *Daihatsu Nehan* Sutra, Tao-sheng's assertion was verified (*Kōsō Den,* T50, 366c). Fa-tao (1086–1147) was a priest of Sung China. When Hui-tsung, the eighth Sung

emperor and a confirmed Taoist, attempted to suppress Buddhism, Fa-tao remonstrated with him and as a result was branded on the face and exiled to Tao-chou (*Busso Tōki,* T49, 421c).

213. T9, 36c.

214. T12, 419a, 666a.

215. Kakutoku appears in the Nirvana Sutra (T12, 383c). A considerable length of time had passed after the death of the Buddha Kangi Zōyaku, and Buddhism was about to perish. Kakutoku alone strove to protect the orthodox Buddhist teachings, and was attacked by many misguided monks and their disciples. The virtuous king Utoku fought to protect Kakutoku and died in the battle. It is said that because of their devotion to Buddhism, King Utoku was reborn as Shakyamuni Buddha and Kakutoku as Kashō Buddha.

216. Rāhula, a son of Shakyamuni, was one of the Buddha's ten major disciples, respected as foremost in inconspicuous practice. The two hundred and fifty precepts are the rules of discipline to be observed by ordained Hinayana monks. Pūrṇa was another of Shakyamuni Buddha's ten major disciples and was known as the foremost in preaching the Law.

217. Wei Cheng (580–643) was a minister who faithfully served Emperor T'ai-tsung of the T'ang dynasty and gave counsel to his government.

218. Fujiwara no Yoshifusa (804–872) was the Minister of the Left and grandfather of the fifty-sixth emperor Seiwa. Having become a court official at an early age, he laid the foundation for the prosperity of the Fujiwara family. Nichiren, in the text, refers to him with the name Chūjin-kō.

219. Hōjō Tokiyori (1227–1263) was the fifth regent of the Kamakura government. He is referred to here as Saimyōji-dono. Hōjō Shigetoki (1198–1261) was the third son of Hōjō Yoshitoki, the second regent. He is referred to here as Gokurakuji-dono.

220. Nichiren's exile on Sado spanned the years 1271 to 1274.

221. Dōzen-bō (d. 1276) was the chief priest of Seichō-ji in Tōjō village, Awa Province, where Nichiren entered the priesthood. The present work was written in his memory.

222. According to the *Urabon* Sutra (T16, 779b) Maudgalyāyana perceived with his divine eyesight that his deceased mother was suffering in the world of Hungry Ghosts. He tried to send her food by means of his supernatural abilities, but the food turned into flames and burned her.

223. A monk mentioned in the Nirvana Sutra (T12, 560b). He is regarded as a son of Shakyamuni, fathered before he renounced the secular world. He entered the Buddhist Order, but later, overcome by distorted views, is said to have fallen into hell.

224. Tōjō Kagenobu (n.d.), known also as Tōjō Saemon-no-Jō Kagenobu was an official hostile to Nichiren.

225. Both Enchi and Jitsujō were priests at Seichō-ji, antagonistic to Nichiren.

226. Both Jōken-bō and Gijō-bō were priests at Seichō-ji who helped Nichiren escape after Tōjō Kagenobu ordered his arrest when Nichiren declared his new Buddhism on the twenty-eighth day of the fourth month, 1253.

227. The opening words of virtually all Buddhist sutras. They serve to indicate that the teachings contained were heard directly from the Buddha.

228. A Buddha to whom Shakyamuni offered flowers when he was carrying out austerities as Bodhisattva Judō in a previous existence. According to the *Jo* (first) chapter of the Lotus Sutra, Nentō Buddha was one of eight sons of a Buddha called Nichigatsu Tōmyō. He practiced the Lotus Sutra under his father's disciple, Myōkō, and attained enlightenment as Nentō Buddha.

229. Daitsūchishō Buddha appears in the *Kejōyu* (seventh) chapter and Unraionnō Buddha in the *Myōshōgonnō* (twenty-seventh) chapter of the Lotus Sutra.

230. Summarizing a passage in the *Hōben* (second) chapter of the Lotus Sutra (T9, 15b).

231. A reference to the true aspect of all phenomena (Jap *shohō jissō*), as revealed in the *Hōben* (second) chapter of the Lotus Sutra (T9, 35c).

232. This passage is quoted in Chishō Daishi's *Juketsu Shū*, T74, 296b, as Fa-yün's words.

233. *Hokke Mongu*, T34, 3a.

234. *Hokke Gengi*, T33, 681c.

235. *Hokke Gengi Shakusen*, T33, 949b.

236. The source for this statement may be the *Daitō Saiiki Ki*.

237. The present text reads "sixty provinces," although the correct number is sixty-six, as stated later in the passage.

238. The province of Dewa in northern Japan is said to have been famous for its hawk and eagle feathers. Gold was first discovered in Japan in Ōshū in the twenty-first year of the Tempyō era (750).

239. The second of the five types of vision. Also called the divine eye, it is possessed by heavenly beings who can see beyond the limitations of darkness and distance.

240. The fourth of the five types of vision. Also called the eye of the Law, it is the eye of the bodhisattva, which can see all phenomena from the viewpoint of Buddhism.

241. A scholar of the Consciousness-Only school. He was born to a Brahman family and was Vasubandhu's elder brother.

242. Eshin Sōzu (Genshin, 942–1017) was a Tendai priest, famed for having compiled the *Ōjō Yōshū*, which greatly contributed to the spread of Pure Land Buddhism in Japan. Yōkan (1032–1111) was a precursor of the Nembutsu teachings who centered his activities in the Kyoto area.

243. These predictions are found in the *Maka Māyā* Sutra (T12, 1013c) and the *Fuhōzō Innen Den* (T50, 307b). The reference to the *Ryōga* Sutra cannot be identified.

244. T9, 31b.

245. *Kanjin* is to perceive in the depth of one's being the truth that is beyond verbal expression. The term is used in contrast to *kyōsō*, or doctrinal study.

246. The Kannon-ji in Tsukushi, Ono-dera (also called Yakushi-ji) in

Shimotsuke, and Tōdai-ji in Yamato were the sites of the three Hinayana ordination platforms officially established in 754, 761, and 762.

247. Emperor Wu (543–578) of the Northern Chou and Emperor Wu-tsung (814–846) of the T'ang both were responsible for persecutions of Buddhism in 574 and 845, respectively. Nichiren refers to Emperor Wu of the Northern Chou by his family name Yü Wen-[yung].

248. Hsiang Yü (232–202 B.C.) and Kao-tsu (247–195 B.C.) were warlords who contended for power in the confusion created by the death of Shih Huang-ti, the first emperor of the Ch'in dynasty. After a lengthy struggle Kao-tsu (Liu Pang) emerged the victor and founded the Han dynasty in 202 B.C.

249. Some ten years after gaining enlightenment, Shakyamuni Buddha established an ordination platform at the Jetavana Monastery in Śrāvastī. To defy him, Devadatta established a rival platform at Mt. Gayāśīrṣa. The text has been substantially amplified here for the sake of clarity.

250. That is, the eternal Buddha.

251. T9, 54c. The fifth five hundred years refers to the beginning of the Latter Day of the Law. *Kumbhāṇḍas* are beings that drain human vitality. They are ruled by Zōchōten, one of the Four Heavenly Kings.

252. The nun Mahāprajāpatī was the younger sister of Māyā, Shakyamuni's mother. When Māyā died, shortly after Shakyamuni's birth, she married Śuddhodana, his father, and raised the young prince. After Śuddhodana's death she renounced the secular life and followed Shakyamuni's teachings. The *Kanji* (thirteenth) chapter of the Lotus Sutra predicts that she will become the Buddha called Beheld with Joy by All Sentient Beings (T9, 36c).

253. Yaśodharā was the wife of Shakyamuni and mother of Rāhula. Twelve years after his awakening, Shakyamuni returned to Kapilavastu and converted her to his teaching. The *Kanji* (thirteenth) chapter also predicts her enlightenment.

254. There are said to be eight hot hells, located in successive layers below Jambudvīpa. The lowest is the hell of incessant suffering, or the Avīci Hell. Associated with each hell are sixteen subsidiary hells; these one hundred and twenty-eight subsidiary hells, together with the eight hot hells, make a total of one hundred and thirty-six hells. They are variously described in the sutras. There are also eight cold hells that Nichiren does not refer to here.

255. Jōken-bō of the Seichō-ji (Kiyosumi-dera) in Awa.

On Various Actions of the Priest Nichiren

1. Po Chü-i (772–846), a Chinese poet-official, is noted for his *Hsin Yüeh-fu* or "New *Yüeh-fu*," a series of poems in *yüeh-fu* or ballad form criticizing social and political ills of the time.

2. The title *daishi* or Great Teacher was awarded by the sovereign to outstanding Buddhist priests, usually posthumously. To receive the title while still alive would be an unusual honor.

3. Pi Kan was a righteous minister to Chou, the evil last ruler of the Yin or Shang dynasty, around the twelfth century B.C.

4. Fu-ch'a (d. 473 B.C.) was the twenty-fifth ruler of the state of Wu. His father was killed by Kou-chien, king of the state of Yüeh, and Fu-ch'a took revenge two years later by defeating him in battle. Kou-chien proposed a peaceful settlement with Fu-ch'a, but really planned to attack the state of Wu again. Wu Tzu-hsü, a loyal minister of Fu-ch'a, discovered the plot and urged the king to kill Kou-chien, but the king would not listen. Instead, he compelled Wu Tzu-hsü to commit suicide in 485 B.C.

5. Sessen Dōji was the name under which Shakyamuni, in a past life, practiced the bodhisattva way. He met a demon in the Himalaya who recited the first half of a four-line verse. Sessen Dōji was prepared to sacrifice his life to the demon in order to hear the second part of the verse (Nirvana Sutra, T12, 450a). The Bodhisattva Jōtai practiced the *prajñāpāramitā* without giving thought to his body, fame, or wealth (*Dai Hannya* Sutra, T6, 1059c). Zenzai Dōji traveled about visiting some fifty teachers and, under the instruction of the ninth teacher he visited, cast himself into a fire in order to gain *samādhi* (*Kegon* Sutra, T10, 348a ff.). Gyōbō Bonji, a name for Shakyamuni in a previous life, tore off a piece of his skin for paper, pulled out a piece of his bone to make a writing brush, and used his blood for ink (*Daichido Ron* T25, 412a). The stories of the bodhisattvas Fukyō and Yakuō appear in chapters twenty and twenty-three of the Lotus Sutra, respectively. The stories of Āryasiṁha and Kāṇadeva appear in the *Fu Hōzō Innen Den* (T50, 321c, 318b).

6. *Hokke Mongu,* T34,118c.

7. *Nehangyō Sho,* T38, 84c. *See* glossary for the terms *shōju* and *shakubuku.*

8. This is not an actual quotation but Nichiren's view of what Shakyamuni must have believed, based on various passages in the Lotus Sutra and other sutras.

9. Hōjō Tokiyori (1227–1263) was the fifth regent and Hōjō Shigetoki (1198–1261), another high official, of the Kamakura shogunate. Nichiren lists them by the names with which they were known after their retirement, Saimyōji-dono and Gokurakuji-dono.

10. Kenchō-ji and Jufuku-ji were Zen temples; Gokuraku-ji belonged to the Ritsu sect; Chōraku-ji and Daibutsu-ji were associated with the Jōdo sect.

11. Hei no Saemon (d. 1293) was an official of the Hōjō regency who was deputy chief of the Office of Military and Police Affairs. Taira no Kiyomori (1118–1181), a military leader and head of the powerful Taira clan, rose to the position of prime minister of the state and virtually ruled the country. He was noted for his arrogant and willful ways.

12. Persons who plotted against the Kamakura government; their plots were discovered and they were put to death. Ryōkō was executed in 1251, Ryōken in 1261.

13. The fifth scroll includes chapters twelve to fifteen; the thirteenth chapter contains a passage stating that the votary of the Lotus Sutra will be attacked with swords and staves.

14. Ryōkan Ninshō (1217–1303), a famous priest of the Ritsu sect, en-

joyed favor with the Kamakura government. He is mentioned earlier among those whom Nichiren was accused of saying should be beheaded.

15. Izumi Shikibu (b. 976?), a famous poet of the Heian period, was noted for her passionate love affairs.

16. Nōin (998–1050) was a poet-priest who lived in Kyoto. The works of Izumi Shikibu and Nōin both include poems praying for rain.

17. The main street in Kamakura, running from north to south. On it is situated the famous Tsurugaoka Shrine, dedicated to the deity Hachiman.

18. Wake no Kiyomaro (733–799), a high-ranking court official, thwarted the attempt of priest Dōkyō to usurp the throne and suffered persecution as a result.

19. This story is cited in the *Tōke Sanne Shō* by Nichikan (*Fuji Shūgaku Yōshū*, v. 3, p. 229), giving *Fusō Ki* as its source. The *Fusō Ki* is presumably *Fusō Ryakki;* the citation is from a section of the work that is no longer extant. Hachiman is said to have given Dengyō the purple surplice, an honor traditionally bestowed on virtuous priests by the imperial court, out of gratitude for enabling him to hear the teachings of the Lotus Sutra.

20. The shrine, the Goryō jinja, was dedicated to the famous eleventh-century warrior Kamakura Gongorō Kagemasa.

21. Shijō Kingo (c. 1230–1300) was a loyal follower of Nichiren during his lifetime.

22. The quotation from the *Daijuku* Sutra is at T13, 379b; from the *Ninnō* Sutra at T8, 832c; and from the *Konkōmyō Saishōō* Sutra at T16, 390b.

23. Rendaino was a burial ground in the northern part of Kyoto.

24. Li Ling (d. 74 B.C.) was a military commander who led the Chinese forces in an attack on the nomadic Hsiung-nu tribes living north of China and was taken prisoner by them. Fa-tao (1086–1147) remonstrated with Emperor Hui-tsung for attempting to reorganize the Buddhist clergy and was exiled to Tao-chou (*Busso Tōki,* T49, 421c).

25. Suzudan was Shakyamuni's name in a past existence when he was born into a royal family. He ascended the throne, but abdicated to follow the hermit sage Ashi (Skt Asita). Ashi was Devadatta's name when he practiced the Mystic Law in a past existence. His story appears in the twelfth chapter of the Lotus Sutra. The story of Fukyō is to be found in chapter twenty of the Lotus Sutra.

26. Lotus Sutra, T9, 39a.

27. Lotus Sutra, T9, 36c.

28. Kokālika, a clansman of Shakyamuni, entered the Buddhist Order but later fell under Devadatta's influence and slandered Shakyamuni's close disciples, Śāriputra and Maudgalyāyana. Sunakṣatra was a monk who was said to have been a son of Shakyamuni's while the latter was still a prince. He devoted himself to Buddhist austerities and attained a limited degree of enlightenment. In his arrogance, however, he thought that he had mastered Buddhism and is said to have fallen into hell alive (Nirvana Sutra, T12, 560b).

29. T9, 5c.

30. For the three obstacles and four devils (Jap *sanshō shima*) *see* glossary.

The *gura* (Skt *kalākula*) are imaginary insects that are said to swell rapidly in strong winds. T46, 49a.

31. The Devil of the Sixth Heaven is Takejizaiten who resides in the sixth of the six heavens of the world of desire. He is described in the *Daichido Ron* (T25, 123a).

32. *Maka Shikan Bugyōden Guketsu,* T46, 406a.

33. Wada Yoshimori (1147–1213), a military leader and chief of military police under Minamoto no Yoritomo, later attacked the Hōjō and was killed in battle. Retired Emperor Gotoba (here referred to as Oki Hōō or the Retired Emperor of Oki) was exiled to Oki Island after the Jōkyū Disturbance of 1221.

34. Minamoto no Yoritomo, who had established the Kamakura shogunate, appointed constables *(shugo)* and stewards *(jitō)* in all provinces to consolidate his power. Hōjō Nobutoki was the constable of Sado Province, and Homma Rokurōzaemon, the steward of Niiho in Sado, assumed the position of deputy governor of the province of Sado.

35. The *Muryōju, Kammuryōju,* and *Amida* sutras, basic scriptures of the Japanese Pure Land sect.

36. Farmers who were *nyūdō* or lay priests. *Nyūdō* are individuals who, though they take religious vows, do not enter a temple but generally continue to live in their own homes.

37. The Chinese Pure Land leader Shan-tao (613–681) was said to have so earnestly desired rebirth in the Pure Land that he attempted to hang himself on a willow tree, but instead fell out of the tree and mortally injured himself. According to legend, when Kōbō Daishi was about to leave China to return to Japan, he threw his three-pronged *vajra* implement in the air; it was later found on top of Mt. Kōya in Japan. On another occasion, when he was debating with eminent Buddhist leaders at court, he is said to have transformed himself into Dainichi Buddha, the Buddha revered by the Shingon sect.

38. No precise information on these priests is available.

39. The image of Amida Buddha enshrined at Zenkō-ji in Shinano which was regarded as being alive.

40. Lotus Sutra (T9, 58a). The clash between the Retired Emperor Gotoba and the Kamakura forces occurred in 1221 and is known as the Jōkyū Disturbance; it clearly established the power of the Hōjō regents.

41. Andō Gorō was a magistrate who exercised jurisdiction over the northern part of Japan in the time of the Regent Hōjō Yoshitoki (1163–1224).

42. Second son of Emperor Gotoba and head of Ninna-ji; he led the prayers against the Kamakura forces at the time of the Jōkyū Disturbance. Dōjo's name does not appear as such in the text.

43. One *ryō* of gold weighs about 37 grams.

44. Setaka, the cherished favorite of the prince-priest Dōjo, was beheaded in 1221 at the time of the Jōkyū Disturbance.

45. The *Jūjūshin Ron* classifies Buddhist and non-Buddhist teachings into ten levels, placing the esoteric doctrines of Shingon at the peak, the Kegon teachings second, and the Tendai teachings based on the Lotus Sutra, third.

The *Hizō Hōyaku,* a three-volume summary of the *Jūjūshin Ron,* says that Shakyamuni of the Lotus Sutra is "still in the region of darkness" (T77, 371c). The *Ben Kemmitsu Nikyō Ron,* a treatise that compares exoteric and esoteric teachings, likens the Shingon teachings to ghee, the finest of the five flavors, and asserts that T'ien-t'ai stole it (T77, 379a).

46. Shōkaku-bō is Kakuban (1095–1143), the precursor of the Shingi school of the Shingon sect. The quotation from the *Shari Kōshiki* is contained in *Kōgyō Daishi Zenshū* v. 2, 1283.

47. In the summer of 962, when Japan was suffering from drought, the emperor ordered Senkan (918–983), a Tendai priest, to offer prayers for rain. It is said that immediately after the imperial envoy reached him, he caused rain to fall (*Honchō Kōsō Den,* DBZ 102, 157).

48. An allusion to the Confucian *Li Chi* or *Book of Rites, Ch'ü-li,* pt. 2.

49. Shōni Sukeyoshi (1198–1281), the *shugo* of Chikuzen, and Ōtomo Yoriyasu (1222–1300), the *shugo* of Buzen.

50. T8, 832b–c. The seven types of calamity in this sutra are: 1) extraordinary changes of the sun and moon, 2) extraordinary changes of the stars and planets, 3) fires, 4) flood, 5) storms, 6) drought, and 7) war. Other sutras have different versions.

51. T16, 443a.

52. T13, 379b.

53. T8, 833c.

54. T9, 36c.

55. The five cardinal sins are: killing one's father, killing one's mother, killing an arhat, injuring a Buddha, and causing dissension in the community of monks. The four major offenses concern precepts relating to killing, sexual misconduct, theft, and lying.

56. These four priests, along with Enchi-bō in the next sentence, all lived in Awa, Nichiren's native province. Judging from this reference, their fate must have been well known, but no historical record remains.

57. Ulūka (Jap Kuru Gedō) was the founder of the Vaiśeṣika school, one of the six philosophical schools of India. He is mentioned in various works. The present story is from the *Shikan Shiki* by Shōshin (DBZ 22, 579).

58. Kapila was the founder of the Sāṅkhya school, another of the six philosophical schools of India. He was said to have transformed himself into a stone because he was afraid of death. But when Bodhisattva Dignāga wrote a verse of admiration on the stone, it cracked into pieces, thereby revealing the falsity of Kapila's teachings a thousand years after his death (*Maka Shikan Bugyōden Guketsu,* T46, 434b).

59. The five precepts prohibit killing, theft, adultery, lying, and intoxicating drink.

60. The twenty-five gods who, on orders from Taishaku, protect those who maintain the precepts. They are described in the *Kanjō* Sutra (T21, 502c–503a). Dōshō and Dōmyō are said to dwell on a person's shoulders from the time of his birth and to report his actions to Heaven. They are described in the *Maka Shikan Bugyōden Guketsu* (T46, 401a).

61. The split into seven pieces is discussed below in the text. In the Lotus

Sutra (T9, 59b), this vow is made specifically by the ten demon daughters of Kishimojin. There the seven pieces are likened to the branches of the *arjaka* tree, that split into seven pieces when they fall.

62. A statement in the *Hizō Hōyaku,* T77, 371c.

63. The seven demons are enumerated in the *Kyakuon Jinshu* Sutra (ZZ1, 3, 5, 388–389).

64. The five major internal organs are the lungs, heart, spleen, liver, and kidneys.

Earthly Desires are Enlightenment

1. Gishin (781–833) was the first chief priest of the Enryaku-ji on Mt. Hiei. A disciple of Dengyō, he accompanied his teacher to China in 804. In 823, one year after Dengyō's death, he began to perform ordination ceremonies at the Mahayana ordination platform newly established at Mt. Hiei and in 824 he was appointed chief priest by imperial decree.

2. Enchō (771–836), a disciple of Dengyō, was appointed second chief priest of Enryaku-ji in 833.

3. Jie Daishi, more commonly known as Ryōgen (912–985), was the eighteenth chief priest of Enryaku-ji. He had many noted disciples and worked for the restoration of the Tendai teachings.

4. Danna refers to Kakuun (953–1007), one of the chief disciples of Ryōgen. Danna-in was the name of the temple on Mt. Hiei at which he lived. Eshin is Genshin (942–1017) who lived at the Eshin-in on Mt. Hiei. He is famed for his compilation of the *Ōjō Yōshū,* the "Essentials of Salvation." Sōga refers to Zōga (917–1003), a disciple who was noted for his shabby appearance and disregard of worldly fame. Eventually he became a teacher of distinction. No details of Zen'yu's life are known.

5. The three important matters (Jap *san daiji*) refer to the Three Great Secret Laws *(sandai hihō):* the object of worship *(honzon),* the invocation of the *daimoku,* Nam-myoho-renge-kyo, and the sanctuary *(kaidan),* that Nichiren found hidden in the *Juryō* (sixteenth) chapter of the Lotus Sutra.

6. Lotus Sutra, T9, 5b.

7. Source not identified.

8. The above passage has been amplified in translation for the sake of clarity.

9. T9, 389c. The five desires result from the contract of the five sensory organs (eyes, ears, nose, tongue, and skin) with the five sensory objects (form, sound, smell, taste, and texture).

10. T46, 1c.

11. T9, 44a.

12. T9, 12b.

13. T9, 32a.

14. Lotus Sutra, T9, 31b.

15. The term Hokke sect is also applied to the Tendai school. Here it refers to Nichiren's teachings.

Winter Always Turns to Spring

1. The story of King Ajātaśatru, described below in the text, appears in the Nirvana Sutra, T12, 480c–481a.
2. A figure in the Nirvana Sutra, not Shakyamuni's close disciple of the same name.
3. Nirvana Sutra, T12, 402c.
4. T46, 4b. The citation in the *Maka Shikan,* almost identical to that in the Nirvana Sutra, is given in the original text along with a restatement by Nichiren, but both have been omitted to avoid redundancy.
5. The ten demon daughters who vow to protect the votary of the Lotus Sutra in the *Darani* (twenty-sixth) chapter of the sutra. T9, 59a.
6. T9, 9b.
7. This story, frequently cited by Nichiren, appears in the Nirvana Sutra, T12, 450a.
8. The wording of the original has been expanded for clarity.

The Embankments of Faith

1. T9, 15b.
2. T12, 381a. A free translation. The text has *shōmon* for "one who truly understands my teachings."
3. This work attacks chiefly the doctrines of the Pure Land (Jōdo) or Nembutsu sect.
4. *Nehangyō Sho,* T38, 80b.
5. Ibid.
6. Ichinosawa Nyūdō (d. 1278) was a lay priest of the Pure Land sect. In the fourth month of 1272, Nichiren was transferred, while still in exile in Sado, from his hovel in Tsukahara to the relative comfort of Ichinosawa's estate.
7. The eight volumes of the Lotus Sutra proper, and the two related sutras, the *Muryōgi* Sutra and the *Fugen* Sutra. In another letter, to a member of Ichinosawa's family, Nichiren expresses misgivings at entrusting a person of Ichinosawa Nyūdō's faith with a copy of the Lotus Sutra, but says that he felt bound to do so by an earlier promise.
8. T9, 34b.
9. Lotus Sutra, T9, 35b.
10. T9, 34b.

On Itai Dōshin

1. An old monetary unit, consisting of 1,000 coins strung together with a cord.
2. Hōki-bō is another name for Nikkō Shōnin (1246–1333), one of the six senior disciples of Nichiren.
3. Sado-bō is another name for Nikō (1253–1314), another one of Nichiren's six close disciples.

4. Atsuhara is a village in the Fuji area of Suruga in which a large number of Nichiren's followers lived and in which persecutions took place.

5. The wording of the original has been expanded for clarity.

6. This story appears in the *Shih Chi* 4.

7. Ben Ajari is another name for Nisshō (1221–1323), one of the six close priest-disciples of Nichiren.

8. Nichiren refers to him as Daizokuō. His story appears in the *Daitō Saiiki Ki,* T51, 888c.

9. Nichiren refers to him as Sessen Geō. His story appears in the *Daitō Saiiki Ki,* T51, 887a.

10. The story of King Ajātaśatru is frequently cited by Nichiren. It appears in the Nirvana Sutra, T12, 480c–481a.

Happiness in this World

1. Lotus Sutra, T9, 43c.
2. Lotus Sutra, T9, 19b.

Letter to Jakunichi-bō

1. The concluding verse in the *Kanji* (thirteenth) chapter of the Lotus Sutra, which describes the three groups of people who persecute the votaries of the Lotus Sutra after Shakyamuni's death. They were defined by Miao-lo in his *Hokke Mongu Ki* (T34, 315a) as: 1) lay people who are ignorant of Buddhism and attack the votaries with swords and staves; 2) arrogant and sly priests who believe they themselves have attained what they have not attained and slander the votaries; and 3) respected priests who fear losing fame or profit and consequently induce secular rulers to persecute practitioners of the Lotus Sutra.

2. This story is described in the *Myōshōgonnō Honji* (twenty-seventh) chapter of the Lotus Sutra.

3. The five major principles (Jap *gojūgen*) used by T'ien-t'ai to interpret the Lotus Sutra in his *Hokke Gengi* (T33, 682a). They are: designation or name, entity, quality, function, and teaching.

4. T9, 52b.

5. T9, 52c.

6. Fan K'uai (d. 189 B.C.) and Chang Liang (d. 168 B.C.) were military strategists and advisors who helped the first Han Emperor Kao-tsu in the founding of the Former Han dynasty.

7. Taira no Masakado (d. 940) led the first major rebellion by a warrior against the central government. Based in Shimōsa, near present-day Tokyo, he led a struggle to gain control of the area. He attacked government offices in Kanto and adopted the title of New Emperor. In 940 he was defeated by forces led by Fujiwara no Hidesato. Fujiwara no Sumitomo (d. 941) was a

court official ordered to suppress Inland Sea pirates in Iyo (present-day Ehime Prefecture). Instead, he joined forces with the pirates and became their leader. Ordered to return to Kyoto, he rebelled, and was eventually forced to flee to Kyushu. Later he returned to Iyo, but was captured and killed.

8. T9, 54b.

GLOSSARY

NOTE: Buddhist technical terms are generally given in their translated form. Titles of texts and the names of figures who appear in sutras appear in Japanese unless otherwise indicated. Names of historical figures are given in the language of the country of their origin with the exception of Indian scholars who made their way to China.

Agon sutras: (Skt *Āgama-sūtra*) A generic term for all Hinayana sutras. T'ien-t'ai classified Shakyamuni's teaching into five periods, according to the order of preaching. The *Agon* sutras belong to the second period. *See also* Five periods.

Ajātaśatru: (Jap Ajase) The son of King Bimbisāra of Magadha, India. Incited by Devadatta, he killed his father, a follower of Shakyamuni, and ascended the throne to become the most influential ruler of his time. Later he is said to have contracted a terrible disease and, out of remorse for his evil acts, converted to Buddhism and supported the First Buddhist Council for the compilation of Shakyamuni's teachings. His story is frequently mentioned by Nichiren.

Ānanda: (Jap Anan) One of Shakyamuni's ten major disciples. He was a cousin of the Buddha and also the younger brother of Devadatta. He accompanied Shakyamuni as his personal attendant for a great number of years and, as a result, heard more of his teachings than any other disciple. Therefore, he was known as the foremost in hearing the Buddha's teachings.

Animality: (Jap *chikushō*) The third of the Ten Worlds. *See also* Six paths, Ten Worlds.

Annen (841–889?): A Tendai priest who studied both the exoteric and esoteric teachings under Jikaku Daishi. He founded a temple known as the Godai-in on Mt. Hiei and wrote widely on the subject of esoteric Tendai teachings.

Anryūgyō: *See* Bodhisattvas of the Earth.

Arhat: (Jap *arakan*) The highest state of Hinayana enlightenment. Also one who has attained this state. It is the highest of the four states to which a *shōmon* can attain.

Āryasiṁha: (Jap Shishi Sonja) According to the T'ien-t'ai classification, the last of the twenty-four successors of Shakyamuni. His efforts to propagate Buddhism led to his execution by Dammira, a king who destroyed many Buddhist temples and murdered scores of monks. The Zen school holds that before his death he passed on his teaching to a twenty-fifth successor or patriarch.

Asura: (Jap *ashura*) A class of fighting demons in Indian mythology who clash continually with the god Indra or Taishaku. *Asuras* live at the bottom of the ocean surrounding Mt. Sumeru. They occupy the fourth of the Ten Worlds. They represent the world of Anger. *See also* Six paths, Ten Worlds.

Aśvaghoṣa: (Jap Memyō) A second-century Mahayana scholar and poet of Śrāvastī, India. Listed as twelfth in the line of patriarchs or successors to Shakyamuni.

Avīci Hell: *See* Hell of incessant suffering.

Benevolent deities: (Jap *shoten zenjin*) This term is used in various contexts. In "The Opening of the Eyes" it refers to the Shinto deities: the Sun Goddess (Amaterasu Ōmikami or Tenshō Daijin), the God Hachiman, and the Mountain God of Mt. Hiei (Sannō). The term is used also in reference to the gods in the Lotus Sutra who assemble from throughout the universe to listen to Shakyamuni preach.

Bodhisattva: (Jap *bosatsu*) The ninth of the Ten Worlds, a state characterized by compassion in which one dedicates one's self to saving others. The bodhisattva vows to postpone his own entrance into Buddhahood until all sentient beings have been saved. *See also* Ten Worlds.

Bodhisattvas of the Earth: (Jap *Jiyu no bosatsu*) The *Yujutsu* (fifteenth) chapter of the Lotus Sutra describes the appearance of an innumerable host of bodhisattvas that well up from the space below the earth and to whom Shakyamuni entrusts the propagation of the Lotus Sutra. Their leader is Jōgyō (Viśiṣṭacāritra, Superior Conduct). The other leaders are Muhengyō (Anantacāritra, Limitless Conduct), Jōgyō (Viśuddhacāritra, Pure Conduct), and Anryūgyō (Supratiṣṭhitacāritra, Conduct of Standing Firm). (Note that the two Jōgyō are written with different characters.) Nichiren identifies himself with the Bodhisattva Jōgyō, the leader of the four.

Bonten: (Skt Brahmā) Also Dai-Bonten (Mahābrahman). A god said to live in the first of the four meditation heavens in the world of form above Mt. Sumeru and to rule the *saha* world. In Buddhism he was adopted as one of the two major tutelary gods, together with Taishaku. Bonten is also the Japanese name for the Brahma Heaven.

Brahma Heaven: *See* Bonten.

Buddhahood: (Jap *butsu*) The highest of the Ten Worlds, characterized by boundless wisdom and infinite compassion. *See also* Ten Worlds.

Buddha land: (Jap *butsudo*) The place where a Buddha dwells; there are countless Buddha lands. The term is also used in the sense of the enlightened state of a Buddha.

Ceremony in the Air: (Jap *kokūe*) One of the three assemblies described in the Lotus Sutra. The description extends from the latter portion of the *Hōtō* (eleventh) chapter through the *Zokurui* (twenty-second) chapter. In the *Yujutsu* (fifteenth) chapter, the Bodhisattvas of the Earth make their appearance; the essential teaching *(hommon)* begins here. In the *Juryō* (sixteenth) chapter, Shakyamuni reveals his original enlightenment in the remote past of *gohyaku-jintengō*. In the *Jinriki* (twenty-first) chapter, he transfers the essence of the sutra to the Bodhisattvas of the Earth led by Bodhisattva Jōgyō, entrusting them with the mission of propagating it.

Chang-an (561–632): (Jap Shōan) Also known as Kuan-ting (Kanjō). T'ien-t'ai's disciple and successor. He recorded T'ien-t'ai's lectures and later compiled them as the *Hokke Gengi, Hokke Mongu,* and *Maka Shikan.* His own works are the *Nehangyō Sho* (Commentary on the Nirvana Sutra) and the *Nehan Gengi* (Profound Meaning of Nirvana).

Ch'eng-kuan (738–839): (Jap Chōkan) The fourth patriarch of the Hua-yen (Kegon) school, known also by his title Ch'ing-liang (Seiryō or Shōryō). He studied various schools under different masters but concentrated his teachings on the *Kegon* Sutra, participating in the translation of the forty-volume version of this sutra. He was greatly honored by several emperors and was awarded numerous titles and high rank.

Chia-hsiang: *See* Chi-tsang.

Chi-tsang (549–623): (Jap Kichizō) Known also as Chia-hsiang (Kajō) after the temple at which he lived. He is often regarded as the first patriarch of San-lun (Sanron) in China. He studied the three treatises of Sanron: *Chū Ron, Jūnimon Ron,* and *Hyaku Ron,* and organized the teachings of this school.

Chih-che: (Jap Chisha) An honorific name given to the Great Teacher T'ien-t'ai. He is also known as Chih-che ta-shih, and most commonly as Chih-i (Chigi). Nichiren on almost all occasions refers to him as T'ien-t'ai.

Chin-kang-chih (671–741): (Jap Kongōchi; Skt Vajrabodhi) The second, after Shen-wu-wei, famous Indian esoteric master to come to China during the T'ang dynasty. Arriving in 720, he gained the support of Emperor Hsüan-tsung. He translated several texts and was the teacher of Pu-k'ung.

Ch'ing-liang: *See* Ch'eng-kuan.

Chishō (814–891): Also called Enchin and Chishō Daishi. The fifth chief priest of Enryaku-ji, the head Tendai temple on Mt. Hiei. In 853 he went to T'ang China, where he studied the T'ien-t'ai and esoteric doctrines. On his return he combined esoteric doctrines with the

Tendai. He also erected a hall for performing the esoteric *abhiṣeka* (Jap *kanjō*) ceremony at the Onjō-ji (Mii-dera) in Ōtsu. Nichiren frequently condemns him for distorting the Tendai teachings.

Dai-Bonten: *See* Bonten.

Daimoku: (1) The title of a sutra, in particular the title of the Lotus Sutra, *Myōhō-renge-kyō*. (2) The invocation of Nam-myoho-renge-kyo, along with the *honzon,* the object of worship, and the *kaidan,* the high sanctuary that, in Nichiren's teaching comprise the Three Great Secret Laws (Jap *sandai hihō*).

Daishi: "Great Teacher." An honorific title awarded to eminent priests in China and Japan by the imperial court, usually after their death. In 866 Saichō was given the posthumous name Dengyō Daishi (the Great Teacher Dengyō) and Kūkai, that of Kōbō Daishi. These are the first instances of the use of this honorific title in Japan.

Daishōnin: Literally, Great Sage, the title given to Nichiren, especially in the Nichiren Shōshū. Other Nichiren schools refer to him as Shōnin (sage) or Daibosatsu (Great Bodhisattva).

Daitsū: (Skt Mahābhijñājñānābhibhū) Also Daitsūchishō Buddha. According to the *Kejōyu* (seventh) chapter of the Lotus Sutra, he was a king who attained Buddhahood in the remote past of *sanzen-jintengō* and expounded the Lotus Sutra at the request of his sixteen sons. Later all sixteen spread the Lotus Sutra as bodhisattvas. The sixteenth son was after many kalpas reborn in the *saha* world as Shakyamuni.

Daitsūchishō: *See* Daitsū.

Dengyō (767–822): The founder of the Tendai sect in Japan. He is often referred to as Saichō; his honorific name and title are Dengyō Daishi (the Great Teacher Dengyō). In the fourth month of 785 he was ordained in the Hinayana precepts at the Tōdai-ji in Nara and in the sixth month established a temple on Mt. Hiei near Kyoto. In 804 he went to China to study at Mt. T'ien-t'ai. Returning the next year, he founded the Tendai sect in Japan. He made continued efforts to establish a Mahayana ordination center on Mt. Hiei in the face of determined opposition from the older sects in Nara. Permission was finally granted shortly after his death, and his immediate successor Gishin completed the ordination center in 827.

Devadatta: (Jap Daibadatta) A cousin of Shakyamuni Buddha, who followed him but later became his enemy out of jealousy. In his arrogance he sought to kill the Buddha and usurp his position. He fomented a schism in the Buddhist Order, luring away other monks. He also goaded Prince Ajātaśatru of Magadha into overthrowing his father, the king, a patron of Shakyamuni. With the new king supporting him, Devadatta made several attempts on the Buddha's life and persecuted his Order. He is said to have fallen into hell alive. However, in the *Devadatta* (twelfth) chapter of the Lotus Sutra, Shakyamuni reveals that in some past existence he himself had practiced Buddhism under a monk named Ashi (Skt Asita) and that this hermit is the present Devadatta. He also predicts that Devadatta will attain enlightenment in the future as a Buddha called Heavenly King.

Devil of the Sixth Heaven: (Jap Dairokuten no Maō) The king of devils, who dwells in the highest of the six heavens of the world of desire. He works to obstruct Buddhist practice and delights in sapping the life force of other beings.

Dragon king's daughter: (Jap Ryūnyo) The daughter of Shakatsura (Skt Sāgara), one of the eight dragon kings said to dwell in a palace at the bottom of the sea. According to the *Devadatta* (twelfth) chapter of the Lotus Sutra, she began to seek enlightenment when she heard Bodhisattva Monju preach the Lotus Sutra in the dragon king's palace. Later she appeared in front of the assembly at Eagle Peak and immediately attained enlightenment without changing her dragon form. The pre–Lotus Sutra teachings generally held that women could not attain Buddhahood and that even men had to practice austerities for innumerable kalpas in order to do so.

Eagle Peak: (Jap Ryōju-sen; Skt Gṛdhrakūṭa) A mountain located to the northeast of Rājagṛha, the capital of Magadha in ancient India, where Shakyamuni is said to have expounded the Lotus Sutra. In English it is often called Vulture Peak, based on its Sanskrit name. Kumārajīva, in his translation of the Lotus Sutra, referred to it as Eagle Peak, and his version has been followed here.

Eight kinds of non-human beings: (Jap hachibu-shū) They are described in the *Hiyu* (third) chapter of the Lotus Sutra. They are: 1) gods; 2) dragons; 3) *yasha* (Skt *yakṣa*), demons, sometimes described as fierce, who are followers of Bishamonten, one of the Four Heavenly Kings; 4) *kendatsuba* (Skt *gandharva*), gods of music; 5) *ashura* (Skt *asura*), fighting demons, said to live at the bottom of the ocean surrounding Mt. Sumeru and who inhabit the fourth of the Ten Worlds; 6) *karura* (Skt *garuḍa*), birds that devour dragons; 7) *kinnara* (Skt *kiṃnara*), gods with beautiful voices; and 8) *magoraka* (Skt *mahoraga*), gods in the form of snakes.

Eight teachings: (Jap hakkyō) One system by which T'ien-t'ai classified the sutras. The eight teachings are subdivided into two groups: four teachings of doctrine *(kehō no shikyō)* and four teachings of method *(kegi no shikyō)*. The first is a division by content, and the second, by method of teaching. The four teachings of doctrine are: 1) the Tripitaka teaching *(zōkyō)*, which corresponds to the Hinayana texts that stress observing precepts; 2) the connecting teaching *(tsūgyō)*, introductory Mahayana teachings for those in the states of *Shōmon, Engaku,* and Bodhisattva; 3) the specific teaching *(bekkyō)*, a higher level of provisional Mahayana taught exclusively for bodhisattvas. The three truths *(q.v.)* are discussed here, but are indicated as being separate from each other; and 4) the perfect teaching *(engyō)*, or true Mahayana which is directed to people of all capacities and holds that all can attain Buddhahood.

The four teachings of method are: 1) the sudden teaching *(tonkyō),* or those teachings that Shakyamuni expounded directly upon his own enlightenment without giving his disciples preparatory knowledge. An example is the *Kegon* Sutra, traditionally regarded as the first teaching he expounded after his enlightenment at Buddhagayā; 2) the gradual teaching *(zenkyō),* or teachings Shakyamuni expounded to his disciples in progressive stages in order to gradually elevate their capacity to understand higher doctrines; 3) the secret teaching *(himitsukyō),* or teachings from which the Buddha's listeners each unknowingly received a different benefit according to their capacity; and 4) the indeterminate teaching *(fujōkyō),* from which the Buddha's listeners each knowingly received a different benefit.

Emanations of the Buddha: (Jap *funjin* or *bunshin*) Buddhas who are different manifestations of a Buddha. The Buddha can divide his body an infinite number of times and appear in innumerable worlds at once in order to save the people there. In the *Hōtō* (eleventh) chapter of the Lotus Sutra, Shakyamuni summons the Buddhas who are his emanations from throughout the universe. They are mentioned at the beginning of the second part of "The Opening of the Eyes."

Emma: (Skt Yama) The lord of hell, who judges the dead for the deeds they did while alive and sentences them accordingly.

Enchin: *See* Chishō.

Enchō (772–837): The second chief priest of the Enryaku-ji on Mt. Hiei. He became a disciple of Dengyō at twenty-seven. He received the bodhisattva precepts in 806 and lectured on various sutras. His posthumous title was Jakkō Daishi.

Engaku: (Skt *pratyekabuddha*) Those who seek to obtain enlightenment without a teacher. Sometimes translated as Men of Realization. They represent the eighth of the Ten Worlds. *See* Ten Worlds.

Ennin: *See* Jikaku.

Essential teaching: (Jap *hommon*) The last fourteen chapters of the Lotus Sutra, from the *Yujutsu* (fifteenth) through the *Fugen* (twenty-eighth) chapters. In his *Hokke Mongu* T'ien-t'ai divided the Lotus Sutra into two parts, the first fourteen chapters, or theoretical teaching, and the last fourteen chapters, or essential teaching. The essential teaching starts when the historical Shakyamuni reveals his true identity as the Buddha who gained enlightenment in the remote past of *gohyaku-jintengō*. *See also* Theoretical teaching.

Fa-tao (1086–1147): (Jap Hōdō) Chinese priest who remonstrated with Emperor Hui-tsung of the Sung dynasty when the emperor supported Taoism and attempted to reorganize the Order of Buddhist priests. Later he was branded in the face and exiled to Tao-chou, south of the Yangtze River. He is frequently referred to by Nichiren.

Fa-tsang (643–712): (Jap Hōzō) The third patriarch of the Hua-yen (Jap Kegon) school and the systematizer of its doctrines. He assisted in the translation of the eighty-chapter version of the *Kegon* Sutra and was greatly honored by Empress Wu and three T'ang dynasty emperors.

Fifth five-hundred-year period: (Jap *go gohyakusai*) The last of the five five-hundred-year periods following Shakyamuni's death. It corresponds to the beginning of the Latter Day of the Law *(mappō)*. According to the *Daijuku* Sutra and other works, this period is one of contention and strife in which Shakyamuni's Buddhism will perish. *See also* Three periods, Latter Day of the Law.

Fifty-two stages of bodhisattva practice: (Jap *gojūni i*) The fifty-two ranks through which a bodhisattva progresses toward Buddhahood. They are described in the *Bosatsu Yōraku Hongō* Sutra (Sutra of the Bodhisattvas' Prior Jewel-like Acts). The fifty-two consist of ten stages of faith *(jisshin)*, ten stages of security or ten abodes *(jūjū)*, ten stages of practice *(jūgyō)*, ten stages of devotion or merit transfer *(jū ekō)*, ten stages of development *(jūji)*, *tōgaku*, the stage almost equal to enlightenment, and *myōkaku*, enlightenment.

Five cardinal sins: (Jap *go gyakuzai*) The five most serious offenses in Buddhism. Explanations vary according to different sutras and treatises. The most common version is: 1) killing one's father, 2) killing one's mother, 3) killing an arhat, 4) injuring a Buddha, and 5) causing dissension in the Buddhist Order.

Five impurities: (Jap *gojoku*) 1) Impurity of the age caused by war, natural disasters, etc.; 2) impurity of thought, 3) impurity of desires, such as greed, anger, or stupidity; 4) impurity of the people, weakened both spiritually and physically by impurities of thought and desire; and 5) impurity of life itself. They are listed in the *Hōben* (second) chapter of the Lotus Sutra; here it states thaat the Buddha appears in an evil world that is defiled by the five impurities.

Five periods: (Jap *goji*) T'ien-t'ai's classification of Shakyamuni's teachings according to the order of preaching. They are: 1) the Kegon period, in which the Buddha expounded his first teachings (the *Kegon* Sutra) after his enlightenment, 2) the Agon period, or period of the *Agon* sutras, in which the Hinayana teachings were expounded, 3) the Hōdō period in which such sutras as the *Amida, Dainichi,* and Vimalakirti were preached, 4) the Hannya period in which the *Hannya,* or Wisdom sutras were taught, and 5) the Hokke-Nehan period, an eight-year interval in which Shakyamuni expounded the Lotus and Nirvana sutras.

Five practices: (Jap *goshu no myōgyō*) The five kinds of practice described in the *Hosshi* (tenth) chapter of the Lotus Sutra. They are to embrace, read, recite, teach, and transcribe the Lotus Sutra.

Five types of vision: (Jap *gogen*) 1) The eyes of common mortals that distinguish form and color, 2) the divine eye that sees things even in the darkness and at a distance, 3) the eye of wisdom, or the ability of people in the two vehicles to judge right and wrong and recognize what must be done, 4) the eye of the Dharma by which bodhisattvas see all phenomena from the viewpoint of Buddhism, and 5) the eye of the Buddha that sees the true nature of life in the past, present, and future.

Former Day of the Law: (Jap *shōbō*) The period when the True Law was taught; the first thousand years after Shakyamuni's death. Frequently referred to as the Period of the True Law. *See also* Three periods.

Four Bodhisattvas: *See* Bodhisattvas of the Earth.

Four categories of Buddhists: (Jap *shishu*) Sometimes called the four kinds of believers. Monks, nuns, laymen, and laywomen.

Four continents: (Jap *shishū*) The continents situated respectively to the east, west, north, and south of Mt. Sumeru, according to ancient Indian cosmology. They are Tōhotsubadai (Skt Pūrvavideha), Saikuyani (Aparagodānīya), Hokkuru (Uttarakuru), and Nanembudai (Jambudvīpa).

Four evil paths: (Jap *shiakushu*) The first four of the Ten Worlds: Hell, Hungry Ghosts, Animals, and Asura. *See also* Ten Worlds.

Four Heavenly Kings: (Jap *shitennō*) The lords of the four quarters who serve Taishaku as his generals and protect the four continents. They are Jikokuten (Dhṛtarāṣṭra), Kōmokuten (Virūpākṣa), Bishamonten (Vaiśravaṇa) and Zōchōten (Virūḍhaka). They are said to live halfway down the four sides of Mt. Sumeru. In the *Darani* (twenty-sixth) chapter of the Lotus Sutra, they vow to protect those who embrace the sutra.

Fourteen slanders: (Jap *jūshi hibō*) Fourteen kinds of slanders against Buddhism described in the *Hiyu* (third) chapter of the Lotus Sutra: 1) arrogance toward Buddhism, 2) negligence in Buddhist practice, 3) arbitrary, egotistical judgment of Buddhist teachings, 4) shallow, self-satisfied understanding, 5) adherence to earthly desires, 6) lack of a seeking spirit, 7) lack of faith, 8) disgust toward Buddhism, 9) mistaken doubt, 10) vilification of Buddhism, 11) contempt for Buddhist believers, 12) hatred toward believers, 13) jealousy toward believers, and 14) grudges against believers. The first ten are slanders against the Law and the latter four are slanders against those who embrace the Law.

Fugen: (Skt Samantabhadra) With Monju, one of the two bodhisattvas who attend Shakyamuni and lead the other bodhisattvas. In the *Fugen* (twenty-eighth) chapter of the Lotus Sutra he vows to protect the sutra and its votaries.

Fugen Sutra: "Sutra of Meditation on Bodhisattva Fugen," a one-volume sutra said to have been preached three months before Shakyamuni's passing. Since this sutra is a continuation of the *Fugen* (twenty-eighth) chapter of the Lotus Sutra, T'ien-t'ai regarded it as the conclusion of the Lotus Sutra.

Fukyō: (Skt Sadāparibhūta) A bodhisattva who appears in the *Fukyō* (twentieth) chapter of the Lotus Sutra. After the death of Ionnō Buddha in the remote past, he propagated a teaching expressed in twenty-four Chinese characters and showed respect toward all people for their innate Buddha nature. People ridiculed him and attacked him with staves and stones, but he continued to practice in this way. Those who slandered him fell into hell, but, after expiating their offense, were reborn with Fukyō and were saved by practicing the Lotus Sutra under his guidance. The name Fukyō means "never despising."

Genshin (942–1017): Tendai priest, known also as Eshin Sōzu, who established a temple, the Eshin-in, on Mt. Hiei. In 985 he compiled the *Ōjō Yōshū*, a work that had considerable influence on the later development of the Pure Land sect in Japan.

Gods of the sun and moon: (Jap *nitten gatten*) The deification of the sun and moon. Nichiren regarded them as Buddhist gods who protect the votaries of the Lotus Sutra.

Gohonzon: The mandala which forms the object of worship in Nichiren's Buddhism.

Gohyaku-jintengō: A time in the extremely remote past when Shakyamuni first attained enlightenment, according to the *Juryō* (sixteenth) chapter of the Lotus Sutra. Also, the length of time that has elapsed since that attainment. Not until the essential teaching *(hommon)* of the Lotus Sutra was expounded did Shakyamuni reveal that his enlightenment had originally taken place long before his lifetime in India. *Gohyaku-jintengō* is explained in the *Juryō* chapter as follows: "Suppose there is one who reduces five hundred, thousand, ten thousand, hundred thousand, nayuta (10^{11}), asōgi (10^{59}) major world systems to particles of dust, and then takes them all to the east, dropping one particle each time he traverses five hundred, thousand, ten thousand, hundred thousand, nayuta, asōgi worlds. Suppose that he continues traveling eastward in this way, until he has finished dropping all the particles. . . . Suppose all these worlds, whether they received a particle or not, are once more reduced to dust. Let one particle represent one kalpa. Then the time which has passed since I attained Buddhahood surpasses this by one hundred, thousand, ten thousand, hundred thousand, nayuta, asōgi kalpas."

Gosho: The individual and collected writings of Nichiren, which include letters of personal encouragement, treatises on Buddhism, and recorded oral teachings.

Great Teacher: *See* Daishi.

Guketsu: The abbreviation of the *Maka Shikan Bugyōden Guketsu*, Miao-lo's annotations on the *Maka Shikan*.

Hachiman: A popular Shinto deity who protects warriors. In the Nara period he was regarded as a guardian of Buddhism and is often called Hachiman Daibosatsu. Hachiman was adopted as a guardian deity by the Minamoto family; Yoritomo erected the Tsurugaoka Hachiman shrine in Kamakura in 1191. Nichiren considered him one of the gods who protect the votaries of the Lotus Sutra.

Hannya sutras: Higher provisional Mahayana sutras belonging to the fourth of the periods of Shakyamuni's teachings, according to T'ien-t'ai's classification. *See also* Five periods.

Heaven: (Jap *ten*) The sixth of the Ten Worlds. The realm of the gods. *See also* Ten Worlds.

Hei no Saemon (d. 1293): An official of the Hōjō regency, also known as Taira no Yoritsuna. He served two successive regents, Hōjō Tokimune (1251–1284) and Hōjō Sadatoki (1271–1311) and wielded tremendous influence in political and military affairs as deputy chief (the chief being the Regent himself) of the Office of Military and Police Affairs. He took an active part in persecuting Nichiren and his followers.

Hell: (Jap *jigoku*) The first and lowest of the Ten Worlds. *See also* Ten Worlds.

Hell of incessant suffering: (Skt Avīci Hell; Jap *mugen jigoku*) The most terrible of the eight hot hells. It is so called because its inhabitants are said to suffer without a moment's respite.

Hōben chapter: "Means." The second chapter of the Lotus Sutra and the key chapter of the theoretical teaching, or the first half of the sutra. In this chapter Shakyamuni declares that Buddhas appear in this world for the sole purpose of enabling people to attain Buddhahood. Earlier teaching set forth the three vehicles of *Shōmon, Engaku,* and Bodhisattva; however, in the *Hōben* chapter Shakyamuni explains that these three vehicles were simply expedients used to lead people to the supreme vehicle of Buddhahood.

Hōdō sutras: Lower provisional Mahayana sutras belonging to the third of the five periods of Shakyamuni's teachings, according to T'ien-t'ai's classification. *See also* Five periods.

Hōjō Tokimune (1251–1284): Hōjō regent to whom Nichiren addressed a letter in 1268 warning of an imminent invasion by the Mongols. The letter was ignored.

Hokke Gengi: "Profound Meaning of the Lotus Sutra." One of T'ien-t'ai's three major works. It gives a detailed explanation of the meaning of the title of the Lotus Sutra, *Myōhō-renge-kyō* (T33, no. 1716).

Hokke Mongu: "Words and Phrases of the Lotus Sutra." One of T'ien-t'ai's three major works. A ten-fascicle commentary on the Lotus Sutra, expounded by T'ien-t'ai and recorded by Chang-an (T33, no. 1718).

Hōnen (1133–1212): Also called Genkū. The founder of the Jōdo (Pure

Land) sect in Japan; it is also referred to as the Nembutsu sect, after the calling of the name (nembutsu) of the Buddha Amida. Hōnen first studied Tendai doctrines, but later turned to the exclusive calling of the Buddha's name. His school and those derived from it gained immense popularity. Nichiren roundly condemns Hōnen throughout his writings.

Hossō sect: (Chin Fa-hsiang tsung) Based on the writings of Asaṅga and Vasubandhu, this school was introduced into China by Hsüan-tsang and developed by his principal disciple K'uei-chi (632–682); Nichiren frequently refers to him as Tz'u-en, the name of his temple. The Hossō teachings were highly detailed and abstruse and the school never gained a substantial following. It was introduced to Japan on four occasions during the Nara period. Dōshō (629–700) of the Gangō-ji is considered the founder of the sect in Japan.

Hsüan-tsang (602–664): (Jap Genjō) A Chinese T'ang dynasty priest, famed for his trip to India to bring back scriptures. He left for India in 629 and studied the Consciousness-Only doctrine at the Nālandā monastery. In 645 he returned to China with many Sanskrit texts, many of which he later translated. His travels are described in the *Daitō Saiiki Ki* (Record of the Western Regions), the source for many of Nichiren's stories. He and his disciple K'uei-chi (also known as Tz'u-en) are regarded as the founders of the Fa-hsiang (Hossō) school.

Humanity: The fifth of the Ten Worlds, the world of human beings. *See* Ten Worlds.

Hungry Ghosts: (Jap *gaki*) The second of the Ten Worlds. *See also* Six paths, Ten Worlds.

Icchantika: (Jap *issendai*) Those of incorrigible disbelief, who have no faith in Buddhism, no aspiration for enlightenment, and thus no prospect for attaining Buddhahood. Some sutras say that *icchantika* are inherently incapable of attaining Buddhahood; later Mahayana texts hold that even an *icchantika* can become a Buddha.

Ichinen sanzen: "A single life-moment, or instant of thought, possesses three thousand realms." A philosophical system established by T'ien-t'ai in the *Maka Shikan* on the basis of the Lotus Sutra. *Ichinen* (one mind or life-moment, sometimes rendered "instant of thought") is the life that is manifested at each moment by common mortals, and *sanzen* (three thousand), the varying aspects and phases it assumes. At each moment, life experiences one of the ten conditions, that is, the Ten Worlds *(q.v.)*. Each of these worlds possesses the potential for all ten within itself, thus making one hundred possible worlds. Each of these hundred worlds possesses the ten factors or suchnesses *(q.v.;* Jap *jūn-yoze)*, thus becoming one thousand factors. Finally each of these factors possesses the three realms of existence *(q.v.;* Jap *sanseken)*, thus equaling three thousand realms.

Ionnō: (Skt Bhīṣmagarjitasvararāja) A Buddha mentioned in the *Fukyō* (twentieth) chapter of the Lotus Sutra. According to this chapter, in the past, two billion Buddhas appeared one after another, all having the same name, Ionnō. Bodhisattva Fukyō appeared during the Middle Day of the Law after the death of the first Ionnō Buddha and revered all people for their inherent Buddha nature.

Itai dōshin: Unity of people with a common cause. *Itai* (literally, different bodies) points to the need for many different personalities and abilities in achieving a given purpose. *Dōshin* (same mind) indicates the importance of uniting in the same spirit or maintaining a common ideal to achieve success. For Nichiren, *itai dōshin* means that people advance together to achieve the common goal of *kōsen-rufu (q.v.).*

Jambudvīpa: (Jap Embudai) In Indian and Buddhist cosmology one of the four continents situated respectively in the four directions with Mt. Sumeru as the center. Jambudvīpa is located to the south and is the place where Buddhism appears and spreads. It is often used in the sense of the entire world inhabited by humanity. *See also* Four continents.

Jikaku (794–866): Also called Ennin or Jikaku Daishi. Third chief priest of the Enryaku-ji. In 838 he journeyed to China where he studied both T'ien-t'ai and esoteric Buddhism. He returned to Japan in 847 and in 854 became head of the Tendai sect. He is frequently condemned by Nichiren for having introduced esoteric elements into the Tendai teachings.

Jōdo sect: Known also as Pure Land or Nembutsu sect. The teaching founded by Hōnen *(q.v.)* that called for recitation of the name of the Buddha Amida to obtain rebirth in his Western Paradise. This teaching achieved great popularity in Nichiren's time and is the object of frequent attacks by him.

Jōgyō: (Skt Viśiṣṭacāritra) Leader of the Four Bodhisattvas of the Earth who appear in the *Yujutsu* (fifteenth) chapter of the Lotus Sutra. In the *Jinriki* (twenty-first) chapter Shakyamuni transfers his teachings to Bodhisattva Jōgyō. Several of Nichiren's writings refer to his own propagation efforts as "the work of Bodhisattva Jōgyō."

Jōgyō: (Skt Viśuddhacāritra, Pure Conduct) *See* Bodhisattvas of the Earth.

Jōjitsu sect: (Chin Ch'eng-shih tsung) A school based on Harivarman's *Jōjitsu Ron,* as translated by Kumārajīva in the fifth century. The school flourished briefly in China and was brought to Japan where it was classified as one of the six Nara sects; however, it never became an independent sect and was studied in conjunction with the Sanron teachings.

Juryō chapter: "The Life Span of the Tathagata." The sixteenth chapter of the Lotus Sutra, regarded as the key chapter of the essential teaching (Jap *hommon*). Shakyamuni reveals here that he first attained enlightenment not in this lifetime but in the remote past of *gohyaku-jintengō,* and that ever since then he has been in the *saha,* or mundane world, teaching the Law.

Kakutoku: Priest who appears with King Utoku in the Nirvana Sutra. A considerable time after the death of the Buddha called *Kangi Zōyaku Nyorai* (literally, Joy Increasing Tathagata), Buddhism was about to perish. Kakutoku tried to protect the orthodox teachings and was harshly persecuted by many misguided priests and their followers. Utoku fought against these slanderous people to protect Kakutoku and died in the battle. It is said that because of their devotion to Buddhism, King Utoku was reborn as Shakyamuni Buddha and Priest Kakutoku as Kashō Buddha. This story is frequently alluded to by Nichiren.

Kalpa: (Jap *kō*) Sometimes rendered as eon. An extremely long period of time. Sutras and treatises differ in their definitions. Kalpas fall into two major categories, those of measurable and those of immeasurable duration. There are three kinds of measurable kalpas: small, medium, and major. One explanation says that a small kalpa is approximately sixteen million years long. According to Buddhist cosmology, a world repeatedly undergoes four stages: formation, continuance, decline, and disintegration. Each of these four stages lasts for twenty small kalpas and is equal to one medium kalpa. Finally, one complete cycle forms a major kalpa. Immeasurable kalpas are described in several ways. For example, a kalpa has been said to be longer than the time required to wear away a cube of stone forty *ri* (one *ri* is about 600 meters) on each side if a heavenly nymph alights on it and brushes it with a piece of cloth once every hundred years.

Kannon: (Skt Avalokiteśvara) Also Kanzeon. A bodhisattva who appears in the *Fumon* (twenty-fifth) chapter of the Lotus Sutra. According to the sutra he assumes thirty-three different forms and manifests himself everywhere in order to save people. Often Kannon appears in the form of a woman and is frequently so depicted in sculpture and painting.

Kanzeon: *See* Kannon.

Kātyāyana: (Jap Kasennen) One of the ten major disciples of Shakyamuni Buddha. He was born to a Brahman family in South India. He was regarded as a skilled debater, and as foremost in the analysis and exegesis of the Buddha's teaching.

Kegon sect: (Chin Hua-yen tsung) Based on the *Kegon* Sutra, according to legend, the first sutra preached by Shakyamuni; it was so abstruse and difficult to understand that he taught next the simpler Hinayana sutras. Tu-shun (Jap Tojun, 557–640) is the first master of the school in China, although Fa-tsang (Jap Hōzō, 643–712) who systematized its doctrines can be considered the real founder. The founder of the Kegon sect in Japan is considered to be Shinjō (Kor Simsang, d. 742), a priest from Silla who had studied under Fa-tsang. The Tōdai-ji in Nara is the head temple of the sect.

Kōbō (774–835): The founder of the Shingon sect in Japan. He is also known as Kūkai or Kōbō Daishi. He was ordained in 793 at the age of twenty and went to China in 804, where he studied the doctrines and rituals of esoteric Buddhism. He returned to Japan in 806 and established a temple on Mt. Kōya. So popular did his teachings become that many of them were later combined with those of the Tendai school. He is frequently condemned by Nichiren.

Kōsen-rufu: Literally, "To widely declare and spread [Buddhism]." The expression kōsen-rufu appears in the Yakuō (twenty-third) chapter of the Lotus Sutra. Nichiren indicates that Nam-myoho-renge-kyo is the Law to be declared and spread widely during the Latter Day of the Law.

Kumārajīva (344–413): (Jap Kumarajū) Famed translator of numerous Buddhist scriptures into Chinese during the Later Ch'in dynasty. Son of a Brahman father and a Kuchean princess, he entered the Buddhist Order at the age of seven. He studied widely in all fields of Indian literature and was fully ordained at age twenty. He spent twenty years in Kucha where he studied Mahayana literature extensively. In 379 he was invited to China, but the Chinese general who had been sent to Kucha, a fervent anti-Buddhist, kept him in Kucha for seventeen years. Eventually he was able to make his way to Ch'ang-an where he and his colleagues established a translation center that produced a large number of important translations in excellent literary Chinese. Prominent among the works was the translation of the Lotus Sutra, Myōhō-renge-kyō.

Kusha sect: (Chin Chü-she tsung) A school based on Vasubandhu's Abidatsuma Kusha Ron, which was translated into Chinese by both Paramārtha and Hsüan-tsang. It flourished briefly in China during the T'ang, but later was absorbed by the Hossō (Fa-hsiang) school. It was introduced to Japan during the Nara period when its doctrines were widely studied.

Latter Day of the Law: (Jap mappō) The period beginning two thousand years after Shakyamuni's death, when his teachings lose their power. One theory holds that it lasts ten thousand years and more. Japanese Buddhists in Nichiren's day believed that the Latter Day had begun in 1052 A.D.

Mahākāśyapa: (Jap Makakashō) One of Shakyamuni's ten major disciples. He was known as the foremost in ascetic practices. After Shakyamuni's death he presided over the First Buddhist Council for compiling the Buddha's teachings. He is counted as the first of Shakyamuni's twenty-four successors.

Major world system: (Jap sanzen daisen sekai) One of the world systems in ancient Indian and Buddhist cosmology. A world consists of a Mt.

Sumeru, its surrounding seas and mountain ranges, a sun, a moon, and other heavenly bodies, extending upward to the first meditation heaven in the world of form and downward to the circle of wind that forms the foundation of a world. One thousand worlds make a minor world system, one thousand minor world systems comprise an intermediate world system, and one thousand intermediate world systems form a major world system. The universe was conceived of as containing countless major world systems.

Maka Shikan: "Great Concentration and Insight," one of T'ien-tai's three major works, compiled by his disciple Chang-an *(q.v.).* It elucidates, among other things, the principle of *ichinen sanzen,* based on the Lotus Sutra (T46, no. 1912).

Mappō: *See* Three periods, Latter Day of the Law.

Maudgalyāyana: (Jap Mokuren) One of Shakyamuni's ten major disciples, known as the foremost in occult powers. Originally a student of Brahmanism, he is said to have become disenchanted with its teachings and to have turned eventually to Buddhism. The *Juki* (sixth) chapter of the Lotus Sutra predicts his enlightenment.

Men of incorrigible disbelief: See *Icchantika.*

Miao-lo (711–782): (Jap Myōraku) Also known as Chan-jan (Jap Tannen). The sixth patriarch of the T'ien-t'ai school, counting from T'ien-t'ai. He is revered as the restorer of the school and wrote commentaries on T'ien-t'ai's major works, contributing to a clarification of the teaching. His principal works are: the *Hokke Gengi Shakusen* (T33, no. 1717), *Hokke Mongu Ki* (T34, no. 1719), and *Maka Shikan Bugyōden Guketsu* (T46, no. 1912).

Middle Day of the Law: (Jap *zōhō* or *zōbō*) The second thousand years after Shakyamuni's death. During this period Mahayana Buddhism spread from India to China, but the teachings gradually became formalized. Also referred to as the Period of the Simulated Law. *See also* Three periods.

Miroku: (Skt Maitreya) A bodhisattva predicted to succeed Shakyamuni as a future Buddha. He is said to have been reborn in the Tuṣita Heaven, where he is now expounding the Law to the heavenly beings. It is said that he will reappear in this world 5,670 million years after the Buddha's death in order to save people. In the Lotus Sutra his persistent questions induced Shakyamuni to expound the *Juryō* (sixteenth) chapter.

Monju: (Skt Mañjuśrī) Also Monjushiri. Leader of the bodhisattvas of the theoretical teaching (Jap *shakumon*). He represents wisdom and enlightenment, and with Fugen is depicted as one of the two bodhisattvas who attend Shakyamuni Buddha.

Monjushiri: *See* Monju.

Muhengyō: *See* Bodhisattvas of the Earth.

Muryōgi Sutra: "Sutra of Infinite Meaning." Serves as an introductory teaching to the Lotus Sutra and is thought of as indicating that the true teaching will be revealed in the Lotus Sutra. In this sutra Shakyamuni states that for the past more than forty years he has not yet revealed the complete truth. This is taken to mean that all the sutras preached before the Lotus Sutra represent provisional teachings.

Mutual possession of the Ten Worlds: (Jap *jikkai gogu*) The principle that each of the Ten Worlds contains all the other nine within itself. This is taken to mean that an individual's life-condition can be changed and that all beings of the other nine worlds possess the potential for Buddhahood. *See also* Ten Worlds, *Ichinen sanzen*.

Myōhō-renge-kyō: (1) Japanese reading of the title of the Chinese translation of the Lotus Sutra, made by Kumārajīva in 406, consisting of eight volumes or rolls and twenty-eight chapters. (2) Conceived of in terms of Nam-myoho-renge-kyo, the "entity of the Mystic Law itself."

Nāgārjuna: (Jap Ryūju) A Mahayana scholar in southern India around the second or third century. He is counted as the fourteenth of Shakyamuni's twenty-four successors. He is the author of many important treatises on Mahayana Buddhism, such as the *Chū Ron* and the *Daichido Ron*.

Nam-myoho-renge-kyo: Regarded as the ultimate Law or absolute reality permeating all phenomena in the universe. It is also the invocation or *daimoku* in Nichiren Buddhism, one of the Three Great Secret Laws *(q.v.)*. *See also* Myōhō-renge-kyō. (Diacritical marks are omitted, and the "u" in "namu" elided to indicate the manner in which the phrase is intoned.)

Nan-yüeh (515–577): (Jap Nangaku) Known also as Hui-ssu (Jap Eshi). T'ien-t'ai's teacher. He entered the priesthood at the age of fifteen and concentrated on the study of the Lotus Sutra. His entire life was devoted to the practice of the Lotus Sutra and the training of disciples.

Nembutsu: The calling of the Buddha's name, in particular that of the Buddha Amida. Nembutsu is practiced by the Jōdo or Pure Land sect. It was advocated by Shan-tao (Jap Zendō, 613–681) in China, whose teachings were embraced by Hōnen *(q.v.)*, the founder of the school in Japan. The term is also used to refer to the sect itself.

Nine great persecutions: (Jap *kuō no dainan*) Also known as the nine great ordeals. The major hardships that Shakyamuni underwent. They are listed in the *Daichido Ron* and are frequently mentioned by Nichiren.

Perfect teaching: (Jap *engyō*) The last of the four teachings of doctrine as classified by T'ien-t'ai. The term "perfect teaching" is often used synonymously with the Lotus Sutra. *See also* Eight teachings.

Pratyekabuddha: See *Engaku*.

Provisional teachings: (Jap *gonkyō*) All the pre–Lotus Sutra teachings. T'ien-t'ai divided Shakyamuni's teachings into two categories: provisional and true. The provisional teachings, which include Hinayana and provisional Mahayana, were expounded during the first forty-two years after Shakyamuni's enlightenment. He taught these doctrines according to the capacity of his listeners as a temporary means to lead them to an understanding of the true teaching. The true teaching, T'ien-t'ai held, was that of the Lotus Sutra.

Pu-k'ung (705–774): (Jap Fukū; Skt Amoghavajra) The last of the three famous Indian esoteric masters to come to China from India during the T'ang dynasty. He arrived in China in 720 and became a disciple of Chin-kang-chih (Jap Kongōchi; Skt Vajrabodhi) and assisted in the translation of Shingon, or esoteric texts.

Pūrṇa: (Jap Furuna) One of Shakyamuni's ten major disciples; he was noted as the foremost in eloquence. Born to a rich Brahman family, he is said to have practiced austerities in the Himalaya. Hearing that Shakyamuni had attained enlightenment, he became the Buddha's disciple.

Rāhula: (Jap Ragora) Shakyamuni's son. Rāhula followed his father in renouncing the world and became one of the Buddha's ten major disciples. He was known as the foremost in inconspicuous practice.

Ritsu sect: (Chin Lü-tsung) A Buddhist sect based on the *vinaya* or rules of monastic discipline. In China it was divided into several schools. Representative is the Nan-shan (Jap Nanzan) school founded by Tao-hsüan (Jap Dōsen, 596–667) that advocated a strict adherence to the precepts. In 753 Chien-chen (Jap Ganjin, 688–763) introduced the teaching to Japan. In the Kamakura period a sect that combined esoteric doctrines with a strict observance of the precepts was established; it is known as Shingon-Ritsu.

Ryōkan (1217–1303): A prominent priest of the Shingon-Ritsu sect who entered the priesthood at seventeen and received the precepts from Eizon (1202–1290), considered the restorer of the Ritsu sect. In 1261 he went to Kamakura where he was named the chief priest of the Kōsen-ji, founded by a Hōjō regent. Later he was named chief priest of the Gokuraku-ji, founded by Hōjō Shigetoki. Nichiren considered him an archenemy and writes disparagingly of his talents.

Sanron sect: (Chin San-lun tsung) A Mādhyamika school based on the three treatises: *Chū Ron, Jūnimon Ron,* and *Hyaku Ron,* it was systematized by Chi-tsang (Jap Kichizō, 549–623) who is often regarded as the founder of the school. There were several transmissions to Japan in the seventh century, but Ekan (Kor Hyekwan) is generally considered the founder in Japan. Sanron is one of the six Nara sects.

Śāriputra: (Jap Sharihotsu) One of Shakyamuni's ten major disciples, known as the foremost in wisdom. The *Hiyu* (third) chapter of the Lotus Sutra predicts that he will in the future become a Buddha named Kekō, Flower Light.

Shakubuku: Propagating Buddhism by refuting a person's attachment to other views and leading him to the correct teaching. The term is found in the *Maka Shikan*. It is contrasted with *shōju,* gradual propagation without refuting attachments. See also *Shōju.*

Shan-wu-wei (637–735): (Jap Zemmui; Skt Śubhākarasimha) Born as a prince in Udyāna, India, he was the first to introduce the esoteric teachings during the T'ang dynasty. He studied the esoteric teachings under Dharmagupta at the Nālandā Monastery. Arriving in China in 716, he engaged in the translation of numerous sutras, including the *Dainichi* and *Soshitsuji* sutras.

Shingon sect: (Chin Chen-yen tsung) The school that taught the esoteric doctrines. Although esoteric texts had been brought to China at an early period, it was not until the T'ang dynasty that three famous Indian masters, Śubhākarasimha, Vajrabodhi, and Amoghavajra, introduced and translated the major sutras of the school. The school flourished briefly in China, but was of much greater importance in Japan. Here it was introduced by Kūkai, Kōbō Daishi, who went to Ch'ang-an in 804 and studied under Hui-kuo, a disciple of Amoghavajra. He established the Shingon sect on his return, building a temple complex on Mt. Kōya. Many Shingon teachings were adopted by the Tendai sect. Nichiren condemns the Tendai priests who followed Dengyō Daishi for having subverted the original Tendai teachings by adding esoteric doctrines.

Shōbō. *See* Three periods, Former Day of the Law.

Shōju: Propagating Buddhism by gradually leading a person without refuting his attachment to other teachings. The term is used in contrast to *shakubuku.* See also *Shakubuku.*

Shōmon: (Skt śrāvaka) One who listens to the Buddha's teaching, and thereby gains enlightenment. The highest stage of the *shōmon* is an arhat. Sometimes translated as Man of Learning. *Shōmon* occupy the seventh of the Ten Worlds. *See also* Ten Worlds.

Six difficult and nine easy acts: (Jap *rokunan kui*) Comparisons set forth in the *Hōtō* (eleventh) chapter of the Lotus Sutra. The six difficult acts are to propagate the Lotus Sutra widely, to copy it, to recite it, to teach it to even one person, to hear of the Lotus Sutra and inquire about its meaning, and to maintain faith in it. The nine easy acts are: 1) to teach innumerable sutras other than the Lotus Sutra, 2) to take up Mt. Sumeru and hurl it across the universe over countless Buddha lands, 3) to kick a major world system into another quarter with one's toe, 4) to stand in the highest heaven and preach innumerable sutras other than the Lotus Sutra, 5) to grasp the sky with one hand and travel around with it, 6) to place the earth on one's toenail and ascend to the Brahma Heaven, 7) to walk across a burning prairie carrying a bundle of hay on one's back without being burned, 8) to preach eighty-four thousand teachings and enable one's listeners to obtain the six supernatural powers, and 9) to enable innumerable people to reach the stage of arhat and acquire the six supernatural powers.

Six non-Buddhist teachers: (Jap *rokushi gedō*) The six most influential thinkers in central India at the time of Shakyamuni. They openly challenged the old Vedic traditions and advocated philosophical and religious concepts of their own. They are given as: 1) Purāṇa-kāśyapa, who rejected morality and denied causality and rewards and punishment for one's acts; 2) Maskari-gośāliputra, who asserted that everything was predetermined by fate; 3) Ajita-keśakambala, known as a hedonist who claimed that since the whole universe was composed of the four elements, earth, water, fire, and metal, this was true also of the human body, and therefore there was no recompense for the good or evil a man practiced; 4) Sañjaya-Vairāṭīputra, a skeptic who rejected all explanations of metaphysical questions; 5) Kakuda Kātyayāna, who denied the laws of causality; and 6) Nirgranthajñātiputra, the founder of Jainism, who championed ascetic practices.

Six *pāramitā*: (Jap *rokuharamitsu*) Six practices for Mahayana bodhisattvas in their progress toward Buddhahood: charity, observing precepts, forbearance, assiduousness, meditation, and wisdom.

Six paths: (Jap *rokudō*) The first six of the Ten Worlds, the realms of transmigration. They are: Hell, Hungry Ghosts, Animals, Asura, Humanity, and Heaven. *See also* Ten Worlds.

Specific teaching: (Jap *bekkyō*) *See* Eight teachings.

Subhūti: (Jap Shubodai) One of Shakyamuni's ten major disciples. He was regarded as the foremost in the understanding of the doctrine of Emptiness.

Sumeru: (Jap Shumi-sen) In Indian and Buddhist cosmology, the mountain that stands in the center of a world system. It is 84,000 *yojana* high; the god Taishaku resides on the summit, while the Four Heavenly Kings live halfway down, one to each of its four sides. In the seas below are four continents, the one to the south being Jambudvīpa, the land where Buddhism spreads, that is, the present world.

Sun Goddess: (Jap Amaterasu Ōmikami or Tenshō Daijin) The chief female deity in Shinto. Nichiren regarded her as a personification of the natural forces that protect those with faith in the Lotus Sutra.

Tahō: (Skt Prabhūtaratna) A Buddha who appears, seated within the Treasure Tower at the Ceremony in the Air, to lend credence to Shakyamuni's teachings in the Lotus Sutra. According to the *Hōtō* (eleventh) chapter of the Lotus Sutra, he lives in the land of Treasure Purity in an eastern part of the universe. While still engaged in bodhisattva practice he pledged that, even after having entered nirvana, he would appear to attest to the validity of the Lotus Sutra, wherever it might be taught.

Taishaku: (Skt Śakra devendra) Generally known as Indra, he is the god of the Trāyastrimśa Heaven (Jap Tōriten). Originally a Hindu god, he together with Bonten are the principal tutelary gods who protect Buddhism. He is served by the Four Heavenly Kings and rules the other thirty-two gods in his heaven at the top of Mt. Sumeru. According to the *Jo* (first) chapter of the Lotus Sutra, he and twenty thousand retainers took part in the assembly at Eagle Peak.

Tao-hsüan (Jap Dōsen, 596–667): The founder of the Nan-shan (Nanzan) branch of the Lü (Ritsu) school that emphasized the *Vinaya*, or monastic rules. From 645 he assisted Hsüan-tsang in his translation work. He compiled several books, including the *Zoku Kōsō Den,* containing the biographies of five hundred eminent priests who lived between 502 and 645.

Tendai sect: (Chin T'ien-t'ai tsung) The school was established by Chih-i (Jap Chigi, 538–597), most frequently referred to by Nichiren by his posthumous name T'ien-t'ai Ta-shih (Tendai Daishi, or the Great Teacher Tendai). The school flourished during the Sui dynasty, fell into decline during the T'ang, although it was revived somewhat by Miao-lo (Jap Myōraku), known also as Chan-jan (Jap Tannen). Its texts were introduced to Japan in the Nara period, but the sect was established in Japan by Saichō (Dengyō Daishi) who founded the Tendai center on Mt. Hiei.

Ten demon daughters: *See* Ten Goddesses.

Ten directions: (Jap *jippō*) The eight points of the compass as well as up and down.

Ten factors: (Jap *jūnyoze*) Also referred to as the ten suchnesses, they are the aspects common to all existence in any of the Ten Worlds. They are mentioned in the *Hōben* (second) chapter of the Lotus Sutra. They are: 1) appearance or form *(nyozesō)*, 2) nature or quality *(nyozeshō)*, 3) substance or entity *(nyozetai)*, 4) power *(nyozeriki)*, 5) activity or influence *(nyozesa)*, 6) cause *(nyozein)*, 7) indirect cause or relation *(nyozeen)*, 8) effect *(nyozeka)*, 9) reward or retribution *(nyozehō)*, and 10) the unifying factor that makes the above nine consistent from outset to end *(nyoze hommatsu kukyōtō)*. See also *Ichinen sanzen.*

Ten Goddesses: (Jap Jūrasetsu-nyo) The ten daughters of Kishimojin (Skt Hārītī), described in the *Darani* (twenty-sixth) chapter of the Lotus Sutra. The mother and daughters vow to protect the votaries of the Lotus Sutra.

Ten Worlds: (Jap *jikkai*) The standard interpretation of the Ten Worlds is as physical places, each with its own inhabitants: 1) Hell *(jigoku),* 2) Hungry Ghosts *(gaki),* 3) Animals *chikushō),* 4) Asura or Fighting Demons *(ashura),* 5) Humanity *(nin),* 6) Heaven *(ten),* 7) *Shōmon, śrāvaka,* one who practices the four noble truths to gain Nirvana, 8) *Engaku, pratyekabuddha,* one who gains enlightenment for himself, 9) Bodhisattva, and 10) Buddha. The Ten Worlds are also sometimes interpreted as potential conditions of life, inherent in each individual.

Thus, the Ten Worlds are rendered as: 1) Hell, 2) Hunger, 3) Animality, 4) Anger, 5) Humanity or Tranquility, 6) Heaven or Rapture, 7) Learning, 8) Realization, 9) Bodhisattva, and 10) Buddhahood.

Tenshō Daijin: *See* Sun Goddess.

Theoretical teaching: (Jap *shakumon*) The first fourteen chapters of the Lotus Sutra as classified by T'ien-t'ai in his *Hokke Mongu*. This portion of the sutra represents the preaching of the historical Shakyamuni who first attained enlightenment during his lifetime in India. The last fourteen chapters of the sutra are classified as the essential teaching *(hommon)*. *See also* Essential teaching.

Three bodies: (Jap *sanshin* or *sanjin*) Also called the three properties: 1) Law or Dharma body (Jap *hosshin*: Skt *dharmakāya*), the body of ultimate reality; 2) the reward or bliss body (Jap *hōjin* or *hōshin*; Skt *sambhogakāya*), the Buddha body received for meritorious actions; and 3) the manifested body (Jap *ōjin*; Skt *nirmāṇakāya*), the body in which a Buddha appears to correspond to the needs and capacities of sentient beings.

Three calamities and seven disasters: (Jap *sansai shichinan*) Calamities and disasters as described in the sutras. There are two kinds of the three calamities: the three greater calamities of fire, water, and wind that destroy a world at the end of the Kalpa of Decline, and the three lesser calamities of high grain prices or inflation (especially that caused by famine), warfare, and pestilence. The seven disasters differ with the sutra. The *Yakushi* Sutra lists them as: pestilence, foreign invasion, internal strife, unnatural changes in the heavens, solar and lunar eclipses, unseasonable storms and typhoons, and drought.

Three evil paths: (Jap *sanakudō*) The three lowest of the Ten Worlds: Hell, Hungry Ghosts, and Animals. *See* Ten Worlds.

Three existences: (Jap *sanze*) Also referred to as the three periods of time: past, present, and future.

Threefold world: (Jap *sangai*) The world of unenlightened beings who transmigrate among the six paths or the first six of the Ten Worlds. The *Kusha Ron* divides this world into three: 1) the world of desire (Jap *yokkai*) which consists of Hell, the realms of Hungry Ghosts, Animals, Asura, Humanity, and parts of Heaven. Here the beings have sexual and other appetites; 2) the world of form (Jap *shikikai*) which comprises part of Heaven. Here the beings have neither sexual nor any other kind of appetite; 3) the world of non-form (Jap *mushikikai*), also part of Heaven, where the beings are free both from desires and material elements and devote themselves to different states of meditation.

Three Great Secret Laws: (Jap *sandai hihō*) One of the most important elements of Nichiren's teaching. The Three Great Secret Laws are the *honzon,* the sacred object of worship, the *daimoku,* the title of the Lotus Sutra itself, and the *kaidan,* the ordination platform. These three Laws are qualified by *hommon no,* indicating that they represent the essential teaching. The object of worship *(honzon)* is the Gohonzon or the eternal Buddha of the *Juryō* (sixteenth) chapter; the *daimoku,* the title of the sutra itself as well as its invocation; and the *kaidan* is the ordination platform, although this latter term was not precisely defined by Nichiren and various interpretations of its meaning have been forwarded.

Three groups of *shōmon* disciples: (Jap *sanshū no shōmon*) The *shōmon* whose enlightenment was prophesied in the first half of the Lotus Sutra. Shakyamuni taught that the ultimate purpose was to obtain Buddhahood rather than some lower state, but his disciples differed in their capacity to understand this teaching. Śāriputra was the first to understand, on hearing it explained in the *Hōben* (second) chapter. He represents the first group and his enlightenment is predicted in the *Hiyu* (third) chapter. Maudgalyāyana, Mahākāśyapa, Kātāyana, and Subhūti through the parable of the burning house in the *Hiyu* chapter; these disciples form the second group and their enlightenment is predicted in the *Juki* (sixth) chapter. Pūrṇa, Ānanda, Rāhula, and others, who finally understood the Buddha's teaching by hearing about their past relationship with Shakyamuni since the remote past of *sanzenjintengō,* as explained in the *Kejōyu* (seventh) chapter, comprise the third group. Their future enlightenment is predicted in the next two chapters.

Three illusions: (Jap *sanwaku*) Also called the three categories of illusion. Classification of illusions established by T'ien-t'ai in the *Maka Shikan:* 1) illusions of thought and desire (Jap *kenshi waku*), 2) illusions as numerous as particles of dust and sand (Jap *jinja waku*), 3) illusions of basic ignorance (Jap *mumyō waku*).

Three obstacles and four devils: (Jap *sanshō shima*) Various obstacles to the practice of Buddhism. They are listed in the Nirvana Sutra and the *Daichido Ron.* The three obstacles are: 1) *bonnō-shō,* obstacles arising from the three poisons, greed, anger, and stupidity; 2) *gō-shō,* obstacles due to bad karma created by committing the five cardinal sins or the ten evil acts. They may also refer to opposition from one's spouse or children; and 3) *hō-shō,* obstacles caused by retribution for actions in the three evil paths. It also may refer to obstacles caused by one's superiors, such as rulers or parents. The four devils are: 1) *bonnō-ma,* obstructions arising from the three poisons; 2) *on-ma,* the hindrance of the five components or aggregates (*go'on* or *goun;* Skt *skandhas*): form, perception, conception, volition, and consciousness; 3) *shi-ma,* the hindrance of death, because fear of death impedes the practice of Buddhism; and 4) *tenji-ma,* obstruction by the Devil of the Sixth Heaven, which usually manifests itself in oppression by men of power. This is the most difficult of all to overcome.

Three periods: (Jap *sanji*) The three periods or stages into which the time following Shakyamuni Buddhas death is divided. These are conventionally described as *shōbō*, the age when the True Law was propagated, *zōhō*, or *zōbō*, the age when the simulated law obtained, and *mappō*, the degenerate age when Buddhism fell into confusion. *The Major Writings of Nichiren Daishonin* renders these terms as the Former, Middle, and Latter Day of the Law, and this terminology has been followed here. The duration of each period differs with the text. Nichiren adopted the view that the Former and Middle Day of the Law each lasted one thousand years, and that the world had now entered the period of the Latter Day of the Law. It was generally believed that the year 1052 marked the beginning of the Latter Day of the Law.

Three poisons: (Jap *sandoku*) Greed, anger, and stupidity.

Three realms of existence: (Jap *sanseken*) sometimes rendered three categories of realm. T'ien-t'ai's elaboration of a concept that appeared originally in the *Daichido Ron:* 1) the realm of the five components or aggregates—form, perception, conception, volition, and consciousness *(go'on-seken)*, 2) the realm of sentient beings *(shujō-seken)*, and 3) the realm of the environment of sentient beings *(kokudo-seken)*. See also *Ichinen sanzen*.

Three schools of the South and seven schools of the North: (Jap *nansan hokushichi*) T'ien-t'ai's designation for the principal systems of comparative classification of the Buddhist sutras in vogue in China during the Northern and Southern dynasties period. These systems are outlined in his *Hokke Gengi*. All three Southern schools characterized the sutras under three categories: sudden, gradual, and indeterminate. The seven Northern schools each had its own classification, but they all gave precedence to the Nirvana or the *Kegon* Sutra. T'ien-t'ai disputed their conclusions with his classification of the five periods.

Three thousand conditions: (Jap *sanzen* or *sanzen no hō*) All phenomena in the universe. See *Ichinen sanzen*.

Three treasures: (Jap *sambō*) The Buddha, the Law, and the Priesthood.

Three truths: (Jap *santai*) Three related aspects of truth, developed by T'ien-t'ai in the *Hokke Gengi* and the *Maka Shikan*. They are: the truth of non-substantiality *(kūtai)*, the truth of temporary existence *(ketai)*, and the truth of the Middle Way *(chūtai)*, where all phenomena are both insubstantial and temporary but yet are basically neither.

Three types of learning : (Jap *sangaku*) Precepts, meditation, and wisdom.

Three vehicles: (Jap *sanjō*) The states and the teachings of *Shōmon, Engaku*, and Bodhisattva. These states were originally encouraged by Shakyamuni, but were rejected in the Lotus Sutra, where the ultimate goal is Buddhahood.

Three virtues: (Jap *santoku*) The virtues of sovereign, teacher, and parent that are possessed by the Buddha.

T'ien-t'ai (538–597): (Jap Tendai) Another name for Chih-i (Chigi), the founder of the T'ien-t'ai school. Nichiren most frequently refers to him as T'ien-t'ai, or the Great Teacher T'ien-t'ai. He entered the priesthood at eighteen and studied the Lotus Sutra at Mt. Ta-hsien. His teacher was Nan-yüeh Hui-ssu (Nangaku Eshi, 515–577). T'ien-t'ai was the great organizer of his school's doctrines. His principal works, the *Hokke Gengi*, the *Hokke Mongu*, and the *Maka Shikan* were all compiled and edited by his immediate disciple Chang-an *(q.v.)*.

Treasure Tower: (Jap *hōtō*) The tower of Tahō Buddha that appears from beneath the earth in the *Hōtō* (eleventh) chapter of the Lotus Sutra.

Tripitaka Master: (Jap *sanzō*) An honorific title given to those who were well versed in the three divisions of the canon. The title was often given to monks from India and Central Asia who came to China and translated Buddhist scriptures into Chinese.

Twenty-four successors: (Jap *fuhōzō no nijūyonin*) The successors of Shak-yamuni. They are listed in the *Fu Hōzō Innen Den* (The History of the Buddha's Successors). They are 1) Mahākāśyapa, 2) Ānanda, 3) Mad-hyāntika (omitted in the *Fu Hōzō Innen Den*, but included in later Tendai works), 4) Śaṇavāsa, 5) Upagupta, 6) Dhṛtaka, 7) Miccaka, 8) Buddhanandi, 9) Buddhamitra, 10) Pārśva, 11) Puṇyayaśas, 12) Aś-vaghoṣa, 13) Kapimala, 14) Nāgārjuna, 15) Kāṇadeva or Āryadeva, 16) Rāhulata, 17) Saṅghanandi. 18) Gayaśāta or Samghayaśas, 19) Kumārata, 20) Jayata, 21) Vasubandhu, 22) Manorhita, 23) Haklena-yaśas, and 24) Āryasiṁha.

Two vehicles: (Jap *nijō*) Teachings expounded for the *shōmon* and *engaku*. The term is also used in reference to the seventh and eighth of the Ten Worlds. *The Major Writings of Nichiren Daishonin* refers to them as Learning and Realization. *See* Ten Worlds.

Tz'u-en (632–682): (Jap Jion) The founder of the Chinese Fa-hsiang (Hossō) school. He is also known as K'uei-chi (Kiki). One of the outstanding disciples of Hsüan-tsang, he collaborated with him on the translation of many important texts, and wrote several commentaries on the Consciousness-Only doctrine.

Vasubandhu: (Jap Tenjin or Seshin) A Buddhist scholar of northern India, thought to have lived around the fourth or fifth century. He originally studied Hinayana and wrote the *Kusha Ron*. He is later said to have been converted to Mahayana by his elder brother Asaṅga and wrote numerous treatises designed to clarify the Mahayana teachings.

Votary of the Lotus Sutra: (Jap *Hokekyō no gyōja*) One who propagates the Lotus Sutra and practices Buddhism in accordance with its teachings. Nichiren considered T'ien-t'ai and Dengyō votaries, and was convinced that he himself fulfilled the sutra's prophecies and served as its votary.

Wise Kalpa: (Jap *kengō*) The present major kalpa in which a thousand Buddhas of great wisdom, including Shakyamuni, will appear in order to save people.

Yakuō: (Skt Bhaiṣajyarāja) A bodhisattva said to possess the power to cure all physical and mental diseases.

Yakushi: (Skt Bhaiṣajyaguru) The Healing Buddha or the Buddha of Medicine who dwells in the Pure Emerald World in the east. As a bodhisattva he made twelve vows to cure all illnesses and to lead all people to enlightenment.

BIBLIOGRAPHY

A. Western-Language Works

The following is a brief listing of translations of Nichiren's works and books concerning him, as well as a list of translations of the Lotus Sutra. No reference is made to articles in academic journals, nor is there any reference to the large scholarly literature in Japanese.

TRANSLATIONS AND STUDIES OF NICHIREN

Anesaki, Masaharu. *Nichiren, the Buddhist Prophet.* London: Oxford University Press, 1916. Reprint. Gloucester, Mass.: P. Smith, 1966.

Del Campana, Pier P. "Sandaihihō-shō by Nichiren." *Monumenta Nipponica* 26(1–2): 205–224, 1971.

Dollarhide, Kenneth, trans. *Nichiren's Senji-sho; An Essay on the Selection of the Proper Time.* Lewiston, N.Y.: Mellen, 1982.

Ehara, N. R. M., trans. *The Awakening to the Truth, or "Kaimokushō."* Tokyo: International Buddhist Society, 1941.

Gosho Translation Committee. *The Major Writings of Nichiren Daishonin.* 5 vols. Tokyo: Nichiren Shoshu International Center, 1979–1988.

Kirimura, Yasuji. *The Life of Nichiren Daishonin.* Tokyo: Nichiren Shoshu International Center, 1980.

Murano, Senchu, trans. *Nyorai metsugo go gohyakusai shi Kanjin sho; or, The True Object of Worship. Revealed for the first time in the fifth of five century periods after the great decease of the Tathāgata.* Tokyo: Young East Association, 1954.

Murano, Senchu, trans. *Rissho Ankoku Ron or Establish the Right Law and Save Our Country.* Tokyo: Nichiren Shu Headquarters, 1977.

Nichiren Shoshu International Center, compiler. *Buddhism and the Nichiren Shōshu Tradition.* Tokyo: Nichiren Shoshu International Center, 1986.

Petzold, Bruno. *Buddhist Prophet Nichiren—A Lotus in the Sun.* Edited by Shotaro Iida and Wendy Simmonds. Tokyo: Hokke Jānaru, 1978.

Renondeau, Gaston, trans. *La bouddhisme japonais [par] Honen, Shinran, Nichiren, et Dogen.* Paris: A. Michel, 1965. (Contains a translation of "The Opening of the Eyes.")

Renondeau, Gaston. *La doctrine de Nichiren.* Paris: Presses Universitaires de France, 1953.

Renondeau, Gaston. "Le 'Traité sur l'état' de Nichiren." *T'oung Pao* 40: 123–98, 1957.

Rodd, Laurel Rasplica. *Nichiren: A Biography*. Tucson: Arizona State University Press, 1978.

Rodd, Laurel Rasplica. *Nichiren, Selected Writing*. Honolulu: University Press of Hawaii, 1980. (This excellent work has, unfortunately, been withdrawn from circulation and is not readily available.)

TRANSLATIONS OF THE LOTUS SUTRA AND RELATED WORKS

The Lotus of the Wonderful Law or the Lotus Gospel. Edited by W. E. Soothill. Oxford: Clarendon Press, 1930.

Muryōgi-Kyō: The Sutra of Innumerable Meanings and Kanfugen-gyō: The Sutra of Meditation on the Bodhisattva Universal—Virtue. Tokyo: Kosei Publishing Co., 1974. (*Muryōgi-kyō* translated by Yoshiro Tamura; *Kanfugen-gyō* translated by Kojiro Miyasaka; both works revised by Pier P. Del Campana.)

Myōhō Renge Kyō, the Sutra of the Lotus of the Wonderful Law. Translated by Bunno Katō. Revised by W. E. Soothill and William Schiffer. Tokyo: Rissho Kōsei-kai, 1971.

Scripture of the Lotus Blossom of the Fine Dharma (The Lotus Sutra). Translated from the Chinese of Kumārajīva by Leon Hurvitz. New York: Columbia University Press, 1976.

The Sutra of the Lotus Flower of the Wonderful Law. Translated by Senchu Murano. Tokyo: Nichiren Shu Headquarters, 1974.

The Threefold Lotus Sutra. Translated by Bunno Katō et al. New York: Weatherhill, 1975.

B. Buddhist Works Cited by Nichiren

The following list contains Buddhist works cited by Nichiren, as well as the sources for many of his stories and allusions where they could be identified. The titles of many Buddhist works are extremely long; thus the name by which they are best known is given, although on occasion the full title is also provided. Nichiren frequently cites works by an abbreviated title; such titles are included in the listing, and are cross-referenced. The readings of the titles of various Buddhist works frequently vary, depending on the sect or school.

Abidatsuma Daibibasha Ron 阿毘達磨大毘婆娑論. T27, no. 1545.

Abidatsuma Honruisoku Ron 阿毘達磨品類足論. T26, no. 1542.

Abidatsuma Hotchi Ron 阿毘達磨発智論. T26, no. 1544.

Agon Kyō 阿含経 Āgama Sutras. T1–2, nos. 1–151.

Amida Kyō 阿弥陀経. T12, no. 366.

Anraku-shū 安楽集, by Tao-ch'o 道綽 (Dōshaku). T47, no. 1958.

Ben Kenmitsu Nikyō Ron 弁顕密二教論, by Kūkai (Kōbō Daishi) 空海(弘法大師). T77, no. 2427. Also called: *Nikyō Ron*.

Binaya Zōji 毘奈耶雑事. T24, no. 1451. Full title: *Kompon Setsu Issai Ubu Binaya Zōji* 根本説一切有部毘奈耶雑事.

Bodaishin Ron 菩提心論. T32, no. 1665.

Bommō-kyō 梵網経. T24, no 1484.

Bosatsu Honjō Manron 菩提本生鬘論. T3, no. 160.

Bosatsu Yōraku Hongō Kyō 菩薩瓔珞本業経. T24, no. 1485.

Buppon Gyōjikkyō 仏本行集経. T3, no. 190.

Busso Tōki 仏祖統記. T49, no. 2035.

Butsuzō Kyō 仏蔵経, T15, no. 653.

Chū Ron 中論. T30, no. 1564.

Chūhen Gikyō 中辺義鏡, by Tokuitsu (Tokuichi) 徳一. Original is lost but significant portions are cited in *Shugo Kokkai Shō*.

Dai Birushana Jōbutsu Kyō Sho 大毘盧遮那成仏経疏, by I-hsing 一行 (Ichigyō). T39, no. 1796.

Daibibasha Ron. See *Abidatsuma Daibibasha Ron*.

Daibon Hannya Kyō 大品般若経. T8, no. 223. Also known as *Maka Hannya Haramitsu Kyō* 摩訶般若波羅密経.

Daichido Ron 大智度論. T25, no. 1509.

Daihatsu Nehan Gyō. See *Nehan Gyō*.

Daihatsu Nehan Gyō Gobun 大般涅槃経後分. T12, no. 377.

Daihōdō Musō Kyō. See *Daiun Gyō*.

Daijikkyō 大集経 T13, no. 397. Also read: *Daijuku Kyō* and *Daishutsu Kyō*.

Daijō Hōon Girin Jō 大乗法苑義林章, by K'uei-chi (Tz'u-en) 窺基(慈恩) Kiki (Jion). T45, no. 1861.

Daijō Kishin Ron 大乗起信論. T32, nos. 1666, 1667.

Daijō Kishin Ron Giki 大乗起信論義記, by Fa-tsang 法蔵 (Hōzō). T44, no. 1846.

Daijō Nyū Ryōga Kyō 大乗入楞伽経. T16, no. 672.

Daijō Shiron Gengi Ki 大乗四論玄義記, by Chün-cheng 均正 (Kinshō). ZZ 1, 74, 1.

Daijuku Kyō. See *Daijikkyō*.

Dainichi Kyō 大日経. T18, no. 848. Full title: *Dai-Birushana Jōbutsu Jimben Kaji Kyō* 大毘盧遮那成仏神変加持経.

Dainichi Kyō Gishaku 大日経義釈, by I-hsing 一行 (Ichigyō) ZZ1, 36, 3–5.

Dainichi Kyō shiki 大日経旨帰, by Enchin (Chishō Daishi) 円珍(智証大師). T58, no. 2212a.

Dainichi Kyō Sho 大日経疏, by I-hsing 一行 (Ichigyō). T39, no. 1796.

Dairon. See *Daichido Ron*.

Daishutsu Kyō. See *Daijikkō*.

Daitō Saiiki Ki 大唐西域記, by Hsüan-tsang 玄奘 (Genjō). T51, no. 2087.

Daiun Gyō 大雲経 T12, no. 387. Full title: *Daihōdō Musō Kyō* 大方等無想経. Also known as *Daihōdō Daiun Gyō*.

Ebyō Shū. See *Ebyō Tendai Shū*.

Ebyō Tendai Shū 依憑天台集, by Saichō (Dengyō Daishi) 最澄(伝教大師). DDZ3, 343–365.

Eizan Daishi Den 叡山大師伝. DDZ5, 1–48 at end.

Fu Hōzō Innen Den 付法蔵因縁伝. T50, no. 2058. Also called: *Fuhōzō Kyō* 付法蔵経.

Fugen Kyō 普賢経. T9, no. 277. Also known as: *Kanfugen-Gyō* 観普賢経.

Fugen Kyō Ki 普賢経記, by Enchin (Chishō Daishi) 円珍(智証大師). T56, no. 2194, Full title: *Bussetsu Kanfugen Bosatsu Gyōbōgyōki* 仏説観普賢菩薩行法経記. Also known as *Kanfugen Gyōki*, 観普賢行記.

Fuhōzō Kyō. See *Fu Hōzō Innen Den*.

Fushō Ki. See *Hokke Mongu Fushō Ki*.

Gejimmikkyō 解深密経. T16, no. 676. Also called *Jimmitsu Kyō*.

Genkō Shakusho 元享釈書. DNBZ 101.

Guketsu. See *Maka Shikan Bugyōden Guketsu*.

Hanju-san 般舟讚, by Shan-tao 善導 (Zendō). T47, no. 1981.

Hannya Shingyō 般若心経. T8, no. 251.

Hannya Shingyō Hiken 般若心経秘鍵, by Kūkai (Kōbō Daishi) 空海（弘法大師）. T57, no. 2203.

Hatsunaion Kyō 般泥洹経, T1, no. 6.

Hizō Hōyaku 秘蔵宝鑰, by Kūkai (Kōbō Daishi) 空海（弘法大師）. T77, no. 2426.

Hōdō Darani Kyō 方等陀羅尼経. T21, no. 1339.

Hoke Kyō Gensan Yōshū 法華経玄賛要集, by Hsi-fu 施復 (Seifu), ZZ1, 53, 3–54, 5.

Hoke Kyō Giki 法華経義記, by Fa-yün 法雲 (Hōun). T33, no. 1715.

Hoke Kyō Mongu Fushō Ki. See *Hokke Mongu Fushō Ki*.

Hoke Kyō Shogisan 法華経疏義纉. ZZ1, 40, 3. Also known as *Tōshun* 東春 and *Hokke Mongu Tōshun* 法華文句東春.

Hokke Denki 法華伝記. T51, no. 2068.

Hokke Gengi 法華玄義, by Chih-i (T'ien-t'ai) 智顗（天台大師）(Chigi, Tendai Daishi). T33, no. 1716. Full title: *Myōhō Renge Kyō Gengi* 妙法蓮華経玄義.

Hokke Gengi Shakusen 法華玄義釈籤, by Chan-jan (Miao-lo) 湛然（妙楽）Tan-nen (Myōraku). T33, no. 1717.

Hokke Genron 法華玄論, by Chi-tsang 吉蔵 (Kichizō). T34, no. 1720.

Hokke Gensan 法華玄讚, by K'uei-chi (Tz'u-en) 窺基（慈恩）Kiki (Jion). T34, no. 1723. Also called *Myōhō Renge Kyō Gensan* 妙法蓮華経玄讚.

Hokke Gensan Yōshū. See *Hoke Kyō Gensan Yōshū*.

Hokke Giki 法華儀軌. T19, no. 1000. Full title: *Jōju Myōhō Renge Kyō Ōyuga Kanchi Giki* 成就妙法蓮華経王瑜伽観智儀軌.

Hokke Gohyakumon Ron 法華五百門論, by Chan-jan (Miao-lo) 湛然（妙楽）Tan-nen (Myōraku). ZZ2B, 5, 4.

Hokke Mongu 法華文句, by Chih-i (T'ien-t'ai) 智顗（天台）, T34, no. 1718. Full title: *Myōhō Renge Kyō Mongu* 妙法蓮華経文句.

Hokke Mongu Fushō Ki 法華文句輔正記, by Tao-hsien 道暹 (Dōsen). ZZ1, 45, 1. Also known as *Hoke Kyō Mongu Fushō Ki* 法華経文句補正記.

Hokke Mongu Ki 法華文句記, by Chan-jan (Miao-lo) 湛然（妙楽）Tannen (Myōraku). T34, no. 1719.

Hokke Mongu Tōshun. See *Hoke Kyō Shogisan*.

Hokke Ron Ki 法華論記. DNBZ 25. (*Chishō Daishi Zenshū*, v. 1).

Hokke Sandaibu Fuchū 法華三大部補註, by Tsung-i 従義 (Jugi) ZZ1, 43, 5–44, 3.

Hokke Shūku 法華秀句, by Saichō (Dengyō Daishi) 最澄（伝教大師）DDZ3, 1–280.

Hōmetsujin Gyō 法滅尽経. T12, no. 396.

Honchō Kōsō Den 本朝高僧伝. DNBZ 102.

Hōshō Ron 宝性論. T31, no. 1611. Full title: *Kukyō Ichijō Hōshō Ron* 究竟一乗宝性論.

Hyaku Ron 百論. T30, no. 1569.

Ichijō Yōketsu 一乗要決, by Genshin 源信. T74, no. 2370.

Jikaku Daishi Den 慈覚大師伝. *Zoku Gunsho Ruijū*, 8, pt. 2, 683–689.

Jimmitsu Kyō. See *Gejimmikkyō.*

Jōjitsu Ron 成実論. T32, no. 1646.

Jōmyō Kyō 浄名経. See *Vimalakirti Sutra*

Jōyuishiki Ron. See *Yuishiki Ron.*

Jūji Kyō 十地経. T10, no. 287.

Jūju Ritsu 十誦律. T23, no. 1435.

Jūjushin Ron 十住心論, by Kūkai (Kōbō Daishi) 空海(弘法大師). T77, no. 2425.

Jūjūbibasha Ron 十住毘婆娑論. T26, no. 1521.

Juketsu Shū 授決集, by Enchin (Chishō Daishi) 円珍(智証大師). T74, no. 2367;
    DNBZ 26, 334–396.

Jūnimon Ron 十二門論. T30, no. 1568.

Kako Genzai Inga Kyō 過去現在因果経. T3, no. 189.

Kakuzenshō: Hokke Hiketsu 覚禅抄:法華秘決. DNBZ 46, 644–676.

Kambutsu Zammai Kyō 観仏三昧経. T15, no. 643. Also known as *Kambutsu Zam-
    maikai Kyō.*

Kammuryōju Butsu Kyō Sho 観無量寿仏経疏, by Chih-i 智顗 (T'ien-t'ai) (天台)
    Chigi (Tendai Daishi). T37, no. 1750.

Kammuryōju Butsu Kyō Sho 観無量寿仏経疏, by Shan-tao 善導 (Zendō). T37, no.
    1753.

Kammuryōju Kyō 観無量寿経. T12, no. 365.

Kanchi Giki 観智儀軌, by Pu-k'ung 不空 (Fukū, Amoghavajra) T19, no. 1000.
    Also known as: *Jōju Myōhō Renge Kyō ōyuga kanchi giki* 成就妙法蓮華経王瑜
    伽観智 and *Hoke Kyō Kanchi Giki.*

Kanfugengyō. See *Fugen Kyō.*

Kanjin Ron Sho 観心論疏, by Kuan-ting (Ch'ang-an) 観頂(章安) Kanjō (Shōan).
    T46, no. 1921.

Kanjō Kyō 観頂経. T21, no. 1331.

Kannen Amida Butsu Sōkai Zammai Hōmon 観念阿弥陀仏相海三昧功徳法門 by
    Shan-tao 善導 (Zendō). T47, no. 1959. Also known as *Kannen Hōmon.*

Kannen Hōmon. See *Kannen Amida Butsu Sōkai Zammai Hōmon.*

Kegon Gokyō Shō. See *Kegon Ichijō Kyōgi Bunzai Shō.*

Kegongyō Sho 華厳経疏, by Ch'eng-kuan 澄観 (Chōkan). T35, no. 1735.

Kegon Ichijō Jūgenmon 華厳一乗十玄門, by Tu Hsun (Chih-yen) 杜順(智儼) (To
    Jun, Chigon). T45, no. 1868.

Kegon Ichijō Kyōgi Bunzai Shō 華厳一乗教義分斉章, by Fa-tsang 法蔵 (Hōzō).
    T45, no. 1866. Also known as *Kegon Gokyō Shō* 華厳五教章.

Kegon Kyō 華厳経 1) old (60v.) T9, no. 278; 2) new (80v.) T10, no. 279.

Kegon Kyō Gōron 華厳経合論, by Li T'ung-hsüan 李通玄 (Ri Tsūgen). ZZ1, 5,
    4–1, 7, 2.

Kegon Kyō Shoshō Gendan 華厳経疏抄玄談, by Ch'eng-kuan 澄観 (Chōkan).
    ZZ1, 8, 3–4.

Kengu Kyō 賢愚経. T4, no. 202.

Kenkai Ron 顕戒論, by Saichō (Dengyō Daishi) 最澄(伝教大師). T74, no. 2376;
    DDZ 1, 25–198.

Kōbō Daishi Goden 弘法大師御伝. *Zoku Gunshi Ruijū*, v. 8, pt. 2, pp. 526–562.

Kokusei Hyakuroku 国清百録, comp. by Kuan-ting (Ch'ang-an) 観頂(章安) (Kanjō, Shōan). T46, no. 1934.

Kongōbei 金剛錍, by Chan-jan (Miao-lo) 湛然(妙楽) (Tannen, Myōraku). T46, no. 1932. Also known as: *Kongōbei Ron.*

Kongōbei Ron. See *Kongōbei.*

Kongōchō Daikyōōgyō Sho 金剛頂大教王経疏, by Ennin (Jikaku Daishi) 円仁 (慈覚大師). T61, no. 2223. Also known as *Kongōchō Kyō Sho.*

Kongōchō Kyō 金剛頂経. T18, no. 865.

Kongōchō Kyō Sho. See *Kongōchō Daikyōōgyō Sho.*

Kongō Hannya Haramitsu Kyō 金剛般若波羅密経. T8, no. 235. Also known as *Kongō Hannya Kyō* and *Kongō Kyō.*

Kongō Hannya Kyō. See *Kongō Hannya Haramitsu Kyō.*

Kongō Kyō. See *Kongō Hannya Haramitsu Kyō.*

Konkōmyō Kyō. See *Konkōmyō Saishōō Kyō.*

Konkōmyō Saishōō Kyō 金光明最勝王経. T16, no. 665. Also known as *Konkōmyō Kyō.*

Kōsō Den 高僧伝. T50, no. 2059.

Kujakkyō Ongi 孔雀経音義, by Kanjō 観静. T61, no. 2244.

Kukyo Ichijō Hōshō Ron. See *Hōshō Ron.*

Kyakuon Jinshu Kyō 却温神呪経. ZZ1, 3, 5.

Kyōji Jō 教時浄, by Annen 安然. T75, no. 2395a.

Kyōji Jōron 教時浄論, by Annen 安然. T75, no. 2395b.

Lotus Sutra. See *Myōhō Renge Kyō.*

Maka Hannya Haramitsu Kyō 摩訶般若波羅密経. T8, no. 223. Also known as *Daibon Hannya Kyō.*

Maka Shikan 摩訶止観, by Chih-i (T'ien-t'ai) 智頡(天台) (Chigi, Tendai). T46, no. 1911.

Maka Shikan Bugyōden Guketsu 摩訶止観輔行伝弘決, by Chan-jan (Miao-lo) 湛然(妙楽) (Tannen, Myōraku). T46, no. 1912. Also known as *Shikan Bugyōden Guketsu* and *Guketsu.*

Māyā Kyō 摩耶経. T12, no. 383.

Memyō Bosatsu Den 馬鳴菩薩伝. T50, no. 2046.

Mitsugon Kyō 密厳経. T16, no. 682. Also known as *Daijō Mitsugon Kyō.* There are two works of the same title, one translated by Divākara (no. 681), the present one by Pu-k'ung 不空 (Amoghavajra, Fukū).

Mongu Ki. See *Hokke Mongu Ki.*

Muryōgi Kyō 無量義経. T9, no. 216.

Muryōju Kyō 無量寿経. T12, no. 361.

Myōhō Renge Kyō 妙法蓮華経. T9, no. 262. The Lotus Sutra.

Myōhō Renge Kyō Upadaisha 妙法蓮華経憂波提舎. T26, no. 1519.

Nehan Gyō 涅槃経. Full title: *Daihatsu Nehan Gyō* 大般涅槃経. T12, no. 374 (Northern 60 v.); T12, no. 375 (Southern, 80 v.). The Nirvana Sutra.

Nehan Gyō Sho 涅槃経疏, by Chan-jan (Miao-lo) 湛然(妙楽) (Tannen, Myōraku). T38, no. 1767.

Nikyō Ron. See *Ben Kenmitsu Nikyō Ron.*

Ninnō Kyō 仁王経. T8, no. 245.

Ninnō Kyō Sho 仁王経疏, by Chi-tsang 吉蔵 (Kichizō). T33, no. 1707.

Nirvana Sutra. See *Nehan Gyō.*

Ōjo Jūin 往生拾因, by Yōkan (Eikan) 永観. T84, no. 2683.

Ōjo Kōshiki 往生講式, by Yōkan (Eikan) 永観. T84, no. 2725.

Ōjō Raisan 往生礼讃, by Shan-tao 善導 (Zendō). T47, no. 1980.

Ōjō Ron Chū 往生論註, by T'an-luan 曇鸞 (Donran). T40, no. 1819.

Ōjō Yōshū 往生要集, by Genshin 源信. T80, no. 2682.

Rokuharamitta Kyō 六波羅密多経. T8, no. 261.

Rōshi Keko Kyō 老子化胡経. T54, no. 2139. Also read *Rōshi Kako Kyō.*

Ryōga Kyō 楞伽経. T16, no. 670.

Saishōō Kyō. See *Konkōmyō Saishōō Kyō.*

Sange Gakushō Shiki 山家学生式, by Saichō (Dengyō Daishi) 最澄（伝教大師）. T74, no. 2377.

Senchaku Shū 選択集, by Hōnen 法然. T83, no. 2608. Full title: *Senchaku Hongan Nembutsu Shū* 選択本願念仏集.

Shakashi Fu 釈迦氏譜, by Tao-hsüan 道宣 (Dōsen). T50, no. 2041.

Shakumon Jikyō Roku 釈門自鏡録, by Huai-hsin 懐信 (Eshin). T51, no. 2083.

Shakusen. See *Hokke Gengi Shakusen.*

Shari Kōshiki 舎利講式, by Kakuban 覚鑁. *Kōgyō Daishi Zenshū*, v. 2, pp. 1281–1294.

Shijūnishō Kyō 四十二章経. T17, no. 784.

Shikan Bugyōden Guketsu. See *Maka Shikan Bugyōden Guketsu.*

Shikan Shiki 止観私記 by Shōshin 證真. DBZ 22, 237–591.

Shinji Kangyō 心地観経. T3, no. 159.

Shingyō Hiken 心経秘鍵, by Kūkai (Kōbō Daishi) 空海（弘法大師）. T57, no. 2203a. Full title: *Hannya Shingyō Hiken.*

Shiyaku Kyō 思益経. T15, no. 586.

Shō-hokke Kyō 正法華経. T9, no. 263.

Shōjōhōgyō Kyō 清浄法行経. Apocryphal work, no longer extant.

Shokyō Yōshū 諸経要集. T54, no, 2123.

Shōmangyō 勝鬘経. T12, no. 353. *Śrīmālā* Sutra.

Shōshinji Donin Kyō 清信士度人経. Full text no longer extant; citation from *Hōon Jūrin*, T53, no. 2122.

Shugo Kokkai Shō 守護国界章, by Saichō (Dengyō Daishi) 最澄（伝教大師）. T84, no. 2362; DDZ2, 151–681.

Shugo Kokkaishu Darani Kyō 守護国界主陀羅尼経. T19, no. 997.

Shuryōgon Gyō 首楞厳経. T15, no. 642. Full title: *Shuryōgon Zammai Kyō* 首楞厳三昧経.

Soshitsuji Kyō 蘇悉地経. T18, no. 893. Full title: *Soshitsuji Kara Kyō* 蘇悉地羯羅経.

Soshitsuji Kyō Ryakusho 蘇悉地経略疏, by Ennin (Jikaku Daishi) 円仁（慈覚大師）. T61, no. 2227.

Sō Kōsō Den 宋高僧伝. T50, no. 2061.

Śrīmālā Sutra. See *Shōmangyō.*

Taizōkai Daihō Taiju Ki 胎蔵界大法対受記, by Annen 安然. T75, no. 2390.

Tembon Hoke Kyō 添品法華経. T9, no. 264. Full title: *Tembon Myōhō Renge Kyō* 添品妙法蓮華経.

Tendai Shikyō Gi 天台四教儀. T46, no. 1929.

Tōke Sanne Shō 当家三衣抄, by Nichikan 日寛. *Fuji Shūgaku Yōshū* 富士宗学要集 v. 3.

Tōshun 東春, by Chih-tu 智度 (Chido). ZZ1, 40, 3. The name by which Nichiren refers to the *Hoke Kyō Shogisan* 法華経疏義纘; also known as *Hokke Mongu Tōshun* 法華文句東春.

Urabon Gyō 盂蘭盆経. T16, no. 685.

Vimalakirti Sutra. See *Yuima Kyō*.

Yakushi Hongan Gyō 薬師本願経. T14, no. 449. Full title: *Yakushi Nyorai Hongan Gyō* 薬師女来本願経.

Yakushi Rurikō Nyorai Hongan Kudoku Kyō 薬師琉璃光如来本願功徳経. T14, no. 450.

Yuga Ron 瑜伽論. T30, no. 1579. Full title: *Yuga Shiji Ron* 瑜伽師地論.

Yuga Shiji Ron. See *Yuga Ron*.

Yuima Kyō 維摩経. T14, no. 475. Vimalakirti Sutra. Also known as *Jōmyō Kyō* 浄名経 and *Yuimakitsu Shosetsu Kyō* 維摩詰所説経.

Yuishiki Ron 唯識論. T31, no. 614. Full title: *Jō Yuishiki Ron* 成唯識論.

Zōbō Ketsugi Kyō 像法決疑経. T85, no. 2870.

Zōichi Agon Gyō 増一阿含経. T2, no. 125.

Zoku Kegon Kyō Ryakusho Kanjō Ki 續華厳経略疏刊定記, by Hui-yüan 慧苑 (Eon). ZZ1, 5, 1–3.

Zoku Kōsō Den 續高僧伝. T50, no. 2060.

Zuiō Hongi Kyō 瑞応本起経. T3, no. 185.

Zui Tendai Chisha Daishi Betsuden 隋天台智者大師別伝, by Kuan-ting (Ch'ang-an) 潅頂(章安) Kanjō (Shōan). T50, no. 2050.

INDEX

108; *Jimmitsu* Sutra and, 113, 225;
Jinriki chapter of, 173, 174, 175–
177, 206, 220, 428*n*25; *Jo* chapter
of, 390*n*199, 430*n*41; *Juki* chapter
of, 380*n*52; *Juryō* chapter of, 72–
77, 97, 102, 103, 153, 165–175,
206, 251, 309, 337, 344, 345,
373*n*66, 382*n*86; *Kambotsu* chapter
of, 135; *Kammuryōju* Sutra vs.,
129; *Kanji* chapter of, 71, 82–83,
122–123, 125, 127, 133, 170, 185,
387*n*152, 398*n*143; *Kanzetsu* chapter of, 125; *Kegon* Sutra and, 108,
112–113, 225, 266; Kōbō and,
273–274, 299, 301, 337; *Kongōchō*
Sutra and, 386*n*152; Latter Day of
the Law and, 128, 173–178, 190,
214–216; merit and, 352; Middle
Day of the Law and, 194–199,
203, 208, 213; moon and, 327–
328; *Ninki* chapter of, 168,
380*n*52; Nirvana Sutra and, 254,
255, 263–264, 289–290, 301–302;
persecution and, 80–91, 136, 147,
258, 303, 312, 329–330, 348;
preparation and, 168, 169; Pure
Law and, 214–215; Shakyamuni
Buddha and, 200, 201, 219–220;
Shingon sect and, 271–275, 285;
shōmon and *engaku* and, 66, 73,
74, 85, 86–91; slander of, 35–36,
40, 51–52, 93–94, 106–115, 128–
129, 136, 254–258, 260, 280–281,
289–291, 308, 316, 339, 345,
350–352, 354, 411*n*66; Ten
Worlds in, 153–154, 160; theoretical teaching of, 169–171, 403*n*50,
405*n*104; Three Great Secret Laws
and, 251; T'ien-t'ai and, 262, 263;
time for preaching and, 183–201;
women and, 121; *Yakuō* chapter
of, 125, 176, 178; *Yakusōyu* chapter of, 135, 261; *Yujutsu* chapter
of, 72–73, 74, 75, 169, 172; *Zokurui* chapter of, 175, 206, 327; see
also *Myō-hō-ren-ge-kyō*
Loyalty, 52–53, 63–64

Madhyāntika, 84, 387*n*157, 429*n*37
Mahādeva, 24, 258, 424*n*265,
428*n*28
Mahākāśyapa, 61, 63, 85, 88, 126,
214, 218, 311–313, 315, 316,
380*n*52
Mahāprajāpati, 61, 316, 381*n*53,
443*n*52
Mahavairocana Buddha, 76, 195,
266, 297, 299–300, 301
Mahayana teachings: Former Day of
the Law and, 169, 182, 191–192;
Hinayana vs., 68, 311–313; Pure
Land and, 22–41; sects of, 253;
spread of, 176–177; time for
preaching and, 186
Maka Shikan (T'ien-t'ai), 54, 107,
401*n*9; Ajātaśātru and, 347; desires and, 345; *ichinen sanzen* and,
149, 150, 151, 153; karma and,
138; Lotus Sutra and, 127, 128;
neglected rites and, 28; persecution and, 329–330; Taoism and,
58; Zen and, 131, 132
Maka Shikan Bugyōden Guketsu
(Miao-lo), 54, 59, 127–128, 131–
132, 138–140, 142, 150–153, 267,
330
Manoratha, 260, 429*n*37
Manorhita, 429*n*37
Mantras, 307–308, 310–311
Mao Pao, 85, 251, 387*n*162, 426*n*2
Maudgalyayāna, 61, 89, 305, 316,
380*n*52, 441*n*222
Māyā, Queen, 185, 203, 232,
443*n*252
Māyā Sutra, 84, 203, 312
Miao-lo (Chan-jan), 11, 54, 80, 172,
209; arrogance and, 123; bodhisattvas and, 99; Buddhas and,
105; evil monks and, 59, 131,
248; Latter Day of the Law and,
178, 179, 190; Lotus Sutra and,
115, 127, 189, 190, 205, 267, 272,
282; mystic powers and, 175; persecution of, 314; Zen and, 131–
132

Land Buddhism and, 6–7, 8; Seichō-ji and, 250–251; slander of, 323, 328, 341–342; Tendai Buddhism and, 6, 11; as votary of Lotus Sutra, 125, 134, 137–138, 317, 341–342, 345–346, 357; youth of, 5–6; Zen and, 6, 8
Nihon Daruma-shū, 5, 377n13
Nikkō, Bodhisattva, 104
Nikkō Shōnin (Hōki-bō), 354, 449n2
Nikō (Sadō-bō), 354, 449n3
Ninna-ji (temple), 284, 418n161
Ninnō Hannya Sutra, see *Ninnō* Sutra
Ninnō Sutra, 13, 20, 33, 71, 159, 229, 237, 339, 369n5; disasters and, 16–18, 38–39, 40, 339; enlightenment of Buddha and, 102; Lotus Sutra and, 159; Nichiren and, 328; persecution and, 288
Ninshō, *see* Ryōkan
Nirvana Sutra, 93–94, 164, 229, 405n97; bodhisattvas and, 374n70; Buddhahood in, 156; Buddhas and, 101, 158–159; enemies of Buddhism and, 301; enlightenment of Buddha in, 74; evil monks and, 20, 21, 124, 127, 130; Fa-yün and, 260–261, 262, 273; heart of, 307; *icchantika* and, 31–32, 123–124; karma and, 139–140; Kōbō and, 273, 301; Latter Day of the Law and, 176; Lotus Sutra and, 128, 135, 175, 194, 254, 255, 263–264, 266, 289, 290, 301, 302; non-Buddhist teachings and, 56; persecution and, 80, 303; *shōju* and *shakubuku* and, 142, 143; slander of True Law and, 29, 31, 33, 35, 40, 69–70, 136, 350; supremacy of, 118–120; Tao-ch'o and, 25; T'ien-t'ai and, 262, 263; transmission of, 168; True Law and, 77
Nisshō, 347
Nittō Junrei Ki (Record of a Pil-

grimage to China in Search of the Law) (Jikaku Daishi), 28–29
Nōin, 324, 439n197, 445n16

Ōjō Raisan (Shan-tao), 372n52
Ōjō Ron Chū (T'an-luan), 22
Ōjō Yōshū (Genshin), 374n71, 397n118, 419n171, 442n242, 448n4
"On Itai Dōshin" (Nichiren), 353–354
Onjō-ji (temple), 19, 131, 218, 283, 302, 371n38, 397n126, 434n122
"On Various Actions of the Priest Nichiren" *(Shuju Onfurumai Gosho)* (Nichiren), 5, 319–342
"Opening of the Eyes, The" *(Kaimoku Shō)* (Nichiren), 9, 50–124, 333
Ōta Jōmin (Gorōzaemon), 180, 408n152

Paramārtha, 203, 415n119
Parents, 50, 51, 52, 54
Pārśva, 126
Persecution, 79–91, 122–124, 135, 136, 138–142, 287–288, 312–315, 320–322, 329–335, 343
Pi Kan, 52–53, 321, 378n4, 444n3
Po Chü-i, 135, 320, 399n151
Prasenajit, King, 17, 89, 370n26
Pu-k'ung (Amoghavajra), 76, 108, 206, 245, 249, 266, 385n122; *ichinen sanzen* and, 163; Lotus Sutra and, 113, 214; rainmaking by, 338; Shingon school and, 195, 267; T'ien-t'ai teachings and, 209, 272, 293–294
Pure Land sect, *see* Jōdo sect; Nembutsu sect
Pure Land teachings, 12; and development of sects, 3–4; enlightenment and, 372n50, 419n32; Hōnen and, 22–27; Nichiren and, 4, 6–7, 8, 182; sutras of, 187; women in, 121; *see also* Nembutsu sect
Pūrṇa, 61, 380n52, 441n216

OTHER WORKS IN THE COLUMBIA ASIAN STUDIES SERIES

The Romance of the Western Chamber (Hsi Hsiang chi), tr. S. I. Hsiung. 1968
Also in paperback ed.

The Manyōshū, Nippon Gakujutsu Shinkōkai ed. Paperback 1969
text ed.

Records of the Historian: Chapters from the Shih chi of Ssu-ma Ch'ien, 1969
tr. Burton Watson. Paperback text ed.

Cold Mountain: 100 Poems by the T'ang Poet Han-shan, tr. Burton 1970
Watson. Also in paperback ed.

Twenty Plays of the Nō Theatre, ed. Donald Keene. Also in paper- 1970
back ed.

Chūshingura: The Treasury of Loyal Retainers, tr. Donald Keene. Also 1971
in paperback ed.

The Zen Master Hakuin: Selected Writings, tr. Philip B. Yampolsky. 1971
Also in paperback ed.

Chinese Rhyme-Prose: Poems in the Fu Form from the Han and Six 1971
Dynasties Periods, tr. Burton Watson. Also in paperback ed.

Kūkai: Major Works, tr. Yoshito S. Hakeda. Also in paperback ed. 1972

The Old Man Who Does as He Pleases: Selections from the Poetry and 1973
Prose of Lu Yu, tr. Burton Watson

The Lion's Roar of Queen Śrīmālā, tr. Alex and Hideko Wayman 1974

Courtier and Commoner in Ancient China: Selections from the History of 1974
the Former Han by Pan Ku, tr. Burton Watson. Also in paperback ed.

Japanese Literature in Chinese, vol. 1: *Poetry and Prose in Chinese by* 1975
Japanese Writers of the Early Period, tr. Burton Watson

Japanese Literature in Chinese, vol. 2: *Poetry and Prose in Chinese by* 1976
Japanese Writers of the Later Period, tr. Burton Watson

Scripture of the Lotus Blossom of the Fine Dharma, tr. Leon Hurvitz. 1976
Also in paperback ed.

Love Song of the Dark Lord: Jayadeva's Gītagovinda, tr. Barbara Stoler 1977
Miller. Also in paperback ed. Cloth ed. includes critical text of
the Sanskrit.

Ryōkan: Zen Monk-Poet of Japan, tr. Burton Watson 1977

Calming the Mind and Discerning the Real: From the Lam rim chen mo of 1978
Tsoṅ-kha-pa, tr. Alex Wayman

The Hermit and the Love-Thief: Sanskrit Poems of Bhartrihari and 1978
Bilhaṇa, tr. Barbara Stoler Miller

The Lute: Kao Ming's P'i-p'a chi, tr. Jean Mulligan. Also in paper- 1980
back ed.

A Chronicle of Gods and Sovereigns: Jinnō Shōtōki of Kitabatake 1980
Chikafusa, tr. H. Paul Varley

Among the Flowers: The Hua-chien chi, tr. Lois Fusek 1982

Grass Hill: Poems and Prose by the Japanese Monk Gensei, tr. Burton Watson   1983

Doctors, Diviners, and Magicians of Ancient China: Biographies of Fang-shih, tr. Kenneth J. DeWoskin. Also in paperback ed.   1983

Theater of Memory: The Plays of Kālidāsa, ed. Barbara Stoker Miller. Also in paperback ed.   1984

The Columbia Book of Chinese Poetry: From Early Times to the Thirteenth Century, ed. and tr. Burton Watson. Also in paperback ed.   1984

Poems of Love and War: From the Eight Anthologies and the Ten Songs of Classical Tamil, tr. A. K. Ramanujan. Also in paperback ed.   1985

The Columbia Book of Later Chinese Poetry, ed. and tr. Jonathan Chaves. Also in paperback ed.   1986

Waiting for the Wind: Thirty-Six Poets of Japan's Late Medieval Age, tr. Steven Carter   1989

Selected Writings of Nichiren, tr. Burton Watson and others, ed. Philip B. Yampolsky   1990

The Book of Lieh-Tzŭ: A Classic of the Tao, tr. A. C. Graham. Morningside ed.   1990

Studies in Oriental Culture

1. The Ōnin War: History of Its Origins and Background, with a Selective Translation of the Chronicle of Ōnin, by H. Paul Varley   1967

2. Chinese Government in Ming Times: Seven Studies, ed. Charles O. Hucker   1969

3. The Actors' Analects (Yakusha Rongo), ed. and tr. Charles J. Dunn and Bungō Torigoe   1969

4. Self and Society in Ming Thought, by Wm. Theodore de Bary and the Conference on Ming Thought. Also in paperback ed.   1970

5. A History of Islamic Philosophy, by Majid Fakhry, 2d ed.   1983

6. Phantasies of a Love Thief: The Caurapañcāśika Attributed to Bilhaṇa, by Barbara Stoler Miller   1971

7. Iqbal: Poet-philosopher of Pakistan, ed. Hafeez Malik   1971

8. The Golden Tradition: An Anthology of Urdu Poetry, ed. and tr. Ahmed Ali. Also in paperback ed.   1973

9. Conquerors and Confucians: Aspects of Political Change in the Late Yüan China, by John W. Dardess   1973

10. The Unfolding of Neo-Confucianism, by Wm. Theodore de Bary and the Conference on Seventeenth-Century Chinese Thought. Also in paperback ed.   1975

Companions to Asian Studies

The Pleasures of Japanese Literature, by Donald Keene   1988

A Guide to Oriental Classics, ed. Wm. Theodore de Bary and Ainslie   1989
T. Embree; third edition ed. Amy Vladek Heinrich, 2 vols.

Introduction to Oriental Civilizations
Wm. Theodore de Bary, Editor

Sources of Japanese Tradition, 1958; paperback ed., 2 vols., 1964

Sources of Indian Tradition, 1958; paperback ed., 2 vols., 1964; 2d ed., 1988

Sources of Chinese Tradition, 1960; paperback ed., 2 vols., 1964

Neo-Confucian Studies

Instructions for Practical Living and Other Neo-Confucian Writings by   1963
Wang Yang-ming, tr. Wing-tsit Chan

Reflections on Things at Hand: The Neo-Confucian Anthology, comp.   1967
Chu Hsi and Lü Tsu-ch'ien, tr. Wing-tsit Chan

Self and Society in Ming Thought, by Wm. Theodore de Bary and the   1970
Conference on Ming Thought. Also in paperback ed.

The Unfolding of Neo-Confucianism, by Wm. Theodore de Bary and   1975
the Conference on Seventeenth-Century Chinese Thought. Also
in paperback ed.

Principle and Practicality: Essays in Neo-Confucianism and Practical   1979
Learning, ed. Wm. Theodore de Bary and Irene Bloom. Also in
paperback ed.

The Syncretic Religion of Lin Chao-en, by Judith A. Berling   1980

The Renewal of Buddhism in China: Chu-hung and the Late Ming   1981
Synthesis, by Chün-fang Yü

Neo-Confucian Orthodoxy and the Learning of the Mind-and-Heart, by   1981
Wm. Theodore de Bary

Yüan Thought: Chinese Thought and Religion Under the Mongols, ed.   1982
Hok-lam Chan and Wm. Theodore de Bary

The Liberal Tradition in China, by Wm. Theodore de Bary   1983

The Development and Decline of Chinese Cosmology, by John B.   1984
Henderson

The Rise of Neo-Confucianism in Korea, by Wm. Theodore de Bary   1985
and JaHyun Kim Haboush

Chiao Hung and the Restructuring of Neo-Confucianism in the Late Ming,   1985
by Edward T. Ch'ien

Neo-Confucian Terms Explained: Pei-hsi tzu-i, by Ch'en Ch'un, ed.   1986
and tr. Wing-tsit Chan

Knowledge Painfully Acquired: *K'un-chih chi*, by Lo Ch'in-shun, ed. and tr. Irene Bloom — 1987

To Become a Sage: The Ten Diagrams on Sage Learning, by Yi T'oegye, ed. and tr. Michael C. Kalton — 1988

The Message of the Mind in Neo-Confucian Thought, by Wm. Theodore de Bary — 1989

Modern Asian Literature Series

Modern Japanese Drama: An Anthology, ed. and tr. Ted Takaya. Also in paperback ed. — 1979

Mask and Sword: Two Plays for the Contemporary Japanese Theater, by Yamazaki Masakazu, tr. J. Thomas Rimer — 1980

Yokomitsu Riichi, Modernist, by Dennis Keene — 1980

Nepali Visions, Nepali Dreams: The Poetry of Laxmiprasad Devkota, tr. David Rubin — 1980

Literature of the Hundred Flowers, vol. 1: *Criticism and Polemics*, ed. Hualing Nieh — 1981

Literature of the Hundred Flowers, vol. 2: *Poetry and Fiction*, ed. Hualing Nieh — 1981

Modern Chinese Stories and Novellas, 1919–1949, ed. Joseph S. M. Lau, C. T. Hsia, and Leo Ou-fan Lee. Also in paperback ed. — 1984

A View by the Sea, by Yasuoka Shōtarō, tr. Kären Wigen Lewis — 1984

Other Worlds: Arishima Takeo and the Bounds of Japanese Fiction, by Paul Anderer — 1984

Selected Poems of Sō Chōngju, tr. with introduction by David R. McCann — 1989

The Sting of Life: Four Contemporary Japanese Novelists, by Van C. Gessel — 1989

The Travels of Lao Ts'an, by Liu T'ieh-yün, tr. Harold Shadick. Morningside ed. — 1990